Using Borland® C++

Lee Atkinson and Mark Atkinson

PROGRAMMING
SERIES

que®
CORPORATION
LEADING COMPUTER KNOWLEDGE

USING BORLAND® C++

©1991 by Que® Corporation

Library of Congress Catalog No.: 90-64404

ISBN: 0-88022-675-7

94 93 92 91   8 7 6 5 4 3 2

Interpretation of the printing code: the rightmost double-digit number is the year of the book's printing; the rightmost single-digit number, the number of the book's printing. For example, a printing code of 91-1 shows that the first printing of the book occurred in 1991.

DEDICATION ▼

To our parents. Thanks for your pride in us.

Publisher, Programming Books

Richard K. Swadley

Publishing Manager

Joseph Wikert

Acquisitions Editor

Gregory Croy

Senior Editor

Rebecca Whitney

Editors

Jodi Jensen
Virginia Noble
Susan Pink

Technical Editor

Greg Guntle

Book Design

Scott Cook

Cover Design

Dan Armstrong

Index

Hilary Adams
Jill Bomaster

Production

Jeff Baker
Claudia Bell
Scott Boucher
Brad Chinn
Martin Coleman
Sandy Grieshop
Betty Kish
Bob LaRoche
Sarah Leatherman
Kim Leslie
Lisa Naddy
Howard Peirce
Cindy Phipps
Tad Ringo
Bruce Steed
Johnna VanHoose
Lisa Wilson
Christine Young

Composed in Garamond and OCRB
by Que Corporation

ABOUT THE AUTHORS ▼

Lee Atkinson

Lee Atkinson is a 20-year veteran of the data processing industry. He has written code professionally in C, Pascal, COBOL, Fortran, PL/I, APL, and a number of assembly languages for machines ranging from the smallest microprocessors to IBM's top-of-the-line mainframes. He is currently an MVS systems programmer for a Mississippi-based regional retail company. He was co-author for Que's *Using C*.

Mark Atkinson

Mark Atkinson was introduced to computer programming in 1969 with a Fortran ballistics program that tracked the Saturn V rocket and astronauts to the moon. He has been involved with computing continuously since that time, including consulting and contract programming for IBM PCs and mainframes in a variety of languages. Based in Mississippi, he is currently a PC technician for the area's largest vendor of office systems. He was co-author for Que's *Using C*.

CONTENT OVERVIEW

Part III   Using Borland C++ with Microsoft Windows

TABLE OF CONTENTS ▼

▼

I   Using Borland C++'s Basic Features

Part II   Using Borland C++'s Object-Oriented Features

Part III   Using Borland C++ with Microsoft Windows

ACKNOWLEDGMENTS

Grateful acknowledgment is made to the following people for their support, guidance, and enthusiasm:

The Que Corporation editorial and production staff. Special thanks are due to Gregory Croy, Jodi Jensen, Virginia Noble, and Susan Pink—you endured us and taught us.

Greg Guntle, our technical editor. Thanks for your keen eye, and for your infectious enthusiasm.

Nan Borreson of Borland International, Inc. We are deeply grateful for the opportunity to write about Borland C++ 2.0, and for your help in providing the materials we needed.

TRADEMARK ACKNOWLEDGMENTS

Que Corporation has made every attempt to supply trademark information about company names, products, and services mentioned in this book. Trademarks indicated below were derived from various sources. Que Corporation cannot attest to the accuracy of this information.

ANSI is a registered trademark of American National Standards Institute.

AT&T is a registered trademark of AT&T, and UNIX is a trademark of AT&T.

IBM is a registered trademark of International Business Machines Corporation. OS/2 is a trademark of International Business Machines Corporation.

Lotus is a registered trademark of Lotus Development Corporation.

Microsoft, MS-DOS, GW–BASIC, and Microsoft QuickBASIC are registered trademarks of Microsoft Corporation. Windows is a trademark of Microsoft Corporation.

Borland C++, Turbo C, Turbo C++, Turbo Assembler, and Turbo Debugger are registered trademarks of Borland International, Inc. Turbo Profiler is a trademark of Borland International, Inc.

THUMB TAB INDEX

1

2

3

4

5

6

7

8

9

Introduction

Welcome to the exciting, changing world of C and C++ programming. The C language *is* changing—it is evolving rapidly into one of the most popular and powerful programming languages in existence. Borland International in particular is playing a significant role in popularizing C and C++. Borland's C++ compiler and development environment make available to *individuals* sophisticated programming tools that once only developers could afford. *Using Borland C++* is, of course, based on this product.

In fact, Borland now offers *two* Borland C++ compiler packages. Borland C++ is still sold individually for less than a hundred dollars. This is Borland's *low-end* package, which contains the C and C++ compilers and the Integrated Development Environment (IDE). The *high-end* compiler package is now known as Borland C++ 2.0, which completely replaces Turbo C++ Professional.

Borland C++ 2.0 features new releases of the C and C++ compilers, a stand-alone debugger, a program profiler, and Turbo Assembler. Also featured is support for building Windows 3.0 executable and Dynamic Link Library (DLL) modules. In addition, Borland C++ contains the Whitewater Group's Resource Toolkit for creating and maintaining Windows resources (icons, menus, dialog boxes, and others). All of these features are covered in this book.

The present explosive growth in popularity of the C language, and its successor language, C++, is the continuation of a phenomenon that quietly began when C was the primary language used by UNIX systems programmers. The C and C++ languages are now also widely known and used by those with desktop PCs (all brands) and mainframe computers (again, all brands). C is quickly becoming *the* language of choice for the serious programmer, whether for the individual or the professional software developer. C++ is also rapidly becoming quite popular. C++ is intimately related to C, yet there are enough differences between C and C++ to speak of two distinct languages. You will discover what those differences are in this book.

Who Should Read This Book?

This book is for you if you belong to one (or both) of the following groups of people:

❏ Those who want to learn more about C programming. This group includes users who know nothing about C or C++, as well as users who have some experience with C or C++. There is enough introductory material in this book to get the beginner started. And there is enough intermediate and advanced material to add significantly to the experienced programmer's fund of knowledge.

❏ Those who specifically want to use Borland's C++ compiler. Borland C++ has its own unique programming environment and its own set of extensions to ANSI standard C. This book introduces you to these subjects.

What This Book Is About

Using Borland C++ has two purposes: to help you learn C and C++, and to show you how to use Borland's C++ programming and development environment.

The primary focus of this book is on the C and C++ languages, particularly as they are implemented in Borland C++. You will probably be more interested in writing C and C++ programs than in reading about the text editor, debugger, or program profiler (although these are covered also). *Using Borland C++*, therefore, is mainly a tutorial introduction to the language.

Of course, you will have some interest in the tools and utilities Borland has packaged with Borland C++. These tools and utilities are the secondary focus of *Using Borland C++*. This book gives you a working knowledge of the major components of the package.

How This Book Is Organized

The Borland C++ package is well documented—almost *too* well, in fact. What you need is a book that begins with the basics, guides you through a jungle of information, and makes sure that you understand the important points—all in an orderly manner convenient for efficient learning. That's what *Using Borland C++* does. It presents the essential material succinctly so that your first experience with Borland C++ will be both pleasant and productive.

This book is a learning tool, not a reference manual. Your needs as a student have been considered, as well as your needs as a programmer. The book is specifically organized to ease your introduction to C and C++, and to the Borland programming environment:

❑ The book is divided into three parts. Part I covers the basic Borland C++ programming environment and the C (non-object-oriented) language. Part II covers the C++ (object-oriented) language. Part III provides a basic introduction to the world of Windows application programming, using the high-end package, Borland C++ 2.0.

❑ The chapters are divided into sections that are carefully designed to contain just the right amount of material to be easily digested.

❑ The chapters themselves appear in an order that does not require you to look ahead to comprehend what is being covered.

❑ The order of presentation is designed to defer the more complicated aspects of C and C++. The languages' foundations must come first, but this does not mean that you will be deprived of the more powerful and technical features of Borland C++.

How To Use This Book

How you approach this book depends on your level of experience with the C and C++ languages. If you have little or no C programming experience, you should start at the beginning and work straight through to the end. That way, you can build your knowledge of C and C++ in the proper order and minimize your confusion. If, however, you already have some C and C++ programming experience, you may want to skip immediately to the topics that interest you. This second approach is recommended if you already have a solid understanding of C language structure.

Whether or not you have prior experience, you should read an entire section at a time. The sections are short enough to be read in one sitting, and they are also sufficiently self-contained so that you do not need to read several sections to understand one point.

Conventions Used in This Book

To get the most out of the book, you need to know something about how it is designed. The chapters contain bold text, italicized text, bulleted lists, numbered lists, figures, program listings, code fragments, and tables of information. All these design features should help you understand the material being presented.

Characters that you are asked to type appear in **bold.** Also in lines that you must type, ***bold italic*** is used for characters that hold the place of a drive or file name (such as ***n:***), or anything else you must substitute.

Italic type is used to emphasize an important word or phrase. You should pay close attention to italicized text. It is used also to introduce new technical terms. An italicized term is followed immediately by a definition or an explanation.

Bulleted lists have the following characteristics:

❑ Each item in a bulleted list is preceded by a shadowed box (the bullet). The bullet is a special flag that draws your attention to important material.

❑ The order of items in a bulleted list is not mandatory. That is, the items represent related points you should understand, but not in a special sequence.

❑ The text for items in a bulleted list is often longer than the text you see in other kinds of lists. Items in bulleted lists contain explanations, not simple actions.

Numbered lists contain actions you should perform, or lists of items that must be kept in a particular sequence. When you see a numbered list, you should do the following:

1. Start at the beginning of the list. Don't skip ahead to later items in the list; order is important.

2. Make sure that you completely understand each item as you encounter it.

3. Read all the items in the list. Don't skip any of them—each item is important.

Figures are pictures or graphics that can help you understand the text. Each figure has a number in the form *c.n*: *c* is the chapter in which the figure appears, and *n* is the number of the figure in a sequence within the chapter. Figure 0.1, which is the first figure in the Introduction, shows how a figure will appear.

Fig. 0.1. A sample illustration.

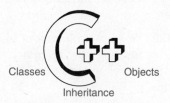

Program listings give the C or C++ source code for a complete program, or perhaps for a program module that can be compiled separately. In either case, source code shown in a program listing can, in fact, be compiled. Listing 0.1, for example, shows the source code for a complete program. (Most complete programs are much longer than this short sample.)

Listing 0.1. `begin.c.` *A sample program listing.*

```
1   #include <stdio.h>
2
3   void main()
4   {
5       puts( "------My program works!!------" );
6   }
```

You should notice a couple of things about listing 0.1. As this listing shows, complete program listings have line numbers down the left side of the page. And program listings, like figures, are numbered (see the heading for listing 0.1). However, the reference numbers for figures and program listings are independent. Note that this Introduction has a figure 0.1 and a listing 0.1.

A *code fragment* also shows C or C++ source code, but the code does not make up a complete program (the fragment cannot be compiled). Code fragments are inserted directly in the text and do not have headings, reference numbers, or line numbers. Code fragments contain enough source code to illustrate a point, but they are short (usually only five or six lines). Note that a special `monospace` type face is used for C keywords, program listings, and code fragments.

The *syntax form* is a special kind of code fragment that shows you the general form used for writing a C statement or declaration. A syntax form looks like this:

```
struct tag_opt { member-list_opt } obj-name_opt ;
```

In a syntax form, the *italicized* characters are placeholders for names and labels of your own choosing, whereas the `regular monospace` items must be written exactly as you see them. Furthermore, the letters $_{opt}$, when shown as a subscript following an item, indicate that the item is optional: it does not have to be present at all.

Tables appear where lists and columns of information are suitable. Tables also have their own headings and reference numbers—again, independent of the numbers for figures and program listings. Table 0.1 shows how a table is presented in this book.

Table 0.1. *The formatting conventions used in* Using Borland C++.

Format Convention	Use
Italic	An eye-catching type style used to emphasize important words or phrases.
Bulleted lists	A list of items with a bullet flagging each item; the sequence of items is not usually important.
Numbered lists	A list of items with numbers flagging each item; sequence *is* important.
Program listings	Complete programs that can be compiled.
Code fragments	A small number of C or C++ source code lines that illustrate a single point; code fragments cannot be compiled apart from other code.
Tables	Information arranged in columnar format; tables may or may not contain explanations or descriptions.

A Note on Practicing C and C++

Many readers of this book will already have some experience in writing C programs. If you have such experience, you need no further explanation about how to learn C.

If, however, you are approaching C and C++ for the first time, you need to know an important point about learning C: it is impossible to learn C or C++ without writing code, compiling your programs, and observing the way they work (or possibly don't work).

Because *practicing* C programming is essential to learning C or C++, a section named "Exercises" appears at the end of each chapter. In that section, you can practice what you have just learned in the chapter. When appropriate, hints and tips on writing the exercise code are provided, but it is up to you to devise a program that does what it is supposed to do. You will know when you have the correct solution: the program will work, and you will have solved a problem on your own. And that is what C programming is all about—finding solutions to *your* problems.

Part I

Using Borland C++'s Basic Features

Getting Started with Borland C++

This chapter helps you install Borland C++ on your computer and shows you how to start taking advantage of the powerful features of Borland C++. First, you learn how to install Borland C++ and configure it for your particular needs. Next, you explore some of the most useful features of the new Integrated Development Environment (IDE). Finally, after becoming familiar with the IDE, you learn how to write a simple C program.

Running the Installation Utility

Installing Borland C++ is an easy task because Borland has an excellent installation utility that relieves you of the strain of installing a large package. Basically, all you have to do is tell the INSTALL program which options you want, and then load each disk when prompted. The rest of the work is done for you.

Installing Borland C++

Before installing Borland C++, you need to check the amount of space available on your hard drive. Borland C++ is a large package: it uses almost 15 megabytes when all the options are installed.

To begin the installation process, put your disk labeled INSTALLATION DISK in a floppy disk drive and type

*n:***install**

where *n:* is the floppy drive that contains the INSTALLATION DISK.

The first screen you see welcomes you to the installation program and informs you that a full installation takes about 15 megabytes of disk space. The second screen asks which disk drive you are using to perform the installation. To respond, just type the correct drive letter and press Enter.

The third screen is the menu for the Borland C++ installation utility. With this menu, you specify what options will be included when you install Borland C++ and where the files will be stored on your hard drive. Figure 1.1 shows the Borland C++ installation utility's main menu.

Fig. 1.1. The main menu of the Borland C++ installation utility.

```
┌─────────────────────────────────────────────────────────┐
│         Borland C++ 2.0 Installation Utility            │
├─────────────────────────────────────────────────────────┤
│  Directories...          [ C:\BORLANDC ]                │
│  Install Examples...     [ C/C++ TD TASM TPROF ]        │
│  Install Options...      [ CMD IDE TD TASM TPROF ]      │
│  Memory Models...        [ S M C L H ]                  │
│  Windows Capability:     [ Yes ]                        │
│                                                          │
│  Start Installation                                      │
└─────────────────────────────────────────────────────────┘
─────────────────────────── Description ──────────────────
 Selecting this option will allow you to select different options. By default
 all of them will be selected.
        Disk Requirement      Windows      No-Windows
           CMD                1530K        1530K
           IDE                2320K        2320K
           TD                 2140K        1465K
           TASM                740K         740K
           TPROF               550K         550K

 F1-Help  F9-Start the installation  ENTER-Select  ESC-Previous
```

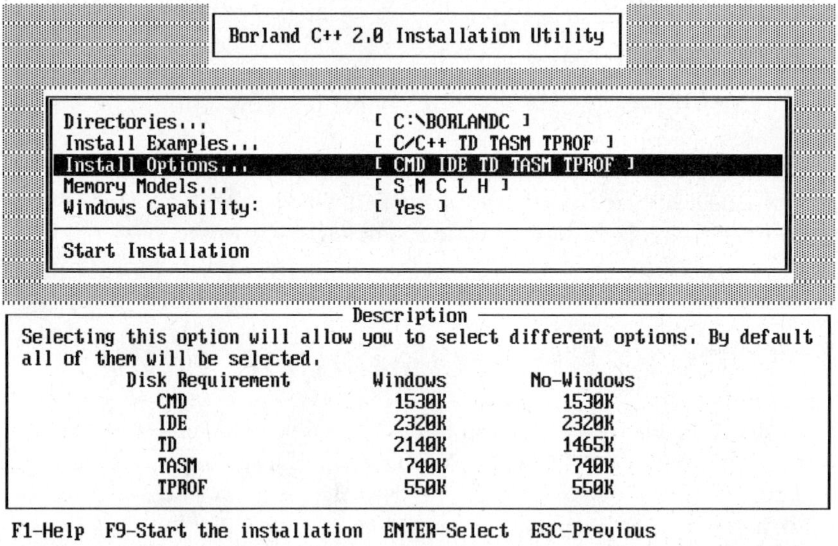

To modify an option on the installation utility menu, use the arrow keys to move the highlight bar to the option you want and press Enter. You are then prompted for the changes you want to make to the menu selection.

In the main menu, the first item enables you to specify where the program and support files for Borland C++ will be placed. Although it's easier to let the installation utility put Borland C++ in the default location, you can specify where *you* want the files to be located.

The installation utility gives you the option of unpacking the program example files. These files are programs that Borland has included to demonstrate some of the uses of Borland C++. If you are running short of disk space or do not need to refer to the example files, you can choose not to have them copied to your hard drive.

One of the most important parts of the installation utility is the selection of memory models you want to install. If you have room on your hard disk, you can choose the default option and install all the memory models. Installing support for all the memory models, however, takes extra room you may not want to use. In that case, you can specify the particular memory models you want to include. Table 1.1 summarizes the characteristics of each memory model.

Table 1.1. Memory model specifications.

Memory Model	Characteristics
Tiny	64K is available for all your code, data, and stack. Near pointers are always used.
Small	64K is available for your code, and 64K is available for your data and stack. Near pointers are always used.
Medium	1M is available for your code, and 64K is available for your data and stack. A far pointer may be used for your code, but the data and stack can use only a near pointer.
Compact	64K is available for your code, and 1M is available for your data and stack. A near pointer is used for the code, and a far pointer is used for the data.
Large	1M is available for your code, and 1M is available for your data and stack. Far pointers are always used.
Huge	Far pointers are used for both code and data. The normal 64K limit for static data is bypassed.

After you set all the items in the installation utility menu the way you want them, you can begin the actual installation. All you have to do at this point is put the disks in the drive when you are prompted. The installation utility takes care of the rest.

When the installation is complete, you need to update the PATH command in your AUTOEXEC.BAT file and the FILES command in your CONFIG.SYS file. For example, you need to add the following drive and path specification to your current PATH command:

PATH=C:\borlandc\bin

To your CONFIG.SYS file, you need to add the following FILES command:

FILES=20

After you reboot your computer so that the revised AUTOEXEC.BAT and CONFIG.SYS files take effect, you can start Borland C++ by typing **bc** at the DOS prompt.

Using the Integrated Development Environment (IDE)

With the new Integrated Development Environment, or IDE, you can do all your programming work in one convenient environment. The IDE integrates all the tools you need so that you can be a productive and efficient programmer. This section introduces you to the Integrated Development Environment and helps you start using its features immediately.

Starting the IDE

Starting Borland C++ is simple. You just change to your Borland C++ directory and type **bc** at the DOS prompt. Starting Borland C++ with this single command works well and takes care of most of your needs. By using the command-line options, though, you can load your program or project file more rapidly and make the IDE use your system more efficiently.

Use the following syntax to start Borland C++ with the command-line options:

bc *sourcename$_{opt}$* |*projectname$_{opt}$* *option$_{opt}$* ...

The *sourcename* can be the name of any ASCII file. Usually, *sourcename* is the name of the C or C++ program you are working with, and *projectname* is the name of the current project file. The *projectname* must have the file name extension PRJ. You can specify a *sourcename* or *projectname*, but not both. The available basic options are /b, /d, /e, /l, /m, /p, /rx, and /x. These are explained in the following list:

❏ /b   (Build All)

The option /b makes Borland C++ recompile and relink *all* the files in your project. During the compile and link processes, any error messages that may be generated are sent to the standard output device. When the compile and link are through, Borland C++ terminates and returns to the DOS prompt.

To determine what project file to build, Borland C++ looks at the command-line parameters first and then at the current file loaded in the editor. Borland C++ first checks the command-line parameters to see whether a file or project is specified. If either is specified, Borland C++ compiles and links that file or project. If the command line does not contain a file name or project name, Borland C++ compiles and links the file currently loaded in the editor.

❏ /d   (Dual-Monitor Mode)

The option /d invokes Borland C++ in dual-monitor mode. You can then use two video monitors at the same time, but they must be in different video modes. For example, the video mode for one monitor can be color, and the mode for the other monitor can be monochrome. For dual-monitor mode to work, Borland C++ must detect the hardware for both monitors. If the necessary hardware is not detected, the /d option is ignored. Dual-monitor mode is useful when you are running or debugging programs and when you are using Borland C++'s DOS shell feature.

In dual-monitor mode, one monitor is *active*, and the other is *inactive*. The active monitor is the one receiving data; the inactive monitor does not receive any data. However, the inactive monitor will still display any data sent to it earlier.

To determine which monitor is active, you use the DOS MODE command. This command lets you select which video mode to use. If you select the color video mode, data will be sent to the color monitor. If you select the monochrome mode, data will be sent to the monochrome monitor. Use the following DOS command to make the color monitor active:

MODE co80

Use this DOS command to make the monochrome monitor active:

MODE mono

When you start Borland C++ in dual-monitor mode, Borland C++ uses the *inactive* monitor and sends the output for your program to the *active* monitor. Therefore, if you run your program from Borland C++ and you want your program displayed in color, you must make the color monitor active *before* you start Borland C++.

Avoid the following conditions when you use the /d option in starting Borland C++:

Changing the mode from Borland C++'s DOS shell

Running programs that directly use the inactive monitor

Running or debugging programs that use two monitors

❑ /e (Expanded Memory)

The /e option makes use of your computer's expanded memory. When allocating memory, Borland C++ swaps out to a hard drive. If you use the /e option, Borland C++ swaps out to your computer's expanded memory. Swapping to memory can improve the performance of Borland C++.

❑ /l (LCD Screen)

The /l option optimizes Borland C++ for an LCD screen. This option may be necessary if you use Borland C++ on a laptop computer.

❑ /m (MAKE.EXE)

The /m option works like the /b option, except that a make is performed instead of a build. With the /b option, *all* files are recompiled and linked. With the /m option, only the out-of-date files are recompiled and linked.

❑ /p (Palette Restore)

The /p option is used for EGA adapters. If your program changes the EGA palette, the /p option causes the palette to be restored when the screen is swapped.

❑ /rx (RAM Disk)

The /rx option makes use of your computer's RAM disk. When allocating memory, Borland C++ normally swaps out to a hard drive. With the /rx option, however, Borland C++ swaps to your RAM disk. Swapping to your RAM disk can increase the performance of Borland C++. The x in /rx specifies which RAM disk to use.

❏ /x   (Extended Memory)

The /x option makes use of your computer's extended memory. When allocating memory, Borland C++ usually swaps out to a hard drive. But if you use the /x option, Borland C++ swaps out to your computer's extended memory. Swapping to extended memory can improve the performance of Borland C++.

Using the IDE's Menus and Windows

The new Integrated Development Environment is more powerful and useful than any previous Borland compiler. With the IDE, you have all the programming tools you need in a single, easy-to-use environment.

In this section, you learn how to use the Integrated Development Environment's menus and windows. Figure 1.2 shows the main parts of the IDE.

Fig. 1.2. The Integrated Development Environment (IDE).

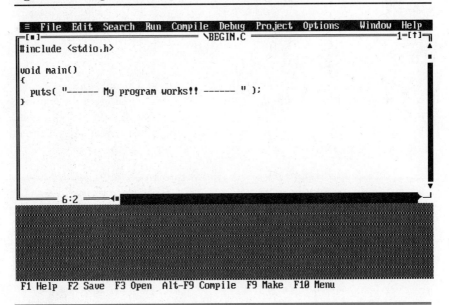

The IDE is composed of three main parts:

1. *The menu system.* The menu system gives you access to Borland C++'s powerful utilities and features. You use these utilities and features by selecting an option from the menu bar. As you can see in figure 1.2, the menu bar is the first line on the screen. The commands on the menu bar access each of the major groups of utilities or features.

2. *The window system.* The window system—the most visible and used part of the IDE—offers a variety of windows. Windows are available for editing a program, debugging a program, and viewing a program's operation. Other windows enable you to select options for utilities or display important messages. Figure 1.2 shows an edit window, where you create and modify your programs. This window contains the file FIRST.C.

3. *The status bar.* At the bottom of the screen, the status bar displays the shortcut keys for the most commonly used commands, tells you what Borland C++ is doing, or gives you hints about the command you have chosen. In figure 1.2, the status bar displays a list of shortcut keys.

The Menu System

The menu system contains the utilities and features necessary for managing your programming tasks efficiently. There are utilities and features for handling files; for editing your program; and for compiling, debugging, and running your own support programs. You can enter the menu system in three ways (the first two with the keyboard, and the third with the mouse):

❑ *The first way to enter the menu system is to move to the menu bar, highlight a command, and select it.* You can move to the menu bar from anywhere in the IDE by pressing the F10 key. Once the cursor is on the menu bar, use the arrow keys to highlight a particular command. After the highlight is on the command you want, press Enter to pull down a menu. You can use the arrow keys to select a command, or you can type the highlighted letter in the command name. When you finish selecting the command, press Enter to execute it. Figure 1.3 shows the pull-down menu for the **Run** command.

Fig. 1.3. *A pull-down menu in the IDE.*

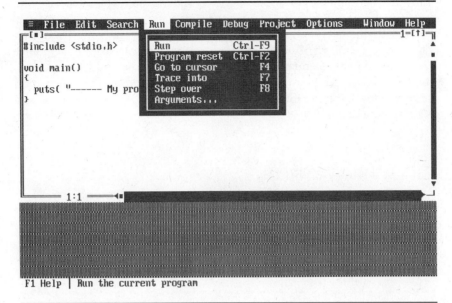

❏ *The second way to enter the menu system is to use an Alt-key combination.* To select a command from the menu bar, hold down the Alt
key and press the highlighted letter of the command. When a pull-
down menu appears, use the arrow keys to move to the command
you want, and then press Enter to select it. Selecting a command can
have three possible outcomes:

 1. The command is carried out.

 2. A submenu is displayed.

 3. A dialog box is displayed that contains a menu offering other
    choices available for the command you picked. You must
    provide in the dialog box the necessary information before the
    command can be executed.

❏ *The third way to enter the menu system is to click the mouse on a
command in the menu bar.* You can choose a command in the pull-
down menus the same way; simply point to the command and
click. If the command you choose pops up a dialog box, you may
need to type some information. However, you can still use the mouse
for many of the selections inside a dialog box. Dialog boxes are
discussed more thoroughly later in this section.

Borland C++ has two sets of menus: a full set and an abbreviated set. The difference between the two sets of menus is that the full set has more options from which you can choose. Although the abbreviated set can handle most of your needs, the full set gives you more control over programming tasks. You can activate the full set of menus in two ways. First, you can select the **O**ptions command from the menu bar and then choose **F**ull menus. Second, you can use the BCINST program to configure Borland C++ to use full menus automatically. For more information on using BCINST, see the next section, "Configuring Borland C++."

The Window System

When you use Borland C++, you will do most of your work inside a window. Several kinds of windows are available in the IDE. They provide areas in which you can write your programs, see the program output, debug problem code, display status information, and keep track of what is happening in your computer. Most of the windows have similar features (see fig. 1.4).

Fig. 1.4. Borland C++ window features.

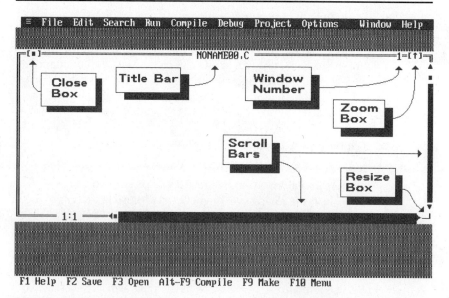

The following basic features are found in a Borland C++ window:

❑ *Close box.* The close box is located in the upper left corner of the window. Clicking the close box with the mouse closes the window. If you don't have a mouse, you can close a window with the **Close** command on the **Window** pull-down menu.

❑ *Title bar.* The title bar, located at the top of the window, displays the window name. Double-clicking the title bar zooms the window; dragging the title bar moves the window.

❑ *Window number.* The window number helps you keep track of the open windows. In Borland C++, you can have up to nine numbered windows. You can get a list of all the open windows by pressing Alt-0 (Alt-zero) or choosing List from the **Window** menu. To work inside a window, you must first make it active. Use one of the following methods:

1. Hold down the Alt key and type the number of the window you want to make active.

2. Select **L**ist from the **Window** menu and then choose the window you want to make active. Or choose **N**ext from the Window menu.

3. Click the mouse anywhere in the window.

The active window will appear on top of all the other windows and will be enclosed in a double-lined border.

❑ *Zoom box.* The zoom box allows you to zoom the window to its largest size. Clicking the zoom box activates the zoom command. Or if you don't have a mouse, you can select **Z**oom from the **Window** menu. If a window is already at its maximum size when you click the zoom box, the window returns to its former size.

❑ *Scroll bars.* Vertical and horizontal scroll bars are on the right and bottom sides of the window. You use the scroll bars to scroll the contents of the window. At each end of the scroll bars are arrows. Clicking the arrows moves the screen one line at a time. Next to the arrows are shaded boxes. Clicking a shaded box moves the contents of the window one page at a time. You can also drag the scroll box to change the contents of the window quickly. The position of the scroll box indicates the location of the information in the window relative to the rest of the document.

❑ *Resize box.* You can drag the resize box to change the size of the window.

One window that you may not be familiar with is the *dialog box*. A dialog box "pops up" for some of the menu commands, enabling you to make several choices about the command you have selected. Any menu command that is followed by an ellipsis (...) generates a dialog box when that command is selected. Figure 1.5 shows the dialog box for the Find command on the Search menu.

Fig. 1.5. *A typical dialog box.*

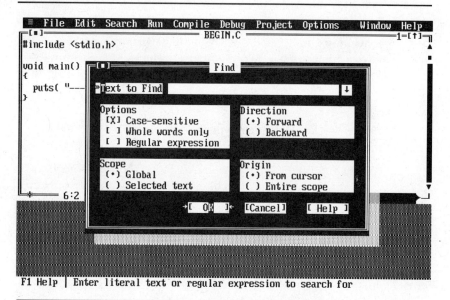

Most dialog boxes contain the following items:

❑ *Input boxes.* You type text into an input box and use the basic editing keys to work with the text you enter. If you need to enter a control code in the input box, you must precede the code with a ⌃P. If the input box is followed by a down-arrow symbol, a history list is associated with the input box. The history list contains entries you have used before in the input box. This feature is useful if you want to repeat or modify a previous command. You activate the history list by pressing the down-arrow key when you are in an input box, or by clicking the down-arrow symbol. If you don't want to use any of the selections in the history list, you can press Esc to exit the list. In figure 1.5, the input box is labeled *Text to Find*.

❏ *List boxes.* A list box lets you select an item from a list without having to leave the dialog box. The displayed list can vary in length. An example of a list box is the file list that is displayed for the **O**pen command from the **F**ile menu.

❏ *Action buttons.* Once you have made your selection from a dialog box or have typed the necessary information, you execute (or cancel) the command with the appropriate action button, which is a small box at the bottom of the dialog box. The standard action buttons are OK, Cancel, and Help (see fig. 1.5). You activate an action button by clicking it with the mouse, or by holding down the Alt key and pressing the highlighted letter in the action box.

❏ *Radio buttons.* You use the radio buttons to choose one—and only one—item from a group of mutually exclusive commands. To "push" a radio button, you can click it with the mouse, or press the Alt key and the highlighted letter in the radio button you want. Or you can use the Tab key to move to a group of radio buttons, and then use the arrow keys to select a particular radio button. Figure 1.5 has radio buttons beneath the Scope, Direction, and Origin options.

❏ *Check boxes.* You use a check box to turn an option on or off. If the check box contains an X, that option is turned on. If the check box does not contain an X, that option is turned off. When several check boxes apply to one topic, they will be grouped together. You can tab to a group of check boxes, use the arrow keys to pick a particular check box, and press the space bar to switch the option on or off. If you have a mouse, clicking a check box will switch it on or off. The Options list in figure 1.5 is a group of check boxes.

Configuring Borland C++

Part of the power of Borland C++ is its versatility. With Borland C++, you are not constrained to a programming environment that Borland thought would be nice. Borland C++ lets you change the programming environment to suit your needs and interests. You can change the Borland C++ environment by using the **O**ptions menu or the BCINST program. The **O**ptions menu is used mainly to customize the features with which you program. The BCINST utility enables you to configure the IDE to your tastes. However, many of the same functions are found in the **O**ptions menu and the BCINST utility. Both give you great flexibility in the way you manage your projects and the way the IDE handles.

Setting the IDE Options

You can make many changes to your programming environment from within the Integrated Development Environment. The facilities to change the environment are found in the menu system, under the Options command. The Options menu is broken into four sections that deal with the menu system, the utilities for building programs, the development environment, and the saving of environment information from session to session. Figure 1.6 shows the Options menu.

Fig. 1.6. The Borland C++ Options menu.

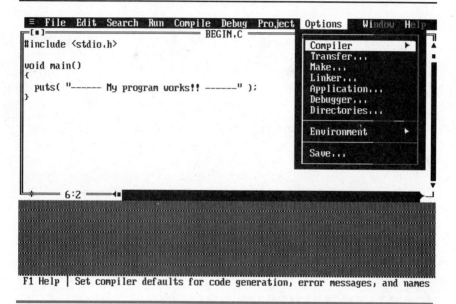

The first section of the Options menu controls the menu system. The only selection here is Full menus, which you use to determine whether complete menus will be displayed. With Full menus turned off, only a limited set of options is displayed when you choose a menu command. This limited set is sufficient for most tasks but lacks the power found with Full menus turned on. With Full menus on, a complete set of options is displayed whenever you choose a menu command. The complete set gives you better control over Borland C++ and enables you to perform more sophisticated functions.

The second section of the Options menu controls the features and utilities you use in your programming projects. Most of this section of the menu is devoted to the setup of the compiler. The Compiler command on the Options menu pops up a menu containing commands that control the compilation of your C and C++ programs:

❑ The **Code Generation** command displays a dialog box that allows you to change the way Borland C++ generates regular C object code.

❑ The **C++** options command allows you to change the way object code is generated but works with C++ code only.

❑ The **Optimizations** command gives you options for various kinds of code optimizations. The main features under this command are the optimizations for code size and code speed. If space is a critical concern, you can optimize for code size. If speed is more important, you can optimize for speed.

❑ The **Source** command displays a dialog box that tells the compiler what kind of source code to expect. Turbo C code lets you use the Turbo C extension keywords. ANSI tells the compiler to use only ANSI C keywords. If ANSI is selected, Turbo C keywords will be treated as identifiers. UNIX V tells the compiler to use only UNIX V keywords. If UNIX V is selected, Turbo C keywords will be treated as regular identifiers. K&R tells the compiler to use only K&R keywords. If you select K&R, UNIX V, or ANSI, the Turbo C keyword extensions will not be recognized but will be treated as ordinary identifiers. You use the **Source** command also to specify the length of identifier names and whether nested comments are allowed.

❑ The **Messages** command enables you to select the kinds of compiler error messages to be displayed, as well as how many error or warnings it takes to cause compilation to abort.

❑ The **Names** command lets you modify the segment, group, and class names for your code, data, and BSS sections. You should leave these selections at their default values until you have a specific need to change them and until you thoroughly understand the results of your changes.

Below the compiler setup options are options for the setup of the other utilities routinely used in the program development cycle:

❑ The **Transfer** command controls the calling of utility programs that you can run while you are still in Borland C++. Borland C++ Professional already has several programs set up. These programs are GREP, Turbo Assembler, Turbo Debugger, and Turbo Profiler. You can add your own programs to this list. With the **Transfer** command, you specify both the program name and the DOS command necessary to start the program. To use these programs, you select them from the [■] command.

❑ The **Make** command controls the operation of the make utility. **Make** lets you specify what error conditions will cause the make to abort its effort to build a program and whether you want to check auto-dependencies.

❑ The **Linker** command lets you change the setup of the linker utility.

❑ The **Debugger** command controls the setup of the debugging routines. With this command, you determine how the debugger operates.

❑ The **Application** command tells Borland C++ what kind of program you are creating. You can make a regular DOS application, a DOS overlay application, a regular Windows application, or a Windows DLL. (Overlay programs are explained and demonstrated in Chapter 7, and Part III helps you create Microsoft Windows applications.)

❑ The **Directories** command lets you specify the location of the library, include, and output directories.

The third section of the **Options** menu focuses on the development environment. When you select the **Environment** command from the **Options** menu, another menu pops up with commands that control how the IDE looks, how the editor works, and how the mouse handles:

❑ The **Preferences** command gives you basic control over the appearance of the IDE and determines what environment information is saved from one session to another.

❑ The **Editor** command gives you a measure of control over the built-in editor. You cannot control all the editor features from this menu, but you can control some basic features that affect the "feel" of the editor.

❑ The **Mouse** command enables you to control what the mouse buttons do and how sensitive the mouse is to a double-click.

Finally, the fourth section of the **Options** menu, containing the **Save** command, determines what information from the IDE will be saved between sessions. You can specify whether or not the environment, the desktop, and the project information will be saved from session to session.

Using BCINST

BCINST is a utility program you can use to customize the configuration of Borland C++. BCINST is not part of the IDE but is a stand-alone program that modifies the BC.EXE file. To start BCINST, move to the directory that contains the Borland C++ executable files and type the following:

bcinst

This command starts the BCINST program and causes BCINST to automatically load the configuration information for Borland C++. Figure 1.7 shows the main menu for BCINST.

Fig. 1.7. The BCINST main menu.

You use the **S**earch command from the BCINST menu to change the default operation of a search. The **S**earch menu contains the following options:

❑ The **D**irection command toggles between forward and backward searches.

❑ The **S**cope command specifies whether a search will look through the whole file or just a selected portion of the file.

❑ The **O**rigin command specifies where a search will start. You can start a search from either the cursor position or the beginning of the file.

❑ The **C**ase Sensitive command lets you specify whether you want a case-sensitive search. Because C, as well as C++, is generally a case-sensitive language, this option is handy.

❑ The **W**hole Words command specifies whether a match for a search string must be a whole word.

❑ The **R**egular Expression command, when turned on, enables you to use wild-card characters in a search string.

❏ The **P**rompt on Replace command lets you specify whether you will be prompted before the replace feature replaces one word with another.

The **R**un command enables you to send a command-line argument to your programs. If a program you create requires a command-line argument, the **R**un command supplies the argument automatically. Your program receives its command-line argument from the **R**un command just as at a DOS prompt. The only limitation is that the **R**un command does not support redirection. When you enter the command-line argument for the **R**un command, you don't have to enter the name of your program.

When you select the **O**ptions command from the BCINST menu, you access the Options menu. This menu has the same commands as the **O**ptions menu in the IDE. The BCINST **O**ptions menu does add one extra command: **S**wap to Memory. With this command, you can set up Borland C++ so that it will use any available extended or expanded memory when it is invoked.

With the **E**ditor Commands option, you can tailor the IDE editor to your preferences. Figure 1.8 shows part of the Editor Commands screen.

Fig. 1.8. The BCINST Editor Commands screen.

```
                         Install Editor
Command name          Primary                   Secondary

Cursor Left         · <CtrlS>              · ▐<Lft>                ▌
Cursor Right        · <CtrlD>              · <Rgt>
Word Left           · <CtrlA>              · <CtrlLft>
Word Right          · <CtrlF>              · <CtrlRgt>
Cursor Up           · <CtrlE>              · <Up>
Cursor Down         · <CtrlX>              · <Dn>
Scroll Up           · <CtrlW>              ·
Scroll Down         · <CtrlZ>              ·
Page Up             · <CtrlR>              · <PgUp>
Page Down           · <CtrlC>              · <PgDn>
Left of Line        * <CtrlQ>S             · <Home>
Right of Line       * <CtrlQ>D             · <End>
Top of Screen       * <CtrlQ>E             · <CtrlHome>
Bottom of Screen    * <CtrlQ>X             · <CtrlEnd>
Top of File         * <CtrlQ>R             · <CtrlPgUp>
Bottom of File      * <CtrlQ>C             · <CtrlPgDn>
Move to Block Begin * <CtrlQ>B             ·
Move to Block End   * <CtrlQ>K             ·
Move to Previous Pos* <CtrlQ>P             ·

←↑↓→-select  PgUp-PgDn-page  ◄┘-modify  R-restore factory defaults  ESC-exit
F4-Key modes:  (*)-WordStar-like  (■)-Ignore case  (·)-Verbatim
```

The Editor Commands screen is divided into three columns. The first column contains a description of all the functions available in the IDE editor. The second column is a list of the *primary* keystrokes for invoking editor commands; a primary keystroke is the main way you invoke an editor command. The third column contains the *secondary* keystrokes, which are alternative ways to invoke editor commands.

The status bar at the bottom of the screen is fairly self-explanatory. The only key whose use may not be obvious is the F4 key, which toggles among three key modes. The key mode determines how the editor control characters that you enter will be interpreted.

The first key mode is the WordStar-like mode. In this mode, any letter or any of the following characters will automatically be entered as a control-character combination:

[ ] \ ^ -

In other words, if you entered the letter *a* to represent a certain function, to get that function in the IDE editor, you would have to press Ctrl-a. Likewise, if you entered the character [to represent a function, to access that function, you would have to press Ctrl-[. The WordStar-like key mode is not case-sensitive. It does not matter whether you enter an *a* or an *A*—the editor interprets either of these the same way. In the Editor Commands screen, if you enter a two-letter code, such as *cd*, it makes no difference to the IDE editor whether you press Ctrl-cd or Ctrl-c Ctrl-d. Both key sequences are interpreted the same.

The second key mode is the Ignore case mode. In this mode, all alphabetic keys that you enter are converted to their uppercase equivalents. This key mode does not automatically add a Ctrl to the key sequences you enter. If you want the key sequence you enter to be a control code, you must enter the Ctrl key yourself. Entering a two-character control code in Ignore case mode, however, may not work the way you expect. For example, if the sequence Ctrl-cd is entered, only that exact sequence will be recognized. The sequence Ctrl-c Ctrl-d would not be recognized.

The third key mode is the Verbatim mode. In this mode, the key sequence you use in the IDE editor must match exactly the key sequence you enter in the Editor Commands screen. If, for example, you enter a Ctrl-Z, you must enter a Ctrl-Z in the IDE editor. In this example, the IDE editor will not recognize Ctrl-z.

Although you can use almost any key sequence you want, the following rules govern the creation of editor commands:

❑ *A key sequence cannot be over six characters long.* Note that some keys count as two keystrokes. These keys are the Alt key with any other key, the cursor-movement keys, and the function keys and their combinations.

❑ *The first character of a key sequence must be a special key or the Ctrl key.* The first character cannot be an alphanumeric key.

❑ *The Esc key must be defined as Ctrl-[.*

❑ *The Backspace key must be entered as Ctrl-H.*

❑ *The Enter key must be entered as Ctrl-M.*

❑ *The predefined help keys, F1 and Alt-F1, cannot be reassigned.* Any of the other function keys can be reassigned. If you try to override a hot (shortcut) key, you will be prompted before any change is made.

BCINST also has options to customize Borland C++ for your video monitor. Following the Editor Commands option on the BCINST menu is the **Mode For Display** option. When you select this option, the **Mode For Display** menu appears. From this menu, you can change the video mode in which Borland C++ starts. Usually, Borland C++ starts in the current video mode. You can change this default if you want Borland C++ to start in a certain mode or if you are having difficulty seeing your display. The **Mode for Display** menu offers the following commands:

❑ The **D**efault command starts Borland C++ in the current video mode (the video mode last used).

❑ The **C**olor command starts Borland C++ in 80-column color mode if you have a color video adapter installed. When you exit Borland C++, Borland C++ resets the video mode to the mode that was current before you started Borland C++.

❑ The **B**lack and White command starts Borland C++ in the black-and-white video mode if you have a color video adapter installed. When you exit Borland C++, Borland C++ resets the video mode to the mode that was current before you started Borland C++. This mode is useful for laptop and composite monitors.

❑ The **L**CD or Composite command starts Borland C++ in the black-and-white video mode if you have a color card installed. When you exit Borland C++, Borland C++ resets the video mode to the mode that was current before you started Borland C++. This mode is useful for laptop and composite monitors.

❑ The **M**onochrome command starts Borland C++ in monochrome mode if a monochrome video adapter is installed.

If you choose any of the video modes that require a color video adapter, BCINST runs a quick video test program. This test program checks for snow when the screen is repainted. You are asked whether snow was present on-screen when the test was run, and your answer determines whether snow detection routines are used. Don't use snow detection unless you need it; snow detection slows down screen-painting considerably.

When you select the **A**djust Colors command, another menu appears. You use the **A**djust Colors menu to customize the screen colors for all parts of the IDE. If you don't like Borland's default screen colors, you can change them to suit your own tastes.

The Save Configuration command lets you save all the changes you have made to the configuration file.

Finally, the **Q**uit command exits BCINST. If you have not used the Save Configuration command, you will be asked whether you want to save the changes that you have made before you exit BCINST.

Writing Your First C Program

Now that you have installed Borland C++ and become familiar with the basic layout of the Integrated Development Environment, you are ready to start programming in C. You need to know what components are necessary to create a C program, and how to enter and run a program in Borland C++.

Understanding C Program Structure

This section shows you what basic components are necessary to create a C program: preprocessor directives, global declarations, the `main()` function, and user-defined functions. When you have finished with the section, you will be able to look at a C program and know what its parts do. Listing 1.1 shows all the major parts of a C program.

The first time you see a C program, it may seem cryptic and confusing. C's syntax is brief, but brevity is what helps make C so powerful and flexible. After you have studied a few C programs, the meaning of most C statements will be obvious. Soon you will see how C's tight syntax speeds program development. The syntax lets you spend more time developing the logic of your program and less time typing program statements. As for C being confusing, good programming practices take care of that problem. Laying out your program in a neat and orderly manner prevents confusion.

Listing 1.1. `begin.c`. *A sample C program.*

```
 1   /* BEGIN.C   This program shows the basic
 2       parts of a C program. */
 3
 4   #include <stdio.h>
 5   #include <stdlib.h>
 6   #include <conio.h>
 7
 8   #define FALSE 0
 9      /* define the macro F to equal 0 */
10   #define TRUE 1
11      /* define the macro T to equal 1 */
12
13   int i = 0;
14
15   void put_msg( void );
16
17   main()
18   {
19     int answer;
20
21     clrscr();
22     printf( "Do you want to see the message?\n" );
23     printf( "Enter 0 for NO, 1 for YES ==> " );
24     scanf( "%d", &answer );
25     if( answer == TRUE )
26     put_msg();
27     else
28       puts( "Goodbye for now." );
29   }
30
31   void put_msg( void )
32   {
33     clrscr();
34     for( i = 0; i <=10; i++ )
35        printf( "Test string # %d.\n", i );
36   }
```

All C programs follow the same basic structure. Even a large, complex C program generally has the same layout as a short program. Figure 1.9 shows the main parts of a C program.

Fig. 1.9. *The basic structure of a C program.*

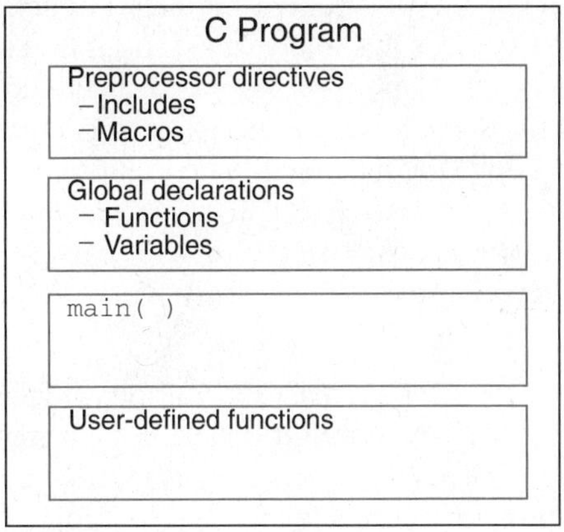

```
                    C Program
    ┌─────────────────────────────────────────┐
    │ Preprocessor directives                 │
    │   −Includes                             │
    │   −Macros                               │
    ├─────────────────────────────────────────┤
    │ Global declarations                     │
    │   − Functions                           │
    │   − Variables                           │
    ├─────────────────────────────────────────┤
    │ main( )                                 │
    │                                         │
    │                                         │
    ├─────────────────────────────────────────┤
    │ User-defined functions                  │
    │                                         │
    │                                         │
    └─────────────────────────────────────────┘
```

The following discussion examines, in turn, the four major parts of a C program. You learn what each part is and how it works. In the discussion, refer to both listing 1.1 and figure 1.9. The program listing shows you actual C code, and the figure shows you how that code fits in the program. Later in the chapter, you learn how all the parts work together in a sample program.

The first two lines of listing 1.1 are a comment, which is included to tell you about the program. A comment is not a required part of the program, nor does a comment perform a programming task. Comments are simply an aid to you, the programmer.

Preprocessor Directives

In a C program, the first part that performs a task consists of the *preprocessor directives*. In listing 1.1, the preprocessor directives are in lines 4–11. These directives instruct the compiler to perform certain tasks before program compilation begins. The most common preprocessor directive that you will see is the #include directive. This preprocessor directive instructs the compiler to include another C source file before compilation begins. Another common preprocessor directive is the #define directive, which is a macro definition. A macro definition in a C program functions much like one in a word processor.

The #include preprocessor directive tells the preprocessor to include another C source file during the program compilation process. The most common use of the include directive is seen in lines 4–6, where #include is used to include a header file.

Header files are composed mainly of function declarations, variable declarations, and macro definitions. A function declaration tells the compiler about a function that will be used but has not been coded at that point in the program. The compiler needs this information about functions that have not been written in order to determine whether the function calls that you made were made correctly. Variable declarations let the compiler know what variables you will be using. And macro definitions supply the replacement text for the macros you use. When you use a macro in your program, the preprocessor replaces the macro you entered with the replacement text found in the macro definition. The following discussion on #define directives explains macros more thoroughly.

#define signals the start of a macro definition, which lets you substitute one string for another. Lines 8 and 10 in listing 1.1 are macro definition statements. These lines tell the preprocessor to replace every occurrence of the word TRUE with 1, and every occurrence of FALSE with 0. In line 25, the preprocessor will replace the macro TRUE with 1. Therefore, when the compiler encounters line 25, the line of code will look like this:

```
if( answer == 1 )
```

Macros can be used in other ways also. Note the following lines:

```
#define FALSE 0
#define SALESTAX 0.06
```

These two macro definitions cause every occurrence of FALSE and SALESTAX in your program to be replaced with 0 and 0.06, respectively. You can even include C statements in macro definitions. See this next example:

```
#define STALL for( i = 1; i < 10000; i++ )
...
STALL;   /* Make program pause */
```

This macro definition substitutes a for( ) loop for the word STALL. Whenever the word STALL is encountered in the program, the for( ) loop is substituted.

Global Declarations

The second major part of a C program consists of global declarations. *Global declarations* tell the compiler about user-defined functions and about variables that are common to all functions in a source file. The global declarations in listing 1.1 are in lines 13 and 15.

As indicated earlier, function declarations tell the compiler about your functions. Specifically, a *function declaration* tells the compiler what type of data your function requires and what type of answer your function will return.

The only function declaration in listing 1.1 is in line 15. This function declaration tells the compiler that the function is not passed a value and that the function does not return a value. Here is a function declaration that requires arguments and returns a value:

```
int sum( int a, int b );
```

This function declaration declares a function named sum( ). The sum( ) function requires two arguments, each of which must be an integer. The function declaration indicates also that sum( ) returns a value. The type of the return value for sum( ) is int, which means that the function returns an answer that is an integer.

The compiler uses the information in the function declaration to verify that function calls are made correctly. After the compiler has passed the function declaration, the compiler checks the function calls to see whether the data types match correctly. The compiler checks the arguments you pass to a function in order to verify that they can be accepted by the function. In addition, the compiler checks to see whether the value returned by a function is used correctly.

Function Declarations, Definitions, and Calls

The first time you come across the terms *function declaration* and *function definition*, you may not realize the distinction between the two. However, each has a special purpose in a C program.

A function declaration tells the compiler about the function, and a function definition tells the compiler what is in the function. The function declaration is usually found near the top of the program, and the function definition is usually found near the bottom.

The function declaration tells the compiler what type of data the function requires and what type of return value it generates. This information is all the compiler needs to start compiling the program. Look at the following function declaration:

```
int product( int a, int b );
```

This function declaration tells the compiler that you will be using a function which requires two integer arguments and returns an integer value.

continues

continued

When the compiler encounters a *function call*, the compiler uses the information from the function declaration to determine if the variables passed to the function are the correct type and if the return value is used correctly. This next example shows a function call:

```
c = product( 3, 5 );
```

The compiler will verify that the values passed to product( ) are integers and that the variable assigned the return value of product( ) is an integer.

Notice that function declarations always end with a semicolon. The semicolon informs the compiler that the function declaration is complete.

A function definition contains the same information as a function declaration, and more. Also included in the function definition is the C code that performs the work of the function. Programming for the function is done in the function definition. The following example shows the body of the product( ) function definition:

```
int product( int a, int b )
{
   int c;
   c = a * b;
   return c;
}
```

Notice that function definitions are not followed by a semicolon. Because the first line of a function definition is followed by the body of the function, a terminating semicolon cannot be used.

It is possible to skip the function declarations. You simply *define* the function at the top of the source file, before any calls are made to the function. If you define the function before it is called, a function declaration will not be needed because the compiler already has all the necessary information to verify that function calls are made correctly. Defining functions at the beginning of a program is legal, but the program may be harder to read.

The global declarations portion of your program can include variable declarations in addition to function declarations. A global *variable declaration* makes that variable available for use to all the functions in the source file. In listing 1.1, line 13 is a global variable declaration for the integer variable i. Notice that i is used in the put_msg( ) function (line 34) even though i is not declared in put_msg( ).

Global variable declarations can cause trouble. In larger programs, you may depend on the value of a global variable but forget that you've changed the value of that variable in another function. Because you can easily lose track of a global variable's value, use as few global variables as possible. If you use a global variable only when you need one, you are less likely to have trouble remembering its value.

The *main()* Function

The third major part of a C program is the main( ) function. Every C program must have a main( ) function. Program execution begins in the main( ) function, and in a well-structured program, execution ends there. In listing 1.1, the main( ) function begins in line 17 and ends on line 29.

Some programs may have only one function—the main( ) function. In a short program, the entire program may fit easily inside the main( ) function. A large program, however, has too much code to fit inside this function. The main( ) function in a large program may consist almost entirely of calls to user-defined functions. Listing 1.1 falls between these two extremes. In begin.c, some of the program's tasks are performed in main( ), and some are performed in the put_msg( ) function. In similar programs, some tasks are carried out in main( ), and longer, logically separate steps are made into user-defined functions.

User-Defined Functions

The fourth part of a C program consists of *user-defined functions*—groups of statements you design to accomplish your programming tasks. User-defined functions can do anything you want them to do. Their only limit is the extent of your imagination.

In listing 1.1, lines 31–36 are the user-defined function put_msg( ). This is a short function that writes a series of messages to the video screen. Notice several points about put_msg( ):

❑ *The function name is preceded by the* type *of the function's return value.* This tells the compiler what kind of value the function will return. The return value can be an integer, a character, or some other data type. In listing 1.1, `put_msg()` has no return value, so the return type is specified as `void`.

❑ *The function name is followed by a* list of arguments *that will be passed to the function.* The argument list is enclosed in the parentheses that follow the function name. This list tells the compiler how many and what kind of arguments the function requires. In listing 1.1, `put_msg()` does not require any arguments; the argument list is therefore `void`.

❑ *The body of the function is enclosed in a set of braces.* In listing 1.1, the body begins with the opening brace in line 32 and ends with the closing brace in line 36. If you forget a brace, the compiler will catch your mistake and generate an error message.

Using the Editor To Write a Program

You are now ready to see how a real program is put together. First, you will use Borland C++ to enter the sample program `order.c`. Second, you will compile and run the program. Practicing with a real program enables you to see what each part of the program does and how all the parts work together.

Listing 1.2 shows the `order.c` program. The numbers on the left are not part of the program, so don't type these numbers when you type the program. They are only an aid in the discussion that follows.

Listing 1.2. `order.c`. *A sample program.*

```
 1   /* ORDER.C   An illustration of the basic parts of a
 2       C program. */
 3
 4   #include <stdio.h>
 5   #include <stdlib.h>
 6
 7   float calc_sub_total( int quantity, float price );
 8   float calc_tax( float sub_total );
 9
10   main()
11   {
12     char name[30];
```

```
13      char product[30];
14      int quantity;
15      float price;
16      float sub_total;
17      float tax;
18
19      clrscr();
20      printf( "\n\nEnter your last name => " );
21      scanf( "%s", name );
22      printf( "\n\nEnter the name of the product => " );
23      scanf( "%s", product );
24      printf( "\n\n Enter the quantity and price => " );
25      scanf( "%d %f", &quantity, &pric e );
26
27      sub_total = calc_sub_total( quantity, price );
28      tax = calc_tax( sub_total );
29
30      clrscr();
31      printf( "\n\nOrder Information\n\n" );
32      printf( "Name: %s\n", name );
33      printf( "Product ordered: %s\n\n", product );
34      printf( "Quantity ordered: %d\n\n", quantity );
35      printf( "Price per unit: $%3.2f\n", price );
36      printf( "Sub total:     $%3.2f\n", sub_total );
37      printf( "Tax:           $%3.2f\n", tax );
38      printf( "Total:         $%3.2f\n", ( sub_total + tax ) );
39  }
40
41  float calc_sub_total( int quantity, float price )
42  {
43    float sub_total;
44
45    sub_total = price * quantity;
46    return sub_total;
47  }
48
49  float calc_tax( float sub_total )
50  {
51    const float tax_rate = 0.06;
52
53    float tax;
54
55    tax = sub_total * tax_rate;
56    return tax;
57  }
```

Writing a program in the Integrated Development Environment is easy. Once you start Borland C++, you need to type the program, save the program, compile it, and run it.

If you start Borland C++ and you don't have an edit screen, you should create one. Use the **New** command from the **File** menu to create a new edit screen. Your cursor will then be placed at the top of the screen.

Borland C++ has many handy editing features built into its program editor. But you do not have to learn all these features to get started quickly. When you are entering your program, you will find that the cursor-movement and text-editing keys work the way you expect. These basic editing keys are all you need to enter the program quickly and correctly.

As you type the `order.c` program, be sure to save it frequently. If you used **File New** to create a new edit screen, you will need to assign a name to your program file. When you are ready to save the program, press F2 to bring up the Save Editor File dialog box. Type the name of the file and press Enter. Don't worry about adding the file name extension; Borland C++ automatically adds it for you.

Now that you have typed and saved your program, you are ready to compile and run it. Borland C++ enables you to compile and run a program with two keystrokes. Just press Ctrl-F9, and Borland C++ does the rest. You will see a status box that tells how much progress the compiler has made on the program. When the compiler is finished, the *user screen* appears. This is where your program is displayed as Borland C++ executes it. You can interact with the program just as if you were running it from the DOS prompt. When the program ends, the IDE editor screen becomes active again. If you want to see the user screen again, just press Alt-F5. This screen will be displayed until you press another key.

The user screen is one of the features that make Borland C++ productive. The screen enables you to see your program run without leaving the programming environment. Your program works just as it would from the DOS prompt, even though the program is running in a window in the Borland C++ IDE. Facilities like the user screen make programming in the IDE more efficient than programming with stand-alone editors, compilers, and debuggers.

Now that you know how to use the IDE to enter and compile a program, it's time to see how the program works. Refer to listing 1.2 as the `order.c` program is discussed.

In listing 1.2, lines 1 and 2 are a brief comment about what the program does. Comments will help other people understand what you are trying to do, and also jog your memory if you haven't looked at the program for a while. In addition to comments, blank lines can make your program easier to read. Using extra blank lines helps you separate the program into logical units. You do not have to worry about the blank lines causing problems because such lines are ignored by the compiler.

Lines 4 and 5 tell the preprocessor to include the `stdio.h` and `stdlib.h` header files. These two header files contain declarations for the standard input/ output and library functions. Because these two header files contain declarations for so many basic functions, they are included in most C programs.

Lines 7 and 8 are the global declarations for the program. Global declarations declare variables and functions that can be used anywhere in the source file. Notice that this program uses only function declarations; there are no global variable declarations.

Each of the function declarations in lines 7 and 8 can be broken into three parts: the return type, the name of the function, and the argument list. The declaration for `calc_sub_total` is in line 7. The first item in line 7, the word `float`, indicates that the `calc_sub_total` function returns a floating-point number. The second item is, of course, the name of the function. The third part of the `calc_sub_total` declaration is the argument list. This list indicates that `calc_sub_total` requires two arguments, one an integer number and the other a floating-point number. The function in line 8, `calc_tax`, returns a floating-point number and requires only one floating-point argument. Notice that each of the declarations ends with a semicolon.

The `main()` function begins in line 10. The empty parentheses following the word `main` indicate that no arguments are passed to this function. The braces in lines 11 and 39 show where the `main()` function begins and ends.

Lines 12–17 are declarations for six variables used in the `main()` function. The first two variables, `name` and `product`, are character arrays. A character array is a *string* of characters that are stored together. Both `name` and `product` are composed of thirty characters. The third variable, in line 14, is the integer variable `quantity`. An integer variable stores a whole number. The last three variables—`price`, `sub_total`, and `tax`—are floating-point variables. Each of the floating-point variables can hold a number that has a fractional part. All the variables declared in lines 12–17 are local to the `main()` function. In other words, the variables declared in lines 12–17 can be used only inside the `main()` function.

Lines 19–25 contain the C code that clears the screen, prompts you for information, and retrieves the information. Each of the statements on these lines is a function call. Each statement calls a function that performs a special task. The `clrscr()` statement is a function call to a function that clears the video screen. The `printf()` statement is a function call that prints formatted information. In this case, the `printf()` statement prints a string on the monitor. The characters `\n` in the `printf()` statement instruct `printf()` to generate a carriage return/linefeed signal. The `scanf()` statement is a call to a function that retrieves information. In the `scanf()` statement, the characters `%s`, `%d`, and `%f` tell `scanf()` to retrieve a string, an integer, and a floating-point number, respectively. The values retrieved by `scanf()` are stored in the variables found in the last part of the `scanf()` statement.

Lines 27 and 28 are calls to user-defined functions, which are functions you create and include in your programs. In a function call, the values of the argument variables are passed to the user-defined function. The values are then used in the user defined-function, and another value is passed back. Look at the following statement:

```
answer = my_func( arg1, arg2 );
```

The user-defined function `my_func()` is passed the values of the arguments `arg1` and `arg2`. `my_func` performs its calculations and returns a value, which is then assigned to the variable `answer`. The function calls in lines 27 and 28 work the same way.

Lines 30–38 simply print the results of all the calculations. Line 30 clears the screen, and lines 31–38 print the report, using the `printf()` function. `printf()` lets you easily format and display data.

Lines 41–47 list the function definition for the user-defined function `calc_sub_total()`. Notice that the first line of the function definition looks just like a function declaration, but without a semicolon. The missing semicolon tells the compiler that the code which follows defines what the function is supposed to do. The compiler looks for opening and closing braces to define what is contained in the function.

The variables in the user-defined function `calc_sub_total()` have the same names as the variables in the `main()` function. The variables in these two functions, however, are completely separate. Only the *values* of the variables are passed from `main()` to `calc_sub_total()`. Passing the values of variables from one function to another is called, naturally, *pass by value*.

Line 46 contains a return statement, which passes the value of its argument back to the calling function. In other words, the return statement in `calc_sub_total()` passes a value back to the `main()` function.

Lines 49–57 contain another user-defined function. At the last matched brace, the compiler knows that it has come to the end of the program. If you do not have opening and closing braces properly matched, your program may not do what you want it to do.

Introducing the Library Functions

The purpose of any computer program is the manipulation of data. A program inputs data, processes the data, and then outputs the results. In C, each of these steps is accomplished with the built-in library functions.

Borland C++ comes with an extensive set of built-in library functions that helps you input, process, and output data. This section shows you how to start using some of the most helpful library functions. First, you see how to get data into your program. Second, you learn how to output the results of your program. Third, you are introduced to functions that let you manipulate the data read into your program.

Using Some Basic Input Functions

For the programs you write to be useful, they must be able to input data. Even a program as simple as the DOS CHKDSK program has provisions for the user to specify options. This section introduces you to the C input functions. You learn how to use two of the most popular groups of input functions.

C has two main families of input functions: the `get...()` functions and the `scanf()` functions. The `get...()` functions read character data—either a single character or a whole string. And the `scanf()` functions input formatted information, which can include numbers and text.

Before you learn about the I/O functions, you need to learn about streams. As you start using the I/O functions, you will see that, generally, you will be controlling streams instead of files. You will see also that controlling a stream is easier than controlling a file.

Simply put, a stream is a representation of a file. Opening a file associates a stream with that file. After the file is opened, you can use I/O functions that control the stream. When you control the stream, you are indirectly controlling the file.

The concept of streams was developed to allow programmers to write programs that could be used on different kinds of computers. Streams let programmers write device-independent programs. A device-independent program is one that can be compiled and run on almost any computer. The reason that a program can be compiled on different computers is that the stream type function calls are usually made the same way in every compiler. The compiler maker gives you a standard stream type I/O function and does the hard work of controlling the I/O hardware for you.

The hiding of the actual control of the I/O hardware is what makes stream type I/O functions so easy to use. The next few sections show you how to start controlling your data by using Borland C++'s stream type I/O functions.

The *get...()* Functions

The first group of input functions includes two functions that read single characters: getc() and getche(). Another function, gets(), reads a whole string. This section covers all three functions.

getc() is a function-like macro that reads a single character from a stream you specify. You use the following syntax for getc():

```
int getc( FILE *stream );
```

This statement simply means that getc() returns an integer value from the stream you specify. The integer value that is returned is the value of the character that was read. The stream argument is a *pointer* to a stream.

Take a look at this example:

```
int char_in;
...
char_in = getc( stdin );
printf( "The input character was %d", char_in );
```

Here getc() has an argument that points to the stream associated with the standard input device, the keyboard. getc() reads a character from the keyboard and stores the integer value of that character in the char_in variable. The printf() statement just prints a short message and the character you entered.

Other functions in the get...() family, such as getche(), do not require a stream argument. Note the following syntax for getche():

```
int getche( void );
```

Notice that the argument list for getche() is void. In other words, getche() does not require any arguments at all. getche() is written so that it always reads a character from the keyboard.

The value returned by getche() is the integer value of the character that was read. The return value is the same as that returned by the getc() function.

The getc() and getche() functions have two important differences. First, the getche() function does not require a stream argument. getche() reads directly from the keyboard. Second, the getche() function bypasses the normal C streams and echoes the input character directly to the screen, using a BIOS (Basic Input/Ouput System) call.

Some functions in the `get...()` family work with strings instead of characters. In C, a *string* is simply an array of characters, such as a name or text stored in a file. By using strings, you can work with groups of characters instead of single characters. `gets()` is a good example of an input function that works with strings.

The `gets()` function reads a string from the standard input device, `stdin`. You use this syntax for `gets()`:

```
char *gets( char *s );
```

`gets()` reads a string from the standard input device and stores that string in the character array pointed to in the function's argument list.

The following example shows how you can use the `gets()` function:

```
char name[30];

printf( "Enter your name => " );
gets( name );
printf( "Hello %s.", name );
```

Here `gets()` inputs your name and stores it in the character array name. `gets()` stores the string it reads in the array *pointed to* in the argument list. Notice that the argument list consists of the variable `name`. At first, you might not think that `name` is a pointer, but remember that the name of an array is a pointer to the first character in that array.

The *scanf()* Function

The other group of input functions is the `scanf()` family of functions. The `scanf()` function has several varieties, but only the basic version is introduced here.

The `scanf()` function performs formatted input. In other words, `scanf()` inputs data in a predefined, or formatted, sequence. The sequence in which data will be input is determined by you.

Listing 1.3 shows a simple program that uses the `scanf()` function to input integer and string data at the same time.

In listing 1.3, lines 8–11 declare the variables to be used in the program. Lines 13–20 print the program instructions and the prompt. In line 21, `scanf()` reads two integers and a string. In the `scanf()` function, the string in quotation marks is called the *format string*. This string tells `scanf()` what kind of data to input. The rest of the arguments in the `scanf()` function call are variables in which the input data will be stored.

Listing 1.3. `scandemo.c.` *A program that demonstrates the* `scanf()` *function.*

```
1   /* SCANDEMO.C - This program demonstrates scanf(). */
2   #include <stdio.h>
3   #include <stdlib.h>
4   #include <string.h>
5
6   main()
7   {
8     int num1;
9     int num2;
10    char operation[4];
11    int comp_result;
12
13    printf( "This program lets you input two numbers and\n" );
14    printf( "the type of mathematical operation \n" );
15    printf( "for the numbers. At the INPUT > prompt,\n" );
16    printf( "enter two numbers and the operation to be\n" );
17    printf( "performed. ADD for addition, SUB for\n" );
18    printf( "subtraction.\n\n" );
19
20    printf( "INPUT > " );
21    scanf( "%d %d %s", &num1, &num2, operation );
22
23    comp_result = strcmp( "ADD", operation );
24    if( comp_result == 0 )
25      printf( "The sum equals %d\n", num1 + num2 );
26    else
27      printf( "The difference is %d\n", num1 - num2 );
28
29    return 0;
30  }
```

`scanf()` requires that you list the address of each variable in which data will be stored. That is why the variables `num1` and `num2` are preceded by the & sign. The & sign indicates that the address of the variable is being used and not the variable itself. Notice that the character-array variable, `operation`, is not preceded by the & sign. The name of a character array is equivalent to the address of the first character of the array. Therefore, you do not have to precede the character array's name with the & symbol to get the address of the array.

In line 23, the string-comparison function, `strcmp()`, compares the input string with the string `ADD`. If the two strings match, the `strcmp()` function returns a value of zero. The value returned by `strcmp()` determines which branch of the `if()` statement, in lines 24–27, will be executed. If the value returned by `strcmp()` is zero, the first branch in the `if()` statement, line 25, will be executed. If the value returned by `strcmp()` is not zero, the second branch of the `if()` statement, line 27, will be executed.

In summary, the `scanf()` function is used to input data. The data that `scanf()` retrieves does not have to be a specific type. You determine the type of data input by `scanf()`. The arguments for the `scanf()` function consist of a format string and a list of addresses of variables. The format string determines what kind of data will be input, and the addresses determine where the data will be stored.

Using Some Basic Output Functions

After your program has processed its data, the program must be able to output the results. You need not only input functions but also output functions. The output functions covered in this section include functions that output characters, strings, and formatted data.

Like the input functions, the output functions are grouped in two families. One family of functions, the `put...()` functions, outputs character and string data. The other family of functions, the `printf()` functions, outputs formatted data.

The *put...()* Functions

This section introduces two `put...()` functions: `putc()` and `puts()`. The `putc()` function writes one character at a time, and the `puts()` function writes a whole string.

`putc()` is a function-like macro that writes a single character to the stream you specify. `putc()` requires two arguments: the first argument tells `putc()` what character it will write, and the second argument tells `putc()` where to write the character. You use the following syntax for `putc()`:

```
int putc( int c, FILE *stream );
```

The first argument in the argument list is the integer value of the character to be output. The second argument is a pointer to the stream where the character will be written. The `stream` is just a pointer associated with a particular file or device. `putc()` does return an integer value. If `putc()` successfully writes the character, the value of the character is returned. If `putc()` is unsuccessful, the value of EOF is returned.

The following example shows how you can use `putc( )`:

```
int c;
...
for( c = 65; c <= 90; c++ ) putc( c, stdout );
```

`putc( )` is called with two arguments, `c` and `stdout`. The argument `c` is an integer variable used as a loop counter in the `for( )` statement. On each loop of the `for( )` statement, `putc( )` writes the character value of `c`, the loop counter. `putc( )` writes the character to the device pointed to by `stdout`, which is a pointer to the standard output device, usually the video screen.

Sometimes, writing a single character is not enough. You may need to write a complete string at one time. In that case, you can use the `puts( )` function.

The following example shows how `puts( )` can write a string to the screen:

```
char my_string[] = "This is a test!"
...
puts( my_string );
```

You can see that the `puts( )` function requires an argument which points to a string. In this case, `puts( )` will write the string that is pointed to by `my_string`. On the first line of the example, `my_string` is declared as a character array, which is a string, and assigned an initial value. The `puts( )` function sends the string to `stdout` and appends a newline character to the end of the string.

The *printf()* Function

The character and string output functions do a good job when you need to output only character-based information. At times, however, you may need to write all kinds of data, not just character data. You then use the `printf( )` function. `printf( )` is just one of the functions found in the `printf( )` family of functions. Although all the functions in the `printf( )` family output formatted data, the functions differ in their arguments and in where the output is sent. See Chapter 6 for more information about the other functions in the `printf( )` family.

With `printf( )`, you can generate formatted output. The function enables you to control the appearance, or format, of your output data.

The syntax for the `printf( )` function looks like this:

```
int printf( const char *format [,argument, ...] );
```

You can see that the argument list for `printf()` is composed of two parts. The first part is the format string, which controls the appearance of the output data. The second part consists of the data that `printf()` will output.

The format string controls how the `printf()` function formats and displays its arguments. This string contains plain text and conversion specifiers. These specifiers determine what kind of data is to be output and in what format that data will appear. The argument list must contain enough variables to match each of the conversion specifiers. If there are not enough variables, the results will be unpredictable.

The next example shows a `printf()` function with a format string that contains regular text and conversion specifiers:

```
printf( "The answer is: %d", sum );
```

In a `printf()` function, the format string is the first argument in the list, and the string is enclosed in quotation marks. Note that this format string contains text information and one conversion specifier. The text in the format string will be printed just as it appears in the `printf()` function call. The conversion specifier, which is preceded by the % character, will be replaced before it is printed. In this example, the conversion specifier will be replaced by the integer value stored in the variable `sum`.

You may have noticed `\n` in some of the `printf()` format strings. `\n` (the newline character) is a special character that tells `printf()` to include the carriage return and linefeed characters when the string is printed. Whenever you need to go to a new line, you can therefore use `\n`.

Using Some Format-Conversion Functions

Format-conversion functions convert a value from one data type to another. The `atof()` function, for example, converts a string to a floating-point number. Another example is the `atoi()` function, which converts a string to an integer.

At first, such functions may not seem useful. Suppose, however, that you have just logged off your favorite bulletin board, and you've got a disk full of financial figures. You probably downloaded the information as some form of text file, and you now have a disk containing information in character format. You can read the information, but you can't add it, subtract it, or perform any computations on it. In this case, you need to read your text file and convert all the character-based numeric information to regular C numeric data types. Borland C++ provides 17 functions and macros to help solve your conversion needs.

The following sections introduce the atoi() and toupper() functions and show how useful they can be in your programs.

The *atoi()* Function

The atoi() function converts a string value to an integer value. The syntax for atoi() looks like this:

```
int atoi( const char *s );
```

You can see from this declaration that the atoi() function requires a pointer to a string as an argument and that the function returns an integer value. The data that atoi() will accept has some limitations. When scanning a string, atoi() looks for the following characters:

❑ *A whitespace character.* Whitespace is composed of space and tab characters; its presence is optional.

❑ *A sign character.* The sign character is optional.

❑ *A string of digit characters.* The string of digit characters ends when a nondigit character is encountered.

The value returned by atoi() is a regular integer value. If atoi() is able to convert the string, it returns the integer value of the converted string. If atoi() is unsuccessful, it returns the value 0.

Listing 1.4 shows how the atoi() function is used in a simple program. strtoint.c reads a string, converts the string to an integer, and then prints the integer value.

Listing 1.4. strtoint.c. *A program that converts a string to an integer.*

```
1   /*    STRTOINT.C  Converting a string value to an integer
2        value.  */
3
4   #include <stdio.h>
5   #include <stdlib.h>
6   #include <conio.h>
7
8   main()
9   {
10    char num_str[6];
11    int  num_int;
```

```
12
13      clrscr( );
14      printf( "Enter an integer number => " );
15      gets( num_str );
16      num_int = atoi( num_str );
17      printf( "\n\nYour integer was %d", num_int );
18  }
```

In listing 1.4, lines 10 and 11 are the variable declarations for the program. Line 10 declares a character array that is six characters long. This array will actually hold only five characters; the last space is used for the terminating null character. Line 11 declares a simple integer variable.

In line 15, the gets( ) function reads a string from the stdin stream. The string is stored in the num_str character array. In line 16, the atoi( ) function converts the string value to an integer value. atoi( ) takes the string in num_str and converts it to an integer value that will be stored in num_int. Line 17 uses the printf( ) function to print the results of the conversion.

The *toupper( )* Function

The toupper( ) function converts lowercase alphabetic characters to uppercase. One use of the toupper( ) function is to convert to uppercase the lowercase letters input by a program's user. Converting input to a uniform pattern can save you much programming time and effort.

Even though toupper( ) converts lowercase characters to uppercase, the function works with *integer* values. The integer values that toupper( ) uses are the ASCII character values. Note the syntax for the toupper( ) function declaration:

```
int toupper( int c );
```

You can see that toupper( ) requires an integer argument and returns an integer value. The argument passed to toupper( ) is the ASCII value of any character between *a* and *z*. The return value is the ASCII value of the corresponding uppercase letter. If the argument is not a lowercase letter between *a* and *z*, toupper( ) does not perform a conversion and returns the value of the argument passed to it.

Listing 1.5 shows one way you can use toupper( ) in a program. upperc.c reads a character from the keyboard, converts it to an uppercase letter, and displays the result.

Listing 1.5. upperc.c. *A program that uses the* toupper() *function to convert lowercase letters to uppercase.*

```
1   /* UPPERC.C   Convert a lowercase letter to an uppercase
2   letter using the toupper() function.   */
3   #include <stdio.h>
4   #include <stdlib.h>
5   #include <conio.h>
6
7   main()
8   {
9      int in_char;
10     int out_char;
11
12     clrscr();
13     printf( "Enter a single character => " );
14     in_char = getche();
15     out_char = toupper( in_char );
16     printf( "\n\nThe uppercase character is: %c",
17             out_char );
18  }
```

In listing 1.5, lines 9 and 10 set up two variables to hold the integer values of the input character and the converted character.

In line 14, the getche() function reads a character from the keyboard and echoes that character to the screen. In line 15, the toupper() function converts the input character to an uppercase letter if possible. toupper() stores the result of its conversion in the out_char variable. Lines 16 and 17 are a printf() statement that displays the converted value.

Exercises

The following exercises give you practice in installing, configuring, and using the IDE.

1. Install the Borland C++ package with all of its memory models. Tell the INSTALL program that you want to install TCTOUR and unpack the program examples.

2. Run the TCTOUR program, which is found in the TOUR subdirectory under the main Borland C++ directory.

3. Use the **O**ptions menu to turn the full menu display on and off.

4. If your monitor supports more than 25 display lines, use BCINST to change the number of lines displayed.

5. Write a program that compares the `getc( )` and `getche( )` functions. Use the `putc( )` function to display the result.

6. Write a program that uses the `puts( )` and `printf( )` functions to display messages.

7. Write a program that uses the `scanf( )` function to read name and age data. Also include `gets( )` to read a comment string. Use `printf( )` to print the results.

8. Write a program that demonstrates the use of the `toupper( )` function.

Summary

In this chapter, you learned how to install, configure, and run Borland C++. You learned some basic C programming concepts, and you became acquainted with many useful functions. The following important points were covered:

❏ *Installing and configuring Borland C++ is easy.* You install Borland C++ and its companion products by using the INSTALL program that came with each of the Borland C++ products. Once Borland C++ is installed, you can use the BCINST program to modify Borland C++'s default values. The **O**ptions menu also lets you configure many of Borland C++'s features.

❏ *You can specify several command-line options when you start Borland C++.* The command-line options enable you to specify what source or project file will be loaded and how Borland C++ will use your computer's hardware.

❏ *The Integrated Development Environment (IDE) is Borland's best programming environment yet.* The IDE contains all the programming tools you need in one easy-to-use package, including utilities for writing, testing, debugging, and managing your programming projects.

❏ *The two main parts of the IDE are the menu system and the window system.* The menu system gives you access to Borland C++'s programming tools. The window system is where you write your program, see the program run, and get information on the program from Borland C++.

❏ *There are four basic parts of a C program: preprocessor directives, global declarations, the* main( ) *function, and user-defined functions.* Preprocessor directives are used to include other source files and to define macros. Global declarations define functions and data that will be used throughout your program. main( ) is the only required function. Program execution always begins with main( ).

❏ *User-defined functions are ones you create.* A user-defined function is a group of C statements you put together to perform a task. Generally, a user-defined function has a single purpose, and all the statements in the function help accomplish that purpose.

❏ *Some functions input characters, strings, and formatted data.* The getche( ) function reads a single character at a time, and gets( ) reads a whole string. If you need to retrieve data of different types, you can use the scanf( ) function. scanf( ) is composed of two parts: the format string and the argument list. The format string lets you specify the kind of data to be retrieved and the order in which the data will be retrieved. The argument list is a list of addresses where retrieved data will be stored.

❏ *Borland C++ has many useful functions to output data, a few of which were introduced in the chapter.* The putc( ) function writes a single character at a time, and the puts( ) function outputs a whole string. One of the most useful functions in C is the print( ) function, which enables you to write many different types of data. Like scanf( ), printf( ) is composed of two parts: a format string and a variable argument list. The format string specifies what kind of data is to be output and the format in which the data will be output. The variable argument list specifies the data to be output.

❏ *Some functions convert data from one format to another.* You saw how the atoi( ) function works, converting a string of ASCII digits to an integer value. And you saw how the toupper( ) function converts lowercase alphabetic characters to uppercase.

2

Understanding the Foundations of C

In the first chapter, you learned how to use the new Integrated Development Environment (IDE) and how to write basic C programs. This chapter focuses on the foundations of the C language. You learn how your program is compiled and executed, how the data in your program is handled, how to write C statements, and how macros are used.

Laying the Foundations

This section helps you understand two important programming concepts: the generation of executable programs from your source code, and the flow of execution in your program. You first see how your program is transformed as its source code is compiled to an executable program. You then see how the flow of execution in your program can be controlled.

Understanding Source, Object, and Load Modules

When you sit down at your computer and type a program, you are creating a source file (the source module)—a program in an English-like language you can understand. At this point, you cannot run the program because the computer does not understand your source file. Processing must be performed to convert the source file to a language the computer can understand. This section explains the process of converting your C program into an executable program the computer can run.

Figure 2.1 illustrates the program-creation process and the type of file created at each step.

Fig. 2.1. The creation of source, object, and load modules.

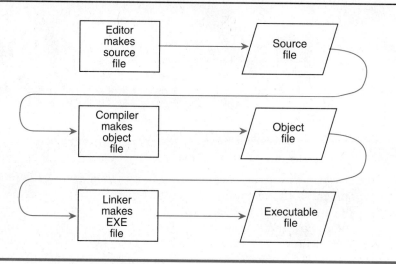

The first step in the program-creation process is to use your text editor to write a C source file (a list of instructions for the computer to follow). The source file is written in C, an English-like language that emulates the way the computer works. The computer, however, cannot understand the English-like instructions you have written.

For the computer to understand the instructions you have given it, you must convert your program from an English-like language to one the computer can understand. This is the job of the compiler. It converts your C language source file into an object module composed of machine-language instructions.

The compiler performs the following actions to convert your C language program into a machine-language program:

❑ *Your source file is read and converted into a series of preprocessing tokens and whitespace characters.* In this phase, special characters are converted, and individual statements occupying two or more lines are spliced together. The preprocessing tokens are simply elements with which the compiler can work. For example, operators, constants, and keywords are tokens. Whitespace characters include space characters, tab characters, and comments. At this point, comments are deleted and replaced by a single space.

❏ *Preprocessing directives are executed.* These directives include instructions like #include and #define. The #include directive instructs the compiler to read in source code from another file. The source code is then put through the same initial processing your program received. Any macros that were defined are expanded at this time.

❏ *Further character and string processing is performed.* Your program is analyzed for correct syntax and semantics. During this phase of compilation, any illegal coding mistakes are caught.

❏ *If no serious errors are found, an object file is created.*

The preprocessor's #include directive enables you to compile more than one source file at a time. The #include directive causes the preprocessor to stop processing your source file and to merge into it the file specified in #include.

The following directive, for example, instructs the preprocessor to halt temporarily the processing of your program:

```
#include <stdio.h>
```

The preprocessor reads the stdio.h header file and includes the C code in that file with your source code. #include is not limited to using header files but can include any file you specify. In Chapter 3, the section "Including Library Functions in Your Program" explores the #include directive in more detail.

At this point, you have your source file, which you can understand, and an object module (a translation of the source file), which the computer can understand. Although the compiler has created a machine-language object module, the computer still cannot execute the object module. One more step must be performed before an executable program is created.

The last step in creating an executable program is to process your object module with the *linker*. The linker combines the object module that the compiler created with special object modules that came with the compiler. The result is an executable program, or a *load module*. The special object modules that are combined with your object module contain an extra set of machine-language instructions. These instructions cause the computer to perform a setup routine that is necessary before your program can be run.

Borland C++ has automated the process of creating executable programs. You don't have to worry about the intermediate steps involved in creating an executable program. Once you have created a source file, you need to execute just one command to have Borland C++ compile and link your program. To compile and link your source file, you select the Make EXE File option under the main menu's Compile command.

Understanding Program Logic and Execution Flow

Usually, your program is executed one line at a time and in sequence. Executing one line after another is fine most of the time. Your program does not always operate in a vacuum, however. When things change, the program needs to adjust to those changes. You can then use conditional instructions (if, if-else, and switch). To perform certain tasks repeatedly, you can use loop instructions (do-while, while, and for).

Using Conditional Instructions

When you are dealing with changing situations, you need to execute different groups of code based on some condition. Two tools can help you handle changing conditions: if and switch. The if statement handles one or two conditions, and the switch statement deals with multiple conditions.

The basic form of the if statement is this:

```
if( expression is true )
    execute statement or group of statements;
```

This pattern indicates that if the expression inside the parentheses is true, the following statement or group of statements is executed. To see how the if statement works, look at an example:

```
if( a > b )
    printf( "A is greater than B" );
```

The expression being evaluated is a > b. If a really is greater than b, the following printf() statement is executed. If a is not greater than b, printf() is not executed.

The question now is, "What tools can you use to evaluate expressions?"

Two basic groups of tools are available. The first group is the *relational operators* (see table 2.1), and the second group is the *logical operators* (see table 2.2).

Table 2.1. *Relational operators.*

Operator	Explanation	Example
>	Greater than	2 > 1
<	Less than	1 < 2
==	Equal to	1 == 1
!=	Not equal to	1 != 2
>=	Greater than or equal to	2 >= x
<=	Less than or equal to	1 <= x

The relational operators compare two values. If the values compare correctly according to the relational operator, the expression is true. For example, the expression 2 > 1 yields a true value. If the values do not compare correctly, the expression is false. The expression 1 > 2 yields a false value because 1 is not greater than 2.

Table 2.2. *Logical operators.*

Operator		Explanation
&&	(AND)	Yields true if both expressions are true
||	(OR)	Yields true if either expression is true
!	(NOT)	Reverses the true or false condition of an expression

When you use logical operators, you can evaluate more than one condition at a time. Each expression is evaluated, and the results of the expressions are logically compared. The following example demonstrates the OR operator:

```
if( ( 2 > 1 ) || ( 2 > 3 ) )
    printf( "The final result was true." );
```

The first expression evaluates as true because 2 is greater than 1. The second expression evaluates as false because 2 is not greater than 3. However, the whole if statement evaluates as true because one of the two expressions *ORed* together is true.

You can also use another form of the `if` statement: `if-else`. The syntax of an `if-else` statement is this:

```
if( expression is true )
    execute the first statement or group of statements;
else
    execute the second statement or group of statements;
```

Like the first type of `if`, the `if-else` statement evaluates the expression in parentheses. If the expression is true, the statement or group of statements following the `if` is executed. Unlike `if`, however, `if-else` adds another piece. If the expression in parentheses evaluates as false, the second statement or group of statements is executed.

The `if-else` statement can be more flexible than the `if` statement. Note the following use of `if-else`:

```
if( line_count < 66 )
    line_count++;
else
    line_count = 0;
```

In this code fragment, the value of the variable `line_count` is checked. If the value of `line_count` is less than 66, the value of `line_count` is incremented by 1. However, if the value of `line_count` is 66 or greater, the value of `line_count` is reset to 0. In that case, `if-else` is more flexible than `if` because `if-else` provides different responses for two different instances.

You may have noticed from this discussion that after an expression is evaluated, the next statement or group of statements is executed. To execute more than one statement, you need to be aware of one thing: if you have multiple statements, you must enclose the group of statements in a set of braces. The reason is that after the `if` statement evaluates an expression, `if` looks to execute only *one* statement.

When you are dealing with more than two conditions, an `if-else` construction will not meet your needs. In that case, you have two alternatives. The first is to write a set of nested `if-else` statements, and the second is to use a `switch` statement.

Writing a series of nested `if-else` statements is legal in C. The compiler won't flag a nested `if-else` as an error or even a warning. Writing a nested `if-else` statement is difficult, however. With many levels, you can easily lose track of what is happening. Instead of using a nested `if-else` statement, you usually can use a `switch` statement, which is easier both to program and to read.

Here is the general form of the `switch` statement:

```
switch( value )
{
    case value: statement or group of statements;
    ...
    default: statement or group of statements;
}
```

The `switch` statement is composed of several parts. The `value` at the top of the statement represents the value of the variable condition you will evaluate. The word `case` is required; it signals the beginning of the code that handles a particular condition. `default` indicates the beginning of the code that is executed if no `case` value matches the conditional value. The `default` selection is optional.

When the `switch` statement finds a `case` that matches the condition, `switch` starts executing the statement immediately following that `case`. Execution continues until the end of the `switch` statement is reached or until a `break` is encountered. Listing 2.1 demonstrates the use of `switch`.

Listing 2.1. `swdemo.c`. *A program that uses a* `switch` *statement.*

```
1   /* SWDEMO.C   A demonstration of the switch statement */
2
3   #include <stdio.h>
4   #include <stdlib.h>
5   #include <conio.h>
6
7   main()
8   {
9       char char_in;
10
11  clrscr();
12
13  printf( "---- Diagnostic Menu ----\n\n" );
14  printf( "A: System Tests\n" );
15  printf( "B: Video Tests\n" );
16  printf( "C: Hard Drive Tests\n" );
17  printf( "D: Keyboard Tests\n\n" );
18  printf( "Enter a letter to select the tests => " );
19
20  char_in = getche();
```

Listing 2.1. *continues*

Listing 2.1. *continued*

```
21   printf( "\n\n\n");
22   char_in = toupper( char_in );
23
24   switch( char_in )
25   {
26     case 'A': printf( "You chose the system tests.\n" );
27             break;
28     case 'B': printf( "You chose the video tests.\n" );
29             break;
30     case 'C': printf( "You chose the drive tests.\n" );
31             break;
32     case 'D': printf( "You chose the keyboard tests.\n" );
33             break;
34     default : printf( "You did not choose a test.\n" );
35       }
36   }
```

Listing 2.1 is a simple menu program. Using a switch statement instead of a series of nested if-else statements makes this code much easier to follow.

Lines 13–18 print the main menu screen. Lines 20–22 read the menu selection and convert it to an uppercase letter if needed. Converting the selection to uppercase lets the switch statement use half the space it would otherwise need.

Lines 24–35 are the switch statement. Line 24 contains the variable to be checked, char_in. Lines 26–32 select the right action for the menu selection. Notice that each case is followed by a break. The break tells the switch statement to stop executing instructions and to jump just past the end of the switch statement. Line 34 is the default selection. The statements following default are executed if the value of the char_in variable does not match any of the cases.

Using Loop Instructions

Some operations need to be repeated over and over. A loop defines a block of code that is repeatedly executed. Depending on the kind of loop you use, the block of code could be executed a set number of times or until a certain condition is met. Borland C++ provides three loop structures: do-while, while, and for.

The `do-while` loop is a *postchecked* loop. This loop executes a block of code as long as a specified condition is true. `do-while` is a postchecked loop because it checks the controlling condition *after* the code is executed. You use the following general form for `do-while`:

```
do statement or group of statements
   while expression is true
```

The `do-while` loop is useful when you have a condition that you do not, or cannot, check before the body of the loop is processed. Consider the following example:

```
do{
   printf( "\n\nEnter a letter => " );
   c = getche();
   c = toupper( c );
   printf( "\nYour uppercase letter is: %c", c);
} while( c != 'X' );
```

Here you are prompted to enter a letter that will be converted to uppercase and displayed. The value of the input character controls the loop. Because the input character is read during the middle of the loop, that character's value cannot be checked until the end of the loop.

The `while` loop is a *prechecked* loop. Like `do-while`, `while` executes a block of code as long as a certain condition is true. However, the `while` loop checks the conditional expression at the beginning of the loop, not at the end. The `while` loop takes the following form:

```
while expression is true
   execute statement or group of statements
```

The `while` loop is useful when the state of the controlling expression could adversely affect the function of the loop. Listing 2.2 shows how you can use the `while` loop to dump the contents of a file.

Listing 2.2. `fdump.c.` *A program that uses the* `while` *loop.*

```
1    /*  FDUMP.C  File dump utility using a while loop */
2    #include <stdio.h>
3    #include <stdlib.h>
4
5    main()
6    {
7            FILE *f_in;
8            char c;
9
```

Listing 2.2. continues

Listing 2.2. continued

```
10          if( ( f_in = fopen( "\\test.txt", "rt" ) ) == NULL )
11          {
12              printf( "Unable to open file. Aborting.\n" );
13              return 1;
14      }
15
16  while( !feof( f_in ) ) {
17          c = fgetc( f_in );
18          putchar( c );
19      }
20  }
```

Listing 2.2 shows how a while loop drives a routine that reads a disk file and prints its contents on the screen. Line 7 declares a FILE object that points to a stream. In line 10, this stream pointer is assigned a value that points to the stream associated with the file TEST.TXT. The fopen() function tries to open the file. If fopen() is successful, it returns a pointer to the file's stream; if fopen() is unsuccessful, it returns NULL. If the fopen() function in line 10 returns NULL, an error message is printed, and the program ends.

Lines 16–19 contain the entire while loop that reads and writes the data file. Line 16 contains the expression that controls the operation of the loop. The feof() function in line 16 checks for the end-of-file indicator on the stream pointed to by f_in. The while loop runs as long as the end of the file is not encountered. In lines 17 and 18, the body of the loop reads a character from the data file and prints that character on the screen. Finally, the brace in line 19 closes the body of the loop.

If you want to execute the loop a certain number of times and the execution does not depend on another condition, you can use a for loop. Here is its structure:

```
for( starting value; condition; changes )
    execute a statement or a group of statements
```

The three values in the control section of a for loop determine how many times the loop will be executed. You can specify these values in many different ways. This discussion focuses on the most common way to control a for loop.

The *starting value* specifies a value at which counting will begin. The *condition* expression limits the for loop to a certain number of iterations, and the *changes* expression indicates how much the starting value will be incremented or decremented on each pass of the loop. Note the following typical for loop:

```
for( i = 48; i <= 122; i++ )
  printf( "\c\n", i );
```

Here the for loop uses the variable i to count from 48 (the *starting value*) to 122 (the value specified in the condition expression). The *changes* expression increments the value of i by 1 on each pass through the loop. If you run this sample code, you will see that the printf() statement uses the value of i to print the ASCII characters from 1 to z.

The next example shows no arguments in the control section of the for loop:

```
for( ; ; )
  printf( "Infinite loop" );
```

If no arguments are present, there is no condition to be met. The loop, therefore, will continue to run forever, or at least until you turn off your computer.

The break statement lets you break out of a switch statement or a loop without completing the rest of the switch or loop. The continue statement lets you start a loop over without executing the statements following the continue statement. These two statements, break and continue, give you extra flexibility in dealing with uncertain events that can occur during loop processing. Both statements are covered in greater detail in the section "Writing Loop-Control Statements" in Chapter 3.

Using the Basic Data Types

The information, or data, used by a C program is categorized by its *type*. The type of a variable tells you what kind of data the variable can contain, as well as the range of values the variable can store. This section examines the basic data types and shows you where and how they are used.

Understanding C's Basic Data Types

Any program you write manipulates some kind of data. The data your program works with comes in different sizes and types. Each type of data requires a different amount of memory for storage. To provide correct answers, your program must therefore know what type of data it is expected to process.

The C programming language has three basic types of data: integer numbers, floating-point numbers, and character data. Each of these basic data types comes in many varieties, providing you with a wide range of values.

Integers

The most basic data type is the integer, which is a numeric data type that represents whole numbers. Whole numbers do not have a fractional part.

When you want to use an integer in a program, you need to declare a variable of type `int`. Here are some examples of integer variable declarations:

```
int loop_counter;

int cookies, cakes;

int cars = 5;
```

To declare an integer, you first list the reserved word `int` and then list the name of the variable you want to use. The word `int` signals your program to set aside enough space for the integer and to assign the name following `int`—in this first declaration, `loop_counter`—to represent that memory space.

The second integer declaration lists two variables, `cookies` and `cakes`. In C, it is legal to declare multiple variables on one line. Such a declaration saves space and typing time. Use your judgment. If you try to put too many declarations on one line, your program may become unreadable.

The third declaration sets up a variable by the name of `cars` and assigns it an initial value. Assigning an initial value to a variable is legal and often useful.

You can use three different modifiers with the reserved word `int` to change the range of values that can be stored in a integer variable. These modifiers are `unsigned`, `long`, and `short`. Table 2.3 lists the various integer types, the number of bytes of memory required, and the range of values each type can store.

Table 2.3. Integer data types, sizes, and ranges.

Type	Size	Range of Values
int	2	−32,768 to 32,767
unsigned int	2	0 to 65,535
short int	2	−32,768 to 32,767
long	4	−2,147,483,648 to 2,147,483,647
unsigned long	4	0 to 4,294,967,295

Floating-Point Numbers

The second C numeric data type is the floating-point number. Unlike an integer, a floating-point number can have a fractional part. Floating-point numbers are also known as real numbers.

You use floating-point numbers when you need to express an exact mathematical quantity. Because floating-point numbers are exact, they are routinely used in scientific and financial calculations. In addition to being more precise than integers, floating-point numbers can represent values of greater or lesser magnitude. In other words, floating-point numbers can represent larger or smaller values than integer numbers.

Declaring a floating-point variable is simple. You just type the reserved word `float` and the variable name. When your program encounters the reserved word `float`, the program sets aside enough memory to hold a floating-point number, and assigns the variable name (following the word `float`) to represent that number.

The next code fragment demonstrates some basic ways to declare floating-point numbers:

```
float radius;
float principal, interest;
float mileage = 5.25;
```

The first declaration is the simplest. It declares a single variable with no initial value. The second declaration shows how you can declare multiple variables on a single line. Again, use discretion when declaring several variables on one line. Cramming too much on the line will make your program hard to follow. The third declaration shows the assignment of an initial value.

Floating-point variables come in different sizes. The larger floating-point types give better precision and range, but they also use more memory. The floating-point types are `float`, `double`, and `long double`. Table 2.4 summarizes the floating-point types, size (byte) requirements, and ranges.

Table 2.4. Floating-point types, sizes, and ranges.

Type	Size	Range
`float`	4	3.4×10^{-38} to 3.4×10^{38}
`double`	8	1.7×10^{-308} to 1.7×10^{308}
`long double`	10	3.4×10^{-4932} to 3.4×10^{4932}

As you can see from the table, floating-point variables can represent very large numbers. The trade-off for using large numbers is the amount of space required to store them. For example, every floating-point variable of type `long double` requires 10 bytes of memory. If your application is limited to a small memory space, be careful about using many large floating-point variables.

Besides providing a greater magnitude of values, `double` and `long double` provide more precise values. Table 2.5 indicates the floating-point types and their precisions.

Table 2.5. *Floating-point types and precisions.*

Type	Precision
float	7 digits of precision
double	15 digits of precision
long double	19 digits of precision

Character Data

As you have seen, C provides two good sets of data types for handling numerical data. But numbers are not the only type of data with which your programs work. Most C programs also use character data. Because character data is important to programming, C provides another data type to handle your character information.

The basic data type for character information is denoted by the reserved word `char`. A variable of type `char` can hold a value that represents a single letter.

Recall that your computer stores information in binary code. It is impossible, therefore, to store a letter directly. To get around this problem, the computer uses a numeric value to represent each letter. A variable of type `char`, then, actually stores a numeric value associated with a particular letter.

Your PC, as well as all PCs like it, uses the ASCII code to represent character data. ASCII, which refers to the American Standards Committee for Information Interchange, developed a widely recognized code that represents 128 different character values.

You use a `char` type variable to store a value representing any of the ASCII characters. An object of type `char` uses one byte of memory. Yet an object of type `char` needs only seven bits of the byte to represent any character. The remaining bit is used as a sign bit. An object of type `char` is therefore equivalent to an object of type `signed char`.

Your PC also uses an extended character set that contains another 128 characters. In all, your computer can use 256 characters. One byte can hold 256 different values if the sign bit is not used. To use both the ASCII and extended character sets, then, you must use an object of type `unsigned char`.

In summary, a `char` type object can represent the ASCII character set. An `unsigned char` type object can represent the ASCII character set and the extended character set.

You should notice that some of the library routines which work with characters actually require you to use an `int` to store the values. For example, the `getche()` function reads a character from the keyboard and returns the value of the character read. The type of the return value is not `char`; it is `int`. `char` and `int` type objects are similar and can usually be interchanged with little trouble.

Knowing Where To Define Data Objects

Now that you know what basic data types are available, you need to know where you can use them. Otherwise, your data will not be useful. This section shows you where you can declare data objects and introduces the concepts of scope and duration. Chapter 3 covers these topics in more detail.

One place that you can declare a data object is at the top of the source file, before the `main()` function. An object declared there becomes a *global variable*—a data object that can be used anywhere in the program. Listing 2.3 shows an example of a global variable.

Listing 2.3. `gvar.c`. *A program that contains a global variable.*

```
1   /*  GVAR.C  Using a global variable */
2
3   #include <stdio.h>
4   #include <stdlib.h>
5
6   int gvar;
7   void funct_1( void );
8
9   main()
10  {
11      gvar = 2;
12      funct_1();
```

Listing 2.3. continues

Listing 2.3. continued

```
13      printf( "In main()\n" );
14      printf( "gvar = %d\n\n", gvar );
15  }
16
17  void funct_1( void )
18  {
19      printf( "In fucnt1()\n" );
20      printf( "gvar = %d\n\n", gvar );
21      gvar = gvar * 2;
22  }
```

In listing 2.3, the only variable, gvar, is declared in line 6—above main() and funct_1(). Because gvar is above and outside both these functions, it can be accessed by both functions. gvar is assigned a value of 2 in line 11. Line 12 calls funct_1(). When the report in funct_1() is executed, you can see that gvar still has a value of 2. In line 21, the value of gvar is multiplied by 2, and control is then passed back to main(). When the report in main() is executed, you can see that gvar has the value it was assigned in funct_1().

The example in listing 2.3 shows that a global variable has *global scope.* The variable can therefore be accessed and used anywhere in that source file. A global variable also has *static duration*, which means that the variable is always available. In fact, room is created for global variables in your object module at compile time.

Global variables are not used much in C programming for two reasons. First, global variables make inefficient use of memory space; they are always available, even when you don't need them. Second, you can easily lose track of their values. A common mistake is to change the value of a global variable and forget that you made the change. The next time you use the global variable, it contains an unexpected value! Mistakes like this can be hard to track.

Most programs use only *local variables*. A local variable, which is declared and used inside a single function, can be accessed in only that function. Even when you call another function that uses a variable with the same name, the value of the variable in the original function remains unchanged. Listing 2.4 shows how you can use—and misuse—local variables.

Listing 2.4. *lvar.c. A program that contains local variables.*

```
1   /* LVAR.C    Using local variables. */
2
3   #include <stdio.h>
4   #include <stdlib.h>
5
6   const PI = 3.1416;
7   void square_1( void );
8   float square_2( float );
9
10  main()
11  {
12     float radius_1 = 5.0;
13     float radius_2 = 7.0;
14     float area_1;
15     float area_2;
16
17     square_1();
18     radius_2 = square_2( radius_2 );
19
20     area_1 = PI * radius_1;
21     area_2 = PI * radius_2;
22
23     printf( "Area 1 = %f\n", area_1 );
24     printf( "Area 2 = %f\n", area_2 );
25
26  }
27
28  void square_1( void )
29  {
30     float radius_1;
31
32     radius_1 = radius_1 * radius_1;
33  }
34
35  float square_2( float    radius_2 )
36  {
37     radius_2 = radius_2 * radius_2;
38     return radius_2;
39  }
```

Listing 2.4, which calculates the area of two circles, demonstrates two ways to use local variables. The area of the first circle is calculated the wrong way, and the area of the second circle is calculated the right way.

Because the radius of the first circle is declared in line 12 in the `main()` function, the variable can be accessed in `main()` only. When the `square_1()` function is called, the value of `radius_1` is unchanged even though `square_1()` manipulates a `radius_1` variable. The `radius_1` variables in `main()` and `square_1()` are completely separate although they have the same name. The result is that the variable `radius_1` in `main()` was never squared, and the value of `area_1` is therefore incorrect.

The handling of the variable values for `radius_2` is performed correctly. Notice that two `radius_2` variables are declared. One variable is declared in `main()`, and the other is declared in `square_2()`. These are completely different variables. The value of `radius_2` in `main()` is correctly calculated because the value of `radius_2` was *passed* to `square_2` properly.

Note the sequence of events in line 18. The function `square_2()` is called. `square_2()` is passed a *copy* of the value of `radius_2` in `main()`. `square_2()` then assigns the passed value to its own `radius_2` variable. The calculation is performed, and a value is finally returned. When the call to `square_2()` is completed, the value returned is assigned to `main()`'s copy of `radius_2`. Because the values of the variables were passed and returned correctly, the value of `area_2` is correct.

Local variables have *local scope*, which means that a local variable can be used in only the function in which it was declared. Local scope is the reason why two functions can have variables with the same name. Furthermore, local variables have *automatic duration*. This means that when a function is called, space is automatically allocated for the variables the function will use. When the function ends, the space for the variables is deallocated automatically. A local variable, therefore, does not retain its value from one function call to the next.

If you want a local variable in one function to have the same value as a variable in another function, you must pass a *value* to the variable in the called function. You saw this done in line 18 of listing 2.4. The function call to `square_2()` passed the value of `main()`'s variable `radius_2` to the function `square_2()`. Inside the function `square_2()`, the value passed to the function was assigned to the `radius_2` variable that is local to `square_2()`.

Writing C Expressions and Statements

Expressions and statements are the building blocks for your C functions and programs. This section explains what expressions and statements are and how you can use them. After you learn about expressions and statements, you learn how to use the C operator set.

Understanding Expressions and Statements

The terms *expression* and *statement* are used throughout this book. In most instances, these terms may seem to be synonymous. However, this is not the case. Expressions and statements have some important differences.

Basically, expressions are the pieces from which statements are made. An expression can be a group of operators and operands that computes a value, or an expression can simply refer to a data object or function.

An expression can contain three parts: operators, operands, and punctuators. *Operators* are symbols that tell the program to perform some type of computation. *Operands* are the arguments that operators require to perform a computation. *Punctuators* help define and organize the relationships of operands and operators.

Expressions can range from simple to complex. A simple expression might consist of just a single operand, and a complex expression might contain several operators and operands. A complex expression might even be composed of subexpressions. The next few lines of code are examples of expressions:

```
a
15
i + 1
j++
x * y + 4 * z
( 1 + j ) * ( x / ( 28 - y ) )
sum( a, b)
```

Notice that expressions can use constants and variables, which can be mixed freely.

The way Borland C++ evaluates the operands in an expression may not correspond to the way the operands are written. Borland C++ tries to rearrange the expression in order to produce better code. However, if an operator specifies an evaluation order for the operands, Borland C++ will not rearrange those operands.

You can use parentheses to force Borland C++ to evaluate an expression in a certain order. Note this example:

```
x = y + ( 2 + 3 )
```

Because of the parentheses, the expression 2 + 3 is evaluated first, and the result is then added to y.

The main difference between expressions and statements is that an expression produces a value. A statement does not generate a value but completes an operation. Expressions are used for the values they generate; statements are used for the effects they cause. Examine these examples:

```
2 + 3
x = 2 + 3
```

Both lines of code are expressions. The first expression's value, 5, is obvious. Notice that the second line of code is also an expression, but what value does it have? This value is also 5, which is assigned to both the variable x and the expression as a whole. The reason that the second line of code is not a statement is that this line does not complete an operation. For the second line of code to become an expression, the line would have to be terminated with a semicolon. The semicolon indicates that an action has been completed and that the effect caused by the expression has occurred.

Now look at these logical operations:

```
10 < 15
result = 10 < 15
```

The value of the first line of code is 1. If the expression were false, its value would be 0. Because the logical operation in the second line of code is true, that subexpression yields a value of 1 also. The value of 1 is assigned to both the variable result and the expression as a whole.

A C statement is terminated by a semicolon. When the compiler encounters the semicolon, it knows that the preceding statement has ended and that another statement is beginning.

If a group of statements is enclosed in a set of braces, the group is treated as a single statement. When encountering an opening brace, the compiler scans the source code for the matching brace that closes the group of statements. Using braces is handy when you need to perform several actions but only one statement is allowed—for example, after an if statement. Only one statement following the if will be executed when the if is true. To execute a group of statements, then, just enclose the whole group in a set of braces.

Borland C++ uses eight different types of statements. They are summarized in table 2.6.

Table 2.6. *Statement types.*

Type	Explanation
Compound	A group of statements enclosed in a set of braces and treated as a single statement.
Expression	A statement terminated with a semicolon. Any side effects of the expression are completed before any other statements are executed.
Labeled	An identification of a location to jump to for goto and switch statements.
Selection	A flow-control statement; the selection statements are if else and switch.
Iteration	A loop-control statement; the iteration statements are while, do, and for.
Jump	A statement that causes an unconditional change in execution flow. The jump statements are break, continue, goto, and return.
asm	A statement used to include inline assembler code.
Declaration	A statement that sets up and possibly initializes data objects.

Introducing the C Operator Set

The *operator set* is a group of tokens defining the basic operations that can be performed on your data objects. Borland C++ provides an extensive set of operators that enhance the speed and ease of programming.

This section covers all the Borland C++ operators and introduces you to operator precedence—the set of rules governing the order in which operators are evaluated. Understanding operator precedence is extremely important in C programming. To produce accurate answers, you have to know how the operators manipulate your data.

The first group of operators is *the unary operators*. A unary operator requires only one operand. Table 2.7 lists the unary operators and their functions.

***Table 2.*7.** *Unary operators.*

Operator	Meaning
+	Unary plus.
–	Unary minus.
!	Not operator (or logical negation).
&	Address operator.
*	Indirection operator.
++	Increment operator. If the operator is prefixed to an operand, a preincrement is performed. If the operator is postfixed to an operand, a postincrement is performed.
– –	Decrement operator. If the operator is prefixed to an operand, a predecrement is performed. If the operator is postfixed to an operand, a postdecrement is performed.
~	Bitwise (1's) complement.

The second group of operators is the *binary operators*. A binary operator, as the name suggests, requires two operators. Table 2.8 lists the binary operators and their functions.

Table 2.8. *Binary operators.*

Mathematical Operators	
+	Addition
–	Subtraction
*	Multiplication
/	Division
%	Modulus
Assignment Operators	
=	Assignment
+=	Assign sum
–=	Assign difference
*=	Assign product

Assignment Operators

/ =	Assign quotient
% =	Assign remainder
& =	Assign bitwise AND
¦ =	Assign bitwise OR
^ =	Assign bitwise XOR
<<=	Assign bitwise left-shift
>>=	Assign bitwise right-shift

Logical Operators

&&	Logical AND
¦¦	Logical OR

Equality and Relational Operators

==	Equal to
!=	Not equal to
<	Less than
>	Greater than
<=	Less than or equal to
>=	Greater than or equal to

Shift and Bitwise Operators

<<	Shift left
>>	Shift right
&	Bitwise AND
¦	Bitwise OR
^	Bitwise XOR

Component Selection Operators

.	Direct component selector
->	Indirect component selector

Conditional Operator

a?b:c	if a then b; else c

Comma Operator

,	Forces evaluation from left to right

Class Member Operators

::	Scope access/resolution
.*	Dereference a pointer to a class member
->*	Dereference a pointer to a class member

As indicated earlier, operator precedence is the set of rules determining the order in which operators are evaluated. If you have only one operator in a statement, you won't have to worry about the precedence rules. However, when you use two or more operators in a statement, operator precedence becomes important. Consider this example:

```
x = 1 + 2 * 3;
```

Notice the two operators + and *. If there were no precedence rules, this simple formula could have two answers. If the addition operator is evaluated first, x equals 9. If the multiplication operator is evaluated first, x equals 7. As you can see from this example, knowing the precedence rules is vital to producing accurate and reliable programs.

Table 2.9 shows the precedence of the Borland C++ operators. The operators at the top of the table have a greater precedence than those at the bottom. In other words, an operator higher in the table is executed before an operator lower in the table.

Each group of operators in the table has a certain associativity. The operators are evaluated from left to right or from right to left.

Table 2.9. Precedence of Borland C++ operators.

Operator(s)	Associativity
() [] -> .	Left to right
! ~ ++ -- +	Right to left
- * & (typecast) sizeof	Right to left
* / %	Left to right
+ -	Left to right
<< >>	Left to right
< <= > >=	Left to right
== !=	Left to right
&	Left to right
^	Left to right
¦	Left to right
&&	Left to right
¦¦	Left to right
?:	Right to left
= += -= *= /= %=	Right to left
&= ^= ¦= <<= >>=	Left to right

Controlling Type Conversions

As you learned earlier in the chapter, each piece of data that your program uses has a certain *type* associated with that data. The type determines what kind of data it is. Data of type int is integer data, and data of type char is character data. A type conversion occurs when data of one type is changed to a different type. Sometimes these conversions are automatic, but at other times, you may need to force a type conversion. In this section, you learn how type conversions work and how to control them.

Understanding Implicit Type Conversions

A *type conversion* is simply the conversion of an object's type. A type conversion occurs, for example, when an object of integer type is changed so that it is handled as a floating-point type, or when an object of type char is converted to type int.

Although you can explicitly cause a type conversion, many type conversions are made automatically by Borland C++. When Borland C++ is responsible for a type conversion, it is called an *implicit* type conversion.

Implicit type conversions occur in arithmetic operations in which objects of two different types are used. Such type conversions cause objects of a lower, or less precise, type to be converted to a higher, or more precise, type. Automatic type conversion results in mathematical operations that are more precise. Another benefit of automatic type conversion is the consistent evaluation of mathematical expressions.

Borland C++ has a set of rules governing the automatic type-conversion process. When a type conversion is required, the basic integer types are converted in one phase, and any other conversions are handled in a second phase.

Table 2.10 summarizes the type-conversion process for integer type objects.

An object of type char consists of a single byte. However, when a char type object is converted to an int type object, two bytes are used. When the conversion takes place, the value of the low-order byte of the new int is the same as for the original char. The value of the high-order byte depends on whether the char object is signed or unsigned. An unsigned char causes the high-order byte of the int to be zero. A signed char causes the high-order byte of the int to be –1. If the original object is of type char, the conversion process depends on the Borland C++ setup. Borland C++ can define a char type object to be signed or unsigned by default.

Table 2.10. *Implicit conversion of integer types.*

Original Type	Converted Type	Conversion Method
char	int	High byte set to zero or sign extended, depending on default char type
unsigned char	int	High byte zero filled
signed char	int	Sign extended
short	int	Same value
unsigned short	unsigned int	Same value
enum	int	Same value

Before evaluating a mathematical expression, Borland C++ performs several steps in a type-conversion process. The first step is to convert char, short, or enum type to integers; the conversions are summarized in table 2.10. The rest of the steps in the type-conversion process are explained in the following list:

1. The expression is checked for an operand of type long double. If either operand is a long double, the other operand is converted to a long double. If neither operand is a long double, the next step in the process is performed.

2. The expression is checked for an operand of type double. If either operand is a double, the other operand is converted to a double. If neither operand is a double, the next step in the process is performed.

3. The expression is checked for an operand of type float. If either operand is a float, the other operand is converted to a float. If neither operand is a float, the next step in the process is performed.

4. The expression is checked for an operand of type unsigned long. If either operand is an unsigned long, the other operand is converted to an unsigned long. If neither operand is an unsigned long, the next step of the process is performed.

5. The expression is checked for an operand of type long. If either operand is a long, the other operand is converted to a long. If neither operand is a long, the next step of the process is performed.

6. The expression is checked for an operand of type unsigned int. If either operand is an unsigned int, the other operand is converted to an unsigned int. If neither operand is an unsigned int, both operands must be of type int.

Arithmetic expressions are not the only places in which implicit type conversions can occur. Automatic type conversion occurs also during assignments and function calls. When an assignment is made, the value type on the right side is converted to the type on the left side. In a function call, the argument to the function call is an expression; therefore, an implicit type conversion can occur just as a conversion can occur for any expression.

Using Explicit Type Conversions

Automatic type-conversion routines handle many of the type-conversion tasks you will encounter. At times, though, you will want to take control of the type conversions yourself.

When you issue a command that causes a type conversion to occur, you have performed an *explicit* type conversion. The explicit type-conversion process is known as *type casting*. The format of an explicit type cast is the following:

```
( type-name ) expression
```

As you can see, any valid C expression can be type cast. To perform the type cast, simply precede the expression with a unary *cast* operator. This operator is made by enclosing the `type-name` in a set of parentheses. The result of the expression appears in the type you specified.

The following code fragment shows a `float` being type cast to an `int`:

```
int i;
float x = 5.9876;
i = ( int ) x;
printf( "i = %d, x = %f", i, x );
```

This code fragment contains two variables: an integer variable and a floating-point variable. The `float` is assigned a value in the second line. On the third line, `i` is assigned the value of the `float` after it has been type cast. The `printf()` statement shows that the fractional part of the `float` was dropped in the type conversion.

The next code fragment shows how a type conversion can provide a function with the proper arguments:

```
int a = 2, b = 4;
double x;
x = pow( ( double ) a, ( double ) b );
printf( "x = %f", x );
```

In this example, a function that requires two `double` arguments is called with two `int` arguments. The two type-cast operators on the third line convert the integer arguments to floating-point arguments. The `pow()` function works correctly with two arguments of type `double`. Here `pow()` returns the value 16.0 as it should.

You should be aware that the values of your variables can change during a type-cast operation. The change in value is obvious when a `float` is converted to an `int`. The `int` cannot hold the fractional part of the `float`. When a `float` is converted to an `int`, the fractional part of the number is lost. The change in value may not be as obvious when an `int` is converted to a `float`. Even though the range of a `float` is large, a `float` cannot store an *exact* value for every number. Therefore, when an `int` is converted to a `float`, the new value may not equal the value before the type cast occurred. The new value will be as close as possible to the original value, but the two values may not be equal.

From these brief examples, you can see that explicit type conversions offer a great deal of flexibility in acquiring and processing data. One of the most useful functions of the type-cast operator is to cast arguments for functions.

Using C Macros

Like macros in a word processor, macros in your C programs can save you time and effort. Macros can also be versatile. You can use a macro, for example, to represent an often-used variable or to work like a function. This section shows you how to start using macros productively in your own programs.

In Borland C++, you can create two kinds of macros: object-like and function-like. When the preprocessor encounters an object-like macro in your source file, the macro is replaced with a value you defined at the beginning of your program. The replacement value can be any C data type, a character, an integer, or a floating-point number. In an object-like macro, the macro is replaced by a data object. When the preprocessor encounters a function-like macro, the macro name is replaced with a piece of code that performs an action. Function-like macros can even be used with arguments. As the name suggests, a function-like macro works similarly to a function.

Defining Object-like Macros

A macro is a string-replacement utility. When a macro name is encountered by the preprocessor, it is replaced with another string that was previously defined. You use the following form for an object-like macro definition:

```
#define identifier replacement-list
```

The #define directive tells the preprocessor that a macro definition is about to begin. The *identifier* is the name of the macro; it is the name that is found in your program. The *replacement-list* replaces the macro name when the preprocessor encounters it in your program.

Note the following object-like macro definition:

```
#define SALES_TAX 0.06
...
total = sales * SALES_TAX;
```

#define signals that a macro definition is about to start. SALES_TAX is the macro name, and 0.06 is the replacement-list. The last line of the example shows how the macro is used. When you want to use the value of sales tax, simply type the macro name **SALES_TAX**. When the preprocessor scans the program, every occurrence of SALES_TAX is replaced with 0.06.

Follow these simple rules in creating macros:

❏ *A #define preprocessor directive signals the beginning of the macro definition.*

❏ *The macro follows the #define directive.* When you name a macro, use the guidelines for naming any other C variable. The macro name cannot contain any spaces. Although uppercase letters are not required, the common practice is to enter the macro in uppercase.

❏ *The replacement string follows the macro name.*

❏ *The macro definition is not terminated by a semicolon.* If you terminate the definition with a semicolon, the preprocessor treats it as part of the replacement string.

❏ *The backslash character (\) enables you to extend the macro definition to more than one line.*

Note that the C compiler is not responsible for handling macros. The C preprocessor does all the necessary work of translating a macro into a form the compiler can accept and use. The preprocessor treats your program as a data file. When scanning the text of your program, the preprocessor replaces each occurrence of a macro name with the predefined replacement-list.

Using macros to define constant values can enhance the performance of your program. Consider this reconstruction of the preceding example:

```
double sales_tax = 0.06;
...
total = sales * sales_tax;
```

Here sales_tax is not a macro, but a double that has been assigned the value 0.06. Because sales_tax is now a variable, the program must look up the value of sales_tax each time it is encountered. Before, when SALES_TAX was a macro, the preprocessor replaced it with the value 0.06. The sales tax amount was therefore coded into the program whenever the amount was used. When the program needed the sales tax amount, the value was already there. Using a macro saved you the time required to look up the value of the variable each time it was used.

The time a macro saves may not be significant in straight line code. When you have calculations inside a loop, though, the savings can be substantial.

Using macros can save you time in other ways. First, macros can save you valuable coding time by making it easy to change constant values. If you use macros to define constants, you have to change only one macro definition to change the value of the constant throughout the program. Second, macros can speed up the debugging process. When you use a macro, you enter a value once instead of many times. Because you make fewer keystrokes, you are likely to make fewer errors.

Macros also make your program easier to read. Instead of scattering obscure values throughout the program, you can use descriptive names, which make more sense to your readers.

The first example in this section showed you how to use a macro to represent a numeric value. In some cases, you may need to use a macro to represent a character or a string instead of a numeric value. Listing 2.5 defines macros that use characters and strings.

Listing 2.5. objmac.c. *A program that uses characters and strings in macros.*

```
 1   /* OBJMAC.C  This program demonstrates the use of object-
 2       like macros that work with characters and strings. */
 3
 4   #include <stdio.h>
 5   #include <stdlib.h>
 6
 7   #define FIRST_CHAR 'H'
 8   #define SECOND_CHAR 'i'
 9   #define COMMA ','
10   #define STRING " this is a macro example."
11
12   main()
13   {
14      putchar( FIRST_CHAR );
```

```
15      putchar( SECOND_CHAR );
16      putchar( COMMA );
17      puts( STRING );
18  }
```

Listing 2.5 shows that object-like macros are not restricted to working with numeric information only. Lines 7–9 are macro definitions for a group of characters. Notice that each replacement-list is enclosed in quotation marks. When the macro substitution takes place, the whole replacement-list replaces the macro name. Thus, the character and the quotation marks in the replacement-list replace the macro name. For example, the macro in the expression

```
putchar( FIRST_CHAR );
```

expands to

```
putchar( 'H' );
```

You can see that every occurrence of the macro name is replaced with a *character constant*. This replacement works correctly in this example because the macro was used in a function call that required a character-constant argument. When you use a single character in a macro replacement-list, make sure that you include the quotation marks only if they are needed.

Line 10 is a macro definition that expands to a string constant. Notice in the replacement-list that the string is enclosed in quotation marks. The macro will therefore be replaced with a string literal. Again, when you use a string in a macro replacement-list, be sure to include quotation marks only when you need them.

Lines 14–17 are a simple series of statements that print all the macro definitions.

You have to be careful in keeping track of your quotation marks when you are defining strings for macros. Remember that anything in the replacement-list is copied during the macro expansion. If you included quotation marks in the replacement string, they will be copied during the expansion. Also remember that in a program any string in quotation marks is treated as a string literal. Note this code fragment:

```
#define STRING "This is my string."
...
printf( "%s", "STRING" );
```

This example does not work as you might expect. Instead of printing the replacement string found in the macro definition, printf() prints the word

STRING instead. The reason is that "STRING" in the printf() statement is treated as a string literal. Therefore, the preprocessor won't treat it as a macro. When you use a macro as an argument to a function, be sure to pay attention to the quotation marks and how they will be interpreted.

After expanding a macro, the preprocessor rescans the result to look for other macros. Because macros are rescanned, one macro can be made of other macros. The next example demonstrates the rescanning feature of the preprocessor:

```
#define NUM_1 10
#define NUM_2 15
#define SUM NUM_1 + NUM_2
...
printf( "SUM is equal to %d", SUM );
```

Here three macros are defined. The first two macro definitions are simple, and the third references the first two. When scanning the program, the preprocessor changes the printf() statement to

```
printf( "SUM is equal to %d", NUM_1 + NUM_2   );
```

The preprocessor then rescans the expanded macro to look for any new macros. In this case, the preprocessor finds two new macros. After the second macro expansion, the printf() statement looks like this:

```
printf( "SUM is equal to %d", 10 + 15 );
```

When you are through with a macro or you want to use the macro name for something else, you can *undefine* the macro. To remove a macro definition, you use the #undef preprocessor directive, which requires the following form:

```
#undef identifier
```

Note this example of the #undef directive:

```
#define MY_MACRO 1
....
#undef MY_MACRO
```

Here the #undef preprocessing directive undefines, or removes, the macro definition for MY_MACRO. After encountering the #undef directive, the preprocessor no longer recognizes MY_MACRO as a valid macro.

Defining Function-like Macros

Macros can have more sophisticated uses than simply supplying constant values. You can write a macro so that it looks and works much like a function. A function-like macro definition contains more pieces than an object-like macro definition. The function-like macro definition also contains a formal argument list. This list enables you to supply values that can change or control the substituted text.

You use the following general form for a function-like macro:

```
#define identifier(identifier-list) replacement-list
```

The #define directive signals the preprocessor that the rest of the information on the line is a macro definition. The identifier is the name of the macro. When the preprocessor encounters the identifier in your program, a macro expansion occurs, and the identifier is replaced with the replacement-list. The identifier-list is a formal argument list. When you use a function-like macro in a program, you should follow the macro name with a number of arguments that correspond to the identifier-list. When the macro is expanded, the arguments you supplied are copied into the replacement-list.

The next code fragment shows a function-like macro that requires a single argument:

```
#define MTOK(m) m * ( 8.0 / 5.0 )
...
double miles, kilometers;
miles = 62.0;
kilometers = MTOK(miles);
```

Here the macro roughly translates miles to kilometers. The macro definition is different from the definition for an object-like macro because of the formal argument list following the macro name. The argument list must start with a left parenthesis and *immediately* follow the macro name. When the macro is expanded, the argument in the replacement-list is replaced with the value of the argument in the identifier-list. The preprocessor expands the last line of this code fragment to

```
kilometers = miles * ( 8.0 / 5.0 );
```

The MTOK() macro was invoked with an argument of miles. As you can see, the preprocessor expanded the macro and replaced the formal argument, m, with the variable miles.

You can use more than one argument in a function-like macro definition. To invoke the macro with more than one argument, all you have to do is separate the arguments with commas. Consider this example:

```
#define WATTS(v,a) v * a
...
int voltage = 120;
int amperage = 5;
int wattage;
wattage = WATTS(voltage,amperage);
printf( "Power consumption = %d", wattage );
```

Notice that both arguments in the formal argument list are used in the replacement-list. The number of arguments in the argument list must always match the number of arguments in the replacement-list.

One useful feature of function-like macros is that they can work with arguments of any data type. Now look at the following example:

```
#define CUBE(x) x * x * x
...
int i;
float y;
i = CUBE(2);
y = CUBE(1.5);
```

The last two lines expand to

```
i = 2 * 2 * 2;
y = 1.5 * 1.5 * 1.5;
```

In this example, a single function-like macro calculates the cube of an integer *and* a floating-point number. Without a macro, you would need two functions to accomplish this same task. The reason that a function is not as versatile is that it can accept arguments of only a certain data type. A macro, however, does not care what argument types are passed to it. As you can see from this example, the macro's arguments are simply copied into the expanded replacement-list expression. Each time the macro is used, the macro is expanded to a new expression. Because a new expression is created, you can supply the macro with arguments of different types each time you use the macro.

When you use function-like macros, you can reference the formal arguments in the replacement-list in three different ways. The first way to reference a formal argument is for it to appear by itself. So far, this is the only way you have seen the formal argument referenced. The second way is to precede the formal argument with the string literal operator (#). The third way is to precede the formal argument with the string concatenation operator (##). The following paragraphs examine the various ways that formal arguments can be used.

In the preceding examples, the argument in the replacement-list appeared by itself. That is why no special character processing occurred during macro expansion. The formal argument in the replacement-list was replaced with the argument you supplied. Review this example of a function-like macro:

```
#define SUM(a,b) a + b
```

The SUM() macro requires two arguments. The arguments in the macro definition, a and b, are the formal arguments. Now examine the expression that uses the SUM() macro:

```
SUM(1,2)
```

This expression uses the SUM() macro and supplies the macro with actual arguments. The actual arguments in this example are the integers 1 and 2. When the macro is expanded, the actual arguments will be copied into the replacement-list. The SUM() macro is therefore expanded to

```
1 + 2
```

This expression is the actual expansion that is placed in your program. The preprocessor has removed the macro name and replaced it with the replacement-list. As you can see, the preprocessor uses the actual arguments when inserting the replacement-list.

The second way to reference a formal argument in the replacement-list is to precede the formal argument with the string literal operator (#). This operator causes the actual argument to appear in quotation marks in the expanded macro. The next code fragment shows one way to use the string literal operator in a printf() statement:

```
#define QUOTE(s) #s
...
printf( "%s\n", "He said " QUOTE("Hi, my name is Joe.") );
```

In this example, the QUOTE() macro is replaced with the macro's argument, which is enclosed in quotation marks. The funny-looking printf() statement therefore prints as

```
He said "Hi, my name is Joe."
```

When scanning the program, the preprocessor converts the QUOTE() macro to a regular string the printf() statement can use. At first glance, you might think that the preprocessor will expand the QUOTE() macro to this:

```
""Hi, my name is Joe.""
```

However, the two quotation marks in a row would cause the compiler to generate an error. The string literal preprocessor command is designed to prevent such an error. Instead of generating the preceding string, the preprocessor generates the following:

```
"\"Hi, my name is Joe.\""
```

The backslash characters tell the compiler that you want to print the actual quotation marks and not delimit another string. Because the backslashes indicate that actual quotation marks will be printed, this string will not generate any errors.

You may have noticed that the argument list for the `printf()` statement is composed of two *data* strings. When the `printf()` was executed, it printed *both* data strings. The reason for both strings being printed is that the data strings were not separated by a comma. The compiler therefore treated both strings as a single string literal. This way of generating a string literal wherever one is required is perfectly acceptable.

The third way to reference a formal argument in a macro replacement-list is to use the argument with the string concatenation operator (`##`). This operator joins two tokens in a macro replacement-list to form a new, larger token. Unlike the string literal operator, the string concatenation operator does not put quotation marks around the expanded macro.

The next code fragment shows how to use the string concatenation operator:

```
#define CAT(a,b) a ## b
...
printf( "%s\n", CAT("my_","macro" );
```

The `printf()` statement prints as

```
my_macro
```

The macro definition for `CAT()` is similar to macro definitions you have seen before—except for `##`, the string concatenation operator. This operator causes the actual arguments for `CAT()` to be concatenated, or joined together. In this example, the arguments `"my_"` and `"macro"` are concatenated into one string. The result is `my_macro`.

After the preprocessor expands a macro with a string concatenation operator, the preprocessor rescans to look for any new macros. Study the next example:

```
#define STR_1 "This is a test!"
#define CAT(a,b) a ## b
...
printf( "%s\n", CAT(STR_,1) );
```

Here the CAT() macro is scanned and replaced with STR_1. After the CAT() macro is expanded, the preprocessor rescans the line, looking for new macros. When it finds the new macro STR_1, it is expanded also. The printf() statement then looks like this:

```
printf( "%s\n", "This is a test!" );
```

Once again, the preprocessor rescans the line. Because no more macros are found, the processing is finished.

The next example shows a string concatenation operator that does not produce the result you want:

```
#define STR_1 "This is "
#define STR_2 "a test"
#define CAT(a,b) a ## b
...
printf( "%s\n", CAT(STR_1,STR_2);
```

This piece of code, when compiled, produces an error. The intended effect of this code fragment is to combine the *expanded* macros STR_1 and STR_2 and to produce the following printed message:

```
"This is a test"
```

But the code fragment cannot generate this message. The preprocessor instead replaces the CAT() macro with

```
STR_1STR_2
```

The preprocessor properly expanded the CAT() macro, but the expansion of the CAT() macro resulted in a meaningless string. When compilation starts, STR_1STR_2 is flagged as an error, and compilation is aborted so that you can fix the error.

Exercises

These exercises give you practice in using the C operators, controlling program execution flow, controlling data types and conversions, and using macros.

1. Write a short program and compile it, using the **Make EXE File** option. As the program is compiling, watch the message windows and notice the status of the compile and link procedures.

2. Write a program that uses an if statement to demonstrate at least three of the relational operators.

3. Write a program that generates a truth table for the logical operators `&&` and `||`. A truth table lists the outcomes of using a logical operator with all possible combinations of operands.

4. Write the beginning of a menu program that uses the `switch` statement.

5. Demonstrate the `while`, `do-while`, and `for` loops.

6. Show that a global variable can be accessed anywhere in a source file and that a local variable can be accessed only in the function in which it was declared.

7. Write an `if` statement that, when true, causes a group of statements to be executed.

8. Write two identical expressions. For one expression, use parentheses to change the order of evaluation.

9. Write several statements that will result in an implicit type conversion for each statement. Notice the change in precision as the type conversions occur.

10. Create a function-like macro that converts temperatures expressed in degrees Fahrenheit to degrees Centigrade.

Summary

This chapter discussed the generation of executable modules, program execution flow, data types and how they are used, C expressions and statements, C operators, and the use of macros. You learned the following important points:

❏ *A source file is the file you create when you write a C program.* An object file is created when the source file is compiled. Although the object file is a machine-language file, it is not an executable file. A load module, or executable file, is created when the object module is processed by the linker. The linker links the object module to other machine-code instructions. The machine code linked to the object module performs the setup necessary to make the object module executable.

❏ *Your program executes one line of code after another until a statement is encountered that changes execution flow.*

❏ *An* if *statement evaluates an expression and can execute one or two different sets of instructions, depending on the evaluation of the expression.*

❏ *You use a* switch *statement when the evaluation of an expression can have several different results.*

❏ *The* do-while *loop is a postchecked loop.* It executes the body of the loop and checks the controlling condition at the end of the loop.

❏ *The* while *loop is a prechecked loop.* It checks the controlling condition before beginning to process the body of the loop.

❏ *The* for *loop executes a loop a certain number of times.* The controlling structure of a for loop has three parts: (1) a beginning condition, (2) a conditional expression that determines when the loop will terminate, and (3) an expression that can change a controlling value on each pass of the loop.

❏ *Three basic data types are available in the C language.* The char data type represents characters. The int data type represents integer, or whole numbers. And the float data type represents real or floating-point numbers.

❏ *You can declare a data object either globally or locally.* A global variable is always accessible anywhere in the source file. A local variable is accessible only in the function in which it is declared. A local variable can be used, therefore, only when the function in which it was created is active.

❏ *An expression represents a value.* The expression can result in a value or can refer to a data object or a function. Furthermore, the expression can contain several operators and operands.

❏ *A statement is composed of expressions, but does not represent a value.* A statement is executed only for its effect.

❏ *The C language contains a rich set of operators.* The secret to mastering the operators is to learn operator precedence—the set of rules governing the order in which operators are executed.

❏ *A type conversion occurs when a data object is converted from one data type to another data type.* An implicit type conversion is performed automatically by the compiler. An explicit type conversion occurs when you perform a type cast.

❑ *C has two types of macros: object-like and function-like.* An object-like macro contains an identifier and a replacement-list. When encountering an identifier in your source file, the preprocessor replaces the identifier with the replacement-list. A function-like macro contains an identifier, an identifier-list, and a replacement-list. The identifier is the macro name that is replaced in your source file, and the identifier-list is a list of arguments used in the replacement-list. The replacement-list is the text that is substituted for the identifier. A function-like macro works much like a regular function.

3

Using C Functions

I n the first two chapters, you learned how to lay the foundation of a C program. This chapter shows you how to build the walls that support the structure of your program. You learn how to use C functions.

Functions are an important part of the C language because they bring together all the components necessary to complete a task. A *function* is an organized package of data and instructions that performs a specific job. Functions are useful because they hide the complexity associated with performing tasks. Consider, for example, `print()`. It's an easy-to-use function that generates formatted output. Using `printf()` saves you the tedious work often associated with generating formatted output.

In this chapter, you learn what functions are and how to use them. More important, you learn how to design and write your own functions. The chapter shows you how to set up a function, pass data to the function, and get answers back from the function.

Understanding the *main()* Function and Library Functions

Every C program has at least one function. A program that does much of anything contains several functions. In this section, you learn how to use the function every program *must* have: the `main()` function. You also become familiar with the extensive set of library functions supplied with Borland C++, and you see ways to use them in your programs.

In C, a function is simply a group of statements. In a well-written program, each group of statements performs a specific task. Ideally, all the statements in a function work together to accomplish a single objective. A good function is easy to design, understand, and maintain.

The C language is built around the modularity of functions. Almost any programming task that requires more than a few lines of code will likely be written as a function. Dividing your program into modular functions enables you to build complex programs quickly and easily.

The functions used in a C program can be broken into three groups; the main() function, the library functions, and the user-defined functions. The main() function is a special function required in *every* C program. You create the contents of the main() function. The library functions are included in the Borland C++ package. Generally, they handle basic programming tasks and the low-level control of your computer hardware. The user-defined functions are ones you create. They are as varied as the programming projects you tackle. This section covers the main() function and the library functions. User-defined functions are discussed in the section "Writing Your Own Functions" later in this chapter.

Writing the *main()* Function

The purpose of the main() function is to serve as an entry point for your program. As you saw in Chapter 2, the linker adds a special segment of code to your program when it is converted to an executable file. The added code performs the setup necessary for the program to be loaded and executed. When the setup code has completed its tasks, the main() function is automatically called. Because main() is automatically executed whenever your program is run, main() has to be included in your program.

Although the rules of the C language require that you have a main() function, they do not require any special code to be included in main(). In fact, main() can include as much or as little code as you want. Listing 3.1 shows a C program with a very short main() function.

Listing 3.1. blank.c. *A program with a short* main() *function.*

```
1   /* BLANK.C   A program that doesn't do a thing! */
2   main()
3   {
4   }
```

The program in listing 3.1 has a main( ) function, as the rules require, but main( ) includes nothing else. The program is perfectly legal even though it doesn't do anything!

The main( ) functions in most programs are much larger than main( ) in listing 3.1. The size of your program determines how much code should be included in main( ). In a short program, you may want to put the code for the whole program in the main( ) function. In a large program, however, placing all the code in the main( ) function would be confusing. In many large programs, the only purpose of the main( ) function is to call the user-defined functions as they are needed.

Every C function—including main( ), library functions, and user-defined functions—has the same basic structure. Figure 3.1 shows the structure of a typical function.

Fig. 3.1. *The structure of a C function.*

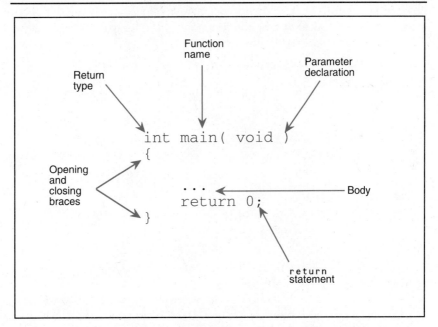

For every function you write, you should specify a return type. The return type indicates the *data type* of the value returned by the function. The compiler uses the return type information to verify that the value returned from a function is used correctly.

You use the function name to refer to the function. This name is the identifier in a function call.

The parameter declaration list declares variables that accept values passed to the function. The variables declared in this list are used to store values passed to the function when it is called. Any other variables used by the function are declared inside the body of the function.

The opening and closing braces define the body of the function. In other words, the braces indicate where the function begins and ends.

The body of the function is a group of C statements. In a well-written function, all the statements in the function body work toward accomplishing a single task. The body of the function can contain variable declarations, regular C statements, and even other function calls.

A special statement contained in the body of a function is the `return` statement. This statement has a dual purpose. First, when the `return` statement is encountered, it indicates that the function has completed its processing. Second, when a function calculates a value, the `return` statement returns the value calculated by the function. The value passed back by the `return` statement should be compatible with the return type of the function.

Note the following code fragment, showing the typical use of a `return` statement:

```
float speed( float size, float rpm )
{
   /* Calculate the speed of a tooth on a saw blade
      rotating at a given speed. The calculated speed
      is expressed in units per second */
   float tooth_speed;

   tooth_speed = ( ( size * 3.1416 ) * ( rpm / 60.0 ) );
   return( tooth_speed );
}
```

The `return` statement returns the value of the variable `tooth_speed`. Notice that the data type of the function matches the data type of the variable `tooth_speed`. When the function is completed, program execution resumes at the point where the function was called. The function call is replaced by the value passed back by the `return` statement.

Many functions are called for the effects they produce. A function executed for a certain effect may not return a value. If a function does not have a `return` statement, function execution terminates at the closing brace. When a function without a `return` statement is compiled, the compiler generates a warning message. The compiler does not generate an error that halts compilation, but simply warns you that the function has no `return` statement.

A function that doesn't return a value can be declared with a `void` type. This type tells the compiler that a return value is not expected. Such a function does not have to contain a `return` statement. If a function declared with a `void` type does have a `return` statement, it has this form:

```
return;
```

Using Library Functions

The Borland C++ function libraries boost your productivity by providing hundreds of ready-to-use functions. These functions are designed to handle basic programming chores and to provide a convenient interface to the computer's facilities. The library functions relieve you of the burden of creating functions that handle low-level programming and interface tasks.

The graphics library, for example, shows how convenient the function libraries are. Borland C++ has an extensive library of graphics functions known as BGI functions. (BGI stands for Borland Graphics Interface.) The BGI functions do the tedious work of controlling your video hardware, and they create most of the images you need. When you use these functions, you can concentrate on your programming project and not worry about basic video programming.

Knowing What Library Functions Are Available

As noted before, there are hundreds of functions in the Borland C++ libraries. Here are the major groups of functions and their general purposes:

❏ *Standard functions.* The standard functions are a group of basic C programming utilities.

❏ *I/O functions.* The I/O functions handle the tasks of moving data in and out of your program. Borland C++ has two different types of I/O functions. One type of function uses C streams to handle data. The other type of function uses the DOS I/O utilities to handle data.

❏ *Classification functions.* Known as the `is...()` family of functions, these functions classify characters. Characters can be classified into various categories, such as uppercase, lowercase, and hexadecimal.

❏ *Conversion functions.* The conversion functions convert data from one format to another.

❏ *Directory-control functions.* These functions enable you to work with DOS directories and paths.

❏ *Diagnostic functions.* With the diagnostic functions, you can trouble-shoot bugs in your program.

❏ *Graphics functions.* The graphics functions control the video hardware in your computer and create many basic graphic images.

❏ *Interface functions.* With the interface functions, you can directly use the DOS and BIOS functions.

❏ *Manipulation functions.* The manipulation functions work with strings and blocks of memory.

❏ *Math functions.* These functions handle almost any calculation you need to perform.

❏ *Memory functions.* The memory functions handle dynamic memory allocation for the small and large data memory models.

❏ *Miscellaneous functions.* These functions handle a variety of programming tasks.

❏ *Process-control functions.* These functions handle the creation and termination of processes that originate inside other processes.

❏ *Standard functions.* These are the general-purpose functions from the `stdlib.h` header file.

❏ *Text-window functions.* The text-window functions are used to send text information to the video display.

❏ *Time and date functions.* These functions handle time and date information.

❏ *Variable argument list functions.* These functions process the variable-length arguments passed to a function.

For a complete list of the functions and macros found in each of these categories, see Chapter 2 of the *Borland C++ Programmer's Guide*.

You can find specific information about the library functions in two ways. The first way is to use the Borland C++ on-line help facility. This facility has a complete list of the library functions. The listing for each function contains a brief description of the function, information about the function declaration, example code, and cross-references to related functions. The second way to find out more about a function is to use the *Borland C++ Reference Guide*, which contains all the information you need in order to use every library function.

Including Library Functions in Your Program

Now that you know what kinds of library functions are available, you need to learn how to use them in your program. Using the library functions is simple. Once you find a function you want to use, you include the appropriate header file in your source code and make sure that you pass any needed arguments to the function.

When you use a library function in your program, you must include the header file associated with that function. A library function's header file contains the declarations of variables, macros, and functions necessary to use the function in your program. The statement that includes a header file looks like this:

```
#include <stdio.h>
```

#include is a preprocessor directive that tells the compiler to merge the specified file into your source file during compilation. The included file is not permanently copied into your source file but is referenced during the compilation of the source file. The angle brackets surrounding the file name tell the compiler to look in the standard library directories for the file of that name. During compilation, the file is included with your source file. In this example, the included file is the stdio.h header file.

Listing 3.2 shows how you can use some of the library functions in a program.

Listing 3.2. txt_demo.c. *A program that uses text-window functions.*

```
1   /* TXT_DEMO    This program uses the text-window functions
2                  to demonstrate the use of the library
3                  functions.*/
4
5   #include <stdio.h>
6   #include <stdlib.h>
7   #include <conio.h>
8
9   main()
10  {
11     int i, j;
12
13     clrscr();
14     textmode( C80 );
```

Listing 3.2. continues

Listing 3.2. *continued*

```
15
16    while( !kbhit() ) {
17      for( i = 0; i <=15; i++ ) {
18        textcolor( i );
19        for( j = 48; j <= 90; j++) cprintf( "%c", j );
20      }
21    }
22  }
```

The program in listing 3.2 uses the text-window functions to generate a multicolor, rolling, ASCII display. The program is composed of three loops. The outermost loop waits for you to press a key to terminate the test. The next loop (the i loop) cycles through the 16 text-mode foreground colors. The innermost loop prints the ASCII characters from 0 (zero) to Z.

The main feature of this program is not its loop structures, however, but its library functions. In line 13, the clrscr() function clears the screen. Notice that clrscr() is not passed any parameters; the reason is that clrscr() is declared with a void parameter list. In line 14, the textmode() function is called. This function sets the video mode—in this case, to an 80-column color display.

Inside the loops, the textcolor() function is called. Notice that the argument passed to textcolor() is the loop-index variable i. The loop index is used with textcolor() so that all 16 text-mode colors can be displayed. Also inside the loops is the cprintf() function. cprintf() has a format string and a variable argument list. The arguments passed to cprintf() cause the function to print the ASCII value of variable j.

To use these special text-window functions, you must include the correct header file in your source file. You can see in line 7 that the conio.h header was included in the source file. Without this header file, the program would not compile correctly. You must always include the correct header file for the library functions in your program.

Writing Your Own Functions

The Borland C++ libraries provide a wide range of useful, specialized utility functions. Still, these functions cannot do everything. By their nature, the library functions perform specialized tasks. For general programming, you need to create your own functions. This section shows you how to create your own user-defined functions and transfer data to those functions.

Writing Prototypes for Your Functions

Function prototypes, or function declarations, tell the compiler about the functions you write. A *function prototype* contains the name of the function, the number and type of arguments passed to the function, and the type of the value returned by the function. The function prototype differs from a function definition in that the prototype does not contain any information about the body of the function—only information about the data passed to and from the function. A typical function prototype looks like this:

```
int my_sum( int a, int b, int c );
```

This function prototype declares the function my_sum( ), which requires three integer arguments when it is called. After my_sum( ) has performed its calculations, it returns an integer value as an answer.

Why do you need to include function prototypes in your program? The answer is that the compiler needs to know what type of data your functions require in order to verify that they are used correctly.

Figure 3.2 shows how the user-defined function declarations and function definitions are arranged in a typical C program. The accepted programming practice is to place function declarations at the top of the program, along with global declarations. Function definitions appear at the bottom of the program.

Fig. 3.2. Typical placement of user-defined function declarations and function definitions.

```
Function declarations
main()
Function definitions
```

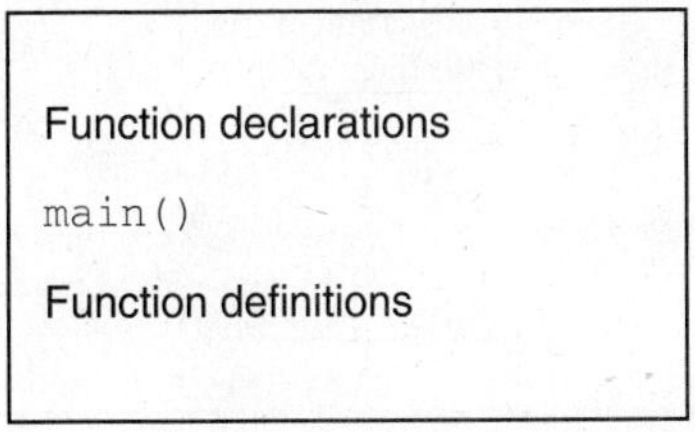

Placing the function declaration at the top of the program enables the compiler to learn what type of information the function requires before it is ever called. If a function call occurred before a function declaration, the compiler would not be able to determine whether the function call was made correctly.

There is a way to get around the need for function declarations. You can avoid writing a function declaration if you define the function at the beginning of the program. The function definition contains not only the information about the data passed to and from the function, but also the complete body of the function. With the function definition at the top of the program, the compiler knows what kind of data the function uses and what the body of the function does.

Defining a function at the beginning of a program has two drawbacks, however. The first drawback is that the program is harder to read. You may have difficulty following the flow of a program when the first function you see is one of the most detailed functions in the program. A program with the most general functions at the beginning is much easier to understand than a program with the most specific functions listed first. The second drawback is that you must be sure to define the most detailed functions first. Defining a function that calls an undefined function will generate an error. Using function prototypes is easier than trying to determine which figure you must declare first.

Figure 3.3 shows the steps in designing and writing a user-defined function.

Fig. 3.3. *The function-creation process.*

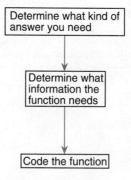

The first step in the function-creation process is to decide what kind of answer you need. Do you need a function that calculates an integer value, returns a character, or generates an answer of some other type? When you have decided what type of answer the function should generate, you'll know what type of data the function will return. The type of the answer returned by the function is the type of the function.

The second step is to determine what data the function requires. You need to decide which values the function needs in order to calculate an answer, and you need to know the data type of the values passed to the function. The argument list in the function declaration contains the information about the type of data passed to the function.

The last step is the writing of the function. In this step, you create the function definition. It contains the body of the function—the group of C statements that form the function.

The information you gathered in the first two steps of the function-creation process is used in the function prototype (function declaration). Here is the exact format of the function prototype:

```
return_type function_name( argument-type argument-name ... );
```

The `return_type` specifies the type of the answer returned by the function. The type can be an `int`, a `double`, or any of the other data types. The `function_name` is simply the name you use to call the function. This name can contain up to 32 characters, including letters, numbers, and the underscore. The only restriction on the function name is that it must begin with a letter or an underscore. The variables in the argument list are those to which data is passed when the function is called. Finally, the `argument-type` specifies the data type of an element in the argument list.

> **Note:** Avoid function names that start with an underscore because Borland C++ uses identifiers that begin with the underscore character.

Now look at the following code fragment:

```
double cube( double x );
```

The function `cube()` has a return type specified as a `double`. This means that the value calculated by `cube()` can be assigned to any variable declared as a type `double`. The argument list for `cube()` contains a variable of type `double`. Therefore, any function calls to `cube()` should pass to it a value that is a `double` floating-point number.

As noted earlier, you can use a special data type, `void`, in function declarations. Declaring a function with a `void` return type signals that the function does not return any kind of value. Look at this example:

```
void show_logo( void );
```

The function declaration for `show_logo()` indicates that it neither requires an argument nor returns a value.

If you write a function prototype and do not include a return type, the compiler assumes that the function returns a value of the default, or integer, type. Note the following code fragment:

```
sum( int a, int b );
```

The compiler assumes that the value returned by the function `sum()` is an integer.

Passing Arguments to Your Functions

In the preceding section, you learned how to create prototypes for your functions. In those function prototypes, you declared variables used to store values that are passed to the functions. In this section, you learn how to pass information to your functions and how to use the variables declared in function prototypes.

The most important concept to remember when you use C functions is that arguments are passed to functions by *value*, not by *reference*. Passing arguments by value means that when you call a function, the called function works with *copies* of the arguments in the function call. Listing 3.3 shows how arguments are passed by value.

Listing 3.3. `loopcnt.c`. *A program in which arguments are passed by value.*

```
1  /* LOOPCNT.C  This program demonstrates how arguments are
2               passed by value.  */
3
4  #include <stdio.h>
5  #include <stdlib.h>
6
7  void loop_count( int i );
8
9  main()
10 {
```

```
11    int i = 2;
12
13    loop_count( i );
14    printf( "In main, i = %d.\n", i );
15  }
16
17  void loop_count( int i )
18  {
19    for( ; i < 10; i++ )
20      printf( "In loop_count, i = %d.\n", i );
21  }
```

In listing 3.3, a function is passed a value that is modified inside the body of the function. Even though the value of the argument is changed in the function's body, the value of the variable in the function call is not changed. The function modifies a *copy* of the variable used in the function call.

In line 11, the integer variable i is declared and assigned a value of 2. The loop_count( ) function is called with the variable i. Immediately after the function call, the value of the variable i is printed. The value of i still equals 2.

The variable i in main( ) has a value of 2 both before and after the call to loop_count( ). This variable has the same value before and after the function call even though loop_count( ) modifies another i variable in the body of the loop. Notice the for statement in line 19. In the for loop, the first statement—the one that specifies an initial condition for the loop—is blank. This statement is left blank because the variable used to control the loop, the variable i, has already been assigned a value. The value of i in loop_count( ) is equal to the value of i in main( ). Even though loop_count( ) modifies the value of i, the value of i in main( ) remains the same.

Figure 3.4 shows how arguments are passed by value and by reference.

From listing 3.3, you can see that passing arguments by value protects the original values of the variables. Most of the time, you will want to leave the original values of the variables unchanged. Passing arguments by value helps prevent program errors caused by unrecognized changes in an argument's original value. Although this method of passing arguments is usually better, you may at times need to change the original value of an argument. In those cases, you can pass arguments by reference.

Fig. 3.4. *Passing arguments by value and by reference.*

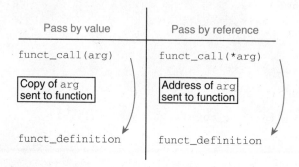

In C, the way to pass arguments by reference is to pass a pointer to the argument. A pointer contains the memory address of the argument. Because the called function has the address of the original argument, the function can change the value of that argument. Listing 3.4 shows the preceding program rewritten to use pointers.

Listing 3.4. `loopref.c`. *A program that shows how to pass arguments by reference.*

```
 1  /* LOOPREF.C   This program demonstrates how arguments are
 2                 passed by reference.   */
 3
 4  #include <stdio.h>
 5  #include <stdlib.h>
 6
 7  void loop_count( int *i );
 8
 9  main()
10  {
11    int i = 2;
12
13    loop_count( &i );
14    printf( "In main, i = %d.\n", i );
15  }
16
17  void loop_count( int *i )
18  {
19    for( ; *i < 10; (*i)++ )
20      printf( "In loop_count, i = %d.\n", *i );
21  }
```

In listing 3.4, the value of the variable used in the function call is changed when the function is executed. Notice that the function prototype in line 7 is different. In listing 3.3, the function prototype declares an integer. In listing 3.4, the function prototype declares a *pointer* to an integer. The symbol * in the function declaration indicates that the variable being declared is a pointer to an integer.

Because the function is declared with a pointer as an argument, the argument passed to loop_count( ) must be an address. In line 13, you can see how the address of main( )'s i variable is passed to loop_count( ). The symbol & in the function call indicates that the address of the specified variable is being passed to loop_count( ).

The version of loop_count( ) in listing 3.4 modifies the value of the variable in main( ). In main( ), the address of the variable i is passed to loop_count( ) during the function call. Because loop_count( ) is passed an address, loop_count( ) modifies the information stored at that address.

In loop_count( ), the value stored in the variable i is a pointer. In other words, the value stored in i is an address. If you looked at the value stored in the variable i in loop_count( ), you would find the address of the variable i in main( ). However, the for statement in loop_count( ) works with an integer value, not an address. The for statement works correctly because the *indirection operator* is used. This operator is specified by the symbol * and causes the value stored at the address indicated by the pointer to be used.

Notice the last part of the for statement in line 19. The indirection operator and the pointer variable are enclosed by parentheses. The parentheses force the indirection operator to execute before the increment operator. Without the parentheses, the increment operator tries to increment the *pointer* value instead of the value to which the pointer points. Incrementing the pointer value instead of the data value can produce strange results.

Type promotions can occur when the argument passed to a function has a less precise type than the function parameters specify. Note the following example:

```
char c;
int d;
...
d = toupper( c );
```

The variable c is declared as type char. However, the toupper( ) function requires an int argument. The type of c in the function call is promoted just as it would be if c were assigned to an integer variable.

Returning Values from Functions

C functions are designed so that a value is usually returned when a function completes its processing. Like any other value in a C program, the value returned by a function has a data type. It can be any of the valid C data types, such as `int`, `char`, or `double`.

Because functions return values, you can use a function wherever a value is required. A function can return a value to be used, for example, as part of a calculation, in an assignment, or even in a function call.

This section shows you how to specify a function's return type when you write the function prototype. You also learn how a function's data type can change the value of the data returned by the function. Finally, you see how functions can be used like data objects.

Defining and Using Function Types

In the C language, every function has a data type. The compiler uses the information about a function's data type to verify that the values returned by the function are used in a legal manner. Usually, the compiler gets its information about the type of a function's return value from the function prototype. Examine this function prototype:

```
int my_calc( int a, int b );
```

The keyword `int` at the beginning of the function prototype specifies the return type of the function. Here `int` indicates that the function returns an integer value.

In many cases, a function returns a value that is one of the fundamental types, such as `char` or `int`. However, a function is not limited to returning values of only the basic types; a function can return any type of value you can legally declare in your program. For example, when you are working with arrays, it is more efficient for your function to return a pointer to an array. You can even return data objects that have data types you create, such as structures.

Listing 3.5 shows a function that works with strings. Because strings are arrays of characters, the function has a return type that is a pointer to a character array.

Listing 3.5. `name_cmp.c.` *A program containing a function that returns a pointer.*

```
1   #include <stdio.h>
2   #include <stdlib.h>
3   #include <conio.h>
4
5   char *long_name( char *first, char *second );
6
7   main()
8   {
9     char *first = "Joe";
10    char *second = "John";
11
12    clrscr();
13    printf( "The longest name is %s.\n",
14            long_name( first, second ) );
15
16    return 0;
17  }
18
19  char *long_name( char *first, char *second )
20  {
21    if( strlen( first ) >= strlen( second ) )
22      return first;
23    else
24      return second;
25  }
```

The program in listing 3.5 uses a function that returns a pointer to a string. The function `long_name()` compares two strings passed to it. After comparing the strings, `long_name()` returns a pointer to the longer of the two strings.

In line 5 of listing 3.5, the `long_name()` function is declared to have a return value that is a pointer to a character array. The compiler knows that `long_name()` returns a pointer to a string because of the `char *` type declaration for the function.

Because the `long_name()` function returns a pointer to a string, `long_name()` can be used anywhere a string can be used. The pointer returned by `long_name()` is used in the `printf()` statement in lines 13 and 14. In that statement, the value returned by `long_name()` points to the string that `printf()` prints.

Notice in listing 3.5 that both the function declaration and the function definition (lines 5 and 19) specify the same return type for the function. If they do not specify the same return type, the compiler generates an error message.

As noted earlier, a function that does not return a value has a void type. The `long_name()` function in listing 3.5 could be rewritten so that it has a void type. The function declaration and function definition for `long_name()` would then look like this:

```
void long_name( char *first, char *second );
...
void long_name( char *first, char *second )
{
  if( strlen( first ) >= strlen( second ) )
    printf( "The longest name is %s.\n", first );
  else
    printf( "The longest name is %s.\n", second );
}
```

Both the function declaration and the function definition begin with the keyword void, indicating that the function does not return a value. Because a void function does not return a value, the function does not need to contain a return statement. However, a function of any other data type should contain a return statement even if the function does not generate a useful value.

In the program examples earlier in this book, the main() functions do not contain return statements. When compiled, each program would generate a warning message. As noted before, this warning does not cause compilation to abort, nor does the warning cause any error in the program. The warning just lets you know that the compiler was expecting a return statement.

The main() function in listing 3.5 has a return statement and does not, therefore, generate a warning when the program is compiled. By default, the value returned in listing 3.5 is an integer. If you do not specify the type of a function, the compiler automatically assumes that the function returns an integer.

Even if a function returns a value, you may not want to use that value. When you call a function, you don't have to use the value returned by the function. In that case, the value is simply ignored.

Notice that the `long_name()` function in listing 3.5 has two return statements. Multiple return statements, which are legal, do not cause problems because the first return that is encountered ends processing in the function. You can use as many `return` statements as you like. However, the `first` return causes program execution to resume immediately following the call to the current function.

A type cast can occur during the execution of a `return` statement. For example, if a function is declared to have a return type of `double`, and the `return` statement returns integers, the integers are promoted to `doubles`. The following code fragment shows how to cast a function's return value:

```
double sum_it( int a, int b )
{
   return a + b;
}
```

In this example, the function `sum_it( )` is declared to return a `double` floating-point value. In the function, however, the `return` statement returns an integer value. Declaring the function's return value as a `double` causes the value passed back by the `return` statement to be type cast from an integer to a `double`. An implicit type cast of a function's return value can cause errors that are difficult to debug. Be careful when you use implicit type casts.

Using Functions Like Objects

When a function call is encountered in a C statement, the called function is executed, and a value from the function is passed back. The program considers the value passed back from the function to be a regular data object that can be used like a variable or constant.

If your program has a statement that uses an integer value, the program won't care whether that integer value is stored in an integer variable or comes from a function with an integer return type. The program treats a function call just like any data object.

The following example shows how a function can be used as a data object:

```
int a, b, c;
int answer;
...
a = 10;
b = 2;
c =3;
answer = a / ( sum_it( b + c );
```

The `sum_it( )` function is used in place of a regular data object. The variable a is divided by an integer value. This value is not a variable or a constant, but the value returned by a function.

Generally, whenever you need a data object, you can instead use a function that returns a value of the correct type. When the function completes its processing, the value returned by the function occupies the same spot in the C statement that the call to the function occupied.

Understanding Storage Classes

In C, a variable has two main attributes. The first attribute is the variable's *type*. You have already learned that the type of a variable determines what kind of object the variable is and how much space it uses. Some of the most common data types are integer, character, and floating point. The second attribute is the variable's *storage class*, which determines when and where a variable can be used.

The term *storage class* covers several specific aspects of variable availability and longevity. In this section, you become familiar with storage classes. You learn what scope, duration, and linkage are and how they affect your data. In addition, you learn how to use the different storage classes to your advantage when you create your own functions.

Although scope, duration, and linkage are interdependent, each describes a different characteristic. Scope determines where a variable can be used in a source file, and duration determines when a variable can be used in a source file. Linkage is important when you have multiple source files to be compiled into one program. Linkage determines whether the same name in different source files refers to the same data object.

Determining a Variable's Scope

Scope indicates where in a program a variable can be used. The C language has four different types of scope:

❑ *File scope.* If a variable has file scope, the variable can be used anywhere in the source file. File scope is equivalent to the global scope you have already seen. Any function in a source file can use a variable that has file scope. You can create a variable that has file scope by declaring the variable outside any function. The declarations for variables with file scope generally appear before the `main()` function.

❑ *Function scope.* If a variable has function scope, the variable can be used only in the function in which the variable was declared. Therefore, only one function in a program will have access to a variable declared with function scope. A variable with function scope is declared at the top of a function definition.

❑ *Block scope.* Block scope, also known as local scope, is slightly different from function scope. A variable declared with block scope can be used only in the block in which the variable was declared. Block scope covers only a block of code, but it doesn't have to be entire function. The following code fragment shows how you can use block scope:

```
main( )
{
   int  i = 10;
   int cnt;
   for( cnt = 0; cnt <=20; cnt++ ) {
     int j = 1;
     printf( "In loop, j = %d.\n", j );
   }

   printf( "Out of loop, i = %d.\n", i );
}
```

Notice the variables i and j. The variable i is declared with function scope and can be used anywhere in the program. The variable j is declared with block scope and can be used only in the for loop in which j is declared. If you try to access j outside the for loop, an error is generated.

❑ *Function prototype scope.* Function prototype scope is a scope you use all the time but never notice. This scope applies to the variables in a function declaration's parameter list. A variable with function prototype scope is accessible only until the end of the function prototype. Thus, variables in a function declaration's parameter list can be used in that parameter list only.

Scope and visibility are similar concepts. Usually, they mean the same thing. In some instances, however, a variable is in scope but not visible. Note the following variation of the preceding code fragment, showing how scope and visibility can differ:

```
main( )
{
   int i = 10;
   int cnt;

   for( cnt = 0; cnt <=20; cnt++ ) {
     int i = 1;
      printf( "In loop, i = %d.\n", i );
   }

    printf( "Out of loop, i = %d.\n", i );
}
```

This code fragment declares two i variables. The first i variable has function scope. The second i variable—the i in the for loop—has block scope. When execution is in the for loop, the i declared at the top of the function is in scope, but the variable is not visible. Only the i variable declared in the for loop is in scope and visible during the execution of the loop. Therefore, even though a variable in scope, the variable may not be visible.

Determining a Variable's Duration

Duration refers to the time a variable is available. A variable's duration determines when memory is allocated for the variable.

In a large program, allocating memory for all the variables for the entire length of the program would be wasteful. C gets around this space problem by allocating memory for a variable only when the variable is used. When a function is called, memory is allocated for the variables in the function. When the function ends, the memory allocated for the function's variables is freed.

Note that there are two kinds of duration:

❑ *auto duration*. This is the default duration of variables declared in a function. When a function is called, memory is allocated for the auto variables. When the function ends, the memory allocated for the auto variables is freed. auto variables make the most efficient use of memory.

❑ *static duration*. This is the default duration of variables with file scope. A static variable is always available because the memory allocated for it is not freed until the program ends. You can even declare the variables in your function to have static duration. You just precede the variable declaration with the static keyword. Look at the following example:

```
void my_func( void )
{
    static int i;
    ...
}
```

The variable i in my_func( ) has static duration. Even after my_func( ) ends, the variable i will still have a section of memory allocated. Thus, the variable i retains its value from one function call to the next. i has static duration but still has function scope. Having function scope means that i can be accessed only from my_func( ); no other function has access to i. The variable i is stored in memory between function calls, but i can be accessed only from my_func( ) when that function is called.

Determining a Variable's Linkage

The linkage of a variable indicates whether it can be accessed from another source file. Three different types of linkage are available:

❏ *Internal linkage.* A variable with internal linkage is visible to all parts of a single source file. Because the variable is visible to the whole file, the variable also has file scope. Variables with internal linkage are declared outside any functions in the source file.

❏ *External linkage.* Like a variable with internal linkage, one with external linkage is visible to all parts of a source file. However, a variable with external linkage is visible also in other source files; such a variable can be accessed in more than one source file. An external variable has file scope. Because of this scope, the variable must be declared outside any functions. To access a variable in another function, you must redeclare the variable and precede the declaration with the extern keyword.

❏ *No linkage.* If a variable has no linkage, it is visible only in the block in which the variable was declared. It cannot be accessed by more than one function.

A variable declared outside any functions has both internal and external linkage by default. Look at the following code fragment:

```
#include <stdio.h>
#include <stdlib.h>

int global_int;

main()
{
...
```

The variable global_int can be used anywhere in the source file because the variable is declared with file scope. global_int can be used in other source files also, if it is declared correctly. For another source file to have access to global_int, that source file must include the following declaration:

```
extern int global_int;
```

If you changed the preceding code fragment to

```
#include <stdio.h>
#include <stdlib.h>

static int global_int;

main()
{
...
```

the variable global_int would have only internal linkage. The static keyword modifies the declaration so that the variable can be used in just one source file.

Using Advanced Program Control Logic

In Chapter 2, you learned how to use C loops to change the flow of execution in your program. You learned how to use the do-while, while, and for loop-control structures. This section shows you some new tools for more precise control of these structures. After you learn better control of your loops, you learn some new ways to change the flow of execution in a program. Finally, you learn a new way to end program execution and a way to start another program from inside your program.

Writing Loop-Control Statements

You have already seen how useful loop-control structures are. They provide a way for you to execute a group of instructions as many times as you want. With loop structures, your program can follow a circular execution path instead of a linear execution path.

All loops have the same basic parts. Each loop contains a section of code that performs setup functions, a section that does the main work of the loop, a section that updates a limiting condition, and a section that checks a limiting condition. Figure 3.5 shows each step in the execution of a loop.

Fig. 3.5. A basic loop structure.

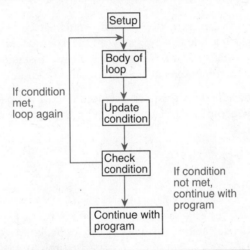

Each of the three C loops—do-while, while, and for—contains the parts of the loop structure shown in figure 3.5. However, the parts of the loop may be in different order.

The do-while, while, and for loops add a great deal of versatility to a program. These loops can handle almost any repetitive task you have. If the standard loop structure cannot handle a particular task, C provides additional statements you can use: goto, break, and continue. With these statements, you can change the flow of control inside your loop structures.

Using *goto*

The `goto` statement causes an unconditional transfer of control. This statement takes the following form:

```
goto label
```

The *label* in the `goto` statement specifies the location where program execution continues. The following code fragment shows how you can use a `goto` statement:

```
for( i = 0; i < 10; i++ ) {
  if( i = 5 ) goto label1;
  printf( "In the for loop, i = %d.\n", i );
  label1: ;
}
```

Although this code fragment does not do much, it clearly shows the use of `goto`. On the first line, in the body of the `for` statement, an `if` statement checks the variable `i`. If `i` is equal to 5, the `goto` statement is executed, and the program resumes execution at the `label1` statement.

In a well-designed program, you seldom need a `goto` statement. Note, however, that you can use `goto` anywhere in a program, not just in loop-control structures.

Using *break*

You use the `break` statement in loop structures and in `switch` statements. In `switch` statements, `break` causes program execution to jump to the end of the `switch` statement. In loop structures, `break` causes program execution to break out of the loop. You saw in Chapter 2 how to use `break` with `switch`. The next code fragment shows how to use `break` in a loop structure:

```
int no_of_cust, i, status;
...
for( i = 1; i <= no_of_cust; i++ ) {
  status = process_cust( no_of_cust );
  if( status == -1 ) break;
}
if( status == -1 )
  printf( "An error occurred during customer processing." );
```

In this code fragment, the `for` loop executes as many times as there are customers. In the body of the loop, the customer-processing function `process_cust()` is called. It returns a –1 if an error occurs during `process_cust()`. If an error occurs, the `for` loop does not need to continue. The `if` statement checks the value returned by `process_cust()`. If the value returned by that function indicates that an error occurred, the `break` statement causes program flow to break out of the `for` loop.

Using *continue*

The `continue` statement causes program execution to resume at the top of the loop. Any statements following the `continue` statement are skipped. The next code fragment shows how you can use `continue` to print the multiples of 5 from 1 to 100:

```
int i;
...
for( i = 1; i <= 100, i++ ) {
   if( i % 5 != 0 ) continue
   printf( "%d is a multiple of 5!\n", i );
}
```

The `for` loop is used to count from 1 to 100. In the body of the loop, the `if` statement determines whether the variable `i` is a multiple of 5. If `i` is not a multiple of 5, the `continue` statement is executed. The `continue` statement causes the `printf()` statement to be skipped and execution to resume at the top of the loop.

The `do-while`, `while`, and `for` loops can handle most repetitive tasks. When you combine the `goto`, `break`, and `continue` statements with these loop structures, you have tools that are even more versatile.

Changing the Flow of Program Execution

When you think of changing the flow of execution in a program, you usually think of using the iteration statements or the conditional statements (`if` and `switch`). But these tools are not the only ones available for changing the flow of execution. You can also use a number of *functions*.

The functions that change the flow of execution in a program can be divided into two groups. The functions in the first group handle the early termination of a program. This group includes the `exit()` and `abort()`

functions. The functions in the second group cause a program to be suspended while another program is executed. This group includes the `spawn...( )` family of functions, the `exec..( ).` family of functions, and the `system( )` function.

Using *exit( )* and *abort( )*

You use the `exit( )` and `abort( )` functions to terminate a program early. The `exit( )` function terminates a program normally, and the `abort( )` function terminates a program abnormally.

The `exit( )` function causes any open buffers to be written, closes open files, and executes any specified shut-down functions. Although the `exit( )` function terminates a program normally, `exit( )` is not used unless a serious error is encountered. In that case, the `exit( )` function shuts down the program in as orderly a manner as possible. This function has the following format:

```
exit( status );
```

In the `exit( )` function call, the *status* parameter indicates whether the program is terminating normally or abnormally. If the program is to terminate normally, the *status* argument is `EXIT_SUCCESS`, a macro which has a value of 0. If the program is to terminate abnormally, the *status* argument is `EXIT_FAILURE`, a macro with a nonzero value. The *status* argument is passed to the process that called the program, letting the calling process know the condition of the program at termination.

You can use the `atexit( )` function with the `exit( )` function to provide a series of up to 32 functions that can be called when the program terminates. When the `exit( )` function is called, any functions *registered* by the `atexit( )` function are executed before the program terminates. The functions registered by `atexit( )` are called on a last-in-first-out basis. Listing 3.6 demonstrates the `exit( )` and `atexit( )` functions.

Listing 3.6. `term.c`. *A program that uses the* `exit( )` *and* `atexit( )` *functions to terminate a program.*

```
1   #include <stdio.h>
2   #include <stdlib.h>
3
4   void term_1( void );
5   void term_2( void );
6
7   main()
```

```
8   {
9     atexit( term_2 );
10    atexit( term_1 );
11
12    printf( "In main, processing normally.\n" );
13    printf( "Beginning termination.\n" );
14    exit( EXIT_SUCCESS );
15    printf( "This statement is never executed.\n" );
16  }
17
18  void term_1( void )
19  {
20    printf( "Program termination eminent.\n" );
21    printf( "In function term_1.\n" );
22  }
23
24  void term_2( void )
25  {
26    printf( "Program termination proceeding.\n" );
27    printf( "In function term_2.\n" );
28  }
```

In lines 9 and 10 of listing 3.6, the atexit( ) function registers two functions. The registered functions are executed when the exit( ) function is called. Notice the order in which the functions are registered. The last function to be executed is registered first, and the first function to be executed is registered last.

In line 14, the exit( ) function is called. This function halts program execution after the registered functions are executed. The registered functions term_1( ) and term_2( ) are called before the program ends. In addition, the exit( ) function closes any open files and writes any open output buffers. This program has no files or buffers to close. Note that the statements following the exit( ) function are never executed.

Like exit( ), the abort( ) function causes a program to terminate. However, abort( ) does not perform any cleanup before halting the program. The abort( ) function simply causes the program to crash. This function is most often used when a catastrophic error has occurred and the only thing you can do is to bomb out of your program. abort( ) is a messy but effective way to end a program.

The following code fragment shows the use of abort() in a program:

```
printf( "Catastrophic errors have occurred.\n" );
printf( "Terminating program.\n" );
abort();
```

As you can see, calling the abort() function is simple. When abort() is executed, it causes an exit code of 3 to be returned to the parent process or to DOS.

Using the *system()*, *exec...()*, and *spawn...()* Functions

The abort() and exit() functions are two useful functions Borland C++ provides for handling extraordinary circumstances. Borland C++ has a second group of functions you can use to change your program execution. The functions in this group, though, are not as severe as abort() and exit(). You use the functions in this second group to run other programs under your application. Running other programs from within your program is a handy feature of Borland C++. You have available the utility of the other program without having to rewrite that program yourself.

This section introduces the system(), exec...(), and spawn...() functions. The system() function lets you run programs or DOS commands from within your program. You use the exec...() and spawn...() functions only to execute programs. The exec...() and spawn...() functions are more versatile than the system() function.

The system() function starts COMMAND.COM and executes a normal DOS command. The function has this form:

```
system( const char *command )
```

The *command* in the system() parameter list can be any valid DOS command, or the name of an executable or batch file. In the following line of code, the system() function calls the DOS CHKDSK.COM program:

```
system( "CHKDSK" );
```

You use the exec...() and spawn...() families of functions to run other programs. The programs run by exec...() and spawn...() are known as *child processes*.

The difference between exec...() and spawn...() is that spawn...() accepts an extra argument, the *mode* argument. This argument specifies how spawn...() behaves when a child process is called. The three possible values for the *mode* argument are these:

❏ P_WAIT

The P_WAIT argument specifies that your program will be temporarily stopped while the child process is executed.

❏ P_OVERLAY

The P_OVERLAY argument specifies that the child process will overlay the memory location of the calling process. Using the P_OVERLAY option with spawn...( ) works the same as with exec...( ).

❏ P_NOWAIT

This argument is currently unavailable. If P_NOWAIT were available, it would let your process continue while the child process runs.

Except for *mode*, the arguments for the spawn...( ) and exec...( ) functions are the same. Both families of functions have a *path* argument and an argument list that will be passed to the child process. The *path* argument is the location and name of the child process. spawn...( ) and exec...( ) use the standard DOS procedures when searching for the child process specified in the *path* argument. Here is a typical spawn...( ) function call:

```
spawnl( P_WAIT, "my_prog", NULL );
```

The spawn...( ) function executes the program my_prog. spawn...( ) searches first for MY_PROG.COM; if it doesn't exist, spawn...( ) then looks for MY_PROG.EXE. The calling, or parent, process is suspended while the my_prog child process is executed. In this example, no arguments are passed to my_prog.

See Appendix C to learn more about the exec...( ) and spawn...( ) functions. You can also find information about these functions in the *Borland C++ Reference Guide*.

Using Variable Argument Lists

Many of the functions you write will require a fixed number of arguments. Passing arguments to one of these functions is simple because the function always uses the same number and type of arguments. All functions are not this simple, however. Consider the printf( ) function. Each call to printf( ) could have different types and numbers of arguments. The printf( ) function has a variable argument list.

In this section, you learn how to use variable argument lists in your functions. Variable argument lists can enhance the utility and compactness of the functions you write. The utility of your functions will be enhanced because they can handle more data as well as different kinds of data. Your functions will be more compact because, with variable argument lists, you can write one function instead of several.

Designing Variable Argument Lists

Although a variable argument list is more complicated than a standard argument list, a variable argument list is still easy to use. It requires more planning than a regular argument list because a variable argument list has to determine how many and what kind of arguments are passed to the function.

To access the arguments in a variable argument list, you use a pointer that points to the arguments in the list. The first step in pulling arguments from the variable argument list is to initialize a pointer to the first argument in the list. Once the argument pointer is initialized, each item in the list can be read as the argument pointer is "bumped down" the argument list.

When designing a variable argument list, keep in mind two important points so that the argument pointer points correctly to the arguments in the list:

❑ *You have to specify how long the variable argument list will be.*

❑ *You have to specify what type of data will be contained in the variable argument list.*

Providing such specific information may first seem to contradict the idea of a variable argument list. You can use one of three ways to provide this information, however, and still use a *variable* argument list.

The first, and most common, way to indicate how much and what kind of data you have is to use a *format string*. A format string uses a set of symbols to indicate the type and number of arguments that follow in the variable argument list. Note the use of a format string in this `printf( )` function:

```
printf( "i = %d, x = %f", i, x );
```

`printf( )` prints two variables of different types. This function knows what kind of information to print because of the format string

```
"i = %d, x = %f"
```

The two characters preceded by the % sign are called *conversion specification characters*. These characters let the `printf( )` function know how many and what type of variables follow in the variable argument list.

The second way to keep track of the variables in a variable argument list is to include a *terminating value*. This value is not used in the function but is placed at the end of the variable argument list to signal that all data has been read. Look at this line of code:

```
sum( num_type, 2, 39, 56, 0 );
```

The value 0 (zero) is the terminating value. Because this example contains a sum( ) function, the 0 value is not needed. Therefore, when you encounter a 0 in the variable argument list, you know that you have read all the numbers you need. The 0 tells you that you can stop fetching numbers to sum.

The drawback to using a terminating value is that all the numbers have to be a fixed type. If you use a terminating value, you cannot mix data types. The computer has to know what data type you want so that the computer can read the proper number of bytes from memory. (Remember that each data type uses a different number of bytes for storage.)

The third way to track the arguments in a variable argument list is to include a variable that tells the function how many data items to read. This method suffers from the same drawback for using a terminating value. All the items in the variable argument list must be the same type.

Using the *va_...( )* Functions

In the preceding section, you learned what a variable argument list is, and you saw how to use a pointer to move down the list and point to the next data item to be retrieved. This section presents the tools you can use with variable argument lists. Borland C++ provides three macros and one data type for manipulating a variable argument list. These tools belong to the va_...( ) family of functions.

The data type defined is va_list. It is used to declare an *argument pointer* that points to the data items in the variable argument list. The macros in the va_...( ) family have this syntax:

```
void va_start(va_list ap, lastfix);
type va_arg(va_list ap, type);
void va_end( va_list ap);
```

va_start( ) sets up the argument pointer to point to the first variable argument in the list. The ap parameter tells va_start( ) which pointer will be used to access the variable argument list, and the lastfix parameter specifies the last fixed argument in the variable argument list. The va_start( ) macro causes ap to point just beyond the argument specified by lastfix. This macro must be executed before either va_arg( ) or va_end( ) can be used.

va_arg( ) has a twofold purpose. First, va_arg( ) returns the value of the object pointed to by the argument pointer *ap*. Second, va_arg( ) updates the argument pointer to point to the next item in the list. The *type* specified in the va_arg( ) parameter list tells va_arg( ) what type of data is being read. The *type* argument tells va_arg( ) whether the data pointed to is an integer, a double, or some other type. The *type* argument also provides va_arg( ) with the information necessary to update the argument pointer correctly.

va_end( ) performs the housekeeping chores necessary for the called function to return correctly. If va_end( ) is not called after all the variable arguments have been read, your program can suffer from strange and undefined errors.

The next two program listings, listings 3.7 and 3.8, show how you can use the va_...( ) family of functions. The first program contains a variable argument list that has the number of arguments specified when the function is called. The second program, which is a variation of the first program, uses a special value to indicate the end of the list.

Listing 3.7. v_list1.c. *A program that uses a variable argument list.*

```
 1   /*   V_LIST1.C   This program uses a variable argument list
 2                    that specifies the number of arguments in
 3                    the list when the function is called. */
 4
 5   #include <stdio.h>
 6   #include <stdlib.h>
 7   #include <stdarg.h>
 8   #include <conio.h>
 9
10   int sum( int no_args, ... );
11
12   main( )
13   {
14      int no_args;
15      int result;
16
17      clrscr( );
18      printf( "This program calculates the sum of a \n" );
19      printf( "group of numbers. You will supply the \n" );
20      printf( "sum function with the number of items to \n" );
21      printf( "sum and a list of integer values. \n\n" );
22
```

```
23    no_args = 5;
24    result = sum( no_args, 3, 5, 18, 57, 66 );
25    printf( "The value of result = %d\n", result );
26
27    return 0;
28  }
29
30  int sum( int no_args, ... )
31  {
32    va_list ap;
33    int result = 0;
34    int i;
35
36    va_start( ap, no_args );
37
38    for( i = 1; i <= no_args; i++ ) {
39      result += va_arg( ap, int );
40    }
41
42    return result;
43  }
```

Listing 3.7 shows a sum( ) function that uses a variable argument list. The sum( ) function uses a variable that stores the number of arguments to be passed to the function.

As you have seen, a variable argument list requires a method of detecting the end of the argument list. In listing 3.7, an extra variable stores a value that equals the number of arguments passed to the function. This extra variable lets you read all the arguments passed to the function without going past the end of the argument list.

Line 10 contains the function prototype for the sum( ) function. This function returns an integer value, which is equal to the sum of the arguments passed to the function. Two specifications are in the argument list for sum( ). The first argument, no_args, is the variable indicating the number of items in the variable argument list. You supply the value of the no_args variable each time you call the function. The second argument is the ellipsis (. . .). It indicates that a variable number of arguments will be passed to the function.

An example of a function call to sum( ) is shown in line 24. Notice in line 23 that the no_args variable is assigned a value which equals the number of arguments passed to sum( ) in line 24.

The sum() function is defined in lines 30–43. An argument pointer, with a va_list data type, is declared in line 32. The argument pointer points to an argument in the variable argument list. In line 36, the va_start() macro loads the argument pointer ap with the address of the first variable argument.

In lines 38–40 of listing 3.7, the for loop steps through the items in the variable argument list. The va_arg() macro returns the value of an item in the variable argument list and increments the argument pointer to the next item in the list. The result variable accumulates the values returned by the va_arg() macro. When the for loop finishes, the value of the result variable is returned to the calling function.

The program in listing 3.8 does not require a variable indicating the number of arguments passed to the function. Instead, the function checks the variable argument list for a terminating value. When one is encountered, the function stops processing arguments.

Listing 3.8. v_list2.c. *Another function with a variable argument list.*

```
1   /*   V_LIST2.C   This program uses a variable argument list
2                    that contains a terminating value. */
3
4   #include <stdio.h>
5   #include <stdlib.h>
6   #include <stdarg.h>
7   #include <conio.h>
8
9   int sum( int first_num, ... );
10
11  main()
12  {
13    int result;
14
15    clrscr();
16    printf( "This program calculates the sum of a \n" );
17    printf( "group of numbers. You will supply the \n" );
18    printf( "sum function with a list of values. \n" );
19    printf( "You must have at least one value, and the \n" );
20    printf( "last value must be zero. \n\n" );
21
22    result = sum( 43, 56, 1, 19, 3 ,0 );
23    printf( "The value of result = %d\n", result );
24
25    return 0;
```

```
26  }
27
28  int sum( int first_num, ... )
29  {
30    va_list ap;
31    int result;
32    int number;
33
34    va_start( ap, first_num );
35
36    result = first_num;
37
38    while( ( number = va_arg( ap, int ) ) != 0 ) {
39      result += number;
40  }
41
42    return result;
43  }
```

The program in listing 3.8 is similar to the program in listing 3.7. This program, however, does not require a value to be passed to the sum( ) function, indicating how many arguments will be in the variable argument list.

Notice the function declaration in line 9 of listing 3.8. Every function with a variable argument list requires that you have at least one fixed argument. In sum( ), the fixed argument stores the first item in the list of items to be summed. In line 36, you can see that the fixed variable is processed separately.

In listing 3.8, the loop that reads the values in the variable argument list is different from the loop in listing 3.7. To loop through the variable argument list, the for loop in listing 3.7 uses the variable that indicates the number of items in the list. In listing 3.8, the while loop gets values from the variable argument list until the terminating value is encountered.

In line 38, the va_arg( ) macro reads a value from the variable argument list, and the value is assigned to the variable number. The value assigned to number is then checked to determine whether the terminating value was read. When the terminating value is read, the while loop ends.

Exercises

These execises give you practice in creating your own functions, passing and returning values from functions, controlling loops, handling errors, and using variable argument lists.

1. Write a program containing functions that return `int`, `double`, and `char` values.

2. Use the Borland C++ on-line help facility to find the header files required for the `clrscr()`, `gettime()`, `modf()`, and `setpalette()` functions.

3. Design and write a function that gets two letters from the keyboard, compares the letters, and tells you which letter has the greater value. Use the function-creation process described in the section "Writing Prototypes for Your Function."

4. Write a function with arguments passed by value. Then write a similar function with arguments passed by reference.

5. Write a function to demonstrate the use of a `static` variable.

6. Design a loop that uses the `continue` statement.

7. Write a program that uses `exit()` to handle a simulated error.

8. Define a function that uses a variable argument list. Use a terminating character to detect the end of the variable argument list.

Summary

In this chapter, you learned more about the use and design of C functions. The following important points were covered:

❏ *The `main()` function is required in every C program.*

❏ *Borland C++ has an extensive set of library functions.* To use a function from the Borland C++ libraries, you must include the appropriate header file in your program.

❏ *A function prototype, or function declaration, tells the compiler about the data sent to and from a function.* This information helps the compiler catch errors that result from the improper use of a function.

❏ *You can pass arguments to a function either by value or by reference.* Passing by value means that a copy of the argument is sent to the function. Passing by reference means that the address of the data variable is sent to the calling function.

❏ *A variable's storage class determines where and when the variable can be accessed.* The three parts that make up a variable's storage class are scope, duration, and linkage. Scope refers to the parts of the program that can be accessed by a variable. Duration indicates the length of time a variable exists. Linkage refers to the accessibility of your data from another source file.

❏ *You use the* `va_...( )` *family of functions to process variable argument lists.*

Using Pointers and Derived Types

Now that you have learned the basic features of C programming, you can write moderately useful programs. This chapter covers some of the most powerful features of the C language and will enable you to write advanced programs. You learn more about C's data types, and you learn how to use the derived and aggregate data types. Perhaps most important, you see how pointers can provide new ways to access functions and data in your applications. A pointer is, strictly speaking, a derived type. However, pointers are so special and useful in C programs that they occupy a category by themselves.

Understanding Standard C Derived Types

This section introduces C's derived types. So far, all you have seen are the basic data types, which declare the fundamental data objects used in C. An object declared with a basic type represents only a single piece of data. An object declared with a derived type, however, can represent several pieces of data, or it can represent a new use for an already familiar type.

Understanding derived types involves expanding your view of how C categorizes and controls data objects. Therefore, in this section, you first learn about C's data typing scheme. With that conceptual foundation in place, you then learn what the derived types are and how they are used by your computer.

Understanding C's Typing Scheme

Only three broad categories of types are at the apex of the C typing scheme: *object types*, which describe variables and more complex data objects; *function types*, which are associated with all C functions; and *incomplete types*, which identify the kind of object being used, but lack sufficient information to determine the object's size. It is important to know these categories of C types, because derived types can cut across the boundaries of type categories.

Beginning students of C are generally surprised to learn that C, at the most fundamental level, knows about only two kinds of data: integers and floating-point numbers. All other basic data types are qualified or derived versions of these two. Some groups of type versions overlap other groups. C recognizes the following broad categories of object types:

❏ The *integral types* are most fundamental to C. The integral types include characters, integers, and enumerations. The integral types also include both the signed and unsigned character and integer types.

❏ The more general group of *arithmetic types* overlaps the integral types. The arithmetic types include all the integral types plus the floating-point types.

❏ The *scalar types* comprise an even more general grouping of types. The scalar types include both the arithmetic types and the pointer types. Because a pointer is a derived type, the scalar types include both basic and derived object types.

C creates the derived types from the categories of types just listed.

Creating New Types from Old

A *derived type* is a modified form of a basic data type. Borland C++ follows the ANSI standard for C in providing two derived object types and a function type:

❏ *Array type*. An array is a collection of many objects, all of which have the same basic type. You can define an array of `int`, an array of `char`, and so on, for all the basic C types. You can also declare an array of the aggregate type `struct` (`struct` is described shortly), resulting in an array of `struct`.

❑ *Function type*. From the perspective of C's typing scheme, a function is a special type of object that returns a value having a type you define. A function that returns an integer, for example, has type function returning `int`. You might also declare a function with type function returning `char*` (a pointer to `char`), function returning `void*` (a `void` pointer), or simply, function returning `void` (a function returning nothing).

❑ *Pointer type*. The pointer is a special object in C. A pointer is an object whose value is the *memory address* of another object. A pointer type may be derived from a function type, a basic type, or an incomplete type (see the sidebar "What Is an Incomplete Type?"). The kind of object being pointed to is called the *reference type* of the pointer. For example, if you define a pointer to `int`, the reference type is `int`. C pointers give you tremendous power and flexibility in managing and manipulating data and functions.

As you have seen, a function is a collection of C statements that performs some task. When a function completes its processing, it generally returns a value to its caller. The kind of value returned is determined by the declaration of the function's type. The type of the value returned by the function determines the function's precise type.

The type of a pointer is determined by the type of the object referenced by the pointer (that is, by the reference type). Borland C++ makes use of the pointer's reference type when the pointer is used for processing array-like objects. The pointer's reference type determines how much the pointer must be incremented to advance to the next object.

Arrays are a hybrid object type, spanning the boundaries of both derived and aggregate types. Arrays are collections of objects that have the same data type. An array is a derived type because it represents a new use for its element type. An array is considered also an aggregate type because it is a collection of similar objects.

Many arrays contain objects declared only as basic data types, but you can declare an array of pointers to objects, an array of pointers to functions, and even an array of structures. Figure 4.1 shows how an integer array is stored in your computer's memory.

As you can see from figure 4.1, an array occupies a contiguous block of memory. The amount of memory used is determined by the number of elements in the array and the space required to store each element. A 10-element `int` array, for instance, occupies less space than a 10-element `double` array. The sizes (and value ranges) of the basic types were given in Chapter 2.

What Is an Incomplete Type?

An *incomplete type* describes instance objects (particular, defined objects) but lacks enough information to determine an object's size. You can take the address of such an object, but you cannot access the object. Only arrays and structures can have incomplete type, as described in the following paragraphs.

An array with a missing size value (subscript bound) has incomplete type. The declaration `extern int ages[]` has incomplete array type, for instance. You can use such a declaration to describe an array of unknown size residing in another source file, or to pass an array of variable size to a function. For multidimensional arrays, only the leftmost subscript bound can be omitted (for example, `extern int stats[][2]` is a list of pairs of statistics, but the length of the list is unknown). An incomplete array type is completed when you initialize the array, like this:

```
int numbers[] = { 1, 2, 3, 4 };
```

If the leftmost bound (or the only bound) is omitted, you can use the array normally—but be sure that you do not refer to elements beyond the end of the array.

A structure declaration with a tag but no member list has incomplete type. That is, a structure declared without its contents has incomplete type. You might want to write such a declaration if all you need to do at the moment is reserve the structure's name for use in a `typedef`, defining the structure's contents later. For example:

```
struct bigrec;                 /* Incomplete struct type */
...
typedef struct bigrec REC;       /* Here's the typedef */
...
struct bigrec {    /* Now complete struct definition */
  double data1, data2, data3, data4
};
...
REC averages;        /* Finally, use struct via typedef */
```

Note that you cannot use an incomplete `struct` type as a function parameter.

Fig. 4.1. *How an array is stored in memory.*

A 4=element integer array
uses 8 bytes of memory.

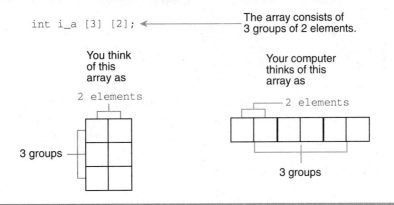

low
address

high
address

2 bytes=
1 element

An array can be declared also with multiple dimensions. You can think of a two-dimensional array as a grid of elements. Each item in the two-dimensional array can be accessed by its row-and-column number. Even though a two-dimensional array is like a grid, the computer stores the elements of the array in a one-dimensional sequence of memory locations, as shown in figure 4.2.

Fig. 4.2. *How a two-dimensional array is stored in memory.*

```
int i_a [3] [2];
```
The array consists of
3 groups of 2 elements.

You think
of this
array as

Your computer
thinks of this
array as

2 elements

2 elements

3 groups

3 groups

You can declare arrays with more than two dimensions. Think of the elements in the arrays as being stored in groups and subgroups. Memory is allocated for an array so that all the elements indexed by the rightmost subscript are in contiguous memory locations.

An *enumeration* is a special integer type, and not really a derived type. It is mentioned here simply because it is syntactically similar to derived type declarations. An enumeration lets you assign mnemonic identifiers to integer values. The classic example is the assignment of values to the days of the week:

```
enum wk_days{ sun, mon, tue, wed, thu, fri, sat };
int day_no;

for( day_no = sun; day_no <= sat; day_no++ )
   printf( "The day number is: %d\n", day_no );
```

On the first line of this code fragment, the `enum` statement assigns an integer value to the name of each weekday. After the enumeration statement, whenever the name of a weekday is used, that name is replaced with the integer value assigned to it in the enumeration. Because each weekday name is assigned an integer value, the assignment expressions in the last two lines do not generate errors.

Understanding C Pointers

The pointer may be the most flexible feature of C—and it may be the most widely misunderstood as well. Programmers familiar with other languages may have found pointers difficult to use. In C, however, you can easily include pointers in your programs, after you master the underlying concept. Of all derived types, the pointer is discussed first because almost all significant C programs use pointers heavily.

The basic concept of a C pointer is easy to understand. A *pointer* is a data object that holds the memory address of another object. Thus, you can deal directly with the pointer, or you can deal with the object *addressed by* the pointer. You can change the value of a pointer, thus changing the location in memory being pointed to. You can change also the value of the object pointed to, accessing the object by means of the pointer.

Now here is a statement that should give you pause for thought: the size of a pointer *object* is not necessarily the same as the size of the *object pointed to*. Hang in there for just a minute. It is important to sort out the ideas of a pointer as an object, and a pointer as a locator for another object.

To highlight that difference, think for a moment about a pointer to a function in a small model Borland C++ program. Because the small model is being used, the pointer requires only two bytes of memory to hold the address of the function. But how big is the function? A function's executable code could occupy thousands of bytes of memory. You can see that there is a considerable difference between the size of the function and the size of the pointer to the function.

Pointers can sometimes speed up the handling of data. You can move the address of a complex data structure more quickly than you can move the data structure itself, simply because pointers are typically much smaller than the objects they point to. Pointers also give you more control over your data: with a pointer, you can access data that does not even reside in the boundaries of your program!

This section explains how you can use pointers. You learn how Borland C++ implements pointers by using the indirection and address-of operators to control indirect addressing.

Understanding Indirect Addressing

Understanding indirect addressing requires that you first understand how *any* object is stored in RAM. A computer's random-access memory (RAM) is arranged as a contiguous series of storage locations. Each location contains enough bits to hold the smallest recognizable object for the machine. On the 80x86 CPU, the smallest addressable location is an 8-bit byte, which is sufficient to store one C character. (On some machines the smallest addressable unit is a *word*, which may be able to hold more than one byte.)

Each RAM location is associated with a number called its *address*. Each data object therefore has a specific address in your computer's memory. When the Borland C++ compiler encounters the variables you declare, it sets aside storage for the variables and keeps track of where the variables were placed in memory. That is, the address of the variable is recorded in the compiler's *symbol table* (see the sidebar "RAM Addresses and the System Loader"). Later references to the same function or variable cause the compiler to use the address stored in the symbol table to access the object. Figure 4.3 illustrates how data objects are stored and accessed directly.

RAM Addresses and the System Loader

Addresses of program variables are known relative to the beginning of the memory segments used during compilation and link editing. For example, `function_a()` might be 256 bytes beyond the start of the code segment, and the integer `counter` might be 16 bytes beyond the start of the data segment.

Actual memory addresses are determined by the DOS loader when the program is run. The process of computing true function and variable addresses at run-time is called *address relocation*.

Fig. 4.3. *Accessing an object through direct addressing.*

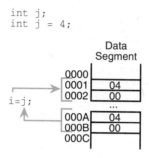

As noted, a pointer is a data object that contains the memory address of another object. A pointer to an integer, for instance, contains the address (that is, the RAM location) of the integer variable. To access the variable being pointed to, the compiler must generate code in two steps. First, the pointer *object* must be fetched to get the address of the target variable. Second, the address from the first step is used to access the variable. This process is called *indirect addressing* and is the method Borland C++ uses to implement pointers in your program. Figure 4.4 shows how a variable can be accessed using indirect addressing (that is, by using a pointer). Listing 4.1 shows how an integer variable can be accessed indirectly, through a pointer.

Fig. 4.4. *Accessing an object through indirect addressing.*

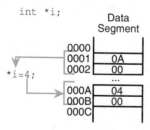

Listing 4.1. p_intro.c. *A program that uses indirect addressing.*

```
1   /* P_INTRO.C   This program demonstrates the use of
2                  pointers and indirect addressing.   */
3
4   #include <stdio.h>
5   #include <stdlib.h>
```

```
 6
 7  main()
 8  {
 9    int i, j;
10    int *i_ptr;
11
12    i = 34;
13    i_ptr = &i;
14    j = *i_ptr;
15
16    printf( "i = %d\n", i );
17    printf( "j = %d\n", j );
18    printf( "i_ptr = %p\n", i_ptr );
19
20    return 0;
21  }
```

In listing 4.1, two integer variables are declared. In line 12, the first integer, i, is assigned the value 34. In line 14, the second integer, j, is assigned, by indirection, the value stored in the first integer. Before the second integer can be assigned a value, however, a pointer must be declared and initialized, as shown in line 13.

In line 10, a pointer to int is declared. The indirection operator (*) indicates that the object being declared is a pointer and not a regular variable. In line 13, the integer pointer i_ptr is assigned the address of the integer variable i. Note that the address-of operator (&) is used to get the address of the i variable. (The * and & operators are discussed in the next section.)

Next, in line 14, the value stored in i is assigned to j by indirection—that is, through the pointer. Now the * indirection operator prefixed to i_ptr indicates that the value stored in the *object pointed to* by i_ptr will be assigned to j. Think about this carefully: an object value, not the pointer's value, is assigned.

The purpose of listing 4.1 is to introduce you to the concept of indirection; this program is only a limited demonstration of pointers and indirection. Using pointers to refer to objects of the basic data types has little value. Pointers are most useful when they refer to complex data structures, and when they are used to manage dynamically controlled data.

You can use a single pointer to flexibly select different data objects. There are many applications of this idea. A common example is "stepping through" the characters in a string quickly, without using array subscripts. Listing 4.2 shows a program that does this.

Listing 4.2. `exchange.c`. *A program that uses a pointer to step through a string.*

```
 1  #include <stddef.h>
 2  #include <stdlib.h>
 3  #include <stdio.h>
 4  #include <string.h>
 5
 6  /* +----------------------------------------------------+
 7     + Exchange two areas of memory with no auxiliary
 8     +    storage used.
 9     +
10     + Calling Sequence:
11     +
12     + mem_exchange( void *s1, void *s2, size_t n );
13     +
14     +   where s1 and s2 can be pointers of any type.
15     +   Two areas of storage, each "n" bytes long,
16     +   are exchanged in place.
17     +
18     +----------------------------------------------------+
19  */
20  void mem_exchange( void *s1, void *s2, size_t n )
21  {
22     unsigned char *p1, *p2;
23
24     p1 = s1;
25     p2 = s2;
26     for ( ; n>0; n-- ) {
27        *p1 ^= *p2;
28        *p2 ^= *p1;
29        *p1++ ^= *p2++;
30     }
31  }
32
33  void main()
34  {
35     char s1[40] = "This is the FIRST string. ";
36     char s2[40] = "This is the SECOND string.";
37     int i1 = 255;
38     int i2 = 127;
39
40     clrscr();
41     printf( "%s\n%s\n", s1, s2 );
```

```
42      mem_exchange( (void *)s1, (void *)s2, strlen( s1 ) );
43      printf( "%s\n%s\n\n", s1, s2 );
44
45      printf( "%d\n%d\n", i1, i2 );
46      mem_exchange( (void *)i1, (void *)i2, sizeof( int ) );
47      printf( "%d\n%d\n\n", i1, i2 );
48  }
```

The `exchange.c` program shown in listing 4.2 demonstrates using pointers to step through strings. It shows you also how to swap the contents of two memory locations without using an intermediate holding area.

The `mem_exchange()` function in lines 20–30 does all the work. The first two arguments to this function are `void` pointers so that callers of this function can use any pointer type. `void` pointers are a new feature of ANSI C and have the following characteristics:

❑ `void` *pointers have the same internal representation and address alignment requirements as character pointers*. Character pointers were, in fact, the generic pointer workhorse of pre-ANSI C. Now `void` pointers fill that role.

❑ *You can assign any pointer to a* `void` *pointer without worrying about pointer types*. Pointer type casting is not required when assigning to or from a `void` pointer.

❑ *Pointers are implicitly converted to and from* `void*` *in four circumstances*. A pointer is implicitly converted to or from `void*` in assignments, function prototypes, comparisons, and conditional expressions. The implicit conversion occurs only if there is a clash between the pointer type used and `void*`.

The program in listing 4.2 takes advantage of this rule. The first two arguments for `mem_exchange()` have type `void*` (see line 20), but you can call the function using any pointer type.

❑ *A* `void` *pointer cannot be dereferenced*. That is, you can manipulate address values with a `void` pointer, but you cannot use it to access a data object (dereferencing a pointer is discussed in the next section).

Because a `void` pointer cannot be dereferenced, `mem_exchange()` declares two local pointer variables with type `unsigned char*` (line 22), and uses them to step through the strings. (This function treats everything as if it were a string.)

`mem_exchange()` swaps the contents of the two memory locations addressed by the `void` pointers `s1` and `s2` by applying to every byte in each area a series of three exclusive OR operations. The order in which the exclusive ORs are performed and the order of the operands for each operation are crucial to the success of the technique.

Suppose, for example, that you have two objects, A and B, and you want to exchange their contents. Using an algebra-like pseudocode, the sequence of operations is as follows:

```
A = A XOR B
B = B XOR A
A = A XOR B
```

In `mem_exchange()`, the same effect as this sequence of steps is achieved by using the powerful C exclusive-OR-and-assign compound operator (`^=`). The series of XORs is seen in lines 27–29. The syntax of line 29 is particularly interesting. Here it is again:

```
29          *p1++ ^= *p2++;
```

This line is not as complicated as it may seem, if you just keep operator precedence in mind. Recall that the indirection operator (`*`) has higher precedence than the postfix increment operator (`++`). (Operator precedence was shown in Chapter 2, table 2.9.) Thus, the right side of the assignment is interpreted as meaning that the object pointed to by `p2` is fetched for use *first*, and only then is the pointer incremented. The same rule applies to the `p1` pointer on the left side. Therefore, the XOR operation is logically completed before the pointers are adjusted to the next byte location.

Because a character string is an array of characters, the technique used in listing 4.2 should apply to arrays in general. It does—you can use pointers to step through any array in the manner illustrated in listing 4.2. Figure 4.5 shows how a pointer can be used to step through the elements of an array.

Fig. 4.5. Using a pointer to access array elements.

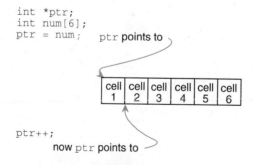

```
int *ptr;
int num[6];
ptr = num;      ptr points to
```

| cell 1 | cell 2 | cell 3 | cell 4 | cell 5 | cell 6 |

```
ptr++;
        now ptr points to
```

The integer array in figure 4.5 has six cells. Two bytes are required to store each integer in the array. When the array is declared, it is assigned a contiguous block of memory that starts, in this case, at the address FF00. Referencing the array name without a subscript returns the starting address of the array. You can see how this works when ptr is assigned the value of num. The ptr pointer is assigned the address of the first element in the array.

If the ptr pointer is incremented by 1, ptr points to the next element in the array. Now ptr holds the address FF02. Note that ptr was incremented by 1, but the *address value* in ptr was incremented by 2. When you increment a pointer, the new value stored in the pointer always points to the next data object. It does not matter whether the data object takes 2 or 20 bytes; when the pointer is incremented, the pointer points to the next data object. Borland C++ uses the size of the pointer's reference type to determine how many byte locations to add when incrementing a pointer by 1.

Using C's Indirection and Address-of Operators

Borland C++ has two special unary operators for working with pointers and address values. You have already seen them, because it is impossible to use a pointer without them. These operators are the *indirection operator* and the *address-of operator*. The indirection operator is represented by the * symbol, and the address-of operator is represented by the & symbol. Now these operators are discussed in more detail.

The indirection operator has a twofold purpose. First, the indirection operator is used to *declare a pointer*. Second, the indirection operator is used to *dereference a pointer*. Dereferencing a pointer means accessing (fetching or storing) the value of the object pointed to.

Note how the indirection operator (*) is used in the following examples of pointer declarations for most of C's basic data types:

```
int *int_ptr;          /* Declare a pointer to int */
char *char_ptr;        /* Declare a pointer to char */
double *flt_ptr;       /* Declare a pointer to double */
const int *ci_ptr;     /* Declare a pointer to const int */
void *any_ptr;         /* Declare a pointer to anything */
```

As you can see, you can declare a pointer for any type of data object. Some of these declarations can even point to arrays. Look at this example:

```
char *char_ptr;
```

`char_ptr` is obviously a pointer to a character type object. But `char_ptr` can be used also as a pointer to a character array. (As you will see shortly, a character array is a string.) You can use any pointer to a basic data type as a pointer to an array of the same type.

The next code fragment shows how a pointer is dereferenced:

```
int *int_ptr;
int i = 6;
int_ptr = &i;
printf( "i = %d", *int_ptr );
```

In this example, a pointer is assigned the address of an integer variable. The pointer is dereferenced in the `printf()` statement, and `printf()` displays the value stored in the integer variable. The pointer is dereferenced (the object is accessed) by the expression `*int_ptr`.

The second unary operator, the address-of operator (&), returns the memory address of its operand. This memory address can be assigned directly to a pointer variable of the correct type. You have seen the address-of operator used several times before. Look at the examples in the following code fragment:

```
char *char_ptr;        /* Declare a pointer       */
char c = 'A';          /* Declare a variable      */
char str[30]           /* Declare an array        */
char_ptr = &c;         /* Get address of variable */
char_ptr = str;        /* Get address of array    */
```

These examples show when the address-of operator is needed and *when it is not.* In the fourth line, the & operator takes the address of the variable c. The address is then assigned to the character pointer variable `char_ptr`. The address-of operator is needed when you want to take the address of a basic data object. In the fifth line, however, the address-of operator is not needed because the address of an array is assigned to a character pointer. Remember that when you reference an array name and you do not supply a subscript, the value returned is the address of the first element in the array. Because you have the address of the first element, you do not need to use the address-of operator. Function names without the function call parentheses also yield the address of the function without using the address-of operator.

The address-of operator cannot be used with a bit-field object or a register variable. A bit-field occurs only in a structure and is discussed later in this chapter. A *register variable* is an `auto` variable that asks the compiler to place the variable in a system hardware register whenever possible. (The `register` keyword is only a hint to the compiler: the variable might not be placed in a system register.)

You should exercise some care to be sure that any pointer you declare is properly initialized before it is used. The compiler will not stop you from using an uninitialized pointer, but the results will be unpredictable.

The value you assign to a pointer can be any valid data address, as well as the NULL value. The NULL value has some interesting features. First, NULL is guaranteed to be unequal to any pointer to an object or function. Therefore, the NULL value will never compare as equal to any valid pointer value in your program. Second, any two NULL values are guaranteed to compare as equal. The NULL values are guaranteed to be equal even if the pointers in which the values are stored are of different types.

Only three arithmetic operations are legal on pointers. You can add integers to pointers, subtract integers from pointers, or subtract pointers from pointers. All other mathematical operations are illegal and pointless. The following list explains the three legal operations:

❑ *Adding an integer value to a pointer.* Adding an integer to a pointer increases the pointer value by the specified number of data objects. For example, if you add 3 to an integer pointer, you will point to the third integer from your current location. You will *not* point to the third byte from your location. Borland C++ always increments by data objects, not by bytes.

❑ *Subtracting an integer value from a pointer.* Subtraction is similar to addition. Subtracting 2 from a `double` pointer causes the pointer to point to a preceding `double` variable. You will not point to a location two bytes in front of your current location. When you perform integer arithmetic on a pointer, Borland C++ makes sure that you move by the specified number of data objects, not by bytes.

❑ *Subtracting one pointer from another.* Subtracting one pointer from another returns the number of data objects between the pointers. You do not get the number of bytes between the objects. When you subtract two pointers, Borland C++ automatically takes the difference in bytes and divides it by the size of the data object. The result of subtracting two pointers can be stored in a variable with the type `ptrdiff_t`.

You can also cast a pointer from one type to another in an expression. A pointer *cast* simply tells the compiler to assume that a different reference type is now being used—the data pointed to does not change, but the compiler handles the data as if it has another type. Pointer casts can be useful when manipulating data in sophisticated ways not ordinarily allowed. Listing 4.3 demonstrates a pointer cast.

Listing 4.3. `uitoh.c`. *A program that prints an* `unsigned long` *integer, byte by byte.*

```
1  /* UITOH.C   This program takes an unsigned integer
2                number and uses a type cast to print
3                each byte of the number in hexadecimal.   */
4
5  #include <stdio.h>
6  #include <stdlib.h>
7
8  main()
9  {
10    unsigned long x = 4096;
11    char *dump;
12    int i;
13
14    dump = ( char * ) &x;
15    for( i = 1; i <= 4; i++ )
16      printf( "Byte %d = %.2x\n", i, *dump++ );
17
18    return 0;
19 }
```

Listing 4.3 uses a pointer cast to print each byte of a multibyte data object—in this case, an `unsigned long` integer. The `unsigned long` is declared and initialized in line 10. A character pointer is declared in line 11. An `unsigned long` integer requires four bytes of memory. However, the `unsigned long` is printed with a `char` pointer that points to one byte at a time. Before the `dump` character pointer can access the data stored in the variable x, a type cast must be performed. The type cast is executed in line 14, where the address of the `unsigned long` integer is obtained. Then the address is type cast to a character pointer, which enables you to access the data in the variable one byte at a time. Because the `dump` pointer points to one byte at a time, `printf()` must be called four times to print the complete value of the x variable.

Using Arrays and Strings

An *aggregate type* is a special derived type. An aggregate is an object that is composed of simpler objects having various other types. Types that can be included in an aggregate object include the basic types, derived types (except for functions), and even other aggregate types. C's aggregate data objects are useful because they can group and control collections of objects *as a unit*, while still permitting access to individual member objects.

There are two kinds of aggregate data objects in C: *arrays* and *structures*. Although a union is not an aggregate type, it has some similarities to structures. Thus, unions are discussed together with structures a little later, in "Using Structures and Unions."

Arrays belong to both the derived and aggregate categories of object types. In this section, you learn how to declare, initialize, and use arrays.

This section shows you also how to use C strings. In C, a string is an array of characters. In fact, the terms *character array* and *string* are synonymous. You learn how to determine the size of an array for a given string, how to initialize a string, and how to assign values to the string.

Declaring and Using Arrays of Objects

An array is a collection of data objects, called array *elements*, that all have the same base data type and occupy a contiguous area of memory. Array elements can have any valid data type. An array declaration has the following form:

```
typename identifier[ size-constant-expression ]
```

`typename` specifies the type of the array's elements. For example, if the element type is `double`, every element in the array is a `double` floating-point number.

The `identifier` is the name of the array. You use this name when you refer to the array in your program. The standard rules for creating a variable name apply to creating a name for the array.

The square brackets enclosing the `size-constant-expression` are called the *array declarator*, and they must be coded as shown. The `size-constant-expression` is an expression that evaluates to a positive integer value, and determines how many elements the array has. If the `size-constant-expression` evaluates to 25, for example, the array has 25 elements. The `size-constant-expression` can be an expression, but it must yield a constant value. You cannot use a variable as the `size-constant-expression`.

Now examine the following declaration:

```
int my_array[100];
```

int is the *element type* of the array, specifying that the elements in the array are integer objects. my_array is the *identifier* of the array. The value 100 indicates how many elements are in the array—it is the array size. In this case, my_array has 100 integer elements.

Later, when you want to access an element in the array, you use an *array index*: the array name my_array followed by a number enclosed in square brackets. The brackets in a reference to an array element are called the array *subscript operator*. Note that the array declarator previously mentioned is, in fact, an array subscript operator (it is just used to indicate size in the declaration) and has the same operator precedence as the subscript operator.

The array index is an expression that evaluates to an integer value, indicating which array element will be accessed. The array index is known also as the *array subscript*. It is important to remember that arrays use a *zero-origin array index*. This means that the first element in the array is element 0, not element 1. When looping through an array, be sure that you start at array element 0.

The following code fragment declares, initializes, and prints an array of integers:

```
int i;
int my_array[100];

for( i = 0; i <= 99; i++ )
  my_array[i] = 100 - i;

for( i = 0; i <= 99; i++ )
  printf( "my_array[%d] = %d\n", i, my_array[i] );
```

In the second line of this code fragment, my_array is declared as an integer array that holds 100 integer values.

The first for statement in the code fragment initializes the array. Note that the array subscript starts with a value of 0. The for loop loops from 0 to 99, or once for every element in the array. As the subscript increases, the corresponding element values in my_array are decreased. The last for loop in the preceding code fragment prints the value of each element in my_array.

Note in the preceding code fragment that a variable can be used as an array subscript. Only the array size must be a constant expression.

Using a multidimensional array is as easy as using a one-dimensional array. The declaration of the array changes only a little—you can declare an array *of array*. You can declare a two-dimensional array, for example, in this way:

```
int my_array[10][3];
```

This array has ten groups of three elements. This declaration is interpreted to mean an array containing ten arrays. Each element is an array that happens to contain three integers (that is, the element type is still int). Each group of three integers is stored together in memory. Thus, when stepping through an array sequentially, the rightmost subscript is exhausted first.

To access a member in a multidimensional array, you use a statement like this:

```
int *i;
...
i = my_array[5][2];
```

You can initialize an array during its declaration, by providing an initializer list. An *initializer list* is a list of values separated by commas and enclosed in braces, as shown in the following line of code:

```
int even_int[5] = { 2, 4, 6, 8, 10 };
```

ANSI-compatible compilers like Borland C++ allow you to leave a trailing comma after the last value in an initializer list. This is convenient if you later want to extend the list (it could prevent a compile-time error). Note that a semicolon is required after the closing brace of an initializer list.

The values in an initializer list are assigned to corresponding array elements from *left to right*. The leftmost value in the string is assigned to even_int[0], and the second value in the string is assigned to even_int[1]. The process continues until all the values are assigned. If you do not supply enough initial values, the remaining elements of the array will be initialized to 0.

If you initialize an array during its declaration, you can optionally omit the *size* of the array (the size expression inside square brackets is also called the *subscript bound*). If you omit the array size expression when declaring an array, the compiler counts the number of elements in the initializer list and automatically allocates enough memory to store the values you provided. You could therefore rewrite the preceding declaration as follows:

```
int even_int[] = { 2, 4, 6, 8, 10 };
```

Even though you did not specify the size of the array, you can still use the array subscript to access any element in the array. Just be sure to note how many elements you assign to the array. Trying to read a value past the end of the array will produce strange results, because the data values will be unpredictable.

You can also use an initializer list with a multidimensional array declaration. Multidimensional array initializer lists can optionally use interior braces to group elements belonging to different indexes. For example, the following code fragment shows two equivalent methods of initializing an array containing three pairs of screen coordinates:

```
    /* Declare the array with fully bracketed syntax */
int screenxy[3][2] = {
  { 0, 0, },
  { 40, 40, },
  { 80, 25, },
};
    /* Declare the array without interior bracketing */
int screenxy[3][2] = { 0, 0, 40, 40, 80, 25, };
```

Notice in the preceding declarations that the initial values are written in the order needed to accommodate the left to right assignment of values used. You could also have omitted the array bound values because the initializer list is given.

Using array subscripts is not the only way you can access array elements. You can also use a *pointer*. Using the name of the array without an array subscript yields the address of the first element in the array. The expression my_array gives the address of the first element in my_array. To access a specific element in the array, you simply add the number of the element you want to the address returned by the array name. The next line of code shows how you can get the value stored in the second element in my_array:

```
i = *( my_array + 1 );
```

my_array written without the subscript operator gives the address of the first element in the array. Adding 1 (remember zero origins) to my_array gives the address of the second element in the array. You do not have to specify the number of bytes to add to my_array. The number of bytes needed for the offset you specify is calculated automatically. The indirection operator, *, returns the value stored at the address calculated in the parentheses.

To get to the fifth element of my_array, you use the expression *(my_array+4). This expression is equivalent to the expression my_array[4]. Array subscript notation is always equivalent to pointer notation in C.

Understanding C Strings

A string is a character array. You can declare a string in the following ways:

```
char str_1[31];
char str_2[] = "This is a demonstration string.";
```

The first declaration, for str_1, sets up a character array that can hold 31 elements. This character array is long enough to hold a 30-character string. str_1 can hold only a 30-character string because every string in C is terminated by the null character. The null character, \0, acts as a *fence* that indicates the end of the string.

The second declaration, for str_2, sets up a character array long enough to hold the string assigned to str_2 plus a null character. As you can see from this declaration, the initializer in a string declaration is a *string literal*, not a list of characters in curly braces. Note that you *cannot* assign a string literal to a string in an ordinary assignment statement.

Figure 4.6 shows how Borland C++ stores a string in your computer's memory.

Fig. 4.6. *How strings are stored.*

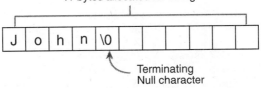

```
char f_name[11] = "John";
```

11 bytes allocated for string

| J | o | h | n | \0 | | | | | |

Terminating
Null character

You don't have to declare strings just barely large enough to hold the initial value. You can declare the string to be considerably longer, and you should if the string will be manipulated in some of the ways shown later in this section.

To get the address of the beginning of the string, you use the name of the string without the braces or an element number. You need to be able to specify the beginning address of the string when you use functions like printf(). When you print a string, printf() requires that you supply only the address of the string. Passing the address of the string increases the speed of your program because only the string's address (not its contents) is passed as an argument. The next line of code prints the contents of str_2:

```
printf( "str_2 = %s\n", str_2 );
```

You can initialize a string outside the string declaration by using the strcpy() function. This function copies the contents of one string into another string. Here is the syntax of strcpy():

```
*strcpy( char *s1, const char *s2 );
```

The contents of the character array pointed to by *s2 are copied into the character array pointed to by *s1. strcpy() returns a pointer to the string s1 (the location of s1 is not changed). It is up to you, the programmer, to arrange matters so that there is enough room in the receiving string. The compiler cannot and will not stop you from copying in a string that is too long (destroying the variables stored just beyond the end of the string).

Actual arguments to the `strcpy()` function can be either string literals or string names (the receiving string, of course, cannot be a string literal). The following code fragment demonstrates the use of `strcpy()`:

```
char s1[30];
char s2[30] = "This is a demonstration.";
...
strcpy( s1, s2 );
printf( "s1 = %s\n", s1 );
```

This code fragment copies the string in the `s2` character array into the `s1` character array. Notice that the arguments for the `strcpy()` function are pointers to the strings being processed. After the `strcpy()` is completed, the `printf()` statement prints the contents of the `s1` string.

Two other useful string-handling functions are `strcat()` and `strlen()`. The `strcat()` function concatenates two strings, and the `strlen()` function calculates the length of the string. Note the format for the `strcat()` function:

```
*strcat( char *s1, const char *s2 )
```

`strcat()` concatenates, or appends, `s2` to the end of `s1`. The terminating null character at the end of `s1` is removed so that the only terminating character will be at the end of the new string. Like `strcpy()`, `strcat()` requires arguments that point to strings. `strcat()` returns a pointer to `s1` when the concatenation is complete.

The following code fragment shows the use of `strcat()`:

```
char first_name[81] = "Bob";
char last_name[20]= "Johnson";
...
strcat( first_name, " " );
strcat( first_name, last_name );
printf( "The name is: %s\n", first_name );
```

The first `strcat()` function adds a blank character to the `first_name` string so that the first and last names are separated correctly. The second `strcat()` function adds the `last_name` string to the `first_name` string. The `printf()` function prints the final result of the concatenation operations.

When you use the `strcat()` function, make sure that the string into which you are copying can hold the entire string. You can use the `strlen()` function to check the lengths of the strings. Listing 4.4 shows how you can use `strlen()` and `strcat()` together.

Listing 4.4. `name.c`. *A program that uses string functions.*

```
1   /* NAME.C        This program demonstrates the strlen() and
2                    strcat() functions. */
3
4   #include <stdio.h>
5   #include <stdlib.h>
6   #include <string.h>
7
8   #define LONG_STR 81
9   #define SHORT_STR 31
10
11  main()
12  {
13     char first_name[LONG_STR] = "Bob ";
14     char last_name[SHORT_STR] = "Johnson";
15     int i;
16
17     i = strlen( first_name ) + strlen( last_name );
18     if( i <= LONG_STR ) {
19       strcat( first_name, last_name );
20       printf( "string length = %d\n", i );
21       printf( "%s\n", first_name );
22     }
23     else
24       printf( "Strings too long.\n" );
25
26   return 0;
27  }
```

In line 17, `strlen()` calculates the lengths of the `first_name` and `last_name` strings. The results of `strlen()` are stored in the variable `i`. In line 18, the value stored in `i` is compared with the maximum string-length value. If the length of both strings is less than the maximum string length, the statements in lines 19–21 are executed. The two strings are concatenated, and the results are displayed.

The `strlen()` function requires an argument that is a pointer to the string whose length is to be calculated. The value returned by `strlen()` has the data type `size_t`. However, the value returned by `strlen()` can be stored in a regular integer, as in line 17.

You can use the strlen() function, and take advantage of the fact that strings are arrays, to insert individual characters anywhere in the string. The following code fragment contains a function that performs this task:

```
#include <string.h>
...
void cinsert( char ccode,char *anystring,int spos )
{
  int p;

  p = strlen(anystring);
  spos = ( spos < 0 ) ? 0 : spos;
  spos = ( spos >= p ) ? p : spos;
  for ( ; p>=spos; p--) anystring[p+1]=anystring[p];
  anystring[spos]=ccode;
}
```

The cinsert() function will insert a character anywhere within a string: at the beginning, in the middle, or at the end. The character to be inserted, ccode, will be placed at the insertion point, defined by the argument spos. Note that spos should have the sense of a subscript: to insert a character at the beginning of the string, set spos to zero. The inserted character will appear in the string *before* the character originally in that same position.

To make room for the new character, all the characters at the insertion point and to the right of it are moved out of the way (by moving them one position to the right). The terminating null character is moved also. Since character movement proceeds from right to left, it is easier to use array subscript notation than pointer notation to access characters in the string. Here is how the function works:

1. The length of the target string is computed first and stored in the local variable p. Note that p used as a subscript at this time would index to the position of the terminating null character. That is exactly right, since the null character should "move out of the way" also.

2. The first conditional assignment statement determines whether the requested insertion point is to the left of the string (that is, whether spos is negative). If it is, the insertion point is coerced to the beginning of the string.

3. The second conditional assignment statement determines whether the requested insertion point is to the right of the string (beyond the null terminating character). If it is, the insertion point is coerced to the right end of the string.

4. The for loop now moves the right-hand fragment of the string one position to the right, to make room for the new character. This is accomplished quite easily, by successively assigning the [p+1] character in the string the value of the [p] character. The string is treated just like any other array by the for loop, subscripting to the desired locations. Many string functions use only pointer notation, but that is only a matter of convenience and suitability for a specific task.

5. Finally, the new character is placed in the string at the insertion point.

The string functions presented here are just a few of those that Borland C++ provides. An extensive library of string functions is accessible when you include the string.h header file in your programs.

Using Structures and Unions

Structures and unions enable you to keep related data together in one object. This section shows you how to create structures and unions, and how to implement them in your programs. Even though a structure and a union may look similar, they are handled differently.

Building Structures from Different Types

Like an array, a structure stores a group of data. However, the *member objects* in a structure do not have to be of the same type. A structure can contain members that are either basic, derived, or aggregate data types. Thus, unlike arrays, structures do not overlap the categories of derived and aggregate types—a structure is strictly an aggregate object.

Although the member objects of a structure may have different types, member objects are usually related functionally. A medical record is a good example of a structure. Such a record contains character arrays for the patient's name, integers for age, and floating-point numbers for weight, as well as many other kinds of information. Structures provide a way to keep all the information together where it is needed. Figure 4.7 shows a typical structure.

The structure object in figure 4.7 contains three member objects. One member in the structure has an aggregate data type, and the other two members have basic data types. The structure member with an aggregate type is name, which is a character array. The other objects, age and weight, have basic data types.

Fig. 4.7. *A structure data type object.*

```
struct med_rec {
    char name [30];
    int age;
    double weight;
}
```

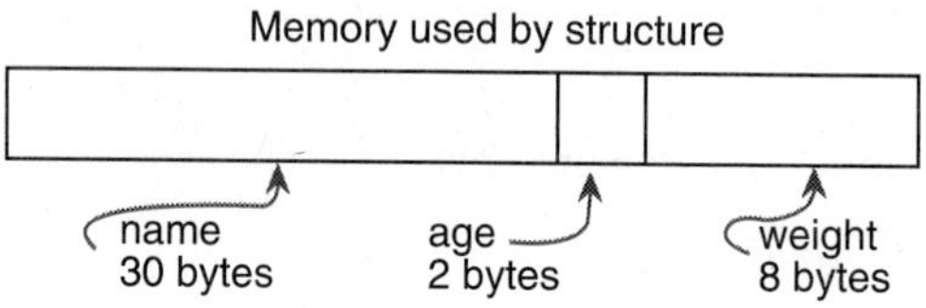

Memory used by structure

name   age   weight
30 bytes   2 bytes   8 bytes

A structure *type* declaration has the following basic form:

```
struct tag-name   {
               opt
    member-list
               opt
} identifier-list    ;
                 opt
```

In the first line, the `struct` keyword signals the compiler that a structure declaration is about to begin. The `tag-name` gives the structure type a name and makes it possible for you to declare a structure type object later in the program. The `tag-name` is optional; you do not have to supply one, but omitting it will prevent declaring later structure *objects* with this specific structure type. The `member-list` contains the data types and names of the member objects that are included in the structure. The `member-list` is also optional, but the structure type is *incomplete* until a member list is declared to complete the declaration (see the sidebar "What Is an Incomplete Type?" earlier in this chapter). Finally, the optional `identifier-list` can define one or more structure *objects* to be used in your program.

The following code fragment is a typical structure declaration that includes a tag name:

```
struct cars{
    char make[31];
    int year;
    double miles;
    double cost;
};
...
struct cars car1, car2;
```

Here `struct` tells the compiler that a structure is being declared. `cars` is the *tag name* used to declare other objects with this same structure type. The declarations between the braces are the member list, containing the data objects in which the structure's information is stored. Any structure objects defined with this type will have type `struct cars`.

Notice on the last line of this code fragment that the `cars` tag name defines two structure type data objects. The data objects defined each contain all the member variables listed in the structure declaration.

If a structure does not use a tag name, all the data objects of that structure type must be declared immediately following the structure declaration. Without a tag name, the preceding structure declaration would look like this:

```
struct {
    char make[31];
    int year;
    double miles;
    double cost;
} car1, car2;
```

You can create a type definition by using the `typedef` keyword with your structure declaration. `typedef` works like a tag name, but its purpose is to define a synonym for *any* existing type name. Here, using a `typedef` enables you to create another name for your structure type. If you rewrote this structure declaration with a `typedef`, you would have the following form:

```
typedef struct {
    char make[31];
    int year;
    double miles;
    double cost;
}   CAR_TYPE;
...
CAR_TYPE car1, car2;
```

You can even use a tag name with the `typedef` statement if you like, but using both is redundant.

You use the *structure member operator* (`.`) to access a member of a structure. To get the `miles` member of the `car1` object, for example, you use this statement:

```
x = car1.miles
```

Here the value stored in the `miles` member of the `car1` object is assigned to the variable `x`.

If you have two objects with the same structure type, you can assign all the values in one structure to the other structure with one statement:

```
car1 = car2;
```

The value of each member in `car2` is assigned to the corresponding member in `car1`. This kind of assignment can be handy for initializing structures from existing structures.

When you are using pointers to locate and control structures, accessing a member object is a little different. To access a member through a pointer to `struct`, you must use the *structure pointer operator* (`->`). The following code fragment demonstrates the use of the structure pointer operator:

```
struct demo_s {
  char d_str[20];
  int d_int;
  double d_flt;
};
struct demo_s d_struct1;
struct demo_s *d_ptr;
d_ptr = & d_struct1;
...
i = d_ptr -> d_int;
```

In the first five lines, a structure is declared. On the sixth line, an object of type `struct demo_s` is declared. This structure type object is `d_struct1`, and the seventh and eighth lines set up a pointer to the `d_struct1` data object. On the last line of the code fragment, the `->` operator is used to fetch the value stored in the `d_int` member of the `d_struct1` structure type object. The value stored in this instance of `d_int` is assigned to the variable `i`.

To determine the size of a structure object, you use the `sizeof` operator. The value returned by `sizeof` may be different from the value you calculate by summing the sizes of the members of the structure. The reason for the discrepancy is that the compiler may insert empty space in your structure to control the alignment of member objects.

Bit-fields are data formats you can use only inside a structure. A bit-field lets you declare signed or unsigned integers from 1 to 16 bits wide. A bit-field also can store multiple values in one byte of information. The declaration of a bit-field variable has this form:

```
type-specifier bitfield-id : width
```

The *type-specifier* determines what type of value is stored in the bit-field. The possible data types are `char`, `unsigned char`, `int`, and `unsigned int`. *bitfield-id* specifies the name of the bit-field. If the bit-field name is left blank, space for the bit-field is allocated but is unaccessible. This feature helps you match hardware registers in which all the available bits are not used. The *width* specifies the size (as a number of bits) of the bit-field. The colon must be coded as shown; it signals that the declaration is a bit-field.

Bit-fields are allocated memory from the low-order bit to the high-order bit within a word of memory. A word of memory is 2 bytes, or 16 bits. Thus, bit-fields are allocated bit sequences from right to left within a word.

Signed integers in a bit-field are stored in 2's-complement form. The leftmost bit of a 2's-complement number is used as the *sign bit*. (A sign bit is 0 if the number is positive, and 1 if the number is negative.) Therefore, if the bit-field type is int, the leftmost bit is a sign bit. If the data type is unsigned, the leftmost bit is a normal bit.

Unions Are Alternate Views of Structures and Objects

A union is a derived type, not an aggregate type. Unions exhibit many of the syntactical and functional characteristics of structures, but use memory differently. Like a structure, a union can declare a group of different data objects, but in a union *only one member is active* at a time. The effect is much like overlaying several foils on a slide projector at once. Every union member thus has an offset of zero from the beginning of the union.

A union type object is allocated enough memory to hold only the largest member found in the union declaration. If a smaller member is active, the remaining space is padding (wasted space). Figure 4.8 shows memory allocation for a typical union object.

Fig. 4.8. How a union uses memory space.

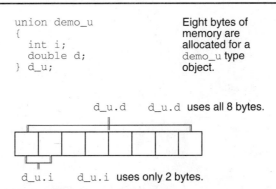

```
union demo_u                Eight bytes of
{                           memory are
   int i;                   allocated for a
   double d;                demo_u type
} d_u;                      object.
```

d_u.d   d_u.d uses all 8 bytes.

d_u.i   d_u.i uses only 2 bytes.

You can see from figure 4.8 that enough memory is allocated to hold only the d member. Because d is declared as a `double`, eight bytes of memory are allocated. These eight bytes are the total memory allocated for the union. Remember that a union declaration allocates memory *only* for the largest object in the union—in this case, d.

Unions are declared using syntax almost identical to that for structures. The only difference is the `union` keyword itself, as follows:

```
union  tag-name_opt  {
   member-list_opt
}  identifier-list_opt  ;
```

The same rules for tag names, member lists, and member identifier lists apply to union declarations, as to structures.

Union members can be accessed with the structure member operator (`.`) and structure pointer operator (`->`), the same as for structures. You must be aware, however, of which member is active at the moment—the compiler makes no effort to keep track of an active member for you.

You can even access a union using two different member names, without reinitializing the union. This action results in the overlay appearance of unions. You can look at the same object in different ways, just by using a different member name. But always remember that the data does not change when you do this; only your perspective changes.

Perhaps the most common use of the ability to view data in multiple concurrent ways with a union is to describe the system registers as both a set of word (integer) objects and a set of byte (character) objects. Borland C++ provides such a union, named REGS, in the dos.h header file. REGS is the union of two structures, WORDREGS and BYTEREGS. Thus, all the required declarations look like this:

```
struct WORDREGS {
   unsigned int ax, bx, cx, dx, si, di, cflag, flags;
};
struct BYTEREGS {
     unsigned char  al, ah, bl, bh, cl, ch, dl, dh;
};

union   REGS  {
    struct     WORDREGS x;
    struct     BYTEREGS h;
};
```

As you can see in the REGS declaration, the x member is a structure describing the word registers, and h is a structure describing the byte registers. The following code fragment illustrates how to use the REGS union to set up a call to the BIOS write-characters video routine (with Borland C++'s int86() built-in function):

```
unsigned ch = '*';
int attr = 7;
int  count = 20;
...
REGS reg;
...
reg.h.ah=9; reg.h.al=ch; reg.x.cx=count; reg.x.bx=attr;
int86(0x10,&reg,&reg);
```

Note in this code fragment that the AX register is set up one byte at a time (using AH and AL). The CX register, however, is initialized with an integer (word) with the expression reg.x.cx = count.

You can write an initializer list with a union declaration, but you must remember that only the first member of the union will be initialized. Consider, for example, the following code fragment:

```
struct itype {
   int a, b;
};
struct dtype {
   double c, d;
};
...
union alltype {
   struct itype;
   struct dtype;
};
```

Given the preceding union declaration, the following lines illustrate valid and invalid uses of a union initializer list:

```
union alltype = { 1, 2 };           /* Okay: First member init */
union alltype = { 3.1316, 6.28 }; /* Invalid: Not first member */
union alltype = { 1, 2, 3.1416, 6.28 }; /* Invalid: 2 members */
```

Using Pointers to Functions

You already know how easily C functions can be called. You simply write the function's name followed by a list of arguments enclosed in parentheses. Calling a function this way is fine for almost all your programming tasks. C provides a more versatile way to call functions, however, that gives you greater control of your program. You can use a pointer to call a function. A pointer to a function is like any other pointer; it stores the address of the function. When the pointer is dereferenced, the function is executed.

Declaring and Initializing Pointers to Functions

Using pointers with functions differs from using pointers with data objects when the pointer is dereferenced. When you dereference a pointer to a data object, you get the value addressed by the pointer. Dereferencing a pointer to a function does *not* retrieve a value: instead, the function is called.

Before a pointer to a function can be initialized or used, it must be declared, as is true for any other pointer type. The declaration of a pointer to a function has this form:

```
type ( *function-pointer ) ( parameter-listopt );
```

type specifies the data type of the value returned by the function. The compiler requires the return type of the function to carry out its type-checking tasks, and particularly to determine whether the pointer is valid for the function pointed to.

The *function-pointer* specifies the name of the function pointer you will use. The * is the indirection operator, and indicates that a pointer is being declared and must be present.

The function-pointer name is enclosed in parentheses because the function call parentheses (the ones enclosing the argument list) have a higher operator precedence than the indirection operator. Therefore, if the function pointer name is not enclosed in parentheses, you declare a function returning a pointer to *type*. Look at the next two declarations:

```
int ( *f_ptr ) ( ... );   /* Pointer to a function
                               returning int */
int *f_ptr ( ... );       /* Function returning a pointer
                               to an integer */
```

The first declaration properly declares a pointer to a function, but the second declaration declares a function that returns a pointer to an integer value. The parentheses in the first declaration force f_ptr to be evaluated as a function pointer.

The *parameter-list* is an optional part of the function-pointer declaration. Omitting a function parameter list, when declaring functions or pointers to functions, means that the function does not expect any arguments (not that they do not matter). If the function does accept arguments, you must specify the type of each argument to satisfy type-checking requirements. (Remember that formal parameter names can be omitted from a prototype, but type names cannot.)

You can declare an array of function pointers by including an array declarator in the function-pointer declaration. Use this syntax:

```
type ( *function-pointer[bound] ) ( parameter-list );
```

This function-pointer declaration is like a regular function-pointer declaration, but with one difference. The *bound* value specifies how many elements are in the array of pointers to function. The square brackets are the array declarator and must be coded as shown.

After you declare the function pointer, you still have to initialize the pointer before it can be used. To initialize the pointer, you must assign the address of the function to the pointer. Using the function's name by itself (without the function-call parentheses and argument list that normally follow a function name) yields the address of the function. You can then assign the address to the function pointer. The next line of code initializes a function pointer:

```
f_ptr = printf;
```

The address of the printf() function is assigned to the function pointer f_ptr. Because printf is a function name, the address-of operator (&) is not needed to take its address.

Calling Functions with a Pointer Reference

Using a pointer to a function to call a function is as easy as dereferencing the pointer. You can call a function through a pointer in two ways. First, when you dereference a pointer to a function, the function is called. Second, you can call the function with normal function call syntax, thanks to the new requirements of the ANSI standard for C. The following code fragment shows how to call a function through a pointer:

```
void ( *my_clr ) ( void );
my_clr = clrscr;
...
( *my_clr ) ();   /* Old way, but still valid */
...
my_clr();          /* New ANSI way, sometimes preferred */
```

The first line of this code fragment declares a function pointer. The function pointer is used with a function that does not require an argument and does not return a value. On the second line, the function pointer my_clr is assigned the address of the clrscr() function. Because my_clr has the address of clrscr(), that function is executed when my_clr is dereferenced. The last line uses the new ANSI method of calling a function through a pointer. This method is preferred for its simplicity and clarity. However, you will often want to use the old syntax to highlight the fact that a *pointer* is being used to call a function (especially if there are many pointers to functions in the program).

Listing 4.5 demonstrates the use of pointers to functions in the context of an entire program.

Listing 4.5. `car.c`. *A program that uses pointers to functions.*

```
 1  /* CAR.C   Using pointers to functions. Declaring,
 2               initializing, and dereferencing function
 3               pointers. */
 4
 5  #include <stdio.h>
 6  #include <stdlib.h>
 7  #include <conio.h>
 8
 9  void calc_mileage( void );
10  void maint_schedule( void );
11  void calc_cost( void );
12
13  main()
14  {
15     void ( *car_ptr[3] ) ( void );
16     int i = 0;
17
18     car_ptr[0] = calc_mileage;
```

```
19    car_ptr[1] = maint_schedule;
20    car_ptr[2] = calc_cost;
21
22    while( ( i < 1 ) || ( i > 3 ) ) {
23      clrscr();
24      printf( "Car Utilities\n\n" );
25      printf( "1.  Gas mileage calculations.\n" );
26      printf( "2.  Preventive maintenance schedule.\n" );
27      printf( "3.  Calculate cost per mile.\n " );
28      printf( "\n\nEnter option => " );
29      scanf( "%d", &i );
30    }
31    ( *car_ptr[i-1]) ();
32
33    return 0;
34  }
35  void calc_mileage( void )
36  {
37    double begin;
38    double end;
39    double gallons;
40
41    clrscr();
42    printf( "--- Calculate mileage ---\n" );
43    printf( "\n\n" );
44    printf( "\nEnter your beginning mileage => " );
45    scanf( "%lf", &begin );
46    printf( "\nEnter your ending mileage => " );
47    scanf( "%lf", &end );
48    printf( "\nEnter gallons of gas used => " );
49    scanf( "%lf", &gallons );
50    printf( "\n\n\n" );
51    printf( "Your mileage was %f miles per gallon.\n",
52            ( ( end - begin ) / gallons ) );
53    return;
54  }
55
56  void maint_schedule( void )
57  {
58    int miles;
59    int result;
```

Listing 4.5. continues

Listing 4.5. continued

```
60
61    clrscr();
62    printf( "--- Maintenance Scheduler ---\n" );
63    printf ( "\n\n\n" );
64    printf( "Enter your mileage to the nearest thousand "
65            "miles => " );
66    scanf( "%d", &miles );
67    printf( "\n\n\n" );
68    if( ( miles % 3000 ) == 0 )
69      printf( "Time to change the oil.\n\n" );
70    if( ( miles % 5000 ) == 0 )
71      printf( "Time to rotate the tires.\n\n" );
72    if( ( miles % 10000 ) == 0 )
73      printf( "Time for a tune up.\n\n" );
74    return;
75
76 }
77
78 void calc_cost( void )
79 {
80    double begin;
81    double end;
82    double allowance = 0.25;
83
84    clrscr();
85    printf( "--- Calculate Cost ---\n" );
86    printf( "\n\n\n" );
87    printf( "\nEnter your beginning mileage => " );
88    scanf( "%lf", &begin );
89    printf( "\nEnter your ending mileage => " );
90    scanf( "%lf", &end );
91    printf( "\n\n\n" );
92    printf( "Your cost of operation is %6.2f",
93            ( ( end - begin ) * allowance ) );
94    return;
95 }
```

In the program in listing 4.5, an array of pointers is used to store the address of each function. The declaration for the array of pointers is in line 15. Notice there that the type of the function and the type of the function's arguments are used in the declaration of the function pointers. This information is necessary for the compiler to check the values passed to and from the function. Even though the parameter list and return type are `void` here, they must still be coded in the function-pointer declaration.

In lines 18–20, the addresses of the functions are assigned to the function pointers. To get the address of a function, you simply reference the name without the function-call parentheses.

In line 31, the appropriate function is called. The expression `i-1` converts the menu selection to a zero-origin array index. For the function to be called, its pointer must be dereferenced. To ensure that the function call is made correctly, enclose the dereferenced pointer in parentheses (the reason is again operator precedence). Be sure also to include an argument list. Without it, the function cannot be called. Even though the functions in this program do not expect arguments, the `void` (empty) argument list must be included in the function call.

Using Pointers with Dynamic Memory

You have seen how memory is allocated for constants, variables, and data structures. When you declare any of these objects, your program automatically allocates the memory needed to store these data items. In particular, these declarations set aside space for variables *in the bounds* of your program. Thus, your EXE file on disk will be larger, for one thing.

Further, internal variables are useful, but they do not enable you to handle a changing amount of data. To handle more data, you can use arrays. In fact, you can declare an array that will hold more items than you plan to use. Declaring an array larger than you need, however, wastes memory space. As programs and data take more room, you have to be careful of the amount of memory you use. Modern PCs may be bigger and more powerful, but so are the applications. Always be aware of the amount of memory space you use.

The best way to deal with varying amounts of data is to use *dynamic allocation*. Dynamically allocated objects enable you to allocate memory for your data while your program is running. They are *dynamic* because the amount of space they require can be determined at run-time. Dynamic objects are more efficient because you allocate and use memory space only when you need it. When a dynamic object is not needed, the space used by the object can be deallocated. The deallocated space is then available for other uses.

This section shows you how to set up and use dynamic objects. You learn how to declare pointers that can be used to access dynamic objects, how to allocate memory for dynamic objects, and how to free the memory so that it's available for other uses.

Your C Program and Dynamic Memory

When you allocate memory dynamically, your computer's memory resources are used more efficiently. Using memory more efficiently sounds like a good idea, but the following example shows just how much difference dynamic memory can make.

A program that handles customer-account information could have a structure like this:

```
typedef struct {
  char first_name[30];
  char last_name[30];
  char cust_street[30];
  char cust_city[30];
  char cust_state[3];
  int cust_zip;
  char account_num[10];
  double account_bal;
  double account_limit;
  int overdue;
} cust_type;
...
cust_type c_array[100];
```

Each character in the structure requires 1 byte, each integer requires 2 bytes, and each `double` requires 8 bytes. An object with this structure type requires 154 bytes of memory. (A byte is wasted aligning the integer `cust_zip` on a word boundary.)

If you have ever kept track of customer information, you know that the structure in this example lacks fields for much of the information you need. Even this small structure, though, shows how much space can be used *in your program* when the array of 100 structures is declared—if you do not use dynamic memory.

The program that contains the preceding structure has over 15K of memory for the array of structures. That much data space is set aside in your program whether you use the entire array or not. If you use only 30 of the array elements, you are left with 11K of wasted memory space. The 15K array takes up space on disk in your EXE file, too.

To avoid wasting so much of your memory resources, you can allocate space for it dynamically—on the C heap. This memory is not contained in your program. When your program begins execution, the program is given a certain amount of memory. The memory outside your program—the heap—is dynamic memory, which is available to you if you use the proper memory-allocation functions. Figure 4.9 shows how a typical program uses memory.

Fig. 4.9. How a C program uses memory.

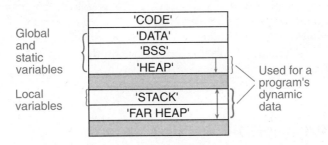

In figure 4.9, the amount of memory allocated to each section depends on the memory model used to compile the program. Even though the actual amounts of memory can change from one memory model to another, all Borland C++ programs use memory in the same basic way.

Your program stores the data it uses in three areas: in the program itself, on the system stack, and on the heap. Global and static variables are stored in the program itself. These variables are placed in the DATA segment (for initialized variables) and in the BSS segment (for uninitialized variables). The space taken up by these variables is a permanent part of your program. You can change the allocation of global and static variables only by recompiling the program.

Local variables (variables local to a function or an interior block of a function) are stored on the system stack. These variables are created, and space is allocated for them, only when the function or block of code begins execution. They are destroyed (and the space is released) when execution exits the function or block. In a sense, local variables are dynamically allocated and destroyed, but this is not what the term *dynamic memory* really means.

The *heap* is the area of memory reserved for use by your program's dynamically created variables. From the heap, you acquire the dynamic memory for the program. To acquire this space, you use the Borland C++ memory-allocation functions.

When you use the heap to store data, you specify exactly how much memory you want. By using dynamic memory, you avoid wasting space and thus save room for other data. Using the heap saves room on your disk, too, because dynamic memory is not contained in your program.

If you acquire memory from the heap, be sure to release the memory when you are through with it. If you do not deallocate the acquired memory, you could run out of memory. Using dynamic memory is more efficient, but only if you use it correctly.

An advantage of using dynamic data is that you don't have to determine how much memory you need when you write your program. You can design the program so that it calculates the amount of memory needed while the program runs. That way, you let the program make the most efficient use of the memory resources available.

Using Dynamic Memory

To use dynamic memory, you follow four steps:

1. Determine how much memory you need.

2. Allocate the memory.

3. Store (and use) a pointer to the acquired memory space.

4. Deallocate the memory when you are through with it.

You can allocate memory space in two ways. First, you can allocate memory for a specified *number of objects*. Borland C++ determines the size of the objects. All you have to do is calculate the number of objects you will use. Second, you can allocate a specified *number of bytes* of memory. For this method, you have to calculate the allocation amount as a product of how much space each object will require and how many objects will be used. Each method is covered here with its corresponding allocation function.

The first function is the `calloc()` function. It requires two arguments, one to specify the number of objects for which you will acquire memory, and the other to tell `calloc()` what *type* of object you will be storing. `calloc()` performs all the calculations necessary to determine exactly how much memory is required. The other function for allocating memory is the `malloc()` function. This function allocates a specified amount of memory. With `malloc()`, you are responsible for determining how much memory is required. Usually, you code a formula that determines how much memory you need.

The function prototype for the `calloc()` function is as follows:

```
void *calloc( size_t nmemb, size_t size );
```

Notice that the declaration for this function does not declare a pointer to a function, but declares a function that returns a pointer. `calloc()` returns a `void` pointer to the allocated memory in the heap. The function returns a `NULL` pointer if the memory could not be allocated.

The `nmemb` argument specifies the number of members for which space will be allocated. You must provide a way for your program to determine how many members need allocated memory. The `size` argument specifies the size of the data object for which you are allocating space.

Borland C++ has an operator you can use to supply a value for the `size` argument of the `calloc()` function. The `sizeof` operator calculates the size of any data object given to it as an operand. The next code fragment shows how the `sizeof` operator works:

```
int i;
char c_a[] = "This is a string.";
float x;
double y = 4;

printf( "i occupies %d bytes.\n", sizeof( i ) );
printf( "c_a occupies %d bytes.\n", sizeof( c_a ) );
printf( "x occupies %d bytes.\n", sizeof( x ) );
printf( "y occupies %d bytes.\n", sizeof( y ) );
printf( "A long double requires %d bytes.\n",
        sizeof( long double ) );
```

The `calloc()` function and the `sizeof` operator are useful tools that can handle most of your dynamic-memory allocation needs. Usually, you will want to allocate memory for a number of data items. The easiest way is to use the `calloc()` function along with the `sizeof` operator to supply the size of the object.

You can also compute the number of bytes required for the dynamic data and request that amount of memory in bytes. This is done using `malloc()`, the second memory-allocation function. Note the following function prototype for `malloc()`:

```
void *malloc( size_t size );
```

The `malloc()` function allocates a block of memory from the heap, and the size of the block *in bytes* is specified by the `size` argument. Like `calloc()`, `malloc()` returns a `void` pointer to the beginning of the allocated block of memory. `malloc()` returns `NULL` if the memory could not be allocated.

After you allocate a block of memory, be sure to test the value returned by either `calloc()` or `malloc()` to determine whether the allocation was successful. You need to provide a routine in your program that handles an unsuccessful allocation attempt.

Once you allocate a block of memory, you need to assign the block's address to a pointer variable of the correct type. This assignment enables you to keep track of where your data is located, and to free the block of memory when you are through with it. (Freeing the block is especially important—if you do not, you can fill up the heap.) The following code fragment shows how you can store the address for an integer array:

```
int *int_ptr;
...
if( NULL == ( int_ptr = calloc( 500, sizeof( int ) ) ) ) {
  printf( "Could not allocate memory, aborting program. " );
  abort();
}
```

The first line of this code fragment declares a pointer to an integer. The pointer is used to keep track of the beginning address of the allocated block of memory. Inside the `if` block, the `calloc()` statement allocates space for an array of 500 integers. The value returned by `calloc()` is assigned to `int_ptr`. If the returned value is `NULL`, `calloc()` was unable to allocate the block of memory successfully. If `calloc()` was unsuccessful, the rest of the `if` block is executed, and the program is aborted.

The `realloc()` function can resize an allocated block of memory. Note the function prototype of `realloc()`:

```
void *realloc( void *block, size_t size );
```

The value returned from `realloc()` is a pointer to the reallocated block of memory. The address of the new block of memory can be different from the address of the old block. If `realloc()` returns `NULL`, the original block still exists, but could not be reallocated.

The `block` argument is a pointer to the block to be reallocated. (Because the argument type is `void*`, you can call this function with any pointer type.) The `size` argument tells `realloc()` how much space is to be used for the reallocated block of memory. The amount of space used for the new block can be more or less than the amount of space used for the old block of memory. If the new size is less than the old size, as much of the old block as will fit is copied to the new block of memory (the block is truncated). If the new size is greater than the old size, the extra space in the new block should be considered uninitialized.

realloc() has two more interesting and very useful features. First, if you call realloc() with the block pointer set to NULL, it acts just like malloc() and allocates the block (if possible). Second, if the size argument is zero but the block pointer is not NULL, the block is freed just as if free() had been called.

Perhaps the most important part of managing the heap is releasing old allocations. If you never release acquired dynamic memory during program execution, you may fill up the heap. Being inconsistent about releasing dynamic memory can be just as bad. If you free only some heap objects, you may fragment the heap. This means that dynamic data objects are scattered throughout the heap, with relatively small free areas between them. But you may find that not one of those smaller free areas is sufficient for the next allocation request.

Therefore, when you are through with a dynamic memory block, you need to free that memory for other uses. The free() function deallocates a block of memory allocated with the calloc(), malloc(), or realloc() function. Here is the function prototype for the free() function:

```
void free( void *block );
```

The block argument is a pointer to the beginning address of the allocated block of memory. This argument is declared as a void pointer so that any type of pointer can be passed to free() as an argument. Because the free() function does not need to return a value, free() is declared as a void function.

Listing 4.6 shows a program that uses the heap to store a two-dimensional array. The unique thing about this array is that the program prompts you to enter the number of elements in the array. This array is truly dynamic because the space for it is allocated during the execution of the program.

Listing 4.6. dyna.c. *A program that uses dynamic memory and arrays.*

```
 1  /* DYNA.C   This program uses dynamic memory to simulate a
 2               two-dimensional array. The number of elements
 3               in the array is specified by the user at
 4               run-time.   */
 5
 6  #include <stdio.h>
 7  #include <stdlib.h>
 8  #include <conio.h>
 9  #include <alloc.h>
10
11  main()
12  {
```

Listing 4.6. continues

Listing 4.6. *continued*

```
13    int *i_ptr;
14    int row;
15    int column;
16    size_t nmemb;
17    int i, j, k = 0;
18
19    clrscr();
20    printf( "\n\nThis program simulates a two "
21            "dimensional array of integers." );
22    printf( "\n\nEnter the number of rows => " );
23    scanf( "%d", &row );
24    printf( "\n\nEnter the number of columns => " );
25    scanf( "%d", &column );
26
27    nmemb = row * column;
28    if( NULL == ( i_ptr = calloc( nmemb, sizeof( int ) ) ) ){
29        printf( "Not able to allocate memory.\n" );
30        printf( "Aborting program." );
31        abort();
32    }
33
34    for( i = 0; i < row; i++ ) {
35        for( j = 0; j < column; j++ ) {
36            i_ptr[ ( i * column + j ) ] = k;
37            k++;
38        }
39    }
40
41    for( i = 0; i < row; i++ ) {
42        for( j = 0; j < column; j++ ) {
43            printf( "%4d  ", i_ptr[ ( i * column + j ) ]  );
44        }
45        printf( "\n" );
46    }
47
48    free( i_ptr );
49
50    return 0;
51 }
```

In line 9 of listing 4.6, the `alloc.h` header file is included. This header file contains the declarations for the memory-management functions. `alloc.h` is required if you want to use the `calloc()`, `malloc()`, `realloc()`, and `free()` functions.

In line 13, the integer pointer `i_ptr` is declared, which points to the beginning of the block of allocated memory. An integer pointer is used so that indexes into the block of allocated memory can be performed correctly.

Lines 19–25 are a routine that prompts the user for the number of elements to include in the array. The ability to specify (or compute) the number of elements at run-time is one of the important benefits of using dynamic allocation. Because the array is allocated dynamically, the user can enter a different size for the array each time the program is run.

Line 27 calculates the number of elements in the array and stores the value in `nmemb`. The value stored in `nmemb` determines how much space will be allocated for the array when `calloc()` is called in line 28. If the `calloc()` call in line 28 is unsuccessful, the `if` statement falls through, and the program terminates abnormally.

The allocated memory is initialized with the values of the array elements in lines 34–39. The elements in the array are initialized on a row-by-row basis, starting at the left of each row and moving to the right. The outer loop is used to step down the array row by row. The inner loop moves across the array column by column.

Because the memory is allocated dynamically, a regular two-dimensional array subscript cannot be used *directly* (hold that thought for a moment). Instead, the address for each element in the array has to be calculated. Line 36 shows the formula that calculates the correct array index. The expression `i * column` calculates the current row position. `column` is the number of columns in each row, and `i` is the number of the current row. Multiplying `i` by `column` gives the offset of the beginning of the current row. Adding `j` to the offset of the current row gives the offset of the current element. This expression calculates the offset of the current element from the beginning of the allocated memory block. The offset of the current array element can be used with the pointer `i_ptr` to determine the exact memory location of the current array element.

Once the exact location of an array element is known, a data value can be stored in, or read from, the array element. In line 36, the value of the variable `k` is assigned to an array element. In the loop in lines 41–44, the `printf()` function in line 43 displays the value of each of the array elements.

Finally, notice the statement in line 48. The free() function deallocates the memory used to store the array. When you are through with a block of memory, be sure to deallocate that memory. Deallocating portions of memory that you no longer need frees the memory for other uses.

Now return to the idea of using array subscripts on a dynamically allocated array. It is true that you cannot use subscripts directly, but you can use subscript notation with a dynamically allocated array. However, you will have to pay the price of using enclosing parentheses and the indirection operator to access the array. Listing 4.7 shows how to do this.

Listing 4.7. newdyna.c. *Using array subscripts with a dynamically allocated array.*

```
 1  #include <stdio.h>
 2  #include <stdlib.h>
 3  #include <conio.h>
 4  #include <alloc.h>
 5
 6  #define MAXX 8
 7  #define MAXY 8
 8
 9  main()
10  {
11    int (*iarray)[MAXX][MAXY];
12    size_t nmemb;
13    int i, j, k = 0;
14
15    clrscr();
16
17    nmemb = MAXX * MAXY;
18    if( NULL == ( iarray = calloc( nmemb, sizeof( int ) ) ) ){
19      printf( "Not able to allocate memory.\n" );
20      printf( "Aborting program." );
21      abort();
22    }
23
24    for( i = 0; i < MAXX; i++ ) {
25      for( j = 0; j < MAXY; j++ ) {
26        (*iarray)[i][j] = k++;
27      }
28    }
29
30    for( i = 0; i < MAXX; i++ ) {
```

```
31        for( j = 0; j < MAXY; j++ ) {
32          printf( "%4d  ", (*iarray)[i][j]  );
33        }
34        printf( "\n" );
35      }
36
37      free( iarray );
38
39      return 0;
40  }
```

The MAXX and MAXY macros are provided (in lines 6 and 7) to control the array bounds (and to simplify the example a little). Note how the pointer to the dynamic array is declared in line 11. This pointer is no longer a simple pointer to int; it is now a pointer to a multidimensional array.

Note carefully that parentheses are used in line 11 to surround the pointer name: (*iarray). The parentheses are required because the subscript operator ([]) has higher precedence than the indirection operator. Therefore, omitting the parentheses would cause the declaration to be interpreted as an *array of pointers to* int, rather than the desired *pointer to an array of* int.

Now that the pointer is properly declared as a pointer to an array of int, reference can be made to array elements using the subscript operator, as shown in lines 26 and 32. Note again, however, that you must still use the surrounding parentheses to force the grouping of operators.

Exercises

The following exercises let you practice using arrays, strings, and structures.

1. Write a program that declares and initializes an integer array. After the array is initialized, add a different value to each element in the array. For element 0, add the value 1; for element 1, add the value 2; and so on.

2. Use the strlen() function to calculate the length of a string you enter. Use the strcat() function to concatenate at least three strings you enter.

3. Create an array of structures with any kind of members you want. Initialize and print the array of structures.

4. Write a program that uses an array of pointers to functions instead of a `switch` statement.

5. Modify the program you created in exercise 3, to place the array of structures on the heap. Here is a thought-provoking question: how are you going to access a member of a structure which is both an array element and located by a pointer? Experiment until you have the method down pat.

Summary

This chapter discussed some of the most important topics in C programming: derived types, aggregate types, and most of all, pointers. The following important points were covered:

❏ *A pointer is a data object that contains the address of another object.* Accessing an object through a pointer is called *address indirection.*

❏ *In a declaration, the indirection operator* `*` *declares a pointer type object.* In the rest of your program, the indirection operator `*` dereferences a pointer.

❏ *When you dereference a pointer, you obtain the value stored at the address pointed to.* It is important to remember the distinction between a pointer used as an object itself (that happens to contain an address) and a pointer used as a locator for another data object (when it is dereferenced).

❏ *The* `&` *symbol yields the address of an object.* This symbol is not needed to take the address of arrays and functions. Referencing an array or function by name alone yields the address of the array or function.

❏ *An array is a data object that contains several members.* All members of an array have the same data type. Arrays can be accessed using subscript notation or using pointer notation: the two methods are equivalent.

❏ *A string is simply a character array.* However, a string does contain a special terminating character: the null character, `'\0'`.

❏ *A structure is a data object that contains several members.* The members of a structure can have different data types.

❏ *A union is a structure-like object in which only one member is active at a given time.* Unions are most frequently used to give an alternate view of an object.

❏ *A function can be referenced and called with a pointer to the function.* Dereferencing a pointer to a function invokes that function. The new ANSI standards permit the function pointer to be used with normal function-call syntax, as well.

❏ *To make more efficient use of your computer's memory, you can use dynamic memory—the C heap.* Memory is then allocated outside your program while it runs. `calloc()` and `free()` are two of the most commonly used functions that handle dynamic memory.

CHAPTER

5

Building, Compiling, and Testing Borland C++ Programs

This chapter shows you how to create larger and more useful programs with Borland C++'s project-management facilities. In earlier chapters, you learned how to use functions to organize and group related C statements. In this chapter, you see how to organize and group related functions into separate source files.

As you create larger, more powerful projects, you will find it difficult to keep all the functions in a single source file. You can keep track of what your project is doing by combining related functions into separate source files. You can then compile these source files separately to create your project. Another benefit of combining related functions into separate source files is that you can easily reuse the groups of functions in other projects.

In this chapter, you learn how to create projects that use several source files. You learn also how to create source files that are composed of groups of related functions. You then see how to combine the source files into powerful projects.

At the end of the chapter, you are introduced to debugging in the Integrated Development Environment (IDE). You learn how to use the built-in debugger to find errors in your program quickly and easily.

Using Several Source Files for One Program

As your programming projects get larger and more involved, you will want to package them in several source files or *modules*. Dividing a project into smaller pieces has the following advantages:

❑ *Following your program's logic is easier.* If all the code for a large project were contained in a single source file, the size of the file would make the program hard to follow. Breaking the program into smaller, logically related pieces makes it easier to see the overall design of the program.

❑ *The process of debugging and modifying your program is easier.* Having your program divided into source files makes isolating a problem easier. You can quickly find which group of functions is causing the problem.

❑ *You can develop libraries of functions.* As you develop large projects, you will probably create functions that can be used extensively. Grouping the useful functions you write into source files makes it easy to use those functions in other projects.

Deciding What To Put in a Source File

Once you have a project that is large enough, you need to decide how to divide your functions into separate source files. You need also to consider how you can easily debug, modify, and reuse those source files. All good engineering is modular.

When you start dividing your functions into source files, be sure to keep related functions in one source file. If, for example, you keep all your data input functions in one source file, you will have only one source file to debug when you have an input problem. With all the related functions in one source file, you do not have to search through pages of listings to find the function you need to fix. Also keep the data needed by a function in the same source file as the function. This strategy helps prevent unintentional changes to data values.

Create groups of functions you can modify easily. For instance, if all the sorting functions for a database project are in one source file, you can make changes to these functions without disturbing other parts of the project. Organize your functions so that all the modifications to a function can be made in one source file.

Divide your functions so that you have groups of functions that can easily be included in other programs. As you develop bigger and more powerful programs, you are likely to create functions that are useful in a number of other programs. Breaking these functions into groups makes it easier to reuse the functions in other programming projects.

However you divide your programs, just remember that you can have only one source file with a main() function. You can place any other functions you want in that source file, but one—and only one—source file can contain a main() function. Some projects are made so that the primary source file contains a main() function whose only purpose is to call all the other functions as they are needed.

Other projects are designed so that the main source file contains all the specialized code for that project. Any other source files are included as needed. The CW program is an example of this kind of design. CW comprises one main source file plus two other source files to handle the keyboard-input functions.

CW is a program that helps you develop your Morse code skills. The program is primarily designed to help you learn Morse code for a ham radio license. In this chapter, however, the CW program is included to illustrate the features of a programming project that uses separate source files.

Listings 5.1, 5.2, and 5.3 present the code for the CW program project. Listing 5.1 is the source code for the cw.c program itself. Listing 5.2 shows source code for the cinsdel.c program. Finally, listing 5.3 shows the source code for stredit.c.

Listing 5.1. cw.c. *A Morse code practice program.*

```
 1   /*
 2
 3       Program CW.C -- Morse code generation and practice
 4
 5   */
 6
 7   #include <stdlib.h>
 8   #include <stdio.h>
 9   #include <conio.h>
10   #include <string.h>
11   #include <dos.h>
12   #include <math.h>
13   #include <time.h>
14
```

Listing 5.1. continues

Listing 5.1. continued

```
15  #include "cinsdel.h"
16  #include "stredit.h"
17
18  #define maxc 44
19  #define FALSE 0
20  #define TRUE 1
21
22  char *codes[] = {
23    "a.-",        "b-...",      "c-.-.",      "d-..",
24    "e.",         "f..-.",      "g--.",       "h....",      "i..",
25    "j.--",       "k-.-",       "l.-..",      "m--",       "n-.",
26    "o--",        "p.--.",      "q--.-",      "r.-.",      "s...",
27    "t-",         "u..-",       "v...-",      "w.--",      "x-..-",
28    "y-.--",      "z--..",      "0----",      "1.----",    "2..--",
29    "3...--",     "4....-",     "5.....",     "6-....",    "7--...",
30    "8--..",      "9----.",     "..-.-.-",    ",--..--",   "?..--..",
31    "--...-",     ":--...",     ";-.-.-.",    "(-.--.-",   ")-.--.-"
32  };
33
34
35
36  int i,j,k; /* GLOBALLY USED SUBSCRIPTS */
37  int ewait; /* WAIT BETWEEN ELEMENTS */
38  int lwait; /* WAIT BETWEEN LETTERS */
39  int wwait; /* WAIT BETWEEN WORDS */
40  unsigned char keystroke;
41  unsigned char port_data;
42  char fname[80];
43  FILE *fspec;
44  char workstr[255];
45
46  void set_window1()
47  {
48  window(2,2,79,9);
49  }
50
51  void set_window2()
52  {
53     window(2,12,79,23);
54  }
55
```

```
56 void fancy_box(int x1, int y1, int x2, int y2)
57 {
58    int i;
59
60    gotoxy(x1,y1); putch(201);
61    for ( i = x1+1; i < x2; i++ ) putch(205);
62    putch(187);
63    for ( i = y1+1; i < y2; i++ ) {
64      gotoxy(x1,i); putch(186);
65      gotoxy(x2,i); putch(186);
66    }
67    gotoxy(x1,y2); putch(200);
68    for ( i = x1+1; i < x2; i ++ ) putch(205);
69    putch(188);
70 }
71
72 void box_it(int x1, int y1, int x2, int y2)
73 {
74    int i;
75
76    gotoxy(x1,y1); putch(218);
77    for ( i = x1+1; i < x2; i++ ) putch(196);
78    putch(191);
79    for ( i = y1+1; i < y2; i++ ) {
80      gotoxy(x1,i); putch(179);
81      gotoxy(x2,i); putch(179);
82    }
83    gotoxy(x1,y2); putch(192);
84    for ( i = x1+1; i < x2; i ++ ) putch(196);
85    putch(217);
86 }
87
88 void dash()
89 {
90    sound(900); delay(150); nosound(); delay(55);
91 }
92
93 void dot()
94 {
95    sound(900); delay(45); nosound(); delay(55);
96 }
97
```

Listing 5.1. continues

Listing 5.1. continued

```
 98  void find_letter()
 99  {
100    i = 0;
101    while ( i < maxc && codes[i][0] != keystroke ) i += 1;
102  }
103
104  void send_letter()
105  {
106    if ( i < maxc ) {
107      for ( j = 1; j < strlen(codes[i]); j++ ) {
108        if ( codes[i][j] == '.' ) dot(); else dash();
109        delay(ewait*5);
110      }
111      delay(lwait*10);
112    }
113  }
114
115  void single_chars()
116  {
117    clrscr();
118    cputs("Strike \\ to Return to Menu.\r\n");
119    cputs("Strike Other Keys to Hear Code.\r\n");
120    keystroke = ' ';
121    while ( keystroke != '\\' ) {
122      keystroke = getch();
123      switch ( keystroke ) {
124        case 32: delay(1000);
125                 putch( ' ' ); break;
126        case 13: cputs( "\r\n" ); break;
127        default:
128                 if ( keystroke != 27 && keystroke != '\\' ) {
129                   find_letter();
130                   putch(codes[i][0]);
131                   send_letter();
132                 }
133      }
134    }
135  }
136
137  void show_chars()
138  {
```

```
139     clrscr();
140     cputs("Strike \\ to Return to Menu.\r\n");
141     cputs("Strike Other Keys to See Code.\r\n");
142     keystroke = ' ';
143     while ( keystroke != '\\' ) {
144       keystroke = getch();
145       switch ( keystroke ) {
146         case 13:  cputs( "\r\n" ); break;
147         default:
148                   if ( keystroke != 27 && keystroke != '\\') {
149                     find_letter();
150                     if ( i <= maxc )
151                       cprintf( "%s\r\n", codes[i] );
152                   }
153       }
154     }
155 }
156
157 void set_stretch()
158 {
159   clrscr();
160   cputs("  Setting this parameter will \"stretch\" "
161         "the amount of time waited\r\n");
162   cputs("between the dots and dashes.  The startup "
163         "value is 5, which will wait\r\n");
164   cputs("an extra 25 msecs. Set it to 0 for a "
165         "[mathematically] normal fist.\r\n");
166   cputs("You may specify a value from 0 to 20.\r\n");
167   cputs( "\r\n" );
168   cprintf( "Enter \"stretch\" parameter: " );
169   cscanf( "%d", &ewait );
170   if ( ewait < 0 ) ewait = 0;
171   if ( ewait > 20 ) ewait = 20;
172 }
173
174 void set_wwait()
175 {
176   clrscr();
177   cputs("  Setting this parameter will wait an "
178         "extra number of milliseconds\r\n");
179   cputs("between whole words.  The startup value "
180         "is 1000, which will wait\r\n");
```

Listing 5.1. continues

Listing 5.1. continued

```
181    cputs("an extra 1 second. Set it to 0 for a "
182        "[mathematically] normal fist.\r\n");
183    cputs("You may specify a value from 0 to 1000.\r\n");
184    cputs( "\r\n" );
185    cprintf( "Enter Word-Wait parameter: " );
186    cscanf( "%d", &wwait );
187    if ( wwait < 0 ) wwait = 0;
188    if ( wwait > 20 ) wwait = 1000;
189  }
190
191  void set_speed()
192  {
193    clrscr();
194    cputs("  This parameter sets the number of words "
195        "per minute that will be\r\n");
196    cputs("transmitted for random code groups, lines, "
197        "and text files.\r\n");
198    cputs("Default set to 3 WPM. If \"stretch\" > 0, "
199        "this will be inaccurate.\r\n");
200    cputs("Likewise, if word-wait time > 0, "
201        "this will be inaccurate.\r\n");
202    cputs("You may specify a value from 1 to 25.\r\n");
203    cputs( "\r\n" );
204    cprintf( "Enter Words Per Minute: " );
205    cscanf( "%d", &j );
206    if ( j < 1 ) j = 1;
207    if ( j > 25 ) j = 25;
208    lwait = floor(6000.0 / (25.0*j) - 10.0);
209    if ( lwait < 0 ) lwait = 0;
210  }
211
212  void speed_menu()
213  {
214    while ( 1 ) {
215      clrscr(); cputs("Strike a NUMBER Key To:\r\n");
216      cputs("  1-Set Words Per Minute\r\n");
217      cputs("  2-Set Character Duration\r\n");
218      cputs("  3-Set Word Wait Time\r\n");
219      cputs("  x-Go Back to MAIN MENU\r\n");
220      keystroke = getch();
221      switch ( keystroke ) {
```

```
222          case '1': set_speed(); break;
223          case '2': set_stretch(); break;
224          case '3': set_wwait(); break;
225          case 'x':
226          case 'X': return;
227       }
228     }
229 }
230
231 void random_chars()
232 {
233   int again;
234
235   clrscr();
236   cputs("I will select a code at random and send it.\r\n");
237   cputs("You type the letter or character you "
238         "think matches it.\r\n");
239   cputs("If you miss one, type + to repeat, "
240         "anything else to go on.\r\n");
241   cputs("Type a \\ to end the random character session.\r\n");
242   keystroke = ' '; k = 0;
243   while ( keystroke != '\\' ) {
244     k = random(maxc);
245     again = TRUE;
246     while ( again ) {
247       keystroke = codes[k][0]; i = k; send_letter();
248       cprintf( "? " );
249       keystroke = getch();
250       if ( keystroke == '\\' ) return;
251       if ( keystroke == codes[k][0] ) {
252         cprintf( "%c is CORRECT.\r\n", keystroke );
253         again = FALSE;
254       }
255       else {
256         cprintf( "INCORRECT. That was %s "
257                  "Type + to repeat.\r\n", codes[k] );
258         keystroke = getch();
259         if ( keystroke != '+' ) again = FALSE;
260       }
261     }
262   }
263 }
```

Listing 5.1. continues

Listing 5.1. continued

```
264
265  void random_groups()
266  {
267    int n;
268
269    clrscr();
270    cputs("I will send groups of 5 random codes.\r\n");
271    cputs("I will also display the codes as they are sent.\r\n");
272    cputs("You copy the codes until a group is finished, "
273          "and then check the screen.\r\n");
274    cputs("Strike Enter to go to the next group.\r\n");
275    cputs("Type a \\ to end the random group session.\r\n");
276    keystroke = ' '; k = 0;
277    while ( keystroke != '\\' ) {
278      for ( n = 0; n < 5; n++ ) {
279        k = random(maxc);
280        keystroke = codes[k][0]; i = k;
281        send_letter();
282        cprintf( "%s%c", codes[k], 219 );
283      }
284      cprintf( "\r\n" );
285      keystroke = getch();
286    }
287  }
288
289  void with_edit()
290  {
291    clrscr();
292    cputs("Type in a line of characters; "
293          "strike Return to send.\r\n");
294    cputs("Type a line with only \\ in it to quit.\r\n");
295    strcpy( workstr, "" );
296    while ( workstr[0] != '\\' ) {
297      strcpy( workstr, "" );
298      edit_text( workstr, wherex(), wherey(), 60, 0, 0 );
299      cputs( "\r\n" );
300      if ( workstr[0] != '\\' ) {
301        for ( k = 0; k < strlen(workstr); k++ ) {
302          keystroke = workstr[k];
303          if ( keystroke == ' ' ) delay(lwait*20);
304          find_letter(); send_letter();
```

```
305          }
306        sound(1200); delay(1000); nosound();
307      }
308    }
309 }
310
311 void send_file()
312 {
313   int slen;
314   char *temp = 0;
315
316   clrscr();
317   cprintf( "What File Name?: " );
318   cscanf( "%s", fname );
319   cprintf( "\r\n" );
320   if ( NULL != ( fspec = fopen( fname, "r" ) ) ) {
321     while ( !feof(fspec) && !kbhit() ) {
322       fgets(workstr, 255, fspec );
323       if ( NULL != ( temp = strchr( workstr, '\n' ) ) )
324         *temp = '\0';
325       slen = strlen( workstr );
326       for ( k = 0; k < slen; k++ ) {
327         keystroke = workstr[k];
328         if ( keystroke == ' ' ) delay(lwait*20);
329         find_letter(); send_letter();
330         }
331       cprintf( "%s\r\n", workstr );
332     }
333     fclose(fspec);
334   }
335 }
336
337 void MAIN_MENU()
338 {
339   while( 1 ) {
340     clrscr();
341     cputs("Strike a Function Key.\r\n");
342     keystroke = getch();
343     if ( keystroke == 0 ) keystroke = getch();
344     switch ( keystroke ) {
345       case 59: single_chars(); break;
346       case 60: show_chars(); break;
```

Listing 5.1. continues

Listing 5.1. *continued*

```
347        case 61: random_chars(); break;
348          case 62: random_groups(); break;
349          case 63: with_edit(); break;
350        case 64: send_file(); break;
351        case 65: speed_menu(); break;
352        case 66: window(1,1,80,25);
353                 clrscr();
354                    exit( 0 );
355      }
356    }
357 }
358
359 /* ----------------- MAIN PROGRAM BODY ------------------ */
360 void main()
361 {
362    randomize();
363    ewait = 5; lwait = 70; wwait = 1000;
364    textbackground( BLUE );
365    textcolor( WHITE );
366    clrscr();
367    fancy_box(1,1,80,10);
368    box_it(1,11,80,24);
369    set_window1();
370    gotoxy(1,1);
371    clrscr();
372    cputs("                          CW Practice\r\n");
373    cputs("\r\n");
374    cputs("          F1-Sound Single Characters    "
375       "F2-See Single Characters\r\n");
376    cputs("          F3-TX Random Characters    "
377       "F4-TX Random Code Groups\r\n");
378    cputs("          F5-TX Lines From Keyboard    "
379       "F6-TX An ASCII Text File\r\n");
380    cputs("          F7-Control TX Speed        "
381       "F8-QUIT\r\n");
382    set_window2();
383    gotoxy(1,1);
384    clrscr();
385    MAIN_MENU();
386 }
```

Listing 5.2. `cinsdel.c`. *A C program that handles keyboard insert and delete functions.*

```
1   #include <string.h>
2   #include <ctype.h>
3
4   void cinsert( char ccode,char *anystring,int spos )
5   {
6     int p;
7
8     p = strlen(anystring);
9     spos=( spos < 0 ) ? 0 : spos;
10    spos=( spos >= p ) ? p : spos;
11    for ( ; p>=spos; p--) anystring[p+1]=anystring[p];
12    anystring[spos]=ccode;
13  }
14
15  void cdelete( char *anystring,int spos )
16  {
17    int p;
18
19    p=strlen(anystring);
20    if ( p>0 && spos>=0 && spos<=p) {
21      while ( spos < p ) {
22        anystring[spos]=anystring[spos+1]; spos++;
23      }
24    }
25  }
26
```

Listing 5.3. `stredit.c`. *A keyboard-input program.*

```
1   #include <stdio.h>
2   #include <string.h>
3   #include <mem.h>
4   #include <conio.h>
5   #include <ctype.h>
6
7   int inserton = 1;
8
9   #include "cinsdel.h"
10
```

Listing 5.3. continues

Listing 5.3. continued

```
11  void eraeol(void)
12  {
13    static holdx, holdy;
14    static char empty[81];
15
16    holdx = wherex(); holdy = wherey();
17    sprintf( empty,"%*c",81-holdy,' ' );
18    cprintf( "%s", empty );
19    gotoxy( holdx, holdy );
20  }
21
22  void edit_text( char *anystring,
23                  int colno,
24                  int lineno,
25                  int maxlen,
26                  int offset,
27                  int upcase
28                )
29  {
30    int X,x,y;
31    int x2,y2;
32    int oldlen, newlen;
33    char extcode,exitcode,ch;
34
35    extcode=0; exitcode=0;
36    X=0;
37    y=lineno; x=X+colno;
38    gotoxy( x, y );
39    cprintf("%s",anystring);
40    X=(offset > 0)?offset:0;
41    x=X+colno;
42    gotoxy( x, y );
43    do {            /* MAIN EDIT LOOP */
44      extcode=0;
45      ch=getch();
46      if (ch==0) { extcode=1; ch=getch(); }
47      if (!exitcode) {
48        if (extcode) {
49          switch ( ch ) {
50            case 60:     /* F2 = Erase EOL */
51                        eraeol();
```

```
52              anystring[X] = '\0';
53              break;
54     case 61:    /* F3 = Kill Line */
55              X=0; x=X+colno;
56              gotoxy( x, y );
57              eraeol();
58              *anystring='\0';
59              break;
60     case 71:    /* HOME */
61              X=0;
62              x=colno;
63               gotoxy( x, y );
64              break;
65     case 75:    /* LEFT */
66              if (X>0) {
67                  X--; x--; gotoxy( x, y );
68              }
69              break;
70     case 77:    /* RIGHT */
71              if (X<strlen(anystring)) {
72                  X++; x++; gotoxy( x, y );
73              }
74              break;
75     case 79:    /* END */
76              X=strlen(anystring);
77              x=X+colno;
78              gotoxy( x, y );
79              break;
80     case 82:    /* INSERT */
81              inserton = !inserton;
82              break;
83     case 83:    /* DELETE */
84              if (X<strlen(anystring) && X>=0) {
85                  cdelete(anystring,X);
86                  eraeol();
87                  cprintf("%s",anystring+X);
88                  gotoxy( x, y );
89              }
90              break;
91     case 115:   /* CTL LEFT = Prev. Word */
92              while (X>0 && anystring[X] != 32) {
93                  X--; x--;
94              }
```

Listing 5.3. continues

Listing 5.3. *continued*

```
 95                        while (X>0 && anystring[X] == 32) {
 96                           X--; x--;
 97                        }
 98                        gotoxy( x, y );
 99                        break;
100            case 116:    /* CTL RIGHT = Next Word */
101                        while (X<strlen(anystring)
102                               && anystring[X] != 32) {
103                           X++; x++;
104                        }
105                        while (X<strlen(anystring)
106                               && anystring[X] == 32) {
107                           X++; x++;
108                        }
109                        gotoxy( x, y );
110                        break;
111            }
112        }                /* end extcode */
113    else {
114       switch ( ch ) {
115          case 13: return;
116                   break;
117          case 4:      /* CTL-D = Erase EOL */
118                   anystring[X] = '\0';
119                   eraeol();
120                   break;
121          case 8:      /* CTL-H or BACKSPACE */
122                   if (X>0) {
123                      X--; x--; gotoxy( x, y );
124                   }
125                   if (X<strlen(anystring) && X>=0) {
126                      cdelete(anystring,X);
127                      eraeol();
128                      cprintf("%s",anystring+X);
129                      gotoxy( x, y );
130                   }
131                   break;
132          default:
133                   if (strlen(anystring)<maxlen) {
134                      if ( upcase && islower(ch) )
135                         ch = toupper(ch);
136                      if (inserton) {
```

```
137                          cinsert(ch,anystring,X);
138                        }
139                        else {
140                          if ( X >= strlen(anystring) )
141                            cinsert(ch,anystring,X);
142                          else anystring[X] = ch;
143                        }
144                        cprintf("%s",anystring+X);
145                        X++; x++;
146                        gotoxy( x, y );
147                      }
148                      break;
149                }
150              }
151          }
152      } while (!exitcode);
153  }
```

The following discussion is a brief description of the CW program. As a program that helps you learn how to send and receive Morse code messages, CW has routines that let you practice receiving codes for single letters or a random group of characters. Another routine lets you practice transmitting characters from your keyboard. Other functions enable you to change the speed at which characters are sent to you.

Listing 5.1 is the source code for the cw.c source file. Lines 1–16 contain the #include directives for the program. Notice in lines 15 and 16 that two user-supplied header files are merged into the program. These two header files contain the declarations needed to support the cinsdel.c and stredit.c source files. Lines 18–44 contain the macro definitions and global variable declarations.

In listing 5.1, the function definitions begin in line 46 and continue through line 357. These definitions are for all the functions except main(). Notice that this source file does not use function prototype declarations because all the functions are defined before they are called.

In lines 88–96 of listing 5.1, you can see the functions used to sound the Morse code dots and dashes. Lines 157–210 contain the functions for changing the way the Morse codes sound.

The main() function for the CW program is in lines 359–386 of listing 5.1. The main() function blocks in the main screen and displays the program's menu. Control is then passed to the MAIN_MENU function defined in lines 337–354. MAIN_MENU scans keyboard input for a menu selection and transfers control to the appropriate function.

Notice that the MAIN_MENU function is locked in an endless loop caused by the while() statement in line 339. Because the while() statement is always true, the menu routine does not end until the exit() function is called in line 354. When exit() is called, the program terminates normally.

Listing 5.2 shows the source code for the cinsdel.c source file. This short file contains the cinsert() and cdelete() support functions used by stredit().

Listing 5.3 presents the source code for another user-supplied support source file, stredit.c. The edit_text() function in this source file provides text string data entry for the CW program. You can inspect the source code for edit_text() to determine what keystrokes are permitted during text string editing. The edit_text() function is powerful enough to meet most keyboard input needs.

Setting Up a Borland C++ Project File

When you have a programming project that uses more than one source file, you need to create a project file. The *project file* is a special list of the source files needed in your project. The project file contains not only a list of the files used in the project, but also information needed to create an executable file. A project file includes the following information:

❏ *The location of the source files on disk.* The location of the resulting executable file can also be specified.

❏ *Source file dependencies.* That is, information is included about which file must be compiled before other files can be compiled.

❏ *Specification of the compiler to be used in compiling a source file.* For now, this is always the Borland C++ compiler. Later, when you see how to mix in assembly language source files, this item will become very important. You can also include command-line arguments that will be passed to the compiler.

❏ *Information about the code size, data size, and number of lines from the last compilation of the project.* Borland C++ inserts this information—you do not have to provide it.

The Borland C++ IDE provides a screen for controlling your project information. The project screen is where you enter and modify the information about your project. Figure 5.1 shows the project file screen for the cw.prj project file.

Fig. 5.1. The cw.prj *project screen.*

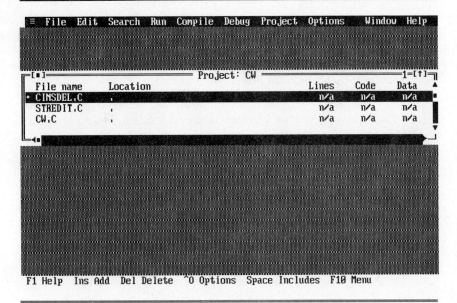

Creating a project requires three basic steps. The first step is to create a new project file, the second step is to add source files to the project file, and the third step is to build the project (make the EXE file).

To access the Borland C++ project-management functions, you use the **P**roject option from the main menu of the IDE. To create a new project file, select the **O**pen command from the **P**roject menu. With the **O**pen command, you can open an existing project or assign a name to a new project. After selecting **P**roject **O**pen, the Load Project File dialog box appears. In the dialog box, type the name and path of the new project file. If you prefer, you can use the **F**iles box to move to the directory that will contain the project file.

After you enter the name of the new project file, you are placed in a Project window like the one shown in figure 5.1. At this point, you have completed the first step in the creation of a project: you have created the new project file. Next, you need to add the source files to be used in the project.

Once you have opened a project file, you can access several other options on the **P**roject menu, including **A**dd item, **D**elete item, **L**ocal options, and **I**nclude files. To begin adding source files to the project, you select the **A**dd item option.

Selecting Add item opens the Add item to Project list dialog box. In this dialog box, you select the files that will be part of your project. There are two ways to select files in this dialog box. First, you can enter the file name in the input box. Second, you can pick a file from the file list box. Once you select a file, use the Add action button to add that file to the project. Select the Cancel action button when you are through adding files to the project. The Cancel button returns you to the main project screen.

When the project window is active, the status line at the bottom of the screen shows several actions you can perform. Table 5.1 lists the actions available and the key(s) you press to perform these actions.

Table 5.1. Actions you can perform from the project window.

Key(s)	Action
F1	Brings up the online help facility for the project-management functions.
Ins	Takes you to the **Add item** of the Project dialog box. This key has the same effect as the **Project Add item** command.
Del	Deletes a file from the project file list.
^O	Opens a dialog box that lets you set more options for a file. (Note that this action requires the key sequence Ctrl-O.)
Space bar	Displays information about the include files required by a program in the project file list.
F10	Takes you to the **Project** menu in the IDE's main menu.

You have now created the project file and added the source files to the project list. The final step, compiling the project, is covered in the section "Compiling and Running Programs with the IDE" later in this chapter. Next, you see how to use functions and variables that are contained in separate source files.

Understanding External References

When you are using multiple source files, the concept of external reference becomes important. External reference has to do with functions in one source file accessing the data and functions in another source file. Without the external reference features of Borland C++, using multiple source files would be impossible.

The referencing of an external object has two parts. First, the object must be defined properly in one file. Second, the object must be declared in each file that references the external object. This section shows you how to set up and use external objects in your programs.

Using the *extern* Keyword

extern is a special keyword used in the declaration of objects that are referenced externally. The extern keyword tells the compiler that the data object you are declaring is an object defined in another source file. extern lets you use objects that were created in other source files. The next line of code shows a variable declared as an external variable:

```
extern double sales;
```

This code declares a double floating-point number. The declaration is different because the variable sales is actually defined in another source file.

Declaring an object and defining an object have a subtle difference. A declaration tells the compiler what kind of data an object works with. However, a declaration does not necessarily reserve storage for the object. A definition is the special declaration that sets aside memory for an object. A definition lets you create an object; a declaration gives you access to that object.

An object can be defined in only one source file. The definition of the object causes space in your computer's memory to be allocated for that object. Because storage space is set aside for the object, it makes sense that the compiler allows only one definition of an object. Once the definition is made, the object can be used in other source files.

Figure 5.2 shows how an external object is defined and declared.

Fig. 5.2. *How an external variable operates.*

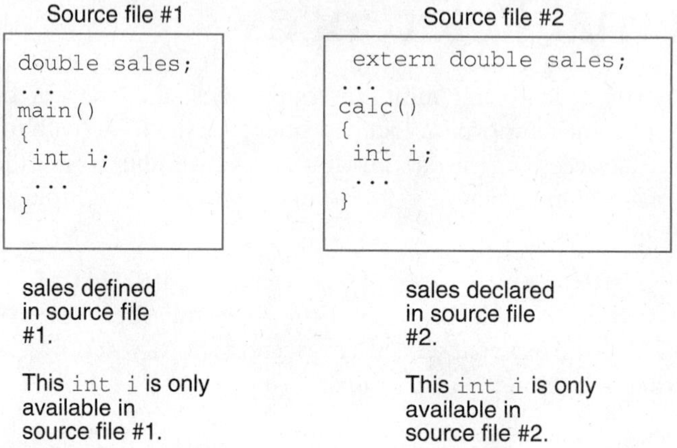

Source file #1

```
double sales;
...
main()
{
  int i;
  ...
}
```

sales defined
in source file
#1.

This int i is only
available in
source file #1.

Source file #2

```
extern double sales;
...
calc()
{
  int i;
  ...
}
```

sales declared
in source file
#2.

This int i is only
available in
source file #2.

Figure 5.2 graphically shows two source files. In the first source file, a global variable, sales, is defined. The definition in the first source file causes memory to be allocated for the double variable. In the second source file, the sales variable is declared as an external variable. The keyword extern signals that the actual data object is defined in another source file. The extern keyword indicates that space is not to be allocated for the sales variable again.

Also notice that an i variable is declared in both source files in figure 5.2. The i variable declared in each source file is unique to that source file. In other words, the i variable in one source file cannot be referenced in the other source file. In fact, the i variable in each source file can be referenced only in the function in which it is declared because i is an auto variable. i comes into existence when the function begins execution, and i is destroyed when the function ends.

A declaration for a variable with the extern storage class specifier references a data object that has *external linkage*. An object having external linkage can be accessed by functions in other source files.

Variables that need to be accessed by functions in other source files are usually declared as global variables. Recall that global variables are declared outside any functions in a source file. By default, global variables have external linkage and are therefore easily accessed by functions in other source files. You simply declare the variable in the other source file with the extern storage class specifier.

Using External Functions

The whole point of creating a project file is to separate your functions into logical and manageable files. This section shows you how to call and use the functions and external data objects in separate files.

In the preceding section, you saw how to share a variable across several separate source files. A variable with external linkage in one source file can be accessed in another source file if you declare the variable with the `extern` keyword. The `extern` keyword lets the compiler know that the variable was created in a different source file.

Calling functions existing in other source files is similar to using variables from different source files. Using external functions requires that you perform two steps: you first define the function in one source file and then declare the function in the other source files.

You do not have to do anything special to define a function to be used by callers in multiple source files. Because a function has external linkage by default, the function is automatically available for use by functions in other source files. Just do not forget to write a prototype declaration for the function in the other source files.

The declaration of a function found in another source file does not require the use of `extern`, as the declaration of a variable does. To use a function residing in another source file, write a normal function prototype declaration that includes the following information:

❏ The return type of the function.

❏ The name of the function.

❏ An argument list that includes declarations for all the arguments passed to the function. The argument list must specify the data type for each of the arguments; specifying a variable name is optional.

Figure 5.3 shows how a function defined in one source file can be declared and used in another source file.

Two source files are shown in figure 5.3. The first source file defines a function that can be called from either the first source file or another source file compiled with it. The function `func1` in the first source file is declared and defined just like any other function. By default, `func1` in the first source file has external linkage and can thus be called by functions in other source files.

The second source file shown in figure 5.3 uses the `func1` function defined in the first source file. Once `func1` is declared in the second source file, function calls to the `func1` function can be made in the usual manner.

Fig. 5.3. *How to reference an external function.*

First source file

```
#include <stdio.h>
...
int func1( int i);
...
main()
{
...
}
...
int func1( int i )
{
...
}
```

func1 is defined in
the first source
file.

Second source file

```
#include <stdio.h>
...
int func1( int i );
...
main()
{
...
j = func1( 2 );
...
}
```

func1 is declared
and used in
the second source
file.

Writing Header Files for External Modules

You have seen that using functions and variables residing in another source file requires that you declare those functions and variables in your source file. If you used many separate source files, keying all those extra declarations would be tedious. With header files, you can avoid all that extra typing.

A *header file* is a special file that contains all the declarations you need in order to use the functions and variables found in another source file. When you want to use functions or variables found in one of the other source files, you simply use the #include macro to merge the declarations for the other source file into the current source file.

Two of the benefits of using header files are speed and accuracy. Including a header file is much faster than typing all the necessary declarations for the functions and variables in another source file. Header files also prevent errors because you have to type the declaration just one time. Once you create a good header file, you do not have to worry about errors caused by typing.

You are already familiar with using the header files for Borland C++'s built-in library functions. This section shows you how to create your own header files that work like the built-in header files supplied by Borland C++.

Deciding What Goes in the Header File

Deciding what to put in a header file is a simple task. The header file for a source file should include any objects you want externally referenced. In other words, a header file should contain declarations for any variables or functions to be accessed from other source files.

When you write declarations in a header for variables that will be used by other source files, do not forget to add the extern storage class specifier to the declarations. This is not necessary for function prototype declarations because functions always have external linkage (unless you qualify the function definition with static).

Figure 5.4 shows how a basic header file is used.

Fig. 5.4. Header files and object declarations.

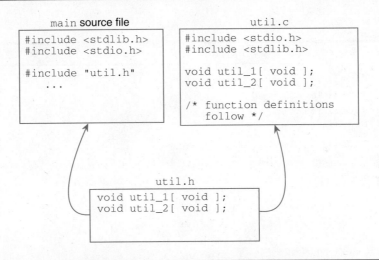

The main source file in figure 5.4 uses the #include macro to merge in the util.h header file. The util.h header file contains declarations for the util_1 and util_2 functions that are defined in the util.c source file. The util.h header file contains declarations for all the external objects that are to be referenced in the util.c source file.

If the util.c source file in figure 5.4 had variables to be externally referenced, declarations for the variables would be included in util.h.

In addition to containing declarations for functions and variables, a header file can contain macro definitions. If macros make your external functions easier to use, include the macros in the header file. When the header file is included in the main source file, the macros will be ready to use.

Including User-Supplied Header Files

To pull in the header files you create, all you need is the #include macro. The following statement merges the file my_hdr.h into your source file:

```
#include "my_hdr.h"
```

Everything in the my_hdr.h file is included in your source file.

In line 16 of listing 5.1, the cw.c source file uses the #include macro to merge the stredit.h header file into cw.c. Listing 5.4 shows the stredit.h header file.

Listing 5.4. stredit.h. *The header file for* stredit.c.

```
1    #include <stdio.h>
2    #include <string.h>
3    #include <mem.h>
4    #include <conio.h>
5    #include <ctype.h>
6
7    extern int inserton;
8
9    void eraeol(void);
10   void edit_text( char *anystring,
11                  int colno,
12                  int lineno,
13                  int maxlen,
14                  int offset,
15                  int upcase
16              );
```

When the code in listing 5.4 is merged into `cw.c`, the `cw.c` source file is able to use the `eraeol()` and `edit_text()` functions defined in the `cinsdel.c` source file. `cw.c` also can reference the `inserton` variable.

Notice that the included header file contains `#include` directives. In lines 1–5 of listing 5.4, several library function header files are included. Nesting `#include` directives this way is perfectly legal. When the preprocessor expands an `#include` directive, the resulting source code is rescanned, to look for more `#include` directives (and macros).

Take another look at line 16 in listing 5.1. Notice that the `#include` directive does not surround the file name with the less-than (<) and greater-than (>) symbols you have seen before. Instead, the `#include` directive encloses the file name in quotation marks.

The quotation marks in the `#include` directive tell the preprocessor that a user-supplied header file is being used. The quotation marks signal the preprocessor to modify its searching algorithm so that the user-supplied header file can be found. The preprocessor searches the current directory first. Usually, that is where the source file is located. If the header file is not found in the current directory, the preprocessor searches each of the include directories.

Using Conditional Compiler Directives in Header Files

Large projects often require that many header files be included during program compilation. When you include several header files, you can declare the same object several times. You can make many of the declarations more than once without any problems. A better practice, though, is to make sure that the declarations are made only once. Borland C++'s set of conditional compiler directives can help you ensure that declarations are made only one time.

The conditional compilation directives are also called the conditional inclusion directives. The purpose of these preprocessor directives is to enable you to include or exclude certain sections of code before compilation takes place. Using the preprocessor's `#if` directive, you can decide which sections of code will be included or excluded. The various forms of the `#if` directive let you perform logical tests before compilation starts.

Note the syntax for the conditional compilation directives:

```
#if [!]constant-expression

#elif [!]constant-expression

#else

#if [!] defined identifier

#if [!] defined ( identifier )

#ifdef identifier

#ifndef identifier

#endif
```

The symbol [!] indicates that the logical NOT can optionally be used in the expression.

In the list of conditional compilation directives, the *constant-expression* can be any expression that evaluates to an integer value. The *constant-expression* can contain arithmetic operators, logical operators, and even other macro expressions. A *constant-expression* that evaluates to a nonzero value is considered to be true. If the *constant-expression* evaluates to zero, however, the expression is considered false.

In the preceding list, the *identifier* used in the #if defined series of directives is a symbol you create. The #if defined directives determine whether the symbol indicated by *identifier* has been previously defined in your source code. *identifier* can optionally be enclosed in parentheses.

With the #if, #elif, #else, and #endif directives, you can create a logical construct that includes or excludes code based on a certain condition. You must be able to express the condition that is to be evaluated as an integer value. A typical #if construct looks like this:

```
#if condition_1
  <first code section>
#elif condition_2
  <second code section>
#else
  <default code section>
#endif
```

When the preprocessor scans the preceding group of #if directives, it evaluates *condition_1* first. If *condition_1* evaluates to a nonzero integer value, the first code section is included for compilation. The other code sections are not included in the compilation of the program.

If `condition_1` yields a zero (false) value, the preprocessor then evaluates `condition_2`. The second code section is included in the program's compilation if `condition_2` evaluates to a nonzero (true) value.

If neither `condition_1` nor `condition_2` evaluates as true, the default code section following the `#else` directive is included during program compilation.

You don't necessarily have to include code in any of these code sections. At times, you may need to create a conditional compilation structure, but you will not want to include any code for some conditions.

The `#endif` signals the end of the `#if` structure. You must include an `#endif` directive for every `#if` directive you use.

Listing 5.5 shows the use of an `#if defined` directive. The code is the `cinsdel.h` header file that is included by the `cw.c` program found in listing 5.1.

Listing 5.5. `cinsdel.h`. *The* `cinsdel.c` *header file.*

```
1  #if !defined _CINSDEL
2  #define _CINSDEL
3  #include <string.h>
4  #include <ctype.h>
5
6  cinsert( char ccode, char *anystring, int spos );
7  cdelete( char *anystring, int spos );
8  #endif
```

In line 1 of listing 5.5, the `#if defined` directive is combined with the logical NOT symbol. The `#if !defined` directive causes the code section that follows to be included only if `_CINSDEL` has *not* been previously defined.

The `#if defined` directive determines whether the specified identifier has been previously defined in your source code. In listing 5.5, the identifier that is checked is `_CINSDEL`.

In listing 5.5, the first action taken if `_CINSDEL` has not been defined is to define it. Once the identifier `_CINSDEL` is defined, the declarations in `cinsdel.h` will not be made if the `cinsdel.h` header file is included again.

Listing 5.5 illustrates another point. You can control the inclusion of header files by placing the `#include` directives inside an `#if` directive. In that listing, the inclusion of the `string.h` and `ctype.h` header files is controlled by the presence of the `_CINSDEL` identifier. Using an `#if` construct like the one in figure 5.5 ensures that your header files will include other header files only one time.

The directive

```
#if defined TEST_OBJ
```

is equivalent to the directive

```
#ifdef TEST_OBJ
```

You can use the `#if defined` directive anywhere you would use the `#ifdef` directive. The next two directives are equivalent also:

```
#if !defined TEST_OBJ
#ifndef TEST_OBJ
```

Compiling and Running Programs with the IDE

Once you create the source, header, and project files, you are ready to compile your program. Without the advanced project-management features of Borland C++, compiling a large project could be a complicated task. But the Borland C++ IDE and project-management functions make building programs easy, whether they are simple or complex.

Once you compile your program, Borland C++ can even run it without leaving the Integrated Development Environment. Running your program in the IDE can save you much time because modifications can be made quickly and recompiling takes only a few keystrokes.

This section shows you how to use Borland C++ to compile and run your program. The instructions work for small C programs as well as large projects.

Compiling and Running Simple Programs

You have already used the Borland C++ compiler to compile your single source file programs. Compiling these programs is simple; all you do is select the Make EXE file command from the Compile menu. Compile Make causes Borland C++ to compile your program and generate an EXE file.

Compiling your project files is just as easy. To compile a project file, be sure that the project has been opened (using **P**roject **O**pen) and then choose **C**ompile **M**ake. Borland C++ compiles all the files in your project and creates an executable file. The F9 key is a shortcut key you can use to start the **C**ompile **M**ake operation.

You may have noticed that the Lines, Code, and Data fields in the project window change after you compile your project. These fields give you information about the files in the project. The Lines field indicates the number of code lines for a source file in the project. The Code and Data fields tell you how many bytes of code and data the compiler generated. Borland C++ automatically updates these fields after you compile your project file.

If Borland C++ detects any errors or questionable conditions during the compilation of your code, Borland C++ creates a message window to inform you of these conditions. The message window is useful because you can use it to place the cursor at the point in the source file where the error was detected.

You can use either the keyboard or the mouse to select an error or warning condition to correct. First change to the message window and then select the condition you want to correct. With the keyboard, use the arrow keys to select an error or a warning condition; then press the Enter key. The cursor is placed at the point in the source code where Borland C++ detected an error. With the mouse, put the mouse pointer on the condition you want to fix and then double-click. Again, the cursor is placed in the source file at the point where Borland C++ detected a problem.

When you are through with the message window, you can remove it in one of two ways. You can click the close box if you are using a mouse, or you can select the **R**emove messages command from the **C**ompile menu. You can select this command with the keyboard or the mouse.

Borland C++ lets you run your program without leaving the IDE environment. To run the program, select the **R**un command from the **R**un menu. (The shortcut key combination for this command is Ctrl-F9.) When you run the program, Borland C++ creates a user screen in which the program executes. While the program is running, the user screen is active by default. When the program ends, Borland C++ switches back to the current edit window. If you want to see the program output again, press Alt-F5. Press any key to return to the edit window when you are through viewing the user screen.

Borland C++ automatically saves the project you are working on when you exit the IDE. When you exit, Borland C++ generates two files: the project file (with a PRJ file extension) and a desktop file (with a DSK file extension). The project file contains all the information about your project. The desktop file contains information about the state of the IDE desktop at the time you exit the program.

Compiling and Running Complex Programs

Borland C++ provides additional features to help you work with the more complex programs you create. In this section, you learn how to use some of these advanced features.

With the Compile menu, you can do more than just create an executable file. Figure 5.5 shows the additional options on the Compile menu.

Fig. 5.5. The Borland C++ Compile menu.

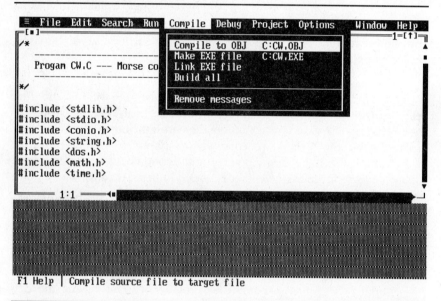

On the Compile menu, the Compile to OBJ option generates an object file. Recall that an object file is a form of your program that has been converted to machine-language instructions. However, an object file is still not an executable file. The object file must be linked with other files before it can be run. With the Compile to OBJ command, you can create an object file that will be linked at a later time.

The Link EXE file command creates an EXE file from the currently selected OBJ and LIB files. The files are linked without a make being performed. In other words, the files are not compiled again; they are simply linked to form an EXE file. If you have LIB files specified in your project file, they are linked into the EXE file. If you do not have any LIB files specified in the project, Borland C++ uses only the default LIB files during the link.

The **B**uild all option causes all the files in the project to be rebuilt. This command builds all files, even if they are up-to-date.

If your program requires command-line arguments in order to operate properly, you can pass them to your program with the **A**rguments command from the **R**un menu. The program receives the arguments you specify just as if you had started it from the DOS command prompt.

Borland C++ also provides a handy utility that lets you keep notes on your project. The Project **n**otes command in the **W**indow menu opens a note window in which you can enter comments about the current project. Every project has its own notes file in which you can store your comments. When you load a project, the notes file is automatically available for use.

Autodependency checking is an advanced and powerful feature of the Borland C++ Project Manager. This feature saves you compile-and-link time and verifies that all the OBJ files for a project are up-to-date. The rest of this section shows you why autodependency checking is needed and how it works.

The purpose of a project file is to separate your program into manageable pieces. When you need to modify or correct a piece of code, you need to work with only one source file of your project. Having your code separated into smaller pieces makes it easier to maintain and upgrade your programs.

In a large project, recompiling and relinking the whole project when you make changes in the individual program modules takes too much time. And it's hard to keep track of files that need recompiling after you make several changes. The Borland C++ Project Manager takes care of both these problems for you.

If you have turned on the **C**heck Auto-Dependencies option from the Make dialog box on the **O**ptions pull-down menu, Borland C++ puts dependency information in the OBJ files that are created. When you perform a make on a project, Borland C++ checks the dependency information in the object files. If any of the source files used by the project have a later date than the one listed in the dependency information stored in the object files, Borland C++ recompiles the out-of-date source files. Because only the out-of-date source files are compiled, the make process takes less time. The autodependency checking also ensures that *all* the modified files in your project are recompiled.

To use autodependency checking, make certain that the date and time are set correctly on your computer. If you are using an older computer that does not have a clock, be sure to set the date and time when you start the computer. If the date and time are not set, the autodependency feature won't work correctly.

Introducing the Integrated Debugger

The Borland C++ Integrated Development Environment contains just about everything you could want to make programming easy and efficient. The IDE even has a built-in debugger to help you track down elusive problems. The integrated debugger is not as powerful as a stand-alone debugger like Turbo Debugger. However, the integrated debugger's features can take care of many of your debugging tasks.

Debuggers are utilities that enable you to execute your program one statement at a time. As you step through the program, you can examine the way it works, and you can inspect the values stored in the program's variables. With other debugger features, you can run your program at full speed until a specified statement is encountered or a certain condition is met.

This section introduces you to the built-in Borland C++ debugger. You will learn how to execute your program line by line, inspect data values, and set breakpoints.

Using the Step over Command To Narrow the Search

The **R**un menu contains several commands you can use to control the execution of your program during debugging. Figure 5.6 shows the options offered through the **R**un menu.

You use the **S**tep over command to execute your program one line at a time. This command does not trace (follow execution) into a function when a function call is encountered, but only lets you single-step through the current function.

To see how the **S**tep over command works, start Borland C++ and open the CW.PRJ project file. Then select the CW.C source file; either press the Enter key or double-click the mouse to load the CW.C source file into an edit window.

When CW.C is in an edit window, you can use the **S**tep over command to step through the program. The shortcut key for this command is F8. When you press the F8 key, the compiler's message window flashes by. The compiler is checking to see whether CW.C is up-to-date. If it is, the cursor is placed at the first executable statement in the source file, which is the beginning of the `main()` function definition. Notice that all the declaration statements and the function definitions before `main()` are skipped. The **Step** over command begins at the first *executable* statement, not necessarily the first statement in the source file.

Fig. 5.6. The Run menu's debugging options.

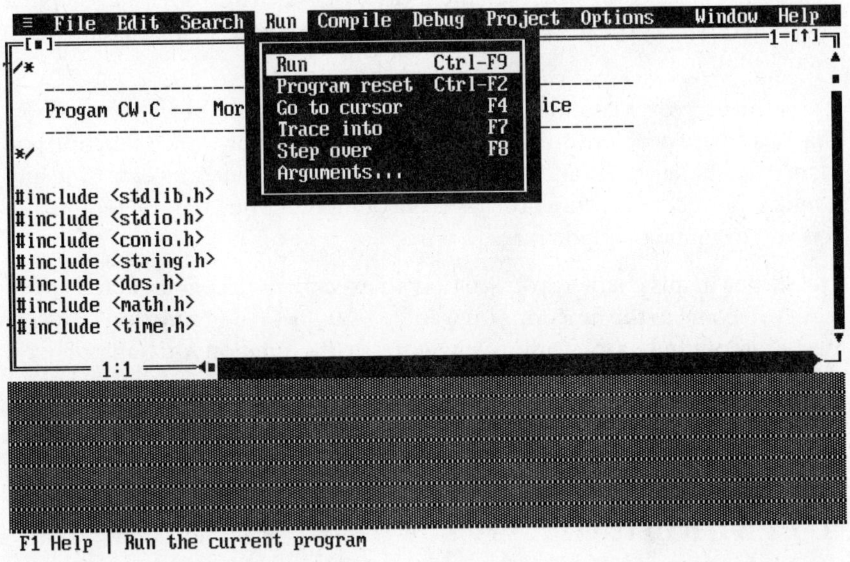

```
 ≡  File  Edit  Search  Run  Compile  Debug  Project  Options    Window  Help
┌[▪]═══════════════════╥═══════════════════════════╥════════════════1═[↑]═┐
/*                      ║ Run              Ctrl-F9  ║                      ▲
  ─────────────────     ║ Program reset    Ctrl-F2  ║ ────────────         ▮
   Progam CW.C ─── Mor  ║ Go to cursor          F4  ║ ice                  
  ─────────────────     ║ Trace into            F7  ║ ────────────         
*/                      ║ Step over             F8  ║                      
                        ║ Arguments...              ║                      
#include <stdlib.h>     ╚═══════════════════════════╝                      
#include <stdio.h>                                                         
#include <conio.h>                                                         
#include <string.h>                                                        
#include <dos.h>                                                           
#include <math.h>                                                          
#include <time.h>                                                          ▼
└──── 1:1 ════◄▪══════════════════════════════════════════════════════════┘
```

```
 F1 Help │ Run the current program
```

Press the F8 key until the cursor is at the beginning of this statement:

```
fancy_box( 1, 1, 80, 10 );
```

While you are pressing the F8 key, notice that the screen flashes. Borland C++ is switching to the user screen every time a statement that writes information to that screen is executed. After the statement is completed, Borland C++ switches back to the edit window.

Now press Alt-F5. You are switched to the user screen. If you have a color monitor, all you see is a blue screen. Press the Esc key to switch back to the edit window. You can use Alt-F5 whenever you want to examine your program's screen output.

The next time you press the F8 key, two things happen. First, the function call is executed. You can verify that the function was executed by switching to the user screen. You should now see a double-lined box in the top part of the screen. Second, the cursor is advanced to the next statement in the `main()` function. The cursor will now be in front of the following statement:

```
box_it( 1, 11, 80, 24 );
```

The position of the cursor, in front of box_it(), indicates that the statement before this one has been executed and that the debugger is waiting to execute box_it(). Even though the fancy_box() function was executed, you were not given the opportunity to step through the statements in the fancy_box().

You did not trace the statements in the fancy_box() function because you used the Step over command. This command steps through the statements in the current function only. Statements in lower-level functions are "stepped over." In this case, because the current function is main(), the statements in main() are traced.

The Step over command from the Run menu is useful when you know that you have a problem in a certain function. If you know which function you want to examine, you don't want to be distracted by the debugger tracing into a function every time a function call is encountered. The Step over command lets you examine one function at a time.

Later in this chapter, you see how to execute the program at full speed until you come to the function you want to examine. If that function is deeply nested, it could take a long time to single-step to the function you want to check.

Using the Trace into Command To Pinpoint the Problem

The Trace into command from the Run menu works similarly to the Step over command. The difference is that the Trace into command traces into a function when a function call is encountered. You can see this difference by stepping back through the CW.C file. This time, you will trace into the functions that are called.

If you already have the CW.C program set up from the last example, you can use another Run menu command to start the program again. Select the Program reset command or press Ctrl-F2 to reset the program so that you can trace through it.

Once you have reset the program, you can use the F7 key (the shortcut key for the Trace into command) to step through the program until you are at the beginning of the following statement:

```
fancy_box( 1, 1, 80, 10 );
```

You may have noticed that you were not able to trace into the library functions supplied with Borland C++. This is normal. The Trace into command works only with the functions you supply.

The next time you press the F7 key, you will see the edit window change to show the `fancy_box()` function. When you pressed the F7 key, the debugger placed you at the beginning of the `fancy_box()` function definition. You can now step through the `fancy_box()` function statement by statement.

When you reach the end of the `fancy_box()` function, the debugger transfers you back to the `main()` function. If you continue to use **Run Trace into**, you can step through the `main()` function, tracing into each function that is called.

Using the **Trace into** command along with the **Step over** command is handy. Use the **Step over** command to trace to a function you want to examine. When you reach the call for that function, switch to the **Trace into** command. This command places you inside the function to be examined. You can then use either of these commands to continue your investigation.

You use the **Step over** command when you want to examine a specific function, but not other functions that are called. You use the **Trace into** command when you need to examine the execution of your program in more detail. The **Trace into** command is helpful when you are tracking a problem whose cause is not known.

Another useful option from the **Run** menu is the **Go** to cursor command. With this command, you can execute your program at full speed until you reach the point in the source file where the cursor is located. You can position the cursor anywhere in the source file. When you select **Go** to cursor, the program runs at full speed until you reach the location of the cursor. Execution of the program then stops, giving you a chance to trace slowly through the rest of the program.

Setting and Removing Breakpoints

With breakpoints, you can execute your program until certain locations in your source file are reached. When a breakpoint is reached, execution stops so that you can begin to examine and trace the program.

A breakpoint can be either conditional or unconditional. When an unconditional breakpoint is encountered, program execution stops. When a conditional breakpoint is encountered, program execution stops only if a condition that you specify is met.

Figure 5.7 shows the breakpoint commands on the **Debug** menu.

Fig. 5.7. The Debug menu and breakpoint commands.

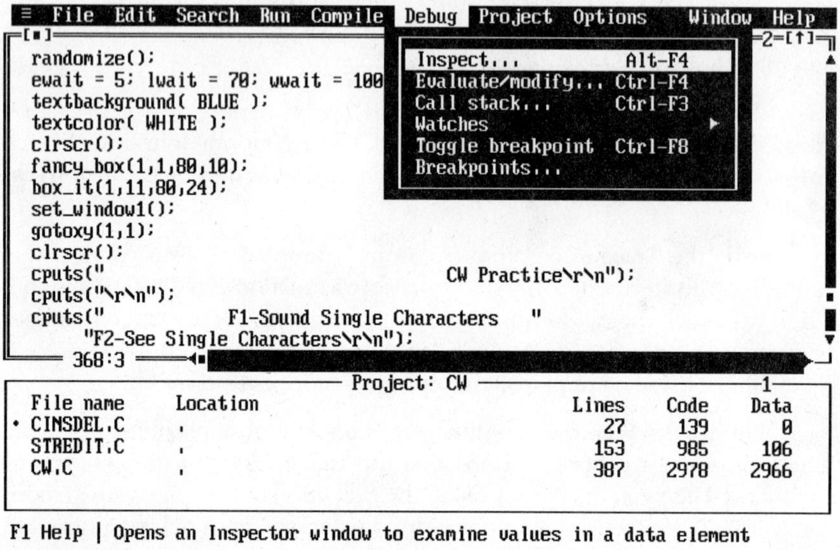

```
≡  File  Edit  Search  Run  Compile  Debug  Project  Options    Window  Help
┌[■]══════════════════════════════╤══════════════════════════2═[↑]═╗
  randomize();                      │ Inspect...      Alt-F4                ▲
  ewait = 5; lwait = 70; wwait = 100│ Evaluate/modify... Ctrl-F4
  textbackground( BLUE );           │ Call stack...    Ctrl-F3
  textcolor( WHITE );               │ Watches                     ▶
  clrscr();                         │ Toggle breakpoint Ctrl-F8
  fancy_box(1,1,80,10);             │ Breakpoints...
  box_it(1,11,80,24);               └────────────────────────────
  set_window1();
  gotoxy(1,1);
  clrscr();
  cputs("                          CW Practice\r\n");
  cputs("\r\n");
  cputs("           F1-Sound Single Characters  "              ▼
     "F2-See Single Characters\r\n");
 ══ 368:3 ═══◄■▓▓▓▓▓▓▓▓▓▓▓▓▓▓▓▓▓▓▓▓▓▓▓▓▓▓▓▓▓▓▓▓▓▓▓▓▓▓▓▓▓▓▓▓▓▓▓▓═╧
┌──────────────────── Project: CW ──────────────────────1─┐
  File name    Location            Lines    Code    Data
 • CINSDEL.C       ,                  27     139       0
   STREDIT.C       ,                 153     985     106
   CW.C            ,                 387    2978    2966

└─────────────────────────────────────────────────────────┘
F1 Help │ Opens an Inspector window to examine values in a data element
```

With the **Toggle** breakpoint command from the **Debug** menu, you can insert an unconditional breakpoint in your program. When you run your program from within the IDE, execution stops when the unconditional breakpoint is encountered. You insert an unconditional breakpoint by placing the cursor at the spot where you want the breakpoint, and then selecting the **Toggle** breakpoint command. You can set more than one breakpoint in your program.

You can also put conditional breakpoints in a program. A conditional breakpoint stops execution only when a certain condition is met. This kind of breakpoint is useful for checking loop bounds or input values. Note the next code fragment:

```
int i;
...
scanf( "%d", &i );
...
```

You may want to place a conditional breakpoint on the line following the scanf() statement. This breakpoint can be used to check the value of the variable i. If the value of i meets a condition you specify, program execution stops.

To insert a conditional breakpoint, position the cursor at the place where you want to check a condition and stop program execution. Next, select the **B**reakpoint command from the **D**ebug menu. From the Breakpoint dialog box that appears, you can control the breakpoints you set. Once you are in the dialog box, choose the Edit button at the bottom of the box. You are then placed in the Breakpoint Modify/New dialog box where you can specify the condition on which you want the breakpoint to suspend execution. When you have entered the condition, choose the box's **N**ew button. You are then returned to the Breakpoint dialog box, where you can choose the O**K** button to return to the IDE.

After you have completed the setup for the conditional breakpoint, you can run your program. If the breakpoint's condition is met, program execution is suspended. You can then use the other debugging commands to examine your source code.

The Evaluate/modify command lets you inspect and change the values of expressions in your program. To select an expression for evaluation, place the cursor at the beginning of the expression. Then select the **E**valuate/modify command. Borland C++ brings up a dialog box showing three fields that display the expression to evaluate, the result of the expression, and the new value you want the expression to have.

The Expression field shows the first character of the expression where your cursor is located. If you want to include more of the expression, press the right-arrow key. More of the expression is copied from the edit window.

Once you have pulled in the expression, you can have the debugger evaluate it by choosing the dialog box's Evaluate button. The value of the expression is shown in the Expression field. Any expression can be evaluated that does not contain any of the following:

❏ A function call

❏ A symbol that was created with the preprocessor's `#define` directive

❏ A variable that is not available in the current scope

You can change the value of the expression by entering a value in the New Value field. To have the debugger place the changed value in your program, press the Modify button found at the side of the dialog box. When you press Esc, you exit the Evaluate and Modify dialog box.

Exercises

The following exercises give you practice in designing multisource file programs, managing projects, and using the integrated debugger.

1. Design a book-cataloging program. In the program, use an array of structures to hold information about a book title, author, and publisher. Make this program a project by separating the functions that input data and the functions that print a report.

2. Write the support functions for the cataloging program. When you are through with a source file, go ahead and write the header file that will be used for the source file.

3. Create the project file for your cataloging program.

4. Compile and test your program.

5. Use the integrated debugger to locate any errors in your program. If there aren't any errors, make some so that you can practice with the debugger.

Summary

This chapter covered complex project design and the fundamentals of program debugging using the Borland C++ integrated debugger. You learned the following important points:

❑ *As your programs get larger, you will want to divide them into modules of related functions.* Dividing your large programs into smaller modules makes maintaining and modifying your programs easier.

❑ *The Borland C++ Project Manager simplifies the task of creating multiple source file projects.* The Project Manager keeps track of the dependencies among your source files. This autodependency feature lets you concentrate on your C code instead of trying to remember which source file you last changed.

❑ *The* extern *keyword signals the compiler that the object you are declaring was defined in another source file.* The extern keyword tells the compiler not to allocate space for the object again.

❏ *You do not have to use the* extern *keyword when you declare functions defined in other source files.* Functions are created with external linkage by default. This means that a function is automatically available for use in other source files.

❏ *When you create a source file that will be compiled with other programs, you need to create a header file for that source file.* The header file is a collection of all the declarations needed to access the functions and variables in the source file you created. The header file is included by other programs that will use the functions and variables in your source file.

❏ *Borland C++ provides a group of conditional compilation preprocessor directives.* One purpose of these directives is to prevent multiple declarations of the same objects. The #if defined and #ifdef are two of the conditional compilation directives.

❏ *Compiling and running complex programs is almost as easy as compiling and running simple programs—thanks to the IDE's project-management facilities.* To compile most programs or projects, you can use the **Make EXE** file command from the **Compile** menu. To run a program in the IDE, use the **Run** command from the **Run** menu.

❏ *Although not as powerful as a stand-alone debugger, the integrated debugger is still useful.* The integrated debugger lets you step through your program, set breakpoints, and evaluate or modify expression values. For many debugging tasks, the integrated debugger is sufficient.

6

Using the Borland C++ I/O Function Library

So far, you have been using basic C input and output functions. These functions read data from the keyboard and send results to the video screen. The functions are useful, but they cannot access or record permanent data. Without the ability to store data permanently, you will have to enter the data manually each time you run your program. The usefulness of a program that cannot permanently store data is, as you may imagine, sharply limited.

This chapter shows you how to use the Borland C++ functions that enable you to access any of your computer's I/O devices, not just the screen and keyboard. You learn first how C handles data and then how to use the Borland C++ I/O library functions. With these functions, you can access the mass storage and other I/O devices on your computer. Using the disk drives and other devices on the computer opens up new worlds of programming possibilities.

Understanding I/O Concepts

Before you start using the Borland C++ I/O functions, you need to know how C handles input and output data. Borland C++ uses *streams* to represent the data that moves in and out of your program. Borland C++ streams let you use your computer's I/O devices without worrying about low-level control of your computer.

This section introduces the primary I/O devices that are available on your computer. After you learn how your computer handles data, you see how Borland C++ associates streams with the devices and files on your system. Finally, you learn about the two basic types of files that Borland C++ uses: binary and text files.

Understanding Files and Devices

Usually, when you work with large amounts of data, the data is stored in a file. A *file* is simply a group of related data. Depending on the type of file you are using, you can read data from the file or write data to the file, and sometimes you can do both.

Every file is associated with some type of device. A *device* is a piece of computer hardware that either stores or transfers information. One device that you are already familiar with is the hard disk in your computer. The hard disk is a mass storage device whose purpose is to store large amounts of information permanently.

Devices can be divided into two groups: permanent and interactive devices. As you know, the hard disk in your computer is a permanent device. Permanent devices store data for a very long time. Examples of other permanent devices are diskette drives, tape drives, and CD ROM drives. Each of these devices has its particular advantages and disadvantages, but all are designed to retain data for extended periods of time.

Interactive devices are generally used to transfer data to or from your computer. Unlike permanent devices, interactive devices store data for only a short period of time. Your video card and display monitor make up an interactive device. Data is sent to your video card, which produces an image on the monitor. The image on the monitor stays there as long as you have power and as long as you don't send other data that erases the screen. The monitor does not store data permanently; once the data on the screen is lost, the data is gone forever (or at least until you re-create it). Some of the other interactive devices attached to your computer are the mouse, keyboard, and modem.

One of the biggest problems with the devices that your computer uses is that they are slow. Even a fast hard disk transfers data much more slowly than the computer can process the data. Because the devices attached to your computer are slow compared to the CPU, many of the devices are buffered. A *buffer* is a special area of memory set aside to store the data being sent to or received from a device.

If the device is sending data to the computer, the buffer stores the information until it is convenient for the CPU to process the data. If the device is receiving data from the computer, the buffer stores the data sent by the CPU until the device is able to accept the data. Using a buffer correctly can greatly improve the performance of your programs. Figure 6.1 shows how a buffer works.

Fig. 6.1. *How a buffer works with the CPU and devices.*

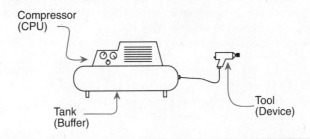

Generally, an I/O buffer serves a similar purpose to that of the tank on an air compressor. The air compressor compresses air and stores the high-pressure air in a tank. When a tool needs air, the tank has a large volume of high-pressure air readily available.

Because the tool remains idle much of the time, running the air compressor continuously would be inefficient. The compressor runs only when the pressure in the tank drops to a specified level. When the compressor does operate, it runs at full speed and efficiency.

An I/O buffer works similarly to the air tank. The I/O buffer stores data until the I/O device is ready to receive the data. When the device is ready, the buffer supplies the device with all the data the device can handle.

The compressor in this example is like the CPU in your computer. Because I/O devices are slow, it would be inefficient for the CPU to send data to the I/O device all the time. Without an I/O buffer, the CPU would be tied up for long periods of time. The buffer allows the CPU to send data in larger blocks, thereby increasing the efficiency of the CPU.

In the compressor example, the air tank represents only an output buffer. Your programs make use of both output and input buffers. An input buffer stores the data sent from a device until the CPU is ready to process the data.

Understanding Files and Streams

For many operations, Borland C++ accesses data files through streams. A stream represents a file and is used to transfer the data to and from the file.

Streams are also a portable way to handle your I/O tasks. Borland C++ has several functions that enable you to manipulate your files directly through DOS interfaces. These functions, however, are not portable to other compilers. But many of the functions that use streams can be ported to other compilers without source code changes. If you need to write portable code, use the I/O functions that control data files through streams.

To associate a stream with a file, all you need to do is open the file. Functions like `fopen()` automatically associate a stream with a file. The following example shows how to use the `fopen()` function:

```
FILE *my_file;
...
if ( ( my_file = fopen ( "text.tst", "w" ) ) == NULL ) {
  printf( "Could not open file.\n" );
  printf( "Exiting program.\n" );
  exit( 0 );
}
...
fclose( my_file );
```

In this code fragment, the `fopen()` function opens the `test.txt` file and prepares to write to the file. Even though `fopen()` automatically associates a stream with the `test.txt` file, you do not manipulate the `my_file` stream object directly. To control the stream, and therefore control the file, you must use the library functions—`printf()`, in this example—that control the `FILE` type data object pointed to by `my_file`.

`my_file` is a pointer to a special data object that holds information about a particular stream. The data object pointed to by `my_file` has the data type `FILE`. To control a stream, you have to use functions that can access and use the data contained in a `FILE` type data object.

A `FILE` type data object contains several pieces of information about a particular stream. Some of the items contained in the `FILE` type data object are the following:

❏ Information about the I/O buffer associated with the file

❏ The size of the stream

❏ An indicator signaling that an I/O error has occurred

❏ A file position indicator that marks the current position in the file

❏ An indicator signaling that the end of the file has been encountered

When you are through with a file, you need to disassociate the stream from the file and close the file. The `fclose()` function performs both tasks. The last line in the preceding code fragment shows how `fclose()` is used.

Standard Borland C++ Streams

Borland C++ provide five standard streams for your program. Whenever you write a C program, you automatically have access to the following five standard streams:

Stream	Purpose	I/O Device
stdin	Input stream	Keyboard
stdout	Output stream	Video monitor
stdprn	Printer stream	Printer port
stdaux	Auxiliary output	Serial port
stderr	Error stream	Video monitor

`stdin` is the basic standard input stream that handles keyboard input. `stdaux`, which can be used for either input or output, enables you to send and receive data from the serial port. The serial port lets you connect your computer to a modem or even to another computer.

Four of the five streams supplied by Borland C++ are standard output streams. `stdout` is the output stream that sends data to your screen, `stdprn` is the output stream that sends output data to the printer port, and `stdaux` is the stream that sends data to the serial or COM port. `stderr` is the standard error stream, which sends error messages to the screen.

Understanding Text and Binary Streams

Opening a file associates a stream with that file. The way you open a file, though, determines what *type* of stream will be associated with the file. Borland C++ has two types of streams you can use with your files: text and binary streams.

The type of the stream used for a file determines the way in which the data in the file will be translated. Functions that work with text streams change, or translate, some of the special characters in the file. Functions that work with binary files do not translate any characters in the file.

When a text stream is read, special characters in the file are converted to an internal format. For example, when a carriage-return character and a linefeed character are read from a file, the two characters are converted to the newline character (\n). Furthermore, when a file is treated as a text stream, a tab character is changed to a series of space characters.

No conversions take place when a file is processed as a binary stream. The data in a binary stream matches the data in the file, bit for bit. When a binary stream reads a carriage-return character and a linefeed character, each of the control characters is included in the stream. A binary stream does not convert carriage-return/linefeed characters to a newline character, as a text stream does. Figure 6.2 shows how a text stream and a binary stream represent the information in a file.

Fig. 6.2. Data representation in binary and text streams.

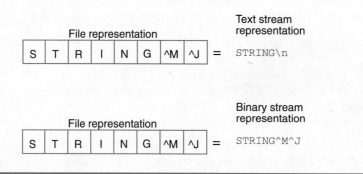

In figure 6.2, you can see how data in a file is represented when the file is opened first as a text stream and then as a binary stream. The file consists of several characters. The first six characters spell the word *string*. The last two characters in the file represent the carriage-return character (^M) and the linefeed character (^J).

When the file in figure 6.2 is opened as a text stream, the carriage-return/linefeed characters are converted to a single character by the functions that work with text streams. A newline character (\n) in the stream replaces the carriage-return/linefeed characters in the file. When the same file is opened as a binary stream, no character conversion takes place. The carriage-return/linefeed characters are treated as separate characters in binary streams.

Text streams are useful for files containing information that can be read directly by people. Binary streams are often used when files are processed by the computer. For example, an object file is opened as a binary stream before the object is linked. Binary streams are used also in reading and writing files that contains numbers stored in the computer's internal format.

Using the Standard Streams for I/O

Borland C++ automatically opens five standard I/O streams for your program. Using these standard streams is easy because you do not have to open any files for the streams. Borland C++ automatically opens the standard streams and makes them available for your use. These standard streams were listed in the preceding section.

In this section, you learn about two groups of powerful I/O functions that can be used with the standard streams. First, you see how to use formatted I/O functions to input and output any of the standard data types. Next, you see how to use character I/O functions to input and output character-based information.

Using Formatted I/O Functions

Borland C++ has two main families of formatted I/O functions: the scanf() input functions and the printf() output functions. Chapter 1 introduced you to these families of functions. You will learn more about using scanf() and printf() in this section.

The scanf() and printf() functions are similar in that both work with formatted data—data arranged in any order you specify. When you use the scanf() function, you specify what type of data will be read and the order in which it will be input. For printf(), you specify the type and order of the data that will be output. Both scanf() and printf() work with any of C's basic data types. For example, scanf() can be used to input floating-point numbers as easily as characters or integers, and printf() can print any of the basic data types in the sequence you want.

Listing 6.1 shows a rudimentary inventory-database program that uses functions from both the scanf() and printf() families to retrieve and display data. This program shows you how to use the formatted I/O functions to create, update, and display a simple inventory database.

Listing 6.1. `fdata.c`. *A program that uses formatted I/O functions for terminal and file I/O.*

```
1   /* FDATA.C  This program demonstrates the use of the
2             formatted I/O functions. Formatted I/O
3             functions are used for both terminal and
4             file I/O.  */
5
6   #include <stdlib.h>
7   #include <stdio.h>
8   #include <conio.h>
9   #include <io.h>
10
11  #define DATA_FILE "data.fil"
12
13  int menu( void );
14  int add( void );
15  int display( void );
16
17  /* main() - The main() function calls functions based on
18             the value returned by the menu() function.
19
20             If main() executes correctly, a value of 0 is
21             returned. */
22
23  main() {
24    int return_value;
25
26    while( ( return_value = menu() ) != 0 ) {
27      switch( return_value ) {
28        case 1:   add();
29                  break;
30        case 2:   display();
31                  break;
32        case 3:   clrscr();
33                  printf( "Enter a correct menu value.\n" );
34                  printf( "Press a key to continue.\n" );
35                  while( !kbhit() );
36                  break;
37      }
38    }
39    return 0;
40  }
41
```

```
42  /* menu() - The menu function displays a menu screen and
43               prompts the user to select a menu item. The
44               user's character input is converted to an
45               integer value.
46
47               menu() returns an integer value that represents
48               a menu selection. */
49
50  int menu() {
51    char char_in[2];
52    int i;
53
54    clrscr();
55    printf( "\n\n\n\n\n" );
56    printf( "1.  Add data to the data file.\n" );
57    printf( "2.  Display the data file.\n" );
58    printf( "0.  Quit.\n" );
59
60    printf( "\n\nEnter your selection ==> " );
61    gets( char_in );
62    i = atoi( char_in );
63    if( i >= 0 && i <= 3 )
64      return( i );
65    else
66      return( 3 );
67  }
68
69  /* add() - The add() function opens a data file, prompts
70             the user for the product information, and adds
71             the product information to the data file. When
72             all the new items are added to the file, add()
73             closes the data file.
74
75             If add() executes correctly, a value of 0 is
76             returned. */
77
78  int add() {
79    FILE    *fp;
80    char    more = 'Y';
81    char    name[30];
82    int     count;
83    float   weight;
84
```

Listing 6.1. continues

Listing 6.1. *continued*

```
 85    clrscr();
 86
 87    if( ( fp = fopen( DATA_FILE, "ab" ) ) == NULL ) {
 88      clrscr();
 89      printf( "\n\nData file could not be opened.\n" );
 90      exit( 0 );
 91    }
 92
 93    while( more == 'Y' ) {
 94      clrscr();
 95      printf( "\n\nEnter product name ==> " );
 96      scanf( "%s", name );
 97      printf( "\nEnter number of items ==> " );
 98      scanf( "%d", &count );
 99      printf( "\nEnter product weight ==> " );
100      scanf( "%f", &weight );
101      fflush( stdin );
102
103      fprintf( fp, "%s %d %f", name, count, weight );
104
105      printf( "\n\n\nEnter another product? Y/N ==> " );
106      more = getche();
107      if( more == 'y' ) more = 'Y';
108    }
109
110    fclose( fp );
111    return 0;
112  }
113
114  /* display() - The display function displays the contents
115                 of the data file that was created or
116                 appended by the add() function.
117
118                 A value of 0 is returned if display()
119                 executes correctly. */
120
121  int display() {
122    FILE    *fp;
123    char    name[30];
124    int     count;
125    float   weight;
126
127    clrscr();
```

```
128    if( ( fp = fopen( DATA_FILE, "rb" ) ) == NULL ) {
129      clrscr();
130      printf( "\n\nData file could not be opened.\n" );
131      exit( 0 );
132    }
133
134    while( !feof( fp ) ) {
135      fscanf( fp, "%s %d %f", name, &count, &weight );
136      printf( "\n\n" );
137      printf( "Product name: %s\n", name );
138      printf( "Product count = %d\n", count );
139      printf( "Product weight = %4.2f\n", weight );
140    }
141
142    printf( "\n\nPress any key to continue." );
143    while( !kbhit() );
144
145    fclose( fp );
146    return 0;
147  }
```

Program execution in listing 6.1 starts in the main() function (line 23). The while statement in line 26 repeatedly calls the menu() function until a value of 0 is returned by menu(). If menu() returns a value of 1 or 2, the corresponding function is called. If menu() returns a value of 3, an error message is displayed, and execution continues.

In the add() function (lines 78–112), scanf() is used to store the inventory data input by the user. Once the inventory data is input and stored in the proper variables, fprintf() writes the data to the disk file.

The display() function (lines 121–147) uses fscanf() to get the product data from the disk file, and uses printf() to display the data on the video screen.

Understanding *scanf()*

This section discusses the use of the scanf() function in listing 6.1. You learn how to format and use the functions in the scanf() family, and you also see what other scanf() functions are available.

The statement in line 98 of listing 6.1 shows a typical use of `scanf()`:

```
scanf( "%d", &count );
```

The `scanf()` function call consists of two parts: the format string and the variable argument list. In this line of code, the format string is the expression `"%d"`. This string tells `scanf()` the order and type of data that you want to read. Here the `%d` specification tells `scanf()` to read an integer value. As you can see, the format string is enclosed in parentheses.

The second part of the `scanf()` function call is the variable argument list. This is a list of addresses where input data is stored. Each item in the format string should have a matching address in the variable argument list. In the preceding line of code, for example, the integer value extracted from the input stream will be stored at the address `&count` (that is, *in the variable* `count`).

When you use any of the functions in the `scanf()` family, remember the following requirements:

❏ *Every format specification in the format string requires an address in the variable argument list.*

❏ *The data type of the conversion specifier in the format string and the data type at the address specified in the variable argument list should match.*

❏ *The variable argument list is a list of addresses.* Each item in the variable argument list should be an address, not a variable.

Look at the next two statements from listing 6.1. The first statement is the `scanf()` function call in line 96, and the second statement is the `scanf()` function call in line 98:

```
scanf( "%s", name );
...
scanf( "%d", &count );
```

The `%s` conversion specifier in the first `scanf()` function call causes a string to be input. The string that is read is stored in the address specified by the variable `name`. Recall that when you use the name of an array without a subscript, you get the address of the array. In the first `scanf()` statement, `name` gives the address where the input string is stored.

The second `scanf()` statement is slightly different from the first in that the address-of operator (`&`) is used in the variable argument list. When the unary address-of operator is used with a variable, the address of that variable is returned. In the second `scanf()` function call, the address-of operator causes the address of the `count` variable to be returned. Whenever you use a variable with a basic data type in a `scanf()` statement, you must use the address-of operator to get the address of the variable.

The format string in the `scanf()` function can contain the following three types of objects:

❑ *Whitespace character.* The valid whitespace characters are the blank, tab, and newline characters. A whitespace character in the format string instructs `scanf()` to read and ignore all the whitespace characters in the input until a nonwhitespace character is encountered.

❑ *Nonwhitespace character.* Nonwhitespace characters are any ASCII characters except the percent sign (%). A nonwhitespace character in the format string causes the `scanf()` function to read and discard a matching nonwhitespace character in the input.

❑ *Conversion specifier.* A conversion specifier causes the `scanf()` function to read a data item of the specified type from the input stream. The data item that is read is stored at an address specified in the variable argument list. All conversion specifiers start with the percent sign (%).

In the following statement, the first conversion specifier tells `scanf()` to read and store an integer value:

```
scanf( "%d %d", &i, &j );
```

The blank character following the first conversion specifier instructs `scanf()` to ignore all whitespace characters until a nonwhitespace character is encountered. Then the second conversion specifier causes `scanf()` to read and store another integer value. Refer to Appendix B for a complete list of the conversion specifiers and options that can be used with the `scanf()` function.

Table 6.1 lists the `scanf()` family of input functions and indicates their uses.

Table 6.1. *The* `scanf()` *family of input functions.*

Function	Description
scanf()	Used with the standard input stream `stdin`.
cscanf()	Reads data directly from the console.
fscanf()	Scans data from the stream you specify.
sscanf()	Reads data from a string.
vscanf()	Works like `scanf()` except that `vscanf()` requires a *pointer* to a list of arguments instead of an argument list.

Table 6.1. continues

Table 6.1. *continued*

Function	Description
vfscanf()	Scans data from a stream you specify. vfscanf() requires a pointer to a list of arguments.
vsscanf()	Inputs data from a string. A pointer to a list of arguments is required.

All the functions in the scanf() family are alike in that they are used to input formatted data. Even though all the scanf() functions perform the same basic purpose, there are different functions for the different streams from which you input data. There are other functions, the v...scanf() functions, that provide alternatives to calling the scanf() functions. The function calls for the v...scanf() functions are different because you pass the function a pointer to an argument list instead of the actual argument list.

The scanf() and fscanf() functions are the simplest of this family of formatted input functions. The display() function in listing 6.1 uses the fscanf() function. Like scanf(), fscanf() reads and stores data. However, fscanf() can input data from any stream you specify. Notice line 135 of listing 6.1:

```
fscanf( fp, "%s %d %f", name, &count, &weight );
```

The first argument in the fscanf() function call specifies the stream from which data is to be read. In this example, fscanf() reads data from the stream pointed to by the FILE type variable fp. In listing 6.1, fp is a variable that holds a pointer to the stream associated with the disk file data.fil (see the macro in line 11). It is from this disk file that fscanf() inputs all the data for the display() function.

The vscanf() functions and its relatives are a little more complicated. Listing 6.2 shows how you can use the vscanf() function. In this example, vscanf() lets you start a data input routine and set up the arguments for a scanf() type function with only one function call.

Listing 6.2. varscan.c. *A program that illustrates the use of the vscanf() function.*

```
1   /* VARSCAN.C  This program shows how the vscanf() function
2              can be used. */
3
4   #include <stdio.h>
```

```
 5   #include <stdlib.h>
 6   #include <stdarg.h>
 7   #include <conio.h>
 8
 9   int input( char *format, ... )
10   {
11     va_list arg_ptr;
12     int item_count;
13
14     clrscr();
15     printf( "Enter two integers and a string.\n" );
16     printf( "Separate the entries with whitespace "
17             "characters.\n\n" );
18     printf( "==> " );
19
20     va_start( arg_ptr, format );
21     item_count = vscanf( format, arg_ptr );
22     va_end( arg_ptr );
23
24     return item_count;
25   }
26
27   main()
28   {
29     int i, j;
30     char str[81];
31
32     clrscr();
33     printf( "This program demonstrates the "
34             "vscanf() function. \n\n" );
35     printf( "Press any key to continue.\n" );
36     while( !kbhit() );
37
38     input( "%d %d %s", &i, &j, str );
39
40     clrscr();
41     printf( "i = %d, j = %d\n", i, j );
42     printf( "str = %s\n", str );
43
44     return 0;
45   }
```

In listing 6.2, the arguments for the `vscanf()` function call are specified in the `input()` function call in line 38. The arguments for the `input()` function are the format string and variable argument list used in the `vscanf()` function call.

`vscanf()` is designed so that it can get its arguments from a variable argument list accessed by the `va_start` and `va_end` macros. In line 20, `va_start` sets `arg_ptr` to point to the variable argument list passed to the `input()` function. In line 21, `vscanf()` is called. The `format` argument in `vscanf()` is the format string passed to the `input()` function. The `arg_ptr` argument in `vscanf()` is the same `arg_ptr` set up by the `va_start` macro. These arguments allow `vscanf()` to access the arguments specified in the `input()` function call.

Understanding *printf()*

Like the `scanf()` function, the `printf()` function consists of two main parts, a format string and a variable argument list. The format string specifies what type of data will be output by the `printf()` function. The variable argument list supplies the data to be output.

The variable argument list for the `printf()` function is optional. It is perfectly legal to use `printf()` without specifying a variable argument list. Line 33 of listing 6.1 shows the use of `printf()` without a variable argument list:

```
printf( "Enter a correct menu value.\n" );
```

This line of code simply uses the `printf()` function to print a message.

If you do use conversion specifications and a variable argument list, you should make sure that the conversion specifications match the variables you provide. A mismatch between the format string and the variable argument list causes odd program behavior. However, you can have more arguments than conversion specifiers without causing any errors.

The `printf()` format string can contain the following two types of objects:

❑ *Plain character.* Plain characters are any ASCII characters. Any plain characters you include in the format string are copied to the output stream.

❑ *Conversion specifier.* Conversion specifiers are instructions to the `printf()` function to output a data item of the specified type. Every conversion specification begins with the percent sign (%). A complete list of conversion specifications and options can be found in Appendix B.

The `printf()` family of functions consists of several output functions. Table 6.2 shows the different functions in the `printf()` family and explains how each function is used.

Table 6.2. *The* `printf()` *family of functions.*

Function	Description
`printf()`	Sends output to the `stdout` stream.
`cprintf()`	Sends output data to the current text window. Note that `cprintf()` does not translate the newline character (`\n`) to carriage-return/linefeed characters.
`fprintf()`	Works like the `printf()` function with one exception. With `fprintf()`, you specify the stream to which output will be sent.
`sprintf()`	Sends output to a string instead of a stream.
`vprintf()`	Like `printf()`, sends formatted data to the standard output stream. However, `vprintf()` is called with a pointer to a variable argument list instead of with the argument list itself.
`vfprintf()`	Called with a pointer to a variable argument list and sends output to the stream you specify.
`vsprintf()`	Sends formatted output to a string. `vsprintf()` is given a pointer to a variable argument list as a pointer.

Note how the `fprintf()` function is used in line 103 of listing 6.1:

```
fprintf( fp, "%s %d %f", name, count, weight );
```

`fprintf()` sends a string, an integer, and a floating-point number to a stream pointed to by the `FILE` pointer variable `fp`. In listing 6.1, `fp` points to the stream associated with the disk file DATA.FIL.

Each argument in the variable argument list for a `printf()` type function is an expression that yields a value compatible with the matching conversion specification in the format string. The arguments in the variable argument list are not limited to variable identifiers. Note the following example:

```
printf( "%d", 2+3 );
```

This is a valid `printf()` function call. The expression 2+3 is an integer expression that can be matched to the `%d` conversion specification. This line of code prints the integer value 5.

Listing 6.3 shows how the `vprintf()` function, which uses a pointer to a variable argument list, is called in a program.

Listing 6.3. `varprint.c`. *A demonstration of* `vprintf()`.

```
 1   /* VARPRINT.C  This sample program shows how the vprintf()
 2                  function can be used to print a program's
 3                  error messages. */
 4
 5   #include <stdio.h>
 6   #include <stdlib.h>
 7   #include <stdarg.h>
 8   #include <conio.h>
 9
10   void msg_print( char *format, ... )
11   {
12      va_list arg_ptr;
13
14      clrscr();
15      printf( "An error has occurred.\n\n" );
16      va_start( arg_ptr, format );
17      vprintf( format, arg_ptr );
18      va_end( arg_ptr );
19   }
20
21   main()
22   {
23      int i = 50;
24
25      clrscr();
26      printf( "This is a demonstration of an error message "
27              "report function.\n" );
28      printf( "\n\nPress any key to continue." );
29      while( !kbhit() );
30
31      msg_print( "Testing message utility i = %d\n", i );
32
33      return 0;
34   }
```

The program in listing 6.3 shows how the `vprintf()` function makes it easy to display error messages. Listing 6.3 has a routine called `msg_print()` that clears the screen, informs you that an error has occurred, and then prints any information you pass to `msg_print()`. Usually, performing all three of these message-display tasks would take two function calls. The first function call would clear the screen and tell you that an error has occurred. The second function call would call `printf()` to print the diagnostic message. With `vprintf()`, though, you can perform all three tasks with one function call.

When `msg_print()` is called, it is passed an argument list just like the arguments passed to the `printf()` function. First, `msg_print()` uses the `clrscr()` function to clear the screen. Second, `printf()` prints a message telling you that an error has occurred. Finally, `vprintf()` prints the information that was passed to `msg_print()`. `vprintf()` performs this task easily because `vprintf()` needs only pointers to the data to be output. The arguments passed to `vprintf()` are pointers to the arguments that were passed to the `msg_print()` function.

Before you can call the `vprintf()` function, some setup is required. First, you need a pointer that can point to the arguments passed to `msg_print()`. Line 12 declares the `va_list` type pointer `arg_ptr`. This pointer can point to the arguments in a variable argument list. Second, the argument list pointer must be initialized to the beginning of the variable argument list. The `va_start()` macro in line 16 sets up the argument pointer `arg_ptr` correctly. `va_start()` needs two arguments, the argument pointer and the name of the last fixed argument. The last fixed argument is the last argument before the variable argument list begins.

Once `va_start()` has been called and the argument pointer is initialized, the `vprintf()` function can be called. Notice that the first argument passed to `vprintf()` in line 17 is the `format` argument that was passed to `msg_print()`. The second argument passed to `vprintf()` is the pointer to the variable argument list that was initialized by `va_start()`. Once `vprintf()` has the arguments it needs, it outputs data just as the `printf()` function does.

When you are through using `vprintf()`, make sure that you call the `va_end()` macro, which ends access to the variable argument list. Failure to call the `va_end()` macro when you are though with the variable argument list pointer can cause your program to behave in strange and undefined ways.

Using Character I/O Functions

This section shows you how to use the Borland C++ character I/O functions. The two groups of functions covered are those that input and output only one character at a time, and those that work with strings. Table 6.3 summarizes the character I/O functions and describes what they do.

Table 6.3. *The character I/O functions.*

Function	Description
fgetc()	The basic character input function that reads one character at a time from the stream you specify.
fputc()	The basic character output function that lets you specify the stream to which character data will be written. fputc() writes one character at a time.
fgetchar()	A version of fgetc() that automatically reads data from the stdin stream.
fputchar()	A function that works like fputc() except that fputchar() writes all data to the stdout stream.
fgets()	A function that reads a *string* from the stream you specify.
fputs()	The string output function that requires an argument specifying the stream to which data will be output.

The fgetc() function reads a single character from the stream you specify. Here is the format for the fgetc() function declaration:

```
int fgetc( FILE *stream );
```

The value returned by fgetc() is the integer value of the character that was read. Even though the value returned is an integer value, it is legal (and common) to assign the returned value to a char type variable. Note, for example, the fgetc() statement in the following code fragment:

```
char c_in;
...
c_in = fgetc( my_stream );
```

This is a perfectly acceptable way to read a character from my_stream and assign the character value to c_in.

The only argument to fgetc() is a pointer to a stream. The stream that is pointed to is where fgetc() will read data. The stream must be open before the fgetc() function is called.

fputc() is the mirror-image function of fgetc(). Whereas fgetc() reads a single character from a stream, fputc() writes a single character to a stream. Note the format for the fputc() function declaration:

```
int fputc( int c, FILE *stream );
```

The fputc() function requires two arguments: the character that will be output, and the stream where the character will be written. The first argument in the fputc() function call is the integer value of the character that will be output. You can pass fputc() a char type object as an argument with no problem. A char type argument is simply promoted to an int type argument.

The second argument in the fputc() function call is a pointer to the stream where data will be written. The stream should be opened in write or append mode before fputc() is called.

Listing 6.4 shows how the fgetc() and fputc() functions can be used together to read a disk file and display the file on the video screen.

Listing 6.4. chario.c. *A program that uses* fgetc() *and* fputc().

```
1   /*  CHARIO.C   This program demonstrates the use of the
2                  character I/O functions fgetc() and fputc().
3                  The program opens a text file and uses the
4                  character I/O function to read and display
5                  the file. */
6
7
8   #include <stdio.h>
9   #include <stdlib.h>
10
11  main()
12  {
13    FILE *file_ptr;
14    char xfer_char;
15
16    if( ( file_ptr = fopen( "text.dat", "rt" ) ) == NULL ) {
17      clrscr();
18      printf( "Could not open data file.\n" );
19      printf( "Calling the exit() function.\n" );
20      exit( 0 );
21    }
22
23    do{
```

Listing 6.4. continues

Listing 6.4. continued

```
24        fputc( ( xfer_char = fgetc( file_ptr ) ), stdout );
25    } while( xfer_char != EOF );
26
27    fclose( file_ptr );
28    return 0;
29  }
```

The heart of the program in listing 6.4 is the do-while loop in lines 23–25. The do-while loop calls the fputc() function as long as the xfer_char variable does not contain an EOF value.

Only one statement—the fputc() function call—is in the loop. At first glance, the fputc() function call in line 24 may look complicated. However, a closer examination shows how simple this fputc() call is.

Every fputc() call requires two arguments—the integer value of the character to output, and a pointer to the stream where the output character will be sent. In line 24, the second argument to the fputc() function call is a pointer to the standard output stream. The stdout stream pointer indicates that fputc() will write data to the video screen one character at a time.

The first argument for the fputc() function call is another function call—a call to the fgetc() function. Remember that fgetc() reads a character and returns its integer value. The integer value returned by fgetc() is the same value that is output by fputc().

In line 24, the assignment of the value returned by fgetc() to the variable xfer_char is made so that the do-while loop can determine when to stop. When the value returned by fgetc() is the end-of-file character, the do-while loop stops.

fgetchar() is a special version of the fgetc() function. fgetc() requires an argument that indicates from which stream data will be read, whereas fgetchar() automatically reads data from the stdin stream. Thus, fgetchar() normally reads data from the keyboard. Note the following example:

```
char in;
...
in = fgetchar();
```

In this code fragment, the fgetchar() function reads a character from the keyboard and assigns the character to the char type variable in.

`fputchar()` works like `fputc()` except that `fputchar()` sends data to the `stdout` stream by default. Here is the format of the `fputchar()` function definition:

```
int fputchar( int c );
```

The integer value passed to `fputchar()` is the value of the character that will be output. The value returned by `fputchar()` is equal to the value of the output character if `fputchar()` wrote the character successfully. If the `fputchar()` function was not successful, it returns the value `EOF`.

In line 24 of listing 6.4, you could use the `fputchar()` function instead of the `fputc()` function. If you used `fputchar()`, the statement would look like this:

```
fputchar( xfer_char = fgetc( file_ptr ) );
```

The program in listing 6.4 would work exactly the same. The `fputchar()` function call would use `fgetc()` to read a character, and would then output the value returned by `fgetc()`.

The last two functions discussed in this section, `fgets()` and `fputs()`, work with strings instead of characters. `fgets()` reads a string from a stream you specify, and `fputs()` writes a string to the stream you choose.

You use the following format for the `fgets()` function:

```
char *fgets( char *s, int n, FILE *stream );
```

The first argument in the `fgets()` function call is a pointer to the string where `fgets()` stores the string that is read. Note the following code fragment:

```
char c_array[81];
...
fgets( c_array, 81, my_stream );
```

The `c_array` argument in the `fgets()` call points to the character array `c_array`.

The second argument in the `fgets()` function call tells `fgets()` when to stop reading characters from the input stream. This second argument, n, tells `fgets()` to stop reading characters from the input stream when $n - 1$ characters have been read. `fgets()` stops reading before $n - 1$ characters are input if a newline character is encountered.

The third and last argument to the `fgets()` function is a pointer to the stream where `fgets()` will read data. The stream pointer has a `FILE` data type.

The value returned by `fgets()` is either a pointer to a string or the null value. If `fgets()` reads a string successfully, `fgets()` returns a pointer to the string (character array) where the input string is stored. If `fgets()` encounters the end of the file, a null value is returned.

The `fputs()` function is the reciprocal function to `fgets()`. `fputs()` writes a string to any stream you choose. You use the following format for the `fputs()` function:

```
fputs( const char *s, FILE stream );
```

The first argument is a pointer to a character array, which contains the string that will be output. The second argument is a pointer to the stream where the output will be sent. Listing 6.5 shows how you can use the `fgets()` and `fputs()` functions.

Listing 6.5. `strio.c`. *A program that uses the* `fgets()` *and* `fputs()` *string I/O functions.*

```
 1   /*   STRIO.C   This program demonstrates the use of the
 2                  string I/O functions fgets() and fputs().
 3                  The program opens a text file and uses the
 4                  string I/O function to read and display
 5                  the file. */
 6
 7
 8   #include <stdio.h>
 9   #include <stdlib.h>
10
11   main()
12   {
13     FILF *file_ptr;
14     char store[256];
15
16     if( ( file_ptr = fopen( "text.dat", "rt" ) ) == NULL ) {
17       clrscr();
18       printf( "Could not open data file.\n" );
19       printf( "Calling the exit() function.\n" );
20       exit( 0 );
21     }
22
23     clrscr();
24     while( NULL != fgets( store, 256, file_ptr ) )
25       fputs( store, stdout );
26
27     fclose( file_ptr );
28     return 0;
29   }
```

Listing 6.5 is a variation of the program in listing 6.4. The program in listing 6.5 reads and writes a whole string with one function call, whereas the program in listing 6.4 inputs and outputs data one character at a time.

The controlling statements for listing 6.5 are found in lines 24 and 25. These two lines make a loop statement that reads one string at a time from the disk file pointed to by `file_ptr`. After a string is read, it is sent to the `stdout` stream for display on the video screen.

In line 24 of listing 6.5, `fgets()` reads up to 255 (256 − 1 = 255) characters from the stream pointed to by `file_ptr`. The characters that are read are placed in the array pointed to by `store`.

If the `fgets()` function does not reach the end-of-file marker, the `fputs()` statement in line 25 is executed. The `fputs()` function writes to the `stdout` stream the string pointed to by `store`.

Using the File Control Functions

Before you use the file I/O functions discussed in this chapter, you need to make sure that the file you are using is opened properly. Otherwise, you will not be able to perform the desired I/O functions. This section shows you how to use the functions that allow you to open and access files on disk drives. It shows you also how to close the files and delete them when they are no longer necessary.

The last part of this section shows you how to control the buffers associated with your files. You can then better control the use of your system resources and the performance of your I/O functions.

Opening, Closing, and Controlling Files

Before you can access a file, it must be opened. Opening a file performs two basic services. First, opening a file determines what kind of I/O can be performed on the file. In other words, the way a file is opened determines whether you can read or write data to the file. Second, opening a file associates a stream with the file. The stream is used to represent the file and to transfer data to and from the file.

In the programs in this chapter, you have seen that the data files are always opened before a file I/O function is called. The function that is used to open the files is `fopen()`. The prototype for the `fopen()` function looks like this:

```
FILE *fopen( const char *filename, const char *mode );
```

The fopen() function has two arguments that specify the file's name and the access mode for the file. The file's name is the regular DOS file name with which you are familiar. The mode argument tells fopen() whether the file can be read from, written to, or both. The file mode also determines whether the file is treated as a binary or text file.

The following fopen() statement attempts to open the file DATA.FIL:

```
file_ptr = fopen( "DATA.FIL", "r+" );
```

Because no path is specified in the file name, fopen() attempts to open DATA.FIL in the current directory. However, if the preceding fopen() statement were

```
file_ptr = fopen( "C:\\DATA.FIL", "r+" );
```

the fopen() statement would attempt to open the data.fil file in the root directory of the C: drive. Notice that the first argument, the file name, is enclosed in quotation marks in the fopen() function call. Quotation marks are used because fopen() expects a string for the file name argument (a string variable *identifier* can also be used here—the compiler generates an address value for the argument either way). Notice also that two backslash characters (\\) are used to indicate the path to the root directory. Because the backslash character is a special editing character, you must use two backslashes in a row so that the actual backslash character is included in your string.

The second argument, "r+", is the mode argument, which determines the way in which the file can be accessed. As for the file name string, you can define a mode string variable and use its identifier here, too. Table 6.4 lists the values you can use for the mode argument.

Table 6.4. Mode argument values for the fopen() function.

Mode Value	Access
r	File opened for reading only.
w	File opened for writing only.
a	File opened in append mode. The file is created if it does not exist. If the file does exist, the file is opened for updating at the end of the file.
r+	File opened in update mode. Update mode opens an existing file for read or write operations.
w+	A new file is created in update mode. Data can be read from or written to the file. If the file already exists, the old file is overwritten.

Mode Value	Access
a+	File opened in append mode. An update can be performed at the end of the file. If the file does not exist, one is created.
t	If a t is appended to the previous mode strings, the file is opened in text mode.
b	If a b is appended to the previous mode strings, the file is opened in binary mode.

The value returned by the fopen() function is a pointer to the stream that fopen() associated with the file. The pointer to the stream is used by the I/O functions to access the file. The following code fragment calls fopen() and assigns the return value to a pointer that the other I/O functions will use:

```
FILE *file_ptr;
...
if( ( file_ptr = fopen( "myfile.txt", "rt" ) ) == NULL )
  printf( "Could not open file\n" );
```

The first line of this code fragment declares a pointer that can point to a stream. The second line calls the fopen() function. The value returned by the fopen() is assigned to the variable file_ptr. file_ptr now points to the stream associated with myfile.txt. On the second line of the code fragment, the value returned by fopen() is compared to the value NULL. If fopen() is unable to open the file successfully, fopen() returns a null value. If a null value is returned, the printf() statement on the third line of the code fragment is executed. The printf() statement tells the user that the file was not opened.

The freopen() function is used to associate another file with an open stream. The declaration for the freopen() function looks like the declaration for fopen(), except that freopen() has one extra argument, as you can see in the function prototype:

```
FILE *freopen( const char *filename, const char *mode, FILE *stream );
```

Here the file name and mode arguments follow the same rules as for the fopen() function. The stream argument is a pointer to a currently open stream.

freopen() associates the file specified by the file name argument with the currently open stream pointed to by the stream argument. When freopen() is called, the stream listed by the stream argument will be closed. All subsequent stream access goes through the file specified by the file name argument.

You use the freopen() function to redirect the stdin, stdout, and stderr streams. The next code fragment shows how the stderr stream can be redirected to the disk file error.dat:

```
if( freopen( "ERROR.DAT", "w", stderr ) == NULL )
  printf( "Could not redirect stderr.\n" );
```

When you are through with a file, you should always close it. Closing the file properly helps prevent data loss. If you get out of your program without closing the files you use, you have no guarantee that those files will be there when you come back.

Borland C++ offers two useful functions for closing your files: fclose() and fcloseall(). The fclose() function closes a single stream and requires an argument indicating which stream you want to close. The following statement closes the stream pointed to by file_ptr:

```
flose( file_ptr );
```

When fcloseall() is called, all open streams (except the standard streams stdin, stdout, stdprn, stdaux, and stderr) are closed. fcloseall() does not require any arguments. The following statement closes any streams you have opened:

```
fcloseall();
```

The only streams left open are the standard streams that Borland C++ opened before your program began.

As your programs grow larger and more complex, you will probably find that you need to create temporary disk files to store data. Borland C++ provides two functions that make the task of creating temporary files safe and easy. Both functions ensure that the temporary file which is created will have a unique name and will not, therefore, overlay any of your files. The temporary file functions are tmpfile() and tmpnam().

The tmpfile() function creates a temporary binary file and opens the file in update mode. tmpfile() does not require any arguments but does return a pointer to the stream that was opened. The following code fragment shows how tmpfile() is called and used:

```
FILE *file_ptr;
...
if( ( file_ptr = tempfile() ) == NULL )
  printf( "Temporary file was not created.\n" );
```

The temporary file that is created with the tmpfile() function is removed automatically when the stream is closed or when your program ends.

The tmpnam() function creates a unique file name. tmpnam() can generate up to 65,535 different file names. The generated file name can be used by the fopen() function to create a temporary data file.

tmpnam() can have either a null argument or a pointer to a character array that can hold the temporary file name. If the argument is a pointer to a character array, the array must be at least L_tmpnam characters long. L_tmpnam is a value that is defined in the stdio.h header file. If tmpnam() has an argument that is a pointer to a string, tmpnam() stores the unique file name in that string. If tmpnam() has a null argument, tmpnam() stores the file name in an internal static object and returns a pointer to the name. The following code fragment demonstrates the use of the tmpnam() function:

```
char file_name[L_tmpnam];
int i;
...
for( i = 0; i <= 50; i++ ) {
  tmpnam( file_name );
  printf( "%s\n", file_name );
}
```

This code fragment is a for loop that calls the tmpnam() function 50 times. Each time the tmpnam() function is called, the file name is stored in the array file_name. On every pass through the loop, the new value of file_name is displayed.

The remove() function deletes a file from your disk drive. All that remove() needs is a character string that is the name of the file you want to remove. When remove() is called with a valid file name, the file is erased. Note this example:

```
remove( "MYTEXT.DAT" );
```

This remove() function deletes the file mytext.dat from the current disk drive.

The rename() function, which renames a file, needs to know both the old file name and the new file name. Both arguments are passed to rename() as character strings. For example, the statement

```
rename( "C:\\AUTOEXEC.BAT", "C:\\AUTOEXEC.OLD" );
```

changes the name of your autoexec.bat file to autoexec.old.

If drive specifiers are given in the rename() argument list, the drive specifiers must match. However, directory specifiers in the old file name argument do not have to match the directory specifiers in the new file name argument. If the directory specifiers are different, the file is moved from the directory listed in the old file name argument to the directory listed in the new file name argument.

Controlling File Buffers

In the earlier section "Understanding Devices and Files," you were introduced to buffers. You learned that a buffer is a section of memory set aside for data to be sent to or received from a device. A buffer can improve the performance of your program because the buffer provides a speed-matching service between the slow devices hooked to your computer and the fast memory your program uses. This section shows you how to use the Borland C++ functions that control the I/O buffers.

The first I/O buffer function is the `setbuf()` function. Note the syntax of the `setbuf()` declaration:

```
void setbuf( FILE *stream, char *buf );
```

The `stream` argument is a pointer to the stream to which I/O buffering will be assigned, and the `buf` argument is a pointer to the character array to be used as a buffer for the stream. If the `buf` argument is null, the stream will be unbuffered. If the `buf` argument does point to a character array, the character array must be at least `BUFSIZ` bytes long. `BUFSIZ` is defined in the `stdio.h` header file.

The `setbuf()` function can be called immediately after any of the following instances has occurred:

❏ The stream is created.

❏ A call to `fseek()` is made.

❏ The stream has been unbuffered.

Now note the following code fragment:

```
char io_buf[BUFSIZ];
FILE *file_ptr;
char in_char;

if( ( file_ptr = fopen( "C:\\AUTOEXEC.BAT", "rt" ) ) == NULL )
  printf( "Could not open file.\n" );
```

```
    setbuf( file_ptr, io_buf );

    do{
      fputchar( in_char = fgetc( file_ptr ) );
    } while( in_char != EOF );
```

This code fragment shows how to set up and use the setbuf() function. The first line declares a character array to be used as a buffer. The character array is declared to be BUFSIZE characters long. Immediately after the stream is opened, the setbuf() function is called. Once the setbuf() function is called, the data that is being read will be fully buffered.

The setvbuf() function is the second I/O buffer function Borland C++ provides. setvbuf() gives you more control over the type of buffer you use and the space allocated to the buffer. The setvbuf() function has the following prototype declaration:

```
int setvbuf( FILE *stream, char *buf, int type, size_t size );
```

The stream argument is a pointer to the stream you want to buffer, and the buf argument is a pointer to the buffer to be used for the stream. If the buf argument is null, the malloc() function is called, and a buffer is allocated for you. The size argument tells malloc() how much space to allocate for the buffer.

The type argument indicates the type of buffering to use. This argument can be one of the following values:

_IOFBF   This value causes the file to be fully buffered.

_IOLBF   This value indicates that the file will be line buffered (a whole text line is gathered, until end-of-line is encountered).

_IONBF   The file will be unbuffered.

The size argument specifies the size of the buffer to be used to buffer the file. This argument should be greater than 0 and less than or equal to 32,767. If type is _IONBF, the size argument is ignored.

Now look at the following code fragment:

```
FILE *file_ptr;
char in_char;

if( ( file_ptr = fopen( "C:\\AUTOEXEC.BAT", "rt" ) ) == NULL )
  printf( "Could not open file.\n" );
```

```
setvbuf( file_ptr, NULL, _IOLBF, 256 );

do{
  fputchar( in_char = fgetc( file_ptr ) );
} while( in_char != EOF );
```

This code fragment shows the setbuf() code fragment modified to use the setvbuf() file buffering function instead. Notice that the buffer pointer argument has been set to NULL. A null buffer pointer causes setvbuf() to automatically call the malloc() function to allocate the buffer space (256 bytes here). In this code fragment, the setvbuf() function has created a 256-byte line buffer for the stream pointed to by file_ptr.

The fflush() function is the third I/O buffer function. fflush() is use with streams that have buffered output. When fflush() is called, all remaining data in the buffer is written to the file. fflush() requires a FILE type argument that points to the stream to be flushed.

Using the Direct File I/O Functions

The I/O functions that have been introduced in this chapter so far have been easy to use. These I/O functions allow you to write programs quickly and easily. However, these simple functions don't give you as much control over I/O events and performance as do the *direct file I/O functions*.

What is direct file I/O? Direct file I/O (or simply direct I/O) is file input and output in which you can position *directly* to the part of the file you want to work with, skipping any intervening file data. Thus, the direct file I/O class of functions provides support for *file positioning* and *reading* and *writing* chunks of data (usually referred to as file *records*).

Because direct I/O usually deals with fixed-length chunks of data, or records, direct I/O is also usually performed using a binary file access mode. It is possible, however, to use the direct I/O functions in text mode.

The direct I/O functions give you more precise control of the data you read and write. Using direct I/O functions can also increase file I/O performance. This section shows you what the direct I/O functions are and how to use them.

Understanding Direct I/O Concepts

When you start using the direct I/O functions, you will develop a better appreciation for the work your computer does for you. Soon you will realize what kinds of information you need to keep track of when working with a file:

❑ *The beginning-of-file position.* Borland C++ (and all other ANSI standard C compilers) record locations within a file as a *relative offset from the beginning of the file* (also called the file *origin*). Thus, the relative position of the origin is zero.

❑ *The current file position.* The current file position is the location in the file where the *next read or write activity* will take place. You can record the current file position at any time, using one of the position reporting functions discussed later in the chapter.

❑ *The end-of-file position.* The end-of-file position is the location *just beyond the last byte* actually used in the file. When reading or writing has progressed to the end-of-file position, an end-of-file *indicator* is turned on in the stream object. It is meaningless to read beyond end-of-file, but you can position to end-of-file and continue writing to extend the file (to *append* data to the file).

❑ *Details about the sizes of the Borland C++ data types.* As you saw earlier in this book, each data type can occupy a different amount of memory. You need to know the type of the data you are using so that you can determine the number of bytes to read or write (especially in binary mode).

❑ *The location and sizes of the buffer or buffers being used.* It is not necessary to "manually" keep track of buffer locations and sizes—unless you take over buffer allocation as explained earlier in this chapter.

❑ *The stream associated with the data file.* The stream (that is the type FILE object) is where much of the control information mentioned in this list is stored.

The I/O functions covered earlier in this chapter kept track of most of this information for you. But with the direct I/O functions, you have to be able to access this information in order to make direct I/O function calls effectively. Although using the direct I/O functions means that you have to be more aware of the way your program works, these functions give you precise control of the input and output of your data.

Consider what happens when you write character data to a disk file. Opening the file requests the operating system (DOS, UNIX, or another system) to set aside some space on the disk (that is, to *allocate space* for the file). The beginning of the allocated space on disk is also the beginning of the file, but your program doesn't have to know the physical disk address. All the program does is to begin writing at the file's origin (zero bytes from the beginning); the operating system handles translation of relative addresses into physical addresses.

When your program writes a character of data (one byte of data) to the file, the output library function automatically increments the *file position indicator*, which is just a number recorded in the FILE stream object noting the current relative address in the file. If your program should request that multiple bytes be written, the file position indicator is adjusted accordingly.

When your program has finished writing data to the file, it must call the file close function. The close function causes any data still in memory to be written out, and requests that the operating system make a record of how much data the file contains (in the file's directory entry and the disk's file allocation tables). Now, when your program terminates, nothing is lost. All the data just written is still there, waiting for you to use it again.

You can, of course, open the file just created, and read and write in it, using the functions already described in this chapter. But what if you want to read only the first 10 bytes and the last 10 bytes in the file? Reading the first 10 bytes is easy: open the file as usual and read 10 bytes. To read the last 10 bytes, however, you must use one of the *file positioning* functions to set the file position indicator 10 bytes before the end-of-file position. Then you can read the last 10 bytes. If your program should now attempt to read more data, the input library function will return only an end-of-file *indicator*. There is a macro for the end-of-file indicator, named EOF, supplied in the stdio.h header. In Borland C++, as in most systems, the value of EOF is −1 (0xFFFF), so that it will not likely be confused with a valid return value (direct I/O functions return the number of bytes read or written).

When a program reads and writes in a file directly in the manner just described, the file is commonly referred to as a *direct file*. This term is really a shorthand term for *direct access file*, meaning that you can read and write any part of the file without having to read or write data located earlier in the file. You can skip over parts of the file and process only those parts necessary at a given time. Note, too, that a file which is treated as a direct file by one program may be treated as a normal text file by another program. That is perfectly all right, as long as the internal structure of the file *is* that of a text file.

Now that you have some idea of what sort of tasks the direct I/O functions can handle, you need to know how to use the functions in your programs.

Reading and Writing Direct Files

The fread() and fwrite() functions are a fast way to move chunks of data to and from your disk drive. fread() reads data from the file and places the data in an area of memory. The fread() function automatically increments the file position indicator (that is, updates the current file position) by the number of bytes just read. Thus, the next read operation will input the next sequential data bytes from the file, unless you use the file positioning functions to change the current position. fwrite() works similarly, but takes data from an area of memory and writes the data to the disk file. fwrite() also increments the file position indicator automatically.

Listing 6.6 shows the fwrite() and fread() functions in the context of a program. Refer to this program listing as you read this section.

Listing 6.6. dirio.c. *A program that uses the* fwrite() *and* fread() *direct I/O functions.*

```
1    /* DIRIO.C  This program uses the fread() and fwrite()
2                functions to create a file that holds an
3                array of double floating point numbers,
4                write the array to disk and then read
5                the array back to memory. */
6
7    #include <stdio.h>
8    #include <stdlib.h>
9    #include <conio.h>
10
11   main()
12   {
13     FILE *file_ptr;
14     double x[3] = { 12.3, 45.6, 78.9 };
15     double y[3];
16
17     clrscr();
18     if( ( file_ptr = fopen( "mynum.dat", "w+b" ) ) == NULL ) {
19       printf( "Could not open file.\n" );
20       printf( "Exiting program.\n" );
21       exit( 0 );
22     }
23
24       if( fwrite( x, sizeof( x ), 1, file_ptr ) == 1 )
25         printf( "Successful write.\n" );
26       else
```

Listing 6.6. continues

Listing 6.6. continued

```
27        printf( "Unsuccessful write.\n" );
28
29      rewind( file_ptr );
30
31      fread( y, sizeof( y ), 1, file_ptr );
32
33      printf( "%6.3f, %6.3f, %6.3f\n", y[0], y[1], y[2] );
34      fclose( file_ptr );
35      remove( "mynum.dat" );
36      return(0);
37  }
```

The actual I/O functions in listing 6.6 take only two lines. All the code from lines 7–23 is setup code for the variables and files. The `fwrite()` call that writes the entire `x[]` array to a disk file is found in line 24 (notice how the `sizeof` operator can be used to get the size of the entire array). The disk file is read from disk and placed in another array by the `fread()` statement in line 31. These two statements move the entire array from main memory to the disk drive and back to another array in main memory. The `printf()` statement in line 33 is there just to prove that the direct I/O statements work.

The `fread()` statement requires four arguments. Its prototype declaration looks like this:

```
size_t fread( void *ptr, size_t size, size_t nmemb, FILE *stream );
```

The first argument for the `fread()` function is `ptr`, which is a pointer to an array in the computer's memory. The array pointed to by `ptr` is where the data read from the disk will be stored. In listing 6.6, the `ptr` points to the `double` array `y[]`.

Note that the I/O area specified in fread() is a *user* area that is separate from any file buffers used by the file. The direct I/O functions perform physical transfers of data to and from the *buffers*, and then copy the data back and forth to the area pointed to by the fread() and fwrite() functions. A user I/O area does not have to be as large as a file buffer. It doesn't even have to be an integral multiple or divisor of the buffer size: all coordination of data movement is taken care of by the library routines.

`fread()`'s second argument is `size`, which specifies the size of each member to be read or written. In listing 6.6, the `size` is specified as the `sizeof( y )`. This means that `fread()` will read an amount of data that is

as large as the array y[]. You can use different size values from one fread()
call to the next. For example, you can read the entire array in listing 6.6 at one
time, and then later read just single array elements (by specifying sizeof
double). Thus, you can read whole records, parts of records, or just single
bytes to suit the logic requirements of your program at any point during
execution.

nmemb, which is the third argument, tells fread() the number of
members to read from the disk file. Because the size argument in listing 6.6
is the size of the entire array in memory, the nmemb argument is set to 1. In this
sample program, you could just as easily have specified sizeof double and
read three members to input the entire array.

The fourth and final argument is the stream pointer, which points to the
stream associated with the disk file you are reading. Notice that the stream
pointed to by file_ptr in listing 6.6 is opened by the if statement found in
lines 18–22. Notice also that the stream is opened in a binary access mode.

fread() returns a size_t count of the number of items actually read.
If end-of-file was reached or there was an error, the count returned will be less
than you requested (it may be zero if nothing was read).

The fwrite() function is the inverse of the fread() function. fwrite()
takes data that is stored in an area of memory and writes that data to a disk file.
Like fread(), fwrite() has four arguments in its prototype declaration:

```
size_t fwrite( const void *ptr, size_t size, size_t nmemb, FILE *stream );
```

In the fwrite() function, the ptr argument is a pointer to an area of memory
from which data is to be written to the disk drive. In listing 6.6, ptr contains
the address of the x[] array. This array contains three double floating-point
numbers that are copied to a disk file.

The size argument indicates the size of each member to be written to
the disk file. The size argument in listing 6.6 is the size of the entire x[] array.
size indicates that fwrite() will copy the entire array to the disk with one
write.

The nmemb function specifies the number of members fwrite() will
output. In listing 6.6, nmemb is equal to 1 because the entire array will be copied
to the disk in one write statement.

Finally, the stream argument is a pointer that points to the stream to
which data will be written.

The fwrite() function returns a size_t count of the number of items
actually written. If there was an error, the count may be less than you requested
or zero.

Many times, the fread() and fwrite() statements are used to process files that contain character data. Listing 6.7 shows how the fread() function can be used to extract information from an exported database file.

Listing 6.7. prtlab.c. *The print-label program, using* fread() *to extract information from a database file.*

```
1    /* PRTLAB.C   This program reads and prints the records in
2                  an address-label database file. The file can
3                  contain a variable number of records.
4
5                  Even though the number of records in the file
6                  is variable, the size of each of the fields in
7                  the records is fixed. The size of each of the
8                  fields is determined by the typedef structure
9                  address_t.   */
10
11   #include <stdlib.h>
12   #include <stdio.h>
13   #include <string.h>
14   #include <stddef.h>
15
16   #define MAXLABS 180
17
18   typedef struct {
19     char name[36];
20     char street[36];
21     char apt[36];
22     char city[36];
23     char state[6];
24     char zip[5];
25     char fill[2];
26   } address_t;
27
28   void null_term( char* str, int length );
29   int compzip( const char*, const char* );
30
31   void main( int argc, char* argv[] )
32   {
33     int j = 0, k = 0;
34     FILE* adrfile;
35     FILE* labels;
36     char adrname[81];
```

```
37      char labname[81];
38      address_t* list;
39
40      if ( argc < 3 ) {
41        puts( "Command format is: prtlab addressfile labelfile" );
42        exit( 0 );
43      }
44
45      if ( NULL == ( list = malloc( MAXLABS*sizeof(address_t) ) ) ) {
46        puts( "Unable to acquire memory for address table." );
47        exit( 8 );
48      }
49
50      strcpy( adrname, argv[1] );
51      strcpy( labname, argv[2] );
52
53      if ( NULL == ( adrfile = fopen( adrname, "rb" ) ) ) {
54        puts( "Can't open input address file." );
55        exit( 8 );
56      }
57      if ( NULL == ( labels = fopen( labname, "w" ) ) ) {
58        puts( "Can't open output label file." );
59        exit( 8 );
60      }
61
62      while ( j<MAXLABS-1 && fread( &list[j], sizeof(address_t), 1, adrfile ) )
63        list[j].fill[0] = ' ';
64        ++j;      /* go to next address record slot */
65      }
66      fclose( adrfile );
67
68      printf( "Read %d address records.\n", j );
69
70      qsort( list, j, sizeof(address_t), compzip );
71
72      for ( k=0; k<j; ++k ) {    /* null terminate line strings */
73        null_term( list[k].name,36 );
74        null_term( list[k].street,36 );
75        null_term( list[k].apt,36 );
76        null_term( list[k].city,36 );
77        null_term( list[k].state,6 );
78        null_term( list[k].zip,6 );
```

Listing 6.7. continues

Listing 6.7. continued

```
 79       }
 80       k = 0;
 81       while ( k<j ) {
 82         fprintf( labels, "%s\n", list[k].name );
 83         fprintf( labels, "%s\n", list[k].street );
 84         fprintf( labels, "%s\n", list[k].apt );
 85         fprintf( labels, "%s   %s     %s\n", list[k].city,
 86            list[k].state, list[k].zip );
 87         fprintf( labels, "\n" );
 88         ++k;
 89       }
 90       fclose( labels );
 91    }
 92
 93    void null_term( char* str, int length )
 94    {
 95       static int i;
 96
 97       str += length - 1;    /* point to last byte */
 98       for( i=length; i>0; --i ) {
 99         if ( *str != ' ' ) {
100            ++str;
101            break;
102         }
103         --str;
104       }
105       if ( i == 0 ) ++str;
106       *str = '\0';
107    }
108
109    int compzip( const char* arg1, const char* arg2 )
110    {
111       return( strncmp( &arg1[offsetof(address_t,zip)],
112                        &arg2[offsetof(address_t,zip)], 5 ) );
113    }
```

Listing 6.7 is a utility program used to format a file of address labels. The input data for the program is a file that consists of a number of fixed-length records. Each of the fixed-length records is a complete address. If you look at the typedef in lines 18–26, you can see how each record is organized.

Lines 62–64 contain the `fread()` function that reads one record at a time from the address file. The records that are read are placed in the `list[]` that is set up in lines 45–48. Note the `size` argument for `fread()` in line 62. `fread()` reads enough data from the disk file to fill an `address_t` type record. Reading this much information allows `fread()` to retrieve an entire address record with one read.

After the `list[]` array is filled, the `qsort()` function is called to sort the entire list of addresses. `qsort()` is called in line 70.

Once the records are sorted, each field in the record is stripped of excess trailing blanks. The `for` statement in lines 72–79 steps through each record in the list. As each record is accessed, the `null_term()` function is called to strip the blanks off each field in the record.

Finally, after the trailing blanks are removed, the `fprintf()` function is called to print a formatted address label. The formatted labels are written to a file on the disk so that they can be printed at a later time.

Using the File Positioning Functions

The direct I/O functions `fread()` and `fwrite()` are useful functions all by themselves. However, these functions are even more useful when they are combined with the file positioning functions.

With the file positioning functions, you can detect your current location in a file and change that location if you want. Being able to change your position in a file gives you greater flexibility in getting the data you want, when you want it. This section shows you how to use the functions that indicate your current position in the file, and the functions that let you change your position.

Obtaining the Current File Position

Borland C++ has two functions that indicate your current file position: `ftell()` and `fgetpos()`. The value returned by `ftell()` is the current file position expressed as a byte offset from the beginning of the file. The value returned by `fgetpos()` is the value of the file pointer for a stream. The exact return value of the `fgetpos()` is irrelevant to you; the return value is needed only by other functions like `fsetpos()`.

fgetpos() is called with two arguments. The fgetpos() prototype declaration shows the arguments and their types:

```
int fgetpos( FILE *file_ptr, fpos_t *position );
```

The file_ptr argument is a pointer to the stream for which you want to determine the value of the current file pointer. position points to an object that holds the current file position. Listing 6.8 shows how fgetpos() is called in a program.

Listing 6.8. getpos.c. *A program that uses the* fgetpos() *function.*

```
 1   /* GETPOS.C  This program uses the fgetpos() function
 2                to determine the current file position. */
 3
 4
 5   #include <stdio.h>
 6   #include <stdlib.h>
 7
 8   main()
 9   {
10     FILE *file_ptr;
11     fpos_t position;
12     char text_out[] = "Extra string stuff.";
13
14     file_ptr = fopen( "junk.txt", "w+" );
15
16     fgetpos( file_ptr, &position );
17     printf( "Current position = %ld.\n", position );
18
19     fwrite( text_out, sizeof( text_out ), 1, file_ptr );
20
21     fgetpos( file_ptr, &position );
22     printf( "New position = %ld.\n", position );
23
24     fcloseall();
25     return 0;
26   }
```

You need to watch for two things when you use the fgetpos() function. First, make sure that you have declared a variable of the type fpos_t (see line 11). The fpos_t type variable holds the current file position value. Second, make sure that you use the address-of operator when passing the position argument to the fgetpos() function (see lines 16–21).

The ftell() function is even simpler to use than fgetpos(). ftell() needs to know only the name of the stream for which you want to determine the current file position. The following code fragment shows the use of ftell():

```
file_ptr = fopen( "junk.txt", "a+b" );
fprintf( file_ptr, "Additional information." );
printf( "The current offset is %ld.\n", ftell(
file_ptr ) );
```

The ftell() function is called in the printf() statement on the last line. The value returned by ftell() is the current file position, which is printed by the printf() statement. Notice that ftell() is given an argument that points to the stream that was opened with the preceding fopen() function.

Setting a New File Position

Knowing the current file position is nice, but being able to change it easily is even better. You use three standard functions —rewind(), fsetpos(), and fseek()— to change the position of the file pointer.

The rewind() function sets the value of the file position indicator back to the beginning of the file. You invoke rewind() by calling it with a stream pointer argument. Note an example:

```
rewind( file_ptr );
```

This statement causes the file position indicator for the stream pointed to by file_ptr to be reset to the beginning of the file.

You use the fsetpos() function with the fgetpos() function. fsetpos() sets the file position indicator back to the value that was stored by fegetpos(). The declaration for fsetpos() looks like this:

```
int fsetpos( FILE *file_ptr, const fpos_t *position );
```

The first argument passed to fsetpos() is a pointer to the stream for which you want to change the file position indicator. The second argument is an fpos_t type variable, which should contain a file position indicator previously stored by the fgetpos() function.

The following code fragment shows how the fgetpos() and fsetpos() functions are used together:

```
FILE file_ptr;
fpos_t position;
...
fgetpos( file_ptr, &position );
...
fsetpos( file_ptr, &position );
```

In this code fragment, `fgetpos()` stores in the `position` variable the current value of the file position indicator. Later, when the `fsetpos()` function is called, the file position indicator is returned to the position indicated by the variable `position`.

Finally, the `fseek()` function is one of the most versatile file positioning functions because it lets you move anywhere in the file. Note the format of the prototype declaration for `fseek()`:

```
int fseek( FILE *stream, long int offset, int whence );
```

The first argument points to the stream you will be working with. The `offset` argument lets you specify the relative number of bytes you want to move the file position indicator. The value of the `offset` argument is combined with the value of the `whence` argument to determine exactly where you want to put the file position indicator. The `whence` argument can have any of the following values:

❏ `SEEK_CUR` `whence` is set to the same value as the file position indicator.

❏ `SEEK_SET` `whence` is set to the beginning of the file.

❏ `SEEK_END` `whence` is set to the end of the file.

Listing 6.9 uses the `fseek()` function to calculate the length of a file.

Listing 6.9. `flength.c`. *A program that uses* `fseek()` *to calculate file size.*

```
1   /* FLENGTH.C   This program uses the fseek() function to
2                  calculate the length of a file. */
3
4   #include <stdio.h>
5   #include <stdlib.h>
6
7   main()
8   {
9      FILE *file_ptr;
10     long file_size;
11
12     file_ptr = fopen( "junk.txt", "r+b" );
13
```

```
14    fseek( file_ptr, 0, SEEK_END );
15    file_size = ftell( file_ptr );
16
17    fseek( file_ptr, 0, SEEK_SET );
18    file_size -= ftell( file_ptr );
19
20    fcloseall();
21    printf( "The file is %ld bytes long.\n", file_size );
22 }
```

In line 14, fseek() sets the file position indicator to the end of the file. In line 15, ftell() stores in the variable file_size the value of the file position indicator. In line 17, fseek() is called again. This time, fseek() sets the file position indicator to the beginning of the file. Then the difference between the end-of-file position and the beginning-of-file position is calculated. The result is stored in the file_size variable.

Handling File I/O Errors

The demonstration programs in this book do not check for many file errors because errors are not much of a problem in these sample programs. However, when you start writing production code, file errors can become critical. You need a way to detect a file error that occurs and to correct the problem before much damage is done. This section shows you some of the Borland C++ functions that detect file I/O errors, report these errors, and deal with the error conditions.

Detecting File I/O Errors

One of the handiest error-detection functions is the feof() function. This function checks a stream to determine whether the end of the file has been encountered. If an EOF indicator is detected, feof() returns a nonzero value; otherwise, feof() returns 0. To use the feof() function, all you need to do is tell feof() which stream you want to check.

The following code fragment shows a common use of the feof() function:

```
while( !feof( file_ptr ) )
  char_in = getc( file_ptr );
```

Here the `getc()` function is executed as long as `feof()` does not detect the end of the file. This code fragment, then, reads the entire file pointed to by `file_ptr`.

The `ferror()` function tests a stream to see whether any error indicators have be set. If `ferror()` detects an error, `ferror()` returns a nonzero value. The stream's error indicator can be cleared with either the `rewind()` or the `clearerr()` function.

This next statement tests the stream pointed to by `file_ptr`:

```
if( ferror( file_ptr )
  printf( "An error has occurred.\n" );
```

If an I/O error has occurred on that stream, the `printf()` function is executed, alerting you that such an error has occurred.

Displaying and Clearing File I/O Errors

Once you have determined that an error has occurred, you need to find out what the error is, and clear it if possible. You use the `clearerr()`, `strerror()`, and `perror()` functions for these tasks.

The `clearerr()` function clears a stream's error and end-of-file indicators. To use `clearerr()`, you simply call `clearerr()` with a pointer to the stream for which you want to clear the error. The statement

```
clearerr( file_ptr );
```

clears the error and end-of-file indicators for the stream pointed to by `file_ptr`.

The `strerror()` function helps you diagnose what error has occurred. `strerror()` takes an integer argument that represents an error code, and returns a pointer to an error-message string associated with that error. The following code fragment shows how you can use the `strerror()` function to display the error messages associated with the error codes 1 to 10:

```
for( i = 1; i <= 10; i++ )
  printf( "%s", strerror( i ) );
```

In this code fragment, `strerror()` successively returns pointers to the message strings associated with the error codes 1 to 10. A pointer to a message string returned by `strerror()` can be passed directly to the `printf()` function.

Finally, the perror() function causes the message associated with the current value of errno to be printed to the standard error device. perror() can take a string argument that will also be printed with the system error message.

Note how the perror() function can be used to display a file I/O error:

```
FILE *file_ptr;

if( ( file_ptr = fopen( "nonexist.txt", "r+b" ) ) == NULL )
    perror( "Sorry Charlie" );
```

In this code fragment, when the nonexist.txt file could not be opened, the perror() function was called. Because an error did exist, the perror() function caused an error message to be printed. The string "Sorry Charlie", which was passed to perror() as an argument, is therefore prepended to the system error that perror() displays.

Exercises

These exercises give you practice in using the following Borland C++ file I/O library functions: character and string I/O functions, formatted and unformatted I/O functions, and direct I/O and file positioning functions.

1. Create a simple file program that uses the scanf() and printf() functions to enter and display data in the file. Take advantage of the formatted I/O capabilities so that your program can handle integer, floating-point, and string data types.

2. Use a text editor to create a text file of moderate size. Then write a program that reads and displays the text file one character at a time.

3. To demonstrate the effects of buffer size, modify the program you created in the preceding exercise.

4. Use the fread() and fwrite() functions to copy a text file.

5. Use the fread() and fwrite() functions to copy a file composed of integer values.

6. Create a small text file and use the fseek() function to print every other character in the file.

7. Use the file I/O error-detection functions on two of the programs you created in this group of exercises.

Summary

In this chapter, you learned how to use the Borland C++ I/O library functions, which enable you to access the mass storage and other I/O devices on your computer. The following important points were covered in this chapter:

❑ *A file is a collection of related data.* A file can be kept on a permanent storage device or transferred by an interactive device. A permanent storage device is an I/O device that can hold data for long periods of time, and an interactive device is an I/O device used to transfer data. An interactive device does not store data for long periods.

❑ *Borland C++ uses streams to represent and transfer data from files.* Opening a file associates a stream with the file. When you open the file, a pointer to a FILE type data object is returned. The FILE type object contains information used to control the stream and manage the file's I/O buffer. Closing the file disassociates the stream from the file.

❑ *Borland C++ has two types of streams: text streams and binary streams.* Certain characters from a file opened in text mode are converted to an internal format as the stream is processed—for example, carriage-return/linefeed characters are converted to the newline character (\n). For a file opened in binary mode, no conversions are performed on the data in the file associated with the stream. A binary stream represents the original file, bit for bit.

❑ *You use the scanf() family of functions to input formatted data.* These functions enable you to specify the type and format of data to be input. The scanf() family of functions expect you to supply a *format string* argument specifying data types to input, and a *list of addresses* indicating where input data will be stored.

❑ *You use the printf() family of functions to output formatted data.* These functions enable you to specify the type and format of data to be output. The print() family of functions expect you to supply a *format string* argument specifying data types to output, and a *list of objects* (not addresses) to be output.

❑ *Borland C++ provides a number of functions that perform character and string I/O.* The ...get...() and ...put...() groups of functions provide for the input and output, respectively, of characters and strings. Some versions of these functions assume that the standard streams will be used, whereas other versions allow you to specify a stream.

❏ *The* `setbuf()` *and* `setvbuf()` *functions provide complete control of file buffering.* These functions can increase the performance of your programs by providing a speed-matching service between the computer's slow devices and its fast memory and CPU.

❏ *The* `fread()` *and* `fwrite()` *functions provide direct I/O service.* Using the `fread()` and `fwrite()` functions, you can control precisely the amount of data transferred at one time. Note that you cannot transfer more than 64K – 16 bytes at a time. 64K is the 80x86 segment size, and DOS requires 16 bytes for a Memory Control Block (MCB).

❏ *The file positioning functions provide complete direct access file service.* You can use `fgetpos()` and `ftell()` to determine the current file position, and you can use `fsetpos()` and `fseek()` to change the current file position.

❏ *Several functions are available for detecting errors in your programs.* The `feof()` function detects the end of the file you are working with, and the `ferror()` function tests a stream for possible error conditions. If you have an error condition, `strerror()` and `perror()` functions can provide diagnostic messages to help you track down the error. The `clearerr()` function is useful when you want to clear any I/O or end-of-file errors posted for a stream.

The next chapter shows you how to use memory models and introduces you to VROOMM technology.

7

Using Memory Models and VROOMM Technology

I f you are new to programming, one of your strangest programming tasks is to learn how to use the computer's memory. The Intel family of 80x86 processor chips uses a *segmented memory addressing scheme.* With a segmented addressing scheme, you cannot use one type of pointer to access every location in memory. Because the computer's memory is divided into 64K segments, to access a particular location in memory, you must know the correct segment address as well as the offset into the segment. If all this sounds confusing, this chapter shows you how your computer uses memory and how you can control it.

The chapter shows you also how to start taking advantage of Borland's VROOMM technology. VROOMM (Virtual Run-time Object-Oriented Memory Manager) technology lets you create programs larger than your computer can normally load. Using VROOMM, you can run a large program by keeping unused parts of it on disk or in extended or expanded memory. When the extra parts of the program are needed, they are loaded and executed. VROOMM technology enables you to create more powerful programs than ever before.

Introducing 80x86 Architecture

To get a grasp of how memory addressing works on Intel's line of processor chips, you need to know something about how the chips were made. Once you understand the design of the processor chips, you can understand more easily how to use segmented addressing.

Understanding Segments, Paragraphs, and Offsets

The 8088 chip used in the original IBM PC is a 16-bit processor with a 20-bit address bus and an 8-bit data bus. The data bus, located on the system board, is the group of circuit traces that are used to transfer data from the CPU to the other devices. The 8-bit data bus on the PC allows only 8 bits (1 byte) of data to be transferred at a time.

The address bus is the series of circuit traces that determine which memory location will be used. The number of memory addresses available is determined by the number of bus lines. You can calculate how many addresses are available by raising 2 (the number of values that can be represented on a single bus line) to a power equal to the number of bus lines available. For the PC, the number of memory locations available is equal to 2 raised to the 20th power, or 1M. (If you have an 8088-based computer, you know that you can use only 640K of memory; the remaining 384K of memory is available only for the system's use.)

The 8088 chip is a 16-bit microprocessor. Naturally, a 16-bit processor works with 16 bits of data at a time. Therefore, the largest integer value that the 8088 can use is 65,535, or 64K. The largest integer value that can be used by the processor determines the largest memory address that can be calculated.

You may be wondering how a CPU that can generate only a 16-bit value can control a 20-bit address bus. The secret is that the address is created with 2 *words* of memory (on the 8088, a word is 2 bytes). One word of memory contains an offset address, and the other word contains a segment address. The offset address is a 16-bit value that can address up to 64K of memory. The segment address is also a 16-bit value; however, because the segment address is considered to be *shifted 4 bits to the left*, the segment adress represents a 20-bit value. The segment and offset addresses can be combined to access any memory location.

Take a look at the following example to see how shifting a 16-bit value 4 bits to the left can generate a 20-bit value:

	Binary Value	Hex Value
Before shifting	0001 0010 0011 0100	1234
After shifting	0001 0010 0011 0100 0000	12340

In this example, the value that would be stored in the segment address register is 1234, the 16-bit value on the first line. By itself, the 16-bit segment address value cannot address a memory location; the 16-bit value must be changed to a 20-bit value. Changing the value is accomplished by shifting the binary value four bits to the left. Shifting the value 4 bits is the same as multiplying the value by 16.

You can see on the second line of the preceding example that once the segment address value is shifted, the result is a 20-bit value. This 20-bit value is the actual address of a location in memory.

When you see a segment address written down, or when you check the value in a segment address register, the value that you see is a 16-bit value. To get the actual segment address, remember to add 4 zeros in binary notation (or 1 zero in hexadecimal notation) to the end of the 16-bit value. The result is the 20-bit segment address.

If you are mathematically inclined, you may have noticed that the segment address can address only every 16th byte of memory. This is true because the 4-bit shift always leaves the last 4 bits equal to zero. Each of these 16-byte blocks are called *paragraphs*.

For addressing a particular location, the segment address must be combined with the offset address. The offset address holds a value that specifies the offset, in bytes, from the segment address. For example, if the segment address equaled 2BC00 (hexadecimal notation) and the offset address equaled 00FF, the actual memory address would equal 2BCFF.

The standard notation for writing a memory address is *segment:offset*. The segment value that is written is the 16-bit value stored in the segment register. The memory location 2BCFF, then, would be written as 2BC0:00FF.

It is possible for offset values to overlap. With overlapping offset values, *different* addresses can refer to the same memory location. For example, the following addresses refer to the same location:

    2BC0:00FF
    2000:BCFF
    2111:ABEF
    2A00:1CFF

The idea that offset values can overlap becomes important when you are working with `far` and `huge` pointers. The next section of this chapter shows you what kinds of pointers are available and how they address your computer's memory.

Advanced Features of the 80286 and 80386

Intel's 80286 and 80386 are newer microprocessors that are much more advanced than the 8088. However, few programs have been produced that take advantage of these chips' enhanced capabilities. Microsoft Windows 3.0 is changing all that. Windows 3.0 dramatically increases your productivity by taking advantage of the advanced hardware features of the 80286 and 80386 chips.

Because Part III of this book explores programming for the Windows 3.0 environment, you should be aware of some of the hardware features that Windows can use.

Like the 8088, the Intel 80286 is a 16-bit microprocessor. Yet the 80286 has extra features that make it more powerful than the 8088. Some of these features are the following:

❏ A true 16-bit data bus capable of moving 2 bytes at a time.

❏ A 24-bit address bus that increases maximum RAM capacity to 16M.

❏ Multitasking capability that permits the processor to run more than one program at a time.

❏ Virtual memory that gives the computer access to more memory than is normally available on the computer. This "extra" memory is stored on disk and moved to RAM when needed. The 80286 virtual memory mode gives the processor access to 1 gigabyte of memory.

The 80386 has even more advanced features than the 80286. These features include the following:

❏ A true 32-bit processor that can process *and* transfer data 4 bytes at a time.

❏ A 32-bit address bus that gives you access to 4 gigabytes of memory.

❏ A virtual memory mode that can access 64 terrabytes by using a 46-bit memory address.

Understanding CPU Addressing Registers

To increase overall performance, the processor keeps often-used information stored inside the processor chip in several registers. The *registers* are special 16-bit memory cells that can be accessed quickly.

The 8088 chip has 14 registers that hold information and memory addresses. Figure 7.1 is a diagram of the registers used in the 8088. Not all the registers are used for addressing purposes. However, the functions of all the registers are explained here in preparation for Chapter 10's discussion on using assembly language with C.

Fig. 7.1. The 8088 internal registers.

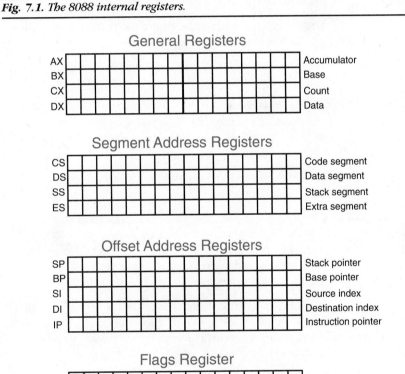

Although the general registers are used for a variety of tasks, each one has some use usually associated with it. Here are some common uses of the general registers:

AX	Used for accumulating values and for mathematical operations
BX	Used in indexing operations
CX	Used in indexing and loop counting
DX	Used for general and mathematical operations

The second group of registers is the segment address registers. Each of these registers stores a 16-bit segment address value. The actual segment address can be determined by shifting the segment address value 4 bits to the left. When combined with an offset value, the segment address value points to a 64K block of memory. The segment address registers and the blocks of memory that they point to are shown in the following list:

CS	The code segment address where the currently executing program is located.
DS	The data segment address where the data for the current program is stored.
SS	The stack segment address for the program's stack area. The stack acts as temporary storage that keeps track of what program functions are called and the values passed to the functions.
ES	The extra segment address used to store program data and to process data transfers between memory segments.

Each of the preceding segment addresses does not have to point to a different segment. In fact, all four pointers can contain the same address. The program's memory model determines whether the segment addresses are the same. Memory models are covered in the section "Using the Six Borland C++ Memory Models" later in this chapter.

The third group of registers consists of the offset address registers. You have already learned that an offset address is combined with a segment address to access a particular memory location. The next list shows what kind of data the offset addresses locate:

SP	The stack pointer is used with the SS (stack segment) register to find the exact location of the top of the stack.
BP	The base pointer is used to index into the stack to find arguments or automatic variables.
SI	The source index register can be used to index into the data segment. The SI register can also serve other general purposes.

DI   The destination index register is used in the same way as the source index register.

IP   The instruction pointer is used as a program counter (PC) for the program currently executing. The instruction pointer points to the next instruction to be executed. This register cannot be directly accessed by Borland C++.

The flags register is a special register that stores information about the current status of the CPU and the instructions that have been executed. On the 8088 processor, the flags register occupies 16 bits. On the 80386 processor, the flags register occupies 32 bits. The extra 16 bits on the 80386 flags register store information specific to the 80386 chip and its processing modes.

Understanding *near*, *far*, and *huge* Pointers

You saw in Chapter 4 that a pointer is a data object containing the address of another data object. You saw also that you can have different types of pointers: pointers to integers, to floating-point numbers, to characters, and even to functions. In this section, you learn that additional types of pointers are available. However, these pointers don't point to different types of objects, but to different locations in memory.

This section shows you that the type of pointer you use depends on whether the object pointed to is in the same memory segment as one of the segment registers. You also learn how to use the near, far, and huge pointers.

Choosing the Pointer Size You Want

Borland C++ has three different pointer sizes: near, far, and huge. The memory model that you use has one of these three types as the default pointer type. However, you can explicitly declare a pointer to be any type you want. This section explains the distinctive features of each pointer type.

A near pointer is the easiest pointer to use and the most limited because it can store only a 16-bit address. Because of its 16-bit address value, the near pointer can address just 64K. Remember that the maximum integer value that can be stored in 16 bits is 65,535. The near pointer's size, then, limits it to accessing one 64K block of memory.

In accessing an actual memory location, the near pointer must be combined with an address in one of the segment registers. That address points to the beginning of a block of memory, and the address in the pointer is an offset into that block. Which segment register is used depends on what type of object the pointer points to. The CS (code segment) register provides the segment address when a near pointer points to a function. The DS (data segment) register provides the segment address when a near pointer points to a data object.

near pointers are easy to use because you do not have to account for segment values when manipulating the functions. Because near pointers do not store segment values, the pointers can be directly compared. Arithmetic operations are also easier on near pointers because calculations do not have to handle segment values.

A far pointer is a 32-bit pointer that can access any memory location. A far pointer contains both a segment value and an offset value. The biggest advantage of far pointers is that they can access code and data segments larger than 64K. Thus, far pointers free your program and data from the 64K limit.

Using far pointers does create some problems. Earlier in the chapter, you saw that a single memory location can have several different *segment:offset* values. For example, the following three *segment:offset* addresses locate the same place in memory:

```
4000:000A
3FFF:001A
3ED2:12EA
```

Suppose that you have three far pointers, each of which contains one of the values in the preceding list. Each far pointer points to the exact same location in memory. However, if you tried to perform a logical comparison on the pointers, the comparison would indicate that the pointers are not equal. The *values* (addresses) stored in each of the three far pointers are not mathematically equal even though the pointers point to the same location. Thus, you have to be sure that the segment values are identical if you compare far pointers. If you need to perform logical comparisons, a near pointer or a huge pointer is easier to use.

Performing arithmetic operations on the address stored in a far pointer may not work the way you expect. When you add a value to, or subtract one from, a far pointer, only the offset value is affected. You cannot change the segment value in the far pointer with a mathematical operation. If the value 4000:FFFF that is stored in a far pointer is incremented by 1, the new value of the far pointer will equal 4000:FFFF, not 5000:0000.

Like a far pointer, a huge pointer contains a 32-bit address and can point to any location in memory. The distinguishing feature of a huge pointer is that the address stored in the huge pointer is normalized.

A normalized pointer is one that has had a conversion performed on the address stored in the pointer. That address has been changed so that as much of the address as possible is stored in the segment value. The offset value, then, contains only the values 0 to F (hexadecimal).

The following example shows how the normalization process works (all values are in hexadecimal notation):

16-bit segment address:	3256
Left-shifted segment address:	32560
16-bit offset address:	00C4
20-bit memory address:	32624
Normalized segment address:	3262
Normalized offset address:	0004

Here the original 16-bit segment address is left-shifted to create a 20-bit segment address, and the original offset address is then added. The actual memory location is indicated by the address 32624. Once the actual address is calculated, the normalization process can start. The normalized segment address is equal to the first 4 high-order digits of the actual address. The remaining low-order digit from the actual address is the offset value for the new normalized address.

A normalized huge pointer has two advantages over a far pointer. First, logical operations can be performed on the huge pointer. Second, the huge pointer's segment value can be changed with a mathematical operation.

The normalization of a huge pointer lets you logically compare huge pointer values. With far pointers, two pointers could point to the same memory location and still have different segment and offset values. Because of normalization, though, any huge pointers that point to the same location compare as equal.

Unlike the far pointer, when the offset value of the huge pointer wraps around, the segment value is also changed. Because the segment value can be changed when you are working with huge pointers, a huge pointer can work with a single object larger than 64K.

The problem with huge pointers is that extra overhead is needed for huge pointer arithmetic. Special functions have to be called when you perform huge pointer arithmetic. Your processing speed is therefore reduced.

Using the *near*, *far*, and *huge* Specifiers

You can declare pointers in your programs either with or without the near, far, and huge modifiers. Using a pointer modifier overrides the default type and creates a pointer of the type you specify. For example, the line

```
char far *char_ptr;
```

declares a far character pointer regardless of the program's default pointer type. But the line

```
char *char_ptr;
```

declares a character pointer that will have the program's default pointer type. If the program is compiled with the tiny memory model, the default pointer type is near. If the program is compiled with the large memory model, the default pointer type is far.

The short program in listing 7.1 uses far pointers to keep track of a disk file that has been stored in the far heap.

Listing 7.1. farmem.c. *A demonstration of the use of* far *pointers.*

```
1    /*FARMEM.C   This program demonstrates the use of far
2                 pointers by allocating enough memory to
3                 hold an entire file. For this program to
4                 work correctly, it must be compiled under
5                 the COMPACT, LARGE, or HUGE Memory Model. */
6
7    #include <stdio.h>
8    #include <stdlib.h>
9    #include <alloc.h>
10   #include <fcntl.h>
11   #include <io.h>
12
13   main(){
14     unsigned long file_size;
15     unsigned long i;
16     int           file_handle;
17     char          *memory_ptr1;
18     char          *memory_ptr2;
19
20
21     if( (file_handle = open("printers.txt", O_RDONLY|O_TEXT)
22         ) == -1 ) {
23       printf( "Could not open file.\n" );
```

```
24      printf( "Exiting program.\n" );
25      exit( 0 );
26    }
27
28
29    file_size = filelength( file_handle );
30    if( file_size > farcoreleft() ) {
31      printf( "Not enough memory to store file.\n" );
32      printf( "Exiting program.\n" );
33      exit( 0 );
34    }
35    else{
36      memory_ptr1 = farmalloc( file_size );
37      memory_ptr2 = memory_ptr1;
38      read( file_handle, memory_ptr2, file_size );
39    }
40
41    for( i = 1; i <= file_size; i++ ) {
42      putchar( *memory_ptr2 );
43      memory_ptr2 ++;
44    }
45
46    close( file_handle );
47    farfree( memory_ptr1 );
48    return 0;
49  }
```

Listing 7.1 shows how the memory model that is used to compile a program affects the pointers declared in the program. Before you examine the Borland C++ memory models, first review the purpose of the program in listing 7.1.

The program farmem.c gets the size of a text file stored on disk, allocates enough memory to store the file in RAM, reads the file, and then prints the file.

Lines 21–26 use the open() function to open a text file stored on the disk drive. If the value returned by open() is equal to –1, open() failed, and the program is aborted.

The filelength() function in line 29 gets the length of the file opened in lines 21 and 22. Then, in line 30, the length of the file is compared to the amount of memory available in the far heap. The farcoreleft() function returns the amount of memory available in the far heap. If there is sufficient memory to store the file, farmalloc() allocates a block of memory just large enough to store the disk file.

In line 38, a single function call to the `read()` function reads the entire disk file and stores the file in the far heap. The `read()` function is able to read the entire file with one function call because the value returned by `filelength()` tells `read()` how many bytes to read from the disk file.

The `for` loop in lines 41–43 steps through the allocated memory block one byte at a time. This technique is not the most efficient way to display the data in the block, but does provide an easy way to manipulate the block's data. Stepping through the block byte by byte makes it easy to come back and modify this program.

Listing 7.1 uses two pointers to index into the block of allocated memory. The two pointers are declared in lines 17 and 18. Although these pointers are declared without any modifiers, both pointers are `far` pointers because the large memory model under which the program was compiled causes all pointers to have a default type of `far`. It would be perfectly legal, but redundant, to code the declarations in this way:

```
char far *memory_ptr1;
char far *memory_ptr2;
```

Whenever you need to declare a pointer of a type that is different from the default type for the program, all you have to do is include the modifier in the declaration. Suppose, for example, that you needed to use a `near` pointer in listing 7.1. The declaration for the pointer would look like this:

```
void near *extra_ptr;
```

Borland C++ has four other pointer modifiers you can use with `near` pointers: `_cs`, `_ds`, `_es`, and `_ss`. Each of these modifiers specifies a segment address to be used with the `near` pointer. The segment address supplied by the modifiers corresponds to the matching segment address register. For example, the `_ds` modifier tells the pointer to use as the pointer's segment address the address stored in the data segment register. The following line of code shows a declaration containing the `_ds` modifier:

```
char _ds my_ptr;
```

Using the Six Borland C++ Memory Models

You have seen several references to memory models in this chapter. A *memory model* is just a compiler option that determines how much memory space to allocate for your program's code and data. This section gives you guidelines on choosing the memory model that is appropriate for your program.

Deciding Which Memory Model To Use

Borland C++ offers six different memory models from which you can choose. Each memory model has different features that affect how much space will be allocated for the code and data in your program. Table 7.1 lists the memory models and indicates their features.

Table 7.1. The Borland C++ memory models.

Model	Description
Tiny	This memory model is the smallest. A program compiled under the tiny memory model can be converted to a COM file. With this memory model, all four segment registers point to the same address. The program's code, data, and stack have to fit within 64K. You use the tiny memory model when you don't have any space to spare.
Small	For the small memory model, the code and data segments are different, but each segment is limited to 64K. The stack is included in the data segment. Many applications work well with the small memory model. Because this memory model uses only near pointers, program performance is increased.
Medium	The medium memory model uses the far pointer for the program's code and uses near pointers for the data. Therefore, the code for a medium model program can occupy up to 1M, but the data is limited to 64K. This model is good for large, complicated programs that do not use data.
Compact	The compact model is a mirror image of the medium model, using near pointers for code but far pointers for data. The program's data can

Table 7.1. continues

Table 7.1. *continued*

Model	Description
	occupy up to 1M of memory, but the program itself is limited to 64K. The compact model is good for shorter programs that handle large amounts of data.
Large	The large model is used for big programs that work with large amounts of data. far pointers are used for both the program's code and data. Therefore, both code and data can occupy up to 1M of memory.
Huge	Like the large memory model, the huge memory model uses far pointers for the code and data. The difference between these two memory models is that the huge memory model sets aside the 64K limit for static data. Static data can therefore use more than 64K. You use the huge model for your largest programs.

You select which memory option you want before you compile your program. To select one of the memory options, choose the Compiler command from the Options menu and then select Code Generation. The dialog box displays a list of radio buttons for the memory models. Just click the memory model you want, and you are ready to compile.

Because each memory model allocates code and data memory differently, each model has a unique set of default pointer modifiers. Figure 7.2 summarizes the default pointer modifiers for each of the memory models. The default segment modifier is listed if the model's pointers are near pointers.

Programming with Mixed Models

A time will probably come when you link a program that has modules compiled under different memory models. When you link these mixed models, problems can occur if you are not careful.

Fig. 7.2. The default pointer and segment modifiers for the six memory models.

Memory Models and Pointer Modifiers

Memory Model	Function Pointer	Segment Modifier	Data Pointer	Segment Modifier
TINY	near	_cs	near	_ds
SMALL	near	_cs	near	_ds
MEDIUM	far	N.A.	near	_ds
COMPACT	near	_cs	far	N.A.
LARGE	far	N.A.	far	N.A.
HUGE	far	N.A.	far	N.A.

Consider what happens when a small module tries to call a function in a large module. From figure 7.2, you can see that the small module, by default, calls functions with near pointers, and that the large module calls functions with far pointers. When a function in the small module calls a function in the large module, the function call is made with a near pointer. But the function called in the large module requires a far pointer. This situation simply will not work.

There is a way to use mixed memory models and have functioning programs. The secret is to use a function prototype that explicitly declares the pointer type for the function. Listings 7.2 and 7.3 show two program modules, each compiled under a different memory model, that can be linked to form a functioning program.

Listing 7.2 is a source file that contains functions called by another program module. Listing 7.2 was compiled to an object file under the large memory model. The functions in listing 7.2 are therefore called with far pointers.

Listing 7.3, which is the main source file for the mixed-model example, contains a main() function that calls the other functions located in listing 7.2. Listing 7.3 was compiled to an object file under the small memory model. The function calls made in listing 7.3 are therefore made with near pointers.

Listing 7.2. `module1.c`. *The first module of a mixed-model program.*

```
 1   /* MODULE1.C  This source code is the first program module
 2                 used in the demonstration of mixed-model
 3                 programming. This module was compiled under
 4                 the LARGE memory model. */
 5   int func1()
 6   {
 7      return 1;
 8   }
 9
10   int func2()
11   {
12      return 2;
13   }
```

Listing 7.3. `module2.c`. *The second module of a mixed-model program.*

```
 1   /* MODULE2.C This source code is the second program module
 2                used in the demonstration of mixedmodel
 3                programming. This module was compiled under
 4                the SMALL memory model. */
 5
 6   #include <stdio.h>
 7   #include <stdlib.h>
 8
 9   extern int far func1();
10   extern int far func2();
11
12   void main()
13   {
14      printf( "%d %d\n", func1(), func2() );
15   }
```

Even though the program in listing 7.3 was compiled under the small memory model, the program is able to call the far functions in listing 7.2 because of the declarations in lines 9 and 10. Listing 7.3 contains declarations that explicitly declare the external functions as far functions. The explicit far function declaration causes far pointers to be used even though the default pointer type is near.

If the external declarations in listing 7.3 were coded as

```
extern int func1();
extern int func2();
```

the linker would generate an error when the project file was compiled.

You also have to be careful about pointers passed as arguments. For example, if the function definition for func1() in listing 7.2 were

```
int func1( int * i )
{
   ...
}
```

the function declaration for func1() in listing 7.3 should be

```
extern int( int far * i );
```

If you have a small model program that needs to link in Borland C++ library routines, you may need to create a special header file. The library routines are large model routines and use far pointers. To use the library routines with your small model program, you need to make a special copy of the header file. In the new copy of the header file, you must declare explicitly all the functions and pointers as far type pointers.

Just remember that the success of mixed-model programming depends on using the right function and pointer declarations. If you throw in an extra measure of care, your mixed-model programs will work.

Creating COM Executable Program Files

COM files are executable files like EXE files, but COM files have strict limits on the size of the code and data. This section explains the advantages of using COM files and how these executable files are created with Borland C++.

Using COM Files

Once you compile and link your source code, you have created an executable file, which has all the parts its needs to be run in DOS. Usually, the executable file you create has an extension of EXE. However, you can create another type of executable file: the COM file.

The size of a COM file is its most distinguishing feature. Because a COM file is compiled under the tiny memory model, all of the COM file's code, data, and stack must fit within one 64K block of memory. This 64K size is somewhat restrictive, but many programs can easily fit in this memory limit.

The biggest advantage of a COM file is its speed. Because a COM file always uses near pointers, all the overhead associated with far and huge pointers is avoided. The reduction in processing time needed for handling far and huge pointers increases the performance of your program.

Listing 7.4 shows a simple filter program that was compiled under the tiny memory model and linked as a COM file.

Listing 7.4. little.c. *A small program compiled and linked as a COM file.*

```
 1   /* LITTLE.C   This program is compiled with the TINY
 2                 memory model in order to generate a COM
 3                 file. The resulting OBJ file must be linked
 4                 with TLINK to create the COM file. */
 5
 6   #include <stdio.h>
 7   #include <stdlib.h>
 8   #include <ctype.h>
 9
10   main()
11   {
12     FILE *file_ptr;
13     char proc_char;
14
15     if( ( file_ptr = fopen( "printers.txt", "rt" ) ) == NULL )
16     {
17        printf( "Unable to open file.\n" );
18        printf( "Exiting program.\n" );
19        exit( 0 );
20     }
21
22     while( proc_char != EOF ) {
23       proc_char = fgetc( file_ptr );
24       proc_char = toupper( proc_char );
25       putchar( proc_char );
26     }
27
28     fclose( file_ptr );
29     return 0;
30   }
```

The program in listing 7.4 is well suited for linking as a COM file. This short filter program reads a file and converts all lowercase alphabetic letters to uppercase.

The heart of the program is contained in the `while` loop found in lines 22–26. The disk file is scanned one character at a time. If the character that is read is a lowercase letter, it is converted to an uppercase letter. The input character, converted if necessary, is then written to the video screen.

The program is suitable for compiling and linking as a COM file because it contains very little code and data. The only two variables in the program are a file pointer and a `char` type variable.

The program in listing 7.4 was written and compiled to an object file in the Borland C++ Integrated Development Environment (IDE). Because the file was to become a COM file, the tiny memory model was selected. The creation of the executable COM file required the use of the TLINK utility.

TLINK is a stand-alone linker that comes with the Borland C++ package. If you are used to the IDE, you may not be familiar with TLINK. However, TLINK is needed for some linking tasks, such as creating a COM file. To create a COM file, you use TLINK with the `/t` option to link your OBJ file. The format for the TLINK command line is the following:

```
tlink option     COx myobjs, exe, map    , mylibs
              opt                     opt          opt
overlay     emu|fp87 mathx     Cx
       opt                opt
```

The following discussion explains how each of the required TLINK parameters is used. None of the optional parameters were needed when the program in listing 7.4 was linked.

`option`, which can be placed anywhere on the command line, tells TLINK which options to turn on. To see a complete list of the options you can use, invoke TLINK without any parameters. A `/t` option tells TLINK that a COM file should be generated.

`COx` specifies which initialization module will be used. Each memory model has a separate initialization module, and you select the correct one by replacing the `x` with the first letter of the memory model name. For example, the medium memory model requires the initialization module parameter `COm`. The initialization module parameter is a required argument.

`myobjs` specifies which object files are to be linked. The object file names are separated from the `COx` argument by a blank space, not a comma. If you have more than one object file to link, the object file names are separated by blanks. You do not have to enter the OBJ extension for the object file names.

The `exe` parameter, another required argument, specifies the name of the executable file that will be created. You do not have to specify the file name extension; it is provided automatically.

The following arguments are optional: `map` specifies the name of the map file that will be created; `mylibs` lists any user-supplied library file; `overlay` indicates whether the overlay manager library will be linked; and `emu|fp87` specifies which floating-point libraries will be used, if any.

`Cx` is a required argument that specifies which run-time library will be used. Each memory model has a different library. The *x* option works the same as in `COx` except that the tiny and small models use the CS.LIB run-time library.

The actual TLINK command that linked the object file for the program in listing 7.4 looks like this:

```
tlink /t \tc\lib\COt little, little, , \tc\lib\CS
```

The paths to the library files were used to ensure that the correct library files were used for the link. Notice that there is no separating comma between the initialization module parameter and the object file name. Notice also that commas are used to delimit the option fields. The commas are needed so that TLINK can distinguish the files.

Understanding the Overlay Manager

For the first few years after the PC was introduced, programs were not too complex. During this period, most programs worked with only 256K of memory. As the programs became more sophisticated, they required more memory. Adding memory was fine, until the 640K barrier was reached. Making programs larger meant that whole programs would not fit in memory at one time. Overlays had to be used to store unused parts of the programs on disk.

Borland has brought a new level of sophistication to overlay programming with its VROOMM technology. Using VROOMM, you can create programs that are more powerful and useful than ever before. This section shows you how to start taking advantage of Borland's new overlay utilities. You learn first how a typical overlay system works and then how Borland's new system works.

Knowing What an Overlay Manager Does

To run a program that has become too large to fit in memory, you must first divide the program into pieces that can be called as needed. Each of these pieces is called an *overlay*. When a program needs to execute a function stored in an overlay, the appropriate overlay is loaded into memory, and the function is executed.

The job of the overlay manager is to decide which overlay needs to be loaded in memory and which overlay can be stored on disk. The overlay manager is responsible for the initial loading of the overlay modules and for the swapping of modules as the program is executing.

Regular overlay systems, although not as sophisticated as Borland's VROOMM, are still quite helpful. A regular overlay system is divided into two groups of functions: the base unit and the overlay units.

The base unit is the stable part of the program that stays loaded in memory as long as the program is executing. The functions in the base unit can be called by any overlay unit that is currently loaded in memory.

The overlay units do not always reside in memory; they are loaded only if they are needed. A function in an overlay unit is able to call functions located in the base unit or other parts of the same overlay unit. However, a function in one overlay unit is not able to call a function in another overlay unit. The reason is that the typical overlay system allows only one overlay unit to be loaded in memory at a given time.

When a typical overlay program begins execution, it allocates only enough memory space to store the base unit and the largest overlay unit. Thus, when a new overlay needs to be loaded, the current overlay must be put away to make sufficient room for the new overlay.

A typical overlay system is better than nothing, but it is still hard to work with. In such a system, each overlay unit must be self-sufficient. The way in which overlays are loaded into memory prevents one overlay from accessing any of the functions in another overlay. The only other unit that an overlay can access is the base unit.

The typical overlay system requires that you have complete knowledge of the interdependencies of your program's functions. To include a function in an overlay unit, you must be sure that the function does not call any function outside its overlay unit or the base unit. Keeping track of *all* the interdependencies of the functions in your program can be time-consuming.

Understanding Borland's VROOMM

Borland has introduced a new overlay manager with Borland C++. This new overlay manager is called VROOMM, for Virtual Run-time Object-Oriented Memory Manager. VROOMM is more sophisticated than other overlay managers because VROOMM is more intelligent.

As noted before, with a conventional overlay manager, one overlay unit cannot call functions in another overlay unit. VROOMM, however, uses a technique called *dynamic segment swapping* that lets a function call any other function, regardless of the segment in which the called function is stored. With a typical overlay manager, the basic division of a program is called a *unit*. With VROOMM, each division of a program is called a *segment*.

Dynamic segment swapping is what makes VROOMM versatile. When a segment is needed, VROOMM attempts to load that segment into the swap area. If enough space is available in the swap area, the new segment is loaded, and your program continues. If enough space is not available, VROOMM looks for other segments that are not being used. Those segments are moved out to make room for the new segment. What if the whole swap area contains active segments when a new segment is called? In that case, VROOMM selects an already loaded segment and removes it to make room for the new segment. Segments are removed until there is enough space to load the new segment. Dynamic segment swapping relieves you of the task of tracking every function's interdependency.

VROOMM has two useful capabilities: changing the overlay buffer size and using extended or expanded memory. When an overlay is loaded, it resides in an *overlay buffer*. This buffer is located between the stack and the far heap. The size of the overlay buffer is usually calculated at program start-up, but the size can be changed by a variable in your program. _ovrbuffer is a global buffer that can hold a value which determines the size of the overlay buffer. Using _ovrbuffer, you can fine-tune your program for size and speed.

The use of extended or expanded memory also enhances the performance of VROOMM. If your computer has extended or expanded memory, segments that are swapped out will be stored there until they are needed again. Storing unused segments in extended or expanded memory is much faster that relying solely on the disk drive for storage.

Figure 7.3 shows how VROOMM uses your computer's memory for a large memory model program. In figure 7.3, memory is allocated for a large model program that uses overlays. Using overlays does not change the way the code, data, stack, and far heap segments are used. The allocation of these four memory areas is determined by the memory model, not by the use of overlays.

However, there are three extra memory blocks used for overlays. The first block is the overlay control information. This block of memory contains information that is used to manage the overlays. The second block contains a stub segment for each overlay segment; the stub segment contains basic information about each of the overlay segments. The overlay information segment and the stub segment are automatically generated by the linker when an overlay program is created. The third block of memory is for the overlay buffer, which is where the current overlays are stored. The overlay buffer is allocated automatically when the program begins and can be set with the _ovrbuffer global variable.

Fig. 7.3. *How VROOMM uses memory.*

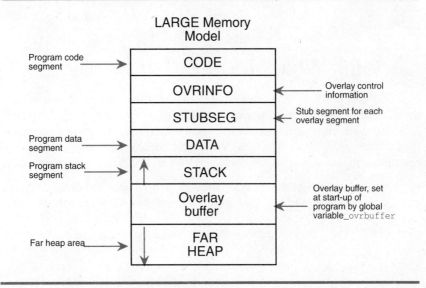

Remember an important point: only the medium, large, and huge memory models can be used when creating an overlay program. The tiny, small, and compact memory models cannot use overlays.

The actual overlay manager is an object file that is combined with your program during linking. If all the program options are set correctly (covered in the next section), the linker will include the overlay manager object module when your executable file is created.

Designing and Creating Overlay Programs

Although the concept of overlay programs is simple, it takes a lot of code to manage an overlaid program. Until Borland C++'s VROOMM became available, using the overlay managers took a good deal of thought and planning. However, VROOMM takes care of most of the details for you. Now you can spend more time developing your program and less time planning your overlay units.

Even though VROOMM is easy to use, some planning is required in setting up and compiling your program. This section shows you how to plan your program and, once you have the program written, how to build the executable file.

Deciding What Modules To Overlay

The nice thing about using VROOMM is that you do not have to spend much time determining what can be overlaid and what can't be overlaid. Dynamic segment swapping makes all your overlays available when you need them. When you call a function, VROOMM makes sure that the module containing that function is used, no matter what other overlay is in memory.

You should give some thought, though, to how your functions call each other. Suppose, for example, that you have the following segments of code:

Segment 1:
```
...
func1()
{
   func2();
}
...
```
Segment 2:
```
...
func2()
{
   func3();
}
...
```
Segment 3:
```
...
func3()
{
   printf( "Last call in chain.\n" );
}
```

Segment 1 has to call segment 2, and segment 2 has to call segment 3. If all three segments were small and could fit in memory, this would not be a problem. But if the segments were large, segments 1 and 2 would probably be moved out of memory by the time that segment 3 was called.

If `func1()`, `func2()`, and `func3()` were all in the same segment, the extra segment swapping would be avoided, and the program would run faster. As you can see from this example, grouping interdependent functions together enhances the performance of your program. When you create a program, you might want to put all the graphics functions in one segment and all the help functions in another segment.

Some functions should not be overlaid. Functions that are designed to be short, fast, or time-critical are better left resident. You should always leave a time-critical function resident to ensure that the function is immediately available when it is needed. Functions that handle system interrupts should not be overlaid either. If an interrupt handler is not in memory when an interrupt occurs, your program will probably blow up.

As you can see, dividing your program into overlay segments is simple. You should group logically related, interdependent functions in overlay segments and leave the time-critical functions and interrupt handlers resident. Dividing your program into logical segments usually results in good overall performance.

Compiling and Linking an Overlay Program

Creating an overlay program is easy when you use the IDE. You design and write overlay projects just as you design and write other C projects. With an overlay project, however, the option settings for the compiler, linker, and project manager are different. Here are the settings required to build an overlay project:

❑ The compiler must have the **Overlay** support option turned on in the dialog box you access with **Options Compiler Code Generation**.

❑ The **Options Linker** menu should have the Overlay box checked.

❑ You use the ⌃**O** Options selection in the project list dialog box to indicate each module that will be placed in an overlay.

Listings 7.5, 7.6, and 7.7 are part of a project that was compiled as an overlay program.

Listing 7.5. `ovrmain.c`. *The main file in the overlay project.*

```
 1   /* OVRMAIN.C   The main file in the overlay program
 2                  project. This file will stay resident
 3                  during the entire program execution. */
 4
 5   #include <stdio.h>
 6   #include <stdlib.h>
 7   #include <conio.h>
 8
 9
10   extern void ovrfunc1( void );
11   extern void ovrfunc2( void );
12
13   int global_i;
14   extern char *ovr1_msg;
15   extern char *ovr2_msg;
16
17   main()
18   {
19     clrscr();
20     printf( "In ovrmain.c. global_i and global_msg have "
21             "not been initialized.\n\n" );
22
23     ovrfunc1();
24     printf( "The first overlay module has been called.\n" );
25     printf( "global_i = %d.\n", global_i );
26     printf( "The overlay message = %s.\n\n", ovr1_msg );
27
28     ovrfunc2();
29     printf( "The second overlay module has been called.\n" );
30     printf( "global_i = %d.\n", global_i );
31     printf( "The overlay message = %s.\n\n", ovr2_msg );
32
33     printf( "Back in ovrmain.c module, ready to exit.\n" );
34     return 0;
35   }
```

The three listings make a simple program. The main program module in listing 7.5 makes calls to the overlay modules, which store values in global variables in the main module.

These three program modules were written and compiled like any normal project. The IDE's option settings determine that the project is turned into an overlay program.

Listing 7.6. `ovrmod1.c`. *The first overlay module.*

```
1   /* OVRMOD1.C This is the first overlay module to
2                be called. The purpose of this module
3                is to set the values of the global
4                variables in ovrmain.c. */
5
6   extern int global_i;
7   char *ovr1_msg;
8
9   void ovrfunc1( void )
10  {
11     global_i = 10;
12     ovr1_msg = "Working in ovrmod1.c";
13  }
```

Listing 7.7. `ovrmod2.c`. *The second overlay module.*

```
1   /* OVRMOD2.C  This is the second overlay module file. This
2                 file is called by the ovrmain.c module. */
3
4   extern global_i;
5   char *ovr2_msg;
6
7   void ovrfunc2()
8   {
9      global_i = 20;
10     ovr2_msg = "Working in ovrfunc2";
11  }
```

The overlay options for the compiler and linker do not change the way you write and compile the programs. However, the project manager does require that you perform an extra step when making a project file. The project manager has to know which program modules will be resident and which modules will be overlays.

In the project file for the three listings, listing 7.5 was specified as a resident segment. This segment is kept in memory at all times. Listings 7.6 and 7.7 were specified as overlays. Because the segments for these two listings are overlays, they are loaded into memory only when they are needed.

This short project simply illustrates how the overlay manager works. A real program that profitably uses the overlay manager would be too large to include in this book. As you create more powerful programs, you will soon discover how useful the overlay manager can be.

Exercises

The following exercises give you practice in creating and compiling programs in different memory models, using pointers in different memory models, and using overlay programs.

1. Create a short program and compile it under the small and large memory models.

2. Make a large model program that uses a pointer to a string. Use the FP_SEG() and FP_OFF() functions to examine the values of the far pointer.

3. Write a program that counts the number of Cs in a disk file. Compile the program to an object file and then use TLINK to link the program to a COM file.

4. Create a mixed-model project that has a large module with at least three functions, and a small module with only a main() function. Have the main() function call each of the functions in the large module.

5. Write an overlay program that keeps the main() function resident and overlays two other functions. Have one overlay dump a text file in all lowercase letters, and have the other overlay dump a text file in all uppercase letters.

Summary

In this chapter, you saw how your Borland C++ programs make use of your computer's memory. The following important points were covered:

❏ *Because the Intel family of processor chips is based on a design that uses a 16-bit processor and a 20-bit address bus, the address of a memory location has to be divided into two parts: the segment address and the offset address.* By itself, the segment address cannot address a particular memory location. An offset address must be added to the segment address in order to access a particular memory location.

❏ *To increase CPU performance, the 8088 processor has a series of registers built that store often-used data.* These registers store, among other things, segment and offset addresses for your program's code, data, and stack memory locations.

❏ *Borland C++ has three types of pointers:* near, far, *and* huge. The near pointer must be used with a segment value in one of the segment address registers. The far pointer can access any memory location, but you cannot reliably compare or perform mathematical operations on far pointers. The huge pointer can access any memory location and can be successfully compared and manipulated. huge pointers can work with objects larger than 64K. However, the normalization of huge pointer requires extra function calls and consequently slows your program.

❏ *Borland C++ has six different memory models you can use when compiling your program.* They are the tiny, small, medium, compact, large, and huge models. The model you use determines how much memory will be available for the code and data in your program.

❏ *Mixed-model programming requires that you explicitly declare the types of the functions and pointers in the external modules.*

❏ *COM files are executable files that have the program's code, data, and stack stored in the same 64K block of memory.* COM files are useful for small programs that do not require much data. Such files are efficient because only near pointers are used.

❏ *VROOMM, the Virtual Run-time Object-Oriented Memory Manager, controls the use of overlays in your program.* An overlay is a program segment that is stored on disk until the program segment is needed. At that time, the segment is read from disk and executed.

❏ *When designing an overlay program, try to keep interdependent functions in the same segment.* Keeping these functions together means fewer overlay swaps and better performance. Interrupt-handling and time-critical functions should not be overlaid. Over-laying an interrupt handler can cause odd program behavior.

The next chapter shows you how to use the Borland C++ video functions. These functions make it easy for you to control both your text and graphic video output.

8

Using the Borland C++ Video Functions

One of the nicest features of Borland C++ is its wide selection of video functions. Borland C++ provides an extensive library of text functions and graphics functions, enabling you to create professional screens quickly and easily.

The purpose of this chapter is to get you up and running with the Borland C++ video functions. The chapter is not designed to be an exhaustive reference on video programming; a complete reference requires more space than is available. The chapter does cover most of the video functions and shows you how to use some of the more popular one.

Understanding the IBM/PC Text Modes

Video monitors work in two basic video modes: graphics mode and text mode. In graphics mode, because you have control of every pixel on the screen, you can display any type of image you want. In text mode, you are limited to displaying characters from the video adapter's character set. The advantages of text mode are the speed and ease with which character output can be formatted and displayed. This section provides an overview of how character data that is sent from your program is displayed on the screen.

307

Surveying PC Video Adapters and Screens

The video display system on your computer consists of two parts: the video adapter and the screen. Inside your computer, the *video adapter* is a group of circuits that translates the data which is output by your program to a video signal the monitor can use.

When your program outputs the letter T, the ASCII value that represents the letter T is sent to the video adapter. The video adapter uses the ASCII code to look up the shape of the letter in the adapter's ROM (read-only memory). The information from the ROM chip tells the adapter which pixels must be turned on in order to display the character on the screen. Finally, the character is displayed at either the current cursor position or a position you specify. Figure 8.1 shows the basic process of displaying a character on the screen.

Fig. 8.1. *How a character is displayed.*

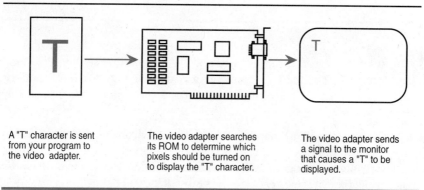

A "T" character is sent from your program to the video adapter.

The video adapter searches its ROM to determine which pixels should be turned on to display the "T" character.

The video adapter sends a signal to the monitor that causes a "T" to be displayed.

The process in figure 8.1 shows how data is displayed on the screen in text mode—the display mode in which only character data can be displayed. See Appendix A for a list of the 256 ASCII characters that can be displayed in text mode.

Borland C++ supports six different text modes. These modes differ in the number of characters displayed on the screen and whether color is used. Table 8.1 lists the six text modes and their distinguishing features.

Table 8.1. *The Borland C++ text modes.*

Mode	Features
BW40	A black-and-white 40-column mode. This mode displays 25 lines, each of which can hold 40 characters. The characters are displayed in black and white.
C40	A color 40-column mode. The screen displays 40 columns and 25 rows of characters in color.
BW80	A black-and-white 80-column mode. The screen displays 80 columns and 25 rows. The characters are displayed in black and white.
C80	A color mode that displays 80 columns and 25 rows.
MONO	A mode that displays monochrome text in 80 columns and 25 rows.
C4350	A special color mode for EGA and VGA adapters. If an EGA adapter is used, the display is 80 columns by 43 rows. If a VGA adapter is used, 50 rows of 80-column text can be displayed.

Understanding Memory-Mapped Screen I/O

So that the image on your monitor appears stable to the human eye, the image is redrawn 60 times every second. Even though an image does not appear to change, the screen is still redrawn every sixtieth of a second.

Fortunately, your program does not have to send data to the display adapter every time the screen is redrawn. When the program sends data to the display adapter, the data is stored in a special section of RAM reserved for *video memory*. Each time the video adapter redraws the screen, the adapter checks the video memory to see what should be put on the screen.

Each display location on the screen has a corresponding location in video memory. If there is a character in a video memory location, that character is drawn at the corresponding location on the video display.

Having a memory location for each location on the video display is the idea behind memory-mapped screen I/O. If you do not specify a memory location, display data that is output by your program is stored at the next available location in video memory. If you want, you can specify the memory address where your data is to be stored. Specifying the memory address lets you put display data at the exact screen location you want.

With the built-in Borland C++ video functions, you can create sophisticated images without having to worry about direct access to video memory. With these video functions, you can place data anywhere on the screen by using the correct row and column address. You do not have to use the actual video memory address. Borland C++ takes care of that for you.

When you are working in text mode, every location on the screen has two memory bytes associated with it. The first byte of memory stores the ASCII value of the character to be displayed. The second byte, called the *attribute* byte, stores information about the way the character is displayed. Figure 8.2 shows how a location in video memory is related to a location on the screen.

Fig. 8.2. *Memory-mapped video.*

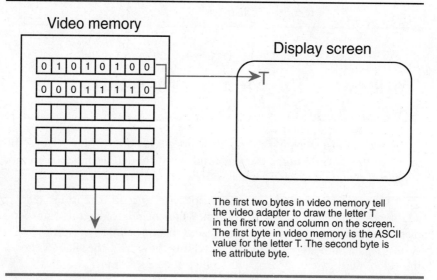

Controlling the Text Screen

The Borland C++ library of functions makes it easy for you to control the appearance of the text-mode screen. Functions are available for selecting the text mode to be used, the background color, and the attributes of the text. You can also set a global variable that uses direct video memory I/O for better performance. This section shows you how to start making use of these text-mode control functions.

Using the Text-Mode Control Functions

The first text-mode control function that you need to call is the textmode() function. This function determines the number of characters that can be displayed and whether color will be used. Note the format of the textmode() function:

```
textmode( int t_mode );
```

t_mode is an integer value that determines which text mode will be used. You can use either an integer value or a symbolic constant for the t_mode argument. The symbolic constants and their integer values are listed in table 8.2. The six text modes shown in table 8.2 are described in table 8.1 in the preceding section.

Table 8.2. *The symbolic constants and integer values for* textmode().

Symbolic Constant	Integer Value
BW40	0
C40	1
BW80	2
C80	3
MONO	7
C4350	64
	−1 (last mode used)

You can call the `textmode()` function with either of these statements:

```
textmode( C4350 );
```

```
textmode( LASTMODE );
```

The first call to `textmode()` sets the text mode to display 43 rows if an EGA adapter/monitor is used, or 50 rows if a VGA adapter/monitor is used. The second call to `textmode()` sets the text mode back to the last text mode used.

If you have a color monitor and you are using a color text mode, you can change the background color. You set the background color with the `textbackground()` function, using the following format:

```
textbackground( int b_color );
```

`b_color` is an integer variable that determines which background color is to be used. You can use a symbolic constant as an argument for the `textbackground()` function.

Table 8.3 shows the symbolic constants and integer values that you can use in functions like `textbackground()` to specify the colors you want. Only eight of the colors listed in table 8.3 can be used as `b_color` arguments to `textbackground()`. The use of each color as a foreground or background color (or both) is noted in table 8.2.

Table 8.3. *The text-mode foreground and background colors.*

Symbolic Constant	Integer Value	Use (F = foreground and B = background)
BLACK	0	F/B
BLUE	1	F/B
GREEN	2	F/B
CYAN	3	F/B
RED	4	F/B
MAGENTA	5	F/B
BROWN	6	F/B
LIGHTGRAY	7	F/B
DARKGRAY	8	F
LIGHTBLUE	9	F

Symbolic Constant	Integer Value	Use (F = foreground and B = background)
LIGHTGREEN	10	F
LIGHTCYAN	11	F
LIGHTRED	12	F
LIGHTMAGENTA	13	F
YELLOW	14	F
WHITE	15	F
BLINK	128	F

If, for example, you make the following function call, the video screen's background color is set to green:

```
textbackground( GREEN );
```

You use the `textcolor()` function to set the color of the displayed characters. Note the format for the `textcolor()` function call:

```
textcolor( int t_color );
```

`t_color` can be any of the symbolic constants listed in table 8.3. An actual call to `textcolor()` looks like this:

```
textcolor( YELLOW );
```

This call to `textcolor()` sets the text, or foreground, color to yellow.

When `textbackground()` and `textcolor()` are used, only the direct video functions that follow these functions are affected. The direct video functions are those that write information directly to the screen, such as `cprintf()` and `cputs()`. Functions like `printf()` and `puts()` are not affected by `textbackground()` and `textcolor()`.

The `lowvideo()`, `normvideo()`, and `highvideo()` functions change the intensity of the text characters that are displayed. `lowvideo()` turns off the high-intensity bit and causes any following direct video functions to display characters in low intensity. `highvideo()` turns on the high-intensity bit and causes text to be displayed in high intensity. The `normvideo()` function displays characters in the video mode that was used before the program began. Note the following code fragment, showing how these three functions are used:

```
textcolor( RED );
lowvideo();
cprintf( "This is a test string.\n" );
normvideo();
cprintf( "This is a test string.\n" );
highvideo();
cprintf( "This is a test string.\n" );
```

The first two statements in this code fragment set the character color to low-intensity red. When the first `cprintf()` statement is then executed, the message is displayed in low-intensity red. The `normvideo()` statement sets the video mode to the one used before the program started. Therefore, the second and third `cprintf()` statements display the message in the color used before the program started, not in red. The second `cprintf()` statement displays a normal-intensity message, and the third `cprintf()` statement displays a high-intensity message.

You use the `textattr()` function to set both the background and foreground colors with one statement. `textattr()` works by changing the values stored in the text attribute byte. The *attribute byte* is the byte that controls the appearance of each text character. This byte is the same one that is manipulated by the `textbackground()` and `textcolor()` functions. The format of the attribute byte is shown in figure 8.3.

Fig. 8.3. *The attribute byte.*

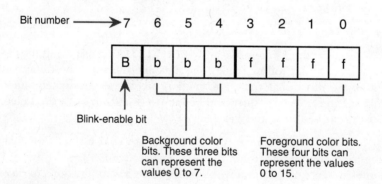

Bit number ⟶ 7 6 5 4 3 2 1 0

| B | b | b | b | f | f | f | f |

Blink-enable bit

Background color bits. These three bits can represent the values 0 to 7.

Foreground color bits. These four bits can represent the values 0 to 15.

Listing 8.1 shows how the `textattr()` function is used.

Listing 8.1. `atrdemo.c`. *A demonstration of the* `textattr()` *function.*

```
1   /* ATRDEMO.C   Text-mode attribute demonstration program.
2                  This program uses textattr() to change the
3                  foreground and background text colors. */
4   #include <stdio.h>
5   #include <stdlib.h>
6   #include <conio.h>
7
8   int main()
9   {
10     int i, j, k;
11
12     for( i = 0; i <= 7; i++ ){
13       for( j = 0; j <= 15; j++ ) {
14         k = i;
15         k = ( k << 4 );
16         textattr( k + j );
17         for( k = 48; k <= 127; k++ )
18           putch( k );
19         cprintf( "\r\n" );
20       }
21     }
22
23     return 0;
24   }
```

The program in listing 8.1 uses the `textattr()` function to change the value of the attribute byte whenever a new line is displayed. The program is composed of three loops. Two of the loops are used to cycle through the background and foreground colors, and the third loop prints a line of characters.

The first loop, in lines 12–21, generates a value that is used to change the background color. Notice in lines 14 and 15 that the value of the outer loop counter is assigned to another variable and then left-shifted four bits. The left shift moves the integer value in the variable four places to the left so that the value will be in the correct bit position in the attribute byte.

The second loop, in lines 13–20, generates a value that is used to change the foreground color. In line 16, the `textattr()` function is called with an argument that adds the value of the second loop counter to the left-shifted value of the first loop counter.

The third `for` loop simply prints a line of characters across the screen. The background and foreground colors of the displayed line are changed by the `textattr()` on every pass through the loop. Because the foreground color is determined by the second loop, the foreground color changes more rapidly than the background color.

Using Direct Console I/O for High Performance

One way to improve your program's performance is to send your display data directly to the video RAM. Sending data directly to video RAM cuts down on the number of calls that have to be made. Therefore, your program speeds up.

Borland C++ has a global variable that determines whether the console output is sent directly to video RAM or is processed by BIOS calls. The variable that controls the console output functions is the `directvideo` variable. If `directvideo` is set to 0, console output is processed by the PC's BIOS functions. If `directvideo` has a value of 1, all console output is sent directly to video memory.

The following statement displays the current value of the `directvideo` variable:

```
printf( "%d", directvideo );
```

The default setting of the variable is 1, indicating that console output is sent directly to video RAM.

The only problem with using direct console I/O is that Borland C++ depends on the computer being 100 percent IBM-compatible. If the `directvideo` variable is set to 1 and the computer on which your program is run is not compatible, the direct writes to video memory may not work. Therefore, if you have to write programs for computers that are not IBM-compatible, it is safer to set the `directvideo` variable to 0. When `directvideo` is set to 0, all video display functions are made with BIOS calls instead of direct memory writes.

Using the Window Functions

To give you more versatility in formatting your screen output, Borland C++ provides window functions with which you can define and use text windows. A *text window* is a rectangular area to which your output is limited. This section shows you how to set up and use the Borland C++ window functions.

The window() function defines a rectangular area on the screen where the output from the direct console I/O functions is sent. When a window is defined, the output from the console I/O functions is displayed only inside the window. Note the format for the call to the window() function:

```
window( int left, int top, int right, int bottom );
```

The arguments passed to the window() function are the *screen* coordinates of the upper-left and lower-right corners of the window. In text mode, the screen coordinates are specified in 1 origin format, which means that the upper-left corner has coordinates 1,1 and not 0,0.

The maximum values of the arguments passed to the window() function depend on the current text mode. If the current text mode is EGA 43 line mode, the largest window has upper-left coordinates of 1,1 and lower-right coordinates of 80,43.

Every program that you write creates a window. If you do not explicitly call the window() function in your program, a window is created by default. The size of the automatically created window is equal to the maximum size of the current text-mode screen. Listing 8.2 demonstrates the use of the window() function.

Listing 8.2. wnddemo.c. *A demonstration of the* window() *function.*

```
 1    /* WNDDEMO.C   This short program creates two different
 2                   windows. The first window uses the entire
 3                   screen. The second window occupies only
 4                   the middle of the screen. The text sent
 5                   to each window is a rolling ASCII pattern.
 6                   The same test pattern is sent to each window.
 7    */
 8
 9    #include <stdio.h>
10    #include <stdlib.h>
```

Listing 8.2. continues

Listing 8.2. continued

```
11   #include <conio.h>
12
13   main()
14   {
15     int i, j;
16
17     textattr( 2 );
18     clrscr();
19
20     for( i = 0; i <= 100; i++ )
21       for( j = 48; j <= 122; j++ )
22         putch( j );
23
24     window( 5, 15, 75, 20 );
25     textattr( 30 );
26     clrscr();
27
28     for( i = 0; i <= 100; i++ )
29       for( j = 48; j <= 122; j++ )
30         putch( j );
31     return 0;
32   }
```

Listing 8.2 is a small program that uses two different windows. The first window is created automatically when the program begins execution. By default, the first window occupies the whole screen. In line 17, the textattr() function is called to set the attributes of the characters to be displayed. The value of 2 passed to textattr() displays green characters on a black background.

The for loops in lines 20–22 and 28–30 print a rolling ASCII pattern. These for loops print the ASCII characters with values from 48 to 122. Notice that there are no newline characters printed in the for loops. The output is allowed to scroll from one line to the next.

The second window that is used is defined by the window() function call in line 24. window() creates a window with the upper-left corner at position 5,15 and a lower-right corner at position 75,20. All the characters output by the putch() function in line 30 will be displayed inside the new window. Everything outside the new window will remain as it was.

Whether text that is displayed in a window will automatically scroll to the next line is determined by the global variable _wscroll. When _wscroll is set to 1, text automatically scrolls to the next line when the current line is full. If _wscroll is 0, text does not scroll to the next line. If _wscroll is 0 and the current line is full, the next character is written at the beginning of the current line. To change the value of _wscroll, you must include the conio.h header file and declare _wscroll as an external integer.

You use the gettextinfo() function to find out what the current text-mode settings are. When gettextinfo() is called, the function stores information about the current text mode in the text_info structure. The text_info structure is defined in this way:

```
struct text_info{
  unsigned char winleft;              /*left coordinate*/
  unsigned char wintop;               /*top coordinate*/
  unsigned char winright;             /*right coordinate*/
  unsigned char winbottom;            /*bottom coordinate*/
  unsigned char attribute;            /*text attribute*/
  unsigned char normattr;             /*normal attribute*/
  unsigned char currmode;             /*BW40, BW80, C40, C80, C4350*/
  unsigned char screenheight;         /*bottom - top*/
  unsigned char screenwidth;          /*right - left*/
  unsigned char curx;                 /*current x coordinate*/
  unsigned char cury;                 /*current y coordinate*/
};
```

The following code fragment uses the gettextinfo() function to get information about the current text screen:

```
struct text_info my_struct;
gettextinfo( &my_struct );
cprintf( "The screen is %d characters tall.\r\n",
         my_struct.screenheight );
cprintf( "The screen is %d characters wide.\r\n",
         my_struct.screenwidth );
```

If the only information that you need is the current cursor position, you can use the wherex() and wherey() functions. These two functions return an integer value equal to the current *x* or *y* coordinate of the cursor. Note the following code fragment:

```
int x, y;
x = wherex();
y = wherey();
```

The wherex() and wherey() functions are used to get the current position of the cursor in the text window. Notice that the return value is the position inside the current text window; the position returned is not necessarily the screen position.

You may have noticed one problem with using windows: when a new screen covers an old screen, the information on the old screen is lost. With the gettext() and puttext() functions, you can get around this problem. gettext() copies the contents of the screen to a block of memory. When you want to redisplay the screen, all you have to do is call the puttext() function. Listing 8.3, which is a modification of listing 8.2, uses the gettext() and puttext() functions to save and restore the first screen.

Listing 8.3. scrsave.c. A program that uses the gettext() and puttext() functions.

```
1   /* SCRSAVE.C   This program uses the gettext() function
2                  to save a screen, and the puttext()
3                  function to restore the screen.
4   */
5
6   #include <stdio.h>
7   #include <stdlib.h>
8   #include <conio.h>
9
10  main()
11  {
12    int i, j;
13    char scr_buf[4000];
14
15    textattr( 2 );
16    clrscr();
17
18    for( i = 0; i <= 100; i++ )
19      for( j = 48; j <= 122; j++ )
20        putch( j );
21
22    gettext( 1, 1, 80, 25, scr_buf );
23
24    window( 5, 15, 75, 20 );
25    textattr( 30 );
26    clrscr();
27
28    for( i = 0; i <= 100; i++ )
29      for( j = 48; j <= 122; j++ )
30        putch( j );
31
32    cprintf( "\r\n\n" );
33    cprintf( "Press any key to continue.\r\n" );
34    while( !kbhit() );
35
```

```
36    window( 1, 1, 80, 25 );
37    clrscr();
38    puttext( 1, 1, 80, 25, scr_buf );
39    return 0;
40  }
```

The program in listing 8.3 uses the `gettext()` function to save the text in the first window before the second window is created. After the information has been displayed in the second window, the first window is restored with the `puttext()` function.

In line 13, a character array is created that can hold all the text in a full-size window. Notice that the array is large enough to hold the text *and* the attribute byte for each character in the window.

Lines 15–20 fill the first window with a continuous sequence of ASCII characters. After the screen has been filled, the `gettext()` function is called, and an image of the screen is stored in the `scr_buf` character array.

Next, in lines 24–30, another window is created and filled with the same type of ASCII character pattern. When the display loop is completed, you are prompted to press a key to continue.

When you press a key to continue, a new full-size window is created and cleared. Once the window is cleared, the `puttext()` function is called, and the text from the original full-size window is restored.

Understanding the IBM/PC Graphics Mode

As noted earlier, you can use two video modes: text mode and graphics mode. In the preceding sections, you learned how to use text mode to handle your character data. You use graphics mode to display your graphical data, such as charts, graphs, drawings, and other images. In this section, you learn what graphics mode is and how to start using it in your programs.

Understanding Pixels and Palettes

The pixel is what graphics mode is all about. A *pixel* is a single dot on your video screen. In graphics-mode processing, you control each pixel on your screen.

Each different type of video adapter and screen supports a different number of pixels. For example, a CGA adapter/display can display a maximum of 640 x 200 pixels, and an IBM 8514 display can display up to 1,024 x 768 pixels. Screen resolution, then, refers to the number of pixels your screen can display.

It is possible for an adapter/screen combination to support more than one resolution. The number of resolutions that can be displayed also depends on the software that controls the adapter and screen. Table 8.4 lists the video adapters and resolutions Borland C++ supports.

Table 8.4. The video adapters and resoulutions supported in Borland C++.

Type	Description	Resolution(s)	# Colors
CGA	Color Graphics Array	320 x 200	4
		640 x 200	2
MCGA	Multi-Color Graphics Array	320 x 200	4
		640 x 200	2
		640 x 480	2
EGA	Enhanced Graphics Adapter	640 x 200	16
		640 x 350	16
HERC	Hercules Monographics	720 x 348	2
ATT400	ATT Video Adapter	320 x 200	16
		640 x 200	2
		640 x 400	2
VGA	Video Graphics Array	640 x 200	16
		640 x 350	16
		640 x 480	16
PC3270	Built-in 3270 Adapter	720 x 350	2
IBM8514	8514 Monitor Support	640 x 480	256
		1,024 x 768	256

Each pixel on the screen has a corresponding memory location. The memory location holds a value that indirectly determines the color of the pixel. This determination is made because the value stored in memory is an offset into a table called a palette. The value in the palette determines the actual color to be displayed.

The *palette* is a list of all the colors that can be displayed on the screen at any given time. Many times, the number of colors listed in a palette is a fraction of the number of colors the screen can actually display. The number of colors in a palette is limited by the amount of video memory available.

The color screens supported by Borland C++ can be divided into two groups by the way that colors are controlled. The first group is the CGA group, which includes the CGA video mode, the AT&T video mode, and the lower-resolution MCGA video modes. The second group is the EGA group, which includes the EGA and VGA adapters.

When you are using CGA-type screens, you can choose either the low- or high-resolution mode. The low-resolution mode displays 320 x 200 pixels in four colors. The high-resolution mode displays 640 x 200 pixels in two colors.

In CGA low-resolution mode, you can display only four colors at one time, determined by the palette you choose. The available palettes in CGA mode are CGAC0, CGAC1, CGAC2, and CGAC3. Each of the CGA palettes contains four different colors. You can select the first color in each of the palettes. Table 8.5 shows the fixed colors in all four CGA palettes.

Table 8.5. The CGA color palettes.

Palette #	Color 0	Color 1	Color 2	Color 3
CGAC0	User-defined	CGA_LIGHTGREEN	CGA_LIGHTRED	CGA_YELLOW
CGAC1	User-defined	CGA_LIGHTCYAN	CGA_LIGHTMAGENTA	CGA_WHITE
CGAC2	User-defined	CGA_GREEN	CGA_RED	CGA_BROWN
CGAC3	User-defined	CGA_CYAN	CGA_MAGENTA	CGA_LIGHTGRAY

You use the `initgraph()` function (covered in the next section) to select the CGA palette you want to use. Once you select the proper palette, you can use the `setcolor()` function to choose one of the colors in table 8.5 as the current drawing color. For example, if CGAC2 is the current palette, either of the following statements sets the current drawing color to green:

```
setcolor( 1 );
```

```
setcolor( CGA_GREEN )
```

In each of the CGA palettes, the first color, color 0, is the background color that can be set by you. Table 8.6 shows the 16 colors from which you can select. This table includes the color numbers and their associated symbolic constants.

Table 8.6. *The 16 CGA background colors.*

Color #	Symbolic Constant	Color #	Symbolic Constant
0	BLACK	8	DARKGRAY
1	BLUE	9	LIGHTBLUE
2	GREEN	10	LIGHTGREEN
3	CYAN	11	LIGHTCYAN
4	RED	12	LIGHTRED
5	MAGENTA	13	LIGHTMAGENTA
6	BROWN	14	YELLOW
7	LIGHTGRAY	15	WHITE

To set the background color, you use the `setbkcolor()` function. This function requires an argument from table 8.6. For example, to specify the background color as blue, you can use either of the following function calls:

```
setbkcolor( 1 );
```

```
setbkcolor( BLUE );
```

Using CGA high-resolution mode is less complicated than using CGA low-resolution mode. In high-resolution mode, each pixel can have a value of either 0 or 1. If the pixel value is 0, the pixel will be in the black background color. If the pixel value is 1, the pixel will be in the foreground color you select. Any of the colors in table 8.6 can be used as a foreground color.

Setting the foreground color in CGA high-resolution mode is a little strange. To set the foreground color, you use the `setbkcolor()` function, which sets the hardware *background* color. You use this function because of a peculiarity in the CGA adapter. If, for example, you wanted to draw a CGA high-resolution figure in yellow, you would use either of these statements:

```
setbkcolor( 14 );
```

```
setbkcolor( YELLOW );
```

In EGA/VGA mode, the palette contains 16 colors you can display at one time. (The only difference between EGA and VGA modes is that VGA has a higher resolution than EGA.) You choose these 16 palette colors from a group of 64 possible colors. By default, the colors in the EGA palette correspond to the CGA background colors. Table 8.7 lists the EGA palette color numbers and the symbolic constant associated with each color number.

Table 8.7. The 16 EGA palette colors.

Color #	Symbolic Constant	Color #	Symbolic Constant
0	EGA_BLACK	56	EGA_DARKGRAY
1	EGA_BLUE	57	EGA_LIGHTBLUE
2	EGA_GREEN	58	EGA_LIGHTGREEN
3	EGA_CYAN	59	EGA_LIGHTCYAN
4	EGA_RED	60	EGA_LIGHTRED
5	EGA_MAGENTA	61	EGA_LIGHTMAGENTA
7	EGA_LIGHTGRAY	62	EGA_YELLOW
20	EGA_BROWN	63	EGA_WHITE

The `setpalette()` function enables you to change each color in the EGA palette. Here is the format of the `setpalette()` function call:

```
setpalette( int p_num, int color );
```

The `p_num` argument specifies which entry in the palette will be changed. The `color` argument is the actual color number of the color to be displayed. Note the following function call:

```
setpalette( 12, 60 );
```

Here the twelfth entry in the EGA palette will be changed so that a light red color is displayed.

You can set all the colors in the palette with the single function `setallpalette()`. This function resets the entire current palette. The format for the `setallpalette()` function call is this:

```
setallpalette( struct palettetype far *my_palette );
```

The argument `my_palette` is a structure containing a new set of color numbers that will be copied to the current palette.

When you use the `setbkcolor( color )` function in EGA mode, the `color` argument is stored in the first entry in the EGA palette.

The `getpalette()` function enables you to find exactly which colors are being used in the current palette. A call to `getpalette()` looks like this:

```
getpalette( struct palettetype far *view_palette );
```

The *view_palette* argument is a *palettetype* structure that has two parts. The first part of the structure is a value that indicates how many colors are in the palette. The second part of the structure is an array of all the actual color numbers for the current palette.

Controlling the Graphics Screen

Before you can use any of the graphics functions, you have to change the screen from text mode to graphics mode. You use the initgraph() function to change the video mode. Note the format of the initgraph() function call:

```
initgraph( int far *graphdriver, int far graphmode,
           char far *pathtodriver );
```

The *graphdriver* argument tells initgraph() which graphics screen driver needs to be loaded for your video adapter. If the *graphdriver* argument is equal to 0, the detectgraph() function is called. detectgraph() checks your hardware and determines the highest graphics resolution that can be used.

When initgraph() is called, the graphics driver specified by *graphdriver* is loaded from disk into memory. Once the driver is loaded into memory, the program is able to control your graphics hardware.

The *graphmode* argument indicates which graphics mode you will be using. For example, if the *graphdriver* argument is set for CGA, *graphmode* can be set to any one of the four CGA modes. If *graphdriver* is set to autodetect the graphics hardware, *graphmode* does not have to be set. When detectgraph() is used, it supplies the arguments for *graphdriver* and *graphmode*.

The *pathtodriver* argument tells initgraph() where the graphics driver files can be found. If the *pathtodriver* argument is NULL, the graphics driver files should be in the current directory.

Table 8.8 lists the values that can be used as the *graphdriver* argument to the initgraph() function.

Table 8.8. The graphics drivers supported in Borland C++.

Driver Name	Numeric Value
DETECT	0 (autodetection mode)
CGA	1

Driver Name	Numeric Value
MCGA	2
EGA	3
EGA64	4
EGAMONO	5
IBM8514	6
HERCMONO	7
ATT400	8
VGA	9
PC320	10

initgraph() should be called with a *graphdriver* argument equal to one of the values listed in table 8.8. Either the numeric value or the name of the driver from table 8.8 can be used as an argument value.

Table 8.9 shows the possible choices for the *graphmode* argument to the initgraph() function.

Table 8.9. *The graphics-mode arguments for* initgraph().

Driver	Graphics Mode	Value	Resolution	Palette
CGA	CGAC0	0	320 x 200	C0
	CGAC1	1	320 x 200	C1
	CGAC2	2	320 x 200	C2
	CGAC3	3	320 x 200	C3
	CGAHI	4	640 x 200	2 Color
MCGA	MCGAC0	0	320 x 200	C0
	MCGAC1	1	320 x 200	C1
	MCGAC2	2	320 x 200	C2
	MCGAC3	3	320 x 200	C3
	MCGAMED	4	640 x 200	2 Color
	MCGAHI	5	640 x 480	2 Color
EGA	EGALO	0	640 x 200	16 Color
	EGAHI	1	640 x 350	16 Color

Table 8.9. continues

Table 8.9. *continued*

Driver	Graphics Mode	Value	Resolution	Palette
EGA64	EGA64LO	0	640 x 200	16 Color
	EGA64HI	1	640 x 350	4 Color
EGAMONO	EGAMONOHI	3	640 x 350	2 Color
HERC	HERCMONOHI	0	720 x 348	2 Color
ATT400	ATT400C0	0	320 x 200	C0
	ATT400C1	1	320 x 200	C1
	ATT400C2	2	320 x 200	C2
	ATT400C3	3	320 x 200	C3
	ATT400MED	4	640 x 200	2 Color
	ATT400HI	5	640 x 400	2 Color
VGA	VGALO	0	640 x 200	16 Color
	VGAMED	1	640 x 350	16 Color
	VGAHI	2	640 x 480	16 Color
PC3270	PC3270HI	0	720 x 350	2 Color
IBM8515	IBM8514LO	0	640 x 480	256 Color
	IBM8514HI	1	1,024 x 768	256 Color

When you select a graphics mode from table 8.9, find the correct graphics driver in the Driver column. Next, locate the resolution and palette you want to use. Finally, use the value from the Graphics Mode column or the Value column as the *graphmode* argument to `initgraph()`.

When you are through with your graphics-mode processing, you can call the `closegraph()` function to return to text mode. This function deallocates any memory that was allocated by the graphics function. The `closegraph()` function then ends graphics mode. `closegraph()` returns the system to the text mode that was used when `initgraph()` was called.

Introducing the BGI Graphics Library

Graphics programming is easy when you use Borland C++. By creating the BGI library, Borland has done all the hard work involved in graphics programming. (BGI stands for Borland Graphics Interface.) The BGI library of functions lets you concentrate on creating your images and frees you from controlling the hardware. This section covers some of the most useful functions from the BGI library. You see how to use the drawing functions and how to control your screen.

Using the Drawing and Filling Functions

The shapes you draw with the BGI library functions can be divided into two major groups: unfilled objects and filled objects. The inside of an *unfilled object* is the same color as the background; you see only the outline of the object. The inside of a *filled object* is set to a color you specify. In this section, you first learn how to use functions that draw unfilled objects. You then learn how to use functions that draw filled objects or fill areas on the screen.

One thing to remember about using the graphics drawing functions is that the graphics-mode screen locations use a zero origin format. In graphics mode, then, the upper-left corner has the *x,y* location of 0,0. In text mode, the upper-left corner has a location of 1,1.

In the BGI library, you can find the following drawing functions to draw unfilled objects:

line()	Draws a line
linerel()	Draws a line a relative distance from the current position
lineto()	Draws a line from the current position to a position you specify
rectangle()	Draws a rectangle
drawpoly()	Draws a polygon
arc()	Draws an arc
circle()	Draws a circle
ellispse()	Draws an ellipse

Listing 8.4 shows how easily you can use these drawing functions. Note that the next three listings were written for a VGA monitor. If you want the programs to work with a CGA monitor or another monitor, you will need to change the values that control the size of the object being drawn.

Listing 8.4. `graph1.c.` *A program that uses the basic drawing functions.*

```
1   /* GRAPH1.C This program shows how easy it is to use
2                  the Borland C++ graphics functions. */
3
4   #include <graphics.h>
5   #include <stdlib.h>
6   #include <stdio.h>
7   #include <conio.h>
8
9   int main()
10  {
11      int graphdrv = DETECT;
12      int graphmode;
13      int x, y;
14      int radius = 30;
15
16      initgraph( &graphdrv, &graphmode, "\\tc\\bgi" );
17
18      for( x = 10; x <= 400; x += 10 ) {
19        y = x;
20        circle( x, y, radius );
21      }
22
23      while( !kbhit() );
24      closegraph();
25      return 0;
26  }
```

The short program in listing 8.4 shows how to call the functions in the BGI library. The program uses a `for` loop to draw a series of circles across the screen.

Before the BGI functions can be called, you must initialize graphics mode. Notice that the `graphdrv` variable in line 11 is defined with the macro `DETECT`. When the `graphdrv` variable is used in the `initgraph()` function call, the value of `graphdrv` causes `initgraph()` to autodetect the best graphics mode. The actual call to `initgraph()` is made in line 16.

Once the graphics mode is initialized, you are ready to call a graphics function. The `for` loop in lines 18–20 causes a diagonal series of circles to be drawn across the screen. The `circle()` function needs *x,y* coordinates that locate the center of the circle, and a value that specifies the radius of the circle. The three-line loop is all you need to draw the whole series of circles.

When you are through with graphics mode, you need to switch back to regular text mode. The switch to text mode is made with the `closegraph()` function in line 24.

Listing 8.5 shows how some of the other drawing functions in the BGI library are called. These include the `drawpoly()`, `ellipse()`, and `line()` functions.

Listing 8.5. `graph2.c`. *A program that uses more BGI functions.*

```
1    /* GRAPH2.C This program shows how functions in the BGI
2                library are called. */
3
4    #include <graphics.h>
5    #include <stdlib.h>
6    #include <stdio.h>
7    #include <conio.h>
8
9    int main()
10   {
11       int graphdrv = DETECT;
12       int graphmode;
13       int i, x, y;
14       int polypoints[] = { 10, 10,
15                            500, 10,
16                            500, 300,
17                            10, 10 };
18
19       initgraph( &graphdrv, &graphmode, "\\tc\\bgi" );
20
21       for( i = 1; i <= 100; i++ ) {
22         x = random( 640 );
23         y = random( 480 );
24         ellipse( x, y, 0, 360, x, y );
25       }
26
27       cleardevice();
28
29       drawpoly( 4, polypoints );
30       line( 0, 450, 640, 450 );
31       while( !kbhit() );
32
33       closegraph();
34       return 0;
35   }
```

The `ellipse()` function in the `for` loop in lines 21–25 uses three groups of arguments. The first group of arguments is the x,y coordinates that locate the center of the ellipse. The second pair of arguments specifies the starting and ending angles of the ellipse. The third set of arguments specifies the ellipse size.

In listing 8.5, the `for` loop draws 100 ellipses of random sizes at random locations. The size and location of the ellipses are controlled by the `random()` functions in lines 22 and 23.

In line 29, the `drawpoly()` function draws a polygon of any shape you want. The number of sides for the polygon is determined by the first argument to `drawpoly()`. Where the polygon's sides will be drawn is determined by the second argument to `drawpoly()`. The second argument is a pointer to an array listing all the x,y coordinates of the points on the polygon. The array of points used by `drawpoly()` is declared and initialized in lines 14–17.

In line 30, the `line()` function is used to draw a line near the bottom of the screen. `line()` has to be told the starting and ending points for the line.

The second major group of drawing functions is the filled-object functions. These functions draw objects that are filled with a pattern and a color you select. The following functions draw filled objects:

`bar()`	Draws and fills a two-dimensional bar
`bar3d()`	Draws and fills a three-dimensional bar
`fillellipse()`	Draws and fills an ellipse
`fillpoly()`	Draws and fills a polygon
`pieslice()`	Draws and fills a pie slice
`sector()`	Draws and fills an elliptical pie slice
`floodfill()`	Fills a bounded region

Using the filled-image functions is as quick and easy as using the unfilled-image functions. Listing 8.6 shows a bar-graph program that uses the `bar3d()` function.

Listing 8.6. `drawbar.c`. *A program that uses a filled-image function.*

```
1   /* DRAWBAR.C  This program draws three 3-D bars, the size
2               of which is determined by the user.*/
3
4   #include <graphics.h>
5   #include <stdlib.h>
```

```
 6    #include <stdio.h>
 7    #include <conio.h>
 8
 9    int main()
10    {
11        int graphdrv = DETECT;
12        int graphmode;
13        int i, j, k;
14
15        clrscr();
16        printf( "Enter 3 numbers from 0 to 9 => " );
17        scanf( "%d %d %d", &i, &j, &k );
18
19        initgraph( &graphdrv, &graphmode, "\\tc\\bgi" );
20
21        i = 450 - ( 30 * i );
22        j = 450 - ( 30 * j );
23        k = 450 - ( 30 * k );
24
25        bar3d(  20, i, 120, 450, 10, 1 );
26        bar3d( 140, j, 240, 450, 10, 1 );
27        bar3d( 260, k, 360, 450, 10, 1 );
28
29        while( !kbhit() );
30
31        closegraph();
32        return 0;
33    }
```

Listing 8.6 is a simple program that draws a scaled bar graph. In line 17, the scanf() function inputs 3 integer values from 0 to 9. The 3 integer values are scaled to size in lines 21–23. Each increment of 1 for the user-supplied integer value increases the height of the bar graph by 30 pixels. Subtracting the height of the bar graph from 450 gives the y coordinate for the top of the bar.

Lines 25–27 are the calls to the bar3d() function. bar3d() requires arguments that specify the left, top, right, and bottom x,y locations of the bar. The last two arguments specify the depth of the 3-D shadow and whether a top is put on the bar. If the last argument is nonzero, a top is put on the bar. If the last argument is 0, no top is placed on the top of the bar.

Borland C++ provides several functions that let you take control of the drawing functions:

`moveto()`	Moves the current position to *x,y*
`moverel()`	Moves the current position by a relative distance
`getlinesettings()`	Gets the current line style, width, and pattern
`setlinestyle()`	Changes the current line style and width
`getaspectratio()`	Gets the current aspect ratio
`setaspectratio()`	Changes the aspect ratio
`getfillpattern()`	Returns the used-defined fill pattern
`setfillpattern()`	Picks a user-defined fill pattern
`getfillsettings()`	Gets the current fill pattern and color
`setfillstyle()`	Changes the current fill pattern and style

A call to the `setlinestyle()` function looks like this:

```
setlinestyle( int linestyle, unsigned upattern, int thickness );
```

The *linestyle* parameter specifies what line style will be used. *upattern* is a 16-bit number you can use to change the line style. For the *upattern* value to be used, the *linestyle* argument must be set to `USERBIT_LINE`. Each bit in the 16-bit *upattern* value corresponds to a bit on the screen. If a bit is on in the *upattern* value, the bit will be turned on when it is displayed on the screen. The *linestyle* argument does not affect arcs, circles, ellipses, or pie slices.

The *thickness* argument indicates whether the drawing lines will be one or three pixels wide. If *thickness* is set to `NORM_WIDTH`, the lines will be drawn one pixel wide. If *thickness* is set to `THICK_WIDTH`, the lines will be drawn three pixels wide.

If, for example, the statement

```
setlinestyle( SOLID_LINE, 0, THICK_WIDTH );
```

were added to listing 8.4 or 8.5, all the images would be drawn with lines that are three pixels wide.

Controlling the Screen and Viewport

When you start drawing on the screen, you will soon find a need to clear the screen and start over. Borland C++ has just the function for clearing the screen: the `cleardevice()` function. When `cleardevice()` is called, the whole screen is erased and is ready to use again.

Your graphics system has from one to four graphics pages you can use. A *page* is a block of memory that hold an entire graphics screen. The page where all the graphics functions send their output is called the *active page*, and the page that is being displayed is called the *visual page*.

Table 8.10 lists the adapters and modes that support more than one video page.

Table 8.10. The adapters and modes that support more than one video page.

Adapter	Mode	Number of Pages
EGA	EGALO	4
	EGAHI	2
	EGAMONOHI	2 (w/256K of memory)
HERC	HERCMONOHI	2
VGA	VGALO	2
	VGAMED	2

The `setactivepage( int page )` function sets the active page where graphics output is sent. `setvisualpage( int page )` selects the video page to be displayed.

In text mode, you can set a *window* area (a rectangular area on the screen) where all the text functions send output. Graphics mode has a similar feature except that the defined area is called a *viewport*.

The `setviewport()` function controls the location of the viewport and the space it occupies. A call to the `setviewport()` function looks like this:

```
setviewport( int left, int top, int right, int bottom, int
          clipping );
```

The position arguments passed to `setviewport()` are absolute screen coordinates. The `setviewport()` function also specifies whether clipping is on. If clipping is on (nonzero), an object that exceeds the size of the viewport will be cut off at the boundaries of the viewport. You use the `clearviewport()` function when you want to erase everything in the viewport.

Using Text in Graphics Mode

Displaying text in graphics mode is different from displaying text in text mode. Because you control every pixel on the screen in graphics mode, you have to control how the letters are drawn when you display text.

The easiest way to display text in graphics mode is to display characters that are already drawn. Using a premade set of characters can save you a great deal of time because you do not have to re-create the characters each time you need them.

A set of premade characters in the same style is called a *font*. The Borland C++ BGI library provides several fonts that you can use to display text information in your graphic images. This section shows how to use the fonts and graphics-mode text functions in Borland C++.

Understanding BGI Fonts

The BGI function library has two families of fonts: the bit-mapped fonts and the stroked fonts. The difference between the two families of fonts becomes evident when you consider how the fonts are created.

A character in a bit-mapped font is made by turning on or off each dot in a rectangular grid. The actual size of the grid (in pixels) can vary depending on the scaling factor used when the character is printed. For example, the built-in bit-mapped font defines each character in an 8 x 8 grid. However, the size of the character that is displayed does not have to occupy an area of 8 x 8 pixels. The font can be scaled so that the displayed size of the font is larger than the defined size.

The stroked fonts are fundamentally different from the bit-mapped fonts. A character in a stroked font is made from a series of vectors that tells the program how to draw the font.

Because of the way stroked fonts are drawn, they can produce better results when they are enlarged. When you scale a bit-mapped font, the basic grid pattern is simply enlarged. When a bit-mapped font is made larger, the appearance of the font becomes more ragged. However, a stroked font can be enlarged with good results. The vectors that define the stroked font create a good image whether the character is large or small.

The Borland C++ BGI package has an 8 x 8 bit-mapped font built in. The bit-mapped font is always available when you use the graphics functions. Each of the stroked fonts is kept in a separate file with a file extension of CHR.

When you create a graphics program, you can leave the stroked fonts on disk or link them into your executable file. If you leave the fonts on the disk, memory will be allocated, and the fonts will be loaded at run time. The BGIOBJ utility can convert the font files into OBJ files that can be linked into your program. Linking the fonts can be useful when you are creating software to be distributed to other people. Making the fonts part of your program will result in easier installations and less chance for users to erase the font files accidentally. The price you pay for linking in the font files is that EXE files will be larger.

Using the Graphics-Mode Text Functions

Borland C++ has several functions that enable you to control the size and appearance of the BGI fonts. Listing 8.7 shows how some of these graphics-mode text-output functions can be used.

Listing 8.7. `showtext.c`. *A program that uses the BGI text functions.*

```
1   /* SHOWTEXT.C    This program demonstrates the use of
2                    the BGI fonts. */
3
4   #include <graphics.h>
5   #include <stdlib.h>
6   #include <stdio.h>
7   #include <conio.h>
8
9   main()
10  {
11     int graph_drvr = VGA;
12     int graph_mode = VGAHI;
13     char test_str[] = "This is a test. This is only a test!";
14
15     initgraph( &graph_drvr, &graph_mode, "\\tc\\bgi" );
16
17     settextstyle( 4, 0, 0 );
18     outtext( test_str );
19
20
21     settextstyle( 2, 1, 0 );
22     outtextxy( 600, 200, test_str );
23
```

Listing 8.7. continues

Listing 8.7. continued

```
24      setusercharsize( 1, 1, 2, 1 );
25      settextstyle( 3, 0, 0 );
26      moveto( 320, 240 );
27      settextjustify( 1, 1 );
28      outtext( test_str );
29
30      while( !kbhit() );
31
32      closegraph();
33      return 0;
34  }
```

Before you can use any of the BGI text-output functions, you must be in graphics mode. In listing 8.7, the `initgraph()` function in line 15 initializes graphics mode. Notice that the arguments passed to `initgraph()` cause the graphics mode to be set to high-resolution VGA mode.

Lines 17 and 18 call the `settextstyle()` and `outtext()` functions. `outtext()` displays text at the current position. The style, size, and direction of the displayed text is determined by the `settextstyle()` function. `settextstyle()` specifies which font will be used, which direction the characters will be printed, and what size the characters will be. The `settextstyle()` function has this format:

```
settextstyle( int font, int direction, int charsize );
```

The `font` argument, which can use symbolic constants or integer values, indicates which of the BGI fonts will be used. The possible `font` arguments are shown in table 8.11.

Table 8.11. The `font` arguments.

Font Name	Integer Value	Description
DEFAULT_FONT	0	Default 8 x 8 bit-mapped font
TRIPLEX_FONT	1	Triplex font (stroked)
SMALL_FONT	2	Small font (stroked)
SANS_SERIF_FONT	3	Sans-serif font (stroked)
GOTHIC_FONT	4	Gothic font (stroked)

The *direction* argument to the settextstyle() function specifies which direction the text will be output. The text can be printed from left to right or from bottom to top. The values used for the *direction* argument are listed in table 8.12.

Table 8.12. *The direction arguments.*

Direction Name	Integer Value	Description
HORIZ_DIR	0	Text is output from left to right.
VERT_DIR	1	Text is output from bottom to top.

The *charsize* argument for settextstyle() specifies the scaling factor for the displayed fonts. For example, if *charsize* equals 1, the 8 x 8 bit-mapped font is displayed in a block that is 8 pixels by 8 pixels. If *charsize* is equal to 3, the bit-mapped 8 x 8 font is displayed in an area that is 24 x 24 pixels. The *charsize* argument can scale fonts up to 10 times their normal size.

If *charsize* is set to 0, the stroked fonts can be scaled with the setusercharsize() function. setusercharsize() requires four arguments. The first two arguments specify the amount by which the width of the stroked characters will be changed. The second two arguments specify the scaling factor that is used for the vertical scaling of the BGI fonts.

The format of the arguments passed to setusercharsize() looks like this:

```
setusercharsize( int multx, int divx, int multy, in divy );
```

If *multx* is 2 and *divx* is 1, the font characters will be twice as wide. If *multy* is 1 and *divy* is 1, the height of the characters will be only half the default size.

The outtext() function, found in line 18 of listing 8.7, prints the string pointed to in the argument list. outtext() starts printing the string at the current screen position.

In line 22, the outtextxy() function starts printing at the location specified in the parameters to the function. Like outtext(), outtextxy() prints the string pointed to in the argument list.

With the settextjustify() function, you can center your text or justify it on the right or left side. With settextjustify(), you can also justify text displayed vertically. In listing 8.7, settextjustify() is called in line 27.

Three other functions enable you to check the parameters of the video mode. The `gettextsetting()` function lets you check the overall graphics-mode parameters. The information gathered by `gettextsetting()` is stored in a structure of `textsettingstype()`. The `textheight()` and `textwidth()` functions return a value that indicates how high and how wide (in pixels) a string of characters will be.

Exercises

The following exercises give you practice in controlling your monitor's display colors, using text windows, and using video graphics drawing functions.

1. Write a program that displays a message in as many different text modes as your monitor supports.

2. Change listing 8.1 so that the blink-enable bit is turned on at least once every time the background color changes.

3. Write a program that displays the contents of a disk file in a window.

4. Write a program that sends the graphics output to a video page that is not being displayed. Once several objects are drawn, display that video page.

5. Write a program that uses the `line...()` functions and input from the cursor keys to create simple line drawings.

6. Write a program that displays a bar chart with legends you create with the `outtext()` and `outtextxy()` functions.

Summary

In this chapter, you learned how to use Borland C++'s text and graphics video display functions. Specifically, you learned the following important points:

❏ *The PC uses a video adapter and a screen to display information.* The video adapter takes the output of your program and generates a signal that causes an appropriate image to be displayed on the screen.

❏ *Borland C++ supports several different video adapters.* Some of the most popular are the CGA, EGA, VGA, and Hercules adapters.

❏ *Two basic types of display modes are available: text mode and graphics mode.* Text mode displays only character data, whereas graphics mode displays any type of image you create. Each of these modes can be divided into several other modes, based on resolution and the number of colors used.

❏ *You can set six different text modes with Borland C++.* The mode you select determines how many characters will be displayed and whether the display will be in color.

❏ *When you are in text mode, each character has its own attribute byte.* This byte determines the foreground and background color for each character displayed. Functions are available for changing the foreground and background colors.

❏ *The* `directvideo` *variable holds a value that indicates whether console output functions write directly to video RAM (which is quite fast) or use BIOS calls to display data.*

❏ *You use the* `window()` *function to create a rectangular area on the screen where all console output will be sent.* The `window()` function requires arguments that indicate the upper-left and lower-right corners of the new window. The `gettextinfo()` function gets the status information for the current text window. `gettext()` and `puttext()` store and retrieve the text information displayed in a window.

❏ *A pixel is a single dot on the screen.* Each pixel has a memory location associated with it. The memory location holds a value that is an offset into a palette table. The palette contains the actual color values of all the colors that can be displayed in the current video mode.

❏ *When you want to enter graphics mode, you use the* `initgraph()` *function.* `initgraph()` needs arguments that specify the type of graphics driver to load, the graphics mode that will be used, and the path to the graphics drivers. `initgraph()` can be called so that it automatically detects the highest-resolution graphics mode that can be used. When you are through with graphics-mode processing, you call the `closegraph()` function to shut down graphics mode.

❏ *There are two basic families of drawing functions: those that draw unfilled objects and those that draw filled objects.* The BGI library includes functions that draw a variety of objects, such as circles, rectangles, ellipses, and 3-D bars.

❑ *A viewport is a rectangular area on the screen to which the output of the graphics functions is limited.* You use the `setviewport()` function to create a viewport. You can tell `setviewport()` how large to make the viewport and where it will be located on the screen.

❑ *Some video adapters support multiple video pages.* A video page is an area of memory large enough to hold an entire graphics screen. You can control which video page will receive the graphics function's output and which video page will be displayed.

❑ *The BGI fonts are collections of characters that can be displayed in graphics mode.* A character in a bit-mapped font is stored as a rectangular grid of bits. The shape of a bit-mapped character is determined by which bits are turned on and off in the grid. A character in a stroked font is stored as a series of vectors that are used to draw the font. You get better results with an enlarged stroked font than with an enlarged bit-mapped font.

Using Turbo Debugger and Turbo Profiler

When you want to produce fast, error-free code, you need to use Turbo Debugger and Turbo Profiler. Turbo Debugger is a stand-alone debugging utility that comes in Borland C++. This utility gives you all the features of the integrated debugger, plus many more. Turbo Profiler is a new utility program that many programmers have never been able to use before. With Turbo Profiler, you can easily analyze the performance of your program. Turbo Profiler provides statistics on what was executed, how often it was called, and how long it took to execute. You have all the data necessary for deciding how to modify your program for increased performance.

Because Turbo Debugger and Turbo Profiler are part of the Turbo family of programming tools, the two utilities are easy to use. Both Turbo Debugger and Turbo Profiler have the same type of interface as Borland C++, so you can start making productive use of them right away.

This chapter shows you how to set up and use Turbo Debugger and Turbo Profiler. You learn how to set up your program so that it will be compiled with the information needed for debugging and profiling. You learn also how to start and use Turbo Debugger and Turbo Profiler, as well as how to find errors and bottlenecks in your program.

Keep in mind that this chapter is only an introduction to Turbo Debugger and Turbo Profiler. The chapter is designed to give you a working knowledge of the most popular features of these utilities.

Setting Up for Debugging

Unlike previous debuggers, Turbo Debugger can be an integral part of your development system. In the past, debuggers were completely separated from the editor and compiler, and consequently, it was harder to start and use the debuggers. Even though Turbo Debugger is a stand-alone unit, it can easily be called from the Integrated Development Environment (IDE).

The first part of this section explains bugs and debugging programs. The second part of the section shows you how to set up your program and Turbo Debugger so that it can be executed from within the IDE.

Understanding Bugs and Debuggers

Bugs are simply malfunctions in your program. These malfunctions can manifest themselves in a number of different ways. A bug that is a *data error* can result in your program's producing the wrong answers. Data errors can occur when you read the wrong data, read data incorrectly, or lose track of your place in a large data structure. Note the following common data error:

```
scanf( "%d", i );   /* This statement does not work right */
```

This scanf( ) function call contains an error that is easy to make but hard to see. When you use the scanf( ) function, remember that you have to supply the address of where the input data is to be stored. To tell scanf( ) the address of a variable with one of the basic data types, you have to precede the variable name with the & symbol. It can be hard to miss an address-of operator error because you know that the scanf( ) function needs the operator and you tend to assume that the operator has been included.

Other bugs are *logic errors*, which are flaws in the program design. A logic error can occur when the program tries to handle something it was never programmed for or when you make a simple typo. Take a look at the following example:

```
int i;
int j = 0;
...
for( i = 0; j = 10; i++ )   /*This loop will never end*/
  printf( "i = %d\n", i );
```

In this code fragment, a logic error is in the for( ) loop. If you look closely, you will notice that the controlling expression for the loop is the expression j = 10, not the correct expression i = 10. The logic error in the for( ) loop will cause it to run forever, or at least until you reboot your computer.

Here are some common errors that programmers make:

❏ *Incorrect use of C operators and punctuators.* Using the assignment operator (=) when you intend to use the equality operator (==) can dramatically change program execution. Another easy mistake is to put a semicolon in the wrong place.

❏ *Untidy errors.* The advice "When you are through with something, put it away!" applies to programming too. For example, if you start allocating memory and you don't free any of the allocated blocks, you can easily run out of memory space.

❏ *Side-effect errors.* It is possible for a function or macro to change the value of data or pointers in your program without your knowledge.

❏ *Unnoticed changes to global variables.* Before a function changes the value of a global variable, make sure that the changed value will not cause problems in the rest of the program.

❏ *Autovariable errors.* Automatic variables are created each time a function is called. An automatic variable ceases to exist when the function ends. Therefore, returning a pointer to an autovariable can cause bizarre results. Reusing a variable name can cause problems if the name is reused in the wrong location.

❏ *Use of integers of different sizes.* Be careful when you assign values to integers of different sizes. For example, you can assign the value of a long int to a short int. However, because the value of the long int is truncated to fit in the short int, the two integer values will not be equal.

❏ *Loop counter errors.* When you create a for( ) loop, use the correct controlling condition expression. For example, the loop

```
for( i = 0; i < 10; i++ )
```

counts from 0 to 9. But the loop

```
for( i = 0; i <= 10; i++ )
```

counts from 0 to 10. The first loop makes 10 passes, and the second loop makes 11.

❑ *Operator precedence.* Remember that C operators are acted on in a definite order. Keep a chart of operator precedence handy when you are writing an expression that uses several operators.

Until recently, finding bugs in programs was difficult. It involved the tedious process of digging through listings and adding extra code to the program to dump the values of variables and to map the flow of program execution. Debugging was a long and involved process.

Now, with a new animated debugger like Turbo Debugger, finding errors in programs is much easier. Turbo Debugger lets you watch your program as it runs. No longer do you have to add reams of `printf()` statements to see what is happening inside the program. Next, you learn the main features of Turbo Debugger and how to compile your program for debugging.

Preparing To Run Turbo Debugger from the IDE

When you get Borland C++, you actually get two debugging utilities. The first utility is the debugger that is part of the Integrated Development Environment. The integrated debugger is handy for basic debugging tasks. The second utility is Turbo Debugger. Turbo Debugger is a stand-alone program, which means that it is a completely separate program from the Integrated Development Environment. The extra features in Turbo Debugger help you track down errors more easily than with the integrated debugger.

Note the following features that make Turbo Debugger powerful:

❑ *Tracing.* Tracing enables you to execute your program one line at a time and thus see the effect of every statement in your program. Animated tracing and stepping are special tracing modes.

❑ *Stepping.* With this feature, you can trace your program one line at a time, without having to trace into called functions.

❑ *Back tracing.* One of the most powerful features of Turbo Debugger, back tracing allows you to execute your program in reverse. By tracing backward, you can *easily* check code that is questionable.

❑ *Animated tracing.* This feature enables you to run your program in slow motion. You can see what statements are executed and how the data changes.

❏ *Viewing.* Viewing gives you a new perspective on your program. You use windows to view almost any part of your program, including the source code, data, stack, and CPU.

❏ *Inspecting.* Inspecting gives you detailed information on your data, even complex data structures.

❏ *Watching.* Watching lets you track the values stored in the variables during the execution of your program.

❏ *Changing.* With Turbo Debugger, you can change the value of a variable while the program is running.

Although Turbo Debugger provides many features, it will not let you edit or recompile your program when you find a program bug. When you find a bug, you must switch back to the IDE to correct the problem and recompile your program.

Not every program can be debugged. Only those programs compiled with the right options can be examined by Turbo Debugger. To work correctly, Turbo Debugger requires that extra information be included in your program's executable file. All you need to do is set an option to have the debugging information included in your program. You first select Options from the IDE menu and then select the Debugger command. When the Debugger dialog box appears, you choose the Standalone radio button from the Source Debugging options (see fig. 9.1). From now on, any program you compile will contain the information necessary for Turbo Debugger to work.

Using Turbo Debugger

This section gets you started in using Turbo Debugger to examine your program. The first part of the section shows you how to load and execute a program under Turbo Debugger. The second part of the section explains how to change the data your program uses.

Running a Program with Turbo Debugger

Because Turbo Debugger is a stand-alone program, it must be started separately from Borland C++. In other words, Turbo Debugger is not automatically loaded when Borland C++ is loaded.

Fig. 9.1. *The IDE Standalone debugging option.*

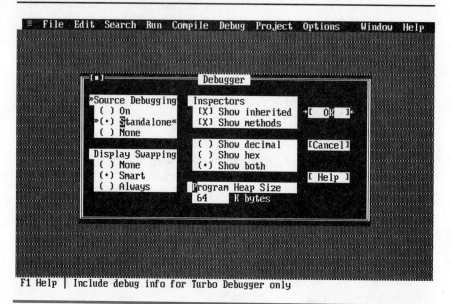

You can start Turbo Debugger in two ways. The first way is to type **td** at the DOS command prompt. Once Turbo Debugger is up, you can load your program and start looking for bugs. However, if you find a bug, you will have to get out of Turbo Debugger, start Borland C++, and fix the problem. The second, somewhat easier, way to start Turbo Debugger is from inside Borland C++. If you select the ∫ symbol, you will see a menu selection to start Turbo Debugger. Figure 9.2 shows the Borland C++ menu that starts Turbo Debugger.

The primary advantage of starting Turbo Debugger from inside Borland C++ is the ease with which you can modify your program when you find a bug. When you are using Turbo Debugger and you find a bug in your program, you still have to get out of Turbo Debugger to fix the problem. But because Turbo Debugger was started from within Borland C++, exiting Turbo Debugger puts you right back in the Borland C++ IDE. As soon as you get out of Turbo Debugger, you are ready to modify and recompile your program.

Once you have started Turbo Debugger, you need the file you want to debug. Loading a file is easy. All you do is use the **File** command to find and load the file. Because the environment of Turbo Debugger is similar to the IDE, loading files in Turbo Debugger is just like loading files in Borland C++.

Fig. 9.2. *Starting Turbo Debugger.*

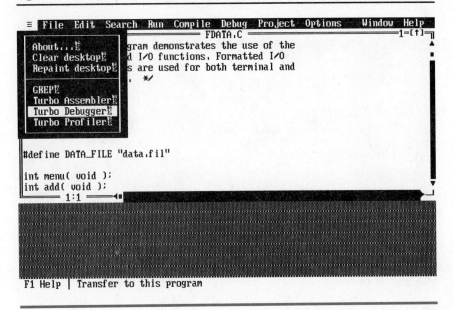

When you choose the **R**un command from the Turbo Debugger's main menu, a pull-down menu appears, indicating a number of ways in which you can run your program. Using the options from the **R**un menu, you can execute your program as slow as one line at a time or as fast as full speed. Figure 9.3 shows the choices from the **R**un menu.

The rest of this section examines the different ways in which you can run your programs under Turbo Debugger. All the menu commands described are found on the **R**un menu in Turbo Debugger. The examples provided use the fdata.c program from Chapter 6.

The **R**un command executes your program at full speed. You are put back in Turbo Debugger only when the program terminates, when a breakpoint is encountered, or when you press Ctrl-Break. A *breakpoint* is an indicator that you can put in the program with Turbo Debugger. The purpose of a breakpoint is to stop program execution so that you can see what is happening.

You do not have to select the **R**un menu from the Turbo Debugger menu bar each time you want to execute the **R**un command or any other tracing command. Instead of bringing up the menu each time, you can use the shortcut keys listed to the right of each command in the pull-down menu. For example, the shortcut key for the **R**un command is F9, and the shortcut key for the **T**race into command is F7.

Fig. 9.3. The Run menu in Turbo Debugger.

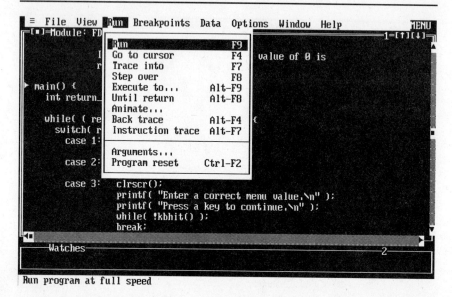

The **Go** to cursor command executes your program at full speed up to the point in the program where the Debugger's cursor is placed. This command is useful when you are checking a program and are interested only in what happens after a certain point in the program.

The **Trace into** command is perhaps the most important command in Turbo Debugger. Using **Trace into**, you can execute one statement at a time. When this command encounters a function call, Turbo Debugger traces program flow into the called function.

Now start Turbo Debugger and load `fdata.exe`. Notice that the cursor is automatically placed on the first *executable* line in the program. As you learned in an earlier chapter, the first executable statement in a C program is the call to the `main()` function. All the comments, macros, and variable declarations before `main()` are not executable statements because these instructions are handled during the compile and link process.

Once you have `fdata.exe` loaded, press F7 to choose the **Trace into** command. When you press F7, the **Trace into** command executes the program up to the `while()` statement at the beginning of `main()`. The `while()` statement controls the execution of the `menu()` function for the `fdata` program. Therefore, when you press F7 again, the cursor moves to the `menu()` function. Continue pressing F7.

Notice that the screen flickers whenever a `printf()` call is encountered. The screen flickers because Turbo Debugger is actually switching screens and displaying the data in the `printf()` call. Displaying this data takes so little time that all you see is the screen flickering.

If you continue to press F7, you are eventually switched to the user screen when the program requests input. This screen is one of the nice features of Turbo Debugger: you can interact with your program while you are debugging it.

When the user screen is brought up and you are prompted for a response, enter the number **0**. This response tells the program that you want to quit. Because there is no need to execute the rest of the program's instructions, press Ctrl-F2. This key combination causes Turbo Debugger to reset the program. The next time you execute any of Turbo Debugger's tracing commands, tracing will start at the beginning of the program.

The **S**tep over command works like the **T**race into command. The only difference is that Step over does not trace into a called function. When Step over encounters a function call, the function is executed at full speed, but Step over does not display the statements in the function.

After you press Ctrl-F2 to reset the `fdata` program, use F8 to step through the program again. This time, you do not see the statements in the `menu()` as they are executed. The only part of the `menu()` function that you see is the user screen prompting you for a menu selection. Enter **0** for the menu selection and continue using Step over to trace through the program until it ends.

The **E**xecute to command runs the program at full speed until the specified address is reached. When you choose Execute to, you are prompted for an address. The address tells Turbo Debugger where to stop program execution. Be aware that it is possible for the Execute to command to execute the whole program and never encounter the address you specified.

Using `fdata.exe`, choose the Execute to command. Enter `menu` when you are prompted for an address for the Execute to command. Once you enter the address, the program runs at full speed until the `menu()` function is encountered.

The **U**ntil return command runs the program at full speed until the function in which you are currently located returns to its caller. This command is handy when you have traced down into a function accidentally.

The **A**nimate command runs the program in slow motion. Selecting Animate is like continually pressing F8 (**T**race into) except that selecting Animate is easier. When you choose the Animate command, you are prompted for the time delay between the execution of each statement. The default value is 3/10 of a second. You can stop the Animate trace at any time by pressing a key on your keyboard.

Back trace is another useful command. It allows you to run your program in reverse. Tracing backward through your program enables you to unravel complicated statements. If you don't know why a statement acts a certain way, you can back up and execute the statement again and again, until you can understand what is happening.

Of course, because a feature like **B**ack trace requires a lot of memory, you are limited in how far back you can trace. If you do not have any EMS memory available, you will be able to trace back only about 400 instructions. If you do have EMS memory available, you will be able to trace back about 3000 instructions.

The **I**nstruction trace command lets you trace one machine instruction at a time. You use this command to trace into machine interrupts and modules that were not compiled with debugging information.

In the **R**un menu, an **A**rguments command is also available. **A**rguments lets you pass command-line arguments to the program you are debugging.

Viewing Data

Tracing through your program is just one of the many features Turbo Debugger offers. Another major feature of Turbo Debugger is its capability to examine all the information associated with your program. You use the **V**iew command to select what type of information you want to examine (see fig. 9.4). Selecting one of the options from the **V**iew menu creates a window that displays all the information for the option you chose. This section examines each of the information windows you can choose under the **V**iew command.

The **B**reakpoints command opens a window in which you can examine the breakpoints you have set. As noted before, a *breakpoint* tells Turbo Debugger to stop the execution of the program so that you can check the program's status.

The Breakpoints window is composed of two panes. The left pane lists all the breakpoints in your program and lets you select a breakpoint to examine. You select one of the breakpoints by using the arrow keys or the mouse. The right pane tells you about the currently selected breakpoint.

While you are in the Breakpoints window, you can pop up another window that lets you add, delete, or modify breakpoints. You pop up the other window by clicking the right mouse button or pressing Alt-F10. Breakpoints are covered in more detail later in this chapter.

The **S**tack command produces a window that displays the current contents of the stack. The last function that was called appears on the top of the stack list. Pressing the right mouse button while the Stack window is current pops up yet another menu window. This menu window enables you to view either the source code for the currently selected function or the variables local to the function. If you don't have a mouse, you can look at the function's source code by pressing Ctrl-I, or look at the function's variable data by pressing Ctrl-L.

Fig. 9.4. The View menu.

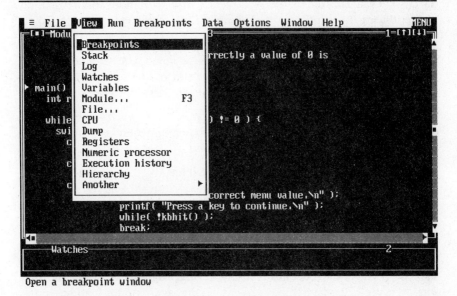

The **Log** command presents a window that shows you the current contents of the log file, which is a list of significant occurrences in your program. Note the following occurrences that trigger an entry to be made in the log file:

❏ A breakpoint is encountered that logs the value of an expression.

❏ You use the **Add** comment option to store a comment in the log file.

❏ You store the contents of a window in the log with the **Dump** pane to log command from the **Window** menu.

The Log window can contain up to 50 lines of information. If you need to record more information, you can write the contents of the log file to disk. To create a disk-based log file, you need to pop up the Log window's local menu. You get that menu either by pressing the right mouse button while you are viewing the Log window, or by pressing Alt-F10.

The Log window's local menu lets you open the log file, close the file, enable or disable logging, add comments, or erase the log. One nice feature of the disk-based log file is that when it is opened, all the messages in the log window are written to disk. This convenient feature lets you create the disk-based log file after the comment that you want to record has been added to the log file.

When you press the Watches command, a window is displayed that shows the current values of the variables you select. You learn more about watching and modifying the values of variables later in this chapter.

The **Variables** command presents a window that shows you all the variables in scope at the current location in the program. The Variables window has two panes. The upper pane displays the value of the global variables. The lower pane shows the values of variables that are local to the current function.

With the **Module** command, you get a window in which you can display the source code for the program you want to debug. When you open a file to debug, the Module window is created for you.

The **File** command opens a window that lets you examine the contents of any file on disk. Once the File window has been opened, you can pop up the local menu by either pressing Alt-F10 or clicking the right mouse button. The local menu presents options for displaying the file in hexadecimal or ASCII format, searching for a string, editing the file, or going to a specific file offset.

The **CPU** command displays a window that shows everything you ever wanted to know about the state of the CPU during program execution. The CPU window is useful for debugging in assembly language, working with programs without debugging information, or finding the most elusive bugs. The CPU window shows the disassembled machine-language instructions, the data from the data segment, and the values in the registers and flags.

When you select the **Dump** command, a window is displayed in which you can examine the contents of a block of memory. With the Dump window, you can look at data in memory in almost any format you want. Some of the formats in which you can display data are byte, word, double words, and floating point.

The **Registers** command presents a window that displays the contents of the CPU's registers and flags. This window is useful when you want to know what is in the registers, but you don't need to see the rest of the CPU window.

If you have a math coprocessor installed, you can use the **Numeric processor** command to display a window in which you can check the operation of the coprocessor.

The Execution history command displays a window that shows you a history of the program instructions which have been executed. This window displays the executed instructions as disassembled machine code. If you pop up the local menu by pressing Alt-F10 or the right mouse button, you can execute the program in reverse. Running the program in reverse enables you to execute a piece of code until you are satisfied that you know how the code works.

The Hierarchy command shows a window you can use for C++ programming. This window displays a tree diagram of the objects or classes in the current module.

Finally, the Another command lets you open an extra dump, file, or module window. In certain instances, Turbo Debugger will automatically open one of these extra windows in response to certain commands you enter.

Using Advanced Debugging Features

Turbo Debugger has two advanced features, changing program values and setting breakpoints, that make your debugging sessions easier and more productive. Turbo Debugger lets you change the values of variables in your program while the program is being debugged. By changing values, you can try various fixes and see their effects immediately. By setting breakpoints, you can stop program execution and examine the status of the program more closely. You can set a breakpoint that stops program execution whenever the breakpoint is encountered or only when a specific value is reached. This section shows you how to start using these two advanced Turbo Debugger features.

Changing Program Values

With the Turbo Debugger's Data menu, you can inspect, evaluate, and modify data in your program. The inspect feature lets you take a close look at the value of a variable or an expression. This feature is especially useful for examining data structures. With the evaluate feature, you can enter an expression and have it evaluated in the same way that the compiler evaluates it. The modify feature lets you enter into your program a new value for an expression.

When you select **I**nspect from the **D**ata menu, an inspector window appears. You use this window to choose and view the expression you want to inspect. If you select a variable or an expression, the variable or expression is automatically displayed in the Inspector window when it is opened. You can choose a variable or an expression with either the cursor keys or the mouse.

Using the evaluate and modify features, you can change the value of an expression or a variable while your program is running in the debugger. When you choose **E**valuate/modify from the **D**ata menu, the Evaluate/modify dialog box appears, containing three fields (see fig. 9.5).

Fig. 9.5. *The Evaluate/modify dialog box.*

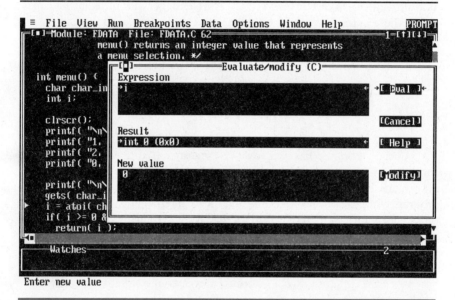

The first field in the Evaluate/modify dialog box is an Expression field. In this field, you enter the variable or expression you want to evaluate. If a variable or an expression is already selected by the cursor when the Evaluate/modify dialog box is opened, that variable or expression appears in the Expression field of the dialog box.

The second field in the Evaluate/modify dialog box is the Result field, which displays the result of the expression in the Expression field.

The third field in the Evaluate/modify dialog box is the New value field. In this field, you enter a new value for the expression in the Expression field.

When you choose the **Modify** button at the right edge of the Evaluate/modify dialog box, the value you entered in the Modify field is placed in your program.

You use the **Watch** command on the **Data** menu to enter an expression that you want to watch while the program is running. The expression you enter is displayed in the Watches window as your program runs.

When you are tracing through a function that is about to return to its caller, you can inspect the return value by choosing the **Function return** command on the **Data** menu.

Setting Breakpoints

You learned earlier that the term *breakpoint* refers to the feature which stops the execution of your program during debugging. Although a breakpoint can simply stop the execution of your program, the breakpoint feature can actually be a great deal more versatile.

To understand the way a particular breakpoint works, note the following three pieces of information:

❑ *Where the breakpoint is located in your program.*

❑ *The triggering condition of the breakpoint.* A breakpoint can be triggered when the breakpoint location is encountered, when an expression evaluates as true, when the value of a data object changes, or when a pass count reaches a predetermined value.

❑ *The status of program execution after a breakpoint is reached.* When a breakpoint is encountered, the program can either stop or continue. If program execution stops, you can examine any part of the program you want. If program execution is allowed to continue, you can specify that the value of an expression be logged or that an expression you supply be executed.

To set a breakpoint, select the **Breakpoints** command from the main menu. You can select the menu command by pressing either the mouse or Alt-B. Selecting the **Breakpoints** command pops up a menu that offers breakpoint options.

The **Toggle** option toggles a breakpoint on and off at the current address in the program module. You can also toggle a breakpoint in the CPU window.

The **At** option lets you set a breakpoint at a specific address in the program. Selecting the **At** option also pops up a Breakpoint options dialog box in which you can set all the breakpoint options (see fig. 9.6).

Fig. 9.6. *The Breakpoint options dialog box.*

The Action radio buttons in the Breakpoint options dialog box determine what happens when a breakpoint is encountered. **Break** causes program execution to stop when a breakpoint is encountered. **Execute** causes the Action expression to be executed when a breakpoint is encountered. **Log** logs the value of an expression to the log file.

The Condition radio buttons determine when a breakpoint will be executed. **Always** causes a breakpoint to be executed every time it is encountered during execution. When Always is selected, you do not have to specify any conditions that will trigger the breakpoint. **Changed memory** tells the debugger to break execution when a data value that you specify changes. The **Expression true** button causes a breakpoint to be triggered only when the supplied expression is true. Finally, **Hardware** is used only with a hardware debugger.

Selecting the **Changed memory**, **Expression true**, or **Hardware** button from the Condition field in the Breakpoints dialog box serves the same purpose as selecting the Changed memory, Expression true, or Hardware options from the **Breakpoints** main menu.

The **Delete all** command on the **Breakpoints** menu clears all breakpoints that are currently set.

Using Turbo Profiler

Using Turbo Profiler should become a new step in your program development cycle. After you have written and debugged your program, you can use Turbo Profiler to analyze your program's efficiency. This utility can show you exactly where your program's time goes, such as the number of times a statement is executed and the amount of time spent executing the statement. By using this information, you can judge the statement's relative efficiency.

This section introduces you to profiling and shows you how to start analyzing your programs. The first part of the section explains the concept of profiling. The second and third parts show you how to set up and profile a program.

Knowing What Profiling Is

Profiling is the statistical analysis of the performance of code in your program. A profiler runs your program and records information indicating which statements are used, how often a statement is executed, and how long each statement takes to execute.

Optimizing and profiling are different processes. The Borland C++ compiler has options you can set that cause your program to be optimized when it is compiled. The optimizing process simply replaces time-consuming function calls with function calls that take less time. The profiling process analyzes your program so that you can change its basic structure and thus make the program more efficient. Figure 9.7 shows the three steps in the profiling process.

You will probably go through the three profiling steps several times as you are fine-tuning your program. After you make one change in the program, you will likely find another area that can be made more efficient. You can repeat these three steps until you are satisfied with the performance of your program.

The first step in the profiling process is to run your program under the profiler's control. Turbo Profiler executes your program and collects information on how the program spends its time and what parts of the program are used.

When Turbo Profiler finishes running your program, the profiler generates data about the performance of the program. Included in this report is information on how many times a statement was executed, how long the statement took, and the overall percentage of processing time devoted to each statement.

Fig. 9.7. The steps in the profiling process.

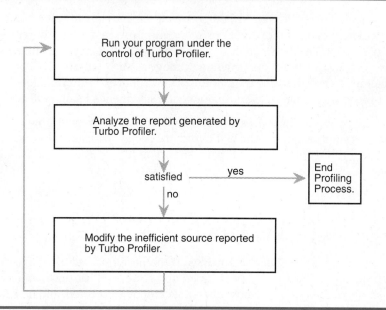

The second step in the profiling process is to analyze Turbo Profiler's report. The report can show you where time is being spent in calling functions or calculating values, which parts of your program are executed, and how often they are used. With a little thought and research, you can learn a great deal about how your program really works.

Once you determine where your program is spending too much time, the third step is to rewrite your source code so that the time-consuming routines will be more efficient. Depending on how your program is spending its time, the task of rewriting your source code can be either simple or complex. At times, you may just need to replace one group of statements with another more efficient group to enhance performance. At other times, you may need to restructure your source code and possibly change the algorithms you use.

The changes you make to your source code can easily be analyzed. All you have to do is recompile and reprofile the program to see whether performance was improved by your changes.

Starting Turbo Profiler

Using Turbo Profiler is a straightforward process, but you need to perform some tasks before you start profiling. First, to get the most useful information from Turbo Profiler, you may need to rearrange the code in your program. Second, to use Turbo Profiler at all, you have to compile your program with the standalone debugging option turned on.

Before you begin profiling, it helps to separate sections of code that you already know need work. Separating code into logical sections makes it easier to see and analyze a particular inefficiency. Separating user-input routines is helpful also. Because user-input routines depend on the speed of the user and not the speed of the computer, profiling the user-input routines does little good. You may even want to replace these routines with a premade set of data from a disk file, with an array, or with random data generated by the computer.

It is important that you compile your program with full debugging information turned on. To turn on debugging information, select Options from the Borland C++ main menu, next pick the Debugger menu item, and finally click the Standalone radio button. Turbo Profiler has to have the debugging information so that the statistics for each line of your *source code* can be shown. When you begin profiling your program, make sure that Turbo Profiler has access to both your EXE file and the source code.

You can start Turbo Profiler in two ways. The way you use depends on the amount of RAM available in your computer. As always, you can simply execute Turbo Profiler by typing **tprof** at the DOS prompt. Starting Turbo Profiler from the DOS prompt requires the least amount of memory. The second way to start Turbo Profiler is from within Borland C++. If you have Borland C++, you can go to the ≡ menu program. Once the menu is displayed, you can transfer control to Turbo Profiler. Starting Turbo Profiler from within Borland C++ requires more memory than starting Turbo Profiler from the DOS prompt.

Once you have started Turbo Profiler, go to the File menu and load the program you want to profile (changing directories, if necessary). Notice that the program you profile is the executable version of the program, not the source code. Turbo Profiler displays the source code and statistics after the executable file has been profiled. Figure 9.8 shows what the Turbo Profiler screen looks like when you first load a program.

Fig. 9.8. The Turbo Profiler screen.

```
≡  File  View  Run  Statistics  Print  Options  Window  Help        READY
┌[■]─Module: PTEST1  File: PTEST1.C 8════════════════════════1═[↑][↓]═╖
│   /* PTEST1.C  This program uses the character I/O functions     ▲
│               to demonstrate the use of Turbo Profiler. */       ■
│                                                                  ■
│                                                                  
│    #include <stdio.h>                                            
│    #include <stdlib.h>                                           
│                                                                  
├► main()                                                          
│    {                                                             
│     FILE *file_ptr;                                              ▼
│     char store;                                                  ▼
└◄───────────────────────────────────────────────────────────────►┘
┌──Execution Profile─────────────────────────────────────2────────╖
│ Total time: 0 sec        Display: Time                          
│ % of total: 100%         Filter: All                            
│      Runs: 0 of 1        Sort: Frequency                        
│                                                                 
│                                                                 
│                                                                 
│                                                                 
└─────────────────────────────────────────────────────────────────┘
F1-Help F2-Area F3-Mod F5-Zoom F6-Next F9-Run F10-Menu
```

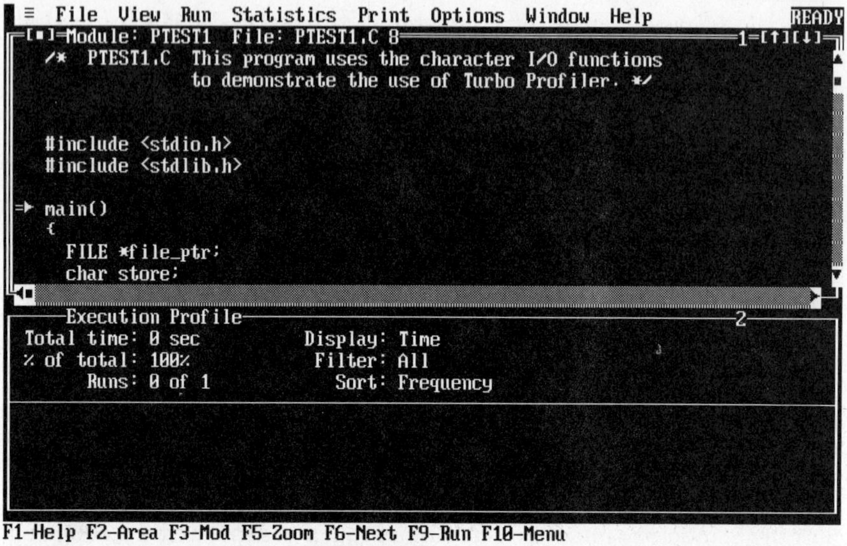

When you load a program, the Turbo Profiler screen is split into two windows. The top window displays the source code for the EXE file you are profiling. In the source code window, the title bar displays some important information about what module is being profiled and the current location in the module. The first name on the source window title bar is the name of the executable module you are profiling. The second name is the name of the source file that contains the code for the executable module. The third item on the title bar is a line-number indicator. This indicator tells you the number of the line where the cursor is located.

The second window on the Turbo Profiler screen is the Execution Profile window. This window displays the report generated by Turbo Profiler, including the statistics for the operation of your program.

Knowing Basic Profiling Information

This section contains a profile of ptest1.c, a short program that displays the contents of a disk file on the screen. Listing 9.1 shows the source code for the ptest1.c program. Note that when you use the ptest1.c program, you need to provide a text.dat file for the program to read.

Listing 9.1. ptest1.c. *The first of two profile test programs.*

```
1   /*   PTEST1.C   This program uses the character I/O functions
2                   to demonstrate the use of Turbo Profiler. */
3
4
5   #include <stdio.h>
6   #include <stdlib.h>
7
8   main()
9   {
10    FILE *file_ptr;
11    char store;
12
13    if( ( file_ptr = fopen( "text.dat", "rt" ) ) == NULL ) {
14      clrscr();
15      printf( "Could not open data file.\n" );
16      printf( "Calling the exit() function.\n" );
17      exit( 0 );
18    }
19
20    clrscr();
21    while( ( store = fgetc( file_ptr ) ) != EOF ){
22      putchar( store );
23    }
24
25    fclose( file_ptr );
26    return 0;
27  }
```

When you load a program that has not been profiled, Turbo Profiler automatically takes care of the following housekeeping tasks for you:

❏ *Scans through your EXE file and locates the main program module.* The source for the main module is loaded.

❏ *Sets the area markers for the program.* Area markers are indicators that tell Turbo Profiler which statements to profile. More information on setting area markers is provided later in the chapter.

❏ *Puts the cursor at the first executable statement in the main program module.* Generally, the first executable statement is the main() function name in the main program module.

Because the `ptest1.exe` program contains only one program module, all that Turbo Profiler has to do is load the `ptest1.c` source code file. Turbo Profiler automatically sets the area markers for every executable line in the program. Setting area markers for all the executable lines indicates that Turbo Profiler will profile each statement in the program. Because the `ptest1` program is short, the default area marker setting works well.

You can tell which statements have been selected with the area markers by looking at the source code window. To the left of each statement is space for a small arrow symbol. If the arrow symbol is present, the area marker is set for the line, and the line will be profiled.

The actual profiling of your program is easy. You simply select the **R**un command from the **R**un menu, and Turbo Profiler does the rest. When you select **R**un and then choose the **R**un command, Turbo Profiler executes your program and starts gathering statistics on the program's operation.

While your program runs, any video output is sent to the user screen. Once the program has completed execution, you are returned to the Turbo Profiler screen. If you want to look at the user screen again, just press Alt-F5 (as in Borland C++). If your program prompts the user for any input, you will be able to enter the necessary information from the keyboard, as you always do. Be aware, however, that waiting for user input can dramatically change the program's statistics. You will see ways to get around this problem later in the chapter.

When Turbo Profiler is through executing your program, the Execution Profile window displays the statistics for the program. Figure 9.9 shows the Turbo Profiler screen after the `ptest1` program is profiled.

The Execution Profile window displays much useful information. The top part of the window displays statistics for the program as a whole. The Total time field indicates how long the program took to execute. The % of total field indicates how much of the program's execution time was spent on the module you are profiling. The Runs field tells you how many times the program was executed. For short programs, you can get better statistics if you run the program several times instead of once.

Also shown in the Execution Profile window is information about display control settings. The Display field tells you what type of statistics the Execution Profile window is displaying. Notice in figure 9.9 that the Display field indicates that statistics on both time and counts are being displayed. The Filter field indicates whether all the statistics are displayed or only a selected group of statistics is displayed. Finally, the Sort field tells you how the statistics are arranged in the Execution Profile window. Later in this chapter, the section "Displaying Profiler Statistics" explains how you can control the profiling statistics that are displayed.

Fig. 9.9. *The Turbo Profiler screen after the* p t e s t 1 *program is profiled.*

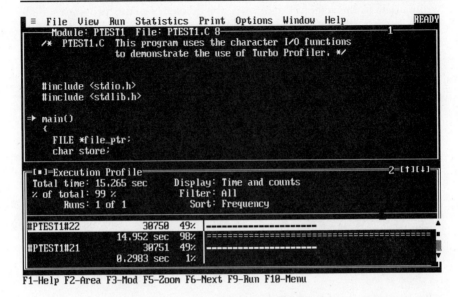

The lower part of the Execution Profile window is what profiling is all about. Displayed here is the statistical information for each line in your program. This information shows you which statements are used most and where the most time is spent.

In figure 9.9, the Execution Profile window displays the time and count data for each line in the program. The time statistics tell you how much of the program's time was spent on each statement. The count statistics tell you how many times each statement was used during program execution. To the right of these statistics, bar graphs give you a quick idea of the relative ranking of each item.

By examining the statistics in figure 9.9, you can see that even though a statement was called many times, that statement may not have taken long to operate. The Execution Profile window indicates that 49% of the instructions executed by the program were made by line 22. (Remember that when an instruction is in a loop, that instruction can be executed many times.) Line 21 accounts for another 49% of the instructions that were executed. However, line 22 took much more of the total execution time than line 21 took. Line 22 used 98% of the program's execution time, whereas line 21 used only 1% or less.

Don't be surprised when you run this program and your execution statistics differ from those statistics listed in the book. The actual values of the statistics depend on the speed of your CPU, the speed of the disk, and the size and type of data files that are used.

If you look at line 22 in listing 9.1, you will see that it is a putchar( ) function. You now know that the ptest1 program is spending 98% of its time writing data to the screen. To improve the efficiency of this program significantly, you would need to change the screen output. The easiest way to do that is to replace character output with string output. Listing 9.2, ptest2.c, shows how ptest1.c was modified.

Listing 9.2. ptest2.c. *The second of two profile test programs.*

```
 1   /*  PTEST2.C   This program is a modification of the  PTEST1.C
 2                  program. This program uses string I/O to
 3                  increase the performance of the program. The
 4                  result can be seen by using Turbo Profiler. */
 5
 6
 7   #include <stdio.h>
 8   #include <stdlib.h>
 9
10   main( )
11   {
12     FILE *file_ptr;
13     char *c_ptr;
14     char store[256];
15
16     if( ( file_ptr = fopen( "text.dat", "rt" ) ) == NULL ) {
17       clrscr( );
18       printf( "Could not open data file.\n" );
19       printf( "Calling the exit( ) function.\n" );
20       exit( 0 );
21     }
22
23     clrscr( );
24     while( c_ptr != NULL ){
25       c_ptr = fgets( store, 256, file_ptr );
26       puts( store );
27     }
28
29     fclose( file_ptr );
30     return 0;
31   }
```

In listing 9.2, the data transfer from the disk file is done one string at a time instead of one character at a time (as with listing 9.1). Running the executable version of listing 9.2 through Turbo Profiler shows how much speed you gain by using string I/O. Figure 9.10 shows the Turbo Profiler screen for the ptest2 program.

Fig. 9.10. The Turbo Profiler screen for the ptest2 program.

```
≡  File  View  Run  Statistics  Print  Options  Window  Help      READY
[■]=Module: PTEST2   File: PTEST2.C 26                      1=[↑][↓]
⇒    clrscr();
⇒    printf( "Could not open data file.\n" );
⇒    printf( "Calling the exit() function.\n" );
⇒    exit( 0 );
     }


⇒    clrscr();
⇒    while( c_ptr != NULL ){
⇒      c_ptr = fgets( store, 256, file_ptr );
⇒      puts( store );
     }

                                                             2
 Execution Profile
 Total time: 10.816 sec    Display: Time and counts
 % of total: 99 %          Filter: All
     Runs: 1 of 1             Sort: Frequency


#PTEST2#26              751   33%  ---------------
                 10.523 sec   97%  ==================================
#PTEST2#25              751   33%  ---------------
                 0.2786 sec    2%  =

F1-Help F2-Area F3-Mod F5-Zoom F6-Next F9-Run F10-Menu
```

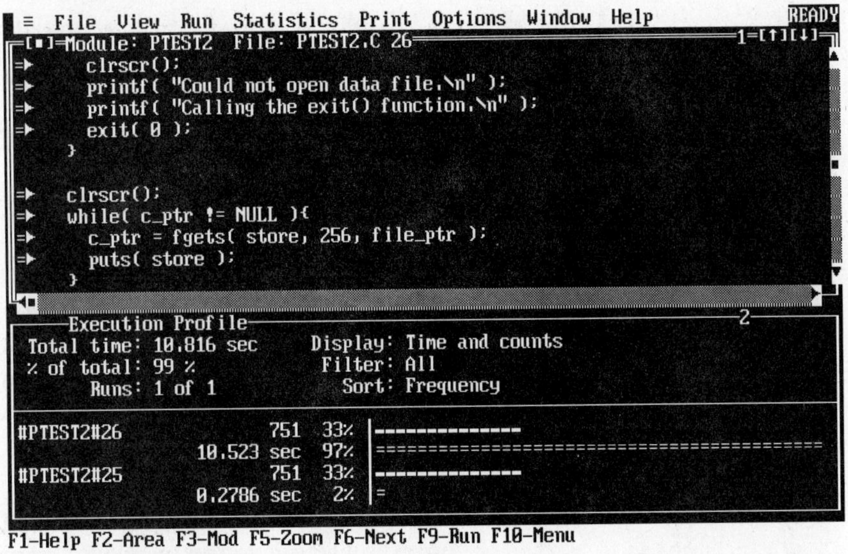

From the Execution Profile statistics shown in figure 9.10, you can see that ptest2.exe still spent 97% of its time in writing data to the screen. However, if you look at the actual time spent displaying information, ptest2.exe is significantly faster than ptest1.exe. Changing from character output to string output increased overall program performance by almost 30%. Notice that character input is almost as fast as string input. The time difference between the character-input statements and the string-input statements is about 2/100 of a second.

Using Advanced Profiling Features

The profiling techniques you saw in the preceding section are fine for small programs. But profiling strategies change as programs get larger. Profiling every line in a large program would take a long time and would probably not tell you what you need to know. When you profile large programs, you need to be able to select exactly what you want to profile and what type of statistics you want to keep.

This section shows you how to use area markers to specify what parts of your program will be profiled. The section shows you also how to organize the information generated by Turbo Profiler.

Selecting Areas To Profile

An area is a part of your program that Turbo Profiler analyzes. An area can be as small as one line or as large as the whole program. In this section, you learn how to set area markers, which tell Turbo Profiler what parts of your program you want analyzed.

When a program loads, Turbo Profiler automatically sets area markers. The type of markers that are set depends on the size of your program. For small programs, like ptest1 or ptest2, Turbo Profiler sets an area marker for every line in the program. For a larger program that may contain several modules, Turbo Profiler sets markers for the program's routines only. (Turbo Profiler uses routines and functions interchangeably.) When area markers are set for all the routines, Turbo Profiler analyzes just the overall performance of each routine, not the performance of each line in the routine. Doing this kind of analysis enables Turbo Profiler to run more quickly.

Turbo Profiler is quite flexible when it comes to selecting an area you want to profile. You can mix and match any combination of single lines, functions, and modules.

To set area markers for individual lines, you can use either the mouse or the F2 key. Selecting area markers with the mouse is quick and easy. You just point to the left of the line where you want the marker set, and then click the left mouse button. Using the F2 key takes a little more work. Before you can set an area marker with F2, you must use the arrow keys to move the cursor to the line where you want the area marker set.

If you want to select a whole area at one time, the **Add** areas menu is more convenient to use. You access the **Add** areas menu through the local menu for the source module window. You bring up this local menu by pressing Alt-F10 or clicking the right mouse button while the mouse cursor is in the source module window. The **Add** areas menu is shown in figure 9.11.

Fig. 9.11. *Selecting area markers with the Add areas menu.*

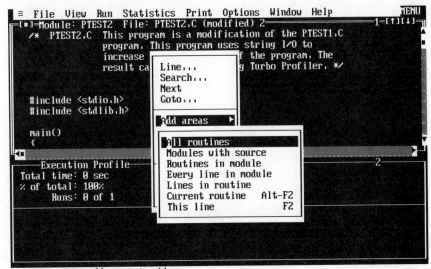

The **All** routines command sets area markers for *all* routines in the program. Even routines for which there is no source code, like library routines, will be analyzed. When you select a routine, Turbo Profiler analyzes the overall performance of the routine. This means that Turbo Profiler keeps track of how many times the routine was called and how long the routine processed, plus other information. When Turbo Profiler is analyzing a routine, the profiler does not keep track of the statistics for each line in the routine.

The **Modules** with source command is similar to the **All** routines command except that only those modules with source code available will be analyzed. The **Modules** with source command causes all the *routines* in the appropriate modules to be analyzed.

With the **Routines** in module command, you can set area markers for the routines in the *current* module only. The current module is the one displayed in the Module window.

Like the preceding command, the **Every line in module** command works just with the current module. This command puts area markers on every executable line in the module displayed in the source window.

The **Lines in routine** command sets area markers for every line in the current routine. The current routine is the routine in which the source window's cursor is located.

The **Current routine** command analyzes the overall performance of the current routine. Turbo Profiler does not analyze each line in the routine.

Finally, the **This line** command sets an area marker for the line where the cursor is located.

Another menu, called **Remove areas**, is also available. This menu looks just like the **Add areas** menu and works similarly except that **Remove areas** lets you *deselect* area markers.

Not only can you select which areas will be profiled, but you also can select what happens when a marked area is encountered. The local menu for the source module window has a selection, **Operation**, that allows you to choose what type of action will be performed when Turbo Profiler gets to an area marker. The **Operation** menu selection pops up a dialog box (shown in fig. 9.12) called the Area options dialog box.

Fig. 9.12. *The Area options dialog box.*

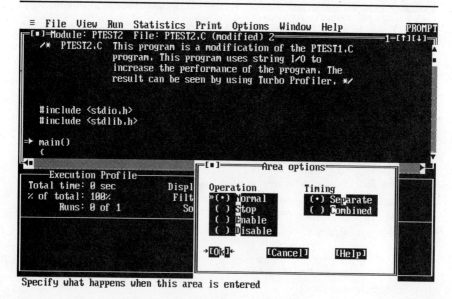

Specify what happens when this area is entered

In the Area options dialog box, four Operation radio buttons are available. You choose one of these buttons to determine what action Turbo Profiler takes when an area marker is encountered.

Normal causes Turbo Profiler to use the default counting procedures. Turbo Profiler gets statistics on execution times and statement counts. Enable turns statistic collection back on if it has been turned off, and Disable turns off statistic collection but lets your program continue to run. After using Disable, you can then use Enable to turn statistic collection back on. Finally, Stop tells Turbo Profiler to stop the execution of your program. When program execution is stopped, you are returned to the Turbo Profiler screen where you can examine the statistics that were collected. After you are through examining the statistics, you can resume program execution.

You use the Timing radio buttons in the Area options dialog box to set the mode for timing statistics. Two buttons, Separate and Combined, are available.

With Separate timing, statistics are collected for each routine individually. If one marked routine calls another marked routine, the execution time of the calling routine does not include the execution time of the called routine.

With Combined timing, the time required for executing both a calling routine and a called routine is reported. The next paragraphs explain how combined times are reported.

If a called routine does not call any other routines, it will have no listing in the Execution Profile window. The only listing will be for the calling routine. The time for the calling routine includes the time required to execute both the calling routine and the called routine.

If a called routine (the middle routine) calls another routine, there will be a listing for the middle routine in the Execution Profile window. However, because Combined timing is on, the time reported for the middle routine may not be what you expect. The time reported for this routine is the time to execute the routine called by the middle routine. The time reported does not include the time required to execute the middle routine.

Displaying Profiler Statistics

There are a number of ways to display the statistics gathered by Turbo Profiler. To choose which information you want displayed, you pop up the local menu for the Execution Profile window. Getting this menu is easy: you either press Alt-F10 when the Execution Profile window is selected, or move the mouse to the lower half of the window and click the right button.

Once the local menu for the Execution Profile window is displayed, you select the **Display** options command. A dialog box then appears (see fig. 9.13).

Fig. 9.13. *The Display options dialog box.*

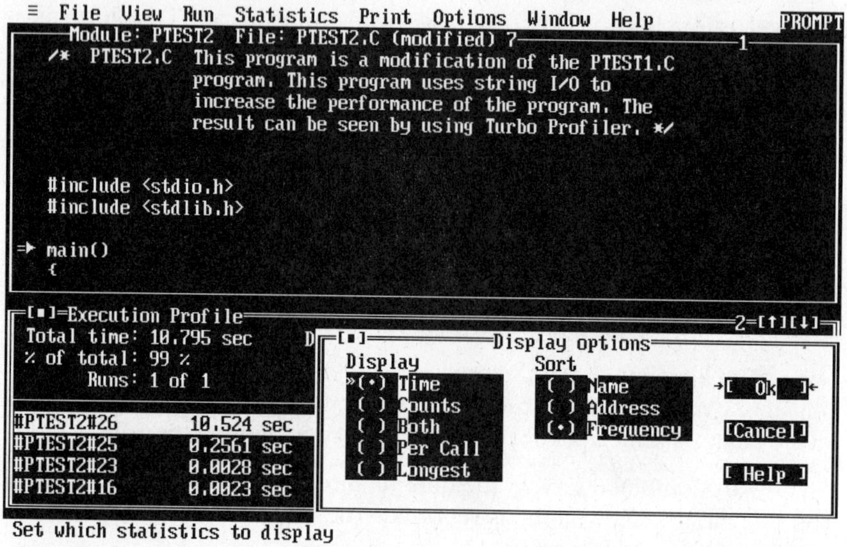

```
 ≡  File  View  Run  Statistics  Print  Options  Window  Help          PROMPT
   ┌─Module: PTEST2  File: PTEST2.C (modified) ?────────────────────1──┐
   │   /*  PTEST2.C  This program is a modification of the PTEST1.C    │
   │               program. This program uses string I/O to           │
   │               increase the performance of the program. The       │
   │               result can be seen by using Turbo Profiler. */      │
   │                                                                   │
   │                                                                   │
   │     #include <stdio.h>                                            │
   │     #include <stdlib.h>                                           │
   │                                                                   │
   │  ⇒ main()                                                         │
   │     {                                                             │
   ├─[■]═Execution Profile══════════════════════════════════2═[↑][↓]══┤
   │ Total time: 10.795 sec   D┌─[■]──────────Display options───────────┐
   │ % of total: 99 %          │ Display         Sort                   │
   │      Runs: 1 of 1         │ »(•) Time        ( ) Name      →[  OK  ]←│
   │                           │  ( ) Counts      ( ) Address           │
   │ #PTEST2#26     10.524 sec │  ( ) Both        (•) Frequency  [Cancel]│
   │ #PTEST2#25     0.2561 sec │  ( ) Per Call                          │
   │ #PTEST2#23     0.0028 sec │  ( ) Longest                   [ Help ] │
   │ #PTEST2#16     0.0023 sec │                                        │
   └───────────────────────────└────────────────────────────────────────┘
    Set which statistics to display
```

The Display options dialog box contains two groups of radio buttons, Display and Sort. You use these buttons to select what profiling information will be displayed and how the information will be arranged.

The Display buttons control what statistics will be displayed. **Time** displays the length of time that program control remained in the specified area. The time displayed is expressed in milliseconds. **Counts** tells you how many times control was passed to the selected area. **Both** lets you display the information from both **Time** and **Counts**. **Per Call** displays the average time that the indicated area had program control. The average time is the **Time** value divided by the **Counts** value. Finally, **Longest** reports the longest time that a particular area had program control.

You use the Sort buttons to select the order in which the statistics are displayed. Options are available for sorting information by area **Name**, **Address** (memory location), and **Frequency**.

The local menu for the Execution Profile window has another menu command, Filter, which lets you add or delete groups of statistics from the Execution Profile report. When you select this command, the Filter menu appears in the Execution Profile window (see fig. 9.14). This menu contains three options.

Fig. 9.14. The Filter menu.

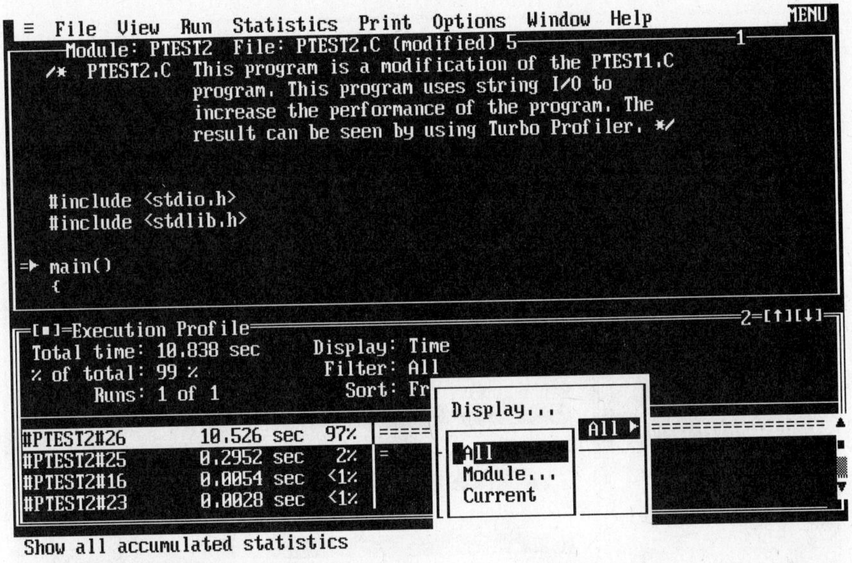

```
  ≡  File  View  Run  Statistics  Print  Options  Window  Help        MENU
  ┌───Module: PTEST2  File: PTEST2.C (modified) 5───────────────1─┐
  │ /*  PTEST2.C  This program is a modification of the PTEST1.C   │
  │          program. This program uses string I/O to             │
  │          increase the performance of the program. The         │
  │          result can be seen by using Turbo Profiler. */        │
  │                                                                │
  │                                                                │
  │   #include <stdio.h>                                           │
  │   #include <stdlib.h>                                          │
  │                                                                │
  │=▶ main()                                                       │
  │   {                                                            │
  └────────────────────────────────────────────────────────────────┘
  ┌─[■]═Execution Profile═══════════════════════════════2═[↑][↓]─┐
  │ Total time: 10.838 sec      Display: Time                     │
  │ % of total: 99 %             Filter: All                      │
  │       Runs: 1 of 1             Sort: Fr┌─Display...──┐         │
  │                                        │          All ▶│ =====▲│
  │ #PTEST2#26      10.526 sec  97% =====  │ ▓All         │       ║│
  │ #PTEST2#25       0.2952 sec  2%   =    │  Module...   │       ║│
  │ #PTEST2#16       0.0054 sec <1%        │  Current     │       ▼│
  │ #PTEST2#23       0.0028 sec <1%        └──────────────┘        │
  └────────────────────────────────────────────────────────────────┘
   Show all accumulated statistics
```

The **All** command restores all the statistics for the program with which you are working. All restores statistics removed by the Module and Current commands.

When you are analyzing a program that contains more than one program module, the Module command is useful. Module lets you filter out the information for all modules but one. When you select this command, you are asked which module you want to examine.

The Current command temporarily filters out the statistics for the current routine. The statistics are not thrown away; they are temporarily hidden. You can restore these statistics with the **All** command.

When you select the Current command, Turbo Profiler recalculates the percentages for all the routines that are left. Current is useful when you want to analyze your program without the effects of a particular routine. You can filter out more that one routine with the Current command.

Choosing Active or Passive Profiling

The profiling mode you use determines what kind of information Turbo Profiler collects and how quickly your program runs under Turbo Profiler. Two profiling modes, active and passive, are available. To choose one of these modes, you first select the **P**rofiling command from the **S**tatistics menu. The Profiling options dialog box then appears (see fig. 9.15).

Fig. 9.15. *Selecting active or passive profiling from the Profiling options dialog box.*

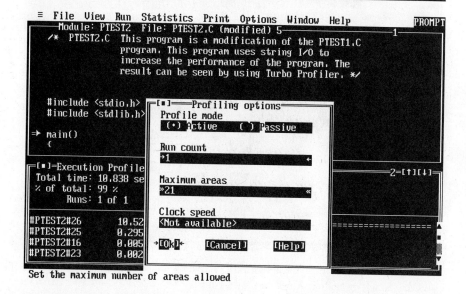

When you select active mode, Turbo Profiler performs a number of functions each time an area marker is encountered. In active mode, Turbo Profiler collects execution times and counts, as well as other information selected from the **S**tatistics menu. Profiling in active mode gives you the most accurate statistics.

However, using active mode has a price—reduced speed during profiling. Active mode requires that Turbo Profiler perform recording functions whenever an area marker is encountered. In a large program with every line selected, profiling can be quite slow.

You can switch to passive mode if you find that your profiling sessions are taking too long. In passive mode, Turbo Profiler regularly checks the status of your program. If your program is in a marked area during a check, the execution timer for that area is incremented. Using passive mode results in no noticeable slow down in program performance.

Like active mode, passive mode requires a price you must pay. Passive mode cannot generate all the information of active mode, and the timer results that you get can be somewhat inaccurate. The only type of information provided by passive mode is timer counts. By its nature, passive mode cannot generate instruction counts. Moreover, because passive mode only samples your program at intervals, it is possible to miscalculate the time an area takes to execute. In fact, if the marked area is fast, passive mode may not even register that the area executed.

Turbo Profiler automatically comes up in active mode, which is the most useful and accurate of the two modes. If you have a large program that takes a long time to run, you may want to switch to passive mode for your analysis.

Exercises

The following exercises give you practice in setting up and using Turbo Debugger and Turbo Profiler.

1. Set the Borland C++ transfer options so that you can start Turbo Debugger while you are still running Borland C++.

2. Write a simple loop program and trace through the program, using the F7 key and the Animate command under Turbo Debugger's Run menu selection.

3. Trace the loop program again. When you have made a few passes through the loop, use Turbo Debugger to change the value of the loop counter. Examine the effects of the change on the program.

4. Write a program that calls a function which adds the first 100 even numbers. Trace through the program by using the Step over, Trace into, and Until return commands.

5. Write a program that contains a structure and an array. Use the Inspect command to view the contents of both.

6. Reload the program that sums the first 100 even numbers. Open a Watches window and watch the value of the accumulator variable as the program is traced with Animate trace.

7. In the even-number program, set a breakpoint that will stop execution when the accumulator value reaches a value of 110.

8. Set the Borland C++ transfer options so that you can start Turbo Profiler from within Borland C++.

9. Load and profile the `ptest1.exe` program. Use the Display options, accessed through the Execution Profile window's local menu, to display each of the different types of statistics available. Be sure that you provide a file for the `ptest1.exe` program to read.

10. Profile `ptest1.c` again, but set the area markers only for the I/O loop.

11. Profile the even-number program you wrote. Profile the program the first time with the Separate timing option selected. Then reprofile the program with the Combined timing option selected.

12. Write a program that calls three or four different looping functions. Profile the program in both active and passive modes.

Summary

In this chapter, you learned how to use Borland's Turbo Debugger and Turbo Profiler. These two programs help you create professional code more quickly and easily. The following important points were covered:

❏ *A debugger is a utility that lets you examine your program while it is running.* A debugger can help you find logic bugs or data bugs. A logic bug is a problem with the basic design of your program. A data bug is a problem with the data your program uses.

❏ *Turbo Debugger is a stand-alone debugger.* This means that it is not part of the Borland C++ Integrated Development Environment. However, Borland C++ has a menu option that lets you transfer control to stand-alone programs such as Turbo Debugger.

❏ *When you trace your program, you run it one line at a time.* Tracing enables you to see the effect of each line in your program.

❏ *Turbo Debugger has a number of tracing commands you can use.* Trace executes your program one line at a time. Run lets you run your program at full speed. Back trace lets you execute your program one line at a time in reverse. You can also choose whether to trace into functions in your program. If you enter a function, you can run at full speed until the function returns.

❏ *You can watch the data values in your program change while the debugger is executing the program.* You can even change the value of the data in your program to see what will happen.

❏ *Breakpoints enable you to interrupt your program so that you can find out what the program is doing.* You can set breakpoints to stop the execution of your program so that you can check the program's status. You can set breakpoints also to log values automatically and continue processing. A breakpoint can be set so that it always stops program execution or stops execution only when a specific event has occurred.

❏ *Turbo Profiler is a stand-alone utility that analyzes the performance of your program.* With Turbo Profiler, you can see exactly which statements are executed, how many times they are called, and how long they take to execute.

❏ *To profile a program, you simply load the EXE version of the program and run it.* Turbo Profiler collects all the statistics you want.

❏ *The program you profile must be compiled with full debugging information turned on.* The debugging information lets Turbo Profiler link the statement in the EXE file with your source file.

❏ *Turbo Profiler knows what to analyze by the area markers you set.* Area markers simply indicate where Turbo Profiler turns statistical collection on and off.

❏ *You can select the type of information to be included in the reports generated by Turbo Profiler.* Two of your options are the number of times an area is executed and the time required for an area to execute. The area's time can be the overall average or the longest time required.

❏ *The Filter command, accessed through the local menu for the Execution Profile window, filters out any unwanted statistics.* Filter lets you look at only the areas that interest you.

❏ *The active or passive modes determine how Turbo Profiler acquires statistics.* In active mode, Turbo Profiler records information every time a marked area is encountered. In passive mode, information is logged at regular intervals. Although active mode records more data more accurately than passive mode, your program is analyzed more slowly.

10

Using Borland C++'s Advanced Features

Turbo C++ and the high-end product Borland C++ 2.0 are amazingly complete and robust compiler packages. These compiler products offer developer-quality software at an individual's price. This is particularly true if you have bought the Borland C++ 2.0 package: you get a compiler that supports K&R C, ANSI C, AT&T 2.0 compatible C++, and Windows 3.0 programming features, plus a number of support programs. Turbo C++ Professional (now replaced by Borland C++ 2.0) is still a very good package—it lacks only Windows programming support.

Part II of this book introduces you to the world of object-oriented programming with C++, and Part III provides your first taste of Windows 3.0 programming with Borland C++ 2.0. This chapter covers some of the advanced features of the Borland C++ compiler, which are extensions to the ANSI C language.

Some other compiler vendors offer products with the features covered in this chapter. Some of these products have all the features presented here. Keep in mind, however, that because these features are *extensions* to the ANSI standard C language, Borland's implementation of them is unique to Borland C++. They are not directly portable to any other brand of compiler. But don't let that stop you from *using* these features. When you design your programs, just remember that these features are not portable, in case you might want to port them to another compiler later.

In this chapter, you learn about the following advanced programming topics:

❏ *Using assembly language with your C programs.* A good C compiler, such as Turbo C++ or Borland C++ 2.0, produces very efficient machine code. That, plus the fact that C is a marvelously powerful and flexible language, tends to make C programmers partial (if not prejudiced). Why use assembly language? By using it, you can get still more power and more use of *all* your computer's capabilities. A program that combines both languages can be an awesome performer. You are introduced to writing assembly language routines, using both inline assembly statements and separately compiled modules.

❏ *Using Borland C++ interrupt functions.* Borland C++ supports a full range of interrupt service routines and facilities. You can cause software interrupts, as well as trap and handle them. Using interrupt services can help you produce a production-quality program. You learn how to use software interrupts and how to trap and handle system-related interrupt events.

❏ *Using the Borland C++ program optimization features.* You can optimize your programs for size or speed. You learn when and how to optimize your programs, and you get a brief tour of compiler optimization strategies.

Using Inline Assembly Language

Inline assembly language is covered first because it is probably the most often-used method of mixing C and assembly language. Borland C++ (and other good compilers, too) produce reasonably efficient machine code, so in most cases you will need to tune only isolated spots in your program in order to provide higher performance or additional function.

Unfortunately, a C book is not the place to teach assembly language programming as such. Part of the language could be covered, but how much coverage would be enough, without leaving you dangling? For a full treatment of assembly language programming, you may want to consult Allen Wyatt's *Using Assembly Language* (second edition, Que, 1990). That book, which is packed with both tutorial and reference information, gives the subject the full-scale treatment it deserves.

This book, however, must concentrate on what you need to know so that you can interface assembly language routines with your C programs, with an emphasis on the C environment.

Understanding the Inline Assembly Environment

Inline assembly statements can appear directly in your Turbo C and Borland C++ programs, so the C language program is the surrounding environment for these statements. You should know two things before you can effectively or correctly use inline assembly statements. First, you must know how to compile a C program containing inline assembly (discussed in this section). Second, you must know what you can and cannot do in inline assembly statements (discussed in the next section).

Compiling a program containing inline assembly statements is only a little more complex than compiling a simple C program. The first requirement, of course, is that you have a copy of Turbo Assembler. If you bought the Turbo C++ Professional product and used the default installation procedure, the assembler was installed in its own directory.

The Borland C++ 2.0 high-end compiler product does things a little more simply. We installed our test copy of the product in the C:\INTEGRA directory, and *all* the program products (C/C++ compiler, assembler, debugger, profiler, and Windows programming tools) were placed in the C:\INTEGRA\BIN subdirectory by the installation procedure. Writing inline assembly statements in a Borland C++ 2.0 is much easier than before, because this compiler has a built-in assembler.

If you want, you can compile Borland C++ 2.0 C programs containing inline assembly with the command-line compiler (TCC) by specifying the -B command-line option. This option causes Turbo C to invoke Turbo Assembler to handle the inline assembly statements. You might use this approach if you are building a project with MAKE files, but the IDE has been used to get the job done here. If you are using the Borland C++ 2.0 compiler, you can use the -B option to invoke the external assembler, or you can omit it and allow the built-in assembler to be used (this second method is *much* faster).

Using the Borland C++ 2.0 IDE to compile a program containing inline assembly requires two extra actions from you: writing the #pragma inline directive and letting the compiler know where to find the assembler. At the beginning of the program, you must write the #pragma inline directive to inform the compiler that the assembler will be needed for inline assembly. Writing #pragma inline is exactly equivalent to using the -B option with the command-line compiler. The #pragma inline directive is illustrated in figure 10.1.

Fig. 10.1. *To use inline assembly statements, you must write the #pragma inline directive to compile from the IDE.*

```
                              TCP
     File  Edit  Search  Run  Compile  Debug  Project  Options   Window  Help
 [■]                             INLINE.C                              2=[↑]
 #pragma inline
 #include <stdlib.h>
 #include <stdio.h>
 void increment( int* arg )
 {
 /*
        LARGE MODEL, far* auto generate
        -------------------------------------------------------
        stack frame: bp -> +0 oldbp
                           +2 ofs ret adrs
                           +4 seg ret adrs
                           +6 ofs of arg pointer
                           +8 seg of arg pointer
        -------------------------------------------------------
 */
    asm {                      /* Get FAR pointer to obj & deref */
       push ds                 /* hang on to DS */
       mov  ax,[bp+8]          /* get seg adrs of arg */
       mov  ds,ax
       mov  si,[bp+6]          /* get offset adrs of arg */
       mov  ax,[si]            /* deref, pick up int */
       inc  ax                 /* increment */
       mov  [si],ax            /* and save it */
       pop  ax
       mov  ds,ax              /* restore DS */
    }
 }

 void main()
 {
    int j = 3;

    printf( "Initial value was %d\n", j );
    increment( &j );
    printf( "New value is %d\n", j );
 }

 ══ 16:1 ═══◄□
```
```
 F1 Help  F2 Save  F3 Open  Alt-F9 Compile  F9 Make  F10 Menu
```

The #pragma inline directive is unnecessary for the Borland C++ 2.0 compiler. Using the directive invokes the external assembler, and omitting the directive allows the built-in assembler to do its work.

Now that the #pragma inline directive has notified the compiler that assembly will take place, you must make sure that the compiler knows where to find the assembler when it is needed. You do this by defining transfer program linkage for the assembler. First select the **Transfer** command from the **O**ptions menu and then set up the linkage as illustrated in figure 10.2, using your own directory for the assembler product.

Fig. 10.2. Inline assembly within the IDE requires that you have the Options Transfer parameters set correctly.

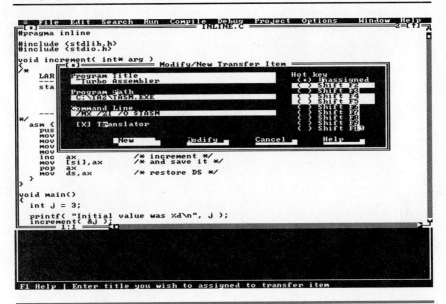

When Turbo Assembler is invoked by the C compiler, any error messages are piped back into the IDE's message window by the TASM2MSG.EXE filter program. If you have set up the DOS path specification properly, that filter program will be located correctly in the \TC\BIN directory. If you are running the IDE under Windows, however, and you have specified a starting directory other than \TC\BIN (a directory containing your source files, for example), you may need to copy TASM2MSG.EXE to the "current" source file directory. If you don't do this, the program build will abort when IDE can't find the filter program.

Transfer linkage does not apply to Borland C++ 2.0 programs when you allow the built-in assembler to be used, because the external assembler is never invoked. Nor is the message filter necessary in this case—there are no messages to pipe. You *should* check to make sure that the DOS Standard or DOS Overlay **O**ptions **A**pplication options are currently selected for Borland C++ 2.0 (unless you are building a Windows application; see Part III of this book for more on that subject).

Using the *asm* Keyword

To insert inline assembly statements directly into your C program, use the asm keyword at the beginning of the statement. Here are several different ways you can code an asm statement:

```
asm assembly statement

asm assembly statement ;

asm assembly statement ; asm assembly statement

asm {

  assembly statement ; assembly statement

  . . .

  assembly statement

  assembly statement

  assembly statement

  . . .

}
```

Because each asm statement counts as a single C statement, you can enclose a series of asm statements in a block, as shown in the preceding examples.

If you are already familiar with either Turbo Assembler or MASM (Microsoft Macro Assembler), you will probably have to adjust to the use of the semicolon as used in inline assembly: the semicolon does *not* signal the beginning of an assembly comment. The semicolon as used in inline assembly means *end-of-line*. Thus, the semicolon can be used to separate multiple asm statements on a single source line. You can write comments on an asm statement: just use the normal C comment syntax (/*-*/ for C or // for C++). Note carefully, however, that no inline assembly statement can be continued to another line.

When you write inline assembly statements in your program, you must become more conscious of memory models and pointer sizes. Although Borland C++ occasionally requires you to be aware of pointer sizes (using graphics library routines in a small model program, for example), you must always be aware of segment arrangements and pointer sizes when mixing C and assembler. Listing 10.1 shows a program that contains inline assembly and that illustrates both memory model dependency and the use of the asm keyword.

Listing 10.1. `inline.c`. *A program that shows the use of inline assembly in a large model C program.*

```
1    #pragma inline
2
3    #include <stdlib.h>
4    #include <stdio.h>
5
6    void increment( int* arg )
7    {
8    /*
9        LARGE MODEL, far* auto generate
10       -------------------------------------------------------
11       stack frame: bp -> +0 oldbp
12                          +2 ofs ret adrs
13                          +4 seg ret adrs
14                          +6 ofs of arg pointer
15                          +8 seg of arg pointer
16       -------------------------------------------------------
17   */
18     asm {                    /* Get FAR pointer to obj & deref */
19       push ds                /* Hang on to DS */
20       mov  ax,[bp+8]         /* Get seg adrs of arg */
21       mov  ds,ax
22       mov  si,[bp+6]         /* Get offset adrs of arg */
23       mov  ax,[si]           /* deref, pick up int */
24       inc  ax                /* Increment */
25       mov  [si],ax           /* and save it */
26       pop  ax
27       mov  ds,ax             /* Restore DS */
28     }
29   }
30
31   void main()
32   {
33     int j = 3;
34
35     printf( "Initial value was %d\n", j );
36     increment( &j );
37     printf( "New value is %d\n", j );
38   }
```

Because the program in listing 10.1 was compiled with the large memory model, the inline assembly must reflect this fact. The comments in lines 12 and 13 indicate that both the segment and offset parts of the return address are pushed on the stack in the large memory model, so that the addresses of argument variables are displaced an extra two bytes in the stack (compared to the small memory model).

Arguments that happen to be pointers are also affected by the memory model. In listing 10.1, the function containing the inline assembly statements expects a pointer to int. Again, because the program was compiled with the large memory model, the resulting pointer is four bytes, not two bytes, long. Three lines of assembly code (lines 22–22) are required to fetch that pointer, and yet another line is needed to dereference the pointer and "pick up" the data variable (by loading it into the AX register).

Coding the correct assembly statements is probably the trickiest thing about mixing C and assembler. It is strictly up to you to write assembly language code that meshes properly with the memory model being used.

You can use all the normal 8086 instructions in your inline assembly statements, including the floating-point instructions. You can use also all the extended string instructions of the 8086 instruction set, including special byte and word forms. The loop and jump instructions are supported, together with the lock and repxxx instruction prefixes. Note that a jump target must be a *C label*, which means that a jump target cannot be written inside a block asm statement.

The data allocation directives (DB, DW, DQ, DT) are available for use with inline assembly, but other assembly directives (such as SEGMENT and ASSUME) are not. You should know that you can use 80186 and 80286 opcodes, if you have set the Code Generation options accordingly on the Compiler menu, but in no case can you use 80386 instructions in inline assembly. Neither Turbo C++ nor Borland C++ 2.0 supports 80386 code generation. You can get around this restriction by writing separately compiled assembler modules, in which you can write any instructions or directives you want. Separate compilation of C-callable assembly routines is covered in the next section.

You may have noticed in listing 10.1 that the DS register is used and later restored. What registers can you use in general, and what are the restrictions on their use? The C function call environment expects you to preserve the BP, SP, CS, DS, and SS registers. If you use or modify them, you *must* be certain that they have been restored to their original values before exiting inline assembly statements. That is why the program in listing 10.1 is careful to restore the contents of DS before allowing the function to return. However, you can use the AX, BX, CX, DX, ES, and flags registers in any way you want: these are considered to be "scratch" registers.

As just noted, certain registers must be restored before returning to C code. Is there ever a time when you should modify those registers? First, there are two registers that you should consider inviolable: the CS and SS registers. Just don't modify these registers (other than indirectly—such as modifying CS through a CALL instruction). You will certainly regret it if you do modify them, unless you are an expert assembly programmer.

Frequently, you will find it necessary to use the DS and ES registers to support certain instruction sequences. Using the ES register is no problem; it is a scratch register anyway. But the DS register is critical to the continued functioning of your C program: restore the DS register. The program in listing 10.1 uses the DS register because the indirect operand instructions in lines 23 and 25 require that DS contain the segment address of the variable being accessed. In this case, the pointer int* is dereferenced when it is loaded into DS:SI. Then the integer object can be accessed through the notation [SI].

Assembly code that does much of anything often uses indirection to access memory locations (just like C programs!). This means that you will have to manipulate segment registers fairly often. Furthermore, you should know which segment registers to manipulate. For your convenience, table 10.1 shows which segment registers are assumed by the various operand formats and their corresponding addressing modes.

The program in listing 10.1 does not make clear that you can generally use the label of any C identifier which is currently in scope when inline assembly statements appear in the code. Such use can make life much simpler in many cases. In this program, for example, you could have written the statements that load the pointer into DS:SI by using the arg label, because that name is in scope for the duration of the increment() function. Those lines would have the following appearance:

```
20      mov   ax,word ptr arg+2   /* Get seg adrs of arg */
21      mov   ds,ax
22      mov   si,word ptr arg     /* Get offset adrs of arg */
```

An exception to this rule crops up when you attempt to refer to the label of a C++ class member variable in inline assembly language. In Part II of this book, you discover that a C++ class has its own unique scope. The labels of member variables are therefore not available to inline assembly statements.

Table 10.1. *Assumed segment registers for operand formats and addressing modes (8088 registers).*

Segment Register	Operand Format	Addressing Mode
(None)	reg	Register operand
(None)	data	Immediate operand (in instruction)
DS	displacement	Direct memory operand
DS	label	Direct memory operand
DS	[BX]	Indirect operand
SS	[BP]	Indirect operand
DS	[SI]	Indirect operand
DS	[DI]	Indirect operand
DS	[BX+disp]	Base relative operand
SS	[BP+disp]	Base relative operand
DS	[DI+disp]	Direct indexed operand
DS	[SI+disp]	Direct indexed operand
DS	[BX][SI]+disp	Base indexed operand
DS	[BX][DI]+disp	Base indexed operand
SS	[BP][SI]+disp	Base indexed operand
SS	[BP][DI]+disp	Base indexed operand

Interfacing Assembly Language Routines

If inline assembly should not prove adequate for your needs in producing fine-tuned, high-performance code, you can go a step further and write complete, separately assembled source modules. You can do this if the logic to be implemented in assembly language is simply too lengthy to fit comfortably in the middle of a C source file. In this section you learn how to call assembly modules from C, and how to call C modules from assembly.

Calling Assembly Routines from C

Writing separately assembled, C-callable modules requires a little more expertise on your part. You must potentially understand all there is to know about the C function call protocol. You must understand the standard C stack frame, calling conventions, and segment naming and ordering conventions. Furthermore, you must know how to return values from assembly language routines to C, and possibly how to call C library functions from an assembly language routine.

Because C passes function parameters on the system stack, one of the most important parts of the C calling environment is the standard C stack frame. The *stack frame* is just that part of the system stack on which C places parameters and return addresses for the function being called—and your assembly language routine *is* a C function. Knowing how the stack frame is organized is the trick. Figure 10.3 illustrates the standard C stack frame for a function expecting two integer arguments; the function is compiled with the large memory model.

Fig. 10.3. The structure of a Borland C++ standard stack frame for a large model program, calling a function with two int arguments.

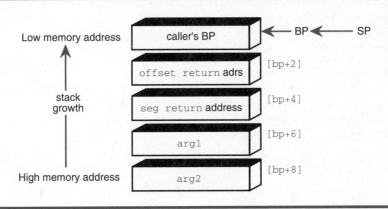

Figure 10.3 illustrates three important points about the stack frame. First, notice that the second argument was pushed on the stack first. This means that function arguments are *scanned from right to left*, as far as calling conventions are concerned, and placed on the stack in that order.

Second, the CALL instruction pushes the return address on top of the function arguments. For a large model program, the return address consists of two "backward back-words," as do all far pointers in memory. That is, the segment address is pushed on the stack first, followed by the offset address, which is placed "on top" of the stack.

Third, your *assembly code* should push the base pointer register (BP) on the stack immediately on entry to the routine, and pop it back off just before returning. This is not optional—failure to do this will corrupt the stack, and things will get really interesting after your assembly routine returns control to its caller.

An extra step is also involved in compiling and linking the complete program when separately assembled modules are involved. You need to provide a project file (assuming that you are using the IDE) in which you name the assembly routines to be assembled and linked together with your main C code.

However, just inserting the name of the assembly language source file into the project list is no longer enough, as it was for C-only projects. You must set *transfer linkage for each assembly source file* in the project list and point it to Turbo Assembler. To do this, you first select the IDE window containing the project file, and then use the arrow keys to move the highlight to the assembly source file name you want.

Next, use the Alt-P and L key sequence (or the mouse) to pop up the Override Options window, as shown in figure 10.4. Then just make sure that Turbo Assembler is selected as the Project File Translator. You don't have to worry about the correct path to the assembler here; you should already have taken care of that by setting transfer linkage with the **Transfer** command on the **Options** menu.

Fig. 10.4. Setting the transfer link option for a mixed-language project file item.

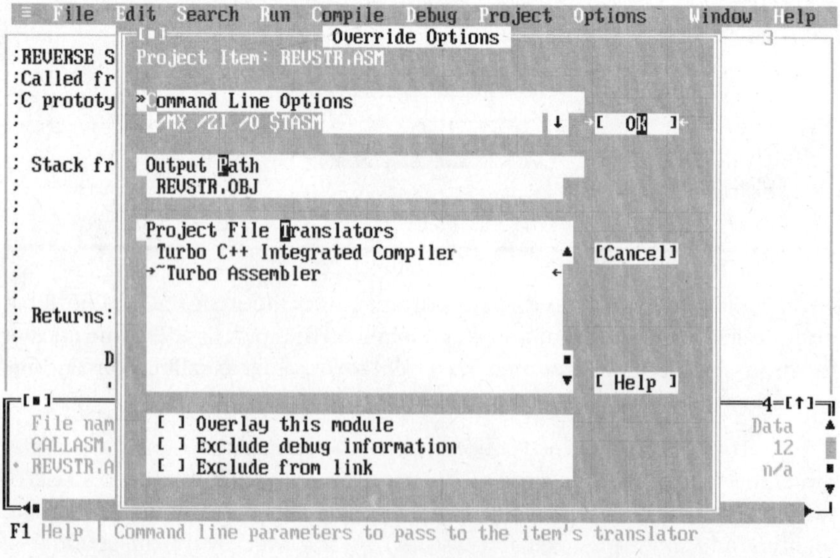

```
 ≡  File  Edit  Search  Run  Compile  Debug  Project  Options  Window  Help
   ┌─[■]─        ┌──────────── Override Options ────────────────┐   ─3─
  ;REVERSE S   Project Item: REVSTR.ASM
  ;Called fr
  ;C prototy    » Command Line Options
  ;               /MX /ZI /O $TASM                      ↓   ┌ [ OK ] ┐
  ; Stack fr
  ;             Output Path
  ;               REVSTR.OBJ
  ;
  ;             Project File Translators
  ;               Turbo C++ Integrated Compiler      ▲    [Cancel]
  ;             » Turbo Assembler                     ←
  ;
  ; Returns:
  ;
        D                                            ■    [ Help ]
   ┌─[■]─                                            ▼                 ─4=[↑]─┐
    File nam   ┌ [ ] Overlay this module                         Data    ▲
    CALLASM.     [ ] Exclude debug information                    12
  • REVSTR.A     [ ] Exclude from link                            n/a     ■
   └◄■                                                                    ▼
  F1 Help │ Command line parameters to pass to the item's translator
```

Now you are set to make a project that contains an assembly language source file. So what can you do with the assembly language function module (remember that it is a C function)? You can do just about anything you want. The full range of Turbo Assembler's capabilities is now open to you. If you are running on an Intel 80386 CPU, for example, you can generate 386 instructions and use all the extended registers. The extended 386 registers are summarized in table 10.2. Note that the 80386 extended registers *contain* their 16-bit counterparts: AX, for example, is the low-order 16 bits of EAX.

Table 10.2. *The Intel 80386 system registers (GPR = General Purpose Register; SEG = Segment Register; SPEC = Special Purpose Register).*

Register Name(s)	Type	Description
AX, EAX	GPR	16- and 32-bit accumulator register
BX, EBX	GPR	16- and 32-bit base register
CX, ECX	GPR	16- and 32-bit count register
DX, EDX	GPR	16- and 32-bit data register
SI, ESI	GPR	16- and 32-bit source index register
DI, EDI	GPR	16- and 32-bit destination index register
BP, EBP	GPR	16- and 32-bit base pointer register
SP, ESP	GPR	16- and 32-bit stack pointer register
IP, EIP	SPEC	16- and 32-bit instruction pointer register
FLAGS, EFLAGS	SPEC	16- and 32-bit flags register
CS	SEG	16-bit code segment register
DS	SEG	16-bit data segment register
ES	SEG	16-bit extended segment register
SS	SEG	16-bit stack segment register
FS	SEG	16-bit unspecified segment register
GS	SEG	16-bit unspecified segment register

When your assembly language module receives control of the CPU (the module is called from a C function), certain assumptions are being made about segment register contents. You must cooperate with these assumptions, or your assembly language module won't get much done (not correctly, at any rate).

A particular assumption is that the segment registers are pointing to the proper code, data, and stack segment locations set up by the C compiler. The most important of the segment registers are, naturally, the CS and DS registers. Table 10.3 shows the value of these registers for each of the memory models supported by Turbo C++ and Borland C++ 2.0.

Table 10.3. Default segment register values on entry to an assembly language function routine.

Memory Model	CS Points To	DS Points To
Tiny	_TEXT	DGROUP
Small	_TEXT	DGROUP
Compact	_TEXT	DGROUP
Medium	*filename*_TEXT	DGROUP
Large	*filename*_TEXT	DGROUP
Huge	*filename*_TEXT	*filename*_DATA

Table 10.3 shows that the tiny, small, and compact models support only one code segment named _TEXT. The medium, large, and huge models support multiple code segments named *filename*_TEXT, where *filename* is the name of the separately (or only) compiled source file. For all the memory models except huge, the DS register points to the DGROUP segment group on entry to your routine. DGROUP contains both the _DATA (initialized global static data) and _BSS (uninitialized global static data) segments. You don't have to modify DS to get access to static global data (unless you borrow DS for another purpose and restore it). For example, if your program has declared a global `action_flag`, you can simply refer to it in this way:

```
            DOSSEG
            .MODEL large
            .DATA
action_flag dw   0                ; global action flag
            .CODE
            PUBLIC _myfunc
_myfunc     PROC
            ...
            mov     ax,action_flag  ; get the flag
            or      ax, 8000h       ; turn on a bit
            ...
            ret
_myfunc     ENDP
            END
```

The `action_flag` variable in the preceding code fragment will be merged (by the linker) into the common global static data segment. Of course, if you want that flag to be available to other modules, you would have to declare it `PUBLIC` here and `EXTRN` in another assembly module, or `extern` in a C module.

In contrast, a huge model program has no DGROUP. Instead, a huge model program has a distinct *filename*_DATA segment and *filename*_BSS segment for *each* separately compiled module. These are `far` data segments. When your assembly language routine is invoked in a huge model program, the assembly language module has its own `far` data segment (if you declare one). You must load DS with the correct value for the `far` data segment, as shown here:

```
        DOSSEG
        .MODEL huge
        .FARDATA
        ...
        .CODE
        PUBLIC _myfunc
_myfunc PROC
        push    ds              ; save original DS
        ...
        mov     ax,@fardata     ; get fardata seg adrs
        mov     ds,ax           ; and load it
        ...
        pop     ds              ; restore DS - REQUIRED
        ret
_myfunc ENDP
        END
```

The same rules concerning the preservation and use of system registers apply to separately assembled modules as they do to inline assembly statements. External identifiers and loading segment registers (especially DS) are considered shortly, but first look at a C program that calls an assembly language module, and the assembly language source itself. The code for `callasm.c` is found in listing 10.2. It is a simple program, whose sole purpose is to call the `revstr()` function to reverse a string in place. The catch, of course, is that `revstr()` is an assembly language module. Worse than that, `callasm.c` uses the small memory model, whereas `revstr()` uses the large memory model.

Listing 10.2. `callasm.c`. *A program that calls an assembly language routine from C with mixed memory models.*

```
1   #include <stdio.h>
2   #include <stdlib.h>
3
4   char Message[] = "Message!";
5
6   int far revstr( char far* str );   /* Don't forget this */
7
8   void main()
9   {
10    revstr( (char far*)Message );
11    printf( "%s", Message );
12  }
```

In listing 10.2, the only acknowledgment of the fact that mixed-model programming is going on here is the prototype declaration for revstr(). The function is explicitly declared to be a far function, and its argument is an explicit far pointer to a string. That's easy enough: it is the same method used to declare the Turbo C graphics library routines, which are always far functions expecting far pointers.

Now look at how this arrangement is handled by revstr() itself. The assembly source code for this external C function is shown in listing 10.3.

Listing 10.3. `revstr.asm`. *A C-callable assembly language routine that reverses a string in place.*

```
1   ;REVERSE STRING function
2   ;Called from C/C++
3   ;C prototype:
4   ;             int far revstr( char far* str );
5   ;
6   ; Stack frame:
7   ;             old_bp          [bp+0]
8   ;             offset return   [bp+2]
9   ;             seg return      [bp+4]
10  ;             offset str      [bp+6]
11  ;             seg str         [bp+8]
12  ;
13  ; Returns:    int strlen( str )
14  ;
```

```
15              DOSSEG
16              .MODEL large
17              .CODE
18              PUBLIC _revstr
19   _revstr    PROC
20              push    bp          ; set up standard stack frame
21              mov     bp,sp
22              push    ds          ; DS gets used, so save it
23              push    si          ; SI/DI may be register vars
24              push    di
25              mov     si,[bp+6]   ; get offset of string address
26              mov     di,si
27              mov     ax,[bp+8]   ; get segment of string address
28              mov     ds,ax
29              push    ds
30              pop     es          ; set up segment for scasb
31              cld                 ; forward direction for scasb
32              xor     ax,ax       ; null search arg
33              mov     cx,256      ; no more than 256 bytes
34   repne      scasb               ; scan the string for a null
35              dec     di          ; we passed it, back off by one
36              mov     cx,di
37              sub     cx,si       ; compute strlen
38              push    cx          ; save strlen
39              or      cx,cx       ; test for null string
40              jz      gohome
41              dec     di          ; point di to last byte of string
42   more:
43              cmp     si,di       ; if pointer regs equal,
44              jae     gohome      ;   then we are done
45              mov     al,[si]
46              mov     bl,[di]
47              xchg    al,bl       ; swap the bytes
48              mov     [si],al
49              mov     [di],bl
50              inc     si          ; step up the string
51              dec     di          ;   and down the string
52              jmp     short more
53   gohome:
54              pop     cx          ; retrieve strlen
55              pop     di          ; reset regs the way they were
56              pop     si
```

Listing 10.3. continues

Listing 10.3. continued

```
57              pop     ax
58              mov     ds,ax
59              pop     bp
60              mov     ax,cx      ; set return value = strlen
61              ret                ; and return to caller
62  _revstr     ENDP
63              END
```

The secret to handling mixed C and assembly language programs with different memory models is in the way you write the assembly language code to handle the standard stack frame. The base pointer (BP) register is used to access argument variables. All you need to do is account for the number of bytes used by return addresses and pointers. In other words, code the assembly language routine however you want, and let the C source prototype declaration handle the required pointer sizes! Of course, the two source modules must expect the same size pointers.

The sample code in listing 10.3 also demonstrates the methods you need for controlling segment naming and segment ordering in a manner compatible with the surrounding C environment. The DOSSEG directive in line 15 indicates to the assembler that DOS segment ordering is to be used at link time. The .MODEL directive in line 16 is nearly self-explanatory: the calling C module was compiled with the large memory model, so the large model is specified here also.

The .CODE directive in line 17 begins the code section of the program, and the PUBLIC directive in line 18 declares the routine name _revstr to be accessible to other modules (most notably, the calling C module). Finally, the PROC directive in line 19 initiates the code for the C-callable function (which happens to be coded in assembly). These are Turbo Assembler's simplified directives, and they generate segment and group names equivalent to those shown in table 10.3. The next part of this section includes more about simplified segment directives and assembly language extensions, in the discussion of variable linkage (public and external variable names).

Look again at listing 10.3 and notice that all references to revstr are prefixed with an underscore: _revstr is the correct form to use within the assembly language module, and revstr is the form to use in the C module. There is no real mystery here. You already know that Turbo C and C++ use prefixed underscores to refer to C identifiers behind the scenes. Well, now you are behind the scenes! You can still use assembler labels that are local to the assembly routine and that do not have a prefixed underscore, but you must remember to use underscores to refer to C identifiers. You can use Turbo Assembler language extensions to avoid this need. That subject is also discussed in the next part of this section.

Before leaving the discussion of revstr(), look at line 60, noting that the AX register is used to return a value to the C caller. Was that an arbitrary choice? Can you return values in any way you want? It is not arbitrary, and there is a standard return location for every C data object type. Table 10.4 summarizes the return locations (that is, where the returned data must be placed before executing the ret instruction) for the C data types.

Table 10.4. Locations for returning values from assembly language routines to C.

Object Type Returned	Place Return Value In
unsigned char	AX
char	AX
enum	AX
unsigned short	AX
short	AX
unsigned int	AX
int	AX
unsigned long	DX:AX (DX = high order, AX = low order)
long	DX:AX
float	8087 TOS reg ST(0)
double	8087 TOS reg ST(0)
long double	8087 TOS reg ST(0)
near*	AX
far*	DX:AX
struct (1–2 bytes)	AX (right justified into AL)
struct (4 bytes)	DX:AX
struct (3 bytes, >4bytes)	Copy to static memory location, return pointer

In table 10.4, the entries indicating that a data type should be returned by placing it in the indicated general-purpose register are straightforward. The method of returning a structure is only a little more complicated: if the structure fits in a register or register pair, return the structure that way; if not, copy it into a static storage area and return the appropriate pointer for the memory model.

The method of returning floating-point values may not be as clear, however, because few assembly language programmers write floating-point code. (The ones that do usually live in a developer's shop—such as Borland's.) What does it mean that a floating-point value should be returned in the 80x87 TOS (top of stack) register?

The 80x87 numeric processor is a computer in its own right, specializing in high-speed floating-point arithmetic. As such, the numeric processor has its own stack. The 80x87 stack has a fixed number of locations (eight of them) named ST(0)—which is TOS—through ST(7). 80x87 stack elements are actually specialized registers, each of which is 80 bits (10 bytes) wide. The trick in using the 80x87 (or an emulation of it like Borland's) is in realizing that operands for 80x87 arithmetic operations are *automatically pushed down onto the floating-point stack* when they are loaded with the fld instruction. An arithmetic operation is then carried out with ST(0) and another operand, and the result is placed in ST(0). Therefore, all you have to do is carry out your computations, refrain from disturbing the 80x87 stack, and return to the caller. Note a short assembly language routine that illustrates how this can be done:

```
;C prototype:
;               double do_fadd( double, double );
;
; Stack frame:
;               old_bp          [bp+0]
;               offset return   [bp+2]
;               double arg1     [bp+4]
;               double arg2     [bp+12]
;
; Returns:    double
; Emulation: 8087 emulation by Turbo C emu.lib
;
            EMUL
            DOSSEG
            .MODEL small
            .CODE
            PUBLIC _do_fadd
_do_fadd PROC
            push    bp                      ; set up standard stack frame
            mov     bp,sp
            fld     qword ptr[bp+4]
            fadd    qword ptr[bp+12]        ; that's all folks!
            pop     bp
            ret                             ; and return to caller
_do_fadd ENDP
            END
```

The preceding code fragment uses the EMUL assembly directive, meaning that the Turbo C floating-point emulation library routines are to be used (those routines will use a real 80x87 if it exists). Beyond that, all that was necessary was to load the first `double` operand into ST(0), `fadd` the other operand, and return (not forgetting C stack frame protocol).

Now you can pass parameters into an assembly language routine and return resulting values to the caller. Can you access variables that exist in other modules—for example, global static data? Because you can access such variables in C-only modules, using the `extern` keyword, you would certainly expect some mechanism to exist for doing the same thing in assembly language. Naturally, there is such a mechanism, which is discussed next.

Suppose that you want to use an assembly routine to sum 10 elements of an integer array and to return an integer value to you. Furthermore, suppose that you want to code the assembly routine so that it can access—using one method—variables in either a DGROUP (up through the large memory model) or a *filename*_DATA `far` data segment (huge model).

The addressing method presented here is, in our opinion, the best because it is simple to implement, and it allows you always to use DS to access the segment, instead of having to use the ES scratch segment register (which is another normal method, but one that requires you to use segment override notation to access variables). The first order of business is to provide the driving C program. That program, `callasm2.c`, is shown in listing 10.4.

Listing 10.4. `callasm2.c`. *A driver program for* `getseg.asm`.

```
1   #include <stdio.h>
2
3   extern int numbers[] = { 1, 2, 3, 4, 5, 6, 7, 8, 9, 10 };
4   extern int sumar( );
5
6   void main( )
7   {
8     printf( "The sum of numbers is: %d\n", sumar( ) );
9   }
```

The program in listing 10.4 is, presumably, to be compiled in either the large or huge memory model. Now you need an assembly language routine that can access the `numbers` array, regardless of which of those memory models is chosen. That is, there are two problems you need to solve: accessing the external data at all; and getting a workable value into a segment register (DS), no matter what else is going on.

First, consider how the numbers array will be stored, using the large or huge memory model. With the large model, all global static data goes into a single DGROUP, and DS will be preset when the assembly routine gets control. Thus, the following directives could be used in the large model scenario:

```
.MODEL large
.DATA
EXTRN    numbers:WORD
...
.CODE
...
lea      si,numbers    ; complete address now in DS:SI
```

If the proposed assembly routine is used with a huge model C program, however, this approach won't work: there is no DGROUP, and the .DATA directive doesn't apply. After some casting about for a solution, you might then fall into the following trap:

```
.MODEL huge
.FARDATA
EXTRN    numbers:WORD
...
.CODE
...
mov      ax,@fardata
mov      ds,ax
lea      si,numbers    ; complete address NOT in DS:SI
```

What is wrong with this code sequence? Nothing is wrong with it, except that the far data segment declared here is the *one belonging to the assembly module*, not to the calling module. In other words, this is the correct method for addressing your own far data segment, but you still do not know which of several possible far data segments belongs to the current caller.

Several other scenarios could be developed, all of them wrong. It will be better instead to go straight to the correct answer. All you have to do is let the compiler and linker do the work of keeping track of segment addresses for you. When it's time to address a specific one of those segments, get its address by using the SEG directive. The assembly program in listing 10.5 shows you how to do this.

The great difference between the program in listing 10.5 and the preceding code fragments is that the EXTRN directive is *declared outside any segment*, so it is dependent on no particular segment. The correct segment address is loaded in DS with the SEG directive, which gets the segment address of the external variable (lines 24–25). Thus, whether the large or the huge memory model is being used to call the assembly routine, you can borrow DS to address an external variable, wherever it may happen to reside.

Listing 10.5. `getseg.asm`. *An assembler routine accessing an array in either* `.DATA` *or* `.FARDATA`.

```
1     ;SUM ARRAY function
2     ;Called from C/C++
3     ;C prototype:
4     ;              int sumar( void );
5     ; Stack frame:
6     ;              old_bp          [bp+0]
7     ;              offset return   [bp+2]
8     ;              seg return      [bp+4]
9     ; Assumes... an array named numbers exists elsewhere
10    ;           which contains 10 elements
11    ; Returns... integer value of sum
12    ;
13             DOSSEG
14             .MODEL large
15             EXTRN   _numbers:WORD
16             .CODE
17             PUBLIC C sumar
18    sumar    PROC C
19             push    ds              ; DS gets used, so save it
20             push    si              ; SI/DI may be register vars
21             push    di
22             mov     cx,10           ; move num items to ctr reg
23             lea     si,_numbers         ; get offset of array
24             mov     ax,SEG _numbers
25             mov     ds,ax           ; and locate its segment
26             xor     ax,ax               ; clear accumulator
27             xor     dx,dx           ; clear running total
28             cld             ; clear direction means go forward
29    top:
30             lodsw
31             add     dx,ax
32             loop    top             ; this is all there is to it!
33             pop     di              ; reset regs the way they were
34             pop     si
35             pop     ds
36             mov     ax,dx               ; put return value in AX
37             ret                         ; and return to caller
38    sumar    ENDP
39             END
```

Notice that the module is declared to have the large memory model, even though it is intended to be used with either large or huge C programs. That is acceptable: large and huge model programs are indistinguishable as far as assembly language is concerned.

Calling C Functions from Assembly Routines

By this time, you have certainly noticed an absence of the old MASM segment directives in the assembly language modules. The reason is that they are terribly difficult to use, compared to Turbo Assembler's simplified segment directives. You can do it the old, hard way, but why should you?

If you do want to use the simplified directives, you should know how the new directives correspond to the MASM directives. Table 10.5 compares Turbo Assembler's simplified directives to the MASM versions.

Table 10.5. Turbo Assembler's simplified segment directives compared to MASM versions.

TASM Directive	Description	MASM Directive
.CODE	Code segment	_TEXT SEGMENT BYTE PUBLIC 'CODE'
.DATA	Init. data seg	_DATA SEGMENT WORD PUBLIC 'DATA'
.DATA?	Uninit. data seg	_BSS SEGMENT WORD PUBLIC 'BSS'
.FARDATA	Init. far data seg	_ *file*_DATA SEGMENT WORD PUBLIC 'DATA'
.FARDATA?	Uninit. data seg	_ *file*_BSS SEGMENT WORD PUBLIC 'BSS'

Combining the information in tables 10.3 and 10.5 gives you just about all the information you need to control segment addressability in your assembly language routines. Given that, plus the fact that you have also seen in listing 10.5 how to write EXTRN assembly declarations to provide access to data in other modules, you are now ready to learn how to access *other modules*. Specifically, you are about to discover how to call C library functions from your assembly language routines.

The sample programs you will be examining demonstrate several things. In addition to showing how to call a C library function, you will see how to use Turbo Assembler's simplified segment directives more fully, and also how to use the *language-independent extensions* to Turbo Assembler.

Presented here is a routine named `tokencpy( )` (notice again the use of C function notation for the assembly module), which illustrates how to call C library functions from assembly language modules. This routine performs a nondestructive scan of a text string; displays the extracted tokens on `stdout`, using a call to `printf( )`; and copies the token into a string provided by the caller. A "nondestructive scan" is one that does not insert null terminating characters throughout the string to be scanned, as does `strtok( )`.

The sample assembly language program is driven by a program named `callc.c`, shown in listing 10.6. There is nothing exceptional about `callc.c` except that the `extern` declaration for `tokencpy( )` explicitly describes the function and its arguments as `far` objects. This allows the C program to be compiled with the small model, even though the assembly language module uses the large memory model.

Listing 10.6. `callc.c`. *A C driver for the* `tokencpy.asm` *module.*

```
 1   #include <stdio.h>
 2   #include <stdlib.h>
 3   #include <string.h>
 4
 5   extern char far* tokencpy( char far* text, char far* token );
 6
 7   void main( )
 8   {
 9     char Message[] = "Testing a line of text tokens today.";
10     char Output[16];
11     char far* text = Message;
12     char far* token = Output;
13
14     do {
15       text = tokencpy( text, token );
16     } while ( *text );
17
18     strcpy( Message, "a+b-c*d/e&f|g" );
19     text = Message;
20     do {
21       text = tokencpy( text, token );
22     } while ( *text );
23   }
24
```

The source for `tokencpy.asm` is shown in listing 10.7. Look at that listing now and see whether you can find instances of the three things mentioned that are illustrated by this sample program: calling C functions from assembly language, language independent extensions, and argument declarations in assembly.

Listing 10.7. `tokencpy.asm`. *A nondestructive scanner that builds a token string and displays it through* `printf()` *before returning.*

```
1   ;TOKEN COPY function
2   ;Called from C/C++
3   ;Calls printf()
4   ;
5   ;C prototype:
6   ;           char far* far tokencpy( char far* line,
7   ;                                   char far *token );
8   ;
9   ; Stack frame:
10  ;           old_bp          [bp+0]
11  ;           offset return   [bp+2]
12  ;           seg return      [bp+4]
13  ;           offset line     [bp+6]  (srcofs)
14  ;           seg line        [bp+8]  (srcseg)
15  ;           offset token    [bp+10] (tokenofs)
16  ;           seg token       [bp+12] (tokenseg)
17  ;
18  ; Returns... char far* line (ptr to new location in source)
19  ;
20          DOSSEG
21          .MODEL large
22          EXTRN  C printf:PROC
23          .DATA
24  fmtstr  db      "%s", 0ah, 0        ; notice newline notation
25          .CODE
26          PUBLIC C tokencpy
27  tokencpy PROC C srcofs:WORD,srcseg:WORD,\
28                  tokenofs:WORD,tokenseg:WORD
29          push    ds                  ; DS gets used, so save it
30          push    si                  ; SI/DI may be register vars
31          push    di
32          mov     ax,srcseg
33          mov     ds,ax               ; seg for source string
34          mov     si,srcofs           ; offset for source string
```

```
35              mov     ax,tokenseg
36              mov     es,ax                   ; seg for token string
37              mov     di,tokenofs         ; offset for token string
38      skipws:
39              mov     al,byte ptr [si] ; skip all blanks and tabs
40              cmp     al,20h
41              jne     short testtab
42              jmp     isws
43      testtab:
44              cmp     al,09h
45              jne     short copystr
46      isws:
47              inc     si
48              jmp     short skipws
49      copystr:                            ; now copy source frag to token
50              mov     byte ptr es:[di],al      ; use seg override
51              or      al,al       ; if null term just copied
52              jz      tokenout
53              call    isop                        ; if operator char
54              je      foundop             ; at beginning of token
55              inc     si
56              inc     di
57              mov     al,byte ptr[si]
58              call    isop                        ; if operator char
59              je      gohome              ;   trailing token
60              cmp     al,20h              ; if more ws appeared
61              je      gohome
62              cmp     al,09h
63              je      gohome
64              jmp     short copystr
65      foundop:
66              inc     si
67              inc     di
68      gohome:
69              mov     al,0                        ; null terminate token
70              mov     byte ptr es:[di],al
71      tokenout:
72              mov     srcofs,si       ; first update source offset
73              pop     di              ; reset regs the way they were
74              pop     si
75              pop     ds
76              lea     ax,fmtstr       ; compute adrs format string
```

Listing 10.7. continues

Listing 10.7. continued

```
77                call    printf C,ax,ds,tokenofs,tokenseg
78                mov     dx,srcseg              ; return seg adrs line
79                mov     ax,srcofs           ; return offset adrs line
80                ret                          ; and return to caller
81   tokencpy     ENDP
82   ;
83   isop         PROC    near ; set zero flag if char is an operator
84                cmp     al,'+'
85                je      endop
86                cmp     al,'-'
87                je      endop
88                cmp     al,'*'
89                je      endop
90                cmp     al,'/'
91                je      endop
92                cmp     al,'%'
93                je      endop
94                cmp     al,'~'
95                je      endop
96                cmp     al,'!'
97                je      endop
98                cmp     al,'='
99                je      endop
100               cmp     al,'&'
101               je      endop
102               cmp     al,'|'
103               je      endop
104               cmp     al,'^'
105               je      endop
106               cmp     al,'.'
107               je      endop
108  endop:
109               ret
110               END
```

As you can see, the program in listing 10.7 has several differences when you compare it to previous samples. The first difference, of course, is the use of the printf( ) library function. The printf( ) function is declared to be EXTRN in line 22 of this listing, and the function is called in line 77.

Now look closely at the call statement in line 77. At first glance, it looks a lot like a normal C function call without the enclosing parentheses. That is because the C character following the function name is a *language specifier*, which invokes the language-independent extensions of Turbo Assembler. This extension allows you to specify arguments in a list, in the same order you would use in a normal C function call. That feature certainly makes life easier.

Language extensions in Turbo Assembler go further than that, however. If you look even more closely at the program in listing 10.7, you will notice that there are *no underscores* in it. Because underscores are still being generated by the compiler, why does this program not have any?

The more readable source format shown in listing 10.7 is enabled by the specification of C language extensions in the EXTRN, PUBLIC, and PROC declarations (in lines 22, 26, and 27). Each of these declarations specifies the C character immediately after the reserved word. The C specification in the EXTRN declaration permits reference to printf() without an underscore. The C specification in the PUBLIC declaration permits reference to the function name tokencpy without underscores. Finally, the same specification in the PROC statement permits reference to the function arguments without underscores.

Furthermore, notice in line 27 that the PROC statement declares the function arguments in the same order in which they appear in a call to this function. The argument declarations here allow you to refer to the arguments in the PROC body without having to explicitly load the BP register, and without having to compute relative offsets from BP to access the argument variables. Notice also that there is no code for pushing or popping BP to establish the standard stack frame. Using the C language extension specifier in the PROC statement causes all this to be done for you.

Using Turbo Assembler's simplified segment directives and the language-independent extensions makes writing assembly language routines for C programs so easy that you can even perform complex BGI graphics in assembly without much effort. Another pair of sample programs demonstrates this important point.

The C program in listing 10.8 is borrowed from the graph2.c program presented in Chapter 8, but is rewritten to invoke the gfx() assembly language function. gfx() does all the graphics work, leaving the C routine only the responsibility for waiting on the keyboard and terminating graphics mode.

Listing 10.8. graph3.c. *A C driver for the BGI graphics assembly language routine.*

```
1    /* GRAPH3.C This program is a rewrite of GRAPH2.C, which
2                    was presented in Chapter 8 */
3
4    #include <graphics.h>
5    #include <stdlib.h>
6    #include <stdio.h>
7    #include <conio.h>
8
9        int graphdrv = DETECT;
10       int graphmode;
11       int i, x, y;
12       int polypoints[] = { 10, 10,
13                            500, 10,
14                            500, 300,
15                             10, 10 };
16       char bgipath[] = "\\tcp\\bgi";
17
18   extern void gfx( );          /* Do it in assembly language */
19
20   int get_rand( int scale ) {
21     return random( scale );    /* random is inline function */
22   }
23
24   int main( )
25   {
26       randomize( );
27       gfx( );
28       while( !kbhit( ) );
29       closegraph( );
30       return 0;
31   }
```

In listing 10.8, the working variables have been moved from within main( ) (which is where they were in graph2.c) to file scope so that these variables will be placed in global static storage. This maneuver greatly simplifies accessing the variables in the assembly routine. The move also provides an opportunity to demonstrate the use of the EXTRN assembly declaration on a larger scale, as you can see in listing 10.9.

Listing 10.9. g f x . a s m . *A program that demonstrates how C language extensions make it easy to use BGI graphics in assembly.*

```
1               DOSSEG
2               .MODEL small
3     ;
4               EXTRN  C  initgraph:FAR
5               EXTRN  C  ellipse:FAR
6               EXTRN  C  cleardevice:FAR
7               EXTRN  C  drawpoly:FAR
8               EXTRN  C  line:FAR
9               EXTRN  C  bar3d:FAR
10              EXTRN  C  get_rand:PROC
11    ;
12              .DATA
13              EXTRN  C  graphdrv:WORD
14              EXTRN  C  graphmode:WORD
15              EXTRN  C  x:WORD
16              EXTRN  C  y:WORD
17              EXTRN  C  polypoints:WORD
18              EXTRN  C  bgipath:BYTE
19    adrsdrv   dd      0
20    adrsmode  dd      0
21    adrsbgi   dd      0
22    adrspoly  dd      0
23    ;
24              .CODE
25              PUBLIC C gfx
26    gfx       PROC C
27              push   si
28              push   di
29              push   ds
30    ;
31              push   ds
32              pop    es         ; start building pointers in _DATA
33              mov    word ptr adrsdrv+2,es
34              mov    word ptr adrsmode+2,es
35              mov    word ptr adrsbgi+2,es
36              mov    word ptr adrspoly+2,es
37              lea    ax,graphdrv
38              mov    word ptr adrsdrv,ax
39              lea    ax,graphmode
```

Listing 10.9. continues

Listing 10.9. continued

```
40            mov     word ptr adrsmode,ax
41            lea     ax,bgipath
42            mov     word ptr adrsbgi,ax
43            lea     ax,polypoints
44            mov     word ptr adrspoly,ax
45   ;
46            call    initgraph C,adrsdrv,adrsmode,adrsbgi
47            mov     cx,100
48   ellipses:
49            call    get_rand C,640
50            mov     x,ax
51            call    get_rand C,480
52            mov     y,ax
53            call    ellipse C,x,y,0,360,x,y
54            loop    ellipses
55            call    cleardevice C
56            call    drawpoly C,4,adrspoly
57            call    line C,0,450,640,450
58            call    bar3d C,100,50,300,400,10,1
59   ;
60            pop     ds
61            pop     di
62            pop     si
63            ret
64   gfx      ENDP
65            END
```

You might notice in listing 10.9 that the assembly module was assembled with the small memory model (as was the C driver program). Remember that all graphics library functions support far calls and far data only. That is why the statements in lines 31–44 for developing far addresses to graphics arguments are necessary. That is also why the FAR specifiers were needed in declaring the external library functions in lines 4–9.

Beyond the necessary machinations for such mixed-model programming, the simplified Turbo Assembler syntax is so clear that little more needs to be said. The calls to graphics functions are transparently obvious, and they have the sterling quality of working as planned.

Using Interrupt Functions

This section leads you through the Turbo C facilities for using 80x86 interrupt architecture. You learn first how to *cause* 80x86 and DOS interrupts and then how to *handle* interrupts caused by other parts of the system.

Understanding 80x86 Interrupt Architecture

80x86 interrupts can be caused by hardware (such as I/O devices) or by software (such as the `int` assembly instruction). When an interrupt occurs, the CPU saves its current status, including the address of the next instruction to be executed, the system flags, and the system registers.

What happens next depends on what *interrupt number* is associated with the interrupt. For hardware interrupts, a support chip generates and supplies the interrupt number. For software interrupts, the interrupt number is supplied by the `int` instruction's operand.

Now the 80x86 CPU uses the interrupt number as an index into a table of *interrupt vectors*; an interrupt vector is nothing more than a `far` (4 byte) pointer. The pointer for an interrupt contains the address of the interrupt service routine (ISR) that will handle the new conditions.

As you might imagine, the interrupt vector table is not placed just anywhere in memory. It has a fixed location at the beginning of RAM, at address 0000:0000. Figure 10.5 shows the relative location of the interrupt vector table, together with the rest of the RAM organization in an IBM PC or a compatible computer.

Because the interrupt vector table occupies the first 1,024 bytes of RAM, there can be a maximum of 256 interrupt vectors. The interrupt vectors are organized in groups, as shown in table 10.6, according to purpose and what kind of ISR will handle the interrupt condition. For complete coverage of specific interrupts and their uses, you may want to consult Terry Dettman's *DOS Programmer's Reference* (second edition, Que Corporation, 1989).

Fig. 10.5. Memory organization, including interrupt vector locations, for the IBM PC and compatibles.

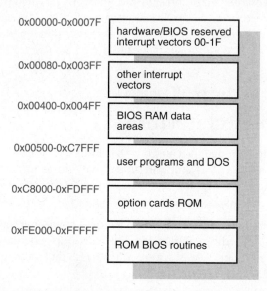

0x00000-0x0007F	hardware/BIOS reserved interrupt vectors 00-1F
0x00080-0x003FF	other interrupt vectors
0x00400-0x004FF	BIOS RAM data areas
0x00500-0xC7FFF	user programs and DOS
0xC8000-0xFDFFF	option cards ROM
0xFE000-0xFFFFF	ROM BIOS routines

Table 10.6. Summary of 80x86 interrupt vector usage on IBM and compatible ISA/EISA and MicroChannel computers.

Interrupt Invoked By	*Interrupt Handled By*	*Interrupt Numbers (Hex)*
Hardware	User, system handler	00-0F
User, DOS	ROM BIOS	10-1F
User	DOS	20-3F
DOS, dvc drvrs	BIOS, device drivers	40-5F
User	(Reserved for users)	60-66
User	LIM EMS driver	67
Hardware	Device drivers	70-77
BASIC	BASIC	80-F0
(Not used)	(Not used)	F1-FF

As you can see in table 10.6, most interrupts are handled by the system: either the BIOS or DOS will do the work. In a few circumstances, your program can "hook" itself into the interrupt vector table and provide the ISR for an interrupt vector. You see how to do that in the section "Using Interrupt Handlers" later in this chapter. But before you move to that more complicated task, you need to consider how to cause system interrupts in a controlled and useful manner.

Using Borland's Interrupt Interfaces

Both Turbo C++ and Borland C++ 2.0 provide two library functions for causing generic 80x86 interrupts, and two functions for causing DOS interrupts. These functions are int86( ), int86x( ), intdos( ), and intdosx( ).

All four of these interrupt-causing functions must use the union name REGS (declared in dos.h) in which to store and read back copies of the system registers. This is important because the system registers must be used to communicate parameters to the interrupt handlers (ISRs) within the BIOS and DOS. The int86x( ) and intdosx( ) functions additionally affect the DS and ES registers through the REGPACK structure (also declared in dos.h), but these functions are not discussed here. This discussion instead focuses on the int86( ) and intdos( ) functions. (Logic involving the modification of DS and ES is best left to assembly language, and you already know how to use that.)

The REGS union has two member structures. The h structure contains unsigned char declarations for all the byte registers (ah, al, bh, bl, and so on). The x structure member contains unsigned int declarations for all the word registers (ax, bx, cx, and the rest). Note that the register variable names are written in *lowercase* letters. Thus, a REGS union object named reg contains a member named reg.h.al, which holds a copy of the system AL register; and a member named reg.x.ax, which holds a copy of the system AX register. Finally, note that assigning a value to reg.x.ax implicitly places a value in reg.h.ah *and* in reg.h.al (remember the overlay nature of unions).

The general sequence for invoking a BIOS interrupt involves first loading the AH system register with a *function code* (a number indicating the specific action to be taken) and then executing the int instruction that specifies the interrupt number as its operand. In the next program, for example, the 0x13 interrupt, function code 0x19 is used to park the heads of a fixed disk drive. The assembly language sequence for accomplishing this action is the following:

```
...
mov     ah,19h      ; function code for park heads
mov     dl,80       ; do it for drive C:
int     13h         ; get BIOS to do it
...
```

When using the Turbo C int86() function, of course, you do not load system registers directly; their values are extracted by the int86() function from the REGS union you set up before calling the function. Nor do you invoke the interrupt directly; the int86() function does that after setting the real system registers properly. Listing 10.10 shows how to use the int86() function to park the heads on all the fixed disk drives on your system.

Listing 10.10. fdpark.c. *A program that uses the* int86() *function to park heads for all system fixed disk drives.*

```
 1   /* FDPARK.C ---- Use INT86() function to park all fixed
 2                         disk drives in the system
 3   */
 4
 5   #include <stdio.h>
 6   #include <stdlib.h>
 7   #include <dos.h>
 8
 9   void main()
10   {
11     union REGS reg;   /* Register structs declared in dos.h */
12     unsigned char driveid = 0;                /* Begin with C: */
13
14     while ( 1 ) {
15       reg.x.ax = 0x1900;
16       reg.h.dl = 0x80 | driveid;
17       int86( 0x13, &reg, &reg );
18       if ( reg.h.ah ) break;    /* Error code means no more */
19       printf( "Parked heads for drive %c:...\n",
20               driveid++ + 67 );
21     }
22   }
```

Notice how the reg object is used in the int86() interrupt call in line 17. Always be sure to pass the *address* of the union to int86(). The first argument is the address of the register variables union used as *input* to int86(): the function will extract the setup values from the first argument. The second argument is the address of the register variables union that will be *output* from int86(): the values of the resulting registers are placed there.

The program in listing 10.10 also illustrates the fact that BIOS interrupt functions often return a status code reflecting the outcome of the operation. In this case, register AH is zero if the head-parking operation was successful, but contains an error code if the operation was not successful. (The logic uses the error code to detect an absence of any further fixed disk drives.) Again, you do not access the system register AH directly. You get the value of that register as reported by int86() from the REGS union.

The head-parking program has some limitations you should know about. Although the program will work with almost all recent computers, some users may have an older computer with a fixed disk drive tacked on to it. BIOS interrupt 0x13, function 0x19 works only for the following personal computers:

❏ The PC/AT with BIOS dated after 11/15/86 or completely compatible computers

❏ The PC/XT with BIOS dated after 1/10/86 or completely compatible computers

❏ The entire PS/2 line of computers and compatibles

If your computer does not fall into one of these groups, fdpark.c won't hurt anything, but it won't *do* anything either.

Because Turbo C++ and Borland C++ 2.0 are such complete packages, there are only a few times when you will need to use the int86() function. Parking fixed disk heads is clearly one of those times. Using the intdos() function is even more rare, but it is discussed here for the sake of completeness.

DOS functions are available to users (meaning programmers) through the 80x86 interrupt number 0x21, with many associated function codes. Because DOS calls fall into a class by themselves, Borland C++ provides the intdos() function, which assumes that the interrupt number is 0x21. Frankly, there is little reason to use this function in ordinary code because the ANSI standard library functions, plus the Borland-supplied additional functions, cover just about every contingency. This is true of the program in listing 10.11, which uses the DOS function code 0x2A to get the system date and the weekday from DOS.

Listing 10.11. `calldos.c`. *A program that uses the* `intdos( )` *function to get the system date and weekday.*

```
1   /* CALLDOS.C ---- Use INTDOS( ) function to get the system
2                          date and weekday
3   */
4
5   #include <stdio.h>
6   #include <stdlib.h>
7   #include <dos.h>
8
9   char *months[] = {
10    "",
11    "January",  "February","March",    "April",
12    "May",      "June",    "July",     "August",
13    "September","October", "November","December",
14  };
15
16  char *days[] = {
17    "Sunday",   "Monday", "Tuesday", "Wednesday",
18    "Thursday", "Friday", "Saturday",
19  };
20
21  void main( )
22  {
23    union REGS reg;   /* Register structs declared in dos.h */
24
25    reg.x.ax = 0x2A00;    /* Set up call code for int. 0x21 */
26    intdos( &reg, &reg );        /* Get the date & weekday */
27    printf( "The current date is %s, %s %d, %d.\n",
28            days[reg.h.al], months[reg.h.dh],
29            reg.h.dl, reg.x.cx );
30  }
```

The `intdos( )` function is almost exactly the same as the `int86( )` function in its use and arguments, except for the name and the absence of the interrupt number. Once more, if you want details on all the DOS interrupts, you can consult Dettman's *DOS Programmer's Reference*.

Using Interrupt Handlers

An interrupt handler is an ISR. That's simple enough. But what if you want to take over the handling of an interrupt, instead of allowing the BIOS code or DOS to do it? Borland C++ provides for this contingency as well, by offering the `interrupt` specifier. You can use the `interrupt` specifier to identify one of your own C functions as an ISR. In this section, you learn what that means and how to do it. You also have a little fun writing an ISR that displays a real-time clock on the screen while your program goes about its other business.

Declaring Interrupt Handler Functions

The general form of an interrupt handler function is the following:

```
void interrupt newint60( int bp,int di,int si,int ds,
                         int es,int dx,int cx,int bx,
                         int ax,int ip,int cs, int flags)
{
    /* Do something in here */
}
```

When an interrupt has caused your ISR to be executed, the system has already pushed the flags, the CS register, and the IP (instruction pointer) register onto the system stack. Code that Turbo C generated and prefixed to your ISR function has also pushed the remaining registers onto the stack, in the order shown in the preceding code fragment (remember that Borland C++ scans argument lists from right to left). You do not have to declare all the system registers for every ISR function. However, you cannot skip any or alter the order shown here: if you need register `ax`, you must declare in the parameter list all the registers before that one.

The body of your ISR function can modify any or all of those registers by assigning new values to the registers arguments passed to the function; this has the effect of altering a register's contents as it sits on the stack. When that register is popped off the stack (when the ISR returns), it contains the new value. Common sense—as well as the restrictions on preserving registers, which were detailed earlier in this chapter—indicate which registers you may safely alter.

Aside from altering system registers in an ISR, you can do a number of useful things in the ISR's function body. You can update variables that are in scope for the ISR function (its own local variables and global static data), read and write data from a communications port, display information on the screen, and even cause further interrupts (nested interrupts). There is one thing that you should *not* do, though, if you want your program to continue running and your disks to remain uncorrupted (unless you are a DOS and an assembly expert). *Do not* attempt to perform disk file I/O.

The reason for this severe restriction is that interrupts occur at unpredictable times—for instance, when DOS is already in the middle of doing other file functions. Furthermore, DOS is a single-tasking (single threaded) operating system, and you may cause that wonderful simpleton to lose track of its internal stack (it actually has two stacks, which is even worse) and completely wreck whatever it was in the process of doing.

There are still many useful things you can do with ISRs, however, as you are about to find out. First, you need to know the basics of setting up the ISR and hooking into the interrupt vector the ISR will be servicing. In broad strokes, you should perform the following tasks when instating your own ISR:

❑ *Preserve the old interrupt vector.* Turbo C thoughtfully provides the getvect( ) function for this purpose. You can save this far pointer in a pointer to function.

❑ *Hook the address of your ISR function into the interrupt vector.* The setvect( ) library function performs this task.

❑ *Before your program exits to the system, restore the old interrupt vector.* Use the setvect( ) function again, with the old ISR address you saved before.

That sounds simple enough. You are ready to put the knowledge to work and write an ISR to demonstrate the techniques. The program in listing 10.12 is named dummy.c because it's pretty dumb, and it doesn't do much. It does implement a primitive form of multitasking, however, by decoding a value in ax and using that value to decide in which of two Turbo C display windows to display an integer value placed in bx. The main( ) function uses int86( ) to generate the 0x60 interrupt, after it has set up the required register values. (0x60 is a user interrupt, so it is legal to use; see table 10.6.)

Listing 10.12. dummy.c. *A dumb program that performs primitive multitasking with user interrupt 0x60.*

```
1    #include <stdio.h>
2    #include <dos.h>
3    #include <conio.h>
4
5    void interrupt (far *oldint60)( );
6
```

```
 7   void interrupt newint60( int bp,int di,int si,int ds,
 8                            int es,int dx,int cx,int bx,int ax)
 9   {
10     if ( ( ax >> 8 ) ) {
11       window ( 20, 12, 26, 20 );
12       delay( 1 );
13       cprintf( "%d\r\n", bx );
14     }
15     else {
16       window ( 10, 12, 16, 20 );
17       delay( 1 );
18       cprintf( "%d\r\n", bx );
19     }
20   }
21
22
23   void main( )
24   {
25     int i;
26     union REGS reg;
27
28     oldint60 = getvect( 0x60 );
29     setvect( 0x60, newint60 );
30
31     clrscr( );
32     for ( i=0; i<4096; ++i ) {
33       reg.x.ax = 0x0000;
34       reg.x.bx = i;
35       int86( 0x60, &reg, &reg );
36       reg.x.ax = 0x0001 | i;
37       reg.x.bx = i;
38       int86( 0x60, &reg, &reg );
39     }
40
41     setvect( 0x60, oldint60 );
42     window ( 1, 1, 80, 25 );
43   }
```

Notice in listing 10.12 that both the a x and b x register variables are used, so all the register variables up to that point in the parameter list are declared. No registers following that point are needed, however, so they are not declared.

The program in listing 10.12 follows all the rules just specified quite nicely. It declares a function pointer in line 5, in which the old interrupt vector is stored (notice the `void` return type and `interrupt` specifier there). Line 28 retrieves the old interrupt value and saves it in the pointer to function, and line 29 sets up the new vector, using your ISR function's address.

The loop in lines 32–39 invokes the 0x60 ISR function, alternately specifying the "left window" (when `ax == 0`) and the "right window" (when `a == 1`). In every case, the value of the loop counter is placed in the `bx` register variable. The resulting effect is quite interesting: the screen displays two integers spooling up toward 4096 simultaneously.

After all the fun is over, the old interrupt 0x60 vector is restored in line 41. Because interrupt 0x60 is reserved for users just like us, the system's ISR was probably a dummy one, but how can your program continue to service the interrupt when it is gone? Failing to restore *any* interrupt vector is to invite a system crash. It is always best to do it by the numbers.

Implementing a Timer Tick Interrupt Handler

This section presents a serious ISR. It intercepts the system clock tick interrupt and uses the opportunity to display a real-time clock in the top left corner of the screen. After you set up the ISR, the rest of the program goes about its business--at the same time that the clock is being continuously updated.

The timer tick interrupt (number 0x08) is one of those interrupts that is hardware generated. When the system interval timer goes off, it activates an interrupt request circuit (a physical electronic circuit) that is gated to the interrupt 0x08 vector. Even more interesting, the BIOS ISR for interrupt 0x08 invokes another, software interrupt: vector 0x1C.

The purpose of interrupt 0x1C is to allow user programs to intercept it and do something useful with it. The BIOS ISR should generally be left alone because it does such things as turning off diskette drive motors that have been left running. (It is possible to intercept interrupt 0x08, but that won't be shown here.)

Figure 10.6 shows the flow of instruction execution when a timer tick occurs. The user program is temporarily suspended, and the interrupt 0x08 ISR is executed; it in turn invokes interrupt 0x1C.

Fig. 10.6. Program execution flow when a timer tick occurs.

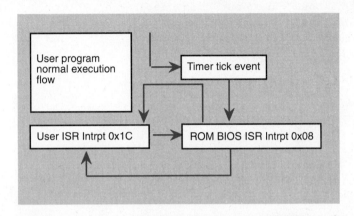

When the real-time clock ISR is finished, execution flow trickles back up through the 0x08 ISR, and finally back to the user program, exactly where it was suspended. The user program then continues running, none the wiser. The net effect, of course, is the appearance of having two programs running at the same time: one for the clock and one for the more mundane code. The program that handles all this, ticker.c, is shown in listing 10.13.

Listing 10.13. ticker.c. An ISR routine that intercepts timer ticks and display a real-time clock on screen.

```
 1   /* ------------------------------------------------
 2       TICKER.C contains an interrupt service
 3       routine (ISR). BE SURE that the test-
 4       stack-overflow Options|Compiler|Code Generation
 5       is turned OFF.
 6       ------------------------------------------------ */
 7   #pragma inline
 8
 9   #include <stdlib.h>
10   #include <stdio.h>
11   #include <dos.h>
12   #include <conio.h>
13
14   void interrupt far (*oldint1c)( );
15
```

Listing 10.13. continues

Listing 10.13. continued

```
16  unsigned char hour, min, sec;
17  unsigned sc0_base = 0xb800; /* base adrs for cga/ega/vga */
18  int todx = 1, tody = 1;
19  char tstring[9];
20
21  void interrupt newint1c( )
22  {
23    static unsigned int count = 18;
24
25    if ( --count == 0 ) {
26      count = 18;
27      asm {              /* Get time function */
28        sti
29        mov   ah,02h
30        int   1ah              /* Invoke BIOS BCD time     */
31        mov   hour,ch
32        mov   min,cl
33        mov   sec,dh
34      }
35      tstring[0] = ( hour >> 4 ) + '0';  /* Unpack BCD time */
36      tstring[1] = ( hour & 0x0F ) + '0';
37      tstring[2] = ':';
38      tstring[3] = ( min >> 4 ) + '0';
39      tstring[4] = ( min & 0x0F ) + '0';
40      tstring[5] = ':';
41      tstring[6] = ( sec >> 4 ) + '0';
42      tstring[7] = ( sec & 0x0F ) + '0';
43      asm {             /* Get it on the screen - quickly */
44        xor   dx,dx
45        mov   ax,tody
46        dec   ax              /* Adjust to 0-origin adrs */
47        mov   si,160
48        mul   si              /* Line offset in AX        */
49        mov   cx,ax           /* Save line offset         */
50        mov   ax,todx
51        dec   ax
52        shl   ax,1            /* Byte offset              */
53        add   cx,ax           /* Total offset CX          */
54        mov   di,cx
55        cli
56        push  es
```

```
57          mov   es,sc0_base     /* ES points to output RAM */
58          mov   cx,8            /* 8 bytes out             */
59          mov   si,0
60       }
61   show_tick:
62       asm {
63          mov   bl,tstring[si] /* Pick up display byte     */
64          mov   bh,70h          /* Normal video attribute  */
65          mov   ax,bx           /* Recover bytes           */
66          stosw                 /* Output, di auto incr    */
67          inc   si
68          loop show_tick
69          pop   ax
70          mov   es,ax
71          sti
72       }
73    }
74  }
75
76  void start_ticker( void )
77  {
78     oldint1c = getvect( 0x1c );
79     setvect( 0x1c, newint1c );
80  }
81
82  void stop_ticker( void )
83  {
84     setvect( 0x1c, oldint1c );
85  }
86
87  void main()
88  {
89     char ch;
90     int quit = 0, i = 1, incr = 1;
91
92     clrscr();
93     gotoxy( 24, 12 );
94     puts( "Strike Esc to stop the demo." );
95     start_ticker();
96     window( 12, 14, 68, 24 );
97     while ( !quit ) {
98        if ( kbhit() ) {
```

Listing 10.13. continues

Listing 10.13. continued

```
 99          if ( 0 == ( ch = getch( ) ) ) ch = getch( );
100          if ( ch == 27 ) ++quit;
101        }
102        gotoxy ( i*5, i );
103        cprintf( "%s", "Hello" );
104        i += incr;
105        if ( i == 10 ) { incr = -1; clrscr( ); }
106        if ( i == 1 )  { incr = 1; clrscr( ); }
107      }
108      stop_ticker( );
109      window( 1, 1, 80, 25 );
110      clrscr( );
111    }
```

One of the most important things to remember about writing an ISR for the timer tick is that *no more timer ticks can occur while your ISR is running*. Therefore, your ISR had better finish its work before the next timer tick occurs, or the system clock will get further behind. Moreover, if you cut it too close, there may be little or no time left over for the main program to do any of its work. All things considered, the faster the ISR runs, the better it will be. For that reason, most of the 0x1C ISR function has been coded with inline assembly.

Perhaps the most interesting feature of this ISR is the invocation of the BIOS 0x1A interrupt to get the current time in BCD (true Binary Coded Decimal—not the kind of number used in the Borland C++ BCD class). The BCD time is unpacked and formatted for display in lines 29–42. The remaining inline assembly is concerned with getting the resulting time string on the screen as quickly as possible.

Exercises

The following exercises reinforce what you have learned about inline assembly, writing separately assembled C-callable modules, and interrupt handlers.

1. Using inline assembly language, write a function that raises one integer to an integral power. The function prototype might look something like this:

```
int ipower( int arg1, int arg1);
```

Use the small memory model, so that `arg1` can be located by `[bp+4]`, and `arg2` can be located by `[bp+6]`. Tip: leave the result in the `ax` register, and return from the function with this statement:

```
return _AX;   /* Use the _AX pseudo-variable */
```

2. Write a separately assembled C-callable assembly language routine that mimics `strcat( )`. Use the large memory model for the assembly module, and use whatever memory model you choose for the C module. If you mix models, be sure to declare the prototype for the assembly function routine in order to guarantee that pointers of the correct size are used.

3. Write another C-callable assembly routine that accepts two `double` arguments, multiplies them together, stores them in a local (`auto`) variable, and calls `printf( )` to display the result. Use the simplified segment directives and language-independent extensions of Turbo Assembler. You can declare the arguments as quadwords, like this:

```
muxproc PROC C arg1:QWORD,arg2:QWORD
```

You can allocate space on the stack for automatic variables by adjusting the stack pointer register, as in this code fragment:

```
sub     sp,8    ; space for double auto
...
fld     arg1
fmul    arg2
fstp    [bp-8] ; store in auto var and pop off ST(0)
fwait
....
add     sp,8    ; dump auto var
...
```

This code fragment shows you also how to multiply the floating-point numbers. Don't forget to code the `EMUL` emulation directive if your computer does not have an 80x87 coprocessor. Before you dump the `auto` variable, you can call `printf( )` with `[bp-8]` as an argument.

4. Modify the `ticker.c` program to allow a user to use the arrow keys to move the real-time clock around the screen. Tip: you will have to unhook your ISR temporarily and reinstate it after adjusting the `todx` and `tody` variables.

Summary

If you want to add the ultimate power to your Turbo C and C++ programs, Borland has provided all the tools you need to do it. This chapter showed you how to use these tools. Specifically, you learned how to

❑ *Write inline assembly statements in your programs.* You can insert assembly statements directly into your programs using the a s m keyword. The new Borland C++ 2.0 high-end package simplifies things further, by providing a built-in assembler.

❑ *Implement fully C-callable assembly language function routines.* With separately assembled modules, you can do just about anything. Turbo Assembler's simplified segment directives and language-independent extensions make this process a snap.

❑ *Call any of the Borland C++ library functions from assembly language code.* You can also call your own C functions from assembly language. Turbo Assembler extensions again make this very easy.

❑ *Use 80x86 and DOS interrupts to provide sophisticated services for your program.* Using interrupts makes available the full power of the system BIOS and the DOS operating system.

❑ *Write an ISR to handle asynchronous (unpredictable) system events.* An interrupt service routine (ISR) lets your program perform sophisticated tasks. You can even implement a small degree of multitasking operation using ISRs.

This is all pretty heady stuff—but there is more to come. In Part II, you learn about object-oriented programming, using Borland C++ at an intermediate to advanced level. And in Part III, you are introduced to the world of Windows 3.0 applications programming, using the Borland C++ 2.0 high-end compiler and its associated utilities. We hope you have the whole weekend free!

Part II

Using Borland C++'s Object-Oriented Features

CHAPTER 11

Using C++ Classes

C++ was originally called "C with classes." The class concept, which is central to C++, gives the language its unique capabilities. Borland C++ supports all the most recent class-definition features. This chapter presents a thorough introduction to C++ class fundamentals.

You should be aware, however, that C++ is not a programming language for beginners. A beginner can learn C++, but even fundamental C++ embodies some rather sophisticated C concepts. From this chapter on, therefore, the text is directed to those users who are at least moderately proficient with standard C and its terminology.

To understand Borland C++, you must understand C++ classes. A *class* is a user-defined *type*. The idea of "class" as a "type" goes considerably further than the `typedef` you have already seen. Recall that the `typedef` is simply a synonym feature provided by C. A C++ class declaration enables you to define a completely new kind of object—a class object—with properties you specify. The difference between C data types and C++ classes is so significant that the terms *data object* and *class object* are used, respectively, to distinguish the two concepts.

As the discussion of classes develops in this and later chapters, you will sometimes see the phrase *C++ base document*. The base document for C++ is a book entitled *The Annotated C++ Reference Manual*, by Margaret A. Ellis and Bjarne Stroustrup (Addison-Wesley, 1990). This book embodies the current standard of C++ practice and is the platform the ANSI X3J16 committee will use to develop a standard for C++. Borland C++ is almost entirely in conformity to this standard.

429

Comparing Derived Types in C and C++

In standard C, *derived types* (arrays, structures and unions, function types, and pointer types) are all derived from the basic data types. You can derive a more complex type from a simpler one by grouping basic type objects together (as in a structure) or by using a basic object type in a new way (as in forming a pointer to an integer). You can also use the `typedef` keyword to associate a new type name with the derived object.

The *structure* is a particularly useful and interesting derived data type for two reasons. First, the structure permits you to group together data objects having many different basic types (even other structures) and to treat the result as a single entity. The standard C structure is a very useful type, even if no further capabilities are added to it. Second, the structure is the underlying basis for the C++ class. What this means will become apparent as you read through this chapter.

There are some things you cannot do with a standard C structure, however. You cannot use a structure directly as part of an expression (although you can write a function that "adds" two structures), and you cannot define a function within a structure (although you can declare a pointer to a function within a structure). You *can* define a C++ class that allows objects of that class to do both of these things, and more.

Redefining "Derived" in C++

With standard C, you can derive new groupings and new uses of predefined data types, but you cannot alter the nature—the fundamental behavior—of any predefined type. Therefore, the type-definition facility of C can never be more than a means of applying new names (synonyms) to something that already exists.

C++ not only allows you to define the existence and contents of a class type, but also requires you to define the type's behavior. Thus, a class can be considered a data type, but a class is not truly a derived type. A class is a *new* type. It is more appropriate to speak of C++ classes as *user-defined* types rather than as derived types.

You can use the features of standard C to approach the functionality of C++ class objects, but C can never match either the power or the elegance of the class object. You can write a function that sums two arrays of integers, for example, but standard C cannot permit the following use of array names:

```
int a[10];
int b[10];
int c[10];
...
c = a + b;   /* ILLEGAL IN STANDARD C */
```

You *can* design a C++ class, however, that will support the use of the addition operator with objects of that class. The following code fragment briefly shows how to define the addition operation for array *class* objects:

```
class arrayplus { // skeleton class declaration
   int data[10];
public:
   arrayplus operator+( arrayplus& );
   ...
};
...
arrayplus arrayplus::operator+( arrayplus& op2 )
{
   int i;
   arrayplus hold; // define a temporary object

for ( i=0; i<10; ++i )
    hold.data[i] = data[i] + op2.data[i];
   return hold;                   // return by value
}
...
arrayplus a, b, c;  // Define some class objects
c = a + b;          // this is legal, now
```

This code fragment contains a number of new features that are explained throughout this chapter and the following chapters. You should be able, however, to detect three things in the code fragment without a detailed knowledge of C++ syntax:

❑ *C++ classes define both the content and the behavior of new (user-defined) types.* In the preceding code fragment, the arrayplus class defines both the structure of an array's data elements and the method used to add two arrayplus objects. The *method* (a technical word borrowed from OOPS) is given in the form of a *member function* (a function that actually belongs to the class). The member function in this case is operator+().

❑ *Class declarations can and do have intimately associated functions that control the behavior of the class.* Standard C structures can contain a pointer to a function, but not embedded function definitions. Nor can a C structure own a function as a class can. You learn how functions are associated with classes in the next section.

❏ *C++ comments differ greatly from C comments.* C++ comments are introduced by two consecutive slashes and are terminated only by the end of the source line. Thus, C++ comments must be either the last thing on a source line or the *only* thing on a source line.

As you can see, you can arrange a C++ class declaration so that an object having that class (that is, having that user-defined type) can be used directly in an expression. Although controlling a class object's behavior is not nearly all that you can do with class definitions, it is one of the most important things you can do with them.

Understanding C++ Encapsulation

It should be clear by now that classes are used to bundle together an object's data structure and the methods for controlling the object's data. This approach to defining objects arises naturally out of the more general theory of OOPS (object-oriented programming systems). Bundling data and methods together is called *encapsulation*.

Encapsulation is an important part of the design of C++. Encapsulation accomplishes three things: (1) it hides complexity, (2) it discourages the programmer from tampering with code that already works, and (3) it promotes the reuse of previously developed code.

C++ encapsulates class objects by using structures (with either the struct or class keyword). Ordinary C structures contain data members that belong to the structure and which cannot be accessed apart from the structure. Class declarations go a step further and permit data *and* member functions, both of which *belong to the class*.

Thus, C++ uses the struct type as a foundation for class objects, but C++ structures and classes can do many things that C structures cannot do. Ownership of functions as well as data gives C++ classes an added "dimension," as shown in figure 11.1.

C++ classes use encapsulation to hide complexity in two ways: by concealing internal data structures and functions, and by providing a user (that is, programmer) interface that does not require knowledge of a class object's internal workings. Just as you do not have to know the bit structure of a floating-point number, or what goes on behind the scenes when floating-point numbers are multiplied together, you also do not need to focus on a class object's internal structure or internal functions in order to use the class object. You need only to call the object's public member functions to "interface" with the object. The concept of encapsulation is illustrated in figure 11.2.

Fig. 11.1. *C structures own data members, but C++ classes own both data members and member functions.*

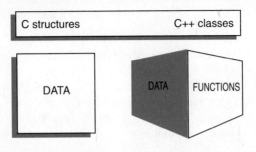

Fig. 11.2. *C++ encapsulation of class objects hides the object's internal workings from a user of the object.*

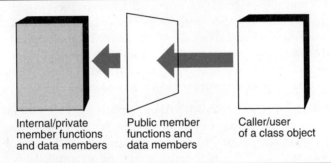

Internal/private
member functions
and data members

Public member
functions and
data members

Caller/user
of a class object

Encapsulation also discourages programmers from unnecessarily tampering with data structures and functions that are already functional. The urge to take shortcuts is sooner or later irresistible to the ordinary programmer (including us, and you too). The danger of modifying data with a shortcut method is simply that you are likely to forget some necessary part of the process, and to corrupt the data.

When data structures and the functions authorized to modify them are placed out of sight through encapsulation, the temptation to tamper with complex structures is reduced. Although encapsulation may at first seem like an irritating restriction, you will find with experience that there are definite benefits involved. Encapsulation really does reduce the incidence of accidental damage to data structures. In the end, the need for debugging large projects can be drastically reduced (but the trade-off is that debugging is correspondingly more difficult).

Encapsulation also provides, in a roundabout way, shortcuts to manipulating data structures. Such shortcuts are possible because class objects are self-contained; you do not have to remember constantly all the complexities of manipulating class objects. The objects themselves take care of handling the data structures.

Finally, the self-contained nature of encapsulated objects encourages the use and reuse of already developed code. C++ classes are easily reusable because class objects tend to be both robust and capable. They are generally robust because it is easier to write sophisticated code in a C++ class than in a plain C program (another benefit of encapsulation). You are therefore more apt to write class declarations that anticipate all uses of the class.

Declaring Classes with *struct*

In the preceding section, you learned that a class object's public member functions provide an "interface" with users of the object (that is, public member functions of a class object can be called by other functions that want to use the object). Thinking of public member functions as an interface to a class object is a helpful notion, but C++ has no formal "implementation definition" or "interface module" as some other object-oriented languages do.

Languages such as Simula do have an interface definition that places user-defined objects in memory outside the main program. The advantage of handling object interfaces this way is that a change made to the class object does not affect the main program. It does not need to be recompiled when changes are made to a class definition.

A formal interface module that must be used to access every class object has a great disadvantage, however: it's *slow*. A lack of execution speed is, in fact, one of the primary reasons that OOPS languages have not become popular sooner.

C++ overcomes the speed barrier by treating user-defined objects in almost exactly the same way that it treats built-in object types. The compiler always knows the size and internal structure of a class object, even if the programmer does not. But treating classes this way means that everything about the class *must be known at compile time*. Interpretation of class code is not done at run time.

Therefore, if any changes are made to a class (even the private, "invisible" parts), any program that uses the class must be recompiled and relinked, or the program will still be using the old version of the class. But the great advantage of this approach is that it allows a main program to access objects *directly*, which is in keeping with the original C philosophy of generating trim, fast run-time code. You do not have to use pointers (or any other additional interface) to an object unless you want to use them.

Although C++ does not place artificial barriers in the way of using class objects, it does observe certain conventions in determining which data members and member functions of a class can be accessed by functions not belonging to the class. A class object has both *private* and *public* members:

❑ *Private data members and member functions can be used only by member functions of the class and by functions that are friends of the class.* Members of a class are private by default when the class is declared with the `class` keyword. You can allow class members to default to `private` access or you can specify them to be private members to hide a class object's complexity. Declaring classes with the `class` keyword is covered in the next section, and friend functions are discussed at the end of this chapter.

❑ *Public data members and member functions can be used by any function.* Members of a class are public by default when the class is declared with the `struct` or `union` keyword. The rest of this section covers the use of `struct` and `union` to declare a class.

Declaring a class with the `struct` or `union` keyword is the most straightforward way to give immediate, direct access to a class and its members. All the members (data and functions) of a C++ `struct` allow public access from anywhere in the program. A class declared with `union` also allows public access by default and has the additional characteristic that only one member is active at a time (in keeping with the notion of unions as overlays of the same area of memory). The following discussion refers only to structures, but the same rules apply to unions too.

In C++, a structure *is* a class and, at the same time, a true structure (avoiding many compatibility problems with C). Comparing C++ structures to C structures is helpful in understanding the additional capabilities of the C++ variety. Recall the general syntax for declaring a structure object:

```
struct tag_opt {member-list_opt} identifier-list_opt ;
```

The `struct` syntax should be familiar to you. You can use it as you would in ordinary C, or you can use it in C++ to define a true class type. When you use `struct` to declare a class, a number of new things begin to happen. Listing 11.1 shows you some of them. Look at the code carefully before continuing to read.

Listing 11.1. `structob.cpp`. *Using* `struct` *to declare a class.*

```
1    #include <stdlib.h>
2    #include <stdio.h>
3
4    struct myclass {
5      int a;
6      myclass();
7      void showclass();
8    } my_obj;
9
10   myclass::myclass()
11   {
12     a = 37; // initialize the object
13   }
14
15   void myclass::showclass()
16   {
17    printf( "The value of my object is %d\n", a );
18   }
19
20   void main()
21   {
22     // ---- Prove that everything in a class
23     // ---- declared with struct is accessible
24
25     my_obj.a = 64;  // ref. just like a C struct
26     my_obj.showclass();
27   }
```

Some parts of the program in listing 11.1 will present no problem to you at all. The `#include` statements in lines 1 and 2 are old friends, and so is the general layout of the `main()` function.

Users familiar with previous versions of Turbo C will probably spot something new, though, in line 20. The `main()` function has been declared as `void`. Many experienced C programmers are accustomed to declaring `main()` with no return type at all. Failure to specify a return type for `main()`, however, causes Borland C++ to generate a compile-time warning message. If you don't mind the warning message, you may certainly code `main()` without a return type.

References to structure members, in lines 25 and 26, appear familiar also. The syntax of a reference to a structure data member is still the same as in ordinary C. But if you look closely at line 26, you will see that the reference made there is to a member *function*—something you cannot include within a C structure.

There are further aspects of the structure declaration in listing 11.1 that are not yet familiar to you. Look first at lines 4–8. The structure is declared in those lines, but remember that this is C++, and the `struct` declaration actually defines a *class*.

Notice particularly that lines 6 and 7 contain function prototypes for the class's member functions. Function prototypes are definitely not allowed in C structures! Several points about member function declarations are not obvious from the sample code:

❏ *C++ classes can declare special functions—constructor and destructor functions—which are not allowed elsewhere in the program.* Constructor functions are used to set up and initialize class objects, and destructor functions are used to destroy class objects (that is, to release their memory if necessary). These functions are covered in the section "Providing Constructor and Destructor Functions" later in this chapter, as well as in Chapter 15.

❏ *Special methods are required for associating class member functions with the class.* The syntax for associating a member function with its class is like nothing you have seen in C. The details for setting up member functions are given in the section "Writing Member Functions for a Class" later in this chapter.

❏ *C++ function prototypes of the form* `function()` *do not imply the old-style (Kernighan and Ritchie) practice of allowing the function definition to assume any function parameters it likes.* In old-style (K&R) C, an empty formal parameter list meant that the corresponding function definition could declare any parameters it was suitable to declare. You just had to make sure that a function call to that function actually passed the expected number and type of arguments.

In C++, an empty formal parameter list has the same meaning as the ANSI standard syntax `function( void )`. In other words, *no* arguments are permitted. This rule also applies to *any* function declared in a C++ program.

❏ *C++ considers old-style function definitions to be an anachronism.* Function definitions of the following form used to be quite common:

```
sum( a, b )
  int a;
  int b:
{
  return a + b;
}
```

In fact, both ANSI C and C++ still permit this form of function definition, but both types of compilers consider the practice to be dangerous and out-of-date. Furthermore, C++ does *not* allow class member functions to be defined with this syntax; you must use the full function prototype for class member functions.

Lines 10–18 in listing 11.1 contain the code defining the class member functions. The class's constructor function (one of those special functions), appears in lines 10–13. This particular constructor function is a simple one: it initializes the integer member variable a. The syntax of the constructor function for a class is distinctive in that no return type is permitted; and the constructor function name is exactly the same as the class name. The most interesting thing about this member function is the way that it accesses the member variable a. Because the function is a member of the class, the function is not required to use the structure member operator (.) that was required in main().

The other member function, showclass(), is shown in lines 15–18. Its sole purpose is to display the value of the member variable a. Like the constructor function, the most distinctive feature of showclass() is that it doesn't need to use the structure member operator to access a member variable.

The last thing you should notice in listing 11.1 is the direct definition in line 8 of a struct object, my_obj, together with the struct declaration. Although such a definition is perfectly legal, class objects are almost never defined in this manner in C++ (regardless of whether the class or struct keyword is used). Normal usage looks like this:

```
struct myclass {    // Declare the class here
   int a;
   myclass();
   void showclass();
};
   ...
void main()
{
   myclass my_obj;    // Declare the class OBJECT here
   my_obj.a = 64;
   my_obj.showclass();
}
```

The main reason for using local object definitions (which, like other local variables, have auto duration) is to avoid the use of global variables. Because C++ class objects are typically much larger than standard C data objects, globally defined class objects take up a lot of memory space in your programs. The goal is to allow class objects to disappear whenever possible, and as soon as possible. Other reasons for using local objects involve issues of performance and garbage collection. Class object behavior and performance are discussed in Chapter 18, in the section "Controlling Object Behavior and Performance."

Other parts of listing 11.1 are obviously worth examining. Elements common to all classes are discussed in the next section. From this point on, classes are declared with the class keyword. This does not mean that classes declared with struct are undesirable—only that they are not as common.

Declaring C++ Classes

The members of a class (both data and functions) declared with the class keyword are private by default; that is, they can be accessed only by member functions (and friend functions) of the class. The fact that class members have by default a private attribute can cause unexpected problems in designing classes. This issue deserves more explanation.

The key concept in understanding the public or private nature of member objects is that the private attribute controls *access* to member objects, *not visibility* of member objects. To help you understand the difference between access control and visibility (that is, classical C *scope*), two C++ programs are presented here. One of them works, but not as expected; the other doesn't even compile correctly.

The first program, named access.cpp, has two classes: cp1 and cp2. The member function show() in class cp2 attempts to access the member variable A in class cp1. The program is shown in listing 11.2.

Listing 11.2. access.cpp. *Access control does not affect this program, but visibility does.*

```
 1   #include <stdlib.h>
 2   #include <stdio.h>
 3
 4   int A; // this is a global data object
 5
 6   class cp1 {
 7     int A; // this is a member data object
 8   public:
 9     cp1() { A = 37; }
10   };
```

Listing 11.2. continues

Listing 11.2. *continued*

```
11
12  class cp2 {
13  public:
14    void show() { printf( "%d\n", A ); }
15  };
16
17  void main()
18  {
19    cp1 X;
20    cp2 Y;
21
22    Y.show(); // this gets to global a
23  }
```

In listing 11.2, the classes cp1 and cp2 are unrelated; they are separate classes. Therefore, when the member function show() of cp2 (written as cp2::show()) attempts to access a variable named A (line 14), it is the global variable A (line 4) that is both visible and accessible to the function, not the intended variable in cp1.

Accessibility is not even possible for the cp1 member variable A in listing 11.2. That variable is completely invisible to the function cp2::show(). You might try to force access to the variable cp1::A by rewriting line 14 and using the scope resolution operator:

```
14    void show() { printf( "%d\n", cp1::A ); }
```

If you do, however, the compiler mistakenly assumes that you are referring to a bit-field object and produces an error message. (Scope resolution is discussed later in several places, including Chapter 13, in the section "Using the Scope Resolution Operator.") In summary, access to the member variable A is controlled by the following considerations:

❑ *A C++ struct or class has its own scope.* Therefore, when the compiler finds a reference to a variable identifier A in a member function of cp2, the compiler first searches the scope of cp2 for the identifier. It is not found there.

❑ *The ordinary scoping rules of C require that the scope surrounding the reference be searched for the identifier referred to.* The surrounding scope, however, *does not include* the members of cp1 because that class has its own scope (which is why cp1::A is completely invisible to cp2). The result is that the global copy of A is found and used.

If the program in listing 11.2 is rewritten so that class cp2 is derived from class cp1, access control becomes the dominant issue. Deriving classes (class inheritance) is explained in Chapter 17. For now, the important thing to know about deriving classes is that the derived class inherits (carries along) many of the characteristics of its base class (the one from which it is derived). If properly declared, the derived class can also have access to the *public* members of the parent class. The rewritten program is shown in listing 11.3.

Listing 11.3. access2.cpp. *Access control is the important issue here because C++* structs *(including classes) have their own scope.*

```
1    #include <stdlib.h>
2    #include <stdio.h>
3
4    int A; // this is a global data object
5
6    class cp1 {
7       int A; // this is a member data object
8    public:
9       cp1() { A = 37; }
10   };
11
12   class cp2 : public cp1 { // inherit from cp1
13   public:
14      void show() { printf( "%d\n", A ); }
15   };
16
17   void main()
18   {
19      cp1 X;
20      cp2 Y;
21
22      Y.show(); // this gets to global a
23   }
```

In listing 11.3, when the member function cp2::show() attempts to access the variable A, the global integer A is not what is accessed. Global A is in fact still visible, but the following new considerations apply in determining which instance of A is meant:

1. A C++ struct or class has its *own scope*. Therefore, no attempt is made to access the global copy of A; the local scope is searched for the referenced identifier first.

2. Because the function `show()` is a member function of `cp2`, the compiler attempts to locate a matching variable identifier within its scope (that is, within the class's *name space*). No such identifier is present in the scope of `cp2`.

3. Because `cp2` is *derived from* `cp1`, and the base class was declared `public` (line 12), the compiler attempts to locate a matching identifier in the `cp1` name space. Such a variable identifier does exist, but it has the private attribute and is not accessible from within a `cp2` member function. Only the public members of the base class (parent class) are available. A compile-time error results.

The critical point in this discussion is that a C++ `struct` or `class` has its *own scope*. It is easy to code yourself into a corner so that you cannot legitimately make reference to a member variable. Object-oriented encapsulation is fully enforced within C++ classes, requiring you to design your classes carefully with regard to visibility and accessibility.

You must be especially careful to choose which class members (data or functions) you want to specify as being `public` members. You learn how to make those choices in the next section. Scope resolution methods and issues are discussed in greater detail in the section "Using the `public`, `private`, and `protected` Keywords" later in this chapter, as well as in Chapters 13 and 17.

Understanding the *class* Declaration

A class is a new type, not merely a synonym for an existing type. Because a class is a new type, you must consider the following points when declaring a class:

❏ *You must decide how the class is to be packaged.* That is, you must determine whether to use the `class`, `struct`, or `union` keyword to declare the class. This decision is influenced by the kind of class-member access control you want to establish for objects of that class, as discussed in the preceding section.

❏ *You must design the internal structure of the new object type.* Deciding which member data objects must be included, as well as how they will be used, is an important part of class design. You must include everything necessary for the efficient use of objects of the class, but you certainly don't want to include unnecessary members (which would uselessly increase the size of class objects).

❑ *You must decide how objects of the new class will behave.* Do you want to be able to use class objects in arithmetic expression? Then you must provide member functions that describe how addition, subtraction, and other operations will work. Do you want class objects to be able to write themselves to the system printer or a disk file? Then you must write member functions that handle such an action.

Clearly, there are many more decisions involved in writing a class declaration than there are in declaring an ordinary structure. Time and practice will assist you in making those decisions, as will the analysis of class declarations that others have written. (You will have ample opportunity to analyze many classes as you read this book.)

Using Class Declaration Syntax

Before you can approach high-level design decisions, however, the mechanics of class declarations must be firmly within your grasp. The best place to begin is with the simplest form of the class declaration. Its general syntax is this:

```
class-key class-name_opt { member-list_opt } obj-name_opt ;
```

Notice that the only *required* parts of the declaration are the `class-key`, the curly braces, and the terminating semicolon. The remaining items can be optional. If `class` is the keyword being used, a class declaration is usually written in the following physical format (indentation and whitespace may vary, as in ordinary C):

```
class class-name {
  data-members
public:
  member-function-prototypes
  inline-member-functions
};
member-function-definitions
```

You now have before you a syntax guideline and a formatting guideline for declaring classes. With these guidelines in mind, note that the syntax controls a class declaration in the following ways:

❑ *The `class-key` may be one of the following keywords:* class, struct, *or* union. The differences between these keywords have already been discussed. Remember that the most important difference between them is access control, not visibility. In the rest of this book, the class keyword is used exclusively.

❏ *The* class-name *becomes a* type name *and is a* reserved word *(a* user-defined *keyword) within the scope in which it is defined.* Just as a struct can have block scope or file scope, so can a class declaration. However, for the compiler, class names have a syntactical significance like that of the keyword int—a significance that goes far beyond that of an ordinary structure tag, because your class name is considered a reserved word for the duration of the program.

Furthermore, it is possible to write an *unnamed class declaration,* one that does not have a class name (like leaving out a structure tag). Class objects defined with unnamed classes are called *singleton objects.* Here are some restrictions on what you can do with unnamed classes and singleton objects:

1. To define a singleton object of the unnamed class, you must use the obj-name (which is otherwise optional) just before writing the final semicolon. Because there is no class name, there is no type name that can be used later to define a normal class object. Note this example:

    ```
    class{  // declare an unnamed class
         . . .
    } anyobject ;   // define a singleton object
    ```

2. An unnamed class may not have constructor or destructor member functions. Because there is no class name, the compiler has no way to associate the correct constructor and destructor functions with the class.

3. A singleton object of an unnamed class cannot be passed as an argument to a function. The compiler is unable to perform proper type checking on a parameter that has no class name. You can get around this restriction by using the variable parameter list ellipsis (. . .) in the called function's prototype. However, the called function can know the object's size only if the object has file or enclosing block scope—in which case there is no need to pass the object as an argument anyway.

4. You cannot return an object of an unnamed class from a called function at all. Again, the reason is that there is not enough information present to permit type checking, and there is no variable list support for returning values.

❏ *The* member-list *specifies the class member data objects and functions.* A class member list is similar to the member list for an ordinary structure, except for the following differences:

1. A member list may contain member function prototypes (or perhaps inline functions—see the section "Writing Member Functions for a Class" later in this chapter).

2. A class member list may be completely empty. Such a class is called an *empty class*. For example, you could declare a class in this way:

```
class some_class {}; // no member data or functions
```

Empty classes are used mostly during program development as placeholders, when you don't yet know what should go into the class declaration. Even though a class is empty, it does not have zero size. An empty class has a small but definite size because of the invisible overhead information necessary for controlling the class.

3. The formatting guideline given earlier in this section does not specify an absolutely required style for writing a member list. It is a common practice to place the data members in the private part of the declaration and to place member functions in the public part. The sample arrangement is not cast in concrete, however. At times, you may need to place some data members in the public part, and some member functions (those that should be used only by other member functions) in the private part.

4. The class member list may also include enumerations, bit-fields, structures, unions, other classes, friend functions, and type names (nicknames). That is, you can include within the member list all the object types you usually include in a `struct` declaration, plus some more object types that are peculiar to C++ classes.

Another class can be declared within an enclosing class declaration. When you write such a *nested class*, remember that a C++ class is a scope, and (in this case) visibility (scope) can become a definite issue. *The nested class is visible only within the scope of its enclosing class.* A nested class can use only type names, static members, and enumerators from its enclosing class (but a nested class can refer to other types indirectly by using pointers, references, and explicit resolved object names). Consider, for example, the following short program:

```
double A;
double Z;
class outer {
```

```
        public:
          double A;
          static double B;
          class inner {
      outer X;       // WRONG. 'outer' not complete yet.

      void f( double C )   // Declare inline function.
      {
        A = C;       // WRONG. Enclosing A not static.
        X.outer::A = C;  // WRONG. Must have a specific
                         //     object, and none can
                         //     exist yet.
        ::A = C;           // OK. Global A accessed.
        B = C;             // OK in ANSI base doc, since
                           //     enclosing B is static --
                           //     will not compile
                           //     in Borland C++.
        Z = C;             // OK. Global Z is visible.
      }
    };
  };

main()
{
  inner obj = 3.1415926; // ERROR: 'inner' not in scope.
                         //    Borland C++ thinks you're
                         //    trying to cast from double to
                         //    inner type.

}
```

The comments in this code fragment tell the tale: a nested class is sharply restricted as to what object references it is allowed to make. You can get around many of the restrictions on nested classes by not using inline functions in the nested class declaration. Experimenting with the previous short program, for example, produced the following piece of code:

```
        double A;
        double Z;
        class outer {
        public:
          double A;
          static double B;
      class inner {
```

```
    public:
      void f(double);
    };
};

void inner::f( double C )    // Declare out-of-line function.
{
  outer X = {0.0};

  A = C;                 // OK now. global A visible.
  X.outer::A = C;        // OK now. Specific object ref.
  ::A = C;               // OK. Global A accessed.
  outer::B = C;          // OK in ANSI base doc & Borland C++.
                         //     This only OK because
                         //     outer::B is STATIC.
  Z = C;                 // OK. Global Z is visible.
}


void main()
{
  inner obj;             // NOT AN ERROR in Borland C++!
                         //    Since the member function
                         //    definition is now outside the
                         //    class declaration, the inner
                         //    class name is no longer local
                         //    to the outer class scope.
  obj.f(3.14);

      }
```

The comments in this new short program imply that it works (it compiles without errors) because this method of defining a member function for a nested class simply slipped by Borland, and the compiler does not quite conform to the base document in this one instance. In any event, the base document views the declaration of a nested class as simply a syntactical convenience. You should rarely, if ever, need to use a nested class declaration.

As mentioned earlier, a *nickname* can be used in a class member declaration. A nickname is a *typedef-name* that names a class.

❏ *An object name is only used following a class declaration to define an object of an unnamed class.* Defining objects of unnamed classes, however, is *not* a recommended or common practice.

Declaring Class Members

Several other rules govern the declaration and use of member objects and functions. Some of the following rules have a basis in standard C, whereas others relate only to C++:

❏ *Member names must be unique within the scope of the class.* This means that you cannot declare data members more than once within the same class. You cannot add a class member to the class by using a declaration outside the class (the member list in the class declaration completes the class entirely). Note that you can use the same identifier more than once in a program *if the identifier is used in different classes.* Member functions are grouped separately in the next rule.

❏ *You can use member function names more than once in the same class only if the combinations of function parameters and return types are sufficiently different.* This strategy is called *function overloading.* Overloading is discussed in Chapter 14.

❏ *A member declaration cannot include an initializer.* This rule may seem too restrictive, until you remember that a *class is a type specification,* not an object definition.

Other rules control what you may do with member object declarations contained in more advanced class declarations. Those rules appear when the advanced uses are covered in succeeding chapters.

Building a LIFO Stack Class

For now, you need to *use* C++ classes, even if you don't understand everything you see. You have enough rules to begin using C++ classes. It's time to apply those rules in a concrete way.

Designing and coding a *useful* class will help you to understand how to build class declarations. The example in the following discussion is a class for generalized LIFO stack objects.

What is a generalized LIFO stack? The answer has three parts. First of all, a stack is an area of memory (RAM) in which temporary variables are stored. (Turbo C auto variables are created on the system stack, and parameter values are placed there as well.)

Second, data on the stack can be stored and retrieved only in a certain sequence. The last object *pushed onto* the stack (placed in the stack's memory) is the first *popped off* the stack (removed from the stack's memory). Older data objects on the stack can be used but not removed before younger data objects are popped off the stack. Thus, the *last-in-first-out* sequencing of objects on the stack yields the acronym LIFO for this kind of memory use.

Third, the stack used by your PC's hardware can (and does) hold all sorts of different data objects. The class used in this discussion should therefore be designed to control a *generalized stack* of objects—a stack that can handle just about anything.

How do you control the memory a LIFO stack uses? To understand how this is done, think of a stack as being similar to a can of three tennis balls. The first ball put in the can is at the bottom, and the last ball put in the can is at the top. Furthermore, the last item pushed onto a stack is said to be on the top of the stack. Figure 11.3 illustrates the memory layout of a LIFO stack.

Fig. 11.3. *A LIFO stack grows from the bottom (high memory address) to the top (low memory address).*

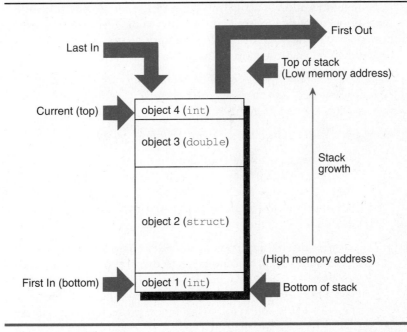

Figure 11.3 shows that stacks are positioned with the "bottom" (first object pushed) at the highest memory address, and the "top" at the lowest memory address. The only reason for this is that diagrams of system memory are traditionally drawn this way. There is no physical reason why you could not arrange stack growth to proceed from low to high memory.

As figure 11.3 illustrates, you need to keep track of several addresses related to the stack and its contents. You need to know how big the stack is; therefore, the addresses of the top and bottom limits are required. Because the top object on the stack is the only object that can be popped off, you need just one more address to control the stack: the address of the top, or current, object. Obviously, you can store all these addresses in C pointers.

In addition to keeping track of the addresses, you need to know the rules for stack control before you can begin coding the stack class declaration:

❏ *Memory for the body of the stack is acquired outside the boundaries of any particular class object.* The purpose of this rule is to keep the size of a stack object small, even though keeping stack contents outside the class object is technically a violation of OOPS encapsulation.

❏ *The pointers used for stack control are named* top, bottom, *and* current *so that their uses will be obvious at a glance.* The top pointer is initially set to the address of the top byte in the stack (the lowest memory address actually in the stack). Both the bottom and the current pointer are set to the address of the first byte *beyond* the bottom byte of the stack (the address of the byte that is one byte higher than the highest address actually in the stack).

❏ *Stack class member functions use only void pointers so that any object, of any size, can be placed on the stack.* (The term *generalized* LIFO stack is derived from this rule.)

❏ *An object is pushed onto the stack in the following manner:*

1. The current pointer is compared to the top pointer to determine whether there is room on the stack for the object being pushed (the object's size is used to perform this calculation). If no room is available, a zero value (*false*) is returned immediately, and no pointer is modified.

2. If there is room for the object, the current pointer is *decremented* by an amount equal to the size of the object, and the object is copied into the memory pointed to by current. Then a nonzero (*true*) value is returned, and the current pointer is left pointing to the last object pushed onto the stack.

❏ *An object is popped off the stack in the following manner:*

1. The current pointer is compared to the bottom pointer to determine whether there are enough bytes still on the stack (a number of bytes equal to or greater than the size of the requested object). If enough bytes aren't available, a *null pointer* value is returned immediately.

2. If a sufficient number of bytes is on the stack to satisfy the request, the current pointer is *incremented* by an amount equal to the size of the requested object, and a pointer to the top object on the stack is returned. Thus, the object just popped off the stack is positioned *above* the current address of the new top object on the stack. That is, the object just popped off is no longer "on the stack."

The LIFO class has two more features that need mentioning before the code is presented. First, a temporary-object allocation member function is also provided so that you can create "local" class objects on the stack, similar to the way that Borland C++ allocates auto variables on the system stack. The allocation algorithm is a minor variant of the push() member function. You delete temporary objects from the stack with the pop() member function. Note that you can create true *class* objects on a LIFO stack; you will see how to do this when listing 11.6 is discussed.

Second, three function-like macros—PUSH, POP, and ALLOC—are provided so that you can call stack class member functions by using a type name to set the object size, instead of having to state explicitly the number of bytes to be pushed or popped.

Because the stack class is useful enough to include in many other programs, compiling the class code separately is worthwhile. To compile the class code separately, you need to arrange the class declaration into two source files: a header file (lifo.hpp), which contains the class declaration and member function prototypes; and a source code file (lifo.cpp), which contains the member function definitions. Listing 11.4 shows the lifo.hpp header file.

Listing 11.4. lifo.hpp. *Class declaration for a LIFO (last-in-first-out) generalized stack object.*

```
1   #include <stdlib.h>
2   #include <string.h>
3
4   class lifo {
5     char *top;
6     char *bottom;
7     char *current;
8     char *work;
9   public:
10    lifo();                      // default constructor
```

Listing 11.4. continues

***Listing 11.4.** continued*

```
11    lifo( unsigned size ); // constructor with parameter
12    ~lifo();                // destructor
13    int push( unsigned bytes, void *obj );
14    void *pop( unsigned bytes);
15    void *get_block( unsigned bytes );
16  };
17
18  #define PUSH(type,obj)  push( sizeof(type), obj )
19  #define POP(type)       pop( sizeof(type) )
20  #define ALLOC(type)     get_block( sizeof(type) )
```

In listing 11.4, lines 1 and 2 contain include directives for `stdlib.h` and `string.h`, respectively. These directives are placed here so that you don't forget, when including `lifo.hpp` itself at a later time, that the includes are required for the correct compilation of the `lifo` class member functions. It won't hurt anything if you also include them elsewhere because Borland has written its standard headers using conditional preprocessing logic to determine whether included code is already present.

The `lifo` class declaration is found in lines 4–16 of listing 11.4. Notice that the `top`, `bottom`, `current`, and `work` pointers are declared above the `public` keyword. Because the `class` keyword (rather than `struct`) is used, all those pointers have private access by default. The `work` pointer might have been declared as a local variable in each member function that needs it. Instead, the `work` pointer was declared as a private member variable; therefore, the pointer is created only once (when a `lifo` object is created) and is shared by all member functions. No further setup overhead is involved in using the `work` pointer when a member function needs it.

The `public` keyword in line 9 introduces the part of the class member declarations that can be accessed by functions outside the class. For the `lifo` class, that part includes all the member functions but none of the member data objects.

The member functions declared in lines 10–12 deserve special mention. The two member functions in lines 10 and 11 have the same name as the class itself. These functions are the *constructor* functions for the class. You use constructor functions to set up and initialize class objects. A common use for constructor functions is to acquire extra memory residing outside the class object (as you will see with the `lifo` class).

Chapter 15 discusses constructor functions (as well as destructor functions), but you should know some things right away. Note the following requirements for constructor functions:

❏ *A constructor function for a class must have the same name as the class.* This requirement is not optional. You can write a class declaration without specifying a constructor (thus allowing the compiler to supply a default constructor), but if you supply one or more constructors, each constructor must have the same name as the class.

❏ *A constructor function declaration cannot specify a return type.* The compiler has its own internal return type for constructors. You cannot code one.

❏ *When you code more than one constructor function declaration, the parameter list for each one must be different from all the others.* In C++, writing more than one function with a single name is called *overloading*. The only way the compiler can distinguish between different "versions" of an overloaded function is to compare parameter lists (and return types too, but they are not permitted in constructors or destructors).

The lifo class declaration features two constructor function declarations. The first, in line 10, is the *default constructor*; it has no formal parameter list and accepts no arguments. For the lifo class, the default constructor is designed to acquire a 2K block of memory to hold stack data. The second constructor function declaration, in line 11, accepts an unsigned integer as an argument, and the corresponding constructor function attempts to acquire a block of memory equal in size to that argument to hold stack data.

You use a destructor function to clean up after a class object has been destroyed—for example, when a local class object goes out of scope. You will need to code a destructor function when you have used the constructor function—for instance, to acquire outside memory (as with lifo class objects). Note the following rules for destructor functions:

❏ *A destructor function for a class must have the same name as the class, except that the first character of the destructor function name must be a tilde (~).* In listing 11.4, the destructor function name is ~lifo(). You can write a class declaration that has no explicit destructor and allow the compiler to supply a default function, just as you can omit the constructor.

❏ *A destructor function cannot specify a return type.* The compiler also has its own special return type for destructor functions.

❏ *A destructor function cannot accept arguments.* Without a parameter list, overloading is not possible. Only one destructor function is therefore permitted in a single class declaration.

The remaining member function declarations are found in lines 13–15 of listing 11.4. These functions include methods for pushing an object on the stack, popping an object off the stack, and allocating space on the stack for an arbitrary object. All these functions will be covered in the discussion of listing 11.5.

The function-like support macros, lines 18–20, appear only in the `lifo.hpp` header file in listing 11.4. The three support macros are `PUSH()`, `POP()`, and `ALLOC()`. They correspond to the member functions `push()`, `pop()`, and `get_block()`, respectively. You can see from these names that C (including C++) is usually a case-sensitive language: `PUSH` is not the same as `push` to the compiler.

The sole purpose of the support macros is to enable you to call the `lifo` member functions by using a type name, instead of having to specify the number of bytes to push, pop, or allocate on the stack. Suppose, for example, that you have declared the following `lifo` class object named `stack`:

```
lifo stack;
```

To push a long integer onto `stack` without the assist macro, you would have to use code like this:

```
long x;
...
stack.push( 4, &x );
```

With the `PUSH()` support macro, however, you could write

```
stack.PUSH( long, &x );
```

which would be expanded by the preprocessor into the following compile-time code:

```
stack.push( sizeof(long), &x );
```

The advantage of the support macros is obvious. You can use type names to specify implicitly the size of the object being pushed or popped, and thus avoid inadvertent size errors. In writing these fragmentary code lines, for instance, we at first mistakenly specified a size of 2 (because of focusing on integers) rather than the 4 bytes required for a long integer.

The preceding discussion of constructor, destructor, and member functions will help you to understand the class member function definitions. The `lifo` class member function definitions are shown in listing 11.5.

Listing 11.5. `lifo.cpp`. *Class member function definitions for* `lifo` *objects.*

```
1   #include "lifo.hpp"
2
3   // ----------------------------------------------------------
4   // Both constructors get space on the free store for a stack
5   // ----------------------------------------------------------
6
7   lifo::lifo()
8   {
9     if ( NULL == ( top = new char[2048] ) ) abort();
10    bottom = current = top + 2048;
11    work = NULL;
12  }
13
14  lifo::lifo( unsigned size)
15  {
16    if ( NULL == ( top = new char[size] ) ) abort();
17    bottom = current = top + size;
18    work = NULL;
19  }
20
21  lifo::~lifo()
22  {
23    delete top;
24  }
25
26  // ----------------------------------------------------------
27  // lifo::push() places a nonspecific object on the stack,
28  //              if there is room for it. Returns 1 if
29  //              successful, 0 if failure.
30  // ----------------------------------------------------------
31
32  int lifo::push( unsigned bytes, void *obj )
33  {
```

Listing 11.5. continues

Listing 11.5. continued

```
34      if ( top > ( current - bytes ) ) return 0;
35      current -= bytes;
36      memmove( current, obj, bytes ); // push object
37      return 1;
38  }
39
40  // ------------------------------------------------------------
41  // lifo::pop() retrieves the next object on the stack.
42  // Returns (void *) on success, NULL on failure.
43  // ------------------------------------------------------------
44
45  void *lifo::pop( unsigned bytes)
46  {
47    if ( bottom < ( current + bytes ) ) return NULL;
48    work = current;
49    current += bytes;
50    return work;
51  }
52
53  // ------------------------------------------------------------
54  // lifo::get_block() allocates n bytes on the stack, but
55  //                   does not push any data. Used to
56  //                   allocate "local object" space.
57  //                   Returns (void *) on success, NULL on
58  //                   failure.
59  // ------------------------------------------------------------
60
61  void *lifo::get_block( unsigned bytes )
62  {
63    if ( top > ( current - bytes ) ) return NULL;
64    current -= bytes;
65    return current;
66  }
```

Implementing the lifo class member functions according to the specifications given earlier is fairly straightforward. A lifo stack is a simple object, and you just need to know how to package the functions. Given the specifications for the class's behavior, the logic of the member functions is self-explanatory.

The member function definitions (declaration parts plus function bodies) are written outside the class declaration for the lifo class. This method is the usual way of writing member functions. The only problem associated with member functions positioned outside the class declaration is this: how to let the compiler know to which class a particular function definition belongs. You can resolve this problem in C++ by prefixing the class name to the function name, using the following syntax:

```
return-type class-name::function-name(parm-list)
{
    ... // function body
}
```

The double colon between the `class-name` and the `function-name` is called the *scope resolution operator*. It is used to determine scope in C++ when a reference to a function or data member would otherwise be ambiguous. You learn more about the scope resolution operator (as well as other methods of packaging member functions) in the section "Associating Member Functions with a Class" later in this chapter. For now, simply note that the scope resolution operator is used in lines 7, 14, 21, 32, 45, and 61 of listing 11.5 so that those functions are associated with the `lifo` class declaration.

You should notice two other features in listing 11.5. First, recall that `lifo.cpp` is intended to be compiled to object code (pardon the pun) separately from any other programs that may use `lifo` objects. Thus, an include for `lifo.hpp` appears at the beginning of this source file (in line 1).

Second, `lifo.cpp` contains two operators you have not seen before. Lines 9 and 16 use the operator `new` to allocate memory on the free store. The `new` operator acquires memory as if `new` were a cross between `malloc()` and `calloc()`. The C++ *free store* is an area of dynamic memory similar to the familiar C heap. (In Borland C++, it *is* the heap, but C++ rules do not require this equivalence.) Both the operator `new` and the free store are covered in detail in Chapter 15. Their general purposes and uses are clear enough at this time.

The other operator new to you is `delete` (see line 23). It performs the companion function to `new`, releasing memory acquired on the free store. The `delete` operator is covered more thoroughly in Chapter 15 also.

Using the *this* Pointer

By now, you should understand how the compiler associates member functions with class declarations. You may be wondering, though, how a *member function* knows which instance of a class object it is dealing with. Detecting the current instance of a class object is a little tricky. Suppose, for example, that you have declared three different `lifo` objects:

```
lifo stack1, stack2, stack3;     // Just like C, right?
int a;                    // Set up something to work with
...
stack2.PUSH( int, &a ); // Now call the member function
```

From the point of view of the *caller* of a member function, it's clear which instance object is meant. You just qualify the reference to the member function with the class (or structure) name, using the structure member operator (`.`). However, it is *not* obvious to the member function `lifo::push()` that `stack2`, in the preceding code fragment, is the object with which `lifo::push()` is dealing. You need some method of steering the member function to the correct object.

The method you use to connect member functions and the current object is simple. The compiler provides, behind the scenes, a special pointer for each class and its member functions. This pointer is made to point to the correct object when a member function is called. The pointer has a special name: `this`. How it selects instance objects is illustrated in figure 11.4.

Fig. 11.4. `this` *is made to point to the correct instance object during a member function call.*

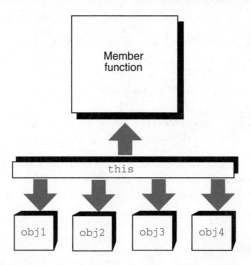

Note the following points about the `this` pointer:

❑ *The* `this` *pointer is handled entirely behind the scenes.* You don't declare `this` yourself, you don't have to initialize it, and you should (normally) not place any address values in it. The compiler secretly generates code that does all the necessary work with `this` before a member function executes.

❏ *C++ makes the use of the* `this` *pointer entirely transparent to the member function using it.* In plain C, whenever you use a pointer to access structure members, you must use the structure pointer operator (`->`) to access the data object. In C++, it is understood that something different—something special—is going on, and the syntax is adjusted accordingly. Note carefully that *within a class member function, access to class data members and other member functions of the same class appears direct and uncomplicated.* Inside a member function, you don't need to use the class or structure name as a prefix to the member name, nor do you need to use structure member operators.

The completely transparent access to member data and functions within the boundaries of the active member function makes writing the member functions simple (as far as member access is concerned, at least). For example, look again at the code for the function body of `lifo::push()` in lines 34–37 of listing 11.5. Both the `current` and `top` members are used, as if they are directly available—and they are. No pointer dereferencing or structure pointer operators are needed. Yet this single member function can service many different instance objects; therefore, copies of `current` and `top` can be unique to each instance object. All copies of instance objects and their member data are distinguished from each other and controlled by the behind-the-scenes action of `this`.

As soon as you are comfortable with the appearance and methods of listing 11.5, move to listing 11.6. This program listing contains the source code for `uselifo.cpp`, which uses the `lifo` class in various ways. Unless you are already experienced with C++, don't expect to understand everything you see yet.

Listing 11.6. `uselifo.cpp`. *A demonstration program that uses a* `lifo` *class object.*

```
1    // ----------------------------------------------
2    // USELIFO.CPP
3    //    To build the executable file for this program, you
4    //    need to set up a project file with these entries:
5    //       USELIFO.CPP
6    //       LIFO.CPP
7    //    You can create lifo stack objects in programs using
8    //    any memory model, but you may run out of heap space
9    //    if you use the small or tiny models.
10   // ----------------------------------------------
11   #include <stdio.h>
```

Listing 11.6. continues

Listing 11.6. continued

```
12   #include <stdlib.h>
13   #include <string.h>
14
15   #include "lifo.hpp"
16
17   //
18   // declare a simple class for use in testing lifo class
19   //
20   class simple {
21     int stuff;
22   public:
23     simple() { stuff = 2; }
24     ~simple() {}  // default destructor
25     void showit() { printf ( "%d\n", stuff ); }
26   };
27
28   //
29   // Overload global operator new()
30   //
31   void* operator new( size_t size, void *ptr )
32   {
33     size = size; // Dummy statement
34     return ptr;  // Here is what we are after
35   }
36
37   main()
38   {
39     unsigned char byte = ' ';
40     char test_str[] = "Well, hello, there!";
41     char *fetch;
42     lifo stack;
43
44     //
45     // Fill up and empty the stack
46     //
47     while ( stack.push( 1, &byte ) ) ;
48     printf( "The stack is full.\n" );
49     while ( NULL != stack.pop( 1 ) );
50     printf( "The stack is empty again.\n" );
51     //
52     // Push and pop something significant
53     //
```

```
54    stack.push( strlen(test_str)+1, test_str );
55    fetch = (char *)stack.pop( strlen(test_str)+1 );
56    printf( "%s\n", fetch );
57    //
58    // Use lifo::getblock() to allocate space on the
59    // stack and create a class object directly in that
60    // spot.
61    //
62    fetch = (char *)stack.get_block( sizeof( simple ) );
63    simple* X;
64    X = new(fetch) simple;
65    X->showit();
66    X->simple::~simple();     // explicitly delete object
67    stack.pop( sizeof( simple ) );      // throw it away
68    //
69    // Now demonstrate the support macros
70    //
71    int one = 1, two = 2, three = 3;
72    int a, b, c;
73    stack.PUSH( int, &three );
74    stack.PUSH( int, &two );
75    stack.PUSH( int, &one );
76    a = *(int *)stack.POP( int );
77    b = *(int *)stack.POP( int );
78    c = *(int *)stack.POP( int );
79    printf( "%d %d %d\n", a, b, c );
80    fetch = (char *)stack.ALLOC( simple );
81    X = new(fetch) simple; // reuse simple object pointer
82    X->showit();
83    X->simple::~simple();      // explicitly delete object
84    stack.POP( simple );                    // throw it away
85  }
```

The program in listing 11.6 contains a mixture of simple and sophisticated code. In the following discussion, every technique in uselifo.cpp is identified, but the main purpose of this program's discussion is to showcase the use of lifo class objects. The more advanced techniques are discussed in later chapters. Overriding operator new() and operator delete(), for example, is covered in Chapter 15.

The comments in lines 1–10 of listing 11.6 are important for this program. The comment lines indicate that lifo.cpp resides in a separate source file; you will therefore need to construct a project file to compile and link uselifo.cpp. A simple project file, consisting of the names uselifo.cpp and lifo.cpp, will be sufficient.

The comments indicate also that you can compile uselifo.cpp with the small model. If, however, you are going to write a more ambitious program (one in which many lifo class objects as well as other class objects are declared and used), you should consider using the large model for the program. The large model will provide a full 64K free store (heap), but the smaller models will not.

Preliminary matters are taken care of in lines 11–35 of listing 11.6. These lines contain the include statements for library functions (*plus* an include directive for the lifo header); a declaration for a different class (a class named simple), which will be used to demonstrate lifo stacks; and a function definition for operator new().

The function definition for operator new() is potentially the most confusing item. If operator new() is supplied by the compiler, why does it need to be redefined? The answer is that operator new(), as used here, is different from the standard global operator new(). Specifically, operator new() will *control the address* at which memory is acquired—in this program, memory will not be acquired from the free store but will be located on the lifo stack object. Once again, such control of the operators new() and delete() is explained more fully in Chapter 15.

Lines 39–42 contain a selection of object definitions. Included are character and string objects, which will be pushed on and popped off the stack, and the lifo class object itself, appropriately named stack. Did you notice in line 42 how simple it is to declare a class object? It's as easy as declaring an int variable; all the real work was done in designing the class header and member function source files.

The first demonstration of lifo class objects appears in lines 45–50. These lines show how to invoke the lifo::push() member function, by pushing characters onto the stack until it is full. Then the lifo::pop() member function is used to pop them all back off again (and to discard them).

Lines 52–60 show how to push a whole string onto the stack, and how to address that string once more when it has been popped. Popping the string off the stack also illustrates why the lifo::pop() routine preserves the address of the current pointer to use as the return value, before adjusting current to its new value. If this were *not* done, the object would be popped and then completely lost.

Lines 57–67 represent fairly sophisticated C++. They show how to allocate space on a lifo stack and how to create, use, and delete another class object in the allocated space. Some of the code from that section of the program is reproduced here:

```
62    fetch = (char *)stack.get_block( sizeof( simple ) );
63    simple* X;
64    X = new(fetch) simple;
65    X->showit();
66    X->simple::~simple();    // explicitly delete object
67    stack.pop( sizeof( simple ) );      // throw it away
```

Line 62 allocates the space on stack in an amount equal to the size of a simple class object. Because fetch is a pointer to char, the resulting void pointer must first be cast to (char *) before it can be assigned to fetch.

Since space allocation for the simple object will be handled explicitly, instead of allowing the global operator new to handle it, line 63 declares only a *pointer* to simple rather than a simple *object*.

The code in line 64 creates the simple object, using the redefined (that is, *overloaded*) global operator new(). Note that this statement causes the simple class constructor to be called (the compiler secretly generates the code to do that) so that initialization can be performed. Remember, too, that the overloaded operator new() is set up to point wherever you like—in this case, to the space on the stack pointed to by fetch.

Line 65 calls a member function of the simple class object. Because this object was created with new(), and because only a pointer to the object was retained, the call must use the structure pointer operator to get to the member function. Don't be confused by this requirement. Logic *inside* the member function still requires *no* dereferencing syntax to access other member functions and variables. The *caller* here must deal with the fact that a pointer is used to locate the object.

Line 66 contains a special function call. The destructor for the simple object is called directly—something you rarely need to do. More about this technique is provided later in the section "Providing Constructor and Destructor Functions," but a question needs to be answered right now. Why call the destructor for a class object when destructor calls are usually automatic (invoked when the object goes out of scope)? You need to call the destructor for the simple object precisely because it was created at a specific address (not on the free store) with an overloaded new() call. A class object created at a specific address will never go out of scope, and cleanup is left entirely to you: the destructor is not automatically called for such an object.

Line 67 completes the program portion in listing 11.6. This line's action is simply to pop off the stack the space used by the simple object, freeing the stack for other use.

The remaining code in listing 11.6 demonstrates the use of the support macros. One of the most interesting aspects of this section of code is the declaration of local variables in lines 71 and 72. You should recall that standard

C permits the declaration of objects local to a block only at the top of the block. C++ is more flexible: you can declare local objects *anywhere within a block*.

As you can see in the code, using the support macros themselves is straightforward. You should remember that the `lifo` member functions return a `void` pointer, which must be cast before assigning its value to another pointer (as in lines 76–78, for example). A `void` pointer can *receive* any pointer type in an assignment without a cast; to *send* a `void` pointer across the assignment operator requires a cast to the receiving pointer type.

Using the *public*, *private*, and *protected* Keywords

You already know that members of a class declared with `class` are private by default, and members of a class declared with `struct` (or `union`) are public by default. You know also that access to member objects can be overridden. You can override access to a class member by using two keywords you already know (`public` and `private`) and one you don't yet know (`protected`). These keywords control access to class members in the following ways:

❑ `public`

Class members that are declared to be `public` (or are `public` by default) can be used (when they are data members) or called (when they are member functions) by any function. The calling function does not need to belong to the class (or any class).

❑ `private`

Class members that are declared to be `private` (or are `private` by default) can be used or called only by member functions of the same class, or by friends of that class (see the section "Using Friend Functions" later in this chapter).

❑ `protected`

Class members that are declared to be `protected` can be used only by member functions and friends of the same class, or by member functions and friends of another class *derived* from the original class.

In other words, the `protected` keyword provides access protection for members *inherited* from a higher class. Class derivation and inheritance are explained in Chapter 17.

The `public`, `private`, and `protected` keywords are called *access specifiers*. You use the following syntax for writing access specifiers:

access-specifier : *member-list*_{opt}

The *member-list* is optional. Even though you can have an empty member list following an access specifier, the colon (`:`) is required. All the member identifiers following an access specifier have the indicated access. You can use any combination of access specifiers in a class declaration; no particular order of appearance is required.

The base document makes a point about access control that is worth summarizing here. The C++ access control mechanism is intended to guard class members against accidental misuse, *not* against deliberate abuse.

Nothing can stop you from taking the address of a class object and casting that pointer to another class. Accessing the object through the second pointer will prevent the compiler from providing type protection according to the original class declaration. Furthermore, nothing can protect a program against the meddling of another (perhaps unscrupulous) programmer who has access to the source code. Such a programmer can change the class declaration, leaving a "back door" entry to presumably protected member objects.

If you usually think of access control as a security measure, think again. You will need some other means of protecting your code.

Writing Member Functions for a Class

In this chapter, you have seen a number of class declarations and their member objects and functions. As the chapter progressed, the explanation of C++ syntax and source code arrangement became more specific. In this section, you learn the explicit rules for declaring and defining class member functions. The rules for declaring and defining friend functions of classes are presented in the last section of the chapter.

Associating Member Functions with a Class

The advances in programming language that are incorporated in C++ have only one purpose: to help the programmer control complexity. For that reason, you will often find that C++ code is used to implement large, complex programs. In such programs, you will most often find separate compilation used to build the final module.

Compiling Member Functions Separately

Because separate compilation is the technique you will probably use the most, the first packaging method presented here is for placing class member function definitions *outside* the class declaration. To simplify the presentation, both the class declaration and the member function definitions are placed together in the next code fragment. However, the comments in the code fragment clearly indicate which parts of the fragment belong in a separate source file. Here is the code fragment, showing how to package member function definitions outside the class declaration:

```
// ----------------------------------------------------------
// Declare a class with member function definitions outside
// the class declaration
// ----------------------------------------------------------

// THIS IS THE PART THAT GOES IN THE HEADER (.HPP) FILE
class A {
  int i;
public:
  void f1( int );        // function declarations only here
  void f2( int );
};
// ****************************************************

// THIS IS THE PART THAT GOES IN THE MEMBER FUNCTION
// DEFINITION SOURCE (.CPP) FILE
                      // function definitions begin here
void A::f1(int arg) // scope resolution operator defines
{                     // which class function belongs to
  i = arg * 2;
}
```

```
void A::f2( int arg )
    {
    i = arg / 2;
    }
```

When class member functions are defined outside the class declaration, you must use the fully qualified function name to identify the function:

```
return-type class::function( parms ) { ... }
```

The class name is specified first, then the scope resolution operator (::), and then the function name. The class name and scope resolution operator indicate to the compiler that the function definition belongs to, and is *in the scope of*, the associated class.

To call a class member function (sometimes loosely called a *method*), you must use the *class member syntax*. This just means that you use the name of a specific class object, followed by the structure member or structure pointer (as needed), and then the function call syntax. Note an example:

```
A stuff; // define stuff with class A
...
stuff.f1( 4 ); // call stuff's f1() member function
```

Keep in mind that member functions must already have been declared in the class declaration, but not yet defined. You can neither redeclare nor redefine a class member function. Furthermore, you cannot add a class member function that was not declared in the class (this would violate all protection and access control).

Finally, you should know that each class member function defined outside the class declaration must have exactly one definition, regardless of the number of source files used to build the complete program. Of course, you can still overload a member function (provide several functions of the same name, but with different arguments and perhaps a different return type).

Declaring Inline Member Functions

You can also package class member functions *inline*. To write an inline member function, you *define* it within the class declaration, instead of simply declaring the function. The following code fragment shows how this is done:

```
// ---------------------------------------------------------
// Declare a class with inline member function definitions
// ---------------------------------------------------------
```

```
// THIS ALL GOES IN THE SAME SOURCE FILE AS THE PROGRAM
// USING THE CLASS
class B {
  int i;
public:
                  // very short functions are suitable for
                  // inline definition, but note restrictions
                  // in the text
  void f1( int arg ) { i = arg * 2; }
  void f2( int arg ) { i = arg / 2; }
};
```

Inline definitions like the one in this code fragment have exactly the same effect as using the `inline` keyword on a member function defined outside the class declaration. For example, the `B1::f1()` member function could be written this way:

```
class B {
  ...
  void f1( int );
};
inline void B::f1() { i = arg * 2 }
```

Requesting the compiler to regard a member function as `inline` (by either method) means that, whenever a call to the function is encountered, you want the function body to be directly inserted into the code. The resulting straight-line code eliminates the overhead of a function call. Function syntax and type checking still apply, however. Note also that you can use `inline` on an ordinary (nonmember) function.

Inline functions are suitable when a function is very short. How short is that? As a rule of thumb, if the function is short enough to strike you as trivial (not unimportant, just very concise), it is short enough to be an `inline` candidate. The presence of too many inline functions can increase the size of a program dramatically, so be conservative in your choices.

The rules for inline functions are slightly different from those for member functions defined outside a class. The most significant difference is that inline member functions may be defined more than once, in several source files. Multiple definitions are possible because the class declaration is most often found in a header file that is included, perhaps several times, in multiple source files.

Note, however, an important restriction on multiple definitions of inline member functions. In every case, the inline member function must be defined in *exactly* the same way. Otherwise, the confusion that would result is obvious. Furthermore, you should understand that coding an `inline` function is only a *request* that the compiler use inline construction. You have no guarantee that the compiler will do so (just as you have no guarantee that a `register` variable will actually reside in a system register).

Specifying Default Arguments for Member Functions

C++ provides another feature for declaring functions that goes beyond standard C: *in a member function's declaration, you can specify default arguments for the member function.* Listing 11.7 contains a simple example of how this is done.

Listing 11.7. `defarg.cpp`. *A program that uses default argument values in a member function declaration.*

```
1   #include <stdio.h>
2
3   class A {
4      int m;
5   public:
6      void incr_m( int = 1 );
7      void show() { printf( "%d\n", m ); }
8   };
9
10  void A::incr_m( int amt )
11  {
12     m += amt;
13  }
14
15  void main()
16  {
17     A obj; // declare an A object
18
19     obj.incr_m( 2 ); // increment by two
20     obj.show();
21     obj.incr_m();    // increment by default amt
22     obj.show();
23  }
```

Line 6 of listing 11.7 shows the member function prototype for `A::incr_m()` with a default argument supplied. Lines 19 and 21 show how you can call the same member function in two different ways—once by supplying an argument, and once by assuming the default argument value.

You can also write default arguments into inline function definitions. You might write line 6, for example, as

```
6      void incr_m( int amt = 1 ) { m += amt }
```

and then delete lines 10–13 (the *out-of-line* member function definition).

The following rules govern the use of default arguments (aren't there always rules?):

❏ *You don't have to supply defaults for all arguments.* Once a default is supplied, though, all subsequent arguments in that same list must have default values. The following examples are *not* meant to be redeclarations of each other:

```
func( int, int );          // OK, no defaults
func( int, int=1, int=2 ); // OK, trailing args have values
func( int, int=1, int );   // ERROR, 3rd arg has no default
```

Trailing *arguments not supplied in a member function call are supplied with values from the defaults (an error occurs if you didn't supply defaults).*

❏ *If a default was supplied in a previous declaration of a member function, you don't have to specify the default again when redeclaring the function.* Example:

```
func( int, int=2 );
func( int=1, int ); // OK 2nd arg already given
```

❏ *You can redeclare a member function prototype, supplying defaults that were not previously supplied.* Example:

```
func( int, int );
func( int=1, int=2 ); // OK, supplies missing defaults
```

❏ *You cannot redefine a default argument that has already been declared.* Example:

```
func( int=1, int=2 );
func( int=1, int=2 ); // ERROR, both args already declared
```

Notice that you cannot redefine a default argument even to the same value.

Providing Constructor and Destructor Functions

Although you learn about constructor and destructor functions (plus some related topics) in Chapter 15, you need to prepare to write C++ classes as quickly as possible. The general rules that apply to these special functions are therefore presented here.

Constructor and destructor functions have been used in this chapter, but without much explanation about them. You have learned only that these functions cannot have a return type, and that they must have the same name as the class (plus a prefixed tilde ~ for the destructor function name). Listing 11.8 shows several styles of constructor functions, giving a more rounded picture of what you can do with them.

Listing 11.8. `constr.cpp`. *A program that contains several different (overloaded) constructors, including a default constructor with default arguments.*

```
1   #include <stdio.h>
2
3   class A {
4     int a, b, c;
5   public:
6     A( int=1, int=2, int=3 );      // constr. 1. (default)
7     A( double, double, double);    // constr. 2.
8     A( long );                     // constr. 3.
9     A( A& );                       // constr. 4. (copy constr)
10    void show() { printf( "%d %d %d\n", a, b, c ); }
11  };
12
13  A::A( int i1, int i2, int i3 )
14  {
15    a = i1; b = i2; c = i3;
16  }
17
18  A::A( double f1, double f2, double f3 )
19  {
20    a = (int)f1; b = (int)f2; c = (int)f3;
21  }
22
```

Listing 11.8. continues

Listing 11.8. continued

```
23   A::A( long n )
24   {
25       a = b = c = (int)n;
26   }
27
28   A::A( A& other ) {
29       a = other.a;
30       b = other.b;
31       c = other.c;
32   }
33
34
35   void main()
36   {
37       A x1;           // use default with def. args (constr 1)
38       x1.show();
39
40       A x2( 3 );   // use only 1 default arg      (constr 1)
41       x2.show();
42
43       A x3( 3, 1 );  // use 2 default args        (constr 1)
44       x3.show();
45
46       A x4( 3.14, 2.414, 6.28 );  // double args(constr 2)
47       x4.show();
48
49       A x5( 53L );                    // long arg (constr 3)
50       x5.show();
51
52       A x6 = x5;          // use copy constructor (constr 4)
53       x6.show();
54   }
```

In listing 11.8, notice that the first constructor function (line 6) is called the *default* constructor. You can specify a default constructor in three ways:

❑ *You can let the compiler generate a default constructor.* The compiler generates a default constructor function, but only if you have provided no other constructor function at all. If you provide any constructors, you need one that can serve as the default (as defined in the next two items of this list). When generating a default constructor for you, the compiler initializes any member data objects to a value of zero (consistent with standard C rules for initialization of basic, derived, and aggregate objects).

❏ *You can provide a constructor function with no arguments.* The oldest, and still most consistent, definition of "default constructor" is a constructor function that accepts *no* arguments. Such a default constructor for the program in listing 11.8, for example, might look like this:

```
class A{
...
A();
...
}


A::A()
{
    a = 0; b = 0; c = 0;
}
```

You can think of this form of default constructor functions as the classical form.

❏ *You can provide a constructor function with all default arguments.* Recent versions of C++ allow a constructor function that has default values for every argument, *and can therefore be called with no arguments at all*, to play the role of default constructor function. This form of default constructor is used in line 6 of listing 11.8.

You should note that the *Borland C++ Programmer's Guide* explicitly states that a constructor with all default argument values is *not* a default constructor, yet the base document explicitly states that it *is*. The difference is probably only one of semantics, however, because the program in listing 11.8 both compiles correctly and runs properly.

The *Borland C++ Programmer's Guide* aptly points out, though, that the classical form of the default constructor (as explained in the second item in this list) and the form with default arguments cannot be used together. The meaning of the two forms used together is ambiguous—the compiler will not be able to determine which one to call. Consider the default constructor call implied by the declaration of obj in the following code fragment:

```
class A{
...
A();
A( int=1, int=2, int=3 );
```

```
...
}
...
void main()
{
    A obj; // Which constructor now?
}
```

The declaration A obj; is the correct format for invoking either form of the A class constructor. Because enough information is not present for the compiler to determine which of the two functions is meant, a compile-time error will result. This is not much of a problem, though. Either form of the default constructor will work; the only practical difference is that the form with all the default values is probably more flexible.

Lines 7 and 8 in listing 11.8 illustrate that you can code (nondefault) constructor functions of several varieties. In other words, you can supply several overloaded constructors. None of the constructor functions can have a return value—that is illegal for *all* constructors—and each version of the function must have clearly different arguments. In this program, the purpose of the overloaded constructors is to allow the declaration of class objects that can be initialized several different ways. Lines 46 and 49 show how to declare objects by using nondefault constructors. Notice that the call arguments are used just as for a normal function call, even though these lines are object declarations that are semantically equivalent to int i.

The last kind of constructor is the *copy constructor*. This form permits a class object to be declared and initialized by copying the contents of another class object. Note the general syntax of a copy constructor:

```
classname( otherclassname & );
```

As used here, the ampersand (&) is called the *reference operator*. A reference has a close family connection to a pointer to an object, but does not require dereferencing as pointers do. (A detailed description of references is provided in Chapter 13.) The copy constructor in listing 11.8 is declared in line 9, and the copy constructor function definition appears in lines 28–32. Line 52 shows a sample of using a copy constructor in declaring a class *object*. For now, just write your copy constructors by mimicking this sample code.

The compiler generates a default destructor function for a class if you don't declare one, just as the compiler generates a constructor function. Like constructors, destructor functions cannot specify a return type. They are different from constructors, however, in several important ways:

❏ *A destructor function has the same name as the class, but the tilde (˜) character appears before the function name.* A destructor function declaration looks like this:

```
class A {
...
public:
...
~A();
};
A::~A() { ... } // destructor function definition
```

The tilde is the same one character that is used for the standard C one's complement operator; the context of the character's use tells the compiler which use is meant. A destructor function can be an inline function.

❏ *The destructor function for a class cannot accept arguments.* Whether you write the destructor yourself or allow the compiler to generate a default destructor, a destructor function cannot accept function arguments.

❏ *A class can have only one destructor function.* This point is really a consequence of the preceding point. If a destructor cannot specify a return type or an argument list, you obviously cannot produce different versions of the destructor function.

Simple class objects (particularly one that does not acquire memory outside the object's boundaries) can usually do quite well with a compiler-generated destructor. If the memory for the whole object is going to be released, whether or not a member integer is first set to zero doesn't matter much.

Other class objects (such as the `lifo` class objects shown earlier in this chapter) will require you to write an explicit destructor function that frees acquired memory or performs other cleanup tasks.

Using Friend Functions

Friend functions are *not* class member functions but are granted access even to private member objects of a class. You use friend functions to keep class object size to a minimum, and to enhance class object performance. These uses of friend functions are covered in detail in Chapter 18, but you need to know now how to declare such functions in order to complete your overview of basic class declarations.

Including Friend Functions in a Class

Declaring a function to be a friend of a class is easy. You just supply a function prototype for the friend function in the class declaration, and you prefix the prototype declaration with the keyword friend. Note the following example:

```
class A {
   int value;
public:
...
friend int peekA( A ); //Here is the friend prototype
};
```

If you write the friend function definition out-of-line, no further special keywords are needed. The function definition for the peekA() function in the preceding code fragment would then be coded like this:

```
int peekA( A obj )
{
    printf( "%d\n", obj.value );
}
```

This second code fragment illustrates two important points about friend functions. First, friend functions *can* access private member variables in the class for which such functions are defined as a friend. Second, you *do* have to use structure member syntax, as shown here, to gain access to class members, and you *do* have to tell the friend function which object is meant (with an argument). There is no automatic assignment of the correct object address to the this pointer, as there is on behalf of member functions. You should also realize that friend functions defined out-of-line are *not* within the scope of the class (as member objects are).

Friend functions may also be defined inline. For example, you can combine the preceding two code fragments by using an inline definition in this way:

```
class A {
   int value;
public:
...
   friend int peekA( A ) //Here is the inline friend
   {
     printf( "%d\n", obj.value );
   }
};
```

The main difference between friend functions defined out-of-line and those defined inline is that inline friend functions *are* within the scope of the class where they are defined.

Note also some important restrictions on which functions can be declared to be friends of a class. You *cannot* declare the following kinds of functions as friends: constructors, destructors, virtual functions, assignment operator functions, and class type cast operator functions. (Assignment and cast operator functions are covered in Chapter 14.)

Whether a friend function is defined inline or out-of-line, you do not have to use the member access syntax (structure member operator or pointer) to call it; a friend function is not a member of the class that declared the function as friend. The `peekA()` friend function defined in the last code fragment, for instance, should be called in this way:

```
main()
{
   A obj1; // declare an A class object
   ...
   peekA( obj1 ); // pass object as arg
}
```

Deciding When To Use a Friend Function

In Bjarne Stroustrup's original book that introduced the new C++ language (*The C++ Programming Language*, Addison-Wesley, 1987), readers were urged to avoid friend functions, with three exceptions. Friends were considered suitable whenever it was necessary to avoid the use of global data, global nonmember functions, or public data members.

Subsequent experience has apparently changed the prevailing attitude toward friend functions. Both the AT&T and Borland C++ implementations of the complex number class, for example, make great use of friend functions. The base document recommends the use of friend functions for a variety of reasons, including these:

❏ *Friend functions can improve the efficiency and performance of class objects and provide (in some circumstances) a cleaner programming interface to class members.* In many cases, using a member function would require passing whole class objects as arguments to and from class member functions. Using friend functions to implement specific kinds of class behavior can avoid much of this inefficiency (as explained in Chapter 19). A function can also be a friend to more than one class, helping to eliminate instances in which a global function would otherwise be necessary to provide a function common to more than one class.

❑ *Friend functions can make more flexible the implementation of overloaded operator functions for classes.* If you define a class on which you want to be able to perform addition, you must also write a function (member or friend) that defines how addition is to be performed on objects of that class. The significance of using friend functions to make such functions more flexible is clearly explained in Chapter 14, in the section "Overloading Operators with C++."

❑ *You can use friend function declarations to provide access to class members for a routine written in another language.* Member functions obviously have to be written in C++ because of the special syntax and scope requirements. However, you may want to write a high-performance service routine in assembler. In that case, you can declare the routine a friend and link it in the finished program later.

In short, use friend functions conservatively, but don't be afraid to use them.

Exercises

The following exercises give you practice in declaring classes, defining member functions, and using class objects.

1. Review the class syntax and formatting guidelines and then answer the following questions: What is the general syntax of a class declaration? How are class declarations commonly formatted in source code? How are class declarations packaged for separate compilation?

2. Review the differences between class objects created with the `struct` keyword and the `class` keyword. When would you choose one keyword over the other, and why?

3. Modify the `PUSH()` macro shown in listing 11.4 so that the second argument in the macro call does *not* require the address-of operator `&`. Remember that the `lifo::push()` member function requires as its second argument a `void` pointer to the object being pushed. Examine the macro closely to see what will actually result from the macro expansion.

4. You might be tempted to modify the `POP()` macro in listing 11.4 so that you don't have to cast the type of object just popped off the stack. The most obvious modification looks like this:

```
#define POP(type)        *(type *)pop( sizeof(type) )
```

This modification won't work, however. No errors are flagged in the header file during compilation, but the source file containing `POP()` macro calls (see listing 11.6, for example) gets a *lot* of errors during compilation. Why doesn't this modification work? (Hint: expand a macro call like `stack.POP( int )` by hand and see what you get.)

5. Review the header file `lifo.hpp` in listing 11.4, observing what members are `private` (by default) and what has been made `public`. Why do you think the class declaration was arranged this way?

6. Write a class declaration with several overloaded constructor functions. Write the default constructor, using all default arguments. Use this class in a C++ program. Repeat the exercise but use a copy constructor instead of a default constructor.

7. Write a class declaration with at least one friend function. Declare a class object and access it through the friend function.

Summary

This chapter covered some of the most important concepts associated with C++. Before continuing with the next chapter, be sure that you understand the following points:

❏ *C++ classes define truly new types, whereas the standard C* `typedef` *provides only a synonym facility.* When you declare a C++ class, you declare not merely the contents of a data structure, but the behavior of that new type as well.

❏ *C++ classes can be declared with the* `class`, `struct`, *or* `union` *keyword.* Classes declared with the `class` keyword permit `private` access to member data and functions by default; the other classes permit `public` access by default.

❏ *Class member functions are always declared within a class and may optionally be defined inline.* Member functions define the behavior of class objects. If a member function is defined out-of-line, you use the scope resolution syntax (the function's *fully qualified name*) to associate the definition with the class to which it belongs:

```
class A {
...
public:
... int show();
```

```
};
...
int A::show() { ... }
```

If you define a member function inline, the fully qualified name is not necessary.

❑ *You declare class objects as you would any other typed object.* for example, you can declare a local class A object in this way:

```
main()
{
   A my_obj; // declare a class A object
}
```

Other ways to create instance objects will be discussed later, particularly in Chapter 15.

❑ *Class member functions can access both private and public member data and functions directly.* Remember that the compiler generates a pointer named this for each instance object. When a member function is called, hidden code sets the this pointer to the correct address for the object. If, however, a member function accesses members of a *different* instance of the same class, the member function must use the member access syntax.

❑ *Nonmember functions can access only public member data and functions, and must use the member access syntax for that purpose.* Some of the member data and functions of a class need to be visible only internally; they should not be accessed by nonmember functions. *Encapsulation* provides protection against accidental (though not fraudulent) access of private members. Furthermore, nonmember functions (other than friend functions) can access private members only through the member access syntax, as shown in this example:

```
class A {
public:
   int i;
   ...
};
...
main()
{
   A someobj;
   ...
   someobj.i = 0;
}
```

In other words, you use the structure member operator (.) or structure pointer operator (->) to access the member. This requirement should not be surprising because classes are based on advanced implementations of structures.

❏ *Friend functions can access both private and public class members, but must still use the member access syntax.* Note the following short program:

```
#include <stdlib.h>
#include <stdio.h>
class A {
  int i;
public:
  friend int report( A obj ) { return obj.i; }
};
main()
{
  A myobj;
  printf( "%d\n", report( myobj ) );
}
```

Friend functions defined out-of-line are not in the class scope; those defined inline are in the class scope. Friend functions can be quite useful, particularly in boosting program performance (see Chapter 19).

If you have mastered these basic concepts, you are ready to begin reading the next chapter, "Creating C++ Objects."

12

Creating C++ Objects

Knowing the rules for declaring classes is something like having a theoretical knowledge of aerodynamics: it doesn't necessarily mean that you can get in an airplane and fly away. A more practical kind of instruction is first necessary. That is what this chapter is about—the practical aspects of using class objects.

The contents of this chapter can be divided into two main categories: creating and initializing class objects. In creating and initializing class objects, you define objects and supply initial values for member data objects. The next chapter, "Accessing C++ Objects," continues the discussion of the practical aspects of using class objects and deals with gaining access to objects.

Defining C++ Objects

The first order of business is the creation of class objects. Because a class defines a new type (not just a synonym), you can at times declare just a class object, much as you declare any other C variable. At other times, you will want an object to persist indefinitely. Then you will need to create the object on the free store, which is analogous to acquiring storage with `malloc()` and `calloc()`.

Simple class object declarations are close to standard C syntax, but more advanced declarations, not surprisingly, exhibit some differences from familiar methods of declaration. Initialization of class objects also has its differences from the familiar initialization methods.

Assigning Storage Classes to Class Objects

Think back for a moment about the rules for C scope, linkage, and duration. Fortunately, almost all of what you learned about these rules in mastering standard C still applies to C++. The great exception is that a C++ class *is* a scope—which by definition could not arise in standard C.

When local, global, and arbitrary objects are referred to in this chapter, the primary concern is the *duration* of class objects (understanding duration in the standard sense). Class object duration is still related to the object's scope, as you have already learned. That is, local objects (objects declared with block scope) by default have auto duration; global objects (objects declared with file scope) by default have static duration.

Furthermore, you can use the *storage class specifiers* (auto, register, static, and extern) with class object declarations in the same way you would use them with, for example, the declaration of an int. Because you are now writing C++, though, the significance of using one of the storage class specifiers may be slightly different from that in standard C. Note the following guidelines for using storage class specifiers in C++:

❑ *You can apply the* auto *and* register *specifiers only to objects declared with block scope.* In Borland C++ (as well as in earlier versions of the Turbo C compiler), an auto object is created on the system stack. That way, the object goes away when the function owning the object returns to its caller. It is therefore a contradiction in terms to apply auto to a global object (which is stored in the data segment).

Because register objects are also auto objects, the same restrictions apply to both kinds of objects. In C++, the register keyword serves merely as a hint that the object is frequently used, and has little to do with placing the variable in a hardware register. Moreover, C++ allows the address of a register object to be taken (that is, the address-of operator, &, can be used on it), which is illegal in standard C. Because of this new capability, most implementations ignore the hint. Borland C++ limits the use of the register keyword to integral object types, and even then it is still only a hint. Turbo C uses hardware registers whenever possible, anyway. Thus, forcing a variable into a register could actually hurt performance by disturbing normal register usage.

Neither the auto nor the register keyword is allowed for class *member* objects. A whole class object may be auto, however.

❑ *You can apply the* static *specifier to objects anywhere.* You can apply the static keyword only to objects and functions—not, for example, to a class declaration. The static keyword can be used at file scope (limiting an object or function to internal linkage only), at block scope (giving a local object static duration), and with a *member* data object within a *global class declaration*. Because a local class declaration will (naturally) go out of scope often, static members are meaningless within such a declaration. (Locally declared classes are severely restricted in what they can do and in what objects they can refer to. The best rule of thumb for handling locally declared classes is not to use them, even though they are legal.)

❏ *You cannot use the extern keyword with class members.* Otherwise, you can use the extern keyword as you always have, with the additional capability of declaring whole class objects extern.

Static data members of a class deserve a little more discussion because they have an interesting characteristic: static data members are not part of any object of that class. This means that a static data member can be referenced through a class object (the member was declared, after all, as a class member) *and* that the static data member can be referenced independently of any particular class object. The following code fragment, for example, is perfectly legal (and usable):

```
class task {
  ...
public:
  static int numberoftasks; // Not a definition!
};
.
int task::numberoftasks = 1; // Here's the definition!
...
void main()
{
  int maxtasks = 16;
  task user1; // declare a class object
  printf("%d\n", user1.numberoftasks );

  printf("Inactive tasks: %d\n",
          maxtasks - task::numberoftasks );

}
```

In this code fragment, the only thing necessary for referring to the static member integer numberoftasks apart from any particular object is to fully qualify the identifier with the class name *classname::identifier*.

You should also notice the comments in the preceding code fragment.

Observe particularly the comment that the declaration of the static object within the class is *not a definition*. With one exception, a static data member must be *defined* elsewhere in the program. The definition of the static member object directs the compiler to allocate space for the object and to initialize it. The one exception arises when you want to allow the member to be *initialized to zero by default*.

The `numberoftasks` static data member is explicitly initialized to 1 in the code fragment. This action illustrates another interesting characteristic: static data members (of a global class declaration) are *initialized just like all other global objects*, but they otherwise obey normal class member access rules. A global object has a default value of zero, and so has a static data member. A global object definition can have an initializer, and so can a static data member. (An ordinary class data member cannot have an initializer.)

A final characteristic of static data members is important: only one copy of a static data member is available, and it is shared by all objects of its class. When all objects of a class must communicate with each other, you can use a static data member instead of an ordinary global variable (which is more susceptible to corruption by uncontrolled access). Additionally, declaring a data member to be `static` helps decrease the size of class objects. Reducing the size of a class object is not a sufficient reason to use static data members, however. Let your program's logistical requirements guide that decision.

You can also declare class member functions to be static. The significance of static member functions is discussed in the section "Understanding `*this`" in Chapter 13.

Defining Arbitrary-Duration Class Objects

Most C++ authorities (including Stroustrup) recommend that programmers avoid global objects whenever possible. The reason is that C++ objects tend to be memory-intensive; using many global class objects can inflate the size of a program. At times, however, the logic of your program simply demands a global object. The alternatives to global objects are, of course, local objects and arbitrary objects. Local objects, which are declared in a block, go away when the block is exited. Arbitrary objects, which you explicitly create, never go away until you explicitly delete them.

C++ arbitrary objects are created with the `new` operator and deleted with the `delete` operator, both of which are unique to C++. Arbitrary objects have the same advantage that global static objects have: they persist for as long as you want them to remain. Furthermore, when you use arbitrary objects, you avoid the disadvantage of inflated program size because they do not exist until they are created during program execution.

You can see how arbitrary objects are used in the following illustration of a class and support program for controlling a Microsoft mouse. The mouse, if used at all during a program, is usually something you will want available throughout program execution. A mouse class object can thus be considered for use as a global static object, but can work equally well as an arbitrary object. Implementing a mouse class object as an arbitrary object is particularly attractive because the private data for the class contains several large structures, and a number of support functions are involved in the class. Furthermore, because there is no need to define more than one mouse object for a given program, there is no corresponding need to declare such objects with the frequency and ease of, say, integer objects.

The mouse class is named msmouse. Note the following characteristics that should be included in this class:

❑ *The class should include a member function that reports the success or failure of mouse initialization.* If the hardware system on which your program is running does not have a mouse, or if the mouse driver software was not installed (or was improperly installed) when the system was booted, the program needs to be able to discover that fact.

❑ *The class should include mouse support for both text and graphics modes.* Using a text mouse is quite common, but mouse support in graphics mode programs has become increasingly necessary in the last couple of years. The program should be able to support a mouse in either mode. Additionally, the program should be able to respond to changes in video modes "on the fly" during program execution; a "reset" member function that can adjust to changing video modes is therefore helpful.

❑ *Mouse coordinates and virtual screens should be completely hidden from the programmer.* The Microsoft mouse software addresses screen RAM in terms of virtual-screen coordinates. A *virtual screen* is an imaginary screen that, as far as the mouse driver is concerned, is never less than 640 by 200 pixels in size. The physical-screen dimensions for a given video mode and screen type vary considerably, requiring the program to convert physical to virtual coordinates, and virtual to physical coordinates. The msmouse class should include member functions that allow the program both to set and to report mouse coordinates *as if they were physical-screen coordinates—*no matter what video mode is active. Thus, the programmer is required to deal with only one set of coordinates while using the mouse.

Although many of the requirements for mouse programming are touched on in the explanation of the msmouse class, you should be aware that mouse-programming technology is fairly complex (especially for some of the advanced features the Microsoft mouse supports). If you want to know more about mouse-programming theory, you should get a copy of *Microsoft Mouse Programmer's Reference* (Microsoft Press, 1989). For other practical examples of mouse programming, you can consult Jack Purdum's *C Programmer's Toolkit* (Que Corporation, 1989), which also has a companion software diskette.

Separate compilation was used to develop and test the `msmouse` class. The three source files involved in demonstrating a mouse object as an arbitrary-duration class object are these: (1) `msmouse.hpp`, a header file containing the class declaration; (2) `msmouse.cpp`, a file containing the member function definitions for the class; and (2) `usemouse.cpp`, a demonstration program that creates and uses a mouse class object. You will need at least the following entries in a project file to compile and link the mouse sample programs:

```
usemouse.cpp
msmouse.cpp
```

The header file `msmouse.hpp` is shown in listing 12.1.

Listing 12.1. `msmouse.hpp`. *A header file that contains the class declaration and support declarations for the Microsoft mouse class.*

```
 1   #if !defined( MSMOUSE )
 2   #define MSMOUSE
 3
 4   #include <dos.h>
 5   #include <graphics.h>
 6   #include <conio.h>
 7
 8   #define callmouse int86( 0x33, &reg, &reg )
 9   #define NOBUTTON      0
10   #define LEFTBUTTON    1
11   #define RIGHTBUTTON   2
12   #define BOTHBUTTON    3
13   #define vmaxx 0
14   #define vmaxy 1
15   #define xsize 2
16   #define ysize 3
17
18   // Screen table can be used to convert mouse to
19   // real coordinates:
```

```
20  //     mousex = ( x - 1 ) * screentab[crtmode][xsize]
21  //     mousey = ( y - 1 ) * screentab[crtmode][ysize]
22  //     x = ( mousex / screentab[crtmode][xsize] ) + 1
23  //     y = ( mousey / screentab[crtmode][ysize] ) + 1
24  // This will take into account the difference between
25  // TC 1-origin and mouse 0-origin coordinate systems
26  // in text modes. Graphics modes already use 0-origin
27  // coordinates.
28
29  extern int screentab[20][4];
30
31  typedef struct {
32    int verify;
33    int crtmode;
34    int cursoron;
35    int buttons;
36    int numpress;
37    int x;         // x and y are in screen coordinates
38    int y;
39    int minx;      // min-max values are in mouse coordinates
40    int maxx;
41    int miny;
42    int maxy;
43    int crtpage;
44  } mstat_t;
45
46  class msmouse {
47    union REGS reg;
48    struct SREGS seg;
49    mstat_t mstat;
50  public:
51    void reset();
52    msmouse();
53    ~msmouse();
54    int initok() { return mstat.verify; }
55    void showcursor();
56    void hidecursor();
57    mstat_t *getposition();
58    void setposition( int = 0, int = 0);
59    mstat_t *getbutton( int );
60    mstat_t *releasebutton( int );
```

Listing 12.1. continues

Listing 12.1. continued

```
61    mstat_t *zonex( int, int );
62    mstat_t *zoney( int, int );
63    };
64
65    #endif
```

The first feature you should notice in listing 12.1 is that the entire header file is controlled by an `#if defined` compiler directive. Using this directive is important when you begin to develop serious multiple source-file programs—and most C++ programs turn out to be serious programs because the OOPS approach encourages you to pack features into an object.

Various support macros appear next in listing 12.1. Lines 8–12 define macros useful for identifying button presses that result from calling the `msmouse::getposition()` member function. (These macros are not used in the demonstration program, listing 12.3, but are provided so that you won't have to code them later.) Lines 13–16 provide macro names for subscripts into the screen conversion table named `screentab` (used to convert to and from mouse virtual-screen coordinates).

Lines 31–44 provide a `typedef` name, `mstat_t`, for a structure that is frequently used by member functions to report mouse status. That structure, `mstat`, is declared as a private data member in line 49 even though several of the member functions return a pointer to it. Returning a pointer to a private member is, strictly speaking, a violation of encapsulation for the class, but there are two good reasons for doing so for this class. First, the structure is used only to report status, not to control or modify the object. Second, the pure convenience of the technique makes using such a pointer desirable.

Member function prototype declarations for the `msmouse` class are shown in lines 51–62 of listing 12.1. These member function declarations aren't notable, except that `msmouse::initok()` is an inline function. `initok()` returns the `verify` flag, which is set to 1 (a true condition) by the constructor *only* if mouse initialization was acceptable.

The next step, of course, is to write the member function definitions for the `msmouse` class. These definitions are shown in listing 12.2.

Listing 12.2. `msmouse.cpp`. *Member function definitions for the* `msmouse` *class.*

```
1    #include <stdlib.h>
2    #include "msmouse.hpp"
3
4    int screentab[20][4] = {
5
6    // -----------------------------------
7    //   vmaxx vmaxy xsiz ysiz    crtmode
8    // -----------------------------------
9        640,   200,   16,   8,    // mode 0
10       640,   200,   16,   8,    // mode 1
11       640,   200,    8,   8,    // mode 2
12       640,   200,    8,   8,    // mode 3
13       640,   200,    2,   1,    // mode 4
14       640,   200,    2,   1,    // mode 5
15       640,   200,    1,   1,    // mode 6
16       640,   200,    8,   8,    // mode 7
17         0,     0,    0,   0,    // mode 8
18         0,     0,    0,   0,    // mode 9
19         0,     0,    0,   0,    // mode A
20         0,     0,    0,   0,    // mode B
21         0,     0,    0,   0,    // mode C
22       640,   200,    2,   1,    // mode D
23       640,   200,    1,   1,    // mode E
24       640,   350,    1,   1,    // mode F
25       640,   350,    1,   1,    // mode 10
26       640,   480,    1,   1,    // mode 11
27       640,   480,    1,   1,    // mode 12
28       640,   200,    1,   1,    // mode 13
29   };
30
31   void msmouse::reset()
32   {
33     reg.x.ax = 0x0F00;
34     int86( 0x10, &reg, &reg );
35     mstat.crtmode = reg.h.al;
```

Listing 12.2. continues

Listing 12.2. continued

```
36      mstat.crtpage = reg.h.bh;
37      mstat.verify = 0;
38      reg.x.ax = 0;        // reset mouse driver
39      callmouse;
40      if ( reg.x.ax == -1 ) {
41        mstat.verify = -1;
42        mstat.cursoron = -1;
43        mstat.buttons = NOBUTTON;
44        mstat.numpress = 0;
45        mstat.x = mstat.y = 0;
46        mstat.minx = mstat.miny = 0;
47        mstat.maxx = screentab[mstat.crtmode][vmaxx] - 1;
48        mstat.maxy = screentab[mstat.crtmode][vmaxy] - 1;
49      }
50    }
51
52    msmouse::msmouse()  // reset mouse, status in AX
53    {
54      unsigned char first_byte;
55      void interrupt far (*oldx33)( ... );
56
57      oldx33 = getvect( 0x33 );
58      first_byte = *(unsigned char far *)oldx33;
59      if ( NULL == oldx33 || first_byte == 0xcf ) return;
60      reset();
61    }
62
63    msmouse::~msmouse()
64    {
65      reg.x.ax = 0;        // reset mouse driver
66      callmouse;
67    }
68
69    void msmouse::showcursor()  // display mouse cursor
70    {
71      reg.x.ax = 1;
72      callmouse;
73    }
74
75    void msmouse::hidecursor()
76    {
77      reg.x.ax = 2;
```

```
78     callmouse;
79   }
80
81   mstat_t *msmouse::getposition()
82   {
83     // Button status data is trapped only if a button
84     // is being HELD DOWN.
85
86     int ofs;
87
88     if ( mstat.crtmode > 3 ) ofs = 0;
89       else ofs = 1;
90     reg.x.ax = 3;
91     callmouse;
92     mstat.buttons = reg.x.bx;
93     mstat.x =
94       ( reg.x.cx / screentab[mstat.crtmode][xsize] ) + ofs;
95     mstat.y =
96       ( reg.x.dx / screentab[mstat.crtmode][ysize] ) + ofs;
97     return &mstat;
98   }
99
100  void msmouse::setposition( int x, int y )
101  {
102    int ofs;
103
104    if ( mstat.crtmode > 3 ) ofs = 0;
105      else ofs = 1;
106    mstat.x = x;
107    mstat.y = y;
108    reg.x.cx =
109      ( mstat.x - ofs ) * screentab[mstat.crtmode][xsize];
110    reg.x.dx =
111      ( mstat.y - ofs ) * screentab[mstat.crtmode][ysize];
112    if ( reg.x.cx < mstat.minx || reg.x.dx < mstat.miny ) {
113      mstat.x = mstat.y = 0;
114      reg.x.cx = reg.x.dx = 0;
115    }
116    if ( reg.x.cx > mstat.maxx || reg.x.dx > mstat.maxy ) {
117      mstat.x = mstat.y = 0;
118      reg.x.cx = reg.x.dx = 0;
```

Listing 12.2. continues

Listing 12.2. continued

```
119     }
120     reg.x.ax = 4;
121     callmouse;
122  }
123
124  mstat_t *msmouse::getbutton( int button )
125  {
126     int ofs;
127
128     if ( mstat.crtmode > 3 ) ofs = 0;
129       else ofs = 1;
130     reg.x.ax = 5;
131     reg.x.bx = button;
132     callmouse;
133     mstat.buttons = reg.x.ax;
134     mstat.numpress = reg.x.bx;
135     mstat.x =
136       ( reg.x.cx / screentab[mstat.crtmode][xsize] ) + ofs;
137     mstat.y =
138       ( reg.x.dx / screentab[mstat.crtmode][ysize] ) + ofs;
139     return &mstat;
140  }
141
142  mstat_t *msmouse::releasebutton( int button )
143  {
144     int ofs;
145
146     if ( mstat.crtmode > 3 ) ofs = 0;
147       else ofs = 1;
148     reg.x.ax = 6;
149     reg.x.bx = button;
150     callmouse;
151     mstat.buttons = reg.x.ax;
152     mstat.numpress = reg.x.bx;
153     mstat.x =
154       ( reg.x.cx / screentab[mstat.crtmode][xsize] ) + ofs;
155     mstat.y =
156       ( reg.x.dx / screentab[mstat.crtmode][ysize] ) + ofs;
157     return &mstat;
158  }
159
160
```

```
161   mstat_t *msmouse::zonex( int minx, int maxx )
162   {
163     int ofs;
164
165     if ( mstat.crtmode > 3 ) ofs = 0;
166       else ofs = 1;
167     reg.x.ax = 7;
168     reg.x.cx =
169       ( minx - ofs ) * screentab[mstat.crtmode][xsize];
170     reg.x.dx =
171       ( maxx - ofs ) * screentab[mstat.crtmode][xsize];
172     callmouse;
173     mstat.minx = minx - ofs;
174     mstat.maxx = maxx - ofs;
175     return &mstat;
176   }
177
178   mstat_t *msmouse::zoney( int miny, int maxy )
179   {
180     int ofs;
181
182     if ( mstat.crtmode > 3 ) ofs = 0;
183       else ofs = 1;
184     reg.x.ax = 8;
185     reg.x.cx =
186       ( miny - ofs ) * screentab[mstat.crtmode][ysize];
187     reg.x.dx =
188       ( maxy - ofs ) * screentab[mstat.crtmode][ysize];
189     callmouse;
190     mstat.miny = miny - ofs;
191     mstat.maxy = maxy - ofs;
192     return &mstat;
193   }
194
```

Lines 4–29 of listing 12.2 contain the screentab coordinate-conversion array. The array contains 20 rows of 4 entries, with each row corresponding to a PC video mode, for modes 0x00 through 0x13 (notice that modes 0x08 through 0x0C are no longer used). Within a row i, the elements screentab[i][vmaxx] and screentab[i][vmaxy] give the resolution of the *mouse virtual screen*, which is always in pixels, even in text modes. Next, the elements screentab[i][xsize] and screentab[i][ysize] give the number of virtual-screen pixels per *physical display location* on the screen.

You must also take into account the fact that mouse virtual coordinates and Borland C++ graphics-mode physical coordinates identify screen positions (both x and y positions) beginning from position 0, whereas Borland C++ text modes identify positions beginning from position 1. Member functions performing coordinate conversion must calculate an adjustment value of 0 or 1, depending on the active video mode. Whether the offset value is added or subtracted from the coordinate depends on the direction of conversion. You can examine the member functions to see how the adjustment value is computed and used.

Suppose, for example, that the screen is running video mode 0x03 (color text, 80x25) and that the member function `msmouse::getposition()` internally determines that the mouse position is on the 0th row and 11th column of the mouse virtual screen. How is the function going to convert these mouse coordinates to text coordinates for reporting to the caller?

First, the x-position, 11, is divided by the `xsize` value for this video mode, and the remainder is thrown away. The result so far is 1, but an adjustment of 1 must be added to the result to convert to a text-origin coordinate. Thus, the text x-position is column 2. A similar operation on the row, or y-position, gives the result of 1. Therefore, the mouse position in physical-screen coordinates (x,y) is (2,1).

You can find further details on how the member functions do their jobs by consulting the mouse technical documentation previously mentioned. All you need to remember is that you *always* communicate mouse coordinates to `msmouse` class objects in terms of the *correct physical-screen coordinates* for the active video mode.

The sequence of calls to `msmouse` member functions is also important. The best way to indicate what sequences are required is to show you. Look now at `usemouse.cpp` in listing 12.3.

Listing 12.3. `usemouse.cpp`. *A program that demonstrates the `msmouse` class in both text and graphics modes, using arbitrary-duration objects.*

```
1   // ------------------------------------------------------------
2   // USEMOUSE.CPP
3   //    Demonstrates the Microsoft mouse class in both text
4   //    and graphics modes. Be sure to compile this program
5   //    with the LARGE MODEL to accommodate graphics FAR
6   //    pointers.
7   // ------------------------------------------------------------
8
```

```
 9   #include"msmouse.hpp"
10
11   #include <stdlib.h>
12   #include <stdio.h>
13   #include <dos.h>
14   #include <conio.h>
15   #include <graphics.h>
16
17   int numitem = 10;
18   char *item[] = {
19    " initok()",
20    " showcursor()",
21    " hidecursor()",
22    " getposition()",
23    " setposition()",
24    " getbutton()",
25    " releasebutton()",
26    " zonex()",
27    " zoney()",
28    " reset()",
29   };
30   char *blurb[] = {
31    "initok() returns -1 if mouse driver initialized OK.",
32    "showcursor() turns on the mouse cursor.",
33    "hidecursor() turns off the mouse cursor.",
34    "getposition() returns TC++ x,y in mouse status block.",
35    "setposition() uses TC++ x,y to set mouse x,y.",
36    "getbutton() gets last TC++ x,y & clicks for button.",
37    "releasebutton() gets TC++ x,y & releases for button.",
38    "zonex() sets x1-x2 range for mouse cursor.",
39    "zoney() sets y1-y2 range for mouse cursor.",
40    "reset() reinitializes mouse after mode change.",
41   };
42
43   void main()
44   {
45     int i;
46     mstat_t *mstat; // pointer to status block
47
48     msmouse *mouse;  // pointer to mouse object
49
```

Listing 12.3. continues

Listing 12.3. continued

```
50      mouse = new msmouse; // create mouse object
51      if ( mouse->initok() != -1 ) {
52        puts("This system does not have a mouse attached." );
53        exit( 0 );
54      }
55
56      textcolor( WHITE );
57      textbackground( BLUE );
58      clrscr();
59      textcolor( BLACK );
60      textbackground( WHITE );
61      window( 10, 5, 70, 15 );
62      clrscr();
63      gotoxy( 1, 1 );
64      for ( i=0; i<numitem; ++i )
65        cprintf("%s\r\n", item[i] );
66
67      window( 10, 17, 70, 25 );
68      textcolor( WHITE );
69      textbackground( BLUE );
70      gotoxy( 1, 1 );
71      cputs("Click the RIGHT BUTTON for GRAPHICS demo.\r\n" );
72      cputs("Click the LEFT BUTTON on item to SELECT.\r\n" );
73      window( 10, 20, 70, 25 );
74      _setcursortype( _NOCURSOR );
75      mouse->zonex( 10, 70 );
76      mouse->zoney( 5, 15 );
77      mouse->setposition( 10, 5 );
78      mouse->showcursor();
79      while ( 1 ) {
80        mstat = mouse->getbutton( 1 );
81        if ( mstat->numpress ) break;
82        mstat = mouse->getbutton( 0 );
83        if ( !mstat->numpress ) continue;
84        i = mstat->y - 5; // scale to index value
85        if ( i >= 0 && i < numitem ) {
86          clrscr();
87          gotoxy( 1, 1 );
88          cprintf("Last item clicked was: %s\r\n", item[i] );
89          cprintf("%s\r\n", blurb[i] );
90        }
91      }
```

```
92
93      window( 1, 1, 80, 25 );
94      mouse->hidecursor();
95      textbackground( BLACK );
96      textcolor( WHITE );
97      clrscr();
98      _setcursortype( _NORMALCURSOR );
99
100     // msmouse.hpp already has graphics.h included
101     // so go ahead with graphics mode demo
102
103     int gdriver = DETECT, gmode, errorcode;
104
105     initgraph( &gdriver, &gmode,"C:\\TCP\\BGI" );
106     errorcode = graphresult();
107     if (errorcode != grOk)  /* an error occurred */
108     {
109         printf("Graphics error: %s\n", grapherrormsg(errorcode));
110         printf("Press any key to halt:");
111         getch();
112         exit(1);                /* return with error code */
113     }
114
115     // -----------------------------------
116     // Important to reset after mode change
117     // -----------------------------------
118     mouse->reset();
119     // -----------------------------------
120
121     // draw a stopsign
122
123
124     int wholescreen[] = {
125       0,0,
126       getmaxx(),0,
127       getmaxx(),getmaxy(),
128       0,getmaxy(),
129     };
130     int gx = getmaxx() / 2;
131     int gy = getmaxy() / 2;
132     int stopsign[] = {
```

Listing 12.3. continues

Listing 12.3. continued

```
133        gx-40,gy-40,
134        gx+40,gy-40,
135        gx+40,gy+40,
136        gx-40,gy+40,
137      };
138      setfillstyle( SOLID_FILL, EGA_BLUE );
139      fillpoly( 4, wholescreen );
140      setfillstyle( SOLID_FILL, EGA_RED );
141      fillpoly( 4, stopsign );
142      setcolor( EGA_WHITE );
143      settextjustify( CENTER_TEXT, CENTER_TEXT );
144      moveto( gx, gy );
145      outtext("STOP" );
146      moveto( gx, gy+80 );
147      outtext("Click the STOP SIGN to end demo" );
148
149      mouse->showcursor();
150      while ( 1 ) {
151        mstat = mouse->getbutton( 1 );
152        if ( mstat->numpress ) break;
153        mstat = mouse->getbutton( 0 );
154        if ( mstat->numpress ) {
155          if ( mstat->x > stopsign[0] &&
156                mstat->x < stopsign[2] &&
157                mstat->y > stopsign[1] &&
158                mstat->y < stopsign[5] ) break;
159        }
160      }
161
162      closegraph();
163  delete mouse;  // don't forget to shut mouse down
164  }
```

The first thing to notice about controlling the mouse is that the constructor function for the class contains all the mouse initialization code. Therefore, a user of the msmouse class needs only to define a mouse object in order to initialize the mouse software. In listing 12.3, line 50 contains this definition, using the new operator to create an msmouse object of arbitrary duration. Because the new operator always returns a pointer of the correct type of object, a pointer for the mouse object is set up in line 48. Even though this code appears within the main() function, the use of the new operator dictates that this object has arbitrary duration, not auto duration.

Lines 51–54 check for the correct initialization of the mouse by calling the `msmouse::initok()` member function. Because the mouse driver returns a value of –1 when the mouse cursor is hidden (invisible), this function returns a –1 if initialization was correct. The mouse cursor is always hidden when you first initialize the mouse; you must "unhide" the mouse cursor later, after you have set the screen the way you want it.

Lines 55–74 set up the display by painting a list of the mouse function and finally by hiding the normal cursor, using Borland C++'s `setcursortype ( NOCURSOR )` function call. The only cursor you will want on the screen is the mouse cursor. Here, at the beginning of the demonstration program, the screen is still in text mode, so text coordinates must be used to communicate with the member functions.

Next, lines 74–77 define the region of the display screen in which the mouse cursor is allowed to appear. This is accomplished with the `msmouse::zonex()` and `msmouse::zoney()` member functions. Once more, remember that the coordinate values you specify in these function calls are physical-screen coordinates, not mouse coordinates. The member functions convert them internally to the correct values before passing on the request to the mouse driver software. After all that has been accomplished, the mouse cursor is finally turned on in line 78.

The code for decoding and interpreting mouse actions is shown in lines 79–91 of listing 12.3. Because the lines are an important logic sequence, they are reproduced here for closer scrutiny:

```
79    while ( 1 ) {
80      mstat = mouse->getbutton( 1 );
81      if ( mstat->numpress ) break;
82      mstat = mouse->getbutton( 0 );
83      if ( !mstat->numpress ) continue;
84      i = mstat->y - 5; // scale to index value
85      if ( i >= 0 && i < numitem ) {
86        clrscr();
87        gotoxy( 1, 1 );
88        cprintf("Last item clicked was: %s\r\n", item[i] );
89        cprintf("%s\r\n", blurb[i] );
90      }
91    }
```

The mouse control and decoding are accomplished with a `while` loop. Notice that the conditional expression for the `while` loop is just 1 (an expression that is always true); logic within the loop must be used to break out at the correct time. That logic depends on which mouse button is pressed.

Right-button presses are checked for in lines 80 and 81. The `msmouse::getbutton()` function (following the Microsoft internal requirements) requests the status of button "1"—the *right button*. Be careful here: this value does *not* correspond to the `LEFTBUTTON` macro shown in line 10 of listing 12.1. The macros defined in listing 12.1 are intended to support the `msmouse::getposition()` function, not button status reporting functions.

The `getbutton()` function reports several things to the caller. Most important, the function reports the number of times the requested button has been pressed since the last call to that function. `getbutton()` returns the address of the status block `mstat` in which the number of button presses was reported. Line 81 then tests that value; if the value is nonzero, the `break` command exits the `while` loop.

The real fun begins in line 82, which requests the left-button status. The left button is the one used to determine which line of the display the user clicked with the mouse. To compute which line was clicked, the minimum and maximum mouse cursor positions allowed must be taken into account. If you look back at line 76, you can see that the mouse cursor is constrained to y coordinates from line 5 to line 15, inclusive.

Because the mouse cursor can be positioned no higher than line 5, line 84 subtracts 5 from the detected vertical mouse position. Mouse coordinates are set and reported *independently* of any windowing that Borland C++ might be doing. If, for example, the mouse was positioned on the top line of that box when the user pressed the left button, the position reported is 5. Then subtracting 5 yields 0, which is a handy number for indexing into the `blurb` array. As you may guess, the `blurb` array contains a list of short explanations of the various mouse functions.

The remaining lines of logic within the `while` loop, lines 85–90, verify that the mouse was indeed clicked on one of the function name lines, and then select and display the corresponding `blurb` entry.

The second half of the demonstration begins only when the right button is clicked (anywhere on the screen). This second phase involves switching to graphics mode and detecting a mouse click within a small area on the screen (a "stop sign" in a red square).

The most important line of code in this part of the program is line 118, where the `msmouse::reset()` member function is called. It is true that the Microsoft RAM-resident mouse driver already knows about the mode change (the driver is hooked into the BIOS interrupt), but the software is not yet aware of it. Hence, a specific function is called that can test the video mode and adjust `msmouse` parameters accordingly.

The detection and decoding loop for the graphics mode demonstration is shown in lines 150–160 of listing 12.3. This loop is constructed almost exactly like the text mode loop, particularly in that physical-screen coordinates are used to detect the mouse cursor location.

Line 163 contains another important line of code. The `delete` operator is used to destroy the `msmouse` object, which was created with `new`. There are two important reasons for not forgetting to delete objects that are no longer needed. The first reason is simply efficient garbage collection. This program has only one object, which lasts for the entire run of the program. In other cases, however, you may need many different objects—so many that memory utilization can become a problem. Additionally, it is bad practice to assume that the operating system will clean up your messes after program termination. The system usually does just that, but in some instances, memory cleanup can be overlooked. Be safe and be sure. If you create it, you clean it up.

The second reason for deleting objects created with `new` is that they remain effective until you delete them. In this case, the mouse stays active for the life of the object. During the development of the `msmouse` class, it became evident (by accident) that leaving the mouse active after a program terminates can lead to some strange errors. Other objects may be hooked into the operating system, or they may be performing some other sensitive function that requires cleanup. The best medicine, once again, is to be sure—delete the object when you are done with it.

Defining Local *(auto)* Class Objects

In this section, you learn how to define local (`auto`) class objects. A useful class, `dbllist`, is presented to illustrate local objects. The `dbllist` class is one that supports the construction and manipulation of doubly linked lists. Note the following features of the `dbllist` class:

❏ *All `dbllist` objects maintain only control information within the class object.* That is, only pointers to the list and the member function prototypes are declared within the class. Thus, you can build practical doubly linked lists that can be as large as the available storage permits, without inflating the size of the object or your program.

❏ *An element in a `dbllist` linked list can be any size.* As for the `lifo` class discussed in Chapter 11, an element body of any size can be handled—even different sizes in the same list. A `typedef` named `dblentry` is provided that contains a `de_size` variable so that individual sizes can be tracked. An element body is assumed to be arbitrarily large; it can be up to 65536 bytes long.

❏ *Elements in a* dbllist *linked list can be either inserted in order or simply appended to the list as the elements appear.* For a list in which order is not important, you can just append the elements to the end of the list as you build it. Or you can build an ordered list by inserting the new elements as you build the list. The insertion logic compares the *entire* element body (not counting control information) to surrounding element bodies to determine the element's position in the list. The list is built in ascending order.

❏ *Complete navigation facilities are included in the* dbllist *class.* Member functions are available for positioning to the head or tail of the list, and for traversing the list either forward or backward.

The header file for the dbllist class, containing support declarations and the class declaration itself, is found in listing 12.4. As you read over the listing, notice again that #if defined() logic is used to prevent redeclaring the class or the companion typedef in multiple source-file programs.

Listing 12.4. dbllist.hpp. *A header file that contains the class declaration for doubly linked list objects.*

```
1    #if !defined( DBLLIST )
2    #define DBLLIST
3
4    #include <stdlib.h>
5    #include <stdio.h>
6    #include <string.h>
7    #include <conio.h>
8
9    typedef struct de_type {
10     struct de_type *prev;
11     struct de_type *next;
12     void *de_body;
13     unsigned de_size;
14   } dblentry;
15
16   class dbllist {
17     dblentry *anchor;
18     dblentry *base;
19     dblentry *hold;
20     dblentry *create( void *, unsigned );
21   public:
22     dbllist();
23     ~dbllist();
```

```
24     void kill();
25     void *gohead();
26     void *gotail();
27     void * gonext();
28     void *goprev();
29     void *append( void *, unsigned );
30     void *insert( void *, unsigned );
31  };
32
33  #endif
```

From the `dbllist` class declaration in listing 12.4, you can see that the class itself is straightforward. The declaration contains some pointers to list elements, as well as a member function in the private portion of the declaration. The other member functions, including a constructor and a destructor, are also fairly simple.

A careful look at the `typedef` for a list element (`dblentry`) shows that the physical construction of the list is not so simple, however. Figure 12.1 shows how the parts of the list are brought together by the class.

Fig. 12.1. *Physical construction of the doubly linked list for the* `dbllist` *class.*

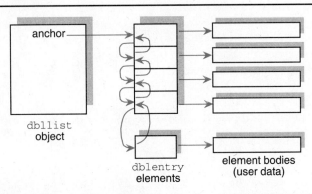

As you can see from figure 12.1, a `dbllist` doubly linked list has three components: (1) the `dbllist` class object, which contains all the control information and member function names; (2) a doubly linked list of `dblentry` structures, each of which contains linkage pointers, size information, and a pointer to the last component; and (3) the element body, which contains any amount of user data you want to store.

Although much of the information is physically outside the class object, the linked-list data is nevertheless well protected because the only access to it is through the class object. Even the means of physically creating a new entry in the list is kept in the private portion of the object (that is, the `dbllist::create()` member function is private). A user of the class can create new objects only indirectly, by means of the `append()` and `insert()` member functions.

Why has the `dbllist` class been arranged this way? The reason is simple. Any useful linked-list data would be impossibly huge for a class object declared locally or globally. If the linked list itself were included within the boundaries of a linked-list class object, you would be able to create such objects only with arbitrary duration—that is, you could use only `new` and `delete` to create and destroy them.

Furthermore, the logistics of handling a completely unpredictable amount of data within the boundaries of a class object would be truly formidable. As the `dbllist` class is designed, however, you can declare such objects anywhere and in any way, without inflating the size of your class objects or your EXE program file. This claim will be proved in a moment, but first look at the member function definitions, shown in listing 12.5.

Listing 12.5. `dbllist.cpp`. *Class member function definitions for the* `dbllist` *class.*

```
1   #include"dbllist.hpp"
2
3   dblentry *dbllist::create( void * data, unsigned bytes )
4   {
5     if ( NULL == ( hold =
          (dblentry *)malloc( sizeof( dblentry ) ) ) )
6       return NULL;
7     if ( NULL == ( hold->de_body = malloc( bytes ) ) ) {
8       free( hold );
9       return NULL;
10    }
11    memmove( hold->de_body, data, bytes );
12    hold->prev = hold->next = NULL;
13    hold->de_size = bytes;
14    return hold;
15  }
16
17  dbllist::dbllist()
18  {
```

```
19    anchor = base = hold = NULL;
20  }
21
22  dbllist::~dbllist()
23  {
24    kill();
25  }
26
27  void dbllist::kill()
28  {
29    base = anchor;
30    while( base ) {
31      hold = base->next;
32      free( base->de_body );
33      free( base );
34      base = hold;
35    }
36    anchor = base = hold = NULL;
37  }
38
39  void *dbllist::gohead()
40  {
41    base = anchor;
42    if ( base ) return base->de_body;
43    else return NULL;
44  }
45
46  void *dbllist::gotail()
47  {
48    if ( base ) {
49      while( base->next ) base = base->next;
50      return base->de_body;
51    }
52    else return NULL;
53  }
54
55  void *dbllist::gonext()
56  {
57    if ( base ) {
58      if ( base->next ) {
59        base = base->next;
```

Listing 12.5. continues

Listing 12.5. continued

```
60          return base->de_body;
61       }
62     else return NULL;
63   }
64   else return NULL;
65 }
66
67 void *dbllist::goprev()
68 {
69   if ( base ) {
70     if ( base->prev ) {
71       base = base->prev;
72       return base->de_body;
73     }
74     else return NULL;
75   }
76   else return NULL;
77 }
78
79 void *dbllist::append( void *data, unsigned bytes )
80 {
81   dblentry *temp;
82
83   if ( NULL == ( temp = create( data, bytes ) ) )
84     return NULL;
85   gotail();
86   if ( !base ) {
87     anchor = base = temp;
88   }
89   else {
90     base->next = temp;
91     temp->prev = base;
92     base = temp;
93   }
94   return base->de_body;
95 }
96
97 void *dbllist:: insert( void * data, unsigned bytes )
98 {
99   dblentry *temp;
100
101                     // if empty list, just add it on
```

```
102
103     gohead();
104     if ( !base ) return( append( data, bytes ) );
105
106                                     // create the new entry
107
108     if ( NULL == ( temp = create( data, bytes ) ) )
109       return NULL;
110
111       // position to entry before which this one belongs
112
113     while ( base->next
114      && memcmp( data, base->de_body, bytes ) > 0 )
115        base = base->next;
116          // if data still greater than last, append it
117     if ( !base->next
118      && memcmp( data, base->de_body, bytes ) > 0 ) {
119        base->next = temp;
120        temp->prev = base;
121        base = temp;
122     }                       // otherwise insert the entry
123     else {
124        hold = base->prev;
125        temp->prev = hold;
126        temp->next = base;
127        base->prev = temp;
128                      // Fix anchor when prepending
129        if ( !hold ) anchor = temp;
130        else hold->next = temp;
131        base = temp;
132     }
133     return base->de_body;
134  }
```

The only private member function in the dbllist class is dbllist::create(). It appears in lines 3–15 of listing 12.5. create() can therefore be called only by other member functions of the class or by friends of the class (in this case, there are no friends). The insert() member function (which creates an ordered doubly linked list) and the append() member function (which creates an order-of-appearance doubly linked list) call create() to set up a new list entry and enter it into the list.

`create()` accepts as arguments a `void` pointer to the user data to be placed in the list, and an unsigned byte size of the object. `create()` first acquires memory for the `dblentry` structure for the element and then acquires memory for the user data. A pointer to the user data and its size are recorded in the `dblentry` structure, and a pointer to the `dblentry` structure is returned to the caller. Notice that no attempt is made at this point to link the entry into the list; that responsibility falls to either `insert()` or `append()`. Notice also that the logic of `create()` allows you to create entries of any size and to mix entry sizes in a single list. Each entry records its own size.

In listing 12.5, look also at the use of the structure pointer operator (`->`) in the `create()` member function. Note various references to `hold->de_body`, `hold->next`, and others. The `hold` variable is a data member of the `dbllist` class. Recall that because member functions of a class have the `this` pointer available to them, structure member and structure pointer operators are unnecessary for accessing member data variables (or functions, for that matter). So why do so many structure pointer operators appear here?

If you examine the `create()` member function code, you can see that the structure pointer operator is *not* used to access the `hold` variable. The `hold` variable is itself a pointer to a `dblentry` structure; therefore, access to a `dblentry` member *does* require the pointer notation. If `dbllist` were an ordinary C structure, for example, you would have to write something like this in order to access `hold` and any structure members it refers to:

```
dbllist obj; // pretend dbllist is an ordinary structure
...
obj->hold->next = NULL; //WAIT! This isn't plain C!
```

Fortunately, this is not plain C, as the comment in the preceding code fragment proclaims. The first structure pointer operator is therefore unnecessary; `this` provides direct access to the class members.. (Because `hold` is a private variable, this code fragment would not compile anyway.) In short, you will see many structure pointer operators in the member functions just because this particular class contains many data members that also happen to be pointers to structures.

Because most of the remaining `dbllist` member functions deal with the ordinary manipulation of doubly linked lists, only three more member functions of `dbllist` need to be mentioned: the `dbllist()` constructor function, the `~dbllist()` destructor function, and the `kill()` member function.

The `dbllist()` constructor function is shown in lines 17–20 of listing 12.5. Because no list element is yet present in the list, this function's sole purpose is to initialize the `anchor`, `base`, and `hold` pointers to a null value.

The anchor pointer either will be NULL or will *always* point to the first dblentry structure in the linked list. That is why this pointer is named anchor: it anchors the entire list. You can always find the beginning of the list by running it backward until there is no further previous-entry pointer, but it's much faster to assign the value of anchor to the pointer locating the current entry.

Locating the current list element is the job of the base pointer. Its value will "float" up and down the list, depending on which direction the list is being run. You can see how base is used by examining the gohead(), gotail(), gonext(), and goprev() member functions in listing 12.5.

The ~dbllist() destructor function is equally simple. All it does is call the dbllist::kill() function to free the storage tied up in each dblentry element and the associated user data. Hidden code generated by the compiler takes care of destroying the dbllist class object itself.

The kill() member function in lines 27–37 is interesting in its own right. Its purpose is to remove all the entries in the list, thus reestablishing an empty list. Why would you want to do this? You might want to repopulate the list with different data when you navigate from a disk directory to a subdirectory. In fact, you will learn how to navigate and repopulate a directory list later (in listings 12.7, 12.8, and 12.9). But first you will see how a dbllist object is declared and used with block scope (a local object with auto duration).

The program usedbl.cpp shown in listing 12.6 declares a dbllist class object that is local to the main() function. The amount of data stored in the list in this sample program is small, but none of the data goes on the system stack (where all auto objects go, whether C or C++) except the dbllist object itself. (There is little danger of overflowing the stack with a large list.)

Listing 12.6. usedbl.cpp. *A program that demonstrates the* dbllist *class, using a local class object.*

```
1    #include"dbllist.hpp"
2
3    void main()
4    {
5      char *word = NULL;
6      dbllist lex;    // Here's the local class object
7
8      clrscr();
9      lex.append("roger", 6 );
```

Listing 12.6. continues

Listing 12.6. continued

```
10      lex.append("dodger", 7 );
11      lex.append("codger", 7 );
12
13      word = (char *)lex.gohead();
14      while ( word ) {
15        printf("%s\n", word );
16        word = (char *)lex.gonext();
17      }
18
19      lex.kill();
20
21      lex.insert("roger", 6 );
22      lex.insert("dodger", 7 );
23      lex.insert("codger", 7 );
24
25      word = (char *)lex.gohead();
26      while ( word ) {
27        printf("%s\n", word );
28        word = (char *)lex.gonext();
29      }
30
31      word = (char *)lex.gotail();
32      while ( word ) {
33        printf("%s\n", word );
34        word = (char *)lex.goprev();
35      }
36    }
```

To compile and link the `usedbl.cpp` program, you need to create a project file with at least the following entries:

```
usedbl.cpp
dbllist.cpp
```

Notice how simply and easily you can create a doubly linked list as a local "variable." All you need is a line of code like the one in line 6 of listing 12.6:

```
dbllist lex; // This is all there is to it!
```

When this statement is executed, the doubly linked list is created (on the system stack), and everything is set up for you, ready to begin populating the list, using the `append()` or `insert()` member function.

Lines 9–11 populate the list with three words (hence, the object name lex) in an order-of-appearance list, using the append() member function. Lines 13–17 then show you how to use the gohead() member function to get to the beginning of the list, and how to use the gonext() member function to run the list forward. What could be easier? After that, the kill() member function in line 19 empties the list for the next part of the demonstration.

Creating an ordered doubly linked list (that is, creating the list in ascending sequence) is just as easy. You use the insert() member function as shown in lines 21–23. Note that the words are not in alphabetical order as they are presented to the insert() function, but they will be in order when lines 25–29 print the list in the forward direction.

The kill() member function does not appear at this point in the program. Instead, the gotail() function is used to position the list for scanning backward. This procedure is demonstrated in lines 31–36 of listing 12.6.

Doubly linked lists are tremendously powerful and flexible. They are frequently used in sophisticated programs, and you will find many opportunities to use doubly linked lists as you get used to them.

Defining Global *(static)* Class Objects

To complete the demonstration of local, global, and arbitrary object declarations, this section shows you how to declare and use global class objects. In the examples provided, you will see how to build a directory object. The dir class is a snap to create because the dbllist class is already available, and Borland has thoughtfully provided Borland C++ with built-in functions for accessing disk directories.

As always, the first thing to do is to write the class declaration and place it in the header file (assuming that you intend to use separate compilation). The header file dir.hpp is shown in listing 12.7.

Listing 12.7. dir.hpp. *A header file that contains the class declaration for the DOS directory class.*

```
1   #if !defined( DOSDIR )
2   #define DOSDIR
3
```

Listing 12.7. continues

Listing 12.7. continued

```
4   #include <dir.h>
5   #include <dos.h>
6
7   #include"dbllist.hpp"
8
9   class dir {
10    struct ffblk dirblock;
11    dbllist *dirlist;
12    int complete;
13    int scanning;
14    char path[41];
15    char mask[13];
16    char search[53];
17    struct ffblk *current;
18  public:
19    dir();
20    dir( char *, char * );
21    ~dir();
22    void reset( char *, char * );
23    struct ffblk *getcurrent();
24    struct ffblk *getnext();
25    struct ffblk *getprev();
26    void navigate();
27  };
28
29  #endif
```

Did you notice that dir.hpp contains an include for dbllist.hpp? If you look a little further (in line 11), you see a *pointer* to a dbllist object. The intention here is clearly to use the doubly linked list class as a base from which to develop the directory class.

Full use will also be made of the built-in Borland C++ directory-access functions, findfirst() and findnext(). You might want to review the operation of these functions in your *Borland C++ Reference Guide*.

The dir class takes advantage of overloaded constructor functions, as discussed in Chapter 11. There are two constructors for the dir class. One is the default constructor, which initializes the object by reading the entire *current* directory, using the file mask "*.*". The other constructor accepts two string pointers (char *) as arguments. The first string specifies the search *path*, which can include drive and directory path information, and can either have or omit a trailing backslash (\) character. (If absent, this character is supplied when the complete search string is built.) The second string can be the file mask and can include up to 12 characters in the format *filename.ext*, with or without DOS wild-card characters (* and ?).

Lines 23–25 show the declarations for the `getcurrent()`, `getnext()`, and `getprev()` member functions. These names are much like the corresponding `dbllist` member functions `gonext()` and `goprev()`. Indeed, the `dir` functions use the `dbllist` functions to get their work done. Note an important distinction between the two classes, however. A `dbllist` linked list is populated with entries by repeated *user* calls to the `insert()` or `append()` function, *after* the object has been created (by either defining it or creating it with `new`). A `dir` class object, though, is completely built by the class constructor. That is, you can create a doubly linked list of directory entries for the directory currently being listed with just the following two lines of code:

```
#include dir.hpp
...
dir workdir();

    // workdir already contains the directory list
    // when you get here!
```

Therefore, the `dir` class member functions `getnext()` and `getprev()` are purely navigation functions for traversing the directory list. There is no `dir` class counterpart to the `dbllist` class `insert()` or `append()` function.

With the difference between the directory class and the doubly linked list class firmly in mind, now look at the code for the `dir` class member function definitions (see listing 12.8).

Listing 12.8. `dir.cpp`. *Class member functions for the* `dir` *class.*

```
1   #include"dir.hpp"
2
3   dir::dir()
4   {
5     complete = 0;
6     scanning = 0;
7     strcpy( path,"" );
8     strcpy( mask,"*.*" );
9     strcpy( search, path );
10    if ( '\\' != search[ strlen( search ) - 1 ] )
```

Listing 12.8. continues

Listing 12.8. continues

```
11       strcat( search,"\\" );
12     strcat( search, mask );
13     dirlist = new dbllist;
14     complete = findfirst( search, &dirblock, 0xFF );
15     while ( !complete ) {
16       dirlist->append( &dirblock, sizeof( struct ffblk ) );
17       complete = findnext( &dirblock );
18     }
19     current = (struct ffblk *)dirlist->gohead();
20     if ( current ) scanning = 1;
21   }
22
23   dir::dir( char *where, char *how )
24   {
25     complete = 0;
26     scanning = 0;
27     strupr( where );
28     strupr( how );
29     strcpy( path, where );
30     strcpy( mask, how );
31     strcpy( search, path );
32     if ( '\\' != search[ strlen( search ) - 1 ] )
33       strcat( search,"\\" );
34     strcat( search, mask );
35     dirlist = new dbllist;
36     complete = findfirst( search, &dirblock, 0xFF );
37     while ( !complete ) {
38       dirlist->append( &dirblock, sizeof( struct ffblk ) );
39       complete = findnext( &dirblock );
40     }
41     current = (struct ffblk *)dirlist->gohead();
42     if ( current ) {
43       scanning = 1;
44       dirblock = *current;
45     }
46   }
47
48   dir::~dir()
49   {
50     delete dirlist;
51   }
```

```
52
53   void dir::reset( char *where, char *how )
54   {
55     dirlist->kill();
56     complete = 0;
57     scanning = 0;
58     strcpy( path, where );
59     strcpy( mask, how );
60     strcpy( search, path );
61     if ( '\\' != search[ strlen( search ) - 1 ] )
62       strcat( search,"\\" );
63     strcat( search, mask );
64     dirlist = new dbllist;
65     complete = findfirst( search, &dirblock, 0xFF );
66     while ( !complete ) {
67      dirlist->append( &dirblock, sizeof( struct ffblk ) );
68       complete = findnext( &dirblock );
69     }
70     current = (struct ffblk *)dirlist->gohead();
71     if ( current ) {
72       scanning = 1;
73       dirblock = *current;
74     }
75   }
76
77   struct ffblk *dir::getcurrent()
78   {
79     if ( current ) return &dirblock;
80     else return NULL;
81   }
82
83   struct ffblk *dir::getnext()
84   {
86
87     if ( !current ) return NULL;
88     temp = current;
89     if ( NULL == ( current =
90       (struct ffblk *)dirlist->gonext() ) ) {
91       current = temp;
92       return NULL;
93     }
```

Listing 12.8. continues

Listing 12.8. continued

```
94     else {
95       dirblock = *current;
96       return &dirblock;
97     }
98   }
99
100  struct ffblk *dir::getprev()
101  {
102    struct ffblk *temp;
103
104    if ( !current ) return NULL;
105    temp = current;
106    if ( NULL == ( current =
107      (struct ffblk *)dirlist->goprev() ) ) {
108      current = temp;
109      return NULL;
110    }
111    else {
112      dirblock = *current;
113      return &dirblock;
114    }
115  }
116
117  void dir::navigate()
118  {
119    char *temp;
120    char tpath[41];
121    char tmask[13];
122
123    if ( !current ) return;
124    if ( dirblock.ff_attrib != FA_DIREC ) return;
125    if ( !strcmp( dirblock.ff_name,"." ) ) return;
126
127    strcpy( tpath, path );
128    strcpy( tmask, mask );
129    if ( '\\' == tpath[ strlen( tpath ) - 1 ] )
130      tpath[ strlen( tpath ) - 1 ] = '\0';
131    if ( !strcmp( dirblock.ff_name,".." ) ) {
132      temp =tpath + strlen( tpath ) - 1;
133      while( *temp && *temp != '\\' ) temp--;
134      *temp = '\0';
```

```
135        strcat( tpath,"\\" );
136      }
137      else {
138        strcat( tpath,"\\" );
139        strcat( tpath, dirblock.ff_name );
140        strcat( tpath,"\\" );
141      }
142      reset( tpath, tmask );
143    }
```

The default and overloaded constructor functions are found in lines 3–21 and lines 23–46, respectively, of listing 12.8. The main difference between the two constructor functions is that the default version uses hard-coded string constants to initialize the search path and search mask, whereas the overloaded version of the constructor function uses the received function arguments to initialize the search path and mask. Both constructor functions initialize the pointer to the directory linked list by simply using the `new` operator to create a `dbllist` object and to get its address:

```
dirlist = new dbllist; // Boy, this is easy!
```

The destructor function for the `dir` class, in lines 48–51, simply deletes the linked list.

The `dir::reset()` function in lines 53–75 is important, but not because of its internal logic or features. This function is similar to the overloaded version of the constructor because this function accepts new values for the search path and mask. The function is different because it begins by calling the `dirlist->kill()` to empty the linked list without destroying the linked list object. `reset()` then rebuilds the list by using the new search values. That is, `reset()` rebuilds the list for what will presumably be a completely different directory.

You have probably already guessed the real significance of the `reset()` member function: it is used to repopulate the directory linked list when you want to "navigate" subdirectories without having to start over. In fact, that is the purpose of the `dir::navigate()` member function shown in lines 117–143 of listing 12.8. The `navigate()` member function assumes that you want to move to either the next lower or the next higher subdirectory in the directory tree. The function assumes also that the directory entry currently being pointed to is the entry for the new target subdirectory.

The `navigate()` member function first checks to see whether its function can be performed (see lines 123–125). `navigate()` performs the following checks:

1. If there is no current directory entry being pointed to, the directory is empty, so get out.

2. If the current directory entry being pointed to does not have the directory attribute, subdirectory navigation is impossible, so get out.

3. If the name field of the current directory entry being pointed to is a single period (.), you are positioned on the placeholder for the directory *two* levels above the one in the linked list. Navigation to this directory is not allowed, so get out.

The rest of the logic in `dir::navigate()` involves only the string manipulation required to rebuild the search path. If the name field of the current entry is "..", the last level of the directory path must be stripped off to get to the next higher level. If the name field of the current entry is anything else (but still a directory-type entry), that name must be suffixed to the search path in order to descend to the next lower level of the directory tree. Finally, `navigate()` merely calls `reset()` with the resulting new search arguments, and away you go!

The list-traversing member functions—`getcurrent()`, `getnext()`, and `getprev()`—need only a little discussion. The `getcurrent()` function returns the address of the `dirblock` structure if the current entry pointer `current` is not `NULL`. In other words, `getcurrent()` assumes that nothing has happened but that you want to get a new copy of the current entry pointer for some reason (there is one good reason, as shown in listing 12.9).

`getnext()` and `getprev()` move to the next or previous directory list entry, respectively, assuming that there is another entry in the indicated direction. If repositioning does occur, the directory block structure (which is an exact copy of the Borland C++ `struct ffblk`) is copied into the `dirblock` structure, which is part of the `dir` class object itself, and the address of `dirblock` is returned to the caller. Notice also that both these functions take precautions to prevent the `current` pointer from "falling off the ends" of the list; `current` will never be `NULL` unless the list is empty.

Once again, all the hard work is finished when you have designed and coded the class declaration and member functions. Using the `dir` class is simple enough, as illustrated by the program `usedir.cpp` in listing 12.9.

Listing 12.9. `usedir.cpp`. *A program that demonstrates the* `dir` *class, using a global class object.*

```
1   #include"dir.hpp"
2
3   dir workdir("c:\\tcp\\pgm","*.*" );
```

```
  4
  5  void main()
  6  {
  7    struct ffblk *entry;
  8
  9  // --------------------------------------------------------
 10  // Display the directory as requested
 11  // --------------------------------------------------------
 12
 13    entry = workdir.getcurrent();
 14    while ( entry ) {
 15      printf(" %-15s %6ld\n", entry->ff_name, entry->ff_fsize );
 16      entry = workdir.getnext();
 17    }
 18
 19  // --------------------------------------------------------
 20  // Find and navigate to the next higher directory
 21  // --------------------------------------------------------
 22
 23    getch();
 24    while( NULL !=
 25      ( entry = workdir.getprev() ) ) ;
 26
 27    entry = workdir.getcurrent();
 28    while ( entry ) {
 29      if ( !strcmp( entry->ff_name,".." ) ) break;
 30      entry = workdir.getnext();
 31    }
 32    workdir.navigate();
 33
 34    entry = workdir.getcurrent();
 35    while ( entry ) {
 36      printf(" %-15s %6ld\n", entry->ff_name, entry->ff_fsize );
 37      entry = workdir.getnext();
 38    }
 39
 40  // --------------------------------------------------------
 41  // Display an altogether different directory
 42  // --------------------------------------------------------
 43
```

Listing 12.9. continues

Listing 12.9. continued

```
44    getch();
45    workdir.reset("\\","*.bat" );
46
47    entry = workdir.getcurrent();
48    while ( entry ) {
49      printf(" %-15s %6ld\n", entry->ff_name, entry->ff_fsize );
50      entry = workdir.getnext();
51    }
52
53  }
```

Using `dir` class objects is so simple, in fact, that only one thing in listing 12.9 needs to be explained. You should supply a pointer to a `struct ffblk` and initialize it with the `getcurrent()` member function in the following circumstances:

❑ *When you first create the `dir` object (by declaring it or creating it new).* You need to pick up the address of the first entry in the list at this time.

❑ *When you use the `reset()` member function to switch to a different directory.* Because the list is reinstated at this time, the old pointers no longer apply.

❑ *When you use the `navigate()` member function to move up or down the directory tree.* Because navigation is just another method of selecting a new subdirectory and resetting, the list is reinstated in this case also.

❑ *When you use the `getnext()` or `getprev()` function until your working pointer is `NULL`.* The `dir` class member functions never allow the *internal* entry pointers to become NULL (unless the list is empty), but such functions may *return* a null pointer if you attempt to run off either end of the list.

The fourth item in the preceding list requires a little amplification. Suppose, for example, that you are traversing the list forward, using `getnext()`. When the internal `current` pointer is already positioned on the last entry in the list, `getnext()` returns `NULL`, but `current` is not changed. Therefore, calling `getcurrent()` initializes your local pointer with a valid address—the address of the last element in the list. The same principle applies, of course, to traversing the directory list backward.

Initializing Class Objects

When you declare an integer data object with an initializer, you can easily see what happens when the integer is initialized. Note, for example, the following line of code:

```
int a = 37;
```

There is no doubt that an integer a is being defined and that the value 37 must be assigned to it.

What must happen when a class object is created and initialized is perhaps not so obvious. Class objects can have constructors, copy constructors, and overloaded constructors. You can use constructors to implicitly convert other types to initialize a class object, and some class objects can take plain initializer lists. These options are discussed in this section.

Using Constructors To Initialize Class Objects

The dir class presented in listings 12.7 and 12.8 illustrates two ways you can use constructors to initialize a class object. The dir class has both a default constructor (which can be called with no arguments) and an overloaded constructor (which can be called with arguments). Remember that you can have more than one overloaded version of the constructor.

The constructor's main job, of course, is to initialize the object—to take a block of memory and shape it into a valid class object. A constructor can do three things toward this end:

❏ *A constructor function can call other member functions of the same class.* You may have designed some member functions whose purpose is to control or modify the object. You can call those member functions freely from the constructor function.

❏ *A constructor function can access all data members, both private and public.* Class member data objects have many of the same characteristics of plain C data objects. Because one of those characteristics is the need for initialization, the constructor should ensure that all member data variables have a legal initial value. Referring to an uninitialized class member *pointer*, for example, can have the same result as referring to any other uninitialized pointer—disaster!

❏ *A constructor function can call any of the compiler's library functions.* You need to be sure that the correct header file has been included in the source module where the call to the library function occurs.

The ability to call any of the standard (or Borland C++ extended) library functions from a constructor is important, even critical. It would not have been possible, for example, to write the `msmouse` class if the `int86()` library function were not available to initialize and control the mouse. Yet C is a "foreign" language to C++. A *linkage specification* is required to allow calls to both C and C++ functions within the same program. A linkage specification tells the compiler which language the called function uses.

The default linkage specification in C++ is to C++ functions, but the Borland C++ standard headers are already set up to prevent confusion and allow free access to all library functions from a C++ program. How Borland C++ does this, along with how you can set up your own header files to do the same thing, is covered in Chapter 14, in the section "Controlling Linkage Problems with Standard C Include Files."

The job of the constructor function is to make sure that every data object and pointer member is given a legal starting value. If the class has multiple overloaded constructors, you must make sure that *each* version does the job *completely*.

Furthermore, a constructor can be invoked in several different ways (which is the same as saying that a class object can be declared in several different ways). The default constructor can be invoked in two ways. You can use the constructor to convert another (basic) object type, and you can invoke the constructor directly. Listing 12.10 shows all these methods.

Listing 12.10. `colorobj.cpp`. *A program that demonstrates the use of constructors in initializing class objects.*

```
 1   #include <stdlib.h>
 2   #include <stdio.h>
 3
 4   #define RED    0
 5   #define BLUE   1
 6   #define GREEN  2
 7
 8   char *colornames[] = {
 9     "Red","Blue","Green"
10   };
11
```

```
12   class colorobj {
13     int color;
14   public:
15     colorobj() { color = RED; }
16     colorobj( int icolor ) { color = icolor; }
17     colorobj( colorobj &other ) {
18       color = other.color;
19       printf("My new color is %s!\n",
20               colornames[color] );
21     }
22   };
23
24   void main()
25   {
26     colorobj c1;                // create a RED object
27     colorobj c2();       // create another RED object
28     colorobj c3 = BLUE; // create BLUE object by conversion
29     colorobj c4 = colorobj( GREEN ); //now call constructor
30     colorobj c5 = c4;    // use the copy constructor
31   }
```

Lines 26 and 27 of listing 12.10 are equivalent. Both these class object definitions cause the default constructor to be invoked. As you can see by comparing these two lines, using the default constructor means that you can either specify an empty argument list or just leave it off altogether.

Line 16 declares a constructor that accepts one argument (an integer specifying the desired color). You can, of course, define a class object by using this constructor in the usual manner:

```
colorobj cobj( RED ); // Use a macro name for argument
```

What is not so apparent in line 16 is that a constructor which accepts a *single argument* means that a *conversion from the argument type to the class type is to be performed*. This in turn means that the preceding line of code is equivalent to line 28 of listing 12.10. You could code line 28 in this way:

```
colorobj c3( BLUE );
```

This line achieves exactly the same result.

Finally, you can invoke the constructor explicitly, as shown in line 29 of listing 12.10. Notice that the constructor/class name on the right side of the assignment in line 29 specifies no object name: the constructor is being called directly. Notice, too, that this is not the same thing as invoking the copy constructor. Even though the right side of the assignment must obviously be copied to the object on the left, the user's copy constructor is not used to do so.

Line 29, when executed, does *not* cause the copy constructor (lines 17–21) to be executed. You can tell this because the copy constructor displays a message on the system console when the copy constructor is executed. Line 30, however, is a classic instance of using the copy constructor to initialize one object from another. In fact, line 30 is included in this sample program simply to demonstrate that the other methods do not involve a user-defined copy constructor.

Using Initializer Lists

Just as you can initialize a plain C aggregate object (structure, union, or array) with an initializer list, you can initialize a class object with an initializer list—if certain stringent requirements are met. To have an initializer list, a class object *cannot* have a constructor function (not even a default one), private or protected members, virtual functions, or base classes (that is, the class object cannot be an object of a derived class). In other words, initializer lists are useful mainly with objects of a class declared with the struct keyword. For example, look at the following class declaration:

```
struct IL {
   int a, b, c;
};
```

The class object shown here meets all the requirements for an initializer list. You can then initialize an IL class object like this:

```
IL threeints = { 1, 2, 3 };
```

An interesting and useful variation on the theme of initializer lists is the *array of class objects*. When you define an array of class objects, you can write an initializer list for the array, and each array element—which is a class object— can have a constructor. Suppose, for example, that you are writing a large and complicated modeling program that requires six lifo arrays (refer to Chapter 11) for various purposes. You can write the array definition like this:

```
lifo request_que[6] = {
   lifo( 4096 );
   lifo( 8192 );
};
```

But wait! The array of lifo objects has six elements, yet only two entries are specified in the initializer list. What happened to the other four initializers?

Quite simply, the compiler will generate the other four initializers with explicit calls to the *default* lifo constructor. The preceding code fragment, then, is equivalent to the following fragment:

```
lifo request_que[6] = {
  lifo( 4096 );
  lifo( 8192 );
  lifo();
  lifo();
  lifo();
  lifo();
};
```

Even though the lifo class has constructor functions, it is not the class for which the initializer list is provided; the initializer list is supplied for the *array*. Note one catch: if you omit any of the initializers, the class being used *must* have a default constructor. Conversely, if the class being used in an array has no default constructor, you *cannot* omit any of the initializers.

Exercises

The following exercises give you practice in defining and using Borland C++ class objects.

1. Get a copy of the *Microsoft Mouse Programmer's Guide* and review the mouse functions available. Extend the capability of the msmouse class to include more of these functions. Don't forget to declare new member functions in msmouse.hpp and to define the functions in msmouse.cpp.

2. To determine the size of a class object, first realize that the class declaration's function prototypes serve two purposes: to provide a prototype declaration and to establish the relationship of the class with an associated member function. Neither inline nor out-of-line member functions physically reside in the class object. A Borland C++ class object's size is thus the sum of the sizes of the data members, and nothing more. Recall also that static data members reside outside an object.

   Armed with that knowledge, make an estimate of the size of a dbllist linked list object and then investigate what circumstances would require you to use global, local, and arbitrary-duration objects. What kind of design consideration is most important in reaching your decision? Here's a tip: storage for the list elements themselves resides *outside* the class object.

3. Add support macros to the `dbllist` class to allow calls to member functions, using a type name rather than a specific byte count. You may want to refer to Chapter 11 to review how such macros were constructed for the `lifo` class.

4. Write another version of the `usedir.cpp` program. Include such features as mouse support and a scrollable window for the directory list, using the Borland C++ `window()` function. Mouse support can consist of scrolling a text file when the user clicks with the left button the file's directory entry, and navigating to a new subdirectory when the user clicks with the right button the file's list entry. This exercise is fairly advanced, so don't get discouraged if it takes a while to write the program.

5. Design and code a class that has several constructors. Write a sequence of code defining objects of that class and invoking the constructors in several different ways.

6. Design and code a class declaration that uses the `class` keyword to declare the class but that can still permit an object definition with an initializer list. What did you have to do to get the code to compile correctly?

Summary

This chapter covered the basics of defining local, global, and arbitrary class objects, as well as how to initialize class objects. You learned the following important points:

❑ *You can define local, global, and arbitrary class objects.* Class objects generally follow the scope and duration rules of other C objects. However, access to class object members is complicated by the fact that a class *is* a scope in C++.

❑ *You can write a variety of constructor functions for initializing class objects.* These functions include default constructors, overloaded constructors, and copy constructors. Furthermore, you can invoke a constructor (that is, define a class object) in various ways: using the default constructor, using a constructor to convert types across the assignment operator, and explicitly invoking a constructor.

❑ *In certain cases—most notably when the class has no constructor— you can initialize a class object by using an initializer list, just as you can for aggregate C objects.*

13

Accessing C++ Objects

You saw in Chapter 12 that declaring class objects involves more technique than declaring plain C objects. *Accessing* class objects is also more complicated than accessing plain C objects. This chapter examines in detail some of the complex methods of accessing class objects and their member components.

Specifically, you learn about the scope resolution operator; look more closely at the C++ scoping rules; learn how to use the `this` pointer to communicate with class objects (as well as how to control `this`); become familiar with the reference operator, its evolution, and its use; and take a look at using class objects as arguments to functions (both member and nonmember).

Using the Scope Resolution Operator

You have already seen in the preceding chapters what the scope resolution operator is and how it works. This section provides more detail on the subject of scope resolution, expanding on familiar topics and introducing advanced topics. You learn about the general uses of the scope resolution operator, the use of scope resolution for syntax control, and the control of ambiguities with the scope resolution operator.

Using Scope Resolution in General

The scope resolution operator (::) was first introduced in Chapter 11, in a discussion of the difference between visibility and access control. This section clarifies some of the concepts presented there.

Recall that the general syntax for using the scope resolution operator is looks like this:

```
classname::membername
```

This form of *membername* is called the *fully qualified member name*, or just the qualified name. The method of writing it is like that of writing a fully qualified file name for DOS—by using the drive, path, file name, and file name extension. In either case, the notation fully specifies which object (or file) is to be referenced. One significant difference, of course, is that a class member can be either a data object or a member function.

You can also use the scope resolution operator to inform the compiler that you want to refer to the *global copy* of a variable or function name, not to a class member version. In this case, you write the scope resolution operator *without* the preceding class name:

```
::objectname
```

An important use for this form of the scope resolution operator is to *unhide* a global function or variable. A function or variable can become hidden (from the perspective of class members) when both a global copy and a member copy of an object exist with the same name. Look, for example, at the following code fragment:

```
int A;
...
class sumpin {
  int A;
public:
  void showit() {
    printf( "%d\n", A );     // display member A
    printf( "%d\n", ::A );   // display global A
  }
};
```

By the same token (if you will excuse the pun), you can contrive a case in which the class name is hidden. You can hide a class name by declaring an object (a nontype, nonclass name, such as an int object), function, or enumeration in the *same scope* with the class declaration. Now you have both an *object* and a *type* with the same name. In this case, the scope resolution operator won't help you much. Scope resolution helps you choose which of several possible objects to use, but it can't unravel the difference between an object name and a type name. In the following short program, the class is hidden (and the program won't compile either):

```
#include <stdio.h>

class A {
public:
  static int qq() { return 37; }
};

int A = 64; // This is the culprit -- it hides class A

void main()
{
  A doodad; // We want a class object, but no dice

  printf( "%d\n", doodad.qq() );
}
```

When you try to compile this program, Borland C++ does fine until it reaches the definition A doodad. The intention is to define a doodad class object, but it is masked by the int A object. The compiler will devoutly declare that doodad is undefined.

If you can't use the scope resolution operator to get out of this scrape, what can you do? Is it still possible to have a class A *and* an integer A? It is possible if you use the class keyword (or the struct or union keyword) to inform the compiler just what kind of object you mean to define. Here is the doodad program rewritten so that it will compile and run correctly:

```
#include <stdio.h>

class A {
public:
  static int qq() { return 37; }
};

int A = 64;  // Still hides the class, but there's a
cure ...

void main()
{
  class A doodad; // This is how you get out of the bind

  printf( "%d\n", doodad.qq() );
}
```

To unhide the class name, you just add the `class` keyword to the declaration: `class A doodad`. Thus, even though the scope resolution operator is not a cure for all ills, it is still nice to have a class A doodad handy, don't you think?

The ANSI base document also allows the use of multiple scope qualifiers to access members of nested classes (within the restrictions given in Chapter 11). For example, the following code fragment ought to be legal:

```
#include <stdio.h>

struct A {
  struct B {
    static double pi;
  };
};

double A::B::pi = 3.1415926;

void main()
{
  printf( "%lf\n", A::B::pi );
}
```

Borland C++, however, will *not* compile this program but will flag the global definition of `pi` as an error, forbidding the use of multiple scope qualifiers. Nevertheless, this syntax is a recent development in C++ and is likely to be supported later.

Using Scope Resolution for Syntax Control

Two uses of the scope resolution operator are related specifically to syntax requirements. You have already seen one of these uses repeatedly in sample code here, and the other use has been presented briefly. Note the following rules for the two uses relating to syntax control:

❑ *You must use the scope resolution operator when defining an out-of-line class member function.* The sole purpose of this rule is to provide a vehicle for informing the compiler of the class to which a member function belongs (other classes may have identical member function names). The syntax is shown in the following code fragment:

```
class book{
...
   int page;
public:
...
int turnpage();    // Member function declaration
};
...
int book::turnpage() // Out-of-Line member function definition
{
   return ++page;
}
```

❏ *You must use the scope resolution operator when referring to a static class data member without using a specific class object.* You should recall that static data members exist independently of any particular class object, and one copy of a static member is common to all objects of that class. These facts explain the behavior of the following short program:

```
#include <stdio.h>
#include <stdlib.h>
#include <string.h>

class star {
public:
   static char name[21];
   star() { strcpy( name, "NONAME" ); }
   star( char *sname ) { strcpy( name, sname ); }
   void tellname() { printf( "%s\n", name ); }
};

void main()
{
   star s1 = "Betelgeuse";
   star s2 = "Rigel";

   s1.tellname();    // Both objects report name as RIGEL
   s2.tellname();

   strcpy( star::name, "Aldebaran" ); //No particular object!
   printf( "%s\n", star::name );
```

```
    s1.tellname();  // Now both objects report name as ALDEBARAN
    s2.tellname();
}
```

Because there is only one copy of the member variable `star::name`, *any* change to that variable (regardless of which object is referenced) changes the name for *all* objects. Additionally, the variable can be referenced independently of any particular class object because of the fully qualified name `star::name`.

Controlling Ambiguities with Scope Resolution

In the last section, you saw how the presence of a class declaration and type definition with the same name in the same scope hides one of the names from the compiler. When a name is hidden, the compiler knows about only one of the declarations. It is also possible to use the same name for a class member that *appears in more than one class* in such a way that the compiler can't determine which member you mean when referring to the member. The compiler considers a reference to that member name *ambiguous*. Most ambiguities of reference occur when you are deriving one class from another.

In fact, all the uses of the scope resolution operator covered in this section look ahead to the subject on derived classes. Even though class derivation is not fully covered until Chapter 17, all the major uses of the scope resolution operator are documented in this chapter.

For now, class derivation can be defined as telling the compiler to create a new class just like an old one—except for a few differences. The old class is called the *base class*, and the new class is called the *derived class*.

All the members of the base class can be accessed *as if* they were members of the derived class *unless* you redefine the base class members in the derived class (this is how you tell the compiler what is different). The basic methods of class derivation are illustrated in the sample program in listing 13.1.

Listing 13.1. `docu.cpp`. *A program that derives classes from other classes.*

```
1    #include <iostream.h>
2
3    class document {
4    public:
5      int pages;
6      void blurb() {
7        cout << "I have " << pages << " pages.\n";
8      }
9    };
10
11   class pamphlet : public document {
12   public:
13     pamphlet() { pages = 10; }
14   };
15
16   class book : public document {
17   public:
18     int chapters;
19     book( int np, int nc ) {
20       pages = np;
21       chapters = nc;
22     }
23     void blurb() {
24       cout << "I have " << pages << " pages and "
25            << chapters << " chapters.\n";
26     }
27   };
28
29   void main()
30   {
31     pamphlet flyer;
32     book uc( 900, 21 );
33
34     flyer.blurb();
35     uc.blurb();
36     uc.document::blurb();
37   }
```

The program in listing 13.1 declares a base class, document, from which the classes pamphlet and book are then derived. A pamphlet needs to record only page count (which is fixed at 10 pages), whereas a book must record both page count and chapter count. Because of this difference between the two derived classes, the blurb() member function must be different for the two classes.

Notice that the basic, uncomplicated blurb() function is defined inline in the base class document (lines 6–8). The base class version of blurb() reports only page count for the document. Because a pamphlet is a document that needs only a page count, no data members are declared within the pamphlet class. A pamphlet, you may notice, can still get to the pages data member, which is declared only in the document base class (line 5).

A book is a more complicated form of document, however. A book must keep track of chapters as well as pages. The book class therefore declares the chapters data member (line 18) and relies on the base class declaration of pages. Furthermore, because the reporting process for a book is usually more complicated, the book class redefines the base class's blurb() member function.

Now consider the use of the scope resolution operator with base and derived classes. Line 35 of listing 13.1 shows a normal call to a book's blurb() function. Both the page count and the chapter count are reported as a result of a call to blurb().

It is possible, however, to report only the page count for a book object if the *base class version* of blurb() can be reached. As illustrated in the function call in line 36, you can indeed reach the base class version by fully qualifying the function name with the base class name.

The blurb() member function shown in listing 13.1 is not really ambiguous. The *derived class's* member function (or data object) is always meant, unless you override the reference by using the scope resolution operator.

Ambiguities can arise quickly, though, when a derived class inherits from *two* base classes instead of one. Suppose that you have a chapter class and a page class, both of which have a size() member function. Partial declarations for these classes might look like this:

```
class chapter {
   unsigned numpages;
public:
   ...
   unsigned size() { return numpages; }
};

class page {
```

In the case of the `shape` and `circle` functions just shown, you might want to access the `shape::draw()` function from within the `circle::draw()` function (perhaps to initialize the screen before drawing the circle). To accomplish this, you can modify the `circle::draw()` function:

```
class circle : public shape {
  int xcenter, ycenter, radius;
  ...
public:
  void draw() {     // this is circle::draw()
    shape::draw(); // call base class version
    circle( xcenter, ycenter, radius );
  }
};
```

You may rarely need to use both versions of a virtual function (or to override the version that is used), but the scope resolution operator enables you to do so.

Understanding the C++ Scope Rules

The concept of the scope of a name in C++ is identical to the concept of scope in plain C. The *scope* of a name is just the part of the program's source code that can refer to the name. In C++, as in plain C, the scope of a name implies something about both its *visibility* and its *duration*.

Specific scope rules in C++ differ somewhat from plain C scope rules, however, because of the added requirement that in C++ a class object has its own scope. This section first examines the differences between C++ and C scope rules and then summarizes C++ scope rules.

Understanding the Differences between C and C++ Scope

C and C++ have several scope and scope-related differences. These differences become important if you must "switch gears" mentally between the two languages. The greatest problem caused by these differences is, of course, that you can forget momentarily whether you are using C or C++ because the languages are so similar. The following list shows the main differences between the two languages:

❑ *C++ scope rules generally follow the ANSI standard scope rules.*
When you are not dealing with classes and class objects directly, or
with one of the exceptions noted in this list, you should handle C++
scoping issues just as you handle C scoping issues.

❑ *C++ allows the declaration of local (`auto`) variables anywhere a C
statement can appear.* Remember that plain C requires the declaration of `auto` variables at the *top of the block* in which they appear.
The following code fragment, for example, is legal in C++ but not in
standard C:

```
void some_function( int number )
{
   int i = 0; // here's a local variable

   while ( number ) {
     --number;
     ++i;
   }

   int j = 0; // here's another local variable

   while ( i ) {
     --i;
     ++j;
   }
}
```

❑ *A C++ function cannot be called before it is declared.* In plain C,
you can call a function that has not yet been declared. The C compiler
assumes that it is to do no type checking of arguments, and also that
the function returns an `int`. In fact, declaring a plain C function *later*
(with different parameters or return type) causes a redefinition
compiler error. A C++ compiler makes no such dangerous assumptions. You *must* declare a function in C++ before you call it.

❑ *A class name can be accidentally hidden by an explicit declaration
of an object within the class.* Because a `struct` or a `class` is a scope
in C++, you can unintentionally hide a type name (a class name) by
declaring an interior object that has the same name as the `class` or
`struct`, or by declaring a nonmember variable in the same scope as
the class having the same name.

Accidentally hiding a class name is not as much of a problem in plain C
(although you can rather easily block visibility to an object of the same type in

an outer scope). For example, the following code fragment (in plain C) shows that a `struct` containing a member with the same name as the `struct` tag does not hide the structure name:

```
#include <stdio.h>
#include <stdlib.h>

struct xxx {
  int xxx;
};

struct xxx obj;

void main()
{
  obj.xxx = 37;
}
```

This code fragment compiles with no errors and runs properly. No conflict occurs between the member integer `xxx` and the structure name `xxx`. A problem can arise, however, because C++ permits you to define your own types, and those type declarations (that is, the class declarations) comprise their own scope. A member variable with the same name as the class can hide the class name, requiring the use of the scope resolution operator in member functions to sort out the intended reference. Alternatively, a nonmember variable in the same scope as the class can also hide the class name, requiring the use of the `class` or `struct` keyword to clarify the reference. Samples of both these cases are shown earlier in this chapter.

Examining the C++ Scope Rules

C++ has four kinds of scope: local, function, file, and class. Note the significance of each kind:

❑ Local scope

C++ local scope is the same as for plain C. A name declared within a block (that is, an `auto` variable) is local to that block. A local variable can be used, after the point of declaration, only within that block and within inner blocks enclosed by it. Note that the *point of declaration* is defined to be directly after the complete declaration but before any initializer for the object. Note, too, that class *objects* can be local "variables" just like anything else. Finally, remember that a C++ local declaration does *not* have to be at the top of the block—such a declaration can be anywhere within the block.

❏ Function scope

Only labels have function scope, and they are in scope only within the function in which they appear. Therefore, the same label name can be used in different functions without confusion.

❏ File scope

File scope is the same as global scope. A name declared outside any block or class declaration has global scope. A global name can be used anywhere within the source file, after the point of declaration.

❏ Class scope

Class scope is new with C++ and does not exist in plain C. The name of a class *member* (object or function) is local to the class. A class member name can be used in the following ways:

1. A class member name can be used directly, without qualification, only by a member function of the same class.

2. A class member name can be referred to by a function outside the class, through the class member operator (`.`). This, of course, is true only if you are not using a pointer to the class object and only if the member has `public` accessibility.

3. A class member name can be referred to by a function outside the class, when the class object is being accessed by a pointer, through the class member pointer operator (`->`). Accessibility rules apply here also.

4. A class member name can be referred to in some circumstances if you use the fully qualified name with the scope resolution operator. Using the `class::member` notation is sometimes needed to resolve ambiguities, as noted earlier in this chapter.

Both the *Borland C++ Programmer's Guide* and the C++ base document summarize the C++ scoping rules under eight points, but the two documents group the points differently. In the list of rules presented here, the base document's arrangement is followed, but more explanation of the rules is provided than in the other documents. These C++ scoping rules deal with both ordinary and class objects:

❏ *C++ names are tested for ambiguity first.* You have already seen that more than one class can use the same member names (because they are different scopes), that function definitions can be overloaded (resulting in multiple functions with the same names but different types), and that class inheritance can cause some ambiguity in the use of names. All these sources of confusion must be resolved first. Only when a name is completely unambiguous will the C++ compiler begin to apply access rules. Finally, when it has been determined that there are no access errors, object type checking is performed.

❏ *Global objects, functions, and enumerations are tested next.* These entities must have the following characteristics:

1. They are declared *outside* any block or class declaration.

2. They *can* be prefixed with the unary scope operator (: :). When the scope operator is used without a class name in front of it, the global copy of the object, function, or enumerator is meant. You will see this use later (particularly in Chapter 15).

3. They *cannot* be qualified with the binary scope resolution operator (*class::name*), and they *cannot* be qualified with either form of the class member operator. (That is, *obj.name* and *ptr->name* are by definition not global names.)

❏ *Class membership is tested next.* If a qualified name (*class::name*, *obj.name*, or *ptr->name*) is used, *name* must be either a member of *class* or a member of another class derived from *class*. Furthermore, if a name such as B->name is used, where B is a class that has overloaded the -> operator, B-> must eventually resolve to A-> (that is, B-> must resolve to a simple pointer to a class object somewhere in the chain). Note, for example, the following code fragment:

```
#include <iostream.h>

class A {
public:
  void blurb() { cout << "Hello!\r\n" ; }
};

class B : public A {
public:
  A* operator->() { return (A *)this; }
};

void main()
{
  B obj;  // Note that this is not a pointer!!
```

```
    obj->blurb(); // Route through operator->() logic
    obj.blurb();  // Do not route through operator->() logic
}
```

The class object `obj` is not a pointer, but the overloaded `operator->()` creates a simple pointer, as if `obj->A::blurb()` had been originally coded. The fact that class `B` here is derived from class `A` is only incidental. The summary of scope rules in the *Borland C++ Programmer's Guide* does not explicitly point out that you can overload the member pointer operator in this way in order to get a pointer to a base class member. However, the compiler handles the code correctly, and the usage conforms to the base document.

❑ *Ordinary local variables are checked next.* These names are not qualified in any of the ways described so far but are used in nonmember functions. If a name is used within a block but not declared within that same block, the compiler first checks to see whether the name is declared in an enclosing block, and only then checks to see whether the name is a global name. As mentioned earlier, local names hide names that are the same (regardless of type) and that reside in enclosing blocks or in file scope. An interesting side effect of this rule is that names in different scopes can never be overloaded versions of one another.

❑ *Local variables in nonstatic member functions are checked next.* This phase of scope resolution proceeds exactly as for ordinary local variables, with one additional restriction. The declaration of a member name can hide member names in base classes, as well as those in enclosing blocks and global names.

❑ *Local variables in static member functions are checked next.* If none of the preceding restrictions apply, a local variable in a static member function must be declared within that static function, must be declared within an enclosing block, must be a static member of the class or a base class, or must be a global name.

❑ *The scope of function arguments is checked next.* The scope of function argument names depends on whether a function *declaration* or a function *definition* is being checked. If a function declaration is being checked, the argument name goes out of scope as soon as the declaration is complete. (That is why formal parameter names do not have to be the same as argument names in the function definition.) If a function definition is being checked, the argument names have scope local to the function. (That is why argument names can be used anywhere in the function body, and also why actual argument names do not have to match formal argument names.)

❏ *The scope of constructor initializers is checked last.* A constructor initializer is a sophisticated feature that allows constructor function arguments to be manipulated. Constructor initializers are covered in Chapter 15. For now, the essential point is that a constructor initializer can refer to the constructor's argument names.

Special circumstances in scoping arise when functions are declared to be friends of a class. Friend functions have the following characteristics:

❏ *Friend functions are not within the scope of the class.* When a function is declared to be a friend of a class (this is done by the class declaration, as explained in Chapter 11), the function is still not within the scope of the class. That is why friend functions must be passed an argument indicating which specific class object the friend function is to manipulate. Note, for example, the following code fragment:

```
class A {
  int priv_data;
  ...
public:
  friend int get_data( A& );
...
};
...
int get_data( A& argobj )
{
  return argobj.priv_data; //must qualify member name
}
```

❏ *Friend functions have access to private and protected members of a class.* The preceding code fragment also illustrates this point. Clearly, friend functions are an important part of the interface to a class object, even though they are not part of the class's scope. Because a class declaration must grant class friendship (it cannot be usurped), there is no violation of the class protection mechanism.

Communicating with C++ Objects

In plain C programs, you have data (which is manipulated), and you have functions (which perform the manipulations). Data and functions are two clearly different things with different purposes.

But even in plain C, there is a slight blurring of the distinction between data and functions. A function has a return type that must be a *data* type, and a function *call* can be placed directly in expressions and statements. Function calls are used the same way variables are. Note the following example:

```
x = sqrt( 3.0 ); /* Take the square root of three */
```

There is an even greater blurring of the distinction between functions and data in C++ because class objects contain both data *and* functions. The structure of C++ encourages you to think of class objects as having some intelligence (only in the computer meaning of the word) and as being able to perform their own data manipulations. In OOP systems generally, the concept is one of "sending messages" to objects instead of calling functions and pointing them at some data.

Even so, you would not expect C++ to be unrecognizable to the C programmer, and it is not. Naturally, the method of sending messages to C++ class objects is simply to call a member function.

Sending Messages to Objects

You are already familiar with the plain C structure member operator (.) and the structure pointer operator (->). Now you need to become familiar with the C++ syntax that allows you to declare functions within a structure or class without having to resort to pointers to functions to do so.

If you have kept up with the developments in ANSI C, you may be somewhat familiar with the C++ syntax for calling a member function. Consider, for example, the following short program, which is 100 percent plain (ANSI) C:

```
#include <stdlib.h>
#include <stdio.h>

void message( void );  /* Prototype the message function */

struct holder {
  void (*router)( void ); /* Pointer to message function */
};

void main()
{
  struct holder mobj;                    /* Declare the struct */

  mobj.router = message;     /* Initialize ptr to function */
```

```
  (*mobj.router)();        /* Call it the classic C way */
  mobj.router();           /* Call it the ANSI C way */
}


void message( void )
{
  puts( "What a funny way to invoke a function!" );
}
```

Notice in this short program that the structure declaration (this is not a class, remember) contains a pointer to a function, coded in the usual manner for C function pointers. Later, in the `main()` function, that pointer is first initialized and then the function is actually called in a way instantly recognizable to pre-ANSI C programmers. The last statement in `main()`, however, introduces something new with ANSI C. Once the pointer to a function is properly set up, the function can be called *without* the older indirection operator surrounded by parentheses syntax.

That isn't very difficult, is it? Well, if you followed that development, you just mastered the basic C++ syntax for calling a member function! You should not be too surprised. Remember that C++ classes are C structures with extended capabilities, and there is no surprise at all.

Generally, then, you can call a class object's member function by using the structure member operator (now called the class member operator) or the structure pointer operator (now called the class pointer operator). Note the syntax for these methods of calling member functions:

```
objectname.memberfunction( mbrfunction args );
objectname->memberfunction( mbrfunction args );
```

It seems that the more things change, the more they stay the same, doesn't it? Now that you know the basic rationale for calling member functions (sending messages to class objects), you can examine a real class, one that does something useful, and see how to communicate with it by calling member functions.

Consider, for example, the `lib` class, which is a library object class. What is a library? A library is a file that contains multiple subfiles (a subfile is called a library *member*). Each member of a library is a file in its own right—it just happens to be contained within the library file. A member of a `lib` file can be anything you want it to be, such as a text file, a binary file, or an EXE file.

You may be asking yourself, isn't this the same thing as the library files that come with my C++ compiler? The `lib` class libraries do have some similarities, but the differences are quite important. The `lib` class in this illustration, then, has been designed to force a file extension of LBR for `lib` files to keep them separate from other LIB files.

Note two ways to distinguish lib library files. They are distinguished first by the way they organize member files internally, and second by the way they handle waste space after a member is deleted.

So that the physical organization of a lib file is maintained, a variation on a familiar technology is used here: doubly linked lists. The variation is that the link addresses are *disk* addresses, not memory addresses. In fact, to organize a library's contents and to manage free (waste) space at the same time, a lib file contains *two* linked lists, as shown in figure 13.1.

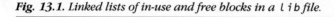

Fig. 13.1. *Linked lists of in-use and free blocks in a* lib *file.*

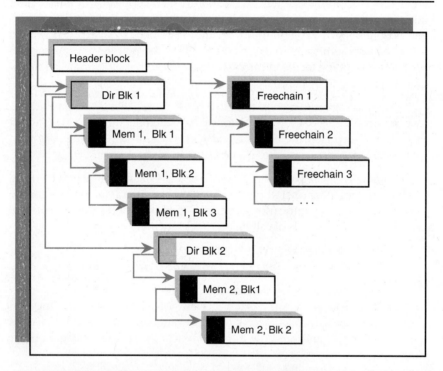

Figure 13.1 shows that the whole library file is anchored by a *header block*. Always the first block in the file, the header block is 19 bytes long. This block contains a disk address pointing to the first *data block*, and another disk address pointing to the first *free block*. All the data blocks are linked together, forming the *in-use chain*; and all the free blocks are linked together, forming the *free chain*. Figure 13.1 does not show all the detail, but the in-use and free chains are in fact doubly linked, much like a linked list kept in RAM.

The free chain is a simple doubly linked list, with no complications. All the empty data blocks (which are created when a member is deleted from the library) are kept in a single list so that one can be recovered and used when a new member is created or when an existing member needs more space. Recovering data blocks in this manner enables you to maintain a *self-reorganizing library* and thus avoid having to copy all the remaining members into another library file to eliminate dead space.

The in-use chain is a little more complicated. It is actually an indeterminate number of sublists woven together. The first of these sublists is the library's *directory*. The address in the header block pointing to the first in-use block actually points to the first directory block. Although there is only one anchor in the header for the in-use chain, there are any number of anchors in the directory entries for the member files. Each member file occupies a discrete linked list of data blocks, anchored by a directory entry but separate from the directory's list. Figure 13.2 illustrates the directory arrangement more clearly.

Fig. 13.2. *Expanded view of a* lib *directory data block.*

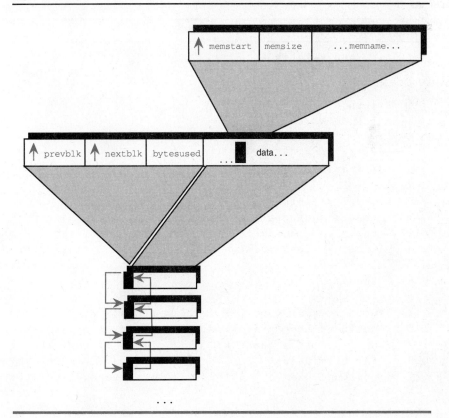

Like the data in a member file, the contents of a directory block reside in a data block. The data portion of the directory's linked list, as shown in figure 13.2, contains a number of directory *entries* (each of which is 21 bytes long). A directory entry contains the following three fields:

❏ *The member's starting disk address.* The starting address of each member is kept in an unsigned long variable, as obtained by the ordinary ftell() function.

❏ *The member's length.* The length of each member is recorded as an unsigned long integer. This means that the size of each member could conceivably be as large as DOS allows a file to be.

❏ *The member's name.* A member name is the same as a DOS file (without drive or path information). This makes good sense because members are loaded from, and extracted to, ordinary DOS disk files.

Little more can be said about lib objects until you examine how the class is put together. Take a look at listing 13.2, which contains the lib.hpp header file for the class.

Listing 13.2. lib.hpp. *A header file for the library object.*

```
 1   #include <stdlib.h>
 2   #include <stdio.h>
 3   #include <string.h>
 4   #include <dir.h>
 5   #include <dos.h>
 6
 7   #define FALSE 0
 8   #define TRUE 1
 9
10   typedef struct {          // 19 byte header
11     char signature[7];          // signature string "LIBV10"
12     unsigned long dir;          // offset of first dir block
13     unsigned long freechain;  // offset of first free block
14     unsigned long eof;          // offset of end of freechain
15   } header;
16
17   typedef struct {          // 128 byte data blocks
18     unsigned long prevblk;      // offset of prevs blk in chain
19     unsigned long nextblk;      // offset of next blk in chain
20     int bytesused;              // bytes used in this block
21     unsigned char data[118];  // data storage for block
22   }datablock;
23
```

```
24   typedef struct {          // 21 byte directory entry
25     unsigned long memstart;   // first block of member
26     unsigned long memsize;    // size of member in bytes
27     char memname[13];         // mem name, with null byte
28   } entry;
29
30   typedef struct {          // struct for libseek and libtell
31     unsigned long blockadr;   // byte address of disk block
32     int blockindex;           // byte index value at location
33   } lib_pos_t;
34
35   // ----------------------------------------------------------
36   // CLASS DECLARATION for lib object
37   // ----------------------------------------------------------
38   class lib {
39     header *hdr;
40     datablock *blk;
41     entry *ent;
42     int incore;               // flag on when unwritten block
43     lib_pos_t diradr;
44     lib_pos_t memadr;
45     FILE *libfile;
46     char *library;
47     int byteindex;
48     unsigned long bytecount; // for comparison to memsize
49     unsigned long curblock;  // disk address of cur datablock
50   public:
51     lib( char *libname );
52     ~lib();
53     void purgeblk();
54     void purgedir();
55     int readblk();
56     int writeblk();
57     int libseek( lib_pos_t *adr );
58     int libtell( lib_pos_t *adr );
59     int readhdr();
60     int writehdr();
61     int readn( unsigned char *buf, unsigned numbyte );
62     int writen( unsigned char *buf, unsigned numbyte );
63     int acquireblk();
64     int releaseblk();
65     int getnextblk();
```

Listing 13.2. continues

Listing 13.2. continued

```
66      int getprevblk();
67      int locate( char *member );
68      void listdir();
69      int addmem( char *member );
70      int delmem( char *member );
71      int listmem( char *member );
72      int extractmem( char *member, char *oname );
73      int unload( char *path );
74    };
75
```

The first thing that you encounter in the `lib.hpp` header file, after the usual `#include` and `#define` directives, is a series of `typedefs` for the various structures used in the `lib` class. The `typedef` declarations provide storage layouts for a `header` type (the overall library header block), a `datablock` type (the linked record used for both data and free blocks), an `entry` type (a directory entry), and a `lib_pos_t` type (for reporting and setting the read/write position within a library member). All these `typedefs` appear in lines 10–33 of listing 13.2.

The `lib` class declaration itself begins in line 38. Structured objects of the types just defined are declared, and several other important variables are declared in the private portion of the class. The integer `incore` is used internally to signal that a `datablock` buffer has received new data and needs to be written physically to disk. The `libfile` and `library` variables are the `FILE` and string objects, respectively, for manipulating and naming the library file.

The `byteindex` variable (line 47) is used internally to note the position of the next read or write, which uses the `datablock` currently in memory. The `bytecount` field appearing next keeps a running count of a member's size as it is being created or read back in. Finally, `curblock` keeps the physical disk address of the current `datablock` being read or written. If any of the member variables named in this paragraph should ever get out of kilter while a library file is being written, the file will be destroyed (so be careful not to misinterpret the use of member variables when modifying this program).

Most of the member function names declared in listing 13.2 at least give a hint about what they do. Glance at the function declarations and then look over the `lib.cpp` source file shown in listing 13.3. Following the listing is an explanation of how the member functions work.

Listing 13.3. `lib.cpp`. *The member functions for the library object.*

```
 1   #include "lib.hpp"
 2
 3   // ----------------------------------------------------------
 4   // lib() --- Constructor for lib object
 5   // ----------------------------------------------------------
 6   lib::lib( char *libname )
 7   {
 8      hdr = new header;
 9      blk = new datablock;
10      ent = new entry;
11      library = new char[81];
12
13      strcpy( library, libname );
14      if ( NULL == ( libfile = fopen( library, "rb+" ) ) ) {
15        if ( NULL == ( libfile = fopen( library, "wb" ) ) ) {
16          this->lib::~lib();   // if nothing works, kill it all
17        }
18        else {
19          strcpy( hdr->signature, "LIBV10" );
20          hdr->dir = OUL;          // initialize the header block
21          hdr->freechain = OUL;
22          hdr->eof = OUL;
23          writehdr();
24          fclose( libfile );  // close-reopen the file normally
25          libfile = fopen( library, "rb+" );
26          byteindex = 0;                // init internal variables
27          bytecount = 0;
28          curblock = OUL;
29          diradr.blockadr = OUL;
30          diradr.blockindex = 0;
31          memadr.blockadr = OUL;
32          memadr.blockindex = 0;
33          incore = FALSE;
34        }
35      }
36      if ( !readhdr() )
37        this->lib::~lib();      // if you can't read header block
38      if ( strcmp( hdr->signature, "LIBV10" ) )
39        this->lib::~lib();         // or signature doesn't match
```

Listing 13.3. continues

Listing 13.3. continued

```
40   }
41
42   // -----------------------------------------------------------
43   // ~lib() --- Destructor for lib object
44   // -----------------------------------------------------------
45   lib::~lib()
46   {
47     delete hdr;  // free all acquired areas
48     delete blk;
49     delete ent;
50     delete library;
51     fclose( libfile );
52   }
53
54   // -----------------------------------------------------------
55   // purgeblk() --- Clear all data from block buffer
56   // -----------------------------------------------------------
57   void lib::purgeblk()
58   {
59     blk->prevblk = OUL;              // clear out the block buffer
60     blk->nextblk = OUL;
61     blk->bytesused = 0;
62     memset( blk->data, '\0', 118 );
63
64   }
65
66   // -----------------------------------------------------------
67   // purgedir --- Clear directory entry buffer
68   // -----------------------------------------------------------
69   void lib::purgedir()
70   {
71     ent->memstart = OUL;
72     ent->memsize = OUL;
73     memset( ent->memname, '\xFF', 13 );
74   }
75
76   // -----------------------------------------------------------
77   // readblk() --- Physical read of block at curblock.
78   //               Do not update curblock
79   // -----------------------------------------------------------
80   int lib::readblk()
81   {
82     byteindex = 0;
```

```
83     if ( 0 != fseek( libfile, curblock, SEEK_SET ) )
84       return FALSE;
85     if ( 1 > fread( blk, sizeof( datablock ), 1, libfile ) )
86       return FALSE;
87     incore = TRUE;
88     return TRUE;
89   }
90
91   // -----------------------------------------------------
92   // writeblk() --- Physical write of block at curblock.
93   //                Do not update curblock
94   // -----------------------------------------------------
95   int lib::writeblk()
96   {
97     byteindex = 0;
98     if ( 0 != fseek( libfile, curblock, SEEK_SET ) )
99       return FALSE;
100    if ( 1 > fwrite( blk, sizeof( datablock ), 1, libfile ) )
101      return FALSE;
102    incore = FALSE;
103    return TRUE;
104  }
105
106  // -----------------------------------------------------
107  // libseek() --- Seek to offset within a particular block
108  // -----------------------------------------------------
109  int lib::libseek( lib_pos_t *adr )
110  {
111    curblock = adr->blockadr;
112    if ( !readblk() ) return FALSE;
113    byteindex = adr->blockindex;
114    return TRUE;
115  }
116
117  // -----------------------------------------------------
118  // libtell() --- Report current block and offset position
119  // -----------------------------------------------------
120  int lib::libtell( lib_pos_t *adr )
121  {
122    adr->blockadr = curblock;
123    adr->blockindex = byteindex;
```

Listing 13.3. continues

Listing 13.3. continued

```
124     return TRUE;
125   }
126
127   // --------------------------------------------------------
128   // readhdr() --- Physical read of header
129   // --------------------------------------------------------
130   int lib::readhdr()
131   {
132     if ( 0 != fseek( libfile, 0, SEEK_SET ) )
133       return FALSE;
134     if ( 1 > fread( hdr, sizeof( header ), 1, libfile ) )
135       return FALSE;
136     else
137       return TRUE;
138   }
139
140   // --------------------------------------------------------
141   // writehdr() --- Physical write of header
142   // --------------------------------------------------------
143   int lib::writehdr()
144   {
145     if ( 0 != fseek( libfile, 0, SEEK_SET ) )
146       return FALSE;
147     if ( 1 > fwrite( hdr, sizeof( header ), 1, libfile ) )
148       return FALSE;
149     else
150       return TRUE;
151   }
152
153   // --------------------------------------------------------
154   // readn() --- read n bytes from member / directory
155   // --------------------------------------------------------
156   int lib::readn( unsigned char *buf, unsigned numbyte )
157   {
158     unsigned i = 0;
159
160     for ( ; numbyte>0; --numbyte ) {
161       if ( byteindex >= 118 )
162         if ( !getnextblk() ) return FALSE;
163       if ( byteindex >= blk->bytesused )
164         return FALSE;              // leave byteindex where it is
165       buf[i++] = blk->data[byteindex++];           // get a byte
166     }
```

```
167    return TRUE;
168  }
169
170  // ----------------------------------------------------------
171  // writen() --- write n bytes to member / directory
172  // ----------------------------------------------------------
173  int lib::writen( unsigned char *buf, unsigned numbyte )
174  {
175    unsigned long oldblock, newblock;
176    unsigned i = 0;
177
178    for ( ; numbyte>0; --numbyte ) {
179      if ( byteindex >= 118 ) {   // chain to next block
180
181        if ( !writeblk() ) return FALSE;   // write full block
182
183        if ( !getnextblk() ) { // no next block, make new one
184
185          oldblock = curblock;            // save old block adr
186
187          if ( !acquireblk() ) return FALSE;
188          newblock = curblock;
189          blk->prevblk = oldblock; // point back from new blk
190          if ( !writeblk() ) return FALSE;
191
192          curblock = oldblock;
193          if ( !readblk() ) return FALSE;
194          blk->nextblk = newblock;  // point fwd from old blk
195          if ( !writeblk() ) return FALSE;
196
197          curblock = newblock;
198          if ( !readblk() ) return FALSE;      // now continue
199        }
200      }
201
202      blk->data[byteindex++] = buf[i++];       // write a byte
203      if ( byteindex > blk->bytesused-1 )
204        blk->bytesused++;                  // update control info
205    }
206    return TRUE;
207  }
```

Listing 13.3. continues

Listing 13.3. continued

```
208
209   // ----------------------------------------------------------
210   // acquireblk() --- Get a free block from Q or create one.
211   //                  curblock will point to acquired block.
212   // ----------------------------------------------------------
213   int lib::acquireblk()
214   {
215     unsigned long newblock;
216
217     byteindex = 0;
218                                     // If there is no free chain,
219                                     // go to EOF and create blk
220     if ( hdr->freechain == NULL ) {
221       if ( 0 != fseek( libfile, 0, SEEK_END ) )
222         return FALSE;
223       curblock = ftell( libfile );
224       purgeblk();            // clear blk buf
225       if ( !writeblk() ) return FALSE;
226       return TRUE;
227     }
228                                     // Take last freechain block
229     curblock = hdr->eof;
230     if ( !readblk() ) return FALSE;
231
232     newblock = curblock;                    // hold it a minute
233
234     if ( blk->prevblk ) {             // try to back up 1 block
235       if ( !getprevblk() ) return FALSE;
236       hdr->eof = curblock;          // note new end of freechain
237       if ( !writehdr() ) return FALSE;
238       blk->nextblk = 0UL;
239       if ( !writeblk() ) return FALSE;
240       curblock = newblock;
241       purgeblk();
242       return TRUE;
243     }
244     else {                       // was only 1 blk in freechain
245       hdr->freechain = 0UL;
246       hdr->eof = 0UL;
247       if ( !writehdr() ) return FALSE;
248       purgeblk();
```

```
249       return TRUE;
250     }
251  }
252
253  // ----------------------------------------------------------
254  // releaseblk() --- Put an existing datablock into the
255  //                  freechain. curblock must point to the
256  //                  block to release.
257  // ----------------------------------------------------------
258  int lib::releaseblk()
259  {
260    unsigned long holdblock;
261    unsigned long oldend;
262
263    holdblock = curblock;
264    byteindex = 0;
265    if ( !hdr->freechain ) {        // if there is no freechain
266      hdr->freechain = curblock;
267      hdr->eof = curblock;
268      if ( !writehdr() ) return FALSE;
269      purgeblk();
270      if ( !writeblk() ) return FALSE;
271      return TRUE;
272    }
273                             // Add after last block of freechain
274    curblock = hdr->eof;
275    if ( !readblk() ) return FALSE;
276
277    oldend = curblock;
278
279    blk->nextblk = holdblock;                    // chain it on
280    if ( !writeblk() ) return FALSE;    // update old endchain
281
282    curblock = holdblock;                  // relocate freed block
283    hdr->eof = curblock;
284    if ( !writehdr() ) return FALSE;
285    if ( !readblk() ) return FALSE;      // and update its link
286    purgeblk();
287    blk->prevblk = oldend;
288    if ( !writeblk() ) return FALSE;
```

Listing 13.3. continues

Listing 13.3. continued

```
289
290     return TRUE;
291   }
292
293   // --------------------------------------------------------
294   // getnextblk() --- Read the next chained datablock
295   // --------------------------------------------------------
296   int lib::getnextblk()
297   {
298     if ( !blk->nextblk ) return FALSE;
299     curblock = blk->nextblk;
300     if ( !readblk() ) return FALSE;
301     return TRUE;
302   }
303
304   // --------------------------------------------------------
305   // getprevblk() --- Read the previous chained datablock
306   // --------------------------------------------------------
307   int lib::getprevblk()
308   {
309     if ( !blk->prevblk ) return FALSE;
310     curblock = blk->prevblk;
311     if ( readblk() ) return TRUE;
312     else return FALSE;
313   }
314
315   // --------------------------------------------------------
316   // locate() --- Find a member in the directory
317   // --------------------------------------------------------
318   int lib::locate( char *member )
319   {
320     if ( !hdr->dir ) return FALSE;
321     curblock = hdr->dir;
322     if ( !readblk() ) return FALSE;
323     libtell( &diradr );
324     while ( readn( (unsigned char *)ent,sizeof( entry ) ) ) {
325       if ( ent->memname[0] == _\xFF  ) {
326         libtell( &diradr );
327         continue;
328       }
329       if ( 0 == strcmp( ent->memname, member ) )
```

```
330        return TRUE;
331      libtell( &diradr );
332    }
333    return FALSE;
334  }
335
336  // ------------------------------------------------------
337  // listdir() --- Display a directory list
338  // ------------------------------------------------------
339  void lib::listdir()
340  {
341    printf( "Directory List for %s\n", library );
342    printf( "==============\n" );
343
344    if ( !hdr->dir ) return;
345    curblock = hdr->dir;
346    if ( !readblk() ) return;
347    while ( readn( (unsigned char *)ent,sizeof( entry ) ) ) {
348      if ( ent->memname[0] == '\0' ) break;
349      if ( ent->memname[0] == '\xFF' ) continue;
350       printf( "%-15s%12ld\n", ent->memname, ent->memsize );
351    }
352    return;
353  }
354
355  // ------------------------------------------------------
356  // addmem() --- Add a new member to library
357  // ------------------------------------------------------
358  int lib::addmem( char *member )
359  {
360    int i;
361    char *ptr;
362    unsigned char ch;
363    FILE *infile;
364
365
366    printf( "LIB: Adding member - %s\n", member );
367
368    // --- open file successfully
369
370    if ( NULL == ( infile = fopen( member, "rb" ) ) ) {
371      fclose( infile );
```

Listing 13.3. continues

Listing 13.3. continued

```
372        return FALSE;
373    }
374
375
376    // --- bypass any path info if present
377
378    i = strlen( member ) - 1;
379    while ( i>0 && member[i] != '\\' && member[i] != ':' )
380      --i;
381    if ( i > 0 ) ++i;
382    ptr = &member[i];
383
384    // --- check to see if it already exists
385
386    if ( locate( ptr ) ) return FALSE;
387
388    // --- find directory entry - note position
389
390    if ( !hdr->dir ) {
391      if ( !acquireblk() ) return FALSE;
392      libtell ( &diradr );
393      hdr->dir = curblock;
394      if ( !writehdr() ) return FALSE;
395    }
396    else {
397      curblock = hdr->dir;
398      if ( !readblk() ) return FALSE;
399      libtell( &diradr );
400      while ( readn( (unsigned char *)ent,sizeof( entry ) ) ) {
401        if ( ent->memname[0] == '\xFF' ) break;
402        libtell( &diradr );
403      }
404    }
405    strcpy( ent->memname, ptr );
406
407    // --- acquire first data block - note position
408
409    if ( !acquireblk() ) return FALSE;
410    ent->memstart = curblock;
411    ent->memsize = 0UL;
412
```

```
413      // --- read file - write member - count bytes
414
415      while ( 0 < fread( &ch, 1, 1, infile ) ) {
416        if ( !writen( (unsigned char *)&ch, 1 ) )
417          return FALSE;
418        ent->memsize++;
419      }
420
421      // --- if incore flag on, write last block
422
423      if ( incore )
424        if ( !writeblk() ) return FALSE;
425
426      // --- close file
427
428      fclose( infile );
429
430      // --- update directory
431
432      if ( !libseek( &diradr ) ) return FALSE;
433      if ( !writen( (unsigned char *)ent,sizeof( entry ) ) )
434        return FALSE;
435      if ( incore )
436        if ( !writeblk() ) return FALSE;
437
438      return TRUE;
439    }
440
441    // ------------------------------------------------------------
442    // delmem() --- Delete a member from library
443    // ------------------------------------------------------------
444    int lib::delmem( char *member )
445    {
446      unsigned long datablk;
447
448      printf( "LIB: Deleting member - %s\n", member );
449
450      if ( !locate( member ) ) return FALSE;
451
452      datablk = ent->memstart;
453
454      purgedir();
```

Listing 13.3. continues

Listing 13.3. continued

```
455      if ( !libseek( &diradr ) ) return FALSE;
456      if ( !writen( (unsigned char *)ent, sizeof( entry ) ) )
457        return FALSE;
458      if ( incore )
459        if ( !writeblk() ) return FALSE;
460
461      curblock = datablk;
462      while ( curblock ) {
463        if ( !readblk() ) return FALSE;
464        datablk = blk->nextblk;
465        if ( !releaseblk() ) return FALSE;
466        curblock = datablk;
467      }
468      return TRUE;
469    }
470
471    // -----------------------------------------------------------
472    // listmem() --- Display a single member
473    // -----------------------------------------------------------
474    int lib::listmem( char *member )
475    {
476      int i;
477
478      printf( "LIB: Showing member - %s\n", member );
479
480      if ( !locate( member ) ) return FALSE;
481      curblock = ent->memstart;
482      if ( !readblk() ) return FALSE;
483      while ( curblock ) {
484        curblock = blk->nextblk;
485        for ( i=0; i<blk->bytesused; i++ )
486          putchar( blk->data[i] );
487        if ( !readblk() ) break;
488      }
489      return TRUE;
490    }
491
492    // -----------------------------------------------------------
493    // extractmem() --- Read a member from the lib and write
494    //                  to a file
495    // -----------------------------------------------------------
```

```
496   int lib::extractmem( char *member, char *oname )
497   {
498     int i;
499     FILE *ofile;
500
501     printf( "LIB: Unloading member - %s\n", member );
502
503     if ( oname[0] == '\0' ) strcpy( oname, member );
504
505     if ( NULL == ( ofile = fopen( oname, "wb" ) ) )
506       return FALSE;
507
508     if ( !locate( member ) ) return FALSE;
509     curblock = ent->memstart;
510     if ( !readblk() ) return FALSE;
511     while ( curblock ) {
512       curblock = blk->nextblk;
513       for ( i=0; i<blk->bytesused; i++ )
514         if ( 1 > fwrite( &blk->data[i], 1, 1, ofile ) ) {
515           fclose( ofile );
516           return FALSE;
517         }
518       if ( !readblk() ) break;
519     }
520     fclose( ofile );
521     return TRUE;
522   }
523
524   // -------------------------------------------------------------
525   // unload() --- Unload entire library
526   // -------------------------------------------------------------
527   int lib::unload( char *path )
528   {
529     char out[81];
530     char holdname[13];
531     lib_pos_t here;
532
533     if ( !hdr->dir ) return FALSE;
534     curblock = hdr->dir;
535     if ( !readblk() ) return FALSE;
536
537     while ( readn( (unsigned char *)ent,sizeof( entry ) ) ) {
```

Listing 13.3. continues

Listing 13.3. continued

```
538
539        if ( !libtell( &here ) ) return FALSE;
540        if ( ent->memname[0] == '\0' ) break;
541        if ( ent->memname[0] == '\xFF' ) continue;
542
543        strcpy( out, path );
544        strcat( out, ent->memname );
545        strcpy( holdname, ent->memname );
546
547        if ( !extractmem( holdname, out ) ) return FALSE;
548        if ( !libseek( &here ) ) return FALSE;
549     }
550     return TRUE;
551 }
552
```

The lib.cpp source file in listing 13.3 contains some tricky code. If you ever want to modify the program, be sure that you completely understand what the existing code does before starting in. Now take a look at the member function definitions to see how they work.

The lib class has only one constructor function, shown in lines 6–40 of listing 13.3. The constructor function accepts as an argument a string pointer to the library's file name. There is no default constructor—that would be pointless.

The constructor's job is simply to open the library file—creating one if necessary—in update mode and to initialize the internal control variables. Notice that the memory for the header, data block, directory entry, and file name string are acquired and maintained outside the boundaries of the lib object. If the library can be successfully opened (or created), the header block is read in, and the *signature* is verified. The signature is just the string "LIBV10", which occupies the first six bytes in the library file.

The lib destructor (lines 45–52) is especially simple. It releases the memory for control structures and closes the library file.

Both the purgeblk() function (lines 57–64) and the purgedir() function (lines 69–74) set something to nulls. The purgeblk() function reinitializes an in-memory data block when a data block is either newly acquired or released. The purgedir() function reinitializes the in-memory directory entry when a member file is being deleted, and also sets the member name to all '\xFF' values. That way, the block can be reused later.

The readblk() function (lines 80–89) performs a physical read of a 128-byte data block (which can contain either member or directory data) from the library. readblk() assumes that some other member function has correctly set the value of the member variable curblock to the physical disk address of the block. Because the block may need to be rewritten after receiving file data, readblk() does not change the value of curblock. Notice that the standard C fseek() and fread() functions are used to read blocks. Notice especially that the incore flag is set *on* (set to TRUE) when a block is read.

writeblk() performs the complementary task of writing a data block to physical disk storage, also using standard C library functions. Notice that whenever a block is physically written, the incore flag is turned off (set to FALSE).

The next two member functions, libseek() and libtell(), perform tasks for a lib file that are similar to those performed by fseek() and ftell() in plain C. The libtell() function (lines 120–125) reports the current read-write position within a member (or directory) by simply capturing curblock and byteindex. Remember that curblock always contains the disk address of the data block currently in memory, and byteindex has the offset (sub-script) of the current byte in that block. The libseek() function (lines 109–115) performs the complementary task by reading in the indicated data block and setting byteindex to the correct value.

Another pair of member functions of critical importance to the lib class is readn(), in lines 156–168, and writen(), in lines 173–207. These functions read and write, respectively, *n* characters from the lib file. These functions are especially important because they provide the main I/O interface to the class.

The self-reorganizing characteristic of lib files is provided by the acquireblk() member function (lines 213–251) and the releaseblk() member function (lines 258–291). acquireblk() gets a data block from the free chain, if one is available, and makes the data block available for use. releaseblk() performs the opposite function of returning a discarded data block to the free chain (blocks are discarded when a member is deleted).

Processing a lib file member in a sequential manner naturally involves reading or writing blocks from the doubly linked chain of data blocks. "Running the chain" can be performed in the forward direction by the getnextblk() function (lines 296–302) and in the backward direction by the getprevblk() function (lines 307–313). These functions are relatively simple compared to the others discussed so far and require only picking up and using address pointers (*disk* addresses) with the same techniques you use for doubly linked lists in memory. To start processing a member file, you need to use the `locate()` member function found in lines 318–334. This member function finds and reads in the directory entry for a member (if, in fact, such an entry exists).

The remaining member functions (from line 336 to line 552) provide higher-level functionality for library objects. They all use the previously described member functions to carry out their tasks. The higher-level service member functions include the following:

❏ `listdir()`

`listdir()` reads the entire library directory and reports each member name and member size on `stdout`.

❏ `addmem()`

`addmem()` adds a new member file to the library. This function fails if the member file name is already present. `admem()` also assumes that there may be drive and path information present in the member name string (so that `lib` users can use wild-card characters to input member names). If such information is present, it is stripped off before the member name is recorded. This member function provides some good sample code for manipulating a library file, including the method for updating the directory when a member is added.

❏ `delmem()`

`delmem()` deletes a member file from the library file. This function's manner of processing the directory is analogous to that used by `addmem()`, except that the directory entry is purged before writing back to disk instead of being filled in with information.

❏ `listmem()`

`listmem()` locates a member file (if it is present in the library) and sends it to `stdout`. Because `stdout` is used, you can redirect output to the printer (using the DOS command-line redirection command >PRN).

❏ `extractmem()`

`extractmem()` is the mirror image of `addmem()`. The `extractmem()` function reads a member file from the library and writes that file to an outside file. As with `addmem()`, it doesn't matter whether the member file read and written by `extractmem()` is text, binary, or something else. All member files are processed in binary mode so that every bit is reproduced faithfully.

❏ unload()

unload(), the last member function in the lib class, is a powerful function that calls extractmem() for *every* member in the library. You might use unload(), for example, if a set of files has been transported (or distributed) in a lib file and you want to recover all the original files.

Many functions are available in the lib class, but it will not be useful without some code that can "drive" it. A driver program, pds.cpp, is provided in listing 13.4. The program name is borrowed from the mainframe computing environment. The acronym *pds* means *partitioned data set*—partitioned, that is, into multiple subfiles, or members.

Listing 13.4. pds.cpp. *A self-reorganizing library program that uses* lib *class objects.*

```
1   #include "lib.hpp"
2
3   // ----------------------------------------------------------
4   // main() --- Driver for testing lib object
5   // ----------------------------------------------------------
6   void main(int argc, char *argv[] )
7   {
8      char lname[81];
9      char mname[81];
10     char oname[81];
11     char action;
12     struct ffblk dosdir;
13     int retn, i;
14     char dirpath[81];
15     char searcharg[81];
16
17     puts( "+--------------------------------+" );
18     puts( "+                                +" );
19     puts( "+ PDS Library Utility Version 1.1 +" );
20     puts( "+                                +" );
21     puts( "+--------------------------------+" );
22
23     if ( argc < 3 ) {
24        puts( "The correct format for the lib command is:" );
```

Listing 13.4. continues

Listing 13.4. continued

```
25        puts( "" );
26        puts( "       pds a lname mname [oname]" );
27        puts( "" );
28        puts( "where a is the action character:" );
29        puts( "    a - add member" );
30        puts( "    d - delete member" );
31        puts( "    x - extract member" );
32        puts( "    u - unload library" );
33        puts( "    l - list directory" );
34        puts( "    s - list member" );
35        puts( "and:" );
36        puts( "    lname - library file name (required)" );
37        puts( "    mname - member name" );
38        puts( "            required unless action=l" );
39        puts( "            (path spec if unloading)" );
40        puts( "    oname - opt. output file for extract" );
41        exit( 0 );
42     }
43
44     action = argv[1][0];
45     strcpy( lname, argv[2] );
46     mname[0] = '\0';
47     if ( argc > 3 ) strcpy( mname, argv[3] );
48     oname[0] = '\0';
49     if ( argc > 4 ) strcpy( oname, argv[4] );
50
51     if ( strchr( lname, '.' ) ) {     // force ext. to .LBR
52       i = strlen( lname ) - 1;
53       while ( i>0 && lname[i] != '.' ) --i;
54       lname[i] = '\0';
55     }
56     strupr( lname );
57     strcat( lname, ".LBR" );
58
59     lib pds( lname );                  // create a library object
60
61     strupr( mname );
62
63     switch ( action ) {
64       case 'a':
65       case 'A': if ( strpbrk( mname, "?*" ) ) {
66                     strcpy( searcharg, mname );
```

```
67                        strcpy ( dirpath, mname );
68                        i = strlen( dirpath ) - 1;
69                        while ( i>0 && dirpath[i] != '\\'
70                                && dirpath[i] != ':' ) --i;
71                        if ( i > 0 ) ++i;
72                        dirpath[i] = '\0';
73                        retn = findfirst( searcharg,&dosdir,0xFF );
74                        strcpy( mname, dirpath );
75                        strcat( mname, dosdir.ff_name );
76                        while ( !retn ) {
77                          if ( !( dosdir.ff_attrib & FA_SYSTEM )
78                              && !( dosdir.ff_attrib & FA_LABEL )
79                              && !( dosdir.ff_attrib & FA_DIREC ) )
80                                pds.addmem( mname );
81                          retn = findnext( &dosdir );
82                          strcpy( mname, dirpath );
83                          strcat( mname, dosdir.ff_name );
84                        }
85                        break;
86                      }
87                      pds.addmem( mname ); break;
88       case 'd':
89       case 'D': pds.delmem( mname ); break;
90       case 'x':
91       case 'X': pds.extractmem( mname, oname ); break;
92       case 'u':
93       case 'U': if ( mname[strlen(mname)-1] != '\\'
94                        && mname[0] != '\0' )
95                      strcat( mname, "\\" );
96                    pds.unload( mname ); break;
97       case 'l':
98       case 'L': pds.listdir(); break;
99       case 's':
100      case 'S': pds.listmem( mname ); break;
101    }
102  }
```

A great deal of code has been presented here (hope you can use it!) to illustrate the simple methods of communicating with member functions. All the calls to member functions in listing 13.4 are of the form *object.function()*. The amazing thing, again, is how much you can do with a fairly simple program once the complex code has been developed and encapsulated in a C++ class.

Understanding *this

The this pointer, which was mentioned briefly in the discussion of the lifo class in Chapter 11, is available to member functions for accessing a particular instance object. Suppose, for example, that you wrote a program that used the following two lib class objects:

```
lib libfile1( "DOCS.LBR" );
lib libfile2( "KEYWORDS.LBR" );
```

Having declared two distinct library objects, now suppose that you want to display the directory for each. You could write these statements to accomplish that:

```
libfile1.listmem();
libfile2.listmem();
```

In both cases, the lib::listmem() function is called. As you may recall from Chapter 11, each access implies that a "behind the scenes" pointer (this) is in place (although you do *not*, in this circumstance, have to do any dereferencing). How does the presence of this affect the operation of listmem()? Look, for example, at line 481, reproduced from listing 13.3:

```
curblock = ent->memstart;
```

How does the member function know which curblock to refer to? There is, after all, a separate copy of the variable for each libfile1 and libfile2. The trick is to understand that the preceding statement is equivalent to the following statement:

```
this->curblock = ent->memstart;
```

The nice thing about the way this works is that you do *not* have to write the pointer reference yourself within a member function when referring to member data (not even if the object was created with new and is being controlled through a pointer).

You rarely use the this pointer with the most current C++ compilers (you formerly had to initialize it yourself in some cases). There are instances, however, in which you need to know that this exists and what it signifies. These instances are covered in the next few sections, which deal with C++ references and the passing and returning of class objects to and from member functions.

Using the Reference Operator

The *reference operator*, as its name implies, enables you to treat a *pointer* to an object as if it were simply an *object*. This concept is extremely important in C++. It vastly simplifies much syntax and makes possible some operations on class objects that would otherwise be difficult or impossible. References can be used on ordinary C objects and on class objects.

Evolving the Reference Operator from the Address-of Operator

Once you understand that a reference uses a pointer behind the scenes, you should not be surprised that the reference operator uses the same character as the address-of operator (&). Then it is only a short step to understanding that the reference generated by the reference operator is merely an alternative name for an object. Consider, for example, the following code fragment:

```
int a = 37;          // declare and init an integer
int& b = a;          // declare a reference to a
```

The first line of this code fragment is just as straightforward as it looks. The second line is straightforward also, if you know that a reference is being declared. You could read the second line as "b is a reference to the integer a."

Notice also where the reference operator appears in the second line of code: the operator is on the left side of the assignment, not in the position of the address-of operator. Furthermore, this code fragment makes it appear as if a is being assigned to b. *That is not the case*. Remember that references deal with pointers, but behind the scenes. Thus, the preceding code fragment is the *working equivalent* of the following code fragment:

```
int a = 37;          // define the integer again
int *b;              // define a pointer
b = &a;              // b contains address of a
```

When you compare these two equivalent code fragments, you can see that a reference is just a pointer in disguise. Moreover, the first code fragment makes another rule clear: *references always bind to objects, not to addresses*. This doesn't mean that addresses aren't being generated and used internally. It only means that *you* don't have to do it, nor do you have to write address notation in the code when using references.

Understanding the Reference Operator

References have two main purposes in C++. Stating these purposes is easy; appreciating their significance may be more difficult. Here are the main purposes for using references:

❑ *You can use references to specify operations for user-defined types.* As an alternative name for an object, a reference can serve as an *object locator* for the object. If you recall your ANSI C theory, this means that using a reference can enable you to use class objects in expressions with operators, and perhaps to stand as lvalues. Using references for this purpose is covered in the section on overloading operators in Chapter 14, and in Chapter 18 in the section on object performance and behavior.

❑ *You can use references to reduce overhead in passing and returning class objects as arguments.* Passing large objects on the stack takes not only stack space but also *time*. If you can avoid placing large amounts of data on the stack, you should do so. References physically place on the stack only addresses of objects. That can mean better performance.

Sometimes these two purposes are at work at the same time: returning a reference to an object from a member function is always efficient, but in some cases it may also be required to implement class operator functions. However, before you go blazing off to write some code that uses the reference operator, you need to know a couple of rules about references:

❑ *You cannot manipulate a reference directly.* This may not make sense immediately because you can manipulate pointer values, and references are disguised pointers. Why, then, can't you tinker with a reference directly? The following code fragment illustrates the reason:

```
double count = 0;          // here is a count field
double& number = count;    // here is a reference to it
...
++number;          // count is now 1 !
```

Remember that a reference is an alternative name, and references always bind to objects. Any reference to `number`, as shown in this code fragment, is an implicit reference directly to `count`.

❑ *You can use a reference to take the address of an object.* This rule also works because references bind to objects. Consider, for instance, this code fragment:

```
int a;       // declare an integer
int& b = a;  // b is reference to a
int *c;      // declare a true pointer to integer
...
c = &b;      // taking address of b same as taking address of a;
             // *c == a
```

Even though the examples here have frankly been trivial, you can do some pretty amazing things with references. In the next section, you get an idea of what those things are. Later on, references will become old friends.

Using Objects as Function Parameters

Class objects, like ordinary C objects, can be passed as arguments to functions and returned from them. This section discusses the use of class objects as function parameters and return values.

Passing Objects by Value and by Reference

You can pass class objects to a function both by value and by reference, just as you can with ordinary arguments in ordinary functions. Passing class objects by value has the same consequences as for ordinary C objects: you get only a copy of the object to work with. For example, look closely at the following short program:

```
#include <stdlib.h>
#include <stdio.h>

class OP {
   int value;
public:
   OP() { value = 37; }
   friend void changeit( OP );
   void show() { printf( "%d\n", value ); }
};
```

```
void changeit( OP someop )
{
   someop.value = 64;
}

void main()
{
   OP x;

   changeit( x );
   x.show();        // displays a value of 37
}
```

In this program, a `friend` function is used so that the private member variable `value` can be accessed. Do you think that the final call to `OP::show()` will display a value of 37 or 64? It will, in fact, display the value 37 because only a copy of the object is placed on the stack and passed to the `friend` function `changeit()`. Only that copy is modified, and the temporary object on the stack is thrown away when `changeit()` returns to its caller. The state of the original object is completely untouched by this operation.

Passing class objects to functions by reference has the same consequences as passing ordinary objects by reference (although the phrase *by reference* now takes on an added dimension). Suppose that the preceding program was coded a bit differently, to allow `changeit()` to accept a reference to an `OP` object:

```
#include <stdlib.h>
#include <stdio.h>

class OP {
   int value;
public:
   OP() { value = 37; }
   friend void changeit( OP& ); // ACCEPT REFERENCE
   void show() { printf( "%d\n", value ); }
};

void changeit( OP& someop ) // REFERENCE HERE TOO
{
   someop.value = 64;
}

void main()
{
```

```
OP x;

changeit( x ); // NO CHANGE, REF'S BIND TO OBJECTS
x.show();       // DISPLAYS A VALUE OF 64 NOW
}
```

In the second version of this program, no longer is a copy of the whole object placed on the stack and passed to the friend function; only a disguised pointer is placed there and passed to friend. Thus, the original object is available to the function, resulting in an altered value of value.

Accessing Other Objects from a Member Function

Obviously, if a member function has a parameter that is also a class object, that member function can refer to the other class object. With class objects, however, you must still take into account the point of declaration of a class as well as some more C++ scoping rules when you write references to other objects. Besides covering how to set up class objects as parameters, these rules deal with accessing other objects from within class objects. The additional scoping rules include the following:

❑ *You cannot refer to objects of a class that has not yet been declared.*
But you can use an incomplete declaration of a class to forward-declare the class to which you want to refer. Consider, for example, the following short program:

```
#include <iostream.h>

class A; // FORWARD-DECLARE THIS CLASS

class B {
  int bval;
public:
  B() { bval = 16; }
  int dosum( A& );
};

class A { // COMPLETE THE DECLARATION FOR CLASS A
  int aval;
public:
  A() { aval = 16; }
```

```
    int getval() { return aval; }
};

int B::dosum( A& aobj ) {
   return bval + aobj.getval ();
}

void main()
{
   A aobj;
   B bobj;

   cout << bobj.dosum( aobj );
}
```

This sample program uses an incomplete declaration of class A so that the argument type in B::dosum() will compile correctly. Notice, however, that the member function definition for B::dosum() is not coded until the declaration for class A has been completed. If dosum() had been coded inline, the function would have referred to members of class A—A::getval() specifically—before their point of declaration. In that case, the program would not compile correctly.

❑ *Class member functions can declare and use local objects that have their own class type.* For example, the class A shown in the preceding program could have contained a member function that declared a local class A object! A class member function can locally define an object of its own class because member functions are invoked on behalf of specific class *objects*, not classes in general. Thus, the local object is a different object, even though the local object has the same class as the member function declaring it. All local objects go out of scope and are destroyed when the member functions returns.

❑ *Class member functions can be passed references to objects of other classes, and can define local objects of other classes.* You can use objects of another class as arguments or local variables provided, of course, that the other class has been completely declared by the time you get around to writing the current class's member function *definition*.

❑ *Member functions or entire classes can serve as friends of a class.* This is a sneaky (but legitimate) way to gain access to an object of another class. You have already seen how friend functions are declared. Whole classes can be declared as friends in the following manner:

```
class A { ... };
class B {
  ...
friend A; // all class A member functions now friends
};
```

Once again, the function body of a member function cannot refer to any part of another class that has not yet been declared.

There are, in fact, even more rules of this kind that deal with class inheritance. For more information on such rules, refer to Chapter 17, "Using C++ Derived Classes."

Using Pointers to Objects

Until now, most of the examples in this book have used either global or local class objects to illustrate class object access. Such objects use the structure member operator (.) to access class members. As you may guess, nothing prevents you from declaring a pointer to a class object. Class objects accessed through a pointer must use the structure pointer operator (->) to access members.

Understanding When Pointers Are Required

In only one instance *must* you use a pointer to access a class object: when the object is created on the free store. As you may recall, objects are created on the free store with the new operator. For example, the following short program uses new to create a class object, and must therefore access the object's member functions by means of a pointer:

```
#include <iostream.h>

class car {
  int drive;
  int cyls;
  int seats;
  int doors;
public:
  car ( int odrive = 2, int ocyls = 8,
```

```
            int oseats = 5, int odoors = 4 );
  void ctell();
};

car::car ( int odrive, int ocyls,
           int oseats, int odoors )
{
  drive = odrive;
  cyls = ocyls;
  seats = oseats;
  doors = odoors;
}

void car::ctell()
{
  cout << "This car has " << drive << " wheel drive, "
       << cyls << " cylinders, " << seats << " seats, and "
       << doors << " doors.\r\n";
}

void main()
{
  car *jaguar = new car;

  jaguar->ctell(); // MUST use a pointer for this access!
}
```

The last line of code in the main() function of this short program shows how to use the structure pointer operator to access a class object through a pointer. The technique is quite simple. The syntax is like the new, simplified ANSI syntax for calling functions through pointers, shown in the section "Sending Messages to Objects" earlier in this chapter.

A question may occur to you at this point. Why can't you use the more familiar calloc() or malloc() function to create class objects? You may, for instance, want to write something like this:

```
car *jaguar = (car *)malloc( sizeof( car ) );
```

There are two problems with this line of code: you must manually cast the pointer returned by malloc() to the car type; and it does not invoke the car class constructor in any way. In other words, you can certainly get sufficient *space* on the stack for a class object with malloc() or calloc(), but you cannot create a *class* object with either of them. The new operator, however, returns the correct type of pointer, and invokes the class constructor as well.

Declaring Pointers and Arrays of Objects

You can do with class objects just about anything you can do with data objects. You can, for instance, declare an array of objects (which does not require new), an array of pointers to objects (which requires new), or a pointer to an array of objects (which requires new).

Consider the most difficult case first: declaring an array of pointers to objects. This grouping is the most difficult to declare and does require the structure pointer operator in order to access a class member. Assume for a moment that you are still dealing with the car class. Look at the following new version of the main() function, using that class:

```
void main()
{
  int i;
  car *jaguar[4];  // array of 4 pointers to objects

  for ( i=0; i<4; ++i ) jaguar[i] = new car;
  for ( i=0; i<4; ++i ) jaguar[i]->ctell();
  for ( i=0; i<4; ++i ) delete jaguar[i];
}
```

The declaration car *jaguar[4] declares an array of pointers to class objects. Because of that, the new operator must be used for *each* array element. That is, new *always* returns a *single* pointer. The use and destruction of each of the class objects follow directly from that fact—you must use the structure pointer operator to access an array element's member function (a class object's member function), and you must use delete explicitly for each object pointed to by the array.

Now suppose that you create another fleet of four expensive cars, but the easy way—a whole fleet at a time. In this instance, you need a true default constructor like this one:

```
class car {
  ...
public:
  car();
  ...
};

car::car()
{
  drive = 2;
```

```
        cyls = 8;
        seats = 5;
        doors = 4;
    }
```

In some circumstances (that is, when deriving classes), a default constructor may be a constructor with *no* arguments (as shown here), or it may be one with *all default* arguments (as shown in the original `car` class). In *this* circumstance—creating an array of objects with `new`—*only* a default constructor function with no arguments will do. Borland C++ will refuse to compile the following `main()` function unless a true default constructor function is provided:

```
void main()
{
    int i;
    car *jaguar;   // ONE pointer to array of objects

    jaguar = new car[4]; // create them all!

    for ( i=0; i<4; ++i ) jaguar[i].ctell(); // no ptr deref!

    delete [4] jaguar; // destroy them all !
}
```

Here the pointer declaration `car *jaguar` has been left alone just to show that `jaguar` is *one* pointer. You could instead replace the fourth and fifth lines with the following single line:

```
    car *jaguar = new car[4];
```

Whether you use one or two lines of code, the result is the same. The `new` operator does the following:

1. `new` creates a contiguous array of class objects on the free store.

2. As each class object is created on the free store, `new` invokes the *default* constructor for the class to initialize the object.

3. `new` finally returns a *single* pointer, which contains the address of the first class object in the array.

The use of subscripts with the `jaguar` array in the `for` loop in the preceding code fragment illustrates another interesting point: even when dealing with arrays of class objects, you can still count on the equivalence of pointers and subscripts. If you recall your basic C theory, `*jaguar`, then, is the same as `jaguar[0]`. Therefore, you can refer to the array elements (which are class objects) as shown in the `for` loop in this code fragment.

Finally, you can get rid of the entire array of class objects with a single use of the `delete` operator. Look at the preceding code fragment carefully to see how this is done. The syntax `delete [4] jaguar` should be read as "delete four instances of the `jaguar` object, all found in a contiguous array."

Exercises

The following exercises give you practice in accessing class member functions, controlling the scope of class members, using C++ references, and using arrays of class objects.

1. Review the rules for using the scope resolution operator, as well as the general rules governing C++ scope. Trying to imagine what kind of code requires these rules may seem like a useless exercise, but the rules will be quite necessary when such code crops up naturally (you will reach that point sooner than you think).

2. Write several class declarations for various kinds of objects that interest you, and practice "sending messages to them" (calling member functions). Create some of the class objects locally and create some on the free store with `new`.

3. Experiment with the reference operator. Use it to access ordinary objects and class objects. Try using it to pass class objects as arguments to functions.

4. Imagine a class of objects that seems to belong naturally in a group or an array. Write the class, making it as full-featured as you can. Create an array of these objects.

Summary

Accessing a C++ object requires some sound knowledge of how class objects are used in C++. In this chapter, you learned the following points:

❑ *The scope resolution operator is used for general purposes, for controlling syntax, and for resolving ambiguities of reference.* You should have a good understanding of how to use the scope resolution operator before you approach Chapter 17 because derived classes frequently will require its use.

❏ *C++ scope rules for class objects go considerably beyond plain C scope rules.* Remember that a class is a scope! C++ scope rules are accordingly more complicated. It is possible to use the same name in different scopes, or to use the same name for a class and a type definition, and thus inadvertently hide one of the names.

❏ *You send messages to objects by calling member functions.* The `this` pointer contains the address of the correct instance object when a member function is entered.

❏ *References are disguised pointers to objects.* A reference provides an alternative name for an object, and references *always bind to objects.* A reference can therefore be an lvalue (be used on the left side of an assignment statement). References will prove to be quite important when you begin to write overloaded operator functions for your classes.

❏ *You can pass a class object to a function, both by value and by reference, and return a class object or reference to a class object from a function.*

❏ *The* `new` *operator can create an array of class objects at one time, calling the* default *constructor for each element (class object) in the array.* The `delete` operator can destroy a whole array of class objects at once.

With this material as background, you are now ready to learn about overloading functions and operators in C++.

14

Using Overloaded Functions and Operators in C++

When you overload a function or operator, you define multiple versions of it. Overloading is one of the distinctive and powerful features of C++.

If you consider C++ from the designer's point of view, it is not surprising that C++ enables you to overload functions and operators. Overloading is required for the C++ user-defined types that are the main feature of C-based OOP systems—you must define not only the object type but also the new type's behavior. Defining member functions that belong to a user-defined type (a class) is a straightforward way to define a class's behavior, and defining how the C operator set is to behave with the class is a natural extension of the concept.

Overloading Member Functions

Overloading member functions is easier to understand than overloading operators on a class basis simply because overloaded functions are declared with a familiar syntax. Overloaded operators are also declared, but not quite in the same way that you declare overloaded member or nonmember functions. This discussion therefore begins with the techniques for overloading member functions.

You have already seen one function for which you might want to provide several versions for a class: the constructor function. It is often convenient to have available several different constructor functions so that objects of the class can be created in different ways.

The idea applies to ordinary member functions as well. It may be convenient or necessary to provide several ways to manipulate class objects. A `temperature` class object, for example, may need two methods of setting a thermostat, depending on whether the Fahrenheit or Centigrade scale is used. This particular example, as well as a need for multiple constructor functions, suggests the more general idea that overloaded functions are appropriate whenever you want to avoid the overhead involved in function argument conversions, or you want to perform the same basic member function with different sets of arguments.

Keeping in mind the notions of conversion avoidance and multiple methods of performing a task, you can begin to discover all kinds of classes that might need or use overloaded member functions. In deciding what functions to overload and how to overload them, you should consider both *calling efficiency* and *calling convenience*.

Understanding C++ Overloading

You have just learned that overloading a function means providing multiple versions of that function. Although the feature is handy, it creates a problem immediately. If you have several versions of a function—`function_a()`, for instance—how does the compiler know at any given place in the source code *which* version of the function you mean to call? This problem is illustrated in figure 14.1.

A number of necessary features were deliberately left out of the functions shown in figure 14.1 to drive home a point. The C++ compiler can distinguish among multiple functions with the same name *only if they have different types*.

You have already learned about function type in plain C. A plain C function is a derived type: specifically, a function has type *function returning type*. That is, a plain C function is typed according to the fact that it *is* a function and also that it returns a given data type.

If C++ were to type functions according to the plain C rule, the compiler designer would have difficulty implementing function overloading. The reason is that changing only the return type is considered a signal that the function has been improperly redeclared. C++ needs something besides the return type in order to distinguish between two functions with the same name. That extra something is the *number and type of arguments*.

Fig. 14.1. Distinguishing among multiple functions with the same name creates a problem for the compiler designer.

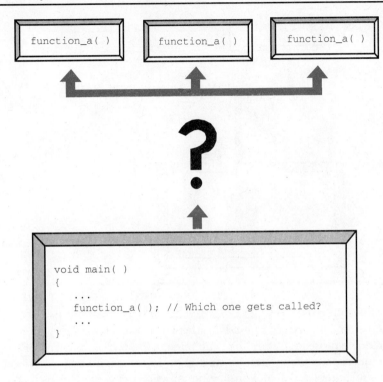

C++ goes beyond plain C in that C++ can match both the return type and the argument list of a function call to the "best matching" declaration. (This is one of the reasons that C++ requires full function prototyping of functions.) Because of this capability, the compiler can determine rather easily which function is intended in a particular function call (see fig. 14.2).

Thus, you can overload functions by declaring multiple functions with the same name and varying the number and type of arguments, or by varying both the return type *and* the arguments. You *cannot* overload functions by varying only the return type.

Now you have seen how to overload a member function and how to write a function call for an overloaded function. How do you suppose the compiler determines which particular function you meant to call? The search for the corresponding function proceeds in this order:

Fig. 14.2. The combination of arguments and return type identifies an overloaded function precisely.

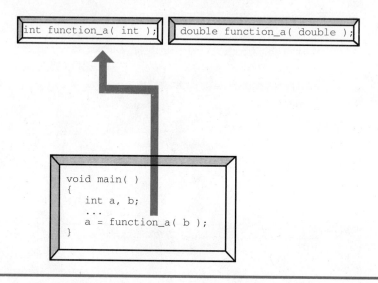

1. *All the functions with the same name and in the same scope as the function call are considered.* Restricting the search for a matching name is more important than you might expect. If overloading of functions in different scopes were allowed, you could easily overload a function by accident. For member functions, this rule means that only other member functions in the same class are considered (remember that a class is a scope!). If there is only one such function, it is selected immediately.

2. *A function with matching return type and arguments is searched for.* If a function call's arguments require no conversion or promotion to match one of the candidates, that function is called immediately.

3. *Possible conversions of the function call's arguments are examined.* If the function call's arguments can be converted in some way to match one of the overloaded function candidates, the matched function is called, using the converted or promoted arguments.

4. *If none of the preceding actions are successful, the call is illegal.* Only after every attempt to match return type and arguments as closely as possible will the function call be flagged as a compile-time error.

Borland C++ uses a "best match" algorithm in searching for a set of conversions or promotions for the function arguments. (Type conversions and promotions are covered in Chapter 2.) The controlling principle used in the best-match search is that the overloaded function requiring the least argument conversion is the best match. Note the rules followed by the compiler for performing the best-match search:

1. *Exact matches are best of all.* Obviously, if no conversion or promotion of arguments is required, the cleanest, fastest code is the result. There can also be no doubt which is the correct function.

2. *Matches requiring only argument promotions are the next best fit.* If promoting integers to more capable integers, or `floats` to `doubles`, is all that is needed for matching a function's argument types, that function is selected (failing an exact match). If several functions can be matched with promotions only, the function with the least number of promotions is best. (The base document says that the selected function must have at least one argument that is a better match than all other possible matches.)

3. *Matches requiring trivial or standard conversions are the next best fit.* Standard conversions (see Chapter 2) and trivial conversions are checked next. Again, the match requiring the least number of conversions is better. Trivial conversions are summarized in table 14.1.

4. *Matches requiring user-defined conversions are the next best fit.* You can write your own cast operator definitions (overload the cast operator) for your classes. User-defined casts can be used in matching arguments for an overloaded function call.

5. *Matches involving functions that use the ellipsis (. . .) are the worst match of all.* The reason is that the ellipsis indicates a variable number of unknown arguments. How can the compiler guarantee that variable arguments will match? Nevertheless, this criterion is used if all else fails.

Table 14.1. *C++ trivial conversions.*

Original Type		New Type	
object	`(T)`	reference	`(T&)`
reference	`(T&)`	object	`(T)`
subscript	`(T[])`	pointer	`(T*)`
call	`(T(args))`	call	`((*T)(args))`
object	`(T)`	constant	`(const T)`

Table 14.1. continues

Table 14.1. *continued*

Original Type		New Type	
object	(T)	volatile	(volatile T)
pointer	(T*)	const pointer	(const T*)
pointer	(T*)	volatile pointer	(volatile T*)

These rules cover just about all the theory of matching function arguments you will ever need. The next section shows you how to *write* overloaded functions.

Declaring Overloaded Member Functions

When Bjarne Stroustrup first introduced the C++ programming language in his 1986 book, people tended to think of function overloading as exotic. Thus, even though *member* functions and class object operators could be overloaded with no extra syntactical requirements, overloading a *nonmember* function required the use of the `overload` keyword in a declaration. Overloaded declarations for a `cube_root()` function, for example, had to be written like this:

```
overload cube_root;      // THIS IS OBSOLETE !!

double cube_root( double );

double cube_root( float );

double cube_root( int );

double cube_root( long );
```

By the time the AT&T 2.0 compilers appeared, though, overloading was regarded as an integral part of the user-defined type (class) definition process. The `overload` keyword is now obsolete (though still tolerated by many compilers, including Borland C++, for the sake of backward compatibility) and will probably soon not be supported at all. Borland C++ allows (and prefers) you to declare overloaded functions without any extra keywords.

Overloading functions is particularly easy within a class declaration; overloading seems to flow naturally from the programming environment. To overload a class member function, you just write more than one prototype declaration for the function name. Listing 14.1 illustrates how to overload class member functions in a simple, uncluttered program.

Listing 14.1. `strings.cpp`. *A program that shows overloading of class member functions.*

```
1   #include <string.h>
2   #include <stdlib.h>
3   #include <iostream.h>
4
5   class string {
6     int length;
7     char data[256];
8   public:
9     string() { length = 0; strcpy( data, "" ); }
10    string( char * );
11    char *search( char );
12    char *search( char * );
13  };
14
15  string::string( char *text )
16  {
17    if ( strlen( text ) < 256 )
18      strcpy( data, text );
19    else
20      strncpy( data, text, 255 );
21    length = strlen( data );
22  }
23
24  char *string::search( char arg )
25  {
26    return strchr( data, arg );
27  }
28
29  char *string::search( char *arg )
30  {
31    return strstr( data, arg );
32  }
33
34  void main()
35  {
36    string hellomsg = "Hello, there, I'm a string!";
37    char *found;
38
39    cout << hellomsg.search( 't' ) << "\r\n" ;
40    cout << hellomsg.search( "string" ) << "\r\n" ;
41  }
```

Notice in listing 14.1 that both the `string::string()` constructor and the `string::search()` member functions are overloaded (lines 9–12). The syntax for overloading these functions is simple, consisting of otherwise ordinary prototype declarations.

The class member function definitions (lines 15–32) are coded just like any class member functions—with the fully qualified names (except for the inline constructor, of course) followed by the formal parameter lists. Lines 39 and 40, within the `main()` function, show how the member functions are called. You just supply the desired argument types, and the compiler generates the call code for the correct version of the function.

Overloading Friend and Nonmember Functions

After member functions, functions that are friends of classes and functions that are not members of classes complete the inventory of the possible kinds of functions you can write in your C++ programs. All these kinds of functions can be overloaded. This section presents examples of overloading both friend and nonmember functions.

Overloading Friends of a Class

Overloading friend functions is nearly as easy as overloading ordinary member functions. The only difference between overloading friend and member functions is that the `friend` keyword is necessary, as it is for any friend function. You just write the friend function declarations, varying the arguments and possibly also the return types, just as for member functions. Friend function declarations are illustrated in the header file `keynew.hpp` (a keyboard handler class) in listing 14.2.

Listing 14.2. `keynew.hpp`. *A header file for the keyboard class, including overloaded friend functions.*

```
1   #define NORM 0
2   #define EXT   1
3
4   #define F1 59
```

```
 5   #define F2 60
 6   #define F3 61
 7   #define F4 62
 8   #define F5 63
 9   #define F6 64
10   #define F7 65
11   #define F8 66
12   #define F9 67
13   #define F10 68
14   #define F11 87    // May not work on some machines
15   #define F12 88    // May not work on some machines
16   #define INS 82
17   #define DEL 83
18   #define HOME 71
19   #define END 79
20   #define UPA 72
21   #define DNA 80
22   #define LFA 75
23   #define RTA 77
24   #define PGU 73
25   #define PGD 81
26
27   #define MAXPUSH 4096
28
29   class keynew {
30     int state;
31     int ch;
32     int lastpush;
33     int pushbuf[MAXPUSH][2];   //LIFO push buffer
34   public:
35     keynew( void );
36     void *operator new( size_t );   // Class operator new
37     void operator delete( void * ); // Class op. delete
38     void next( void );      // Get next state and character
39     void nexte( void );     // Get next state, character, echo
40     void push( int, int ); // Push state and character
41     void loadmac( char * );
42     friend int keystate( keynew & );   // Overloaded
43     friend int keystate( keynew * );   //    friend
44     friend int keyval( keynew & );     //       function
45     friend int keyval( keynew * );     //          prototypes
46   };
47
```

The overloaded friend functions in listing 14.2 are in lines 42–45. There are two versions of the `keynew::keystate()` function and two versions of the `keynew::keyval()` function. One version of each function accepts a reference to a `keynew` class object. The other version accepts a pointer to a `keynew` class object.

Before turning to the `keynew` class, you might want to notice the `MAXPUSH` object-like macro in line 27. `MAXPUSH` defines the size of the push buffer array— an array for recording both the key state (normal or extended ASCII) and the key value. Furthermore, the array is an array of `int`, not `char`. Because `MAXPUSH` is set to 4096, 16K of RAM are set aside for the push buffer. The point here is that you will probably want to create `keynew` objects only on the free store (with `new`), rather than globally (directly in the program) or locally (on the stack). An alternative, of course, is to reduce the size of the push buffer.

The friend function definitions for the `keynew` class are equally simple. You do not have to fully qualify the function names because friend functions do not belong to (are not in the scope of) their associated classes. You write the function definitions directly, as always, providing the required number of overloaded definitions. Both the member and friend function definitions for the `keynew` class are shown in listing 14.3.

Listing 14.3. `keynew.cpp`. *Class member functions for the keyboard class.*

```
 1   #include <stdlib.h>
 2   #include <stdio.h>
 3   #include <string.h>
 4   #include <conio.h>
 5
 6   #include "keynew.hpp"
 7
 8   keynew::keynew( void )
 9   {
10      state = NORM;
11      ch = '\0';
12      lastpush = MAXPUSH;
13   }
14
15   void *keynew::operator new( size_t size )
16   {
17      return ::new unsigned char[size]; // Call global new
18   }
19
20   void keynew::operator delete( void *objptr )
```

```
21  {
22     ::delete objptr;                         // Call global delete
23  }
24
25  void keynew::next( void )
26  {
27     if ( lastpush < MAXPUSH ) {    // Get it from push buffer
28        state = pushbuf[lastpush][0];
29        ch = pushbuf[lastpush][1];
30        ++lastpush;
31     }
32     else {
33        state = NORM;
34        ch = getch();
35        if ( !ch ) {
36           state = EXT;
37           ch = getch();
38        }
39     }
40  }
41
42  void keynew::nexte( void )
43  {
44     if ( lastpush < MAXPUSH ) {     // Get it from push buffer
45        state = pushbuf[lastpush][0];
46        ch = pushbuf[lastpush][1];
47        ++lastpush;
48     }
49     else {
50        state = NORM;
51        ch = getch();
52        if ( !ch ) {
53           state = EXT;
54           ch = getch();
55        }
56     }
57     if ( !state ) putchar( ch ); // if not ext ASCII
58  }
59
60  void keynew::push( int kstate, int kval )
61  {
```

Listing 14.3. continues

Listing 14.3. continued

```
62    if ( lastpush > 0 ) {
63      --lastpush;
64      pushbuf[lastpush][0] = kstate;
65      pushbuf[lastpush][1] = kval;
66    }
67  }
68
69  void keynew::loadmac( char *msg )
70  {
71    char *p;
72    int i;
73
74    p = msg + strlen( msg ) - 1; // Push down kybd macro
75    for( i=strlen(msg); i>0; --i ) push( 0, *p-- );
76  }
77
78  int keystate( keynew &kybd )   // Overloaded friend
79  {                              //  functions start
80    return kybd.state;           //    *** HERE ***
81  }
82
83  int keystate( keynew *kybd )
84  {
85    return kybd->state;
86  }
87
88  int keyval( keynew &kybd )
89  {
90    return kybd.ch;
91  }
92
93  int keyval( keynew *kybd )
94  {
95    return kybd->ch;
96  }
```

The function definitions for the overloaded keynew friend functions are found in lines 78–96 of listing 14.3. The function bodies, like the function declarations, merely reflect the different kinds of arguments accepted by the different functions.

To complete the demonstration, listing 14.4 shows a main program that uses the keynew class. The program's sole purpose is to load text data into the push buffer, using the keynew::loadmac() member function, and then to extract the data again.

Listing 14.4. testnew.cpp. A program that tests and exercises the keyboard class.

```
1   #include <stdlib.h>
2   #include <stdio.h>
3   #include <string.h>
4
5   #include "keynew.hpp"
6
7   main()
8   {
9     int i;                    // Declare an ordinary object ...
10    keynew *kybd = new keynew;  // Create keyboard object
11
12  char *msgs[] = {
13    "This is a keyboard object message block."
          " It was created\n",
14    "just to test the keyboard macro facility."
          " You don't have\n",
15    "to do anything, just watch the message roll"
          " up on the screen.\n",
16    "To exit the program, strike Enter.\n",
17  };
18                              // Load the macro lines backwards, so
19                              // they will read forward
20
21    for ( i=3; i>=0; --i ) kybd->loadmac( msgs[i] );
22
23                      // Call to keyval() uses overloaded friend
24
25    do { kybd->nexte(); } while ( keyval( kybd ) != 13 );
26  }
```

In listing 14.4, look at line 25—the point of interest here. The keyval() function is called, using the object name kybd as an argument. Because kybd is a pointer to a keynew object, the corresponding overloaded friend function is invoked (the function defined in lines 93–96 of listing 14.3).

Overloading Nonmember Functions

Declaring overloaded nonmember, nonfriend functions is the simplest form of function overloading. Because C++ functions *must* at least be declared before they can be called, you need merely to write the multiple declarations for the different versions of the function. The `cube_root()` function mentioned earlier in this chapter is a good example of this kind of overloaded function declaration. You write the declarations like this:

```
double cube_root( double );
double cube_root( float );
double cube_root( int );
double cube_root( long );
```

This time, notice that the `overload` keyword is nowhere in sight. Because Borland C++ is compatible with the latest *de facto* standards in C++, the `overload` keyword is obsolete.

You should consider two additional issues when overloading functions, whether they are member, friend, or nonmember functions. These issues are the handling of *functions with default arguments* and the handling of *functions with unused formal arguments*.

Because functions with default arguments and functions with unused formal arguments are unique to C++, questions about handling them do not arise when you write plain C programs. The following short program (which compiles and runs under Borland C++) incorporates examples of default arguments and unused formal arguments in one function:

```
#include <iostream.h>
#include <stdlib.h>

int f1( int = 0, int = 0 );

void main()
{
   cout << f1() << "\r\n" ;
}

int f1( int value, int )
{
   return value;
}
```

This program shows only one nonmember function, but the following discussion applies to member and friend functions as well.

Notice that the function f1() has two default arguments. Therefore, for purposes of argument matching for overloaded functions, C++ assumes that there are *three* overloaded functions with different numbers of arguments. This makes sense when you realize that f1() can legally be called in the following three ways:

```
f1();
f1( 0 );
f1( 0, 0 );
```

Generally, then, a function with *n* default arguments is considered (for argument-matching purposes) as *n+1* functions having the same name and different numbers of arguments. The point, naturally, is that if you write a call to a function with default arguments so that argument conversions are necessary, a complicated matching sequence (and a needlessly inefficient call) might result.

Now notice that the function *definition* for f1() does not name the second (unused) formal argument. A couple of things are going on here. First, even if an unused formal argument is unnamed, a call to that function must still specify an argument to be passed to the function. Next, the short program just shown has default arguments, which masks the first fact. The important point to understand is this: although unused formal arguments do not appear in the function body, they *do* participate in argument matching for overloaded functions.

Understanding Type-Safe Linkage

Because the overload keyword is now obsolete, the C++ compiler has more responsibility in detecting overloaded functions and sorting out the calls to such functions. That is, the compiler must provide *type-safe linkage* to functions. The solution to any design problems that may result is *function mangling* (the C++ method of typing functions). Making some changes in the way linkage is handled in C++ programs may be required also. Both these subjects are discussed in this section.

Understanding Function Mangling

What's in a name? Everyday wisdom holds that a name is only a surface label and does not change the internal substance of a person or thing. This is only partly true for the compiler designer and, indirectly, for the compiler user.

What's in a C++ name? Function overloading makes it appear—at the source-code level—that you can have the same name for several different functions. This is true only at the source-code level, and then only *apparently* true. In the more technical language of the base document and of compiler design theory, overloading function names is just a *syntactical convenience* for the programmer. When processing source code, the compiler must generate a *unique name* for every distinct object and function. Otherwise, the compiler could never locate the precise object or function again.

A unique internal name is provided during compilation through the process of *function mangling*. The internal name (which exists on the symbol table during compilation) consists of the function name, return type, and signature. A function's signature is nothing more than its argument list. The signature is what primarily distinguishes a particular overloaded function. The signature is unique because of the exact number and type of arguments for the function. Forming unique internal identifiers for an overloaded function name is illustrated in figure 14.3.

Fig. 14.3. *Each mangled name for an overloaded function constitutes a unique identifier and type for the function during compilation.*

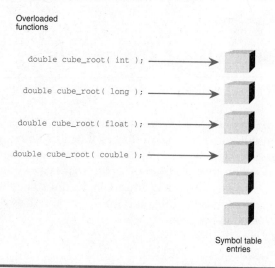

Overloaded functions

```
double cube_root( int );
double cube_root( long );
double cube_root( float );
double cube_root( couble );
```

Symbol table entries

Recent C++ compilers, including Borland C++, provide a feature that guarantees calling the correct version of an overloaded function. This feature is called *type-safe linkage*, which is implemented through nothing less than function mangling.

A problem now arises. How can the compiler know beforehand which functions are overloaded (and therefore need mangling) and which functions are not? The compiler cannot know, but there is a solution to the problem: Borland C++ and comparable C++ compilers mangle *all* functions.

You might think that mangling all functions would solve every possible problem related to redefining and overloading functions. Unfortunately, that is not the case.

On two occasions, function mangling can fail to keep track of which function is intended to be called by a given function call. You can easily introduce errors when redeclaring functions in multiple source-file programs and when including modules from other languages.

Problems caused by accidental redeclaration of a function across two source files are most severe when porting a program from one compiler to another compiler (which may implement types somewhat differently). Such redeclaration can also cause mild problems for a single compiler, even a robust one like Borland C++. Suppose, for example, that you have one source file which contains a function to deal with characters (signed characters, by default, in Borland C++). The first source file might look like this:

```
#include <stdio.h>

void dchar( char c )
{
    printf( "%d\n", (int)c );
}
```

The dchar() function is simple enough; it displays only the numeric value of the character code passed to it. What could go wrong with such a simple function, especially when type-safe linkage is there to protect you? To find out, compile the short source file separately, and then edit and compile the following source file that calls the dchar() function:

```
#include <stdio.h>

extern void dchar( unsigned char );

void main()
{
    dchar( 128 );
}
```

All appears well—until you actually try to run the linked program. Instead of displaying the value 128, as you would expect from examining the source code in the second file, the output actually displays -128. An unintentional conversion of type occurred, leading to an unexpected interpretation of the numeric value involved. Function mangling never had a chance to prevent the problem.

The best cure for this kind of problem is prevention, and the best prevention is well-managed header files. Edit the extern declarations once, in an .H or .HPP header file, and use #include to include the header in other source files. Of course, this strategy still doesn't guarantee that you will never make an error, but it certainly reduces the chances of an error.

Controlling Linkage Problems with Standard C Include Files

The second problem with function mangling and type-safe linkage occurs when you mix modules from other languages with C++ modules. Surprisingly, plain C must be considered a different language for this purpose. It may seem reasonable to expect to call plain C standard library functions directly, but that just won't work—unless something is done to make it work.

You cannot call these library functions directly because of function mangling. A mangled function name is not the same as an unmangled name (which does not contain return type and signature data). Therefore, if C++ mangles *all* function names, how can it ever find, say, the standard printf() function during linkage editing? The answer is that the compiler can't. The linkage editor ends up trying to match names (conceptually) like this:

```
int_printf_vargs ?== printf
```

Clearly, there has to be some way to turn mangling off when you want to reference plain C function names (such as *all* the standard library functions) in separately compiled modules. Of course, there is a way. To see what it is, use the Borland C++ editor to look at some of the standard C header files in the \include directory. The method of turning off function mangling is called *alternate linkage specification*. If, for example, you examine the stdlib.h header supplied with Borland C++, you will see declarations structured something like this:

```
/*        stdlib.h        */

    ... Preliminary macros and definitions go here.

extern "C" {

    ... Function declarations go here.

    ... Since function names declared here are known
    ... NOT to be mangled, the linkage editor will be
    ... able to find them when linking in plain C
    ... modules.

}
```

The general syntax for specifying alternate linkage for single declarations is fairly simple:

```
extern "C" double get_area( double circum );
extern "C" double get_circum( double area );
```

Or you can specify alternate linkage for a whole group of declarations at once by surrounding them with curly braces, just as you would for a compound C statement:

```
extern "C" {
    double get_area( double circum );
    double get_circum( double area );
}
```

In most cases, you will use the extern "C" linkage specifier in your own header files. Linkage specifiers are not restricted to header files, however. From time to time, you may need to use the single-declaration form of the specifier directly within a program source-code file. As with all things C, some rules govern the use of linkage specifiers:

❑ *"C++" is the default linkage and is always required to be present in every C++ compiler.* This rule simply means that function mangling in "on" by default in a C++ program.

❑ *You cannot invent your own linkage strings.* From the point of view of the compiler designer, the value of the "C" and "C++" linkage strings is somewhat arbitrary; the compiler doesn't "care" what strings are used. Once they are set in place (by the designer), they are fixed: if you try to invent a string unknown to the compiler, an error results.

❏ *Linkage specifiers can appear only at file scope.* You cannot write a linkage specifier locally, within a function, like this:

```
int dosumpin( int arg1 )
{
    extern "C" double sumpinelse( double ); // ILLEGAL !!
    ...
}
```

Although you can, as you may recall, use the extern keyword within a function body to declare ordinary linkage elsewhere within the source file, use of the alternate linkage specifier is strictly illegal within a function body. This restriction is used in C++ to avoid requiring compilers to incorporate multiple linkages in different scopes.

❏ *Linkage specifications do not create a new scope.* You may recall that a block statement, enclosed in curly braces, creates a local scope in both C and C++. Despite the similarities to block statement syntax, the compound form of the linkage specifier—extern "C" {...} —is not a block statement and does not create a local scope.

❏ *Linkage specifications are transmitted to inner scopes.* This rule means that a linkage specification applied to a class applies to all *non*member functions and data objects declared within the class. Moreover, a linkage specification applied to a function applies to functions and objects declared (not defined!) within the contained function.

❏ *Multiple declarations for the same function, both with and without explicit linkage specification, can exist in the same source file.* If this occurs, you must write the declaration with explicit linkage specification first, followed by the declaration without any linkage specification. You can use this feature to "phase in" a new C++ version of a function while still maintaining an older, plain C version. The declarations for two such functions are packaged in this way:

```
extern "C" void dosumpin( int ); // Declare old version

void routeold( int arg )
{
        // Establish external linkage to outer declaration
        // to old dosumpin()
    extern void dosumpin( int );

        // Now call the old version
```

```
      dosumpin( arg );
}


// -------- Now set up new C++ version --------
// The new version provides return status information

int dosumpin( int );   // C++ version


...

void main()
{
   int i;

   routeold( 2 );       // Call the old C version
   i = dosumpin( 2 ); // Get return info from new version
}
```

❑ *You can write a linkage specifier for an entire* #include *file.*
Usually, you will write linkage specifiers for various declarations
inside header files. If, however, you do not want to modify the
contents of a header file, you can declare alternate linkage for the
whole header:

```
      extern "C" {
         #include "myheader"
      }
```

❑ *Only one of a group of overloaded functions can have "C" linkage.* It
requires only a moment's thought to figure this one out. Overloading
is the "reason for being" for function mangling. If you turn it off for
more than one overloaded function, you end up with two *different*
functions having *exactly* the same name—resulting in the expected
compiler error.

❑ *Functions and objects declared within a linkage specification act as
if they were explicitly declared* extern, *unless they were explicitly
declared* static. You can naturally assume that declarations surrounded by a linkage specification are found in another source
module—hence, the assumption of extern linkage. You may recall,
however, that the static keyword forces internal linkage. Therefore,
even though you can declare an object or function static within the
{} of a linkage specification, the linkage specification is effectively
ignored for those static objects or functions.

Overloading Operators with C++

Operators are a critically important part of the C and C++ languages. Operators give you the power and flexibility to manipulate data in an astonishing number of ways, as you saw in Chapter 2.

The introduction of user-defined types, or classes, in C++ raises new issues about the operator set. Specifically, if it is the programmer's responsibility to define the behavior of a new type, as well as its data content, how are C operators affected by the new environment? The answer is simple: you must define how the operator set works with your new classes. This process is called *operator overloading*. It is similar to function overloading because a single operator can now have different significance for different objects. Furthermore, if you do not overload a particular operator for a class, it cannot be used with objects of that class. It's all up to you. In this section, you learn how to overload C operators for your classes.

Understanding Operator Overloading

You can, and indeed must, overload an operator before it can be used with objects of your just-invented new class. This does not mean, however, that you can invent new operators of your own. *You can overload only a subset of the existing C++ operator set*. Most of the C++ operators (which are in themselves a superset of the plain C operators) can be overloaded. Table 14.2 shows which C++ operators you can overload.

Table 14.2. C++ operators that can be overloaded.

new	delete					
+	–	*	/	%	^	&
¦	~					
!	=	<	>	+=	–=	*=
/=	=					
=	&=	¦=	<<	>>	<<=	>>=
==	!=					
<=	>=	&&	¦¦	++	––	,
–>*	–>					
()	[]					

Four of the operators in table 14.2 have both binary and unary forms, depending on where in an expression they are used. These are the addition or positive (+), subtraction or negative (–), multiplication or dereference (*), and AND or address-of (&) operators.

Two of the operators shown in table 14.2, the increment (++) and decrement (––) operators, can be used in either a prefix (++*object*) or postfix (*object*++) position. Note carefully that even though you can overload these operators to accept many different types of arguments, you cannot distinguish between their prefix and postfix use. You can overload the ++ operator in Borland C++ in the following way:

```
#include <iostream.h>

class A {
public:
  int data;
  A& operator++();
}

A& A::operator++()
{
  ++data;
  return *this;
}
```

As you can see from the preceding code fragment, nothing inherent in it distinguishes the difference between prefix and postfix notation. You can verify this notation for yourself. Create a source file with the class just shown and follow it with this `main()` function:

```
void main()
{
  A x = {2};
  A y;


// Borland C++ 2.0 has no way to distinguish
// the following two operations. They both behave as if
// the prefix increment notation were used.

  y = ++x;
  cout << y.data << "\r\n";
  y = x++;
  cout << y.data << "\r\n";
}
```

The resulting program was compiled and tested. For both prefix and postfix use, the code acted as if only the prefix increment operator had been used.

On this issue, Borland C++ is slightly behind the cutting edge of C++ developments. The latest documentation requires C++ compilers to provide support for distinguishing prefix and postfix notation. Listing 14.5 contains a program that will work on the latest AT&T C++ compilers but will *not* compile under Borland C++.

Listing 14.5. `incrovld.cpp`. *A program that contains* `operator++()` *functions that can distinguish prefix and postfix notation on non-Borland C++ compilers.*

```
1   #include <iostream.h>
2
3   class A {
4   public:
5     int data;
6     A& operator++();     // For PREFIX notation
7     A& operator++(int); // For POSTFIX notation
8   };
9
10  A& A::operator++()
11  {
12    ++data;
13    return *this;
14  }
15
16  A& A::operator++(int) // Notice unused arg
17  {
18    data++
19    return *this;
20  }
21
22  void main()
23  {
24    A x = {2};
25    A y;
26
27    y = x++;
28    cout << y.data << "\r\n";
29  }
```

In listing 14.5, look at lines 6 and 7, which contain *two* prototypes for the `operator++()` function. The first, in line 6, is the only form that Borland C++ accepts. This prototype has no arguments (or one argument, if you count the implicitly present `this` pointer). The form is used for prefix incrementation in those compilers that support detection of prefix and postfix syntax.

The second prototype, in line 7, takes one argument (two, counting `this`), which must have type `int`. When the postfix notation is detected, this is the version of the overloaded function that is invoked. The integer argument is always zero, and may be ignored (see line 16). That is, the notation `object++` is treated syntactically as if it were `object + 0` when it is found in an expression.

Although Borland C++ does not yet support prefix and postfix increment operators, most other compilers do not support them either. Still, the base document states a requirement for such support, and some compilers do support them. The discussion is included here for completeness and so that you will have a head start when the feature does appear in Borland C++.

Four C++ operators and two preprocessing operators cannot be overloaded. These operators are shown in table 14.3.

Table 14.3. *C++ operators that cannot be overloaded.*

Operator	Description
.	Structure or class member access operator
.*	Pointer to member operator
::	Scope resolution operator
?:	Conditional (ternary) operator
#	Preprocessing stringizing operator
##	Preprocessing string concatenation operator

The class member (`.`), pointer to member (`.*`), and scope resolution (`::`) operators all have predefined meanings that would be difficult or impossible to change dynamically. These operators are therefore excluded from the list of overloadable operators. And the C++ designers simply felt that the conditional or ternary (`?:`) operator was not worth the effort of overloading. Finally, overloading preprocessing operators is a practical impossibility, as they are not used during the actual compilation process.

Because the pointer to class member operator (.*) is rarely seen, and almost never explained, this operator is shown in action in listing 14.6.

Listing 14.6. `ptrmbr.cpp`. *A program that uses a pointer to a class member.*

```
1   #include <iostream.h>
2
3   class A {
4     int value;
5   public:
6     A( int );
7   };
8
9   A::A( int which )
10  {
11    switch ( which ) {
12      case 1 : value = 1;
13              break;
14      case 2 : value = 2;
15              break;
16      case 3 : value = 3;
17              break;
18      default: value = 1;
19              break;
20    }
21  }
22
23  void display( A& arg )
24  {
25    int A::* type;
26    type = &A::value;
27
28    cout << arg.*type << "\r\n";
29  }
30
31  void main()
32  {
33    A x = 3;   // type 3
34
35    display( x );
36  }
```

The use of the pointer to member operator in listing 14.6 is admittedly somewhat contrived. Still, it illustrates the syntax required and the procedure used to bring the parts together. The `.*` operator is put to work in the `A::display()` function found in lines 23–29.

The first thing to understand is how the pointer to member *variable* is itself declared (see line 25). The declaration has three parts:

❑ *The type of the member pointed to.* This is not the type of the pointer variable (obviously), but the type of the data object or function pointed to. In the program in listing 14.6, the type is `int` because that is the type of `A::value`.

❑ *The pointer to member declarator.* In the construction

    classname::*

the name that follows identifies a pointer to member. Remember that the purpose, for the moment, is to declare a *pointer variable* although it is not an ordinary pointer.

❑ *The pointer to member identifier.* This is just the name of the pointer to the member object. In listing 14.6, the name of the pointer variable is `type`.

To put the pointer to member to use, you need some way to initialize the pointer to member variable. The method for doing this is found in line 26. The expression `&A::value` takes the address of the member object. The following syntax is the general form for taking the address of a class member:

    &classname::membername

Its construction is not really surprising. The address-of operator (`&`) does just what a C programmer would expect, and the fully qualified name of the member object is required to prevent ambiguous references.

You must also dereference the pointer to member to access the object to which it points. The syntax for doing this is a little different from that in plain C (see line 28 of listing 14.6). You use the following general form:

    objectname.*ptr_to_member_name

When dereferenced, as shown in line 28, the pointer to member refers to an ordinary member object. It is then an *object locator*, used in the same way as for dereferencing ordinary pointers. As an object locator, it can be used as either an lvalue or rvalue.

Note some additional considerations when you write overloaded operator functions. Table 14.4 shows characteristics of various kinds of overloaded operator functions. These characteristics pertain to class inheritance, virtual overloaded operator functions, return types, function accessibility, and default generation.

Table 14.4. *Characteristics of the overloaded operator functions.*

C++ Operator	Can Be Inherited	Can Be Virtual	Can Have Return Type	Member or Friend	Generated by Default
( )	yes	yes	yes	member	no
[ ]	yes	yes	yes	member	no
->	yes	yes	yes	member	no
op=( )	no	yes	yes	member	memberwise
new	yes	no	void*	static member	no
delete	yes	no	void	static member	no
other ops	yes	yes	yes	either	no

The first six entries in table 14.4 give the characteristics of user-defined functions for special operators; the last entry gives the characteristics for all remaining operators.

Of the operators shown in table 14.4, the assignment operator is unique. It cannot be inherited; all the others can. It is the only operator for which the compiler generates a default overloaded function. If you do not declare an overloaded assignment-operator function, the compiler generates one that copies the class object, member by member.

Although restrictions on operator function linkage are not shown directly in table 14.4, some restrictions are implied. The first four operators—( ), [ ], ->, and =—must be *nonstatic* member functions. The new and delete operators *must* be static functions; they are assumed to be even if you don't code the static keyword in the function declaration. The static storage class for new and delete is dictated by the fact that these two operators, apart from all the others, must already exist *before* the class object has been completely constructed and initialized. The rest of the operators can be either static or nonstatic, and either member or friend functions.

All the operator functions in table 14.4 can also be declared as virtual functions, with the exception of the class `new` and `delete` operators (that is, not global `new` and `delete`). The class `new` and `delete` operators have the additional requirement that the return types shown in the table are mandatory.

Declaring Overloaded Operator Functions

Before jumping directly into examples of overloading operators, you should pause and take stock of what will be required of you (what you should already know) and what you want to accomplish. This section covers some fairly complicated ground. If you aren't adequately prepared to approach the subject of overloading operators, your time will not be well spent.

Setting the Stage for Operator Functions

You should already have a clear idea of what a member function is, what the C++ operators (the ordinary ones) do, and how functions pass and return values. Most important, you should have a strong grasp of C++ references, how to form them, and what they do. Remember that *references bind to objects*, not addresses (even though addresses are at work behind the scenes).

For our part, we have found, while learning C++ and trying to explain it to other programmers, that several important questions must be answered for the person learning to overload operators:

❏ *How do you declare overloaded operator functions?* Without a knowledge of the fundamental syntax involved and its significance, operator overloading becomes a hopeless muddle in the mind of the would-be C++ practitioner. The syntax is fairly simple, but it is rather strange looking.

❏ *What arguments are passed to operator functions?* How many arguments can an overloaded operator function accept? Is the number different for friend and member functions? Should the arguments be objects, pointers, or references—and how do you know when to choose each of these? As you can see, this particular discussion is important, as well as a source of potential confusion.

❏ *Should you return objects or references?* Does it make any difference whether you return objects or references? What if you are returning a *class* object? How is efficiency of execution affected? And do you need to know how the C++ compiler parses expressions? This topic is important also. Miss the boat here, and you will find yourself wondering what happened (with no hope of finding out).

❏ *When should you use friend functions, and when should you use member functions?* And does the choice make any real difference? Using friend functions in the right places can affect program performance. There are also some wrong places to use friend functions.

❏ *How do you handle cast operators?* Yes, you can even overload cast operators in C++. This topic has not yet been raised, so you will need to know about basic syntax, return types, linkage—the works.

Understanding Overloaded Operator Function Syntax

Answers to all of the preceding questions, beginning with the first, are provided in this section and the next several sections. Listing 14.7 contains a program that illustrates how to overload operators.

Listing 14.7. Savings.cpp. A program that overloads the ! and = operators.

```
 1   #include <stdio.h>
 2   #include <stdlib.h>
 3   #include <string.h>
 4
 5   class savings {
 6     double total;
 7   public:
 8     savings() { total = 0.0; }           // CONSTRUCTOR FUNCTIONS
 9     savings( double amt ) { total = amt; }
10     savings( int amt ) { total = (double)amt; }
11     savings( long amt ) { total = (double)amt; }
12     double operator!();                  // REPORT FUNCTION
13     savings& operator=( savings& );   // ASSIGNMENT OPERATORS
14     savings& operator=( double );
15     savings& operator=( int );
16     savings& operator=( long );
17   };
18
19   double savings::operator!()
```

```
20   {
21      return total;
22   }
23
24   savings& savings::operator=( savings& otheracct )
25   {
26      total = otheracct.total; // Notice ref to other object
27      return *this;            // Notice return of ref. type
28   }
29
30   savings& savings::operator=( double amt )
31   {
32      total = amt;
33      return *this;
34   }
35
36   savings& savings::operator=( int amt )
37   {
38      total = (double)amt;
39      return *this;
40   }
41
42   savings& savings::operator=( long amt )
43   {
44      total = (double)amt;
45      return *this;
46   }
47
48   void main()
49   {
50      savings account1( 100.01 );
51      savings account2, account3;  // using default constr
52
53                   // The following syntax requires the return of
54                   // a reference from assign op
55      account3 = account2 = account1;
56      printf( "The savings account now has $%10.2lf dollars\n",
57              !account3 );
58   }
```

Listing 14.7 shows constructor functions and operators overloaded in such a way as to allow the creation or manipulation of a savings object with double, integer, long, or other `savings` objects. Because you are already familiar with constructor functions, turn immediately to the operator functions. The declarations for the overloaded operator functions are found in lines 12–16. Here is the general form of the declaration:

```
returntype operator@( arg   );
                         opt
```

In this declaration, `operator` is a keyword to be coded exactly as you see it here, and @ represents the particular operator you are overloading. The argument *arg* is required only for binary operators.

The *returntype* that you specify for an overloaded operator function depends on what you want the operator to do. Line 12, for example, shows that `savings::operator!()` returns a `double`, indicating the amount of money in the savings account. This particular operator function is, in fact, a good example of the flexibility allowed in defining operator behavior for a class. Because the NOT function usually associated with the ! operator has little significance for the `savings` class, that operator has been "borrowed" to report a value.

Note, however, that such flexibility does *not* mean that you can take liberties with the normal syntax for an operator, any more than you can invent new operators. You can see, for example, in line 57 of listing 14.7 that the operator is written in the usual manner:

```
!account3
```

`account3` is a `savings` class instance object.

Looking again at the syntax for the declaration of an overloaded operator, notice next that the operator keyword is required in the declaration. Although you may substitute a particular operator for the @ in the syntax form, you must code *some* legitimate operator in that position.

Specifying Arguments for Overloaded Operator Functions

Now consider the significance of the optional argument shown in the syntax form. What does it mean? Are other arguments available? The `savings::operator!()` declaration has no arguments, whereas each of the `savings::operator=( arg )` declarations in lines 13–16 of listing 14.7 has one argument.

To understand what arguments are made available to operator functions, you need to recall what happens to *any* member function when it is called. (The use of friends for operator functions, which is slightly different, is discussed later in this section.) The significant point is that a member function *always* has the `this` pointer as its implicit first or only argument. How this affects the implementation of `savings::operator( savings& )`, for example, is shown in figure 14.4.

Fig. 14.4. `operator=( arg )` *has two arguments, one of which is the* `this` *pointer.*

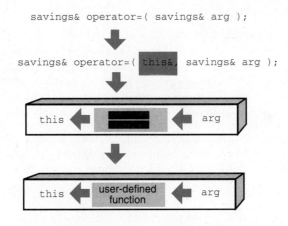

As you can see in figure 14.4, an `operator=()` function with one argument coded *actually* has two arguments: the object on the left side of the assignment is pointed to by `this`, and the object on the right side of the assignment is described by the coded argument (a reference to a `savings` class object in fig. 14.4). Because of this arrangement, the function definition for this particular assignment overload is coded like this:

```
savings& savings::operator=( savings& otheracct )
{
   total = otheracct.total; // Notice ref to other object
   return *this;            // Notice return of ref. type
}
```

Within the function body, the operand on the left is located by the current member variable `total`. The operand on the right is located by the class object passed as an argument to the function, so that access to the operand requires the qualified name `otheracct.total`.

Specifying a Return Type for an Operator Function

The returned value is important also. The comments near the end of listing 14.7 indicate that the syntax of the statement in line 55 requires that the assignment-operator overloaded functions return a reference instead of an object. You can see in lines 27, 33, 39, and 45 that this is precisely what the functions do. However, the syntax of multiple assignment (a = b = c) does not strictly require returning a reference. You could, if you wanted, return an object by value. So why return a reference?

Look closely at *what* reference the `operator=()` functions return: it is a reference to the object pointed to by `this`. Thus, only an object locator (the reference, which is a disguised pointer) for the operand on the left is needed, and the object referred to already exists. The reference to the left-side operand then becomes the right-side argument in the next assignment operator to the left. That is, returning a reference in such a case is very efficient.

Consider the alternative of returning an object by value. The following code fragment shows how you would have to recode the `savings` class to return objects by value from the operator overload functions:

```
class savings {    // POOR METHOD FOR OVERLOADING =
  ...
public:
  savings operator=( savings );
  ...
};
...
savings savings::operator( savings& otheracct )
{
  total = otheracct.total; // still a reference!
  return *this;            // Return whole object
}
```

The most obvious thing about this new version of the `savings` class is that now the whole object must be copied onto the stack and returned to be used in further evaluating the expression a = b. Moving whole objects, particularly large ones, on and off the stack can be expensive both in stack space and execution time.

With multiple assignments in one expression, however, you can still leave the *argument* defined as a reference. Even though a rightmost assignment returns an object, remember that *references bind to objects*. Therefore, in an expression of the form a = b, b can be either a value or a reference because either one is an object locator. All this is just another way of saying that references can be viewed as merely providing an alternative name for an *object*.

Note one final point about the `operator=()` functions for the `savings` class: they are member functions, not friend functions. This requirement was shown in table 14.4. Overloaded operator functions *must* be nonstatic member functions.

Now consider overloaded functions for the `+=`, `-=`, and other compound assignment operators. These functions should be coded with references for return values, even though the compound assignment operator only modifies an existing object. You might think that for such expressions as

```
savings account;
...
account += 256.65;
```

it is perfectly acceptable to write the following `void` return type:

```
void savings operator+=( double );
```

After all, the `account` object is simply updated, and that is the end of the matter. Right? Wrong! Suppose that you used a `void` return type as shown, and you then write something like this:

```
printf( "After deposits, you have $%10.2lf dollars.\n",
        !(account += 256.64) );
```

What happens? As you may recall, the `%10.2lf` conversion specifier means that `printf()` expects a `double` for its first argument after the format string. If `void` is the return type, the preceding line does not compile. If it does compile, you will find that a `void` is not the same as a `double`. If, however, you declared `operator+=()` to return a reference to a `savings` object, the expression `!(account += 256.64)` will be correctly evaluated in the following manner:

1. First, the interior expression `account += 256.64` is evaluated. That is, the compiler generates code to call `operator+=(double)`, which in turn results in a reference to a `savings` object.

2. Next, the `!` operator (which is overloaded!) is applied to the resulting reference to a `savings` object. This operator, remember, returns a `double`—which is just what the `printf()` function expects.

Overloading Operators with Friend Functions

There are all sorts of instances, however, in which it is preferable to use friend functions—for example, when you use compound assignment operators (+=, -=, and so on). Only the simple assignment operator must be a member and cannot be inherited. Compound assignment operators can be friends, and they can be inherited.

Why use friends to overload operators? There are various reasons in various contexts for using friend functions. The reason in the context of operator overload functions is *flexibility*. That is, friend functions allow you to specify arguments for *both* the left- and right-side operands of an operator, so that user-defined conversions can be applied to both operands.

Member operator functions, however, expect only one argument and *assume* that the left operand is *this. Thus, the left operand cannot be converted in this case and must be a lvalue. The significance of this restriction for object behavior is discussed in detail in Chapter 18. In the meantime, use friend functions wherever you can. If you examine Borland C++'s include file complex.h, for example, you will discover that almost all the functions are friends—all that are possible, in fact.

Before examining some examples of friend functions that overload operators for the savings class, consider how using friend functions will affect the argument list structure (the signature). The main thing affecting the design of friend operator functions is that friend functions are not in the scope of the class for which they are declared. That is, *there is no* this *pointer supplied automatically*.

How, then, does a friend operator function "know" what the current object is? It doesn't, unless you tell it. The implied first operator in figure 14.4 (shown earlier) cannot be implied in a friend function—the operator must be explicit. The general form for declaring friend operator functions is this:

```
friend returntype operator@( arg ,arg     );
                                      opt
```

The first argument corresponds to the left-side operand of the operator, and the second argument corresponds to the right-side operand of the operator. Overloaded friend functions for binary operators always require *two* arguments because of the missing this pointer. Friend functions and unary operators are covered in the next section.

You can further expand the savings class by adding operator functions for the subtraction (-) and compound subtraction (-=) operators. We picked this precise pair of operators so that the different effects of the return types can be highlighted. Here are the declarations and functions for these operators:

```
class savings {
  ...
public:
  friend& savings operator-=( savings&, savings& );
```

```
    friend& savings operator-=( savings&, double );
    friend savings operator-( savings&, savings& );
    friend savings operator-( savings&, double );
};
...
savings& operator-=( savings& curr, savings& other )
{
  curr.total -= other.total; // Use global -=
  return curr;                // Return ref to left-side op
}


savings& operator-=( savings& curr, double amt )
{
  curr.total -= amt;          // Use global -=
  return curr;                // Return ref to left-side op
}


savings operator-( savings& curr, savings& other )
{
  savings TEMP;  // Declare a local temporary object

  TEMP = curr;   // Hold left-side operand
  TEMP -= other; // Cheat -- use overloaded -=
  return TEMP;   // Tricky, huh?
}
savings operator-( savings& curr, double amt )
{
  savings TEMP;  // Declare a local temporary object

  TEMP = curr;   // Hold left-side operand
  TEMP -= amt;   // Cheat -- use other overloaded -=
  return TEMP;   // Tricky, huh?
}
```

All four of the preceding overloaded operator functions are friends. There is no reason at all *not* to make them friends, and the goal of efficient objects is a good reason *to* make them friends. Notice that the function names are *not* qualified by the `savings::` syntax. That syntax does not apply to friend functions.

After you have examined the friend operator functions in the preceding code fragment, note the arguments and the return types. Did you notice that wherever a *class* object is an argument, a reference to it is coded? A good rule of thumb is this: *always* use a reference to a class object in the argument list.

That rule is important for two reasons. First, as you learned earlier, you can "call" the operator function (by writing an expression with the particular operator) with either objects or references to an object with impunity—either choice works because references bind to objects. Second, and vastly important, remember that if you pass the argument by value, you can *modify only the copy of it on the stack*—you cannot reach the original object (just as in ordinary C, right?). This restriction might cause problems that are hard to debug.

When passing *ordinary objects* to operator functions, however, you may not want to use references. For anything less than structures, you can pass ordinary objects by value almost as efficiently. They don't require *too* much stack space or execution time, and they may even save execution time because no disguised pointer is processing for them. In the preceding code fragment, for example, `double` objects are passed by value.

The return types for the new `savings` operator functions are even more interesting. Both versions of the `operator-=()` function still return references, for all the reasons stated earlier. In the case of the `-=` operator, returning a reference is useful for two additional reasons. First, the left-side operand (first argument) is modified, and the returned value or object locator should reflect that modification. Second, returning a reference permits efficient behavior (fast execution times) of the class object and flexible use of the operator (remember the `printf()` example earlier).

The `operator-()` functions, however, return by *value*. Not only that, but you have little choice in the matter. If you think about it for a moment, you will realize that "return by value" is required because an expression such as `a - b` yields a result that is *not* stored in either `a` or `b`. Both simple assignment and compound assignment modify the value of the left-side operand, which is where the result is stored. But this is not the case for ordinary arithmetic and shift operators. Where, then, do you put the result? You put it in a temporary "variable" and then pass *a copy of it* back to the compiler-generated code that is evaluating the parsed expression. Whew!

Now look, one line at a time, at the code for the `operator-()` function (the one with the `double` second argument). The first thing you see is the declaration of a savings object *within* the friend function:

```
savings operator-( savings& curr, double amt )
{
    savings TEMP;   // Declare a local temporary object

    TEMP = curr;    // Hold left-side operand
    TEMP -= amt;    // Cheat -- use other overloaded -=
    return TEMP;    // Tricky, huh?
}
```

Won't this cause a recursive creation of `savings` objects? No, it won't. First, this function is a friend function and not part of the `savings` scope. Second, even if this were a member function, it still would not cause recursive creation of objects because it is not in the *constructor* function. The `TEMP` object, then, is a legitimate `auto` object that happens to have type `savings`.

The next line of code in the `operator-()` function places the value of the left-side operand (first argument) in the `TEMP` object. The value of the left-side operand can now be used without disturbing the contents of the original object. Furthermore, the overloaded assignment operator `operator=(double)` is the means of carrying out the transfer.

Next, the just-defined `operator-=(double)` function is used to subtract the right-side operand from the `TEMP` object. `TEMP` now has a value equal to *leftoperand − rightoperand*.

Finally, the `TEMP` object is returned by value. Wait! Won't that constitute a reference to a vanishing local variable? Not at all. The return value is only a *copy* of `TEMP`, and that copy will survive the destruction of `TEMP` when it goes out of scope.

In summary, then, use the following criteria in deciding whether to use references or values for return types for the arithmetic and shift operators:

❏ *If the operator is to modify the left-side operand, return a reference to the left-side operand.* This rule does not apply to unary operators, as shown in the next section.

❏ *Otherwise, create a local object of the class for use as a temporary variable, modify the temporary copy, and return it by value.* Neither the left- nor the right-side operand is modified this way, and returning by value prevents passing back a pointer (disguised or otherwise) to an out-of-scope and nonexistent `auto` object. This rule *does* apply to unary operators.

Defining Cast Operator Functions

Recall that five questions were presented earlier in this chapter. Four of these questions have now been covered. The fifth question is, how do you handle user-defined cast operators for class objects? For an answer, consider once again the example of the `savings` object. Provided here, for brevity, is the cast operator function for a cast to type `long`. This cast might not be useful in the real world because it truncates fractional parts (we have no cents, anyway), but the code aptly illustrates how to set up the class for user-defined casts:

```
class savings {
  ...
public:
  ...
  operator long(); // no return type, no arguments
};
...
savings::operator long()
{
  return (long)total; // Use global (long) cast
}
```

As you can see, a user-defined conversion (cast) of this kind is quite simple. You just specify the targeted type name as the operator, and be sure to return that type. Within the conversion function in the preceding code fragment, the global cast to long is used (that is, an ordinary cast). Of course, for other conceivable conversions—savings to string (char *), for example—considerably more code may be required.

Note that a user-defined conversion function cannot have a return type in the declaration part, even though the return verb is used to pass back a value of the desired type. The operator function name (a cast *is* an operator) already identifies the type. Notice also that user-defined cast operator functions must be *member* functions. They are clearly associated closely with their class—so that friend functions are not permitted.

Nor can a user-defined function have any explicit arguments. Only the implicit and ever-present this can be used by the function. This makes sense: what else would you want to convert, except an object of the class containing the conversion function?

Overloading Binary and Unary Operators

Binary operators, such as addition or subtraction, are characterized by having two operands: the left- and right-side operands mentioned previously. Overloaded operator functions are called, as needed, when the compiler-generated code for evaluating expressions that involve class objects is executed. The compiler-generated code passes arguments to the overloaded functions—arguments that correspond to the operands being used at that point in the evaluation.

The first argument, which may be the implicitly present this pointer, corresponds to the left-side operand being evaluated. The second argument, which is always explicitly coded in the function declaration (except for cast functions), corresponds to the right-side operand.

This manner of supplying function arguments for corresponding operands leads naturally to the syntax you must use to declare the operator functions for binary operators, depending on whether a member function or friend function is used. The following rules apply:

❏ *Overloaded functions for binary operators, implemented as member functions, require one explicit argument.* The `this` pointer is implicitly supplied to member functions as the first or only argument. The implicit `this` pointer therefore corresponds to the left-side operand of a binary operator. The explicitly supplied argument is the right-side operand.

❏ *Overloaded functions for binary operators, implemented as friend functions, require two explicit arguments.* Because friend functions are not in the scope of the class that declares them as friends, there is no `this` argument. Two explicit arguments are required, corresponding to the left- and right-side operands of a binary operator.

Similar considerations apply to unary operators although, of course, unary operators have by definition only one operand. The following rules apply to arguments for overloaded unary operators:

❏ *Overloaded functions for unary operators, when implemented as member functions, require zero explicit arguments.* The `this` pointer is still, as always, implicitly supplied so that no other arguments are necessary.

❏ *Overloaded functions for unary operators, when implemented as friend functions, require one explicit argument.* Because friend functions are not in the scope of the class declaring them as friends, an argument is required to locate the only operand of a unary operator.

As you saw earlier in this chapter, the latest AT&T C++ compiler requirements (found in the base document) permit extensions to these rules in order to distinguish the prefix and postfix use of the increment (++) and decrement (--) operators. Borland C++ 2.0 does not support this distinction at this time. Keep it in mind, though—they will get around to it.

In the preceding section, you learned that you should implement functions for unary operators by using a locally declared temporary class object in order to avoid modifying the contents of the current operand. Is that always true? It is true in all but two cases, and then only if you return a class object or a reference to a class object from the function. Consider the sample expressions shown with each unary operator in table 14.5.

Table 14.5. *Unary operators with sample expressions.*

Operator	Operator Name	Sample Expression(s)
+	Unary +	`a = +b;`
–	Unary –	`a = -b;`
*	Pointer declarator, dereference	`char *text;` `a = *b;`
&	Address-of	`a = &b;`
~	One's complement	`a = ~b;`
!	Logical NOT	`a = !b;`
++	Increment	`++a; a++;`
--	Decrement	`--a; a--;`

For each of the unary operators shown in table 14.5, except the increment and decrement operators, you do *not* want the action of the operator to change the value or state of its operand. You do want the operator to return a desired value, *based on* the original state of the operand. You would not want the address-of operator, for example, to replace an object's *value* with a *pointer*. With the ++ and -- operators, however, you do want to replace the original object's value.

What about using temporary local class objects in unary operator functions? The following code fragment shows two overloads for the unary - operator for the savings class:

```
                    // member functions, unary operator,
                    // take zero arguments
savings savings::operator-()
{
  savings TEMP;

  TEMP = *this;        // Get a copy of operand
  TEMP.total *= -1.0;  // Negate internal value
  return TEMP;         // and return by value
}

double savings::operator-()
{
  return -total;       // Don't need TEMP here
}
```

The `operator-()` function returning `double` in this code fragment obviously needs no help from a temporary variable. There is no danger of modifying anything permanently. The `operator-()` function returning `savings` does need that help, though, because there is no way to get a *whole object*, with its member data negated, into a position to be returned without a temporary object.

The `operator-()` function could have modified `this->total` (by writing `total *= -1.0`). But then there would be no way to set `total` back to its original state after returning. Such a modification would surely cause unexpected results later in the program.

Overloading the Subscript and Function Call Operators

Two additional operators can be overloaded that have not yet been discussed. These are the *subscript operator*, `[]`, and the *function call operator*, `()`. Both are considered binary operators, and in most ways are handled in a normal manner. Because they have sufficiently interesting characteristics, however, these operators are covered separately in this section.

Note that overloaded functions for both `[]` and `()` must be nonstatic member functions. Friends are not allowed in these cases.

Using an Overloaded Subscript Operator

You can define a class for which the array subscript operator function, `operator[]()`, is overloaded. Thus, you can treat objects of that class as arrays, even if the member data in such an object is not actually an array. Still, the most helpful way to think of such a class is as a means of encapsulating and protecting a normal array, and of building extra function into array objects.

Listing 14.8 shows a program, `array.cpp`, which illustrates the use of `operator[]()`. This program appears also in Que's *Using C* but is repeated here because of the combination of interesting elements the program brings together. `array.cpp` shows you how to overload the subscript operator so that an individual array element can be used as an *lvalue* (stand on the left side of an assignment), how to declare and use a constructor function that has a variable argument list, how to write a copy constructor function, and how to implement a nifty little algorithm to reverse the order of array elements in place. This program also returns your attention to a whole, working C++ program that does something useful, thus reminding you of how all the pieces come together.

Listing 14.8. `array.cpp`. *A program that illustrates* `operator[]()` *overloaded functions.*

```
1   #include <stdlib.h>
2   #include <stdio.h>
3   #include <stdarg.h>
4   #include <string.h>
5
6   class array {
7     int value;
8     int numelem;
9     int *elem;
10    char *name;
11  public:
12    array( char *, ... );
13    array( array & );
14    ~array( void );
15    void *operator new( unsigned );
16    void operator delete( void * );
17    int &operator[](int);
18    void reverse( void );
19    void display( void );
20    int sum( void );
21    void newname( char * );
22  };
23
24  array::array( char *sname, ... ) // variadic declaration
25  {
26    va_list ap;
27    int work;
28    value = 0;                 // sum starts at zero
29    numelem = 0;
30    name = new char[strlen(name)+1];
31    strcpy( name, sname );  // init name string
32    va_start( ap, sname );  // Just count them this time
33    while ( 0 <= (work = va_arg( ap, int ) ) ) ++numelem;
34    va_end( ap );
35    if ( numelem > 0 )       // If there were any elements
36    elem = new int[numelem];
37     va_start( ap, sname);   // now load the array
```

```
38    for ( work=0; work<numelem; ++work )
39      elem[work] = va_arg( ap, int );
40    va_end( ap );
41  }
42
43  array::array( array &copy )     // copy constructor
44  {
45    int i;
46
47    value = copy.value;    // ref op makes -> op unnecessary
48    numelem = copy.numelem;
49    name = new char[strlen(copy.name)+1];
50    strcpy( name, copy.name );    // init name string
51    elem = new int[copy.numelem];
52    for ( i=0; i<copy.numelem; ++i )
53      elem[i] = copy.elem[i];
54  }
55
56  array::~array( void )
57  {
58    delete elem;
59    delete name;
60  }
61
62  void *array::operator new( size_t size )
63  {
64    return ::new unsigned char[size];
65  }
66
67  void array::operator delete( void *objptr )
68  {
69    ::delete objptr;
70  }
71
72  int &array::operator[]( int n )
73  {
74                              // Returning a reference ensures
75                              // that the [] op can be used on
76                              // either side of the = operator
77    if ( n<0 || n >= numelem ) return elem[0];
78    return elem[n];
```

Listing 14.8. continues

Listing 14.8. continued

```
79   }
80
81   void array::reverse( void )
82   {
83     int a, b;
84      a = 0;
85     b = numelem - 1;
86     while ( b > a ) {
87       elem[a]^=elem[b];
88       elem[b]^=elem[a];
89       elem[a]^=elem[b];
90       ++a; --b;
91     }
92   }
93
94   void array::display( void )
95   {
96     int i;
97      for ( i=0; i<numelem; ++i ) {
98        printf( "%s[%d]=%d ", name, i, elem[i] );
99      }
100    printf( "\n" );
101  }
102
103  int array::sum( void )
104  {
105    int i;
106
107    value = 0;
108    for ( i=0; i<numelem; ++i ) value += elem[i];
109    return value;
110  }
111
112  void array::newname( char *n )
113  {
114    delete name;                      // Deallocate old name
115    name = new char[strlen(n)+1];     // Allocate new name
116    strcpy( name, n );                // Copy it in
117  }
118
119  main() {
```

```
120                    // Define an object on the stack
121    array x( "X", 1,2,3,4,5,6,7,8,9,0,-1 );
122
123    x.display(); // Send various messages to object
124    printf( "The sum of X's elements is %d\n", x.sum() );
125    x.reverse();
126    x.display();
127    x[0] = 99;   // Use the overloaded [] operator
128    x[1] = 101;  // You couldn't do this if op[]()
129    x[2] = x[1]; // returned other than int&
130    x.display();
131
132    array y = x; // Use the copy constructor
133    y.newname( "Y" );
134    y.display();
135  }
```

The `int& array::operator[]( int )` declaration for the overloaded function appears in line 17 of listing 14.8. Nothing is particularly unusual about the declaration. You should notice that the argument for the function is required to be `int`, which is in keeping with the normal type of an array subscript.

Nor is there anything strange about the `operator[]()` function body. Its purpose is to return the *array[argument]* element, but the function body does go a little further (in the pursuit of encapsulation and protection) by checking the subscript value for correct range. If the subscript is out of range, it returns the zero element rather than aborting the program or trying to fetch the wrong data. This feature alone makes constructing an `array` class worthwhile.

Now pay special attention to the return type of `array::operator[]()`. It returns a *reference* to an integer. Why is this important? Even if you returned an `int` by value, an expression such as

```
a = arr[0]; // syntactically same as a = constant int
```

would still execute correctly. But what if the reference to an array element appeared on the *left* side of the assignment (as it does in lines 127–129)?

You need to go back to C theory to understand what happens then. The rule is that an *lvalue*—an *object locator*—must appear on the left side of an assignment. Is that beginning to sound familiar? A reference *can* be an object locator (lvalue). But an integer value returned from a function cannot be an lvalue. Therefore, because the return type for `array::operator[]()` is a reference, an expression such as

```
x[1] = 101;   // See line 128
```

modifies the value of `array::x.elem[1]` instead of producing a compile-time error. (`array::elem` is actually a pointer to `int`; see line 9. Remember, however, that pointer and subscript notations are equivalent.) Once again, the correct use of references is crucial to the smooth functioning of the class.

The nondefault constructor for the `array` class is found in lines 24–41 of listing 14.8. Although writing a constructor function with a variable argument list may at first seem peculiar, nothing prevents it, as long as you control the arguments correctly. In the case of the `array` class, you are allowed to create an `array` object with as many or as few elements in the argument list as you want. Note that the object declaration in line 121 specifies a `-1` as the last argument to "fence" off the argument list. By watching for that value, the constructor can first count the elements (line 33) and then initialize the array (lines 38–39). You might want to expand the class's capabilities by providing another constructor that accepts a single integer argument specifying the number of elements for which to allocate space.

The code for reversing the current element order is found in the `array::reverse()` member function (lines 81–92). This function uses the simple expedient of a `while` loop that accesses elements from the front and back of the array at the same time, and uses exclusive ORs to exchange their values with no temporary storage. You can exchange any two variables by using three successive exclusive ORs, as shown in these statements:

```
a ^= b;   // step 1
b ^= a;   // step 2
a ^= b;   // step 3
```

The order of the successive statements and the order of the operands within each statement are required to perform this trick.

Handling multidimensional arrays with the subscript operator, `[]`, is a problem. Remember that an overloaded function can accept only one argu-ment (for member functions) or two arguments (for friend functions). In either case, the required syntax for the function limits the right-side operand to just one argument. Thus, there is no legal way to define a class so that `obj[]...[]` can be defined. In the next section, you learn how to get around this problem, using overloaded function call operators.

Using an Overloaded Function Call Operator

Overloading the function call operator, ( ), for a class enables you to access a class object with a minimum of coding. The general form for declaring an overloaded function call operator is this:

```
returntype operator()( args );
```

Once you have overloaded the function call operator for a class, you can call a member function "behind the scenes." Note, for example, the following code fragment:

```
class A {
   ...
   char describe[80];
public:
   ...
   A& operator()( char *arg ) {
      strcpy( describe, arg );
      cout << arg;
   }
void main()
{
   A myobj;
   ...
   myobj( "A new description string." );
}
```

Here you can set a new member value for the class A object myobj with a simple function call syntax, using only the object name. That is, the member function call syntax myobj.function(...) is not needed when the proper function call overload has been defined.

Overloading the function call operator enables you to do more than just simplify the syntax of the member function call. You can use the feature to expand the functionality of the class as well. In the preceding section, for example, you saw how to use the function call operator to permit the implementation of multidimensional arrays.

You can approach the task of encapsulating a multidimensional array in several ways, using function call operator overloads. The obvious method is to define the class with member data that is a fixed-size multidimensional array. That is relatively easy and differs little from the array.cpp program shown in listing 14.9.

Another alternative is to use the added functionality of default function arguments, plus algorithms to simulate multidimensionality based on a physically one-dimensional array. Using these techniques, you can define a class that has from one to three dimensions, with each dimension permitting any number of elements to be stored. The program `marray.cpp`, shown in listing 14.9, demonstrates such a class.

Listing 14.9. `marray.cpp`. *A program that uses function call overloading to provide multidimensional array capability.*

```
 1   #include <iostream.h>
 2   #include <stdlib.h>
 3   #include <stdio.h>
 4   #include <stdarg.h>
 5   #include <string.h>
 6
 7   class marray {
 8     int vecsize[3]; // size of each dimension, can be 0
 9     int numelem;
10     int mux1, mux2;
11     int* elem;
12   public:
13     marray( int = 0, int = 0, int = 0 );
14     ~marray();
15     int& operator()( int = -1, int = -1, int = -1 );
16   };
17
18   marray::marray( int a, int b, int c )
19   {
20     if ( !a ) a = 1; // Make sure at least 1 elem exists;
21     numelem = a;
22     if ( b ) numelem *= b;
23     if ( c ) numelem *= c;
24     elem = new int[numelem];
25     vecsize[0] = a;
26     vecsize[1] = b;
27     vecsize[2] = c;
28     mux1 = a;          // multipliers to linearize subscript
29     mux2 = mux1 * b;
30   }
31
32   marray::~marray()
33   {
```

```
34    delete elem;
35  }
36
37  int& marray::operator()( int a, int b, int c )
38  {
39                      // If any subscript == -1, display array
40    if ( a == -1 || b == -1 || c == -1 ) {
41       int i, j, k;
42       for( i=0; i<vecsize[0]; ++i ) {
43         for( j=0; j<vecsize[1]; ++j ) {
44           for( k=0; k<vecsize[2]; ++k ) {
45             cout
46             << elem[ i + j*mux1 + k*mux2 ]
47             << "   " ;
48           }
49           cout << "\r\n";
50         }
51         cout << "\r\n";
52       }
53       return elem[0]; // dummy return after display
54    }
55                      // Otherwise, return ref to indicated elem
56    if ( a >= vecsize[0] || b >= vecsize[1] || c >= vecsize[2] )
57       return elem[0];
58    else
59       return elem[ a + b*mux1 + c*mux2 ] ;
60  }
61
62  void main()
63  {
64    marray x( 3, 3, 3 );  // three dim, 2 each dim
65
66    int i, j, k, p = 1;    // init element values
67    for( i=0; i<3; ++i ) {
68      for( j=0; j<3; ++j ) {
69        for( k=0; k<3; ++k ) {
70          x( i, j, k ) = p++;  // Here it is !
71        }
72      }
73    }
74
75    x();                       // Show it off
76  }
```

In line 8 of listing 14.9, the integer array `vecsize[3]` is declared as member data for the class. The idea is to permit the construction of an array that has one, two, or three dimensions, with the elements for each dimension being considered a vector (one-dimensional array). The values of `vecsize` elements contain the number of elements each vector can hold.

Furthermore, all but the first vectors can contain zero elements, allowing the class to avoid allocating space for an array of maximum size when you want fewer than three dimensions.

The member variables `mux1` and `mux2` are scaling variables for use in simulating multidimensionality over the physically one-dimensional data area. The goal here is to mimic normal C usage in which all the elements for the righmost subscript are stored contiguously. Figure 14.5 illustrates how physical storage layout compares to subscript usage.

Fig. 14.5. *Elements are stored so that contiguous elements exhaust the rightmost subscript first.*

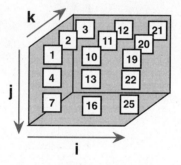

Figure 14.5 shows that a three-dimensional array, using subscripts i, j, and k, can be conceived of as a series of "planes" of elements numbered by subscript k. Each plane is composed of i columns and j rows of elements, or $i * j$ elements.

Notice that to get to the first element of the second row, first plane, you must skip over exactly i elements. To get to the first element on the second plane, you must skip over $i * j$ elements (over the whole first plane). Hence, the `muxn` variables are precomputed in the constructor function in lines 28–29 of listing 14.9 in just this manner.

The multiplier values computed in the constructor functions are used later, in lines 46 and 59, to allow quicker calculation of the one-dimensional equivalent subscript number during access of the array.

The meat of the program in listing 14.9 is almost anticlimactic. All the real work of setting up the array and the means of access, as for a multidimensional array, has already been done (including the reference return type!). Accessing an element of the array, as in line 70, is marvelously simple. The only difference between line 70 and ordinary C-style multidimensional subscripting is that the function call operator is used rather than subscript brackets.

You may want to study listing 14.9 in more detail. Look more closely at the way in which default function arguments are used, for example, to reduce the number of overloaded functions required and to tell the constructor how many dimensions are needed (and their sizes).

Exercises

The following exercises give you practice in overloading member and nonmember functions, and in using both member and friend functions to overload C operators for use with your class objects.

1. Devise a class that does something you find interesting, overloading at least one of its member functions. You might for example, write a `parts` class and provide an overloaded `parts::update()` function. The `update()` function might accept a string argument for updating the part description, a `long` to update the part number, an `int` to update the part count, and a `double` to update per-item cost of a part.

2. Modify the code for the `lib` class (discussed in Chapter 13) to support the compound addition operator. That is, write the `lib::operator+=()` function so that an expression such as

   ```
   lib A, B;
   ...
   A += B;
   ```

   results in all the members from B being added to the library A. This project is not as trivial as it might seem, so be careful—and keep a backup copy of the original code!

3. Expand the operator functions defined for the `savings` class. Be sure to include both binary and unary operators. Pay close attention to the need for friends of member functions, argument number and types, and return types (if any). Experiment with the class and see what you can make it do. For example, why not overload the `&` operator to

cause a savings object to store itself on disk? (Hint: store only member data and in a format you want. Don't try to write the object as a whole to a file.) Use the | operator to reload from a disk file.

4. Invent a class that does something *you* are interested in, giving it a full, robust set of operator functions.

Summary

C++ overloaded functions and operators provide much of the same power and flexibility for C++ classes that the original operators provide for plain C data objects. The great difference is that you must define in C++ what a class member function or overloaded operator will do. The plain C operators, of course, are built-in and have a fixed significance. This chapter presented most of the syntax and theory you need for harnessing overloaded functions and operators. The following points were covered:

❑ *You learned the basic concepts of overloading.* When you write overloaded functions, you are providing your class with multiple versions of the function or operator. The compiler matches a call to an overloaded function (or operator, for that matter) to the correct function definition. To make the match, the compiler examines both the *return type* and the *signature* (that is, the argument list) of the function. You can vary the signature, or the signature and return type, but not just the return type of an overloaded function.

❑ *You can overload any kind of function and most of the operators.* You can have several versions of member functions, friend functions, or nonmember functions. If you have used an older C++ compiler in the past, remember that the overload keyword formerly required for nonmember functions is now obsolete.

❑ *Type-safe linkage is a standard feature in current C++ compilers and is implemented through function mangling.* Function mangling is performed for *all* function names, by default, and consists of forming a unique internal identifier from the name, signature, and return type. If you need to include plain C standard functions (which is almost always the case), you can turn off function mangling by using the extern "C" {...} linkage specifier.

❑ *Overloaded operator functions have special requirements and restrictions placed on them.* Some operator functions must be members; others can be friends of the class. Some operator functions can return whatever type you want; others require a specific return type. Cast operator functions cannot specify any return type at all. The number of arguments for operator functions depends on whether the operator being overloaded is binary or unary. Finally, whether you can use references for argument and return types, as well as where you use such references, is an important consideration in designing overloaded operator functions.

15

Using C++ Constructors and Destructors

C++ constructor and destructor functions are central to the implementation of user-defined types (classes). The `malloc()` and `calloc()` functions can acquire heap storage equal to the correct size of a class object, but these functions do nothing about initializing the member data or establishing linkage with the member functions of a class object. Furthermore, you may want to associate working memory with the object that is outside the boundaries of the class object, but the standard library's memory allocation routines can do nothing about that. Finally, a corresponding cleanup activity must take place when a class object is destroyed (by going out of scope or being deleted), but the standard library functions can't help there either.

All these initialization and termination activities for class objects are relegated to the constructor and destructor functions for a class. A *constructor* function declared for a class is automatically invoked when an object of that class is created. A *destructor* function declared for a class is automatically invoked when an object of that class is destroyed (for example, when a local object goes out of scope and is removed from the system stack). Under certain circumstances, you can call these functions directly. These functions are so important to the operation of the class that the compiler will generate default functions for you, should you not declare any. Compiler-generated constructor and destructor functions have the `public` attribute.

A compiler-generated default constructor is sufficient to make a chunk of storage into a true class object but is otherwise relatively useless, except for the simplest of classes (classes declared with `struct` perhaps). The default action of a compiler-generated constructor is to initialize member data to zero values or null pointers (linkage to member functions was accomplished invisibly at compile time).

A compiler-generated destructor is comparably simple: the `delete` operator is used to free the object's storage. That action is sufficient if the constructor has not acquired memory areas outside the boundaries of the object.

Your constructors and destructors may need to do many more things than the compiler-generated default versions are capable of doing. This chapter covers many of the advanced uses of constructors and destructors, as well as other related topics.

Specifically, the chapter shows you how to declare constructors and destructors and how to overload constructors functions. You learn when and why to call constructor and destructor functions, including how to make direct calls to these functions.

The chapter shows you also how to write initializer lists for constructor functions. The method you use is a convenient carry-over from plain C's method of writing initializers for aggregate objects, and it will prove vital later, when you learn how to derive classes. The chapter shows you not only how to write copy constructors but also how to recognize when you will need them. They are needed more frequently than you might expect in real-world classes.

Finally, the chapter shows you how to use the global `new` and `delete` operators and how to use these operators overloaded by class. For these tasks, you need an understanding of C++'s free store. You see also how to overload the global `new` and `delete` operators.

Understanding Constructor and Destructor Calls

To understand how and when constructor and destructor functions are called, you must know and understand the rules for declaring these functions. You must know also how these functions are used for objects having different scopes and storage classes. This section covers these topics.

Declaring Constructors and Destructors

Constructor and destructor functions, like all other functions, must be declared and defined before they can be used. The declarations and definitions must also conform to certain rules that are unique to constructor and destructor functions. Both kinds of functions should be declared in the `public` part of the class declaration.

Declaring Constructor Functions

You declare and define constructor functions according to the following rules:

❏ *A constructor function must have the same name as the class for which the function is declared.* That is, `class A {...}` must have a constructor function `A()`, if you declare one at all. The purpose of a constructor function is to turn a chunk of raw memory into a class object. The constructor function body does not need to allocate space for the object: the space already exists by the time the constructor function is invoked. A constructor function is implicitly invoked when a class object is declared (that is, when a class object is *created*).

❏ *A constructor function cannot have a return type.* The Borland C++ compiler, like all other C++ compilers, generates its own special (and invisible) return type for a constructor function. You must write the declaration without a return type, as in the following example:

```
class A {
  ...
public:

  ...
  A( args_opt );  // Declare a constructor function
  ...
};
```

You can define a constructor function inline, but you should do this only when the function is short and simple. When the definition appears out-of-line, it is written in the usual manner for out-of-line member functions, except for the return type. The preceding declaration would require this corresponding definition:

```
A::A( args_opt )
{
    ... // Function body goes here
}
```

❏ *Because a constructor function can have arguments, overloading is permitted.* If the function has a distinguishable signature, the compiler will have no difficulty in mangling the function name. Overloading is useful if there are several different combinations of initial data types you want to use in creating an object of a class.

One special case of constructor overloading should be mentioned: using a constructor to convert data types. Such a constructor implementation is called *conversion by constructor* and can be quite handy. It is a special alternative to overloading cast operators, as discussed in the preceding chapter.

Conversion by constructor requires that you code a constructor function which either accepts a single argument or specifies enough default arguments so that the constructor can be invoked with just one argument. For example, to specify conversion from int to class A, you need to declare at least the following constructor:

```
class A {
    ...
public:
    A( int );  // constructor for conversion from
int
};
```

Assuming that the constructor function definition appears somewhere in your program, you can then create class A objects by conversion from int:

```
void main()
{
    int a;
    ...
    A obj1( a ); // This is the first form of call
    A obj2 = a;  // This is an entirely equivalent form of call
}
```

Note that a conversion constructor differs from the copy constructor described later in this list, although the assignment operator can invoke the constructor as shown in the preceding code fragment because a whole object is not copied to another. Constructor conversion of type creates a *new* object, even if the argument's type is a different class. The objects handled by copy constructors have the *same* class.

❑ *A constructor function can have default arguments.* You have already
   seen this feature in some of the sample code in previous chapters.
   Remember that the argument default values appear in the *declaration*
   of the constructor function, not in the definition. The syntax looks like
   this:

```
class A {
   ...
public:

   ...
   A( int = 1, int = 2, int = 3 );
   ...
};
   ...
A::A( int arg1, int arg2, int arg3 )
{
   ...
}
```

Having default arguments is not exactly the same as having no arguments (having no arguments defines a default constructor, not default
arguments). The difference between no arguments and default
arguments is most notably apparent in the way you declare objects of
the class:

```
A obj;  // the form used with NO arguments, default constr.
A obj();            // declaration allowing default values
A obj( 1, 2, 3 );    // functionally same as second object
```

A quick summary is in order here. First, if you are going to declare
objects with aggregate initializer lists, such as

```
struct twoclass { int a; int b; };
   ...
twoclass classobj = { 1, 2 };
```

the class cannot contain a constructor at all. Second, if you are going
to declare arrays of class objects, as in

```
class myclass { ... };
   ...
myclass bunch[20];
```

you must use a default constructor (because you have no way to
specify an argument list for each element). In this case, *default* can
mean either a constructor with no arguments or a constructor with *all*

default arguments. Either way, the constructor can be called without specifying arguments. This means that if you code any constructor at all, you should provide a default (the compiler does not generate one if you write any constructors).

Third, other constructors can have whatever arguments you want, with or without default values. This final point has some rather strange variations when you are using class inheritance (deriving classes), but that discussion is deferred until Chapter 17.

❏ *You cannot take the address of a constructor function.* You can take the address of an ordinary member function and call the function through the pointer to member operator. Forming a pointer to a member function is similar to forming a pointer to a member data object (see the sample program shown in Chapter 14). The following short program (which compiles and runs) illustrates the technique:

```
#include <iostream.h>   // a strange hello program

class A {
public:
   void display();
};

void A::display()
{
   cout << "Hello, there!\r\n";
}

void main()
{
   void (A::*dptr)();   // pointer to member function
   A *thing = new A;    // pointer to class object

   dptr = &A::display;
   (thing->*dptr)();
}
```

Although ordinary member functions can be handled through pointers, it is illegal and impossible to take the address of a constructor function. Note that a pointer to a member function is internally similar to Turbo C's near pointer. A pointer to a member function (or object) is recorded only in terms of its offset from the beginning of the class object; thus, the pointer can be used with more than one object of the class.

❏ *A constructor function cannot be declared* `static, const, or volatile`. A constructor function must be a nonstatic member function because constructor functions cannot exist apart from particular objects. (Remember that `static` member functions can exist apart from specific objects and can be called before any object exists.) The other two specifiers also clearly do not apply to constructors. However, you can define `const` or `volatile` *objects* that also happen to have constructors.

❏ *A constructor function cannot be inherited.* It is unique to its class. If a constructor could be inherited, a number of problems would result, including accidental failure to initialize derived class objects, and invisible changes made to the meaning of copy constructors. Why would these problems occur? When a derived class object is initialized, the base class constructor is invoked first, and then the derived class constructor is invoked. If constructors could be inherited, you could accidentally create a derived class that had no explicit constructor.

❏ *When a class declaration contains member objects that are themselves objects of other classes, the member objects' constructors are executed before the constructor for the containing object.* Consider, for example, how the constructors for classes A and B in the following code fragment are used:

```
class A { ... };
class B {
  ...
  A workobj;
public:
  ...
};
...

B visibleobj; // Create B object with default constructor
```

When the class B `visibleobj` is created (by being declared), A's constructor is executed first on behalf of `workobj`, and only then is B's constructor function body executed.

❏ *A copy constructor, like a default constructor, can be compiler-generated.* The copy constructor for a class is the special case in which the argument is a reference to an object of the same class. Consider this example:

```
class A {
  ...
  int var;
public;
  ...
  A( A& );
};
...
A:A( A& other )
{
  var = other.var; // just for an example
}
```

Note carefully that the copy constructor's single argument must be a *reference* to an object of the same class. This requirement is necessary because passing an object by value implies creating a copy of the argument to place on the stack. But creating that copy invokes the copy constructor, which creates another copy, and so on, causing infinite recursion of the copy constructor function.

Copy constructors are useful when you want to create a new object with reference to an existing object, as in the following code fragment:

```
void main()
{
  A obj1;
  A obj2 = obj1;  // obj2 is a copy of obj1
}
```

A copy constructor is generated for you only if you do not declare one yourself. If a memberwise copy of the object is acceptable, a compiler-generated copy constructor is sufficient. If the object has special requirements, such as maintaining a block of memory outside the boundaries of the object itself, you should write your own copy constructor.

❏ *A* `union` *can declare a class in C++, but an* object *of a class having constructors cannot be a member of a* `union`. This rule exists because unions are viewed as overlays of the same area of storage. That is, a union can contain many different members, but they all occupy the same area of storage—only one member is "active" at a time. There can be no guarantee, therefore, that the member which happens to be a class object will be active at a given time. There is also no guarantee that its constructor function will actually be called.

❑ *Class member functions can be called from within a constructor function, and class member objects can be referenced from within a constructor function.* C++ programmers who are familiar only with Borland C++, or with other AT&T 2.0 compatible compilers, may take this rule for granted. After all, the `this` pointer is the first (or only) implicit argument for constructor functions, just as for all other member functions. However, that was not always true with previous versions of the C++ compiler. In some cases, you had to explicitly initialize `this` before you could access class members.

The rationale used by previous compilers was simple: a constructor function differs from all others in that a constructor takes a chunk of raw memory—not a complete class object—and transforms the raw memory into a working class object. Borland C++ and other recent C++ compilers now consider this usage obsolete because you can overload the `new` and `delete` operators on a *per class* basis. Thus, there is never a time, *in the constructor function*, when `this` is not valid. For a detailed discussion of overloading the `new` and `delete` operators with class objects, see the section "Overloading `operator new()` and `operator delete()`" later in this chapter.

Declaring Destructor Functions

The rules for destructor functions are similar to those for constructor functions. You declare and define destructor functions according to the following rules:

❑ *A destructor function has the same name as its class, except that the name is preceded by the tilde (˜).* That is, you declare a destructor in the following manner:

```
class A {
  ...
public:
  ...
  A();    // constructor for A
  ˜A();   // destructor for A
};
```

The destructor function may be inline. If it is out-of-line, you write the function definition in this way:

```
A::˜A()
{
  ... // destructor function body
}
```

The destructor function's purpose is the opposite of that of the constructor function: the destructor transforms a class object into a chunk of raw data. In other words, the destructor "deinitializes" an object. The destructor function body does not need to explicitly free storage occupied by the class object itself, but may need to free storage that a member function acquired outside the class object's boundaries.

❏ *A destructor function cannot have a return type.* Just as for a constructor function, the compiler generates its own internal type for a destructor function. You are not allowed to code a return type.

❏ *Unlike a constructor function, a destructor function cannot have arguments.* Because a destructor has no arguments and thus no signature for function mangling, you cannot overload a destructor. The question of default arguments, of course, is not applicable to destructor functions.

❏ *You cannot take the address of a destructor function.* You have no need to access a destructor function through a pointer because the function is used only to destroy a class object.

❏ *A destructor function must be a nonstatic member function of its class.* That is, a destructor cannot be declared to be `const`, `volatile`, or `static`. Like a constructor function, though, a destructor function can be defined for classes that have `const` or `volatile` *objects*.

❏ *A destructor function cannot be inherited.* Here the same problems exist for destructors as for constructors. If a destructor could be inherited, the correct destructor might not be executed.

❏ *A destructor function can be a `virtual` function.* You may recall that the virtual-function facility is a kind of "pass through" mechanism guaranteeing that the correct version of a function (that is, the one belonging to the derived class) is executed. Thus, virtual destructors are permitted. In fact, declaring destructor functions `virtual` when deriving classes is often a good idea.

❏ *When a class declaration contains member objects that are themselves objects of other classes, the body of the containing class's destructor is executed before the destructors for the contained objects.* Consider, for example, how the destructors for classes A and B in the following code fragment are used:

```
class A { ... };
class B {
  ...
  A workobj;
public:
  ...
  ~B();
};
...
B* visibleobj = new B; // Create a B object
...
delete visibleobj;     // Now destroy it
```

When the class B `visibleobj` is destroyed (in this case, by being deleted), B's destructor is executed first, and only then is A's destructor invoked on behalf of `workobj`. The order of execution is exactly opposite that of constructor function execution.

❏ *A* `union` *can declare a class in C++,* *but an* object *of a class having destructors cannot be a member of a* `union`. The reasons for this rule are the same as those for constructor functions: there can be no guarantee that the destructor function will actually be executed.

❏ *Class member functions can be called from within a destructor function, and class member objects can be referenced from within a destructor function.* There is, of course, no question that the `this` pointer already exists at the time a destructor function is invoked for an object. Thus, calls to member functions, as well as references to member data, are possible.

You now have before you all the rules that *constrain* the use of constructor and destructor functions. The rest of this chapter shows you what constructors and destructors can do, and presents some important related topics.

Using Constructor Initializers

You have already seen how a class with no constructor can have objects initialized by an aggregate initializer list. In other words, you can declare a class that can be initialized in this manner:

```
#include <stdlib.h>
#include <stdio.h>

struct A {            // struct means all members public
  int a, b;           // There is no constructor, either
  void display();
  void operator()();  // overload function call () op
};



void A::display()
{
  printf( "a = %d, b = %d\n", a, b );
}

void A::operator()() // Define function call operator
{
  display();
}

main()
{
  A obj1 = { 16, 64 };                // initializer list

  obj1();     // Use overloaded function call operator
}
```

You can go beyond the aggregate initializer list form, however, by providing a *constructor* initializer list directly in the definition for the constructor function. Using a constructor initializer list, you can have both an initializer list (although not an aggregate style list) *and* any constructor functions you want. Constructor initializer lists can be important later on, when you build constructors for derived classes. The following short program shows how to write a constructor initializer list:

```
#include <stdlib.h>
#include <stdio.h>

class A {
  int a, b;
public:
  A(int, int);
  void display();
  void operator()();  // Overload function call () op
};
```

```
                   // Define initializer list for constructor

A::A( int i = 0, int j = 0 ) : a(i), b(j) {}

void A::display()
{
  printf( "a = %d, b = %d\n", a, b );
}

void A::operator()() // Define function call operator
{
  display();
}

main()
{
  A obj1;               // Take advantage of default args
  A obj2( 16, 64 );         //Use init list for this one

  obj1();     // Use overloaded function call operator
  obj2();                 // to display object values
}
```

You should be aware of several differences between the preceding program's constructor function and ordinary constructor functions. First, you should notice the syntax of the constructor function definition:

```
class::class( args ) : initlist { functionbody }
```

The punctuation must be coded as shown in this line. You must include *comma separators* between items in the initializer list, but not following the last item. The colon (:) that follows the declaration part and precedes the initializer list is always required, as is the list itself.

Next, you should understand that the default arguments shown in the preceding short program have nothing to do with the initializer list specifically. If the default arguments were not specified, the only thing that would happen is that the compiler would produce an error message saying that no constructor function could be matched to the declaration A obj1; in main(). Note, too, in this short program that the default argument values are supplied in the declaration part of the function definition, not in the function prototype declaration. Default arguments can appear in either place.

The syntax of each item in the initializer list is important also. The syntax determines how class members are matched with their initializing values. Note the following syntax:

```
memberobject( expression ), ...
memberobject( argument ), ...
```

As shown here, the most general form of an item in an initializer list consists of a member object to be initialized, followed by an expression within parentheses. You do not have to supply an item in the list for *every* member data object: some of the objects can be initialized by code in the constructor function body. In other words, the number of items in the initializer list does not have to match the number of member data objects in the class.

The expression within the parentheses of an item in an initializer list can be just that—an expression. It *can* be one of the constructor's function arguments, but it doesn't have to be. You can use an expression containing any names that are currently in scope and visible.

You may have noticed in the preceding short program that the function body for the constructor function is null, composed only of opening and closing curly braces (`{ }`). This is perfectly legal. This particular program has no need for any further logic because the initializer list takes care of setting up all the member data objects. But the function can just as well have any code in it that is legal for ordinary constructors.

As noted before, the availability of constructor initializer lists proves extremely useful when deriving classes from other classes. One instance of class derivation requires the use of constructor initializers: building one class from another class by *composition*—that is, including *objects* of one class in another class.

There is only one problem with including an object of another class in the declaration for the current class. A member data object that is also a class object *cannot be declared with an argument list for the constructor function*. A class member *class object* is therefore normally constrained to using a default constructor. The following code fragment, for instance, is illegal:

```
class A { ... };

class B {
  A myobj( 22, 33 );   // ILLEGAL, args not permitted!
  ...
};
```

Because a member object cannot have an argument list, you might be wondering whether you can incorporate a class object as member data and also provide constructor arguments for the member object. You can—by using the constructor initializer list. The following short program illustrates the technique:

```
#include <iostream.h>

class X {
  int value;
public:
  X( int arg = 37 ) { value = arg; }
  void show() { cout << value << "\r\n"; }
};

class Y {
  int value;
  X obj1;      // can't have arguments here!
public:
  Y( int arg, int oarg ) :  value(arg), obj1(oarg) {}
  void show() {
    cout << value << "\r\n";
    obj1.show();
  }
};

void main()
{
  Y myobj( 37, 64 );

  myobj.show();
}
```

In this program, class Y is built by declaring, among other things, a class X member object. Notice that the object declaration X obj1 has no argument list, conforming to the rule. But an argument is still going to be passed to the X(int) constructor (the *nondefault* constructor). The argument can be passed to the X constructor because the Y constructor has an initializer list containing the initializer item obj1(oarg). The combination of class object declaration and constructor initializer is the functional equivalent of the following declaration:

```
X obj1 = oarg;
```

You should recognize the form of the preceding line of code: an X constructor accepts one argument, and a corresponding object declaration provides an integer value. Therefore, the X constructor is a *conversion constructor*, as described earlier in the chapter.

This example clarifies the reason for the constructor initializer list's syntax: the syntax is constructed precisely so that class objects can be used as class members, while still allowing contained objects to be initialized with a nondefault constructor.

When Are Constructor Functions Called?

Constructor functions are obviously not executed by the compiler. Generally, constructor functions for a class are invoked when an object declaration of that class is encountered during execution. That is, constructor functions are executed as they are encountered at run-time. This sounds simple enough (although there are special considerations for base and derived class constructors, as discussed in Chapter 17), but you should know exactly when and under what circumstances constructors are called. With that knowledge, you can perhaps avoid stumbling into a dark pit while writing one of your C++ programs.

This section, then, shows how and when constructors are called for local objects, global objects, arbitrary objects, unnamed objects, and temporary objects. Also provided are a few comments about how and when copy constructors and constructors for arrays of class objects are called, as well as comments about causing recursion (possibly infinite recursion) during execution of a constructor function.

In normal programming practice for both C and C++, you should avoid the use of global variables or objects, preferring local objects whenever possible. You can, naturally, declare a class object locally (with block scope) just as you can declare ordinary data types. A constructor for a local object is not called until the object declaration is reached during execution within the block, as shown in figure 15.1.

Recall that in C++ a local declaration for an object does not have to appear at the top of the block. Because such a declaration can appear anywhere within the block, a constructor call is also possible from anywhere within a block.

Unlike a local object, a global class object (one with file scope) must behave like an ordinary data type. That is, such an object must be initialized before the `main()` function executes. Thus, a constructor function can be called even before `main()`, as shown in figure 15.2.

Fig. 15.1. *A class constructor call for a locally declared object.*

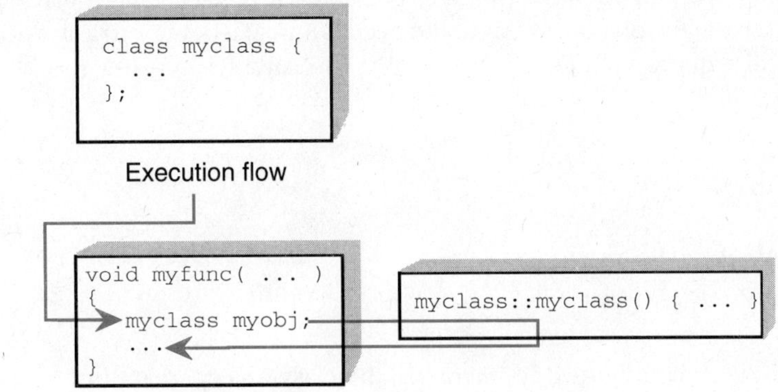

```
class myclass {
  ...
};
```

Execution flow

```
void myfunc( ... )
{
  myclass myobj;
  ...
}
```

```
myclass::myclass() { ... }
```

Fig. 15.2. *A class constructor call for a globally declared object.*

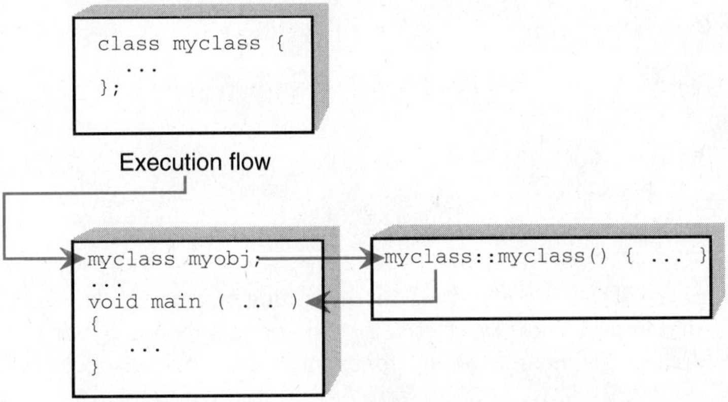

```
class myclass {
  ...
};
```

Execution flow

```
myclass myobj;
...
void main ( ... )
{
  ...
}
```

```
myclass::myclass() { ... }
```

You should not be surprised that code is executed before `main()`. A good deal of program initialization has to be done before any function, including `main()`, can be called. Calling the constructors for global class objects is just a part of the start-up process. If you are curious about what goes on before `main()` is executed, you can use the Borland C++ IDE editor to look at the file `\tcp\examples\startup\c0.asm`, substituting whatever main subdirectory you instructed the installation program to use for Borland C++ in place of `tcp`.

An arbitrary class object (that is, one with arbitrary duration and created by the `new` operator) has its constructor called at whatever point in program execution the `new` operator is used to create the object. Normally, you will use `new` to create the object directly in the declaration of a pointer to a class object. A typical sequence of declarations might, for example, look like this:

```
class A { ... };
...
void main()
{
  A* myobj = new A; // Declare pointer, create object,
                    // and call constructor
}
```

In the preceding code fragment, the class object created by `new` is an arbitrary duration object and exists physically on the free store. In contrast, the *pointer* to the object—the variable `myobj`—is a local variable existing on the system stack and within the scope of `main()`. The implication is that the pointer declaration and the creation of the class object do *not* have to appear in the same line of code. You can just as well write this:

```
class A { ... };
...
  A* myobj;          // Just declare the pointer
...
void main()
{
  myobj = new A;     // Create object and call constructor
}
```

This sequence of statements works, but the coding practice is not normal. The pointer declaration and object creation are often separated, but they are generally placed in the same scope—for example, both placed within `main()`.

You can also cause a class's constructor to be called by explicitly invoking it. There is only one way to do this: you place the constructor call on the right side of an assignment statement. The syntax looks like this:

```
class A { ... };
...
A myobj = A( args );
```

In other words, the expression on the right consists of the class name (not an object name) followed by a parenthesized argument list. Note that the parentheses are required in this kind of object declaration, even if the default constructor is used. A normal object declaration that uses the default constructor does not require empty parentheses (for example, `A myobj;`). The following short program demonstrates explicit calls and the required placement of parentheses:

```
#include <iostream.h>

class A {
  int value;
public:
  A( int arg = 0 ) : value( arg ) {} // two forms in one lick
  void dump() { cout << value << "\r\n"; }
};

void main()
{
  A obj1 = A();                          // Use default form
     // empty parentheses required for default constructor
  A obj2 = A( 37 );                      // Use argument form

  obj1.dump();
  obj2.dump();
}
```

An explicit call to a class's constructor function, such as one of the calls shown in the preceding short program, causes an *unnamed temporary object* to be created. The resulting object is then copied into the object being declared on the left side of the assignment statement. This process uses the copy constructor function if the objects are class objects, as they are in the preceding program.

The use of temporary objects raises another issue related to constructor calls. Constructors for temporaries are called at the time the temporary objects are created, as are all other constructors. But the base document and the *Borland C++ Programmer's Guide* say nothing about *which* constructor is called. The base document leaves the decision up to the implementation, whereas the Borland C++ documentation only states that temporaries are in fact used from time to time. Presumably, the constructor used will be the default constructor (although we have been unable to verify that).

Arrays of class objects present another variation on the theme of constructor calls. You have already learned that declaring an array of class objects causes the default constructor to be executed for the object in each array element. But in what order are the constructor calls made? All arrays are created in an area of contiguous memory, in order of ascending memory address. And that is the order in which the constructors are called, because the call is made as each object is created.

Finally, consider a class object being declared as a member object in another class. At what time is the constructor for the included object called? Clearly, the constructor cannot be called before an object of the containing class is created. But the constructor body for the included object is executed *before* the constructor body for the containing class.

In the case of a constructor with an initializer list, you can easily see why the included object's constructor is executed first. Note, for example, the following code fragment:

```
class A { ... };
...
class B {
...
  A someobj;  // included class object
public:
  B( int arg = 0 ) : someobj( arg ) { ... }
...
};
```

The initializer list item `someobj(arg)` causes the class A constructor to be invoked before the class B constructor function body is reached. It is interesting to note that Borland C++ follows the spirit of the base document's rules for constructor call order, if not the letter. Borland C++ will generate code to execute a contained class object's constructor function first *only* if there is a physical dependency that requires it. That is, in the preceding code fragment, the A class constructor will be executed first only if the B class constructor contains a call to one of A's member functions or refers to A's public member data.

Even when there is no constructor initializer list, the compiler generates code that behaves *as if* the contained object's default constructor is physically called first.

Now consider a problem you might encounter when writing constructor functions—that of accidentally causing infinitely recursive constructor calls. You learned earlier that a copy constructor can accept as an argument only a *reference* to an object of its own class. The reason for this restriction is that passing an object to a copy constructor by value could cause just such infinite recursion. Is it possible to cause infinite recursion of a constructor function in some other way?

There certainly is a way to cause constructor recursion. The method consists of fooling the compiler into allowing you to create a new object of a class before the constructor gets through in the first place. Although the compiler can check the syntax of the copy constructor declaration, the compiler is not intelligent enough to interpret the significance of where you place object declarations. The following short program, for instance, causes infinite recursion of the constructor function (the program runs, but it will cost you a system boot to see it):

```
#include <iostream.h>

class A {
  int value;
public:
  A() {
    A myobj;    // DANGER! Here is the culprit!

    value = 37;
    cout << value << "\r\n";
  }
};

void main()
{
  A someobj;   // Get it started
}
```

This program is appropriately named `lockup.cpp`—and that is precisely what it will do to your computer. Figure 15.3 shows the logic flow of a program with a constructor that locally declares an object of its own class.

Fig. 15.3. The execution flow that results when a constructor function calls itself.

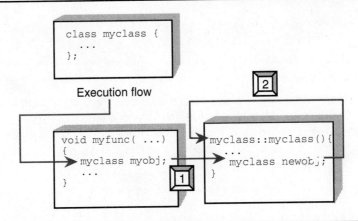

The cure, of course, is to observe the rule that you should never declare within a constructor function an object of the same class. At first, it might seem that the cure *should* be to modify the compiler to prevent such a declaration. To do that, however, you would need to eliminate the ability to declare an object of an *incomplete type*. In other words, you would no longer be able to declare objects in the following manner:

```
class A;  // Forward-declare class A
...
class B {
  A workobj; // Declare an A object here
...
};
...
class A {
  ... // Complete A's declaration now
};
```

Providing the ability to declare objects of an incomplete type (known as forward-declaration), as shown in the preceding code fragment, may seem needlessly complex. Forward-declaration is, in fact, a valuable feature in the design of complex classes. You can, for example, declare two classes that refer to each other.

Most frequently, one class will refer to another class in order to declare the first class (or specific member functions of the first class) as friends of the second class. The code sequence looks like this:

```
class A;  // forward-declaration
class B {
  friend class A; // Declare whole class a friend
  ...
};

class A {  // Complete declaration for A
  ...       // All A members can refer to B members
};
```

A more subtle way in which classes can refer to one another is for both classes to declare as a friend a function that accepts arguments of *both* classes. A common operator function is typical here. Class A and class B might both declare a friend function that "sums" an A object and a B object, returning a simple integer, for example, like this:

```
class A;  // Forward-declare this one

class B {
  ...
  friend int operator+( A&, B& );
  ...
};

class A {  // Complete A class declaration
```

```
      ...
      friend int operator+( A&, B& );
      ...
   };
   ...
   int operator+( A& aobj, B& bobj )
   {
      // Sum numbers somehow here
      // and return an int
   }
```

You should exercise caution, though, when designing mutually referential classes. Just as declaring a constructor that contains an object declaration of its own class can cause infinite recursion, mutually referential classes can cause an infinite loop. For example, the following short program compiles and runs, but only stops running when memory is exhausted:

```
#include <iostream.h>

class A;

class B {
  int value;
  A *aobj;
public:
  B();
  void show();    // declaration only here, inline won t work
};

class A {        // Finish A s declaration first
  int value;
  B *bobj;
public:
  A();
  void show();    // declaration only here, could be inline
};

// Member function definitions can be in any order,
// since there is now a declaration for everything

A::A()
{
  value = 37;
  bobj = new B;
```

```
}

void A::show() {
  cout << value << "\r\n";
}

B::B()
{
  value = 37;
  aobj = new A;
}

void B::show() {
  cout << value << "\r\n";
}

void main()
{
  A testobj;          // This causes recursion again

  testobj.show();  // Execution never gets here
}
```

The declaration A testobj; in function main() gets the ball rolling by invoking the default constructor A::A(). But that constructor function creates a B class object with operator new, invoking the B class constructor. However, the B class constructor also creates an A class object, and recursion has inescapably begun.

When Are Destructor Functions Called?

As noted earlier, destructor functions perform the inverse task of constructor functions: destructors turn class objects into raw chunks of memory. Destructors are also the mirror images of constructors in that destructors are called whenever a class object is destroyed.

For *locally declared* class objects, the containing scope terminates when the current block is exited. The current block may be just a block statement, or the block may be a function body. In the latter case, the class object goes out of scope—and is destroyed—when the function returns to its caller. Calling the destructor for a local object is illustrated in figure 15.4.

Fig. 15.4. The destructor for a local object is called when the containing scope terminates (at the end of the block or when the function returns).

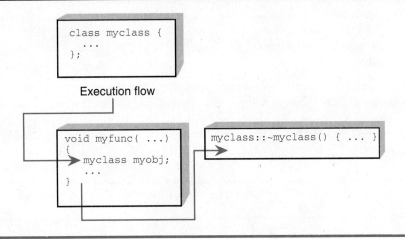

Figure 15.4 shows that the destructor for a local object is automatically invoked after the return mechanism is executed (the return statement or end-of-block is encountered) but *before* any other scope is entered.

The destructor for a *global* class object is invoked when file scope terminates. Note that this timing also applies to objects declared locally within a function or block but modified with the static keyword.

You can terminate file scope in three ways. First, you can let program execution "fall through" the bottom of the main() function. This method is functionally identical to the second method: terminating program execution by executing the exit() function. The exit() function can, of course, be executed from anywhere in your program. In both these methods of terminating file scope, the compiler-generated cleanup code (including the code to invoke destructors) can be executed.

The third method of stopping program execution is very dangerous for all objects, including class objects. This method consists of calling the abort() function. The method is dangerous because there is no guarantee that any cleanup will be done; the program may just stop execution immediately. Both ANSI C and C++ 2.0 standards allow a compiler to generate abort() code that essentially does nothing at all.

Borland C++, in fact, does do something when abort() is called. Borland C++ calls the internal routine _exit()—notice the leading underscore—

with a return code of 3, and displays a message on the `stderr` stream that execution was abnormally terminated. The `_exit()` function does nothing except pass on the return code of 3 to DOS or to the parent process. `_exit()` does *not* close any open files, flush output buffers, or call any registered `atexit()` functions. Nor are destructor functions invoked. If your class objects require some sort of extra processing before being destroyed, you are in trouble.

Using the `abort()` function guarantees that there will be *no* orderly cleanup of class objects because the execution path that involves calling registered `atexit()` functions is bypassed. And the `atexit()` registered functions are called *before* the destructors for any global or static class objects, as illustrated in figure 15.5.

Fig. 15.5. *Functions registered by* `atexit()` *are called before the destructors for global and static objects.*

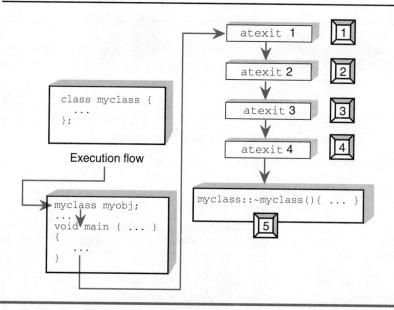

Destructor functions for *arrays* of class objects are handled in mirror-image fashion, compared to constructor calls for arrays. Although the constructors for an array of class objects are called in ascending order of memory address, the destructors for an array are called in the reverse order of the objects' creation. In other words, the destructors are called backwards.

You can cause the destructor functions for arbitrary duration objects (those created with new) to be executed whenever you want. You simply use the delete operator, as shown in the following code fragment:

```
class X { ... };  // Declare a class
...
void main()
{
  X* anobj = new X; // Create arbitrary duration object
  ...              // Things happen here
  delete anobj;    // Kill it at your pleasure
  ...              // More things happen here
}
```

You can certainly create arrays of arbitrary objects and still delete them without regard to the current scope. The following code fragment does just that:

```
class X { ... };        // Declare a class
...
X* anobj = new X[22]; // Pointer to 22 X objects is global

void myfunc();          // Function declaration
...
void main()
{
  myfunc();             // Go execute myfunc()
}

void myfunc()           // Descend to a local scope
{
  delete anobj [22]    // Kill all 22 X objects
}
```

When you delete an array of arbitrary duration objects, you choose the timing, but you still follow the rules for calling destructors for arrays of objects. The destructors are called in reverse order of the objects' (the array elements') creation.

You can cause program recursion in a destructor function, too, just as in a constructor function. In the case of a destructor, however, the mechanism involves calling the exit() function from within the destructor function.

Specifically, exit() causes global and static objects to go out of scope, triggering their destructor functions (local objects are not destroyed in this case). If the destructor in which you call exit() is a global or static object, calling exit() causes the same destructor to be called again—destruction of the object is not yet complete. That leads again to the exit() call, and recursion is established.

Finally, you can explicitly call the destructor function for an object. The following trivial program shows the syntax required for calling a destructor function directly:

```
#include <iostream.h>
#include <string.h>

class tool {
  char descr[41];
  int catlgnum;
public:
  tool( int = 0, char* = "" );
  ~tool() {}
  void tell();
};

tool::tool( int assigncat, char* name )
{
  strcpy( descr, name );
  catlgnum = assigncat;
}

void tool::tell()
{
  cout << "Tool number " << catlgnum << " is a "
       << descr << " device.\r\n";
}

void main()
{
  tool wrench( 1, "Turn nuts and bolts" );

  wrench.tell();
  wrench.tool::~tool();
}
```

This short program illustrates a couple of points about explicit destructor calls. First, although it is not apparent from just looking at this code, you must actually define a destructor function: the compiler-generated one will not do. Borland C++ will not recognize the destructor call unless you have defined a destructor. It can be an entirely empty function, like the one in the preceding program, but a defined destructor must be there.

Second, you must use the fully qualified name for the destructor function. In the preceding example, the class member operator (.) is used in the last line of main() to call the destructor. Had wrench been a pointer to a class object, you would have written the following:

```
wrench->tool::~tool();
```

The fully qualified class destructor function name, following the member name and operator, is always required. Otherwise, it would be possible to write expressions that confuse the one's complement operator (~) with the destructor name character (also ~).

You may recall from Chapter 11 that the program in listing 11.6 used the lifo stack class to create a simple class object (on a lifo stack) at a specific memory address. (The technique was presented without much explanation at the time.) Later in the same program, an explicit destructor function call was used to remove the class object. That use, in fact, is one of the rare times you might need to call a destructor function directly. You might profitably return now to Chapter 11 and review listing 11.6 with a more educated eye for what is going on there.

Overloading Constructor Functions

The constructor functions for a class are clearly an important part of the class's design. This section provides an expanded discussion of constructor design logistics.

Specifically, the section focuses on the issue of providing multiple constructors (overloading them) for a class. Also covered are some of the considerations that determine what logic must be put into the various kinds of constructors (that is, default and nondefault).

Writing a Default Constructor Function

If the process of constructing and initializing a class object is complex enough to require you to overload the constructor function in several different ways, you should provide your own version of the default constructor. This recommendation is especially true on three occasions:

❑ When the class object has special initialization requirements that go beyond what a compiler-generated constructor will do

❑ When you create class objects with the `new` operator or with arrays of class objects

❑ When you need to create an object at a particular memory location

What kinds of objects might have special initialization requirements? Almost any kind of object might have them. Think of the classes that you can define as falling into one of three categories: object-like objects, value-like objects, and action-like objects. (Note that no new technical terms are offered here, but descriptive phrases are provided.) Objects falling into any of these three categories could have special initialization requirements:

❑ *Object-like objects* include objects that control large amounts of data. These objects are focused more on data than behavior, although they do have a behavior. A large table of data that must be kept in main memory is an example of such an object. The `dbllist` class you saw earlier in this book is another example.

Class objects belonging to the object-like category may require large amounts of memory for storing relatively extensive data, as in the case of the `dbllist` class. Any constructor for this class, including the default constructor, must be able to acquire such memory. Additionally, pointers to the acquired memory must be initialized—a null pointer won't do. Special attention must also be given to copy constructors for this category of objects because you will usually not want two objects to point to the same area of acquired memory.

❑ *Value-like objects* are objects whose significance centers on some particular arithmetic value. The Borland C++ `complex` class is an example of such an object. Value-like objects have important data content and behavior (such as the full range of arithmetic operations).

Special initialization requirements for this category of objects are likely to include the setting of initial values for internal *state variables* associated with the object, and the controlling of the object's behavior.

❑ *Action-like objects* are objects whose most significant characteristic is what they *do*, not what they contain. You might design, for example, a `command` class that routes execution to the appropriate service function, based on a command string.

This category of objects is least likely to require special handling when a class object is created. However, each class has its own characteristics, and action-like objects may need starting values for state variables or other setup actions carried out.

The default constructors you provide for classes with objects either created by `new` or declared in arrays are important also. You can provide an initializer list to be passed to the constructor for an object created with `new`, as in the following short program:

```
#include <iostream.h>

class A {
  int value;
public:
  A() { value = 37; }
  A( int arg ) { value = arg; }
  void tell() { cout << value << "\r\n"; }
};

void main()
{
  A* aptr = new A ( 64 ); // Similar to A x( 64 );

  aptr->tell();
}
```

However, you will more often use the `new` operator to specify only a type name. In the preceding short program, for example, `aptr` is usually initialized with this declaration:

```
A* aptr = new A;
```

If objects created with `new` have any of the special initialization requirements previously discussed, a default constructor is quite important. Creating arrays of objects presents a similar problem, but you do not have the flexibility of using a nondefault constructor for class objects created in arrays. Default constructors for objects declared in an array are essential.

Classes that are to have objects created at a particular place in memory (specific address) must receive the same design attention as classes that are created with `new`. In fact, placing an object at a specific memory location involves overloading the global `new` operator, as shown in the following program:

```
#include <iostream.h>

//
// Declare a simple class
//
class simple {
  int stuff;
public:
  simple( int arg = 16 ) { stuff = arg; }
  ~simple() {}              // Default destructor
  void showit() { cout << stuff << "\r\n"; }
};


//
// Overload global operator new()
//
void* operator new( size_t size, void *ptr )
{
  size = size; // Dummy statement avoids compiler warning
  return ptr;  // Here is what we are after
}


void main()
{
  void *fetch;              // Working pointer

                           // Get a block of memory using
                           // original global new
  fetch = (void *)( new unsigned char[ sizeof(simple) ] );

  simple* X;               // Pointer to simple object

  X = new(fetch) simple( 37 );   // Create object
  X->showit();
  X->simple::~simple();    // Explicitly delete object
  delete fetch;            // Release memory
}
```

As the preceding short program shows, you can overload global `new` (this subject is covered at the end of the chapter) and still use an initializer list to pass arguments to the constructor. Note this line from the preceding program:

```
X = new(fetch) simple( 37 );   // Create object
```

However, you must still be careful to provide a way of handling special initialization requirements even if initializers cannot be used. Every possible use of the object must be accounted for in actual practice. That is why the constructor in this short program is given default arguments—so that the constructor can be used as either a default *or* a nondefault constructor.

Writing Other Constructors

Providing your own version of a default constructor for a class instead of allowing the compiler to generate a constructor is important, but overloading the constructor in other ways is often equally important. Note three reasons (all discussed in earlier sections of this chapter) to provide a fairly rich set of overloaded constructor functions for a class:

❏ To avoid constructor argument conversions when performing the best-fit match

❏ To permit several different sets of constructor arguments to be used in creating class objects

❏ To provide for conversion of other types to the class's type by constructor conversion

There may be other reasons to provide a rich set of overloaded constructor functions, but these are probably the most important. There is, however, a trade-off in declaring many overloaded constructor functions. On the one hand, a rich constructor set can contribute significantly to high-performance programs (by eliminating many instances of extra overhead). On the other hand, because each constructor function takes up code space, your program will be correspondingly longer. Generally, the extra code space is not overwhelming, and most programmers prefer high-performance code.

By designing your class and its constructor carefully and thoroughly, you can often eliminate much of the extra code space required by a rich constructor set. You can do this by isolating the initialization code that is common to *all* constructors and placing that code in its own separate function (perhaps in the `private` part of the class declaration). Each different constructor can then call the common initialization routine, and you won't have to repeat the code needlessly. A framework for such a class might look like this:

```
class A {
  ... // state variables, private data
  void common( int required_parm ) { ... } // common code
public:
  A()
  {
    common( arg );
    ... // other init code
  }
  A( char *descr )
  {
    common( arg );
    ... // other init code
  }
  A( int arg, double darg )
  {
    common( arg );
    ... // other init code
  }
```

Occasionally, a programmer tries to use a direct constructor call in an effort to separate the common initialization code. That is, the programmer makes the mistake of packaging the common code as the basic constructor for the class. Note this example:

```
#include <string.h>
#include <iostream.h>

class A {                                           // BAD CODE !!!
  int main_value;
  char descr[41];
public:
  A( int arg = 37 ) : main_value(arg) {
    strcpy( descr , "No description" );
  };
  A( char *text ) {
    A( 64 );         // Try to call this object's constructor
    strcpy( descr, text );
  }
  A( double arg ) {
    A( (int)arg );                          // Drop the ball again
    strcpy( descr, "It was a double" );
  }
  void blurb() {
```

```
      cout << "Value = " << main_value << "\r\n";
      cout << descr << "\r\n";
   }
};

void main()
{
   A obj( "Different text" );

   obj.blurb();
}
```

This program appears to have some fairly sophisticated code, on the surface. The code would be sophisticated—if it worked correctly. The program compiles without error and runs without blowing up. So what is wrong?

The second and third constructors call the first constructor directly, which is legal. The only thing that was forgotten in writing this program is that the syntax `class(args)` doesn't just call the constructor but *first creates a temporary unnamed object.* Therefore, the second and third constructors are merely spinning their wheels uselessly by creating a temporary class object that is thrown away as soon as the statement is complete.

Thus, the object declaration in `main()` gives the appearance that it will invoke the second constructor, which will set `main_value` to 64, and then copy the argument string into `descr`. Although the string is indeed copied, you will find, if you run this program, that `main_value` for *this* object contains garbage. The value 64 is assigned, but it is assigned to the variable in a temporary class object that disappeared.

In summary, then, it is wise to separate common initialization code into a single (perhaps `private`) member function. However, don't try to get fancy by making that function a constructor. Your program will compile with no sign that anything is wrong, but it won't do what you expect it to do.

Deciding When You Need a Copy Constructor

The copy constructor is a special form of overloaded constructor function that you must consider when designing your classes. The problem with copy constructors is that you often need them, but it is not always obvious *when* you need them. The following code fragment illustrates this point:

```
class X {
  int data;
public:
  X() { data = 64; }                     // Default constructor
  X( int arg ) { data = arg; }     // Conversion constructor
  X( X& other ) { data = other.data; }  // Copy constructor
};

void main()
{
  X obj1 = 2;     // Use conversion constructor

  X obj2 = obj1; // Obviously the copy constructor
  X obj3(obj2);  // Copy constructor but not obvious
}
```

What is going on in this program is quite clear—until the last line of main() is reached. The declaration of obj3 in that line uses the alternative form of declaring a class object with initialization from another class object. The syntax doesn't jump out at you and indicate that the copy constructor is going to be used. However, because the constructor argument is a reference to another object of the same class, the copy constructor is in fact used. If you have allowed the compiler to generate the copy constructor, the result may not be what you want.

In deciding when you need a copy constructor, you should also consider initialization tasks. If any of the special initialization requirements mentioned earlier exist for a class, the compiler-generated copy constructor may not be adequate. Generally, it is best to provide a copy constructor yourself. If an object is then initialized by copying another object of the same class, there will be no possibility of incorrect setup.

Using *operator new()* and *operator delete()*

In C++, the operators new and delete enable you to create dynamic objects of arbitrary duration. You can also use these operators to acquire memory for any kind of plain C object, much like allocating memory on the heap with malloc() and calloc().

Objects created with new reside on the *free store*. Objects on the free store are removed with the delete operator. In fact, Borland C++ uses the heap to implement the free store, but the differences in handling warrant treating the free store as a separate conceptual entity. Understanding the new and delete operators is central to the efficient use of C++'s free store.

This section shows you how to use and overload the new and delete operators. Stroustrup, the designer of C++, believed that memory allocation was such an important part of C++ programming that the facilities for memory allocation were implemented as built-in operators instead of standard library routines. As a result, program *execution* of C++ programs that use these operators tends to be slightly faster, whereas program compilation with new and delete (rather than with the library functions) tends to be slower.

Using *new* and *delete* in General

You can use the new and delete operators to allocate space for any C data objects, not just to create class objects. The rules for using new to acquire space on the free store are quite simple:

❏ *The new operator is a unary operator.* It has a single operand, positioned to its right. Note this example:

```
int* data;
...
data = new int;
```

The operand for new can be, as you will soon discover, considerably more complex than the one shown here.

❏ *The operand for new is a type name.* Beginning C++ programmers can easily be tempted to code an *object* for the new operand, when in fact it should be a *type name*. The purpose of new is not to acquire, say, an integer but to allocate sufficient space for one. The following short program illustrates this point:

```
#include <iostream.h>


void main()
{
  int* value;        // pointer to an integer

  value = new int; // Allocate space on free store
  cout << value << "\r\n";;
  delete value;    // Destroy integer
}
```

❑ *The* new *operator returns a pointer of the correct type.* Because the operand must be a type name, new already knows what kind of pointer is required. One of the nice features of new is that you don't have to cast the pointer to the correct type, as you would when using malloc(), which always returns a void pointer. Note that new returns a *null pointer* if space cannot be found on the free store.

❑ *The* new *operator automatically calculates the size of the object for which* new *is allocating memory.* This feature is also handy because you do not have to use the sizeof() operator to compute the size required. The resulting code looks cleaner.

❑ *You can use* new *to allocate space for more complex objects, such as arrays, on the free store.* To use new to allocate memory for a string or an array, simply write the type name and then the array size enclosed by the array declarator ([ ]). The following short program demonstrates this use of new:

```
#include <string.h>
#include <iostream.h>

void main()
{
    char* str;              // pointer to a string

    str = new char[41]; // Allocate array on free store
    strcpy( str, "Here is another hello program.\r\n" );
    cout << str;
    delete str;              // Destroy string
}
```

Notice that when new allocates memory for an array, new returns only a pointer to the first element of the array. This is not a problem, however, because the plain C equivalence of pointers and subscripts applies in C++ also.

❑ *You can create multidimensional arrays of objects with* new, *but with some restrictions.* You can write multidimensional size declarators like this:

```
    intptr = new int[2][2][2];
```

None of the array sizes can be omitted (that is, you cannot refer to an incomplete array type). All the dimensions except the first one must be *constants*. The first dimension can be any legitimate expression, such as the following:

```
int i = 2;
intptr = new int[i][2][2];
```

❏ *References cannot be created with* new. A reference is an lvalue, but not strictly an object. Therefore, new cannot return a pointer to a reference—and new must return a pointer.

❏ *Objects created with* new *are not automatically initialized to any value*. The contents of such an object are garbage, unless you do something about it. You can specify an initializer with new, but only for simple objects, not for arrays. Consider this example:

```
int* i = new int( 37 ); // Set int to 37
```

Using parentheses for the initializer enables you later to specify constructor arguments with new. (Surely, you guessed that was coming!)

Objects created with new on the free store have *arbitrary duration*. (This point has been mentioned before in other contexts.) Arbitrary objects are neither precisely static nor global—they exist until you destroy them with delete. An important side effect of the nature of arbitrary duration objects is that C++ does not guarantee to automatically delete them at any time. You must take care of deleting them yourself. Failing to delete an object, however, is not usually considered an error but is wasteful and can lead to a shortage of storage later.

The rules for using the delete operator are also simple:

❏ *Like* new, *the* delete *operator is a unary operator.* delete works on an operand (or operands) to its right. You use the following general syntax for delete:

```
::opt delete pointer
::opt delete [size] pointer
```

The preceding syntax forms incorporate an exception to the formatting rules that have been used throughout the book. The square brackets around the *size* token form the subscript operator and must be coded as shown here.

Prefixing the scope resolution operator guarantees that the global operator delete is used. (You will learn how to overload delete for a class in the following sections.) The *pointer* must be one that was returned by new, and the [*size*] declarator destroys an array of objects created with new. The following code fragment shows how to code each form of the syntax:

```
double* x = new double; // Create and point to a simple double
delete x;               // Kill the double
...
int* i = new int[256];  // Create array of 256 ints
delete [256] i;         // Kill the whole array
```

❏ *You use the* delete *operator only to free storage acquired by* new. Trying to delete memory allocated by malloc(), for example, is an error. Using delete 0, however, is guaranteed to be harmless. (In other words, you won't blow up your program by deleting a null pointer.)

❏ *You cannot* delete *a pointer to a constant.* Specifying a pointer to a constant with delete implies that you are trying to destroy the constant object, and constants by definition cannot be modified.

As you can see, the rules for using new and delete with plain C data objects are simple. The process is uncluttered by constructor or destructor calls because they do not apply to ordinary data objects. Yet using new and delete with class objects is almost as easy, as discussed in the next section.

Dynamically Creating and Deleting Class Objects

You can use the new and delete operators to create and destroy class objects, and you can use these operators within constructor and destructor functions. To avoid infinite recursion, however, do not use new with the same class type as that of the constructor function containing it.

All the rules for using new and delete with ordinary data objects apply also to using these operators with class objects. You should note some additional considerations, however. When using new to create class objects on the free store, observe the following points:

❏ *Using* new *with a class type causes a constructor for the class to be invoked.* This is the primary difference between using new with data types and with class types. If the class type alone is used, the class's default constructor is called. Note the following code fragment:

```
class radio { ... };
...
radio* jambox = new radio; // Create object and call default
                           // constructor for class
```

The `new` operator both allocates space on the free store for `jambox` and calls the `radio` class default constructor.

❑ *When class objects are created with* `new`, *the* `new` *initializer may be a list of arguments.* This list can be used as arguments for a constructor call. Arguments matching rules apply, so that you can control which overloaded constructor will be invoked. Look at this example:

```
class twocon {
  ...
public:
  twocon ( int );
  twocon ( long, char * );
...
};
                                    // Call second constructor
twocon* objptr = new twocon( 4L, "A string" );
```

❑ *When arrays of class objects are created with* `new`, *only the default constructor can be used.* This point has been mentioned before, but it should be repeated here. Declaring an array of class objects, either with `new` or in some other way, restricts constructor calls to the default version. Remember that because the default constructor can be a constructor with *all default arguments*, the constructor function can be called without arguments. The default constructor is called for each element of the array.

When you use `delete` to destroy class objects on the free store, note these additional considerations:

❑ *When* `delete` *is applied to a class object on the free store, the object's destructor function is automatically invoked.* There can, of course, be only one version of the class destructor function because destructors cannot accept arguments.

❑ *Do not use* `delete` *to destroy a class object created at a specific memory location with an overloaded* `new`. The reason for this restriction is quite simple: `new` didn't create the class object—you did. Even if you acquired the specific memory for the object with global `new`, the allocation was for a plain C object (such as an array of characters). The correct method of destroying a specifically placed object is to call the *destructor* directly and then separately release the storage occupied by the object.

❑ *Using* `delete` *to destroy an array of class objects on the free store automatically invokes the destructor function for each array element.* The syntax for deleting an array of class objects is the same as for plain C objects:

```
class simple {
  char* str; // Point to string outside object
public:
  simple() { str = new char[41]; }
  ~simple() { delete str; }
};


void main()
{
  simple* sarray = new simple [16];    // Array of 16

  delete [16] sarray; // Call destructors for all 16
}
```

Borland C++ currently requires that the array size declarator contain an expression giving the actual array size, as shown in the last statement of the preceding code fragment. This requirement is another instance in which Borland C++ has not yet caught up to the latest specifications in the base document. According to the base document, the form just shown is an anachronism (an obsolete feature) to be supported by the compiler as an extra feature. It would be no surprise if Borland C++ eventually allowed the more general—and less prone to error—form required by the base document. Because the new form does not require the expression giving the array size, you could code the last line in the preceding fragment in this way:

```
delete [] sarray; // Call destructors for all 16
```

As you can see, a considerable amount of programming power is inherent in the global `new` and `delete` operators. There are very few things related to the creation of class objects on the free store that you cannot do with these operators. But because there *are* some things you cannot do with `new` and `delete`, C++ allows you to overload them. Overloading `new` and `delete` is discussed in the remaining sections of this chapter.

Overloading *operator new()* and *operator delete()*

The new and delete operators discussed so far are an integral part of the C++ language. They are called the *global* new and delete operators, and they are available at any time. You can also provide new and delete operators unique to each of your classes. These operators are known as *user-defined* new and delete operators.

Because you already know how to overload operators for a class, it won't surprise you to learn that overloading either the global or the user-defined new and delete operators involves writing the overloaded function definition for the new version of the operator. Specifically, note the following points:

❏ *The use of operator* new *or operator* delete *in an expression causes the corresponding function to be called.* In other words, using operator new causes the function operator new() to be called, and using operator delete causes the operator delete() function to be called.

❏ *A size argument having type* size_t *is the required first (or only) argument for every version of* operator new()*. The* operator new() *function always returns a void pointer (*void*). That is, you must at least define the function with the following declaration part:

```
void* operator new( size_t size ) { ... }
```

Note that if you declare *only* the size_t argument for global new, you are not overloading the new operator—you are completely redefining it. The first argument must be a size_t type object, but you will generally add other, optional arguments, as discussed later in this section.

❏ *A void pointer (*void*) is the required first argument for* operator delete()*. The* operator delete() *function always returns* void *(nothing).* That is, you must at least define the function with the following declaration part:

```
void operator delete( void* obj ) { ... }
```

Here `obj` is a pointer to the object being deleted. The `operator delete()` function can optionally have a second argument specifying the size of the object to be deleted:

```
void operator delete( void* obj, size_t size ) { ... }
```

You can use the optional argument for any purpose you want. It is not generally needed, but some circumstances may arise in which you will need such an argument.

Overloading the Global Operators

You might want to overload the global operators `new` and `delete` for two reasons: to place a class object at a specific memory location (already mentioned briefly), or to take full control of free-store garbage collection and recovery from failures of `new`. Most of the important theory concerning overloading (or overriding) the `new` and `delete` operators, however, is presented in this section and is critical background for that later discussion.

You can create a class object at a particular memory location—for example, one you allocated with `malloc()`—because C++ recognizes the use of operator `new` with *placement syntax*. When you use placement syntax, you simply provide a pointer to the area in which the object is to be constructed. The global `new` operator with placement syntax looks like this:

$$::_{opt} \text{new}(locationptr) \ type \ [number]_{opt}(initializers)_{opt}$$

Note in this syntax form that the prefix scope resolution operator, the array size declarator (which must be surrounded with subscript operator brackets, if used at all), and the list of initializers are all optional.

Earlier in the chapter, you saw a sample program in which a class object was constructed in place. That short program is repeated here for convenience. Because your primary concern (for the moment) is the construction of a single class object in place, the array size declarator has been left out temporarily. The following short program illustrates the technique required for constructing a class object at a particular location:

```
#include <iostream.h>


//
// Declare a simple class
//
class simple {
```

```
   int stuff;
public:
   simple( int arg = 16 ) { stuff = arg; }
   ~simple() {}                          // Default destructor
   void showit() { cout << stuff << "\r\n"; }
};

//
// Overload global operator new()
//
void* operator new( size_t size, void *ptr )
{
   size = size;   // Dummy statement avoids compiler warning
   return ptr;                    // Here is what we are after
}

void main()
{
   void *fetch;                           // Working pointer

                              // Get a block of memory using
                              // original global new
   fetch = (void *)( new unsigned char[ sizeof(simple) ] );

   simple* X;                    // Pointer to simple object

   X = new(fetch) simple( 37 );          // Create object
   X->showit();
   X->simple::~simple();         // Explicitly delete object
   delete fetch;                         // Release memory
}
```

The catch to using new with placement syntax is that no corresponding function is available until you define one. You are therefore required to overload operator new().

In the preceding program, notice first *how* the global operator new() function is overloaded. The function accepts an object size and location pointer, in accordance with the rules outlined in the preceding section. One important consequence of this selection of arguments is that this function is indeed an overload of new, not a complete replacement for global operator new(). You can therefore use the original global new in the usual manner—as is done in main().

With the overloaded `operator new()` in place, constructing the class object in place is a straightforward procedure:

1. *Declare a `void` pointer that will be used to locate the class object.* The pointer should be `void*` because that is the type which will be required for using the overloaded `new` operator and for releasing the acquired memory.

2. *Acquire the memory necessary to hold the object.* The memory you acquire at this point has nothing to do with classes (yet). You can use either a library function like `malloc()` or the original global `new` to allocate the memory. Notice how the `sizeof()` operator is used in the preceding sample program to ensure that the correct amount of memory is allocated.

3. *Declare a pointer to a class object of the desired type.* Do not initialize the pointer yet; just declare it. (The constructor will do the initialization.) In the preceding short program, the declaration amounted to `simple* X`, nothing more.

4. *Now use the overloaded `new` operator with placement syntax to construct the class object.* The first `void` pointer you declared is now used with `new` to cause the class constructor to build the object at the specified spot:

   ```
   X = new(fetch) simple( 37 );
   ```

   Notice in this particular statement that an initializer value is also specified. The action caused by this statement is the reason you did nothing earlier to initialize the class object pointer. `new` both invokes the constructor and returns the pointer to the object here.

5. *Use the object however you want.* The resulting class object is a *true* class object and can be used accordingly. In the example here, one of the member functions is invoked.

6. *Call the destructor function explicitly.* There is no `delete` for the *class object* in this procedure. If you don't call the destructor explicitly, it is not called at all. If the object has special requirements (such as additional memory acquired within the constructor), you may want to leave a number of loose ends dangling.

7. *Release the memory used to hold the object.* You can accomplish this step with a call to the standard library function `free()` or with global `delete`, as in the preceding program.

The procedure outlined represents a cookbook-style approach to constructing class objects at a precise location, but the procedure works—every time. And even though it is very simple, it is quite important. You will, in fact, need it again later in this section.

You may have noticed in the preceding discussion that nothing was said about overloading `delete`. The reason is that no corresponding syntax exists for "in place `delete`." Is there any time when you need to overload `operator delete()`? Yes, there is—when you *override* (not just overload) `operator new()`.

Overriding the original global `operator new()` and `operator delete()` functions is a process fraught with danger; you can stumble into all kinds of deep, dark holes. Not least among your worries is the fact that overriding the global functions means that you have accepted the *whole load* for allocating memory on the free store—no other global routines except yours exist then. Although any decision to override these functions should be weighed carefully, there may be times (such as allocation recovery and garbage collection) when overriding is necessary. Therefore, you need to know the basic techniques for overriding `new` and `delete`, as well as the effects of overriding the global operators when you use them with *basic data types* and with *class objects*.

Consider first how overriding `new` and `delete` affects free store allocation for the basic data types. When you override the global functions, you must understand two things:

❏ *Overriding the global functions defeats all the internal memory management schemes.* The `new` and `delete` functions supplied with the compiler perform tasks you don't notice on the surface, such as tracking the size, number, and type of memory allocations. All that is now up to *you*. Furthermore, you should not mix your `new` function with Borland C++'s `delete` function. Provide *both* functions so that you can release memory in a manner compatible with the way in which memory was acquired—for example, by using `malloc()` and `free()`.

❏ *Borland C++'s `delete` function differs slightly from the AT&T base document specification.* The base document states that to override global `delete`, you *must* declare your version of the function to accept a `void*` pointer to the memory to be released, and you *can* add a second argument specifying the size of the memory area. To override the Borland C++ global `delete`, you *must* specify both, as in this example:

```
void operator delete( void* arg, size_t size ) { ... }
```

If you fail to specify both arguments, you will have indeed defined a function—one that is never used.

Because constructor calls are not an issue when you use your own global new and delete, the process of overriding the global operators is simple. One reason that you might want to do this is to provide for preinitialization of the acquired memory (which original new doesn't do). The following short program illustrates this technique:

```
#include <stdlib.h>
#include <iostream.h>

void* operator new( size_t size )
{
  void* ptr;

  ptr = malloc( size );
  if ( !ptr ) return ptr;     // Return null if failed
  memset( ptr, '\0', size ); // Do init for user
  return ptr;                 // Return ptr by value
}

void operator delete( void *obj, size_t size )
{
  free( obj );
}

void main()
{
  char* str;
  str = new char[41];
  delete str;          // All works for plain C objects
}
```

Even though the plain C data type in the preceding code is actually a complex type (a string), only one call to your operator new() is made when this program is run. The size parameter passed to the function in this example is 41, which is the number of bytes indicated in the new array size declarator. The overridden delete function performs the necessary freeing of storage. Note two things about the size parameter passed to your global operator delete(): first, the size parameter is useless here; and second, its value is equal to the *size of the pointer argument*, not of the object pointed to. We have been unable to determine whether this is true for all compilers, but it is certainly true for Borland C++ (as we determined with the debugger).

Consider next the effects of overriding the global new and delete operators when you use them with class objects. Overriding these operators works well for creating class objects, as long as you don't define any arrays of class objects. The following short program shows no apparent differences between defining class objects and defining plain C objects:

```
#include <stdlib.h>
#include <iostream.h>

void* operator new( size_t size )
{
  void* ptr;

  ptr = malloc( size );
  if ( !ptr ) return ptr;     // Return null if failed
  memset( ptr, '\0', size ); // Do init for user
  return ptr;                 // Return ptr by value
}

void operator delete( void *obj, size_t size )
{
  free( obj );
}

class simple {
  int a, b, c, d, e;
public:
  simple() : a(37),b(37),c(37),d(37), e(37)
      { cout << "Hello!\r\n"; }
  ~simple() { cout << "Goodbye!\r\n"; }
};

void main()
{
  simple* oneobj = new simple;
  delete oneobj;  // All still OK for ONE class object
}
```

In the preceding short program, the expression delete oneobj causes the class destructor to be invoked, followed by the overridden version of operator delete(), just as it should be. Should you be so bold as to override global new and delete, and also attempt to create an *array* of class objects, you will find yourself in deep trouble.

Using operator new to construct an array of class objects always causes the global new function to be used. So far, so good, but that isn't all. Note what happens when Borland C++ encounters the array size declarator with new, as shown here:

```
ptr = new classobj[num];
```

Borland C++ doesn't just call `operator new()`. Borland C++ *first* invokes a routine (undocumented, of course) named `_vector_new_()` that creates storage-management information, and *then* invokes `new` and the appropriate constructors.

The tricky part is that, even if you have overridden `new`, constructing an array of objects seems to proceed normally, including invoking your `new` routine to allocate the correct amount of contiguous memory for the array, and calling each constructor. When your program attempts to execute `delete []` `ptr`, however, things go awry—quickly.

In such cases, the program doesn't usually blow up. It just invokes *your* global `delete` too many times, and with the wrong addresses. This happens because an internal routine named `_vector_delete_()` is expecting to traverse the management information previously created, but it isn't there.

The management information is not there for a good reason: Borland C++, like all other C++ compilers, does not support creating vectors (arrays) of class objects when you override `new` and `delete`. As in the situation that exists when constructing class objects at a specific address, you should *not* use `delete` on an array of class objects created with *your* global `new` function. It's illegal.

You may be asking, can you use your `new` and `delete`, and still construct arrays of class objects at all? You certainly can, and the trick is to use the placement syntax for `new` again. Surprised? If you look back at the general syntax shown earlier, you can see that nothing stops you from using both a placement pointer *and* an array size declarator. The following short program shows you how to use both:

```
#include <iostream.h>

void* operator new( size_t size, void* where )
{
  size = size;
  return where;
}


class simple {
  int a, b, c;
public:
  simple() : a(37),b(37),c(37) { cout << "Hello!\r\n"; }
  ~simple() { cout << "Goodbye!\r\n"; }
};
```

```
void main()
{
  int i;
                          // Pointer to memory for array of objects
  void* oarray;


                                    // Acquire memory independently
                                    // for array of objects


  oarray = new unsigned char[ 10*sizeof(simple) ];


                              // Now create array of objects IN PLACE
                              // and invoke all constructors


  simple* bunch = new(oarray) simple[10];


                                    // Be careful here, using
                                    // pointer-subscript equivalence


  for ( i=0; i<10; ++i ) bunch[i].simple::~simple();


                                    // Now "manually" get rid of
                                    // object storage memory
  delete oarray;                    // ::delete object memory
}
```

The procedure for constructing arrays of class objects with your global new overloaded function (but not delete) is nearly as simple as that for placement of class objects. You need to perform the following steps to construct an array of class objects with your new:

1. *Overload, but do not override, global new.* Providing a function definition to support the placement syntax (as is required) does not completely replace global new. It only provides support for specific placement, nothing more.

2. *Set up the void* pointer that will locate the array.* Do not initialize it yet.

3. *Acquire the memory for the whole array.* As before, you can use standard C library routines or ::new for this purpose. Initialize the void* pointer with the result. Notice in the preceding program how the result of applying the sizeof() operator is multiplied by the number of elements in the proposed array.

4. *Declare a pointer to the class object, and initialize it with* new *by using* both *placement syntax and the array size declarator.* Because the placement syntax guarantees that you have taken over storage management, the data otherwise created by _vector_new_() is not required. The constructors for each class object are still properly called.

5. *After using the array of class objects, write a loop in which you directly call the destructor function for every class object in the array.* This step is similar to the direct destructor call for a single in-place class object.

6. *Use the correct method to release the block of memory holding the array.* Again, you can use either the library functions or global delete. delete will not be confused by the appearance of destroying a vector because you have not used an array size declarator. You are *not* destroying a vector, only a chunk of memory.

If you are getting the feeling that overloading and overriding global new and delete can be tricky business, and that there should be a better way to handle at least some of these rather sophisticated requirements, you are right. There will always be instances in which you will need to use the techniques outlined in this section. But there is a better way to satisfy many of these needs without much of the confusion and difficulty: you can overload new and delete on a per-class basis. This topic is discussed in the final section.

Overloading the Operators for a Class

You can overload the new and delete operators for each class you define (if you want) by simply including as member functions the operator overload declarations. Fortunately, the syntax is identical to the syntax you have already seen in this chapter, with one exception. You cannot use the array size declarator with a class-specific user-defined new function. Arrays of objects (class and otherwise) are always allocated with global new, if new is in fact the means you use.

You do not need to make any modifications to the declarations or techniques you have already learned, except to the notation for declaring class member function definitions. This alteration is shown in the following short program:

```
#include <iostream.h>

class X {
```

```
    int a, b, c;
public:
  ~X();
  void* operator new( size_t size );   // static function
  void* operator new( size_t size, void* ptr );
  void operator delete( void* ptr );
};

  X::~X() { }

  void* X::operator new( size_t size )   // static function
  {
    void* ptr;
    cout << "Standard class new called.\r\n";
    ptr = (void*) ::new unsigned char[size];
    return ptr;
  }

  void* X::operator new( size_t size, void* ptr )
  {
    size = size;    // Look familiar?
    cout << "Placement class new called.\r\n";
    return ptr;
  }

  void X::operator delete( void* ptr )
  {
    cout << "Class delete called.\r\n";
    ::delete ptr;
  }

void main()
{
  X* obj1 = new X;
  delete obj1;

  X* obj2;
  void* buf = (void*) ::new unsigned char[ sizeof(X) ];
  obj2 = new(buf) X;
  obj2->X::~X();
  ::delete buf;
}
```

You should still observe the rule of thumb of providing class-specific new and delete overloaded functions in pairs. If you changed allocation methods by writing a new function, you should probably write also a corresponding delete function that releases acquired memory in the same way that it was acquired.

Class-specific new and delete functions are always static member functions, even if you do not declare them with the static storage class specifier. This is true because new must be called before an object exists (there is no this pointer before the constructor is reached), and delete is called after the object has been destroyed. Note that class-specific delete cannot be overloaded—you are allowed to declare only one delete function.

You can overload new however you want, as long as the first argument is always a size_t object size argument. For example, you may want to pass a flag parameter to a class-specific new function as shown in the following code fragment:

```
#include <iostream.h>

class X {
  int a, b, c;
public:
  ...
  void* operator new( size_t size, int flag );
};
...
  void* X::operator new( size_t size, int flag )
  {
    void* ptr;
    cout << "Overloaded class new called.\r\n";
    cout << "Flag was " << flag << "\r\n";
    ptr = (void*) ::new unsigned char[size];
    return ptr;
  }
...

void main()
{
  X* obj1 = new(64) X;
  delete obj1;
}
```

In this code fragment, note that the `new` operator in `main()` has an initializer. This notation, called the *parenthesized form* of operator `new`, is nothing more than the function call method of invoking an overloaded `new`, passing it extra parameters. (The `size_t` parameter is implicit—do not write it directly into the function call.) When there are many overloaded `new` functions, the correct function is selected through best-fit signature matching, as for any other overloaded function.

Except in declarations of arrays of class objects, a class-specific `new` function will always be called when an object of that class is created with `new`, if the class declared one. If the class did not declare an overloaded `new` function, the compiler resorts to the global `new` or `delete` function. Member functions of the class can use its overloaded `new` and `delete` by default, or they can use the scope resolution operator to access the global `new` and `delete` operators (`::new` and `::delete`). In fact, the overloaded operators in the preceding examples resort to global `new` and `delete` to acquire and release memory.

Exercises

Because the exercises here are longer and more difficult than those for other chapters, only two exercises are provided.

1. Now you know how to overload just about everything in a C++ class. Design and write a class that is *very* rich in member functions, overloaded operators, and overloaded constructors (don't forget the copy constructor), and that can be created either with or without `new` and `delete`.

2. This exercise is much tougher than it might seem! *Practice* overloading `new` and `delete`. All but the very shortest code fragments in this chapter were compiled, run, and tested. To see how the code works, type in some of the code fragments and run them yourself. Then write some code of your own that performs the `new` and `delete` techniques presented.

Summary

In this chapter, you learned some important C++ programming techniques for using constructor and destructor functions. Before moving to the next chapter, review your grasp of these points:

❏ *All C++ classes have constructor and destructor functions.* If you do not provide them, the compiler will generate default versions for you. You should understand how and when constructor functions are called.

❏ *You learned the methods for overloading constructor functions, as well as the reason for overloading them.* Remember that a destructor function cannot be overloaded.

❏ *The copy constructor is used when a class object is initialized by copying another object of the same class.* The compiler will also generate for you a default copy constructor that copies a class object on a member-for-member basis. If your class contains pointers to special areas outside the object, or other special requirements, you should write your own copy constructor.

❏ *You can both overload and override global* `new` *and* `delete`. You should understand especially when such actions can get you into deep trouble (some practice will help here).

❏ *Recent C++ compilers now permit you to overload* `operator new()` *and* `operator delete()` *on a per-class basis.* You learned how to provide extra parameters for a class-specific `new` function and how to pass the extra arguments to the function. Remember that class `new` and `delete` are *not* used when an array of class objects is being created; the global versions are always used for this purpose.

16

Using C++ Streams

Following in the footsteps of its parent C language, C++ has no input/ output facilities—no built-in facilities, that is. Like C, C++ has a standard I/O library, known as the C++ stream library, that can fulfill most of your needs for I/O immediately and can be extended easily.

Introducing C++ Streams

An experienced C programmer cannot avoid forming mental associations when he hears the term *C++ stream*. The C concept of handling I/O as a flowing stream of characters that move in and out of a program is inescapable. This association is partly fortunate and partly misleading.

C and C++ streams have many similarities, including the idea of a stream of characters flowing in and out of a program. This basic concept is indeed behind both the C and the C++ I/O libraries. C and C++ streams have many startling differences, too, which you must see and understand clearly. The most radical difference is the syntax that C++ streams use to get the job done.

With Borland C++, you can use both C and C++ streams in the same program. The type-safe linkage feature of the compiler permits this without confusing the compiler about what library routine is to be used. Which library you *should* use at any point is another matter. That decision may be based on personal taste or on a real need.

Much of the C++ literature you see today touts the C++ stream library as a simpler and thus more efficient way to handle I/O. In our opinion, that may have been true with earlier compilers, when C++ streams were much more primitive and therefore simpler to use. Some other examples of C++ literature, such as the *Borland C++ Programmer's Guide*, treat the subject in a more considered and accurate manner, referring to the *improved flexibility and elegance* of C++ streams.

What, then, is the truth about Borland C++ streams? First, the Borland C++ implementation of AT&T 2.0 streams is largely compatible with the existing standards of practice. That is why programs written with Borland C++ streams should almost always be portable to other conforming compilers. Some future incompatibilities are possible, particularly in `fstream.h`, but the reason is that Borland is attempting to stay right on the cutting edge of C++ language development.

Second, C++ has several predefined standard streams that correspond to the plain C standard streams. Using the standard C++ streams for ordinary console I/O *is* quite easy, and the programmer's job is therefore easier at that level. The standard C++ streams are handy for quick console I/O, which is why you have seen them frequently in the sample code of preceding chapters. These standard C++ streams are still handy, even when you begin to use some of their more advanced features.

Third, some of the more advanced features for manipulating the stream state and the data format can get pretty esoteric in C++. Some of these features may actually take more code to implement I/O procedures in your programs. Really sophisticated I/O programming requires relatively more knowledge of class internals than with standard C I/O.

Are C++ streams worth the effort of learning a whole new approach to I/O? Yes, they are. Your initial reaction to C++ streams may be that they are unnecessary because the standard C library functions are available and you already know how to use them. If nothing else is true, however, C++ streams are an integral part of the C++ environment. They can be quite helpful, and you may not be able to read someone else's code if you *don't* learn about them.

Comparing C++ Streams to Standard Streams

Certain behind-the-scenes activities involved in I/O programming do not change, whether you are using standard C library functions or C++ streams. You are already accustomed to the standard C facilities for I/O: a file buffer for holding data; a `FILE` object, which is a structure holding important information about the stream (including the location of the buffer area); and the constellation of library routines that use the file buffer and the `FILE` object to perform I/O.

All these facilities are present in C++ streams as well; it may take just a little getting used to before you recognize them as such. C++, naturally enough, uses class objects both to implement and to encapsulate I/O support facilities, as well as to add more sophistication and "intelligence" to them.

A C++ `streambuf` class object is the parallel facility to the ordinary C buffer. A `streambuf` object does more than simply hold data. It also provides logic for moving characters in to and out of the buffer (including a parallel function to `ungetc( )`), for flushing the buffer, and for disk file stream buffers, for opening and closing the file.

The `ios` class is the parallel to the `FILE` object of plain C. No objects of the `ios` class are ever created, however; it is used as a base class from which to derive input and output classes that do have objects. The purpose of the `ios` class is to contain information about the state of the stream, including any error data, and to contain a pointer to the associated `streambuf` object for the stream. Figure 16.1 illustrates the nature of these two low-level classes.

Fig. 16.1. *The* `streambuf` *class controls the data buffer and drives character I/O. The* `ios` *class provides stream status and error information.*

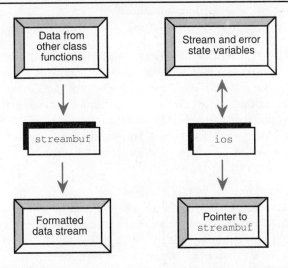

Just as for standard C I/O, some distinction between the input and output processes must be made in C++ stream classes. Borland C++ makes this distinction by deriving two new classes from the `ios` class (see Chapter 17 for details on base and derived classes). These two new classes are the `istream` class (for input) and the `ostream` class (for output). Furthermore, facilities for performing both input and output on the same stream are provided by deriving the `iostream` class from both `istream` and `ostream`, using multiple inheritance. Figure 16.2 shows a schematic of the derivation of these classes.

Fig. 16.2. The `ios` class is a base for `istream` and `ostream` classes. The `iostream` class is derived from both `istream` and `ostream`.

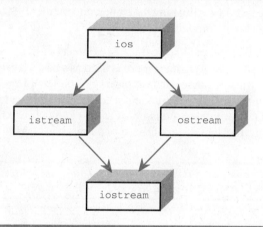

The Borland C++ header file `iostream.h` contains the declarations for all the classes mentioned so far, and it is the only header that you need to include for simple console I/O. (Format conversion and manipulation are covered in the section "Using C++ Stream Manipulators" later in this chapter.) `iostream.h` contains declarations also for the four predefined C++ standard streams (`cin`, `cout`, `cerr`, and `clog`). The standard streams are class *objects* with type `istream` or `ostream`, as appropriate. Figure 16.3 illustrates the standard C++ streams.

In fact, Borland C++ takes the process one step further. A class `istream_withassign` is derived from `istream`, and `ostream_withassign` is derived from `ostream`. The `withassign` classes provide copy constructors and overloaded assignment operators for class objects. The standard streams are objects of the `withassign` classes, but it is more convenient to simply speak of the `istream` and `ostream` classes (as long as you know what is meant).

Fig. 16.3. *The standard C++ stream objects and their classes.*

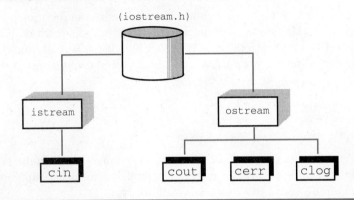

The Borland C++ standard streams perform tasks that are nearly parallel to those of the plain C standard streams. Thus, there is a natural correspondence between the C++ standard streams and the plain C streams. Table 16.1 summarizes the functional correspondence of C++ streams, C streams, and DOS handles.

Table 16.1. *Standard C++ streams, C streams, and DOS handles.*

C++ Stream	C Stream	DOS Handle Used by Plain C `stdio`
`cin`	`stdin`	0
`cout`	`stdout`	1
`cerr`	`stderr`	2
`clog`		
	`stdaux`	3
	`stdprn`	4

It should be emphasized that C++ streams at the AT&T 2.0 level do not use the predefined DOS handles, although version 1.2 streams did. Version 2.0 C++ streams use their own unique file handles and buffering schemes. The `cin` and `cout` streams are line buffered, as are the counterpart `stdin` and `stdout`. The `cerr` stream is line buffered, whereas ANSI C requires `stderr` to be unbuffered. The `clog` stream is a fully buffered version of `cerr` and has no direct counterpart among the plain C standard streams.

Using C++ Streams for Standard I/O

To use the `cin`, `cout`, `cerr`, and `clog` streams in your programs, you do not need to declare any stream objects. These standard stream objects are already declared in the `iostream.h` header file. Just `#include` the header near the beginning of your program, and begin using the streams, as shown here:

```
#include <iostream.h>
...
cout << "Hello,there!\r\n" ;
```

You have already seen the `cout` stream used many times in the sample programs and code fragments in this book, although without explanation. The standard input stream, `cin`, is used in a similar way:

```
#include <iostream.h>
...
char c;
cin >> c; // Get a character from stdin
```

Obviously, the stream classes have overloaded the `<<` and `>>` operators for use with stream objects. The overloaded shift-left operator (`<<`) is called the output stream *inserter* because it "inserts" data into the outflowing data stream. Similarly, the overloaded shift-right operator (`>>`) is called the input stream *extractor* because it "extracts" data from an inflowing data stream and brings it into the program's data areas. Figure 16.4 illustrates how the overloaded `<<` operator function declaration corresponds to the operator's use with `cout`.

Fig. 16.4. *The relationship between the* `<<` *inserter operator and the overloaded* `operator<<( )` *function declaration.*

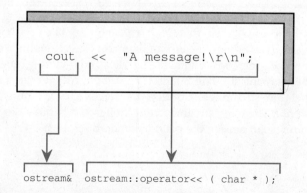

If the stream classes were defined so that only one data item at a time could be inserted or extracted, as shown in the preceding code fragments, the C++ stream would not be very useful. Fortunately, however, the stream classes are defined so that you can cascade, or *chain*, several insertions or extractions in one statement. Note the following example:

```
#include <iostream.h>
...
int a, b, c;
cin >> a >> b >> c; // Extract/input 3 data values
cout << a << b << c; // Now insert/output them
```

In this code fragment, the cin stream is reading your keystrokes from the keyboard (ignoring whitespace), converting the character data to integers, and placing the results in the three variables. Furthermore, cin is preserving the order of appearance of variables and data. That is, the first integer you type is placed in a, the second is placed in b, and the third is placed in c. The items inserted or extracted are handled in order, *from left to right*, just as you would intuitively expect.

The cout stream performs the companion output (insertion) of the three variables, also from left to right. In the preceding code fragment, only variable names are inserted or extracted. cout also allows you to insert any expression, constant, or variable identifier into the stream, as long as the type is supported by the class. For example, you might use the following code:

```
#include <iostream.h>
...
cout << "The answer is " << a << "\r\n";
```

In this fragment, cout produces output on the screen with the following appearance:

```
The answer is 16
```

Presumably, the value of the integer a is 16. The supported data types for cout are shown in table 16.2.

Notice in the preceding code fragment how the inserter operator (<<) is used between the items. Because each inserter "sends" just one value, a statement such as the following is in error:

```
cout << "The answer is " a "\r\n";  // WRONG
```

Notice also that to cause the output string to perform the carriage-return and line-feed action, you need to terminate the insertion sequence with "\r\n". This looks strange if you are accustomed to using only "\n" to terminate a string—for example, a printf() format string. However, cout does not provide (in this particular usage) translation of the newline character to the carriage-return/linefeed characters.

Table 16.2. `cout` data types.

Type	Signed	Unsigned	Default Display Format
`int`	Yes	Yes	Decimal integer
`short`	Yes	Yes	Decimal integer
`long`	Yes	Yes	Decimal integer
`char`	Yes	Yes	Text character
`float`	N.A.	N.A.	Fixed point, 6 digits Precision, rounded
`double`	N.A.	N.A.	Fixed point, 6 digits Precision, rounded
`long double`	N.A.	N.A.	Fixed point, 6 digits Precision, rounded
`char*`	N.A.	N.A.	Text string
`void*`	N.A.	N.A.	Pointer value, xxxxxxxx or xxxxxxxx:xxxxxxxx

For both `cin` and `cout`, control of whitespace is basically up to you. The `cout` stream has a default field width of zero, meaning that as much space as is needed to represent the output is used, but no whitespace is inserted automatically between items. Therefore, if the integers in the preceding fragment had values of 1, 2, and 3, and you write

```
cout << a << b << c;
```

the resulting output appears as

```
123
```

even though the source code statement is nicely spaced out for easy reading. Similarly, the statement

```
cin << a << b << c;
```

works just as well for all the following formats of keyboard input except the last:

```
1 2 3            // This is fine
1   2   3        // and so is this
1[tab]2[tab]3    // Tabs are whitespace, too
123              // wrong, no separation
```

The last input line would provide only a value of 123 for the variable `a`, and `cin` would continue to wait for the rest of the values to be entered. `cin` is a lot like `scanf()` in that respect; that is, you can type each value on a separate line, pressing Enter after each value.

`cin` is unlike `scanf()` in that you cannot include literals in the sequence of extractors and expect to have them exactly skipped over; `cin` by default skips over whitespace, but that is all. The following statement, for example, would yield quite unexpected results:

```
cin >> "A=" >> a;
```

In this line of code, you have fooled `cin` into expecting to receive a pointer to the constant string (which is invalid anyway), followed by an integer value. It just doesn't work out right.

The `cin` stream expects to read input character data for the various types in a format compatible with the way you write constants in a source program, with some slight exceptions. Table 16.3 shows the extractor types that `cin` can accept. Notice that table 16.3 has no entry for the `void*` type. Even if you could type a pointer value, what would it point to?

Table 16.3. *The input data types for* `cin`.

Type	Signed	Unsigned	Default Display Format
`int`	Yes	Yes	Source integer constant
`short`	Yes	Yes	Source integer constant
`long`	Yes	Yes	Source integer constant
`char`	Yes	Yes	Text character
`float`	N.A.	N.A.	Floating-point constant
`double`	N.A.	N.A.	Floating-point constant
`long double`	N.A.	N.A.	Floating-point constant
`char*`	N.A.	N.A.	Text string (not a line)

You must observe some constraints in typing data for `cin`. The most notable constraint is that you cannot use type suffixes as you can in your program's source code. That is, if `cin` is expecting a `long` integer as input, you cannot respond with the character `123L`. Note the following example:

```
long k;
...
cin >> k;  // You type 123, not 123L
```

Specifying the `char*` type may not work the way you expect, either. Suppose, for instance, that you write the following declaration and statement:

```
char str[41];  // a place to hold a string
...
cin >> str;    // Read a string
cout << str;   // Write it back out
```

This code fragment makes it look as if you can type a whole string of characters, press Enter, and see the entire string displayed. But that's not so. `cin` skips whitespace, but it also stops gathering characters for the expected type when whitespace is encountered again. For the preceding code fragment, if you type

```
hello, there!
```

`cout` in turn displays exactly what `cin` extracted. In this case, the result is

```
hello,
```

and nothing more.

Obviously, you will have some problems if you expect to control each character of whitespace with `cin` and `cout`. Inserters and extractors, taken by themselves, don't quite measure up to the task. For that reason, the stream classes provide member functions (as opposed to overloaded operators) that *can* deal with whitespace one character at a time, or a whole line at a time. There are functions for handling pure binary data, too. Table 16.4 shows the `istream` and `ostream` member functions for handling all characters, whole strings, and binary data. `cin` and `cout` are only two specific class objects that can use the member functions. You can declare your own stream objects, including file streams, which can also access those member functions.

Table 16.4 does not show the `signed` and `unsigned` type modifiers for each `char` type, yet overloaded versions of each applicable function with these modifiers do exist. Of course, any of these functions can fail—by reaching an end-of-file (EOF) condition, if nothing else. Handling EOF and error conditions is covered in the next section. The functions in table 16.4 operate in the following ways:

❑ `istream& get( char*, int, char='\n' );`

This version of the `get()` function reads characters into the `char*` buffer until it has either read `int` – 1 characters or encountered the terminating character (newline by default). Note the following code sequence:

```
#include <iostream.h>
#include <iomanip.h>
  char str[41];
...
   istream.get( str, 40, '\n' );
```

For this code sequence, you could type the string **"a   b   c"** and press Enter, with the whitespace (or even binary characters) preserved. That is, the resulting string internally would have the following format:

```
"a    b    c\0"
```

This means that the terminating character is *not* read in, but the null character *is* inserted to complete the string.

Table 16.4. Stream class member functions for special I/O.

Standard Stream	Function Prototype
istream	istream& get(char*, int, char='\n');
istream	istream& read(char*, int);
istream	istream& getline(char*, int, char='\n');
istream	istream& get(char&);
istream	int get( );
istream	int peek( );
istream	istream& putback(char);
istream	istream& ignore(int=1, int=EOF);
ostream	ostream& put(char);
ostream	ostream& write(const char*, int);

❏ `istream& read( char*, int );`

The `read( )` function operates similarly to `get( )`, except that no terminating character is recognized. Exactly `int` characters will be read, and they may consist of ordinary characters, whitespace characters, or binary characters. Note the following example:

```
#include <iostream.h>
#include <iomanip.h>

  char str[41];
...
   cin.read( str, 40 );
```

This code sequence reads 40 characters into `str`. If you press Ctrl-C for one of those characters, the internal character value would be 0x03. This function is more useful when used with file streams.

❏ `istream& getline( char*, int, char='\n' );`

The `getline( )` function operates just like the `get( )` function for a string, except that the terminating character *is* read in before the `'\0'` character is appended. Note this code sequence:

```
#include <iostream.h>
#include <iomanip.h>

  char str[41];
...
  cin.getline( str, 40, '\n' );
```

When you use the preceding code to input the typed characters a b c followed by a press of Enter, the result is the following internal sequence of characters:

```
"a b c\n\0"
```

The `getline( )` member function can be useful for either the `cin` standard stream or a file stream (`fstream`) being read in text mode.

❏ `istream& get( char& );`

This is the single-character version of the `get( )` function. This function can be used to input any ordinary, whitespace, or binary character. Note the following example:

```
char C;
...
cin.get( C );
```

You can use the single-character `get( )` function with standard or file stream objects. Its primary purpose is to retrieve binary data. Note that you can mix text and binary input in a stream, by using a code sequence like this:

```
char c;
...
cin >> c; // Use the extractor to skip whitespace first
cin.get( c ); // Now get ANY second character
```

❏ `int get( );`

Like the single-character `get( )`, this version of `get( )` reads almost any character, but returns an integer rather than a reference to an `istream`. Furthermore, when the `cin` stream uses this version of `get( )`, the function waits for you to press Enter before returning the

character to the stream, and also interprets a Ctrl-C character as a
system Break action. (This is not true for fstreams associated with
disk files.) The normal use of the function looks like this:

```
char C;
...
C = cin.get( );
```

❑ int peek( );

You can use the peek( ) member function to get a look ahead at the
next character in the streambuf without actually extracting it. This
function may seem to have little use with cin (and is more useful
with file streams), but peek( ) can be used to good effect with
standard input. Consider, for example, the following short program:

```
#include <iostream.h>
#include <iomanip.h>

void main( )
{
    char c;

    cin >> c;
    cout << "First character was " << c << "\r\n";
    c = cin.peek( );
    cout << "Next character will be " << c << "\r\n";
}
```

Obviously, peek( ) expects that there is more than one character
waiting in streambuf. But the statement

```
cin >> c;
```

appears to allow only one character to be input at the keyboard. The
catch is that *any* invocation of cin allows you to type as much as you
want, until you press Enter—the characters will be stored in
streambuf and extracted as needed. If in response to the preceding
program, for example, you type the characters abc and then press
Enter, the program produces the following display:

```
First character was a
Next character will be b
```

What if you type only the single character a and immediately press
Enter? What will peek( ) report then? The first message reports the
character a, but the second message contains only the constant part of
the string. What, then, is in c after the call to peek( )? The answer is
determined by the fact that peek( ), like get( ), retrieves *binary*
data. The variable c simply contains the newline character '\n'.

❏ `istream& putback( char );`

You can push a character back into `streambuf` (unextract it, so to speak) with `putback( )` if the program logic decides that the time wasn't really right for extracting it. You might rewrite the preceding short program in the following equivalent way:

```
#include <iostream.h>
#include <iomanip.h>

void main( )
{
    char c;

    cin >> c;
    cout << "First character was " << c << "\r\n";
    cin.get( c );

    ... // Logic decides to unget the character here

    cin.putback( c );
}
```

You will probably use the `putback( )` function, like the `peek( )` function, in applications for scanning and parsing text (such as in a compiler or interpreter).

❏ `istream& ignore( int=1, int=EOF );`

The `ignore( )` function skips over the next `int` characters in `streambuf`. This is a binary mode function, and it is stopped only by an EOF condition if there aren't enough characters in the buffer to complete the operation. Suppose, for example, that you type the text

```
hello there [Enter]
```

into a program that ignored the first six characters from `streambuf`, as shown here:

```
#include <iostream.h>
#include <iomanip.h>

void main( )
{
    char str[41];

    cin.ignore( 6 );
    cin.get( str, 40 ); // Use default fence character
    cout << str << "\r\n";
}
```

Because `ignore( )` attempts to discard characters from `streambuf`, `streambuf` fills itself with the message characters. The `ignore( )` function skips over six of them, including the blank the between words. The resulting output consists only of the string `"there"`.

❑ `ostream& put( char );`

The stream `put(char)` function is the mirror image of the stream `get(char)` function: `put(char)` inserts a binary character into `streambuf` (the character can also be text or whitespace). You can use this function with standard streams or file streams, as you can many of the other member functions. The use of `put(char)` looks like this:

```
#include <iostream.h>
#include <iomanip.h>

void main( )
{
   char c

   cout.put( c );
}
```

❑ `ostream& write( const char*, int );`

Stream `write( )` inserts exactly the stated number of characters from the `char*` buffer into `streambuf`. Although `write( )` can be used with standard streams, it is most useful for file streams, as is stream `read( )`. Note that `write( )` does not take into account or transform newline characters or other text characters. You use `write( )` in this way:

```
#include <iostream.h>
#include <iomanip.h>
void main( )
{
   char buffer[256];
   cout.write( buffer, 256 ); // Insert all 256 characters
   }
```

You should understand that inserters, extractors, and the stream member functions can be used with files (`fstreams`). Many of the member functions, in fact, find their greatest usefulness when applied to `fstreams`. The use of `fstreams` is covered later in this chapter, in the section "Using C++ File I/O Streams."

A few final points should be made about the nature of the << and >> stream operators. There aren't many deep pits you can stumble into, but there are definitely some things you ought to think about concerning these operators (especially when you begin to overload them yourself a little later).

First, remember that you cannot invent new operators for overloading in a class. For stream implementation, the existing shift operators are used. Second, be aware that you cannot change the predefined precedence and associativity of an operator when overloading it. A couple of questions are important here. Why are the shift operators used? And what difference does operator precedence and associativity make to the various stream classes?

The shift operators are used for two reasons. The first reason is that they have *relatively low precedence in the operator set*. This means that the number of instances in which you must use grouping parentheses is reduced to a minimum. It would be inconvenient to be forced continually to resort to parentheses to keep insertion and extraction expressions straight. For example, consider what would happen if the addition operator had lower precedence than the shift-inserter-extractor operators. You would have to write expressions like this:

```
cout << "The value is " << ( a + b); // error for example
```

In fact, you would always have to write expressions like this. Stream manipulation could become quite messy if you used many complex expressions.

Just three operators, which you can use intermingled with inserters and extractors, have lower precedence than the shift operators. These three operators are the AND (&), the exclusive or XOR (^), and the inclusive or OR (|) bitwise operators. When one of these operators appears in an insertion or extraction, you must parenthesize them in this manner:

```
cout << "The value is " << ( a & b ); // You MUST do this
```

If you fail to parenthesize such an expression, you receive the rather cryptic compiler error message `Illegal use of pointer`. In other words, Borland C++ attempts to interpret the ampersand (&) as the address-of operator, with disastrous results.

The second reason for using the shift operators for overloading as inserters and extractors is that the shift operators are *left associative*. That is, operands are associated with the operators from *left to right*. It is this fact that allows insertions and extractions to be chained together, while still preserving the order of the data values. Note, for example, the statement

```
cout << a << b;
```

which is interpreted as calls to the operator << function as

```
( cout.operator << (a) ).operator << (b);
```

In other words, the `cout` object and the variable a are operated on first, with a reference to an `ostream` being returned. Then the resulting reference to an `ostream` and the variable b are operated on. The point, of course, is the expression *was* interpreted left to right—the variable a was "sent" (inserted into a `streambuf`), followed by the variable b.

Handling C++ Stream Errors

When the application of an overloaded stream operator or a stream member function fails, the stream is placed in an *error state*. The `ios` class declaration contains a `protected` variable `ios::state`, which has type `int`. An error state is indicated by setting a particular bit in `ios::state`. (Remember that `ios` is a base class for all streams, so its members are available to all streams.)

When a stream has been placed in an error state, you must do something about it before attempting to insert or extract data from that stream. Two problems then face the C++ stream programmer: determining when an error state exists and correcting the problem. This section shows you how to handle both these tasks.

Detecting C++ Stream Error States

The possible error states that can be recorded for a stream are named in a `public` enumeration called `ios::io_state`. The enumerators (that is, members of the enumeration list) are often called status "bits," even though they are integer values in the enumeration. `ios::io_state` enumerators are in fact integer bit *masks*, which can be used to test or set specific bits within the integer variable `ios::state`. What all this means becomes more apparent when you see the `io_state` enumeration itself:

```
class ios {
public:
  enum io_state {
    goodbit  = 0x00;  // No bits means no error
    eofbit   = 0x01;  // End of file was reached
    failbit  = 0x02;  // Previous insertion/extraction failed
    badbit   = 0x04;  // Last requested operation was invalid
    hardfail = 0x08;  // Error was not recoverable
  };
  ...
};
```

Because io_state is a public declaration, you can refer to the enumerators anywhere in your program, by writing the enumerator name with scope resolution to the ios class. Thus, you can write statements like this:

```
int eofmask;
...
eofmask = ios::eofbit;
```

You will in fact have cause to use io_state enumerator names in detecting stream errors. The question is *how* to use them. You might be tempted, for example, to write code like the following fragment:

```
#include <iostream.h>
#include <iomanip.h>

void main( )
{
   if ( cin.ios::state & ios::eofbit )
     cout << "Standard input is at EOF.\r\n";
}
```

This fragment looks good on the surface, and it would correctly test the value of the io_state end-of-file flag—if only the code would compile! It does not compile correctly because ios::state is a protected variable: it can be accessed only by members and friends of ios, and by members and friends of classes *derived* from ios, but not by any other functions. Figure 16.5 shows the results of trying to compile the preceding code.

Well, how *do* you test the error status of a stream? There are several methods—including an overloaded operator, a type conversion (cast) function, and several member functions—that you can use to test the error state of a stream.

The overloaded operator and cast functions that can be used are all the more elegant because they are simple and sophisticated at the same time. You can overload the NOT (!) operator and the void* cast operator so that a class object identifier can be used in a Boolean expression directly. Examine the following code fragment to see how this is done:

```
class A {
public:
     operator void* ( ) { return this; }
   int operator!( ) { return 1; }
};
void main( )
{
   A a;

   if ( a ) cout << "Oops!\r\n"; // Needs void* cast
   cout << !a << "\r\n";         // operator!( )
}
```

Fig. 16.5. *Accessing the* `io_state` *bit flags directly is illegal.*

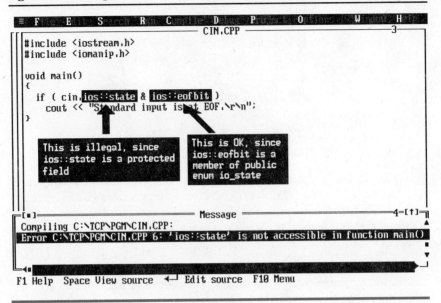

The preceding code fragment simplifies the issue by arbitrarily always returning a nonzero integer or void pointer (representing a *true* condition). The comments in the code fragment indicate which operator function is needed to allow the statement to compile and work properly. The reference to the object a, incidentally, works because signature matching can convert the object reference to a `void*` pointer. The workings of the `operator!()` function are more familiar.

The `ios` class declares and makes available to its derived classes just such operator functions. The `ios` operator functions perform in the following ways:

❑ `ios::operator void*()` returns a null pointer if there has been an error, and a nonnull pointer if no error has occurred. This operator function therefore provides *normal* Boolean logic for error testing.

❑ `ios::operator!()` returns a nonzero integer (a *true* indication) if there has been an error, and a zero integer (a *false* indication) if no error has occurred. This operator function therefore provides *inverted* Boolean logic for error testing.

Thus, you can easily write a functional replacement for the DOS TYPE.COM program by using the stream name in a Boolean expression, as shown in the following code:

```
#include <fstream.h>

void main()
{
  ifstream tfile( "fstream.cpp" );
  unsigned char c;

  while ( tfile.get( c ) ) cout.put( c );
}
```

This is a complete and functional program! It certainly illustrates how simple you can make file I/O when you use C++ streams. Remember that the get(char) function returns a reference to the stream object, so that the conditional expression in the while statement is using the void* cast operator to test the stream state.

You can also use the operator!() implementation to test for stream errors directly, rather than to test for good I/O. For example, you can write the following code:

```
#include <iostream.h>
#include <string.h>
...
char str[] = "Here is a message\r\n";
cout.write( str, strlen( str ) );
if ( !cout )
  cerr << "Uh, oh! I/O problem!\r\n";
```

ios::operator void*() and ios::operator!() provide a slick, easy way to test for stream errors. What they don't do is tell you exactly what the error is. The stream classes also provide member functions for more detailed error reporting and correcting—a subject that is discussed next.

Using the Stream State Member Functions

Six member functions are declared in the ios class (thus making them available to all derived stream classes), which provide more precise error analysis and control of the error state flags. These functions are summarized in table 16.5.

Table 16.5. *Stream state member functions for analyzing and correcting stream I/O errors.*

Function	Description
`int rdstate()`	Returns the value of `ios::state` flags vector
`int eof()`	Returns true if `ios::eofbit` is on
`int fail()`	Returns true if `ios::failbit`, `ios::badbit`, or `ios::hardfail` is on
`int bad()`	Returns true if `ios::badbit` or `ios::hardfail` is on
`int good()`	Returns true if no bits are on
`void clear(int f=0)`	Sets io_state bits to *f*

In the preceding section, you saw how *not* to access the `ios::state` bits. Using the `rdstate()` and `clear()` functions, you can access the bits correctly. With these functions, you can test the error flags yourself, as well as do something about the error. The following code fragment shows one way of performing this task:

```
#include <iostream.h>
#include <iomanip.h>

void main()
{
  int statflags;
...
  statflags = cin.rdstate(); // Get all the error bits
  if ( statflags & ios::badbit ) {  // Test invalid operation
    cout << "Invalid I/O request, error reset.\r\n";
    cin.clear( 0 );  // Set all flags off
  }
  else {
    cerr << "Can't handle that error. Terminating.\r\n";
    abort();
  }
}
```

The preceding code sequence shows how to do the task the hard way, though. To accomplish the same thing, you can more profitably use a combination of the overloaded operators (discussed in the preceding section) with the `eof( )`, `fail( )`, `bad( )`, and `good( )` functions. Using these functions, you could rewrite the preceding code fragment much more cleanly, like this:

```
#include <iostream.h>
#include <iomanip.h>

void main( )
{
...
  if ( !cin ) {           // Go handle some error
    if ( cin.bad( ) ) {   // Test invalid operation
      cout << "Invalid I/O request, error reset.\r\n";
      cin.clear( 0 );    // Set all flags off
    }
    else {
      cerr << "Can't handle that error. Terminating.\r\n";
      abort( );
    }
  }
}
```

Controlling Data Formats with C++ Streams

C programmers have long considered the `printf( )` group of functions (if not the `scanf( )` group) just about the handiest thing since sliced bread. The `printf( )` function is capable of complex formatting of output data, and `printf( )` can do it in the approved, concise C manner (some might read that as "cryptic").

There is no doubt that `printf( )`—and yes, `scanf( )` too—is a powerful and flexible I/O tool. In the C++ stream examples you have seen so far, there has been nothing comparable to the facilities present in `printf( )` for precise control of data formatting. The capability is there, however, and in this section you learn how to use C++ streams to format data in just about any way you want.

Using Inserters and Extractors for Built-In Types

Certain formatting conventions are assumed as defaults by the built-in stream inserter and extractor functions. These default values do not require the inclusion of another header file—iostream.h remains for the moment the only one you need. The conversion base, field width, fill character, and floating-point precision have default values as noted in the following list:

❏ The *conversion base* is the number system that displays the data. This value defaults to 10, which means that the decimal number system is used. If you change the conversion base (and you will soon learn how), it stays changed and does not revert back to the default after a stream is used.

❏ The *field width* is most useful for formatting output data. A typical instance in which output field width is needed is a report featuring columnar data. You can, however, set the field width for input operations, although some caution is needed. Suppose, for example, that you type the string of characters abcdefg as input to the following code fragment:

```
#include <iostream.h>
#include <iomanip.h>

void main()
{
    int wide;
    char a[10], b[10];

    wide = cin.width(3);
    cin >> a >> b;
    cout << a << ' ' << b << "\r\n";
}
```

The resulting output is split into these two pieces:

```
ab cdefg
```

Note that the width() function specifies a three-byte field width, yet only the first two characters appear before the space. This happens because room is needed for the trailing '\0' character in order to terminate the first string. Deliberately setting the width for input *numbers* can be even trickier. For instance, the following code fragment might make you think that you can simply type a single sequence of four digits and have cin split it into two numbers:

```
int wide;

int a, b;

wide = cin.width(2);
cin >> a >> b;
cout << a << ' ' << b << "\r\n";
```

But cin does not work that way. cin reads numeric characters until it receives a nonnumeric character for *each* of the two variables. The width specification of two bytes has no effect on the operation whatever.

The most important thing to remember about setting the output (inserter) field width is that it is set back to the default size after *one* insertion. The default width is 0, which means that cout uses as many output characters as needed to represent the entire value.

❑ The *fill character* is, by default, a space. You can change the fill character (to a period, for example), and the stream will retain the new fill character value.

❑ The *floating-point precision* used by a stream defaults to the same as that used by printf( ). That is, there are six significant digits in the fraction part of the floating-point number, with the rightmost digit rounded instead of truncated. The precision also stays changed if you modify it.

In the ios base class, six member functions are defined for controlling the conversion base, field width, fill character, and precision. Three of these functions just report the current values; the other three functions first report current values and then change the values. Table 16.6 shows these six format-control functions.

Table 16.6. The six format-control member functions in ios.

Function Prototype	Action Taken
`int ios::width( )`	Reports field width only
`int ios::width( int )`	Reports and changes field width (once)
`char ios::fill( )`	Reports the fill character only
`char ios::fill( char )`	Reports and changes the fill character
`int ios::precision( )`	Reports precision only
`int ios::precision( int )`	Reports and changes precision

The following short program illustrates the use (with the `cout` stream) of all six of the stream member functions shown in table 16.6. Study the program carefully to see how the combination of values affects the appearance of the resulting output. In fact, it is a good idea to go ahead and type this short program into the Borland C++ editor, compile the program, and run it so that you can see exactly what happens. Here is the program:

```
#include <iostream.h>
#include <iomanip.h>

void main( )
{
  int wide, precise;
  char filler;

  // Just report the formatting values

  wide = cout.width( );
  precise = cout.precision( );
  filler = cout.fill( );

  cout << "Default width is " << wide << " bytes.\r\n";
  cout << "Default precision is " << precise << " digits.\r\n";
  cout << "Default fill char is '" << filler << "'.\r\n";

  // This time, change them, saving old values

  wide = cout.width(10);
  precise = cout.precision(3);
  filler = cout.fill('.');

  // Observe the results of these two lines carefully

  cout << 37 << 3.1415926 << "\r\n";
  cout << 37 << setw(10) << 3.1415926 << "\r\n";
}
```

C++ streams can control a number of other formatting features as well. You control these features by setting bits in the formatting flags variable. This field is similar to the error-status flag variable, except that it is a `long` rather than an integer. Because the formatting flags variable also has the `protected` access attribute, you cannot access the variable directly.

There is, however, a `public` enumeration containing all the possible mask values for the formatting flags. Table 16.7 summarizes the formatting bit masks. The table shows the enumerator names as you would refer to them in your code.

Table 16.7. *Formatting flags bit masks from* `ios` *enumeration.*

Enumerator Name	Hex Mask Value	Action When Bit Is On
`ios::skipws`	0x0001	Skips whitespace for input
`ios::left`	0x0002	Left-justifies output
`ios::right`	0x0004	Right-justifies output
`ios::internal`	0x0008	Pads after sign or base indicator
`ios::dec`	0x0010	Decimal display conversion
`ios::oct`	0x0020	Octal display conversion
`ios::hex`	0x0040	Hexadecimal conversion
`ios::showbase`	0x0080	Forces display of base indicator
`ios::showpoint`	0x0100	Forces use of decimal point (`floats`)
`ios::uppercase`	0x0200	Hex display is uppercase
`ios::showpos`	0x0400	Adds plus sign to positive integers
`ios::scientific`	0x0800	Engineering notation (`1.2345E2`)
`ios::fixed`	0x1000	Fixed-point notation (`123.45`)
`ios::unitbuf`	0x2000	Flushes all streams after insertion
`ios::stdio`	0x4000	Flushes `stdout` and `stderr` after insertion

As indicated in table 16.7, turning a mask bit on in the formatting flags variable causes the corresponding formatting convention to be used.

Before moving on to a discussion of the `ios` class member functions that affect the formatting flags, you should know that the `ios` class declaration contains three constant `long`s, allowing you to select only a *part* of the whole set of formatting flags. Table 16.8 shows these constant variables (again, as you should refer to them in your code), together with an indication of which groups of flag bits the variables select. A little patience is necessary here; table 16.8 will make better sense when you see the format-control member functions.

Now that you have before you all the formatting flag names and flag-group names, note the `ios` member functions that control the formatting flags. These functions are shown in table 16.9.

Table 16.8. *ios class constants for selecting flag groups.*

Variable Name of Flag Group	Flag Bits Selected
ios:basefield	Dec, oct, and hex conversion flags
ios::adjustfield	Left and right justification, internal padding
ios::floatfield	Scientific and fixed-point notation flags

Table 16.9. *ios class member functions that control the formatting flags.*

Function Name and Return Type	Action
long ios::flags( )	Reports all only
long ios::flags(long *flags*)	Reports all, sets all
long ios::setf(long *group,* long *bits*)	Reports all, sets group
long ios::setf(long *flags*)	Reports all, sets masked
long ios::unsetf(long *flags*)	Reports all, clears masked

Table 16.9 shows that, except for the unsetf( ) function, the stream flags control functions appear in pairs that report only, and report and set flags, respectively. The flags(long *flags*) function is the most dangerous because it does not merge in flags—it replaces the flags variable wholesale. When you use this function, you must be careful not to disturb the settings of flags you do not mean to modify. For example, to use the flags(long *flags*) function to set the ios::hex flag on, you must write code like this:

```
#include <iostream.h>

void main( )
{
    ostream console( 2 ); // Send to stdout
    long hold_flags;
    hold_flags = console.flags( );

    console.flags((hold_flags ^ ios::dec)
                    | ios::hex | ios::showbase);

    console << console.flags( ) << "\r\n";
}
```

In this short program, `ostream console` is defined to avoid modifying the flags for `cout`. Notice that the first action here is to use the report-only `flags()` function to get the bit settings for all the flags before any modifications are made. The result is placed in the variable `hold_flags`, which is in turn used to develop the new bit settings.

The manner in which you manipulate the bits shown in the preceding short program is also important. You must first turn off any conflicting bits (the `ios::dec` flag here), using the exclusive or XOR (^) operator. You must also turn on the new bits, using the inclusive or OR (|) operator. You must take complete control of flag values when using the `flags()` functions. These functions enable you to do anything at all to the flag values—even if it is wrong. Finally, the last line of the preceding short program hex-dumps the new flag settings.

The `setf()` and `unsetf()` functions provide a much safer way to change formatting flag settings because these functions don't just overlay the entire flags variable. Instead, these functions deal only with the flags that are turned on in the *mask*, which forms an argument to the functions. For example, to turn off the `dec` flag and to turn on the `hex` and `showbase` flags, you can write the following (much simpler) code sequence:

```
#include <iostream.h>

void main()
{
  ostream console( 2 ); // Send to stdout

  console setf( ios::hex ); // Just do it!

}
```

There are two reasons why `setf()` (either version) and `unsetf()` are much safer than the `flags()` functions: `setf()` and `unsetf()` won't allow you to set conflicting flags, and you can set only one flag at a time. The next code fragment illustrates this feature by setting the `fixed` flag and then immediately setting the `scientific` flag. The intervening hex dumps of the flags field show that no conflicts were allowed to develop:

```
  ostream console( 2 ); // Send to stdout
...
  console.setf( ios::showbase );
  console.setf( ios::hex, ios::basefield );
...
  console.setf( ios::fixed, ios::floatfield );
  console << console.flags() << "\r\n";
  console.setf( ios::scientific, ios::floatfield );
  console << console.flags() << "\r\n";
```

The preceding code fragment also shows you how to use the flag-group name fields listed in table 16.8 when you call `setf()`. The first parameter to this version of `setf()` is the bit name, which you have already seen. The second parameter is the flag-group field name from table 16.8. This form of `setf()` allows only flag bits indicated by the group name to be manipulated.

The primary use of the `unsetf(long flags)` function is to return a flag bit to its default setting (by clearing it), as shown here:

```
ostream console( 2 ); // Send to stdout
...
    console.unsetf( ios::showbase ); // Clear showbase
```

Because the `setf()` functions do not allow conflicting values to be set, `unsetf()` is not frequently required, although some instances require it.

Overloading the << and >> Operators

Because the purpose of C++ is to deal with class objects, the stream classes would hardly be complete or useful without some means of performing I/O on your own class objects. Input or output of a class object is achieved by overloading the << or >> operator.

The question that immediately arises about overloading these operators concerns the fact that a class, once it is completely defined, can be neither added to nor subtracted from. In other words, you cannot add new member functions to a complete class declaration. How, then, can you overload the << and >> operators?

Only one option remains: you can overload only the *global* versions of the shift operators. This may sound dangerous, but it really is not, given the presence of type-safe linkage with full function signature matching. If you define the overloaded functions correctly, there is no danger of impeding the normal use of the shift operators.

Another issue you must consider is the determination of exactly what part of a class object will participate in the I/O activity. If, for example, you are writing your `widget` class to standard output, is it meaningful to send the entire object, including function pointer and member data used strictly for internal purposes? Probably not.

Generally, you will arrange I/O for class objects so that only significant member data participates in the I/O. This rule is also the secret of reading and writing class objects on disk files for permanent storage. You must go to the trouble of setting up I/O for the class object so that only those parts which *should* be read or written are included. If you stop to think about it, that is exactly what is done in the program `pds.cpp` in Chapter 13—a `lib` *file* is the significant data part of a `lib` *object*.

The best way to see how all these points come together in a program is to write one. A sample program is therefore developed here, which performs stream I/O on a class object one step at a time. First, you must take care of housekeeping matters, including the `#include` directives and the class declaration itself:

```
#include <iostream.h>
#include <iomanip.h>

class widget {
  int size;
  double price;
public:
  widget() { size = 0; price = 1.00; }
  void setsize( int s ) { size =s; }
  void setprice( double p ) { price = p; }
  int getsize() { return size; }
  double getprice() { return price; }
};
```

These lines of code include the `iostream.h` header, which is always required, and the `iomanip.h` header. `iomanip.h` is required because the program later uses the `setw()` stream manipulator to set the output field width temporarily. (Manipulators, which are function-like operators, are described in the next section.)

The class declared in the preceding lines of code is that catchall friend, the `widget`. It is used here because the most useful of all widgets, the `doodad`, will be declared as a class object. Notice that the `widget` class has member functions for setting and reporting the private data member values. These member functions are necessary because the operator functions that are about to be overloaded are not members of the class, and therefore do not have access to private members.

The next order of business, therefore, is to overload the `<<` and `>>` global operators so that they can recognize a widget parameter and return the appropriate stream type. This task is accomplished in the following lines of code:

```
istream& operator>>( istream& instr, widget& thing )
{
    int size;       // local versions of these
    double price;

    cout << "Enter a size from 0 to 10, "
            "a blank, and a price "
            "from 1.00 to 100.00.\r\n";
    instr >> size >> price;
    thing.setsize( size );        // And now do it
    thing.setprice( price );
    return instr;
}

ostream& operator<<( ostream& outstr, widget& thing )
{
    outstr << "This widget's size and price are: ";
    outstr << "Size "
            << thing.getsize( )
            << " and price $"
            << setprecision(2)
            << thing.getprice( )
            << "\r\n";
    return outstr;
}
```

You can see how the input stream operator>>( ) function first inputs and holds the data values, and then uses the widget class access member functions to set the private data values. The output stream operator<<( ) does its work in a similar manner, except that the private data reporting functions can be referenced directly in the stream expression (because they return basic types).

Notice especially how the function arguments and return types are set up for the operator functions. The first argument is a *reference* to a stream of the proper type, and the second argument is a *reference* to a class object of the proper type. Both operator functions return their respective stream types.

That's all there is to it. The only task that's left is to use the overloaded operator functions with a widget class object. The following main( ) function declares a widget class doodad (what else would it be?), and then uses the overloaded stream operators with the cin and cout streams to input and output a doodad:

```
void main( )
{
  widget doodad;   // A  doodad is a widget, naturally
  cin >> doodad;   // Input a doodad
  cout << doodad; // and display a doodad
}
```

The process of learning C++ is a complex and sometimes long one. It is often easy to focus on a new subject so completely that you momentarily forget other useful things you have already learned. Learning C++ streams is complicated, so be careful to keep knowledge already gained fresh in your mind.

You already know, for example, about friend functions, including the fact that they can be used to overload class operators. But did you think of applying that knowledge here? It can noticeably increase the efficiency of overloading the inserter and extractor operators. Here is the complete short sample program for overloading << and >>, implemented this time with friend functions:

```
#include <iostream.h>
#include <iomanip.h>

class widget {
  int size;
  double price;
public:
  widget() { size = 0; price = 1.00; }
  friend istream& operator>>( istream&, widget& );
  friend ostream& operator<<( ostream&, widget& );
};

istream& operator>>( istream& instr, widget& thing )
{
  cout << "Enter a size from 0 to 10, "
          "a blank, and a price "
          "from 1.00 to 100.00.\r\n";
  instr >> thing.size >> thing.price;
  return instr;
}

ostream& operator<<( ostream& outstr, widget& thing )
{
```

```
outstr << "This widget's size and price are: ";
outstr << "Size "
       << thing.size
       << " and price $"
       << setprecision(2)
       << thing.price
       << "\r\n";
return outstr;
}

void main()
{
    widget doodad;  // A doodad is a widget, naturally

    cin >> doodad;  // Input a doodad
    cout << doodad; // and display a doodad
}
```

In this version of the program, the overloaded operator functions are still declared at file scope (they are global functions, not class member functions), but because they are now friends of the class, they can access private member data directly. Therefore, it is possible to eliminate four class member functions and to simplify the coding for the operator functions.

Using C++ Stream Manipulators

The stream member functions provide a powerful method of controlling errors and formatting. So far, however, you have seen only two operators for performing I/O with streams: the inserter operator <<, and the extractor operator >>. Wouldn't it be nice if there were additional operators that you could use directly in stream I/O expressions like

```
stream << (do formatting) << ... ;
```

and that could perform nearly all the format-control tasks of the member functions? It would be nice, indeed. Fortunately, such operators do exist. They are called *manipulators*, and they have a function-like syntax. This section introduces you to the C++ manipulators and shows you how to define manipulators of your own.

Understanding C++ Manipulators

To say that the C++ manipulators have a function-like syntax simply means that some of them (not all) can have arguments. For example, corresponding to the now familiar `ios::width()` member function is a `setw()` manipulator. The following code fragment shows you how to set output field width, both by using stream member functions and by using the `setw()` manipulator:

```
cout.width( 10 );  // Set output field width to 10
cout << 37;        // output 37 in 10-position field
...
cout << setw(10) << 37; // Do it in one expression
```

Stream manipulators come in two varieties: those with arguments and those without arguments. Stream manipulators without arguments are already declared in `iostream.h`. You do not need to do anything more than include that header to use those manipulators. The `hex` manipulator, for example, performs the same task as the `ios::setf( ios::hex )` function call, as shown here:

```
cout << hex << 37; // Displays hex 25
```

Stream manipulators with arguments are more properly called *parameterized manipulators*. The declarations for the parameterized manipulators are very complex and reside in their own header file. To use parameterized manipulators, you must therefore include the header file `iomanip.h` in any program that uses these manipulators.

Operator associativity has a bearing on how you must write stream manipulators, just as it does on evaluating the results of insertions and extractions. Manipulators also associate from left to right, so that you must write a manipulator *before* (to the left of) any variables you want the manipulator to affect. Note this example:

```
cout << 16 << hex;  // ERROR! hex manip does nothing
cout << hex << 16;  // hex format for integer 16 and
                    // following expressions
```

The beauty of manipulators, of course, is their simplicity and ease of use in stream expressions.

Using Manipulators To Change States and Attributes

The principal task of stream manipulators is to modify a stream's formatting bit states and attributes (and thus the stream's behavior), and to do so by being included directly in a stream I/O expression. For this purpose, there are seven nonparameterized manipulators and six parameterized manipulators. The manipulators supplied by Borland C++ cover a wide range of I/O formatting possibilities but, as you will see, not *all* possibilities.

The seven nonparameterized manipulators are shown in table 16.10. Three of these manipulators are used for setting the formatting flags, whereas the remaining four manipulators produce a direct effect on the stream. Notice in table 16.10 that some of the manipulators apply to both istreams and ostreams, and others apply only to one of these.

Table 16.10. The simple stream manipulators.

Manipulator	Use	Description
dec	outstream << dec instream >> dec	Uses decimal conversion base
hex	outstream << hex instream >> hex	Uses hex conversion base
oct	outstream << oct instream >> oct	Uses octal conversion base
ws	instream >> ws	Eats whitespace ("sink" operator)
endl	outstream << endl	Inserts newline char, flush
ends	outstream << ends	Inserts string null '\0', flush
flush	outstream << flush	Flushes all data to output device

The hex, dec, and oct manipulators do the same job as the corresponding ios::setf() function call. This is very good when applied to output streams, but these manipulators can sometimes be dangerous when applied to input streams. Suppose that you have written the following statements in your program:

```
int a;
...
cin >> hex >> a;
```

That looks simple enough, right? It isn't as simple as it looks, unfortunately—because it doesn't work for the hex digits A through F. Suppose that you type the hex number F F (decimal 255), for example. What would the value of the integer a be after the last statement in the preceding code fragment? Borland C++ invariably interprets that input as the number 85 (decimal value). Here is how Borland C++ arrives at that result:

1. The first F is encountered in the cin stream (it doesn't matter whether F is uppercase). Because hex conversion is in progress, cin knows that this is a valid hex number.

2. Because the variable a that is being built is an integer, the first digit (which, remember, has decimal value 15) is scaled to the decimal digit range by subtracting 10 from it:

```
15 - 10 = 5; partial result = 50 hex = 80 decimal
```

3. The second digit is encountered in the input stream and treated to the same scaling process as the first digit, leaving a second digit of 5.

4. The partial results are added—80 + 5—to yield the final answer, which is decimal 85.

It is important to note that the preceding process does *not* produce an error state. You cannot detect the error by means of the stream's state flags. For this reason, you might be well advised to consider *always* performing numeric input in the decimal base. If you *must* allow the user to type hex characters, you can read them as a string and perform the numeric conversion internally, using program logic.

Octal conversions work better because the allowed range of octal digits is completely within the range of decimal digits. For *either* conversion, cin can detect digits outside the *conversion* range (more than hex F or 7 octal). You can detect range problems with the methods you have already learned. When inputting numbers other than decimal numbers, you should include some sort of error-detection method, such as the following:

```
unsigned int j = 1;

if ( cin >> oct >> j ) {}
   else cout << "Error on input." << endl;
cout << j << endl;
```

With code like this in place, you will be informed should you accidentally enter an invalid number.

All the parameterized manipulators require some numeric value so that their appearance in the stream expression is meaningful. The parameterized manipulators are shown in table 16.11.

Table 16.11. *The parameterized stream manipulators.*

Manipulator	Use	Description
setbase(*n*)	*outstream* << setbase(*n*) *instream* >> setbase(*n*)	Sets conversion base to 0,8,10,16. 0 is default.
resetiosflags(*n*)	*outstream* << resetiosflags(*long*) *instream* >> resetiosflags(*long*)	Clears the format flags named by long parameter.
setiosflags(*n*)	*outstream* << setiosflags(*long*) *instream* >> setiosflags(*long*)	Sets the format flags named by long parameter.
setfill(*n*)	*outstream* << setfill(*int*)	Sets fill char to int (can be char const). Does not apply to input.
setprecision(*n*)	*outstream* << setprecision(*int*)	Sets floating-point precision to int digits.
setw(*n*)	outstream << setw(int) *instream* >> setw(*int*)	Sets field width to int bytes. For input, only meaningful with characters/strings.

The setbase( ) manipulator sets the conversion base for output. A zero parameter sets the default: decimal display on output, and normal C rules for literal integers on input. The setbase( ) manipulator, in fact, can take over the jobs of the discrete hex, oct, and dec manipulators. Using setbase( ) allows you to determine *programmatically* which number base you want to use. Choosing the number base at program run time is illustrated by the following code fragment:

```
unsigned int j = 1;
int newbase = 8;    // Define octal base

if ( cin >> setbase(newbase) >> j ) {}
  else cout << "Error on input." << endl;
cout << j << endl;
```

As you can see here, the manipulator's parameter can be an expression (which includes an identifier, of course). This feature can prove helpful for dynamically choosing I/O formats.

The other predefined manipulators also parallel or duplicate other formatting functions. Again, the nice thing about manipulators is that they can appear directly and conveniently in stream I/O expressions.

Finally, as if all these features do not provide enough flexibility for you, you can define your own nonparameterized manipulator functions. They can do whatever you want them to do, as long as you observe the following conventions in writing your own functions:

❏ For manipulators that will have a direct effect on stream behavior, accept an argument that is a reference to the stream type, and return a reference to the stream type.

❏ For manipulators that will affect flags only (in other words, that don't insert or extract data), accept an argument that is a reference to an ios class object, and return a reference to that same ios class object.

For example, you could write a function for a finish manipulator:

```
ostream& finish( ostream& ostr )
{
  ostr << endl << "The end." << endl;
  return ostr;
}
...
cout << finish;
```

On a more useful level, the program in listing 16.1 provides some nonparameterized manipulators of both kinds mentioned previously. These manipulators provide handy functions not found among the predefined manipulators. Listing 16.1 shows you how to set up such manipulators.

Listing 16.1. `manip.cpp`. *A program that includes user-defined stream manipulators.*

```
1
2    #include <iostream.h>
3    #include <iomanip.h>
4    #include <conio.h>
5
6    ostream& eject( ostream& ostr )
7    {
8      clrscr( );
9      gotoxy( 1, 1 );
10     return ostr;
11   }
12
13   ios& engineering( ios& iosobj )
14   {
15     iosobj.setf( ios::scientific, ios::floatfield );
16     return iosobj;
17   }
18
19   ios& fixpoint( ios& iosobj )
20   {
21     iosobj.setf( ios::fixed, ios::floatfield );
22     return iosobj;
23   }
24
25   ios& indicatebase( ios& iosobj )
26   {
27     iosobj.setf( ios::showbase );
28     return iosobj;
29   }
30
31   void main( )
32   {
33     char ch;
34
35     cout << "This here is some text." << endl;
36     ch = getch( );
37     cout << eject << "This here is some more text." << endl;
38     ch = getch( );
39
40     cout << hex << indicatebase << 37 << endl;
41     cout << engineering << 3.1415926 << endl;
42     cout << fixpoint << 3.1415926 << endl;
43   }
```

The first thing you should notice about listing 16.1 is how the user-defined manipulators are used in lines 35–42. The new manipulators are used immediately in the `ostream` expressions, as are any other manipulators or inserters. Furthermore, those manipulators whose definitions require references to `ios` class objects do *not* require any cast expressions or unusual support when used in the stream expressions (see lines 40–42).

The inclusion of the `iomanip.h` header in line 3 of listing 16.1 is not strictly necessary because the program uses no parameterized manipulators. Then why is it there? It's there simply because it is a good practice always to include the `iostream.h` and `iomanip.h` headers in programs that will use C++ stream I/O. Including them doesn't hurt anything and could prevent puzzling linker errors caused by the absence of one of these headers.

You can also define your own parameterized manipulators if you are willing to spend a little more attention on implementation details. To write user-defined parameterized manipulators, observe the following procedure:

1. *Be certain that `iomanip.h` is included in the source file.* You will get nothing but compiler errors if you forget this header. The importance of `iomanip.h` for user-defined parameterized manipulators is explained shortly.

2. *Write any necessary support functions.* The manipulator functions themselves may need to call support functions, or a support function may need to be called before the manipulator is used. An instance of the second case is shown in the next sample program.

3. *Define the parameterized manipulator functions.* Observe the following requirements when you design the manipulator functions:

    A. *The return type must be a reference to the appropriate stream type.* For example, when you write a manipulator function that will be applied to an `ostream`, the return type must be `ostream&`.

    B. *The first argument type must be a reference to the appropriate stream type.* For example, when you write a manipulator function that will be applied to an `istream`, the declaration part will now begin to appear as `istream& funcname( istream& istr, ... )`.

    C. *The second, and last, argument must be either a `long` or an `int`.* The declarations in `iomanip.h` provide support for only two arguments, the second of which is restricted to `long` or `int` types, as are found in the predefined parameterized manipulators shown in table 16.11.

4. *Write an applicator declaration for each user-defined parameterized manipulator.* The `iomanip.h` header provides class declarations that can be used to "apply" your manipulator function to a selected stream type. An applicator declaration is actually the declaration of a class *object*, with a constructor argument that is a pointer to your function. Exactly how you write an applicator declaration is explained in the discussion of the next sample program.

If the preceding procedure seems confusing, the best way to understand it is to see it in action. The program `manipprm.cpp` in listing 16.2 shows you how to write the code for each step in the procedure.

Listing 16.2. `manipprm.cpp`. *A program with user-defined parameterized manipulators implemented through applicators.*

```
1    #include <iostream.h>
2    #include <iomanip.h>
3    #include <conio.h>
4
5    // ------------------------------------------------------------
6    //              You already know about this one.
7    // ------------------------------------------------------------
8
9    ostream& eject( ostream& ostr )
10   {
11     clrscr();
12     gotoxy( 1, 1 );
13     return ostr;
14   }
15
16   // ------------------------------------------------------------
17   // definexy() builds a long from x, y screen coordinates
18   // so that the manipulator can accept one parameter.
19   // ------------------------------------------------------------
20
21   long definexy( int x = 1, int y = 1 )
22   {
23     return ( (long)x << 16 ) + y;
24   }
25
26   // ------------------------------------------------------------
27   // Enumerators define handy names for left or right
28   // adjustment flags for ostream. The values match those
29   // in the iostream.h declaration for ios::left, ios::right.
```

Listing 16.2. continues

Listing 16.2. continued

```
30   // --------------------------------------------------------------
31
32   enum { adjleft = 2, adjright = 4 };
33
34   // --------------------------------------------------------------
35   // Manipulator sa() function definition. Notice that it has
36   // one more argument than operator<<() overload function.
37   // --------------------------------------------------------------
38
39   ostream& setadjust( ostream& ostr, int edge )
40   {
41     ostr.setf( edge, ios::adjustfield );
42     return ostr;
43   }
44
45   // --------------------------------------------------------------
46   // Manipulator goxy() function definition. The parameter
47   // should be a long developed by definexy().
48   // --------------------------------------------------------------
49
50   ostream& positionxy( ostream& ostr, long position )
51   {
52     gotoxy( position >> 16, position & 0x0000FFFFL );
53     return ostr;
54   }
55
56   // --------------------------------------------------------------
57   // Applicator declarations for the sa() and goxy()
58   // parameterized manipulator functions. Generic
59   // applicator classes for longs and ints are declared in
60   // iomanip.h. Note that generic.h is used for declaring
61   // and implementing generic classes for now, and will
62   // most likely go away when class templates are finally
63   // provided in later releases of C++.
64   // --------------------------------------------------------------
65
66   oapply_int sa(setadjust);
67   oapply_long goxy( positionxy );
68
69   // --------------------------------------------------------------
70   //                Now put all that to use.
```

```
71   // -------------------------------------------------------
72
73   void main( )
74   {
75      long screenloc;
76
77      cout << eject << sa(adjleft) << setw(20)
78           << 16 << 32 << 64 << endl;
79
80      screenloc = definexy( 24, 12 );
81      cout << goxy(screenloc)
82           << "Take a look at this message!"
83           << endl;
84   }
```

The program in listing 16.2 defines and uses two parameterized manipulators: sa( ), for setting left or right output alignment of fields; and goxy( ), for positioning the cursor on the screen. Of these two manipulators, goxy( ) is the most complicated, following every step of the procedure previously outlined for writing parameterized manipulators. Its implementation is discussed here in detail; feel free to analyze sa( ) on your own.

When you consider the steps necessary to implement the manipulator goxy( ), you will quickly see that it cannot be implemented directly because cursor positioning requires two integer arguments. Remember that the manipulator function can have only one int or long as the second argument. The solution is just as obvious as the problem: write a support function that converts the cursor position into a single long value to be used as the manipulator's parameter. That task is carried out by the definexy( ) function, shown in lines 21–24 of listing 16.2. The x-coordinate is shifted to the high-order bytes of the long, and the y-coordinate is placed in the low-order bytes (by simply adding it to the result). You must call this function before using the goxy( ) parameterized manipulator.

The manipulator function is defined next, in lines 50–54. Notice that the name of the function is positionxy( ) so that it can be differentiated from both the manipulator name and the gotoxy( ) function name supplied by Borland C++. positionxy( ) is defined for an ostream because little else is meaningful; and the function's second argument is a long, which will contain the long cursor address variable. The function body does little more than separate the x and y components of the desired cursor address once more and, using the results, invoke the Borland C++ gotoxy( ) function.

So far, the program has only disconnected parts, none of which affects stream operation. It is the applicator declaration, in line 67, that ties them all together. Look closely at that line again:

```
oapply_long goxy( positionxy );
```

This line of code declares a class *object* named `goxy`, which has type `oapply_long`. The `oapply_long` constructor accepts an argument that is a pointer to a function of the specific type outlined in the previous procedure. Now the applicator object `goxy` can be used as a manipulator in a stream expression, because the object has been initialized with the address of the function to be called when the `goxy( )` manipulator appears.

The program in listing 16.2 uses only an `ostream` applicator. Fortunately, this is not the only applicator class available. You can define parameterized manipulators for any streams, using one of the applicator types shown in table 16.12.

Table 16.12. *Applicator classes declared in* `iomanip.h`*.*

Applicator Class Name	Stream Type	Manipulator Function Prototype Required
smanip_int	istream,ostream	istream& *func*(istream&, int);
		ostream& *func*(ostream&, int);
smanip_long	istream,ostream	istream& *func*(istream&, long);
		ostream& *func*(ostream&, long);
imanip_int	istream	istream& *func*(istream&, int);
imanip_long	istream	istream& *func*(istream&, long);
omanip_int	ostream	ostream& *func*(ostream&, int);
omanip_long	ostream	ostream& *func*(ostream&, long);
iomanip_int	iostream	iostream& *func*(iostream&, int);
iomanip_long	iostream	iostream& *func*(iostream&, long);

How does the applicator actually work? In other words, how does its presence cause the desired action to take place when the user-defined manipulator appears in a stream expression? Although it is not necessary for you to know how this is done, it is an interesting application of C++ class technology, and it certainly won't hurt to remove the mystery. The `goxy()` parameterized manipulator function is invoked when the manipulator is used, in the following four steps:

1. *The* `oapply_long` *class defines a member function that overloads the* `()` *function call operator.* Thus, when a stream expression such as

   ```
   cout << goxy( loc ) << ... ;
   ```

   is encountered, the `oapply_long operator()()` function is invoked.

2. *The* `oapply_long operator()()` *function creates an* `omanip_long` *class object, passing to its constructor the function address (* `positionxy`, *in this case) and the* `long` *parameter value.* When the `omanip_long` constructor has finished its work, `oapply_long operator()()` returns that `omanip_long` class *temporary* object *by value.*

3. *The stream operator* `<<` *is now applied.* That is, the stream operator is applied to the result of evaluating `goxy(arg)`. The result, you may recall, was a temporary `omanip_long` object. This part of the stream expression evaluation causes the `omanip_long operator<<()` function to be called.

4. *The* `omanip_long operator<<()` *function is nothing more than a globally overloaded* `<<` *operator, which you have already seen in this chapter.* `operator<<()` is declared as a `friend` function and does nothing other than invoke the user-defined manipulator function—which is `positionxy(long)` in listing 16.2.

Because all of this information does not appear in the Borland C++ product documentation, you are probably wondering where the information came from. A simple inspection of the `iomanip.h` header file produced this information. If you need a really detailed understanding of how to design parameterized manipulators of your own, you need to do the same thing. But be prepared to spend some time doing detective work. The declarations in `iomanip.h` are written with the macros declared in `generic.h` (which simulates the proposed class template mechanism discussed in Chap-ter 18). The result is a *very* cryptic mess, typical of the old-style C code that was noted for its compactness but not its readability.

Using C++ File I/O Streams

Most of this chapter has dealt with standard streams, which perform I/O on the system console (screen and keyboard). That is as it should be, not because *file* streams are unimportant, but because standard streams are the easiest and therefore the best introduction to a strange new world.

By now, you are familiar with inserters, extractors, overloaded stream operators, simple manipulators, parameterized manipulators, and user-defined manipulators of all flavors (see how much you have learned in just one chapter?). It is time to apply stream concepts to files and to expand your working knowledge of streams in general.

Just as the `istream`, `ostream`, `iostream`, and `streambuf` classes are fundamental to standard stream I/O, file I/O has its own unique set of classes. Table 16.13 shows the stream classes associated with file I/O and how they are derived.

Table 16.13. *Stream classes for file I/O support.*

Stream Class	Derived From
filebuf	streambuf
fstreambase	ios
ifstream	fstreambase, istream
ofstream	fstreambase, ostream
fstream	fstreambase, iostream

As you can see from the table, the manner in which the file stream classes are derived is an excellent clue as to how they are used. Because the parallels to standard streams are in fact so exact (just about everything you have already learned applies directly to file streams), you will be concentrating mainly on the new features that appear in file streams, as well as focusing on `fstream` objects.

To use file streams, you must include the `fstream.h` header in your program. Then, naturally, you must declare `fstream` objects with which you want to perform input or output. You can declare an `fstream` object in three ways:

❏ *You can declare an* fstream *object without constructor initializers at all.* Using this form of declaration, you get a valid fstream, but it isn't connected to any particular file. You will have to open the file explicitly, later in the program. This is the simplest declarator, and it looks like this:

```
fstream myfile; // Declare the stream, worry later
```

❏ *You can declare an* fstream *object with an integer constructor initializer.* The integer initializer must be a valid DOS handle for a file that is already open. This form of the declarator is most appropriate for defining an fstream for use with one of the predefined DOS handles, as shown here:

```
of sysprint(4);  // Connect to the system printer PRN
```

Notice that this declaration is explicitly for an output file stream with class ofstream. To use this feature with a disk file (fstream), you must open the file yourself, using the Borland C++ open( ) or sopen( ) function, and use the resulting DOS handle to declare the stream, as shown in the following short program:

```
#include <fstream.h>
#include <iostream.h>
#include <stdlib.h>
#include <io.h>
#include <fcntl.h>
#include <sys\stat.h>
void main( )
{
  int handle;

  if ( -1 == ( handle = open( "fstream.cpp", O_RDONLY ) ) ) {
    cerr << "Error opening input file." << endl;
    abort( );
  }

  fstream infile( handle );  // Declare with existing handle
  if ( !infile ) {
    cerr << "Error declaring fstream." << endl;
    abort( );
  }

  char ch;
  while ( infile.get(ch) ) cout << ch;
  close( handle );
}
```

As you can see, using this method for anything but the predefined DOS handles is a good deal of trouble, especially when `fstream` constructors exist that do all the work for you.

❏ *You can declare an* `fstream` *object with a file-name string and open-mode constructor initializers.* For disk files, this is perhaps the best way to declare the `fstream` object. The preceding short program can be considerably simplified with the following syntax, while retaining all of its utility:

```cpp
#include <fstream.h>
#include <iostream.h>
#include <stdlib.h>

void main( )
{
            // Declare with file-name string and open mode
  fstream infile( "fstream.cpp", ios::in );
  if ( !infile ) {
    cerr << "Error declaring fstream." << endl;
    abort( );
  }
  char ch;
  while ( infile.get(ch) ) cout << ch;
}
```

If you choose to use the first method of declaring an `fstream` object— using the default constructor—you will have to open the stream explicitly, as just mentioned, in order to supply a file name and connect the stream to a physical file. Here is the code sequence for performing this task (using the `lifo.cpp` source file shown in Chapter 11):

```cpp
#include <fstream.h>
#include <iostream.h>
#include <stdlib.h>

void main( )
{
  fstream infile;

  infile.open( "lifo.cpp", ios::in,
filebuf::openprot );
  if ( !infile ) {
    cerr << "Error opening stream." << endl;
    abort( );
  }

  char ch;
  while ( infile.get(ch) ) cout << ch;
}
```

The `fstream` member function `open()` has an argument list much like that of the third constructor's argument list. The function prototype for the `open()` function is this:

```
void fstream::open( const char* name, int mode,
                    int prot = filebuf::openprot );
```

Only the third parameter—the file-protection mask—has a default value. This parameter is the easiest one to discuss because the default value is the only possible value at this time. You may as well let it default and go about your other business.

The second parameter of the `fstream::open()` function is known as the *open mode*. The open mode should be one of the `ios::open_mode` enumerators shown in table 16.14 (or several OR'd together, as discussed shortly).

Table 16.14. `fstream` *open-mode enumerator names and uses.*

Enumerator Name	Description of Use in `fstream::open()`
`ios::in`	Opens for input (default for `ifstream`)
`ios::out`	Opens for output (default for `ofstream`)
`ios::app`	Opens in append mode: writes at end-of-file
`ios::ate`	Opens and then seeks to EOF
`ios::trunc`	Creates file, or trunc to 0 length if exist
`ios::nocreate`	Does not create if no file exists (fails if no file exists)
`ios::noreplace`	Does not trunc to 0 length if file exists (fails if file exists)
`ios::binary`	Opens in explicit binary mode

The open-mode enumerators obviously correspond largely with the plain C `fopen()` mode strings. Just as you can combine mode-string characters with `fopen()`, you can combine open-mode enumerators by ORing them together. Because some of the open-mode enumerators differ from `fopen()` mode strings, be cautious when specifying an open mode for `fstream::open()`.

The `ios::in` and `ios::out` open modes open the `fstream` for input and output operations, respectively. As with their plain C counterparts, the open modes can be combined to allow update (combined reads and writes) processing on an `fstream`. The following code fragment illustrates this:

```
fstream iofile( "mydata.dat", ios::in | ios::out );

        // or opening the stream later ...

fstream iofile;
...
iofile.open( "mydata.dat", ios::in | ios::out );
if ( !iofile ) { // do something about it }
```

Note that using the `ios::out` open mode alone truncates the length of an existing file to zero bytes, effectively overwriting the file.

When you use the `ios::app` mode, you should observe the same *caveat* that applies to plain C files opened in append mode. Write operations *always* occur at the end-of-file position, no matter what other open modes you may specify. You can open an `fstream` for both input-mode and append-mode writes in this way:

```
file inandapp( "weird.fil", ios::in | ios::app );
```

You can both read the file normally and perform repositioning operations within it. But write operations still *always* occur at the end of the file. Including append mode in the open operation prevents truncating an existing output file to zero length and overwriting the file.

Using the `ios::ate` open mode (open, then position to EOF) actually performs the operation that novice C programmers are tempted to think append mode accomplishes (but doesn't). Using the at-end mode does not disturb the stream's capability to write elsewhere in the file; at-end mode only performs the often-useful task of opening the file in some other mode or modes, and automatically performing the repositioning operation. Note, for example, the following code fragment:

```
char* fname[] = "todays.dat";
fstream iofile( fname, ios::in | ios::out | ios::ate );
```

This code opens the file named "`todays.dat`" ready to write new transaction data at the end of the file, but leaves it still able to update other records in the file, as well.

`ios::nocreate` and `ios::noreplace` are an interesting pair of open modes that do not have direct parallels in plain C open mode strings. With `ios::nocreate`, opening an output file should fail if the file does not already exist. In contrast, with `ios::noreplace`, opening an output file should fail if the file *does* already exist, unless either `ios::app` or `ios::ate` is also specified.

An `fstream` is opened in text mode by default. You must specify the `ios::binary` open mode in order to process a file in true binary mode. If you do not use this open mode, the file will be subject to having the end-of-line characters (carriage return and linefeed) transformed into a newline character, even if you do not use the formatted stream inserters and extractors.

Reading and Writing *fstream* Files

Reading and writing fstream files are carried out much the same as for the standard streams. However, you won't have much occasion to use simple inserters and extractors with fstream files. You will usually process an fstream with the get( ), put( ), read( ), and write( ) functions, as shown in the following code fragment:

```
#include <fstream.h>
#include <iostream.h>
#include <stdlib.h>

void main( )
{
  fstream infile;
  char hold[255];

  infile.open( "lifo.cpp", ios::in, filebuf::openprot );
  if ( !infile ) {
    cerr << "Error opening stream." << endl;
    abort( );
  }

  while ( infile.getline( hold, 256 ) ) cout << hold;
  }
```

One of the significant reasons for this practice is that extractors, for instance, don't detect an end-of-file condition properly in an fstream. Suppose that you write the last line of the preceding code fragment like this:

```
      char ch;
      while ( infile << ch ) cout << ch;
```

Although this line would work perfectly with cin, the program loops infinitely, continuously sending the closing brace (}) of the lifo.cpp source file to the display. This condition exists because the extractor operator simply sends the last valid character it encountered when it can retrieve no more from the streambuf.

In those cases in which you have opened the stream in binary mode, you will be reading and writing whole records at a time. You can accomplish these tasks with the `read()` and `write()` functions described earlier in this chapter. The following short program illustrates the method:

```
#include <fstream.h>
#include <iostream.h>

char names[4][20] = { // an array of fixed-size records
  "Washington",
  "Lincoln",
  "Jefferson",
  "Adams",
};

void main()
{
  int i;
  fstream namefile;

  namefile.open( "names.dat", ios::out );
  for ( i=0; i<4; ++i ) namefile.write( names[i], 20 );
  namefile.close();

  char hold[20];
  namefile.open( "names.dat", ios::in );

  for ( i=0; i<4; ++i ) {
    namefile.read( hold, 20 );
    cout << hold << endl;
  }
  namefile.close();
}
```

In binary mode, there is little logistical difference between processing an `fstream` and processing a plain C file with `fread()` and `fwrite()`.

File Positioning with C++ Streams

To process an `fstream` in update mode, you must be able to reposition the read and write locations within the file. The `fstream seekg()`, `seekp()`, `tellg()`, and `tellp()` member functions, as well as the `typedef streampos`, are available to assist you in this task.

The `tellg()` and `tellp()` member functions report the current read and write locations in the file, respectively. These functions return a type `streampos` result, and neither function requires arguments. You can report the current "get" or read position, for example, like this:

```
fstream iofile;
streampos currget;
...
currget = iofile.tellg( );
```

The variable currget now contains the position of the next read operation, recorded as an offset from the beginning of the file. Later in the program, you can reposition back to this same location in the file, using currget as an argument for the seekg( ) member function, in the following manner:

```
iofile.seekg( currget, ios::beg );
```

As this line of code indicates, the ios class declaration contains an enumeration of seek directions named seek_dir. Table 16.15 shows the seek direction enumerator names and their significance.

Table 16.15. *ios::seek_dir enumerators.*

Seek Direction Enumerator	Meaning
ios::beg	Seeks relative to file beginning
ios::cur	Seeks relative to current position
ios::end	Seeks relative to end-of-file

The seekg( ) and seekp( ) member functions reposition the file's current read and write locations, respectively. Both functions return nothing and take two arguments. The first argument is the number of bytes to reposition in the file, relative to the location given by the second argument. This *offset* value can be negative, if such a value does not locate the current position before the beginning of the file (for obvious reasons). The second argument specifies a location within the file, using one of the seek direction enumerators shown in table 16.15.

Armed with this information, you can rewrite the earlier namefile program to update the second and fourth names. That short program looks like this after rewriting:

```
#include <fstream.h>
#include <iostream.h>
#include <stdlib.h>
char names[4][20] = {
  "Washington",
  "Lincoln",
  "Jefferson",
  "Adams",
```

```
};

char newnames[2][20] = {
  "Roosevelt",
  "Wilson",
};

void main( )
{
  int i;
  char hold[20];
  fstream namefile;

  // Open for update but trunc first and rewrite
  namefile.open( "names.dat", ios::in | ios::out | ios::trunc );
  for ( i=0; i<4; ++i ) namefile.write( names[i], 20 );

  // Now change the second and fourth names

  namefile.seekp( 20, ios::beg );
  namefile.write( newnames[0], 20 );
  namefile.seekp( -20, ios::end );
  namefile.write( newnames[1], 20 );

  // Position to beginning of file and read it all

  namefile.seekg( 0, ios::beg );
  for ( i=0; i<4; ++i ) {
    namefile.read( hold, 20 );
    cout << hold << endl;
  }
  namefile.close( );
}
```

Although C++ streams may seem intimidating when you first approach them, you can now see how they can make life easier for the C++ I/O programmer. This statement is especially true in programs that do complicated, direct access, binary file I/O.

Using and Converting Old C++ Streams

Because C++ is a rapidly developing language, significant differences in the available compilers have appeared within relatively short periods of time.

The AT&T 2.0 C++ compiler is presently the working standard, and the base document (*The Annotated C++ Reference Manual* by Ellis and Stroustrup) includes discussions on experimental features soon to be incorporated.

Borland C++ supports the AT&T 2.0 standard, but because this level of the compiler is fairly recent, support for the not-so-old version 1.2 C++ streams is also present. This section deals with how to use the version 1.2 streams and, perhaps more important, how to convert old streams to new ones.

Many of the old stream facilities work with version 2.0 streams, but there may be differences that prevent using these facilities with the new `iostream` library. Therefore, if you must use old streams for the purpose of porting old code to the Borland C++ compiler, you should probably use old streams exclusively. If so, be sure to include the `stream.h` header and avoid the use of any of the headers mentioned in this chapter.

Furthermore, you must explicitly direct the linker to use the old stream object libraries. (The linker won't use the old libraries automatically; to do this, you must use a project file or the command-line compiler.) Even worse, the decision as to which memory model to use is up to you; you must select the correct old stream library to match the memory model of your program. Table 16.16 shows the old stream library file names, along with the memory model supported.

Table 16.16. Old stream libraries and memory models.

Old Stream Library	Memory Model Supported
`oldstrms.lib`	Small
`oldstrmm.lib`	Medium
`oldstrmc.lib`	Compact
`oldstrml.lib`	Large
`oldstrmh.lib`	Huge

Differences between Old and New C++ Streams

After you have installed Borland C++ on your system, you will find a text file named OLDSTR.DOC in the Borland C++ base directory. This text file contains a brief reference manual on using version 1.2 streams. If you plan to use these streams, you should print this file and read it carefully (unless you are already an old hand at version 1.2). This section summarizes the major differences between version 1.2 and version 2.0 streams.

First, version 1.2 has only three predefined streams. These are the `cin`, `cout`, and `cerr` streams; `clog` does not exist. The version 1.2 streams are directly connected to `stdin`, `stdout`, and `stderr`, respectively.

Formatted stream I/O facilities are also rather limited. The `hex`, `dec`, and `oct` manipulators are present but are implemented differently; they return a pointer to a `char*` circulating buffer, not a reference to an `ios` class object. You can, however, overload the `<<` and `>>` operators to support I/O of user-defined types, just as you learned in this chapter.

Parameterized manipulators were not heard of in version 1.2 streams, although the `generic.h` header used to declare generic classes existed in a more primitive form. The concept of applicator functions existed at that time, too, although not in the same form as implemented in Borland C++. Nor had applicator functions been used to implement parameterized types.

There was a stream-conversion function, known as `form()`, that closely mimicked `sprintf()`. The prototype of `form()` was the following:

```
char* form( char* formatstring, varargs );
```

The format-string usage was identical to that of `sprintf()`; only the calling conventions were different. You used `form()` in the following way:

```
cout << form( "The value of a is %d\r\n", a ) << ...
```

The `form()` conversion function is no longer supported in version 2.0 compatible C++ compilers, but it was a handy function. If you want to regain the utility of `form()` without reverting to version 1.2 stream libraries, you can just declare it yourself, like this:

```
#include <iostream.h>
#include <stdio.h>
#include <stdarg.h>

char* form( char*, ... );  // prototype form()

void main()
{
  double a = 3.1415926;

  cout << form( "The value of a is %6.4lf\n", a ) ;
}

char* form( char *format, ... )
{
  va_list arg_ptr;
  static char ibuf[256]; // Make it safe and quick
```

```
    va_start( arg_ptr, format );
    vsprintf( ibuf, format, arg_ptr );
    va_end( arg_ptr );
    return ibuf;
}
```

Most of the basic stream facilities are present in a subset form in the old stream libraries, and the two releases have a great deal of continuity. You may find it profitable to read OLDSTR.DOC simply for the background knowledge available concerning some of the more esoteric version 2.0 stream facilities. Digging around in the respective header files can be quite instructive also, but be sure to *compare* the two releases; don't just depend on version 1.2 documentation.

Converting to the New C++ Streams

This section summarizes the guidelines for converting to the new C++ streams; these guidelines are found in the *Borland C++ Programmer's Guide*. When converting your programs from version 1.2 to version 2.0 compatible streams, consider the following points:

❑ *Most of the old* `streambuf` *class public members are now protected.* Programs that formerly accessed those members directly are now compelled to use the standard interface member functions, operators, and manipulators. This change is a good one because it enhances the protection provided by encapsulation.

❑ *You should now use the* `strstream` *and* `strstreambuf` *class objects for in-core formatting.* The older `streambuf` class permitted the use of character arrays instead of the buffer for in-core formatting, just as `sprintf()` does. Use the new string-oriented stream classes for this purpose.

❑ *Creating a stream with a file (DOS) handle must now be done with file streams only.* Formerly, you could declare a stream in this way:

```
    istream cinput(2); // Use DOS handle
```

This declaration is now obsolete. You should instead declare such a stream in this manner:

```
    ifstream cinput(2);
    // or
    fstream cprn(4);
```

❏ *C++ standard streams are no longer directly connected to plain C standard streams.* C++ standard streams have their own file handles and unique buffering schemes. If, for some reason, you need to connect C++ and plain C streams (for example, to avoid buffering problems), you can use the `ios::sync_with_stdio()` member function:

```
cout.sync_with_stdio();
```

This line of code connects `cout` and `stdout`, but slows the performance of `cout` considerably.

❏ *Assigning one stream object to another is now possible only if the left-operand stream object is a* `withassign` *class object.* You learned earlier in this chapter that the standard C++ streams actually have types `istream_withassign` and `ostream_withassign`. These derived classes contain the overloaded assignment operator for their objects. Thus, you cannot assign a standard stream to one of your streams, unless your stream is a `withassign` object, as in these lines:

```
ostream_withassign myout = cout; // Assign it
myout << data;                   // and use it as if cout
```

This concludes the discussion of C++ 2.0 compatible streams as implemented in Borland C++. Although a great deal of material was covered, every *possible* aspect of stream programming was not considered, of course. Still, you are sufficiently armed to learn more about streams by experimenting on your own.

Exercises

The knowledge you have gained in this chapter will evaporate quickly if you do not put it to use. Use the following exercises in C++ stream manipulation to reinforce that knowledge—and do not hesitate to write C++ stream programs of your own devising.

1. Write a program that uses the `cin` and `cout` streams. Include such features as chained inserters and extractors, manipulators, and overloaded `operator<<()` and `operator>>()` functions.

2. Write another program that is a "file filter" program. Use only `cin` and `cout` streams with the `get()` and `put()` functions, or with the `read()` and `write()` functions to copy one file into another in strict binary mode. This arrangement will require the program's users to indicate which files to copy from and to by using command-line redirection.

3. You can declare a file stream and supply the DOS handle you want associated with it as a constructor argument. For example, you could simply define a `cprn` "standard printer" output file stream, as in the following code:

```
#include <iostream.h>
#include <fstream.h>

void main( )
{
  ofstream cprn(4);  // stream to send output to printer

  cprn << "The number is " << 37 << "\r\n";
}
```

The standard DOS handle for the COM1 communications port is 3. Define an `fstream` capable of input and output, and write a simple communications and keyboard loop.

4. Use the stream member functions and manipulators to create a formatted report with multiple columns. You might want to use the `dir` class from Chapter 12 as a source of input data. You will have to set up a Borland C++ project file for this program, including your program's name, `dir.cpp`, and `dbllist.cpp`.

5. Define an `fstream` object for an input/output file. Read the file in binary mode, retrieving data records from it (read them into a `struct`, for example). Transform the input data in some way and update the records in place.

Summary

C++ stream classes are richly functional, providing nearly all the I/O capability you are likely to need in your programs. Streams also provide all this functionality with type-safe linkage, so that such errors as the one in the following code fragment, which uses `printf( )`, are not possible (or at least very difficult to engineer):

```
#include <stdio.h>
#include <stdlib.h>

void main( )
{
  int a = 1;
  char msg[] = "The value of a is: ";

  printf( "%s%d\n", a, msg );  //BACKWARD ARGS
}
```

The *compiler* does not interpret the format string—that is done only at run time by the `printf()` library function. Therefore, plain C can have no way of knowing that the arguments are specified backward here. The program compiles completely free of errors but produces garbage at run time.

The corresponding C++ stream implementation is much more difficult to foul up, as you can see from the following line of code:

```
cout << msg << a << endl;
```

The drawback to C++ streams is that their internals are complex and difficult to learn—yet you must have at least some familiarity with stream internals to control and use them effectively. At the beginning of this chapter, you were advised to learn about C++ streams so that you could read another programmer's C++ code. By now, you may have other (and better) reasons for wanting to learn C++ streams.

In this chapter, you were presented with a mind-boggling assortment of new facts and techniques. Before you continue with the next chapter, be sure that you have learned the following important points:

❑ *The basic stream I/O mechanism consists of the overloaded shift operators << and >>, called an inserter and an extractor, respectively.* Inserters are used for "inserting" data into output streams, and extractors are used for "extracting" data from input streams.

❑ *Inserters and extractors can handle all the built-in types.* You can use all the usual C data types in C++ stream expressions, with no extra preparation required.

❑ *The stream operators can be overloaded to support input and output of user-defined data types.* Overloading the << and >> operators at file scope allows you to extend easily the I/O capabilities of C++ streams to handle I/O for your class objects.

❑ *You can detect and correct C++ stream errors, using the stream state member functions and operators.* The overloaded NOT (`!`) operator and `void*` cast operator enable you to use Boolean expressions to detect the existence of an error condition. With the `rdstate()` and `clear()` member functions, you can analyze the error and, in most cases, clear it as well.

❑ *The `ios` class members control formatting attributes.* You can set the formatting flags, as well as the width, precision, and fill character, by using the `ios` class member functions. Calls to stream member functions are not part of a stream I/O expression.

❏ *Manipulators control formatting state and behavior.* Manipulators can be either simple or parameterized, and can either set formatting flags or have an immediate effect on stream I/O. Manipulators do appear directly in stream I/O expressions.

❏ *You can define your own simple manipulators.* You can write your own manipulator functions to control formatting states or to perform special I/O tasks. The function name becomes the manipulator name. Manipulator must have specifically required return types and arguments.

❏ *You can define your own parameterized manipulators.* User-defined parameterized manipulators are considerably more complex than simple manipulators. Defining parameterized manipulators requires an understanding of generic classes, applicator declarations, and the Borland C++ implementation of iomanip.h. The applicator class object name becomes the manipulator name, and the name of the implementation function can be anything you want.

❏ *File streams support direct access (random read-write) operations.* You can reposition a file, update it, and process it in true binary mode by using the file stream classes.

❏ *Borland C++ supports AT&T version 2.0 compatible streams.* Support is also available for the older version 1.2 compatible streams. Using the older streams requires an understanding of the two implementations of stream I/O. You can, and should, convert older stream logic to new stream logic, but the two versions have a great deal of continuity.

If you have mastered C++ stream programming, you are well on the way to becoming a sophisticated C++ programmer. In fact, you are ready for the topics of code reuse, polymorphism, and late binding of object types. If these topics sound intriguing, continue with the next chapter.

17

Using C++
Derived Classes

A good working definition of an Object-Oriented Programming System (OOPS) is that it is a programming system which supports three features: abstract data typing, type derivation, and polymorphism. Earlier chapters have already covered abstract data typing—C++ classes—in some detail. This chapter introduces type derivation and polymorphism.

In C++, type derivation most often means *class derivation*, the process of deriving new classes from old ones. Class derivation is also sometimes referred to as *class inheritance* because the *derived class* (the new class) inherits many of its properties from its parent, or *base class* (the old class).

To a lesser degree, new classes can be created from old ones by simply grouping the old ones together as members of the new class. This process is called *code reuse by composition*, or just *composition*. Because composition is simpler than true derivation, class composition is covered first.

Reusing Code
without Inheritance

Programmers are often told (constantly, in fact), "If it ain't broke, don't *fix* it!" Software doesn't "break" itself. Programmers do, when they unnecessarily meddle with code that already works. Modifying code in order to reuse it is an efficient way to "break" working software.

The controlling principle of both composition and derivation, then, is to reuse existing code wherever appropriate, *with little or no modification if possible*, to create new code that has more functionality than the original code. The resulting software isn't necessarily *safer* than the original (the new code uses the original code, after all); the new code is just more functional.

Class composition is a way of creating new classes without modifying existing code at all. Class derivation is a way of creating new classes with minimal modifications, and with improved isolation and control of the changed parts. Much of the discussion in this chapter is devoted to access and ambiguity control in composing and deriving classes. These are the programming activities that present the greatest opportunity for confusion.

Understanding Code Reusability

You may not have considered that you are already familiar with the concept of code reuse, simply because you are a C programmer. You reuse code quite naturally and easily each time you use one of the predefined C library functions. These functions (which may be standard C functions or a vendor's extension to the language) are already compiled and placed in the library files you loaded when you installed your compiler. When you declare one of the predefined header files, you have also directed the linkage editor to include the appropriate module from one of Borland C++'s LIB files, as shown in figure 17.1.

In plain C, you can write a function or group of functions just once and then use it (from object modules or libraries) over and over again. That is an efficient way to go about building programs. Once a function or module has been written, however, you can reuse it only in its *original form*; what that function or module does is not flexible and cannot be changed (except by recoding it, of course).

C++ classes give you not only the same efficiencies of reuse but also the capability of using the class in different, flexible ways—all without having to recode the classes. That is what class composition and class derivation are all about.

Reusing Code by Composition

Reusing class code without benefit of class derivation (that is, without class inheritance) is called *class composition*. Class composition is one of the two major ways that C++ programmers can take advantage of encapsulation, which isolates and protects code that already works.

Fig. 17.1. Reusing code by including library functions.

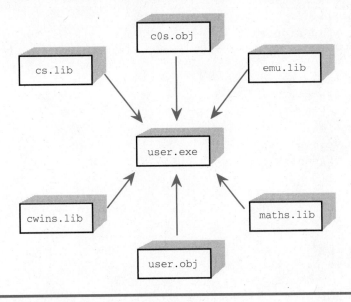

Class composition is the simplest way of reusing class code, involving only the declaration within a class of an object of another class. Figure 17.2 illustrates this concept.

Fig. 17.2. Reusing code by composing classes.

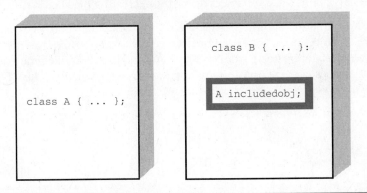

Remember that a class declaration is just that—a user-defined type declaration. Therefore, an object of class B declared within class A is just a declaration until you create a class A *object*. The following short program demonstrates what this means:

```
#include <iomanip.h>

class A {
public:
  void display() {
    cout << "This is a class A object." << endl;
  }
};
class B {
  A compose;
public:
  void display() {
    compose.display();  // Call A::display
  }
  void unique() {
    cout << "This belongs to class B." << endl;
  }
};

void main()
{
  B testobj; // declare a composite class object

  testobj.unique();  // Use the unique member function
  testobj.display(); // Do it another way
}
```

In the preceding short program, class A is completely declared before being referred to in class B. Then class B is declared, with an included class A object. The main() function contains a class B object declaration, creating the class B object.

Note that the complete declaration of a contained (enclosed) class is necessary before an object of that class can be used either to compose or to derive another class. Forward declaration only of the enclosed class results in compile-time errors because the compiler does not yet know the size or contents of the enclosed class. For example, the following code fragment does not compile correctly:

```
class A;    // Name the enclosed class
...
class B {
  A compose;  // fatal error
  ...
};
```

You may recall that forward declaration of a class name *is* sufficient to designate the named class as a friend of the later class, because a friend declaration does not require the compiler to know anything about the size of the friend's type.

In the preceding short program, the compiler is allowed to generate the constructor functions, but you should remember that the constructor for class B is executed first, and then the class A object will be instantiated (by executing its constructor).

You should remember also that only the *default* constructor (one with no arguments or all default arguments) can be called for a class object declared within another class. That is, you can't declare an *enclosed* class object with constructor function arguments. Why does this restriction exist? The answer is that it is not really a restriction. As mentioned in the preceding paragraph, the *enclosed* object is not instantiated until the *enclosing* class declaration is used to create an object. Until then, everything remains just a user-defined type (class) declaration.

You may recall from the discussion of constructor functions in Chapter 15 that there is a way around this apparent restriction. You can use *constructor initializers* in the enclosing class's constructor function definition to pass arguments to the enclosed class object's constructor function. You can rewrite the previous short program by using constructor initializers in the following manner:

```
#include <iostream.h>
#include <iomanip.h>

class A {
  int stuff;
public:
  A( int anum = 0 ) {  // Here is the constructor
    stuff = anum;
  }
  void display() {
    cout << "This is a class A object with value "
         << stuff << endl;
  }
};

class B {
  A compose;
public:
  B( int bnum = 37 ) : compose( bnum ) {} // Make the end run!!
  void display() {
```

```
      compose.display();
    }
  void unique() {
    cout << "This belongs to class B." << endl;
  }
};
void main()
{
  B testobj( 64 ); // Call constructor with args
  testobj.unique();      // Call the member functions
  testobj.display();
}
```

In the preceding short program, the class A constructor is defined so that the only argument has a default value, qualifying the constructor as a default constructor. The class A object `compose` is declared exactly as before, with no arguments in the constructor call.

The class B constructor differs from the previous version, however, in that it now has a constructor initializer list that passes the B constructor's argument on to the A constructor—by way of the class A *object* `compose`.

Class scope and access control rules do not change just because an object of a class is declared within another class. In the preceding short programs, for example, class B functions have no special access to private data in class A. The following code fragment, for instance, does not compile because B attempts to access private data in A:

```
class A { ... };
class B {
  A compose;
public:
  B( int bnum = 37 ) : compose( bnum ) {}
  void display() {
    compose.display();
    compose.stuff = 0;  // ERROR: access violation
  }
...
};
```

In all the preceding examples of code, therefore, class B is a user of class A objects, just like any other nonclass function would be. A class B composite object, then, includes all the functionality of class A, plus its own added functionality, with no modifications whatever having been made to class A code.

Using Single Base Classes

You can also create new classes from old ones by *deriving* them. The new class being created is called the *derived class*, and the one from which it is derived is called the *base class*. The whole process is accordingly called *class derivation*.

There is a distinct parent-child relationship between base and derived classes. In fact, members of the base class are said to be *inherited* by the derived class, so that you can accurately refer to derivation as *class inheritance*. When there is only one base class, *single inheritance* takes place. (Later, the chapter covers multiple base classes and multiple inheritance.) How class members are inherited and what this means for scope and access issues are the subjects of this section, which contains some fairly extensive sample programs.

Understanding Inheritance

Class derivation is much like class composition in that the result of derivation is a combination of the members and capabilities of more than one class. Class derivation is more like class "concatenation" than class "enclosure," however. Figure 17.3 illustrates what this means.

Fig. 17.3. *Members from both base and derived class declarations are found in a derived class.*

```
class A {
    int a;
    ...
};
```
→ `int a;`

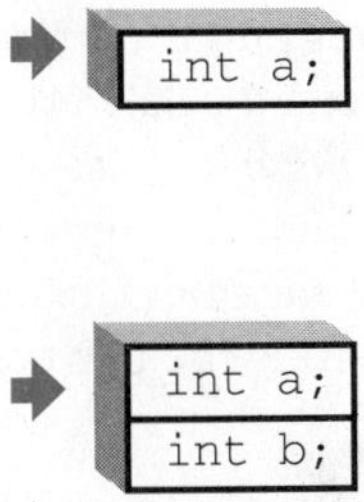

```
class B : public A {
    int b;
    ...
};
```
→ ```
int a;
int b;
```

As figure 17.3 shows, an object of a derived class can be viewed as a concatenated collection of *sub*objects, consisting of a base class object, plus a subobject containing members declared only in the derived class.

Most similarities between composite and derived classes vanish at this point, however. Scope and access issues are largely different for derived classes.
```

In particular, a derived class does not declare a base class *object* within its own declaration.

Declaring Base and Derived Classes

How, then, are derived classes declared? The syntax required for deriving a class is reminiscent of that of a constructor initializer list. The simplest form for deriving a class from a base class is this:

```
class base { ... };
...
class derived : base { ... };
```

As was true of composite classes, a class that is merely named (not yet fully declared) cannot be used as a base class. The reasons for this restriction are exactly the same as for composite classes: in order to put the subobject types together, size information is required, and that information is not yet available when a forward declaration has been used.

It is important to understand that private members of the base class *remain private*: they are inaccessible even to the member functions of the derived class, and certainly not to nonmember functions. The only way available for circumventing this restriction is to declare friend functions explicitly within the base class, which, as you recall, can access private data and function members. The derived class can use only such friend functions to access private base class members.

Furthermore, *all* base class members are considered private members of the derived class, if only the syntax explained so far is used. That is, nonmember functions can access the derived class in the normal ways, but they *cannot access any base class member*. Base class members become private derived class members by default. If you want to allow nonmember functions to access public base class members *through* the derived class, you must use an access specifier in declaring the derived class:

```
class base { ... };
...
class derived : public base { ... };
```

The access specifiers available are public, private, and protected. The base class access specifiers have the following effects on access to base class members through the derived class:

❏ *Declaring a base class* `public`

The `public` access specifier causes the `public` members of the base class to become `public` members of the derived class, causes `protected` members of the base class to become `protected` members of the derived class, and leaves the `private` members of the base class `private`.

❏ *Declaring a base class* `protected`

The `protected` access specifier causes `public` members of the base class to become `protected` members of the derived class, causes `protected` members of the base class to become `private` members of the derived class, and leaves `private` base class members inaccessible to all except the base class.

❏ *Declaring a base class* `private`

The `private` access specifier causes both the `public` and `protected` members of the base class to become `private` members of the derived class. `private` members of the base class are, as always, `private` to the base class.

In most cases, you will want to make the `public` members of the base class `public` in the derived class as well (although this is by no means *always* true). Suppose that you rewrite the preceding short programs with the A and B classes using derivation. You can see the base class access specifier in action in the following new code:

```cpp
#include <iostream.h>
#include <iomanip.h>

class A {
public:
  void display() {
    cout << "This is a class A object." << endl;
  }
};

class B : public A {
public:
  void display() {
    cout << "This is a class B object." << endl;
  }
  void unique() {
    cout << "This belongs only to class B." << endl;
  }
};
```

```
void main()
{
 B testobj; // Declare a derived class object

 testobj.unique();      // Use the unique member function
 testobj.display();     // Do it one way
 testobj.A::display();  // Do it the other way

 A* otherobj = new B;   // Declare a B, cast it to A
 otherobj->display();   // and get A message
}
```

In this version of the workhorse demonstration program, class B is derived from class A, using the `public` access specifier. The `main()` function then defines a derived class object, `testobj`, and calls member functions in three different ways, as shown here:

```
 testobj.unique();      // Use the unique member function
 testobj.display();     // Do it one way
 testobj.A::display();  // Do it the other way
```

The first two of these member function calls refer to members of the derived (B) class and work exactly as you would expect them to. The third function call, however, is able to access a member function of the base class directly because the base class was declared `public`. In fact, the only reason that the scope resolution operator is required at all in this third function call is that the function name is duplicated in each class. And that raises the next issue for discussion.

Assuming that a particular base class member is accessible to a derived class (or perhaps even to nonmember functions), you must consider what happens when there is an *overlap of names* in the derived class. That is, if there are members in both base and derived classes with exactly the same name (and the same signature if the member is a function), how does the compiler sort out which member is to be used?

In case of an exact overlap of this kind, the compiler assumes that the derived class's member name *hides* that of the base class. Therefore, the derived class's member will be accessed, unless the scope resolution operator is used to construct a fully qualified member name, as it was in the preceding example.

The occurrence of name overlap in base and derived classes does not mean that ambiguous names exist—the hiding mechanism ensures that there is no ambiguity. Moreover, even if the overlap appears to occur for two member functions that have different signatures, this does not mean that the function is overloaded. There are merely two distinct functions, one belonging to each class.

Conversion member functions of a class (user-defined cast operators) are a somewhat special case when you consider name hiding under derivation. Conversion functions don't specify a return type and cannot have arguments (they are unary operators). Consequently, a conversion function in a derived class will not hide a conversion function in the base class unless they have identical target types. Note this example:

```
class A {
   int var_a;
public:
   operator int() { return var_a; }
...
};

class B : public A {
   int var_b;
public:
   operator int() { return var_b; }  // Hide A operator int()
...
};
```

In this code fragment, because the type converted to in both base and derived classes is the same, the derived class's operator int() function hides the base class version. In contrast, you can accidentally introduce ambiguities into the code if the target types of the conversion functions do *not* match, but can be confused. The following code fragment illustrates this problem:

```
class A {
   int var_a;
public:
   operator int() { return var_a; }
...
};

class B : public A {
   int var_b;
public:
   operator void*() { return (void*)&var_b; }
...
};
```

With conversion functions defined as in this code fragment, the compiler won't know what to do with the following piece of code:

```
B obj_b;    // derived class object
...
if ( obj_b ) ... // Both void* and int can be tested here
```

In this case, a void pointer can be tested for null, and an integer can be tested for zero, with equal validity. The compiler therefore won't know which conversion function to pick. This circumstance is not as farfetched as you might think. You may recall that the void* conversion was used with stream classes to allow for testing the stream state easily. Such conversions are quite useful, and you may indeed encounter this problem.

Now return your attention to the preceding complete short program. The last two lines in the main() function there illustrate another interesting and important fact: a pointer to a derived class can be converted to a pointer to its base class if the base class is both accessible and unambiguous. Here are the two lines of code again:

```
A* otherobj = new B;    // Declare a B, cast it to A
otherobj->display();    // and get A message
```

The first of these lines creates a derived class object on the free store, returns its pointer, and implicitly converts the pointer to a pointer to the base (A) class. There is no problem so far, but what if you now call the display() function again? Which version of display() will be invoked? The A class function will be invoked. Why this is the case is easy to understand if you recall the subobject structure of the derived class object. The pointer is merely adjusted to point to the base class subobject.

Conversion in the reverse direction—*from* pointer to base class object *to* pointer to derived class object—is another matter. If the compiler were to allow conversions such as the following one, trouble would result sooner or later:

```
A* baseobj = new A;
B* deriveptr = (A*)baseobj;   // ERROR: direction illegal
```

Although it is true that all derived class objects contain a base class subobject, it is *not* always true that a base class *object* is a subobject of anything. It is entirely possible to use a base class both to define objects directly and to use it as a base for deriving another class. A pointer to a base class object can therefore point *only* to a base class object; such a conversion, then, would lead to a type mismatch. The conversion is therefore illegal *according to* the C++ ANSI base document.

There is a catch here, however. As the base document itself points out, few compilers check for bad casts such as the one in the preceding code fragment. Unfortunately, the Borland C++ compiler is one that doesn't perform such checks: it *does* allow the preceding cast to compile (and perhaps even to run). Why should Borland C++ permit such technically illegal actions? The answer is *maximum flexibility* for the programmer.

Borland has designed its C++ compiler pretty much on the assumption that Borland C++ programmers know what they are doing. Thus, although Borland C++ will indeed catch and flag a blunder such as the implicit cast attempt

```
B* deriveptr = new A; // ERROR: Cannot assign A* to B*
```

the compiler will nevertheless allow the earlier code fragment to compile unmolested. The Borland C++ compiler allows a cast from *base* to *derived* class pointer type especially to permit the *recasting* of a class pointer to its *original type*. That is, you can cast from derived class pointer to base class pointer and then back to derived class pointer. Note the following example:

```
A* baseptr;
B* deriveptr = new B;
B* derive2;
...
baseptr = (A*)deriveptr; //Cast to a base pointer
derive2 = (B*)baseptr;   // and back to a derived pointer
```

Now consider another point. Because casting a pointer to a derived class object into a pointer to a base class object is more than just a syntactical convenience—a pointer to a subobject results—then casting first to a base class pointer and then to some other type (such as char*) may not yield the pointer value you are expecting. Consider the following code fragment, for example, in which the class A and B objects are also used:

```
B* ptr = new B;    // pointer to derived class object
char* p1;          // working pointers to base
char* p2;          // and derived subobject locations
...
p1 = (char*)((A*)ptr);   // Convert to base*, then char*
p2 = (char*)ptr;         // Convert straight to char*
if ( p1 == p2 ) ...      // Condition may fail
```

This code fragment results in two pointers to char*, but their contents are probably different. That is, casting to a base pointer and then casting to another type again (for example, char*) does *not necessarily* yield a pointer to the complete derived object. Both p1 and p2 do have type char*, but one points to the base class subobject, and the other points to the complete derived object. The further conversion to char* does not change the address value of the pointer, but the conversion to base pointer did change that value.

The reason that the resulting pointer contents are *probably* different is that there is no guarantee as to the order of appearance of the subobjects in a derived class object. The base class subobject might be placed first, in which case the preceding pointer comparison would in fact succeed. But the base class subobject may not be first, in which case the comparison would fail.

Finally, consider what can and cannot be inherited. You have already learned how access specifiers control a derived class's accessibility to base class members, but the present topic goes beyond that. Some members of the base class cannot be inherited at all, although most can be inherited.

Restrictions on the inheritance of overloaded operators in a base class are the easiest to deal with. All the operators that can be overloaded, except the `operator=()` (the assignment operator), can be inherited. The assignment operator cannot be inherited because its action depends entirely on the specific structure of the class object: the structure of a base class object is not the same as the structure of a derived class object.

You must exercise some care in designing assignment operators for base and derived classes. If you do not code any assignment operator functions, recall that the compiler will generate one that performs a bitwise copy of the source object. That works fine, whether the object has base or derived type; everything gets copied one way or another.

Because the assignment operator is not inherited, though, you will most likely design base and derived classes, *each* of which has its own assignment operator function. Although such functions are present in the base class declaration, they are not necessarily used when a derived class object's `operator=()` is invoked. To illustrate this point, suppose that you have coded a base class in this way:

```
#include <iostream.h>
#include <iomanip.h>

class A {
    int a1, a2;
public:
A( int v1 = 32, int v2 = 64 ) {   // base constructor
    a1 = v1;
    a2 = v2;
}
 A& operator=( A& otherobj ) {      // Assign op here
    a1 = otherobj.a1;
    a2 = otherobj.a2;
    return *this;
}
 void display() {
    cout << "Base class values are "
        << a1 << ' ' << a2 << endl;
}
};
```

Everything seems fine so far: the base class has a valid operator=() function that will serve well for objects of class A. But now suppose that you write a class derived from this one. You might, for example, write the following code:

```
class B : public A {
  int b1, b2;
public:            // Derived constructor uses ctor-initializer
                   // with base CLASS name to pass ctor args
  B( int v1 = 0, int v2 = 0, int v3 = 37, int v4 = 57 )
                                          : A( v1, v2 ) {
    b1 = v3;
    b2 = v4;
  }
  B& operator=( B& otherobj ) {          // Assign op here
    b1 = otherobj.b1;
    b2 = otherobj.b2;
    return *this;      // A class data not taken care of
  }
  void display() {
    A::display();
    cout << "Derived class values are "
         << b1 << ' ' << b2 << endl;
  }
};
```

This code fragment also looks good on the surface. The problem with it is that invoking the assignment operator for a class B object does nothing whatever to provide for copying the base class subobject's member data—so it doesn't get copied. Therefore, when the main() function shown next copies one derived class object into another, base class members are displayed as unchanged:

```
void main()
{
  B obj1;
  B obj2( 1, 2, 3, 4 );

  obj1 = obj2;             // Use the assign operator
  obj1.display();    // Base class member still 0, 0
}
```

Such an accidental failure to copy all members in both the base and derived class subobjects is called a *slicing copy* operation, which is a particularly dangerous trap when you are using class derivation. To get the base class member data updated during the assignment operation, you have to do something explicit about it. In this sample code, you would need to modify the class B (derived) declaration in the following manner:

```
class B : public A {
   int b1, b2;
public:            // Derived constructor uses ctor-initializer
                   // with base CLASS name to pass ctor args
   B( int v1 = 0, int v2 = 0, int v3 = 37, int v4 = 57 )
                                        : A( v1, v2 ) {
     b1 = v3;
     b2 = v4;
   }
   B& operator=( B& otherobj ) {            // Assign op here
     A *temp;                        // Provide base pointer

     b1 = otherobj.b1;
     b2 = otherobj.b2;
     temp = (A*)this;               // Convert to base pointers
     *temp = otherobj;               // Invoke base class op=()
     return *this;   // all members, base and derived copied
   }
   void display() {
     A::display();
     cout << "Derived class values are "
          << b1 << ' ' << b2 << endl;

   }
};
```

In other words, the solution is to use the explicit conversion to a base pointer on the `this` pointer, and then to force the use of the base class's assignment operator function. Notice that in the expression

```
*temp = otherobj;
```

the left-side operand is a base class object, and the right-side operand is a derived class object. This usage is permissible, as long as the base class is `public`. If it doesn't suit you to use this odd-looking construction, you can alternatively form base class pointers to both sending and receiving objects. Note this example:

```
A *temp1, *temp2;  // base class pointers
...
temp1 = (A*)this;  // receiving object
temp2 = (A*)&otherobj; // sending object - notice
adrs op
...
*temp1 = *temp2;
```

The list of member functions that cannot be inherited is a little more extensive. The following functions cannot be inherited:

❏ *Constructor functions.* Constructor functions depend on the internal structure of class objects, as do assignment operator functions. Constructor functions are thus not inherited.

❏ *Destructor functions.* Destructor functions are not inherited for exactly the same reason that constructors are not inherited. Destructor functions can, however, be *virtual* functions, which is even better than inheritance (for destructors). Virtual destructor functions are discussed a little later in this chapter.

❏ *Friend functions.* Friend functions are not inherited simply as a protective measure against accidental access violations. If friend functions were inherited, you could derive a class from a `private` base class and still have access to all base class members, `private` and otherwise.

A Practice Project: Extended Memory Support

It is now time to take a breather from theory and put that theory to use in a concrete setting. This section shows you how to develop a base class named `xmsmgr` that enables you to use the full 4G (gigabyte) address space of extended memory on an 80386 PC.

From the `xmsmgr` base class, another class, `swapbuf`, is then derived, which uses extended memory to "swap out" large areas of the far heap (and actually release them while the data is swapped out). The `swapbuf` class is then tested in the context of moving the contents of an entire text file to extended memory temporarily, and then swapping the file data back into the far heap.

Understanding the Extended Memory Specification (XMS)

For all its power, the Intel 80x86 CPU (central processing unit), which provides the horsepower for the IBM PC and compatible computers, is a wondrously complex and difficult beast. As if the growing rift between ISA

(Industry Standard Architecture) and MicroChannel architecture is not enough to confuse the issue, the Intel 80386 now supports a maximum theoretical 4G address space—but not in a linear manner. The segmented architecture that has plagued assembly language programmers from the beginning now makes the use of all that memory space difficult, to say the least.

But segmented architecture doesn't make using extended memory impossible, fortunately. In fact, you don't have to know much assembly language, or anything at all about switching between real and protected mode CPU operation, to get significant use and value from extended memory. It will help considerably, though, to understand at least the basic divisions of the 80386 address space, as well as the nature of XMS, before you leap into code that uses extended memory services.

The Extended Memory Specification (XMS) is a definition of a software interface that allows programs running in real mode to make use of extended memory. XMS is the result of a joint effort of Microsoft, Lotus Development, Intel, and AST Research to define a standard interface to extended memory services. XMS is typically implemented as an installable device driver, which is called an Extended Memory Manager, or XMM. The Microsoft DOS driver HIMEM.SYS is the XMM assumed by the `xmsmgr` and `swapbuf` classes. Note that you must be running DOS 3.0 or later to use any of these facilities.

Now what about the memory itself? The aggregate collection of all the possible RAM addresses that your computer can control is called the system *address space*. (Most computers naturally don't have the maximum possible RAM *installed*.) At the simplest level, the 80386 address space is divided into *conventional memory* (the first 1M) and *extended memory* (beyond conventional memory, up to a theoretical 4G). Most computers today, but not all, have a *practical* limit of 16M. Note that DOS can use only 640K of conventional memory directly (that is, without the help of a driver), even though most modern computers come from the factory with at least 1M.

It is the memory above 640K, both conventional and extended, with which HIMEM.SYS is concerned. HIMEM.SYS governs three distinct areas of memory:

❑ *Upper memory.* Upper memory, allocated as upper memory blocks (UMBs), is the area of conventional memory from 640K to 1,024K (1M).

❑ *High memory area (HMA).* The HMA extends from 1,024K to 1,088K. A program either uses or does not use the HMA. It is allocated only as a whole unit. The HMA physically is in the extended memory part of RAM.

❏ *Extended memory.* Extended memory proper is that part of extended memory above the HMA, with a theoretical limit of 4G of RAM. Extended memory is allocated in chunks called extended memory blocks (EMBs). Each EMB has an associated integer handle by which it is identified. HIMEM.SYS supports up to a maximum of 128 EMB handles. Because an EMB can control up to 32M, extended memory can range up to 4G (4,096M).

The xmsmgr class about to be presented here uses only EMBs. Figure 17.4 shows the relationship of an xmsmgr class object to HIMEM.SYS and extended memory. All interaction with extended memory takes place through the services of HIMEM.SYS.

Fig. 17.4. *An* xmsmgr *class object allocates and controls up to 128 EMB handles.*

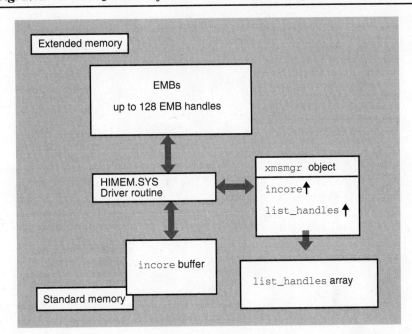

Because the xmsmgr class provides for an array of up to 128 EMB handles, you can use a single xmsmgr object to control all the extended memory if you want. Users of extended memory do not have to know what a particular EMB handle value is: xmsmgr reports the array subscript in which a handle is stored, not the handle itself, thus simplifying extended memory use.

Building the XMS Manager Class

Deciding what extended memory services to provide is the first step in designing the xmsmgr base class. The xmsmgr.hpp class header is the best summary of services. This header is shown in listing 17.1.

Listing 17.1. xmsmgr.hpp. *A header file for the* xmsmgr *class.*

```
 1  #if !defined(XMSMGR)
 2  #define XMSMGR
 3
 4  #include <iostream.h>
 5  #include <iomanip.h>
 6  #include <stdlib.h>
 7  #include <stdio.h>
 8  #include <dos.h>
 9  #include <string.h>
10  #include <alloc.h>
11
12  typedef struct {
13    unsigned long emb_length;
14    unsigned source_handle;
15    unsigned long source_offset;
16    unsigned dest_handle;
17    unsigned long dest_offset;
18  } xmsparms;
19
20  typedef int Boolean;
21  #define FALSE 0
22  #define TRUE  1
23
24  class xmsmgr {
25    enum xms_err { notimpl = 0x80,
26                   vdisk    = 0x81,
27                   a20err   = 0x82,
28                   generr   = 0x8e,
29                   unrecov  = 0x8f,
30                   nohma    = 0x90,
31                   hmainuse = 0x91,
32                   hmamin   = 0x92,
33                   hmanotal = 0x93,
34                   a20enab  = 0x94,
35                   allxms   = 0xa0,
```

```
36                    emmhandl= 0xa1,
37                    invhandl= 0xa2,
38                    srchandl= 0xa3,
39                    srcoffs = 0xa4,
40                    dsthandl= 0xa5,
41                    dstoffs = 0xa6,
42                    invlen  = 0xa7,
43                    overlap = 0xa8,
44                    parity  = 0xa9,
45                    notlock = 0xaa,
46                    islock  = 0xab,
47                    lockcnt = 0xac,
48                    lockfail= 0xad,
49                    smallumb= 0xb0,
50                    noumb   = 0xb1,
51                    umbseg  = 0xb2,
52                    xmshandl= 0xff
53       };
54       long xmsaddr;
55       unsigned largest_free_xm;
56       unsigned total_free_xm;
57       Boolean installed;
58       unsigned char errcode;
59       unsigned (*list_handles)[128][2];
60     public:
61       xmsmgr();
62       ~xmsmgr();
63       inline    operator void*() { return (void*)installed; }
64       inline int operator!() { return !installed; }
65       void query_xms();
66       inline unsigned query_largest_free_xm() {
67                 return largest_free_xm;
68       }
69       inline unsigned query_total_free_xm() {
70                 return total_free_xm;
71       }
72       inline unsigned char readerr() { return errcode; }
73       inline void clearerr() {
74                 installed = TRUE;
75                 errcode = 0;
76       }
```

Listing 17.1. continues

Listing 17.1. continued

```
77    char* xmserr();
78    int alloc_emb( size_t kbytes );
79    void free_emb( int listnum );
80    Boolean stow( char far* send, size_t listnum,
81           unsigned long bytes, unsigned long ofs);
82    Boolean fetch( char far* receive, size_t listnum,
83                   unsigned long bytes, unsigned long ofs);
84  };
85
86
87  #endif
```

The `xmsmgr` base class provides a basic subset of XMS memory management services, but in an encapsulated form that makes these services more readily available to users of the class. `xmsmgr` member functions and their use (aside from the constructor and destructor functions) include the following:

❑ `void query_xms();`

This function is normally used only internally (by the `xmsmgr` constructor) and places values in the `private` member variables `largest_xm_free` and `total_xm_free`. The function is `public`, however, so that it can be accessed by a user of the class.

❑ `unsigned query_largest_free_xm();`
  `unsigned query_total_free_xm();`

These two functions report the largest and total extended memory area available, as determined last by `query_xms()`. These are the two functions meant to be the user interface to XMS size queries.

❑ `unsigned char readerr();`
  `void clearerr();`

`readerr()` returns the error code posted by one of the action member functions (such as allocation, deallocation, or data movement functions) so that it can be examined directly by a user of the class, if necessary. `clearerr()` resets the posted value of the error code so that, if possible, XMS operations can continue. These functions are not exercised in any of the following sample code, but are provided for completeness. The code presented here uses the overloaded operator functions for determining class object state (remember stream states?). These operators are covered shortly.

```
296        mov    ds,dx
297        or     ax,ax     // Test the result
298        jz  badnews
299        jmp goodnews
300     }
301     goodnews:
302     return TRUE;
303
304     badnews:
305     errcode = _BL;          // Save error code
306     installed = FALSE;      // and signal error
307     return FALSE;
308  }
```

Once you get past the inline assembly language, the xmsmgr member functions are straightforward. They pass requests to, and receive responses from, HIMEM.SYS in the manner indicated in the list of member functions provided earlier. A couple of quirks in the code may need some additional comment, however.

First, look at the xmsmgr constructor function in lines 5–41 of listing 17.2. This function acquires space on the free store (using new) for the list_handles array. Now new returns a single pointer to a simple type, but list_handles is a doubly subscripted array. The cast in line 15 is therefore necessary to avoid a type mismatch. The cast expression(unsigned (*)[128][2]) appears complicated but isn't really. The expression should be read as "A pointer, (*), to a doubly subscripted array, [128][2], whose elements have type unsigned."

Second, notice also in the constructor function that there are two initial invocations of interrupt 0x2F. This interrupt, called the *DOS multiplex interrupt*, is used to communicate with multiple TSR (Terminate and Stay Resident) programs (among which are drivers like HIMEM.SYS). The first invocation of 0x2F is used to determine whether HIMEM.SYS is indeed present. If so, the second invocation acquires the far address of the direct entry point to HIMEM.SYS and stores it in a long named xmsaddr. From that point on, HIMEM.SYS is invoked by a far call, rather than the much slower interrupt method. The calling sequences required for HIMEM.SYS are one of the reasons for using inline assembly language in this class.

Third, notice that a temporary long variable is created locally within each function that is to call HIMEM.SYS, and the global xmsaddr is copied into the temporary variable just before inline assembly makes use of it. The reason is that inline assembly has a problem with accessing variables outside the scope in which the a s m keyword invokes inline assembly. In other words, this device is a cheap work-around to a scope problem.

Putting the xmsmgr class directly to work is no problem, although the main purpose is to use this class as a base for the swapbuf derived class. Listing 17.3 contains one of the test programs used to verify the correct operation of xmsmgr, and the program incidentally illustrates how to use many of the class's member function calls.

Listing 17.3. testxms.cpp. *A test driver for the* xmsmgr *class.*

```
1   #include "xmsmgr.hpp"
2
3   void main()
4   {
5     xmsmgr bigblock;
6
7     if ( !bigblock ) {
8       cout << bigblock.xmserr() << endl;
9       exit(0);
10    }
11
12    cout << "The largest free XMS block is "
13         << bigblock.query_largest_free_xm()
14         << " Kilobytes." << endl;
15    cout << "Total free XMS is "
16         << bigblock.query_total_free_xm()
17         << " Kilobytes." << endl;
18
19    delay( 1000 );
20
21    unsigned blk;
22    if ( -1 == ( blk = bigblock.alloc_emb( 64 ))) {
23      cout << bigblock.xmserr() << endl;
24      exit(0);
25    }
26
27    char far* incore;
28    incore = (char far*) farmalloc( 32768UL );
29
30    long filesize;
31    FILE* testfile;
32    testfile = fopen( "lib.cpp", "rb" );
```

```
33    filesize = fread( incore, 1, 32760, testfile );
34    fclose( testfile );
35
36    if ( -1 == bigblock.stow( incore, blk, filesize, 0 )) {
37      cout << bigblock.xmserr() << endl;
38      exit(0);
39    }
40
41    long j;
42    char far* ptr = incore;
43    for ( j=0; j<filesize; ++j ) *ptr++ = '\0';   // Make sure
44
45    if ( -1 == bigblock.fetch( incore, blk, filesize, 0)) {
46      cout << bigblock.xmserr() << endl;
47      exit(0);
48    }
49
50    ptr = incore;
51    for ( j=0; j<filesize; ++j ) cout << *ptr++;
52
53    farfree( incore );
54  }
```

Just about the only thing that the program in listing 17.3 doesn't explicitly demonstrate is the use of the `free_emb()` function. Instead, the class destructor is allowed to run the `list_handles` array, making any necessary `free_emb()` requests before the `list_handles` array itself is released.

Deriving a Swap Buffer Class

The `xmsmgr` class does all the hard work, leaving `swapbuf`, the class derived from it, only a little more to do. The `swapbuf` constructor allocates only one EMB, so that all member functions can assume that the correct EMB handle is in `xmsmgr::list_handles[0]`. Implementing `swapbuf` involves a small handful of `private` variables, a constructor and destructor, and the member functions `swapout()` (move far heap data to EMB, releasing heap pointer) and `swapin()` (move data from EMB back to far heap—possibly at a new location). The simplicity of the class can be seen in its header, shown in listing 17.4.

Listing 17.4. `swapbuf.hpp`. *A header file for the* `swapbuf` *class.*

```
1   #if !defined(SWAPBUF)
2   #define SWAPBUF
3
4   #include <alloc.h>
5
6   #include "xmsmgr.hpp"
7
8   class swapbuf : public xmsmgr {
9     void *swaploc;
10    unsigned swapsize;
11  public:
12    swapbuf( int = 64 );
13    ~swapbuf();
14    int swapout( void far* );
15    void* swapin();
16  };
17
18  #endif
```

The most complicated thing about the `swapbuf` header file is that the constructor function assigns a default value of 64 to its integer argument. Otherwise, the only notable feature is that `swapbuf` declares `xmsmgr` to be its `public` base class.

The implementation of the `swapbuf` member functions is naturally just a *little* more complicated than the class header makes it seem. Look over the `swapbuf` member functions in listing 17.5.

Listing 17.5. `swapbuf.cpp`. *Member functions for the* `swapbuf` *class.*

```
1   #include "swapbuf.hpp"
2
3   // -------------------------------------------------
4   //              SWAPBUF CONSTRUCTOR defaults to 64K
5   // -------------------------------------------------
6
7   swapbuf::swapbuf( int kbytes )
8   {
9     swaploc = NULL;
10    swapsize = 0;
```

```
11      if ( kbytes < 0 || kbytes > 64 ) kbytes = 64;
12      if ( xmsmgr::operator!() ) return;
13      alloc_emb( kbytes );   // Assume list element 0
14   }
15
16   // ------------------------------------------------
17   //              SWAPBUF DESTRUCTOR frees EMB
18   // ------------------------------------------------
19
20   swapbuf::~swapbuf()
21   {
22      free_emb( 0 );
23   }
24
25   // ------------------------------------------------
26   //              SWAPOUT returns 0=failure, 1=success
27   // ------------------------------------------------
28
29   int swapbuf::swapout( void far* obj )
30   {
31      struct farheapinfo node;
32
33      if ( xmsmgr::operator!() ) return( 0 ); // if no EMB exists
34      if ( farheapchecknode( obj ) < 2 )        // heap error
35         return( 0 );
36      node.ptr = NULL;             // Get ready to find heap object
37      while ( farheapwalk( &node )  == _HEAPOK ) { // Look for it
38         if ( node.ptr == obj ) break;
39      }
40      if ( node.ptr != obj ) return( 0 );
41      swaploc = obj;                          // Note where it was
42      swapsize = node.size - 16;          // and how big it was
43               // Note that a far heap node has a 16-byte header
44      if ( !stow( (char far *)obj, 0, swapsize, 0 ) ) {
45         swaploc = NULL;
46         swapsize = 0;
47         return( 0 );
48      }
49      farfree( obj );                      // Here is the good part!
50      return( 1 );
```

Listing 17.5. continues

Listing 17.5. *continued*

```
51  }
52
53  // ----------------------------------------------
54  //         SWAPIN returns NULL=failure, POINTER=success
55  // ----------------------------------------------
56
57  void* swapbuf::swapin()
58  {
59    void* holdit;
60
61    if ( NULL == swaploc ) return NULL;
62    if ( NULL == ( holdit = farmalloc( swapsize ) ) )
63      return NULL;
64    if ( !fetch( (char far *)holdit, 0, swapsize, 0 ) )
65      return NULL;
66    return holdit;
67  }
```

The `swapbuf` constructor function (lines 7–14) sets the `private` members `swaploc` to `NULL` and `swapsize` to zero (nothing is yet swapped out). Next, the base class `operator!()` function is used to verify the state of the `xmsmgr` subobject; notice how the scope resolution operator is used to ensure that the correct operator is invoked. The `swapbuf` constructor also assumes that the base class constructor has *already been called*. In fact, it has been called. This aspect of class derivation is again covered later in this chapter. Finally, the constructor function calls the base class `alloc_emb()` function to acquire a single EMB, which will be the swap buffer. The class destructor function (lines 20–23) is even simpler—it just calls the base class `free_emb()` function to deallocate the swap buffer's EMB.

The `swapout()` member function (lines 29–51) is a bit more interesting. The purpose of this function is to locate the requested allocation on the far heap, relocate it to the swap buffer, *free the far heap memory it used*, and invalidate the pointer that originally located it. Next, you will see in some detail how the function does all that.

Before any far heap manipulations can be carried out, you must first create a structure having type `farheapinfo`. The one used here (line 31) is called `node`. Then, after verifying a usable `xmsmgr` state, the `farheapchecknode()` built-in Borland C++ function is used to verify that the pointer argument passed to the function does in fact refer to a valid far heap allocation. If that function returns a value less than 2, the heap was empty, the heap has been corrupted, or the pointer does not refer to a valid node in the heap.

Next, as another double check (remember that a heap node is about to be destroyed), the logic in lines 36–41 "walks" the entire heap, searching for the node requested by the pointer argument. If the node is found, processing continues; otherwise, the function returns zero immediately. Assuming that all is still well, the node size is extracted from the node's 16-byte header and stored in lines 41–43 (and that is the other reason to find the node this way).

The real meat of the swapout() function is in lines 44–48. This is where the xmsmgr base class function stow() physically copies the far heap data to extended memory. If stow() completes successfully, the Borland C++ farfree() function actually releases the heap memory for this node. This thing had better work right!

The swapin() member function (lines 57–67) performs the reverse task. The most exciting thing about this function is that it first allocates space once more on the far heap and then copies the contents of the swap buffer's EMB back into the far heap. If successful, this function returns a pointer with which the user's pointer into the heap can be reinitialized. Otherwise, the function returns NULL.

The swapbuf test and verification program is almost exactly like that for the xmsmgr class. The program in listing 17.6 reads an entire text file into the far heap, swaps the text file out, swaps it back in, and sends it to the system screen for visual verification. The great difference here is that the heap area is temporarily destroyed, and, of course, using the swapbuf class makes the whole program much simpler.

Listing 17.6. testswap.cpp. *A test driver for the swapbuf class.*

```
1    #include <iostream.h>
2    #include "swapbuf.hpp"
3
4    void main()
5    {
6      swapbuf xfile( 32 ); // Swap buffer with 32K
7
8      if ( !xfile ) {
9        cout << xfile.xmserr() << endl;
10       exit(0);
```

Listing 17.6. continues

Listing 17.6. *continued*

```
11    }
12
13    char far* incore;
14    incore = (char far*) farmalloc( 32768UL );
15
16    long filesize;
17    FILE* testfile;
18    testfile = fopen( "lib.cpp", "rb" );
19    filesize = fread( incore, 1, 32760, testfile );
20    fclose( testfile );
21
22    cout << "File buffer address: "
23        << hex << (void far *)incore << endl;
24
25    if ( !xfile.swapout( incore ) ) {
26      cout << "Swap out failed." << endl;
27      exit(0);
28    }
29    incore = NULL;                // Mark it out of use
30
31    cout << "File buffer address: "
32        << hex << (void far *)incore << endl;
33
34    if ( NULL == ( incore = (char far *)xfile.swapin() ) ) {
35      cout << "Swap in failed." << endl;
36      exit(0);
37    }
38
39    cout << "File buffer address: "
40        << hex << (void far *)incore << endl;
41
42    long j;
43    char far* ptr = incore;
44
45    delay( 2000 );
46
47    ptr = incore;
48    for ( j=0; j<filesize; ++j ) cout << *ptr++;
49
50    farfree( incore );
51 }
```

Using Virtual Functions

Earlier in this chapter, you learned that a pointer to a derived class object can be converted to a pointer to a base class object. That feature of C++ is quite useful but can cause some problems. Specifically, if both the base class and the derived class declare a function with the same name and signature, the pointer manipulations just alluded to can cause the wrong copy of the function to be executed. C++ *virtual functions* can help avoid this sort of problem.

Using Late Binding and Virtual Functions

The virtual function mechanism can be viewed as a "pass through" mechanism intended to guarantee execution of the correct copy of identical functions appearing in both a base and a derived class. Consider, for example, what happens when you *don't* use virtual functions in the following short program:

```
#include <iostream.h>
#include <iomanip.h>

class A {
public:
  void hello() { cout << "My name is A." << endl; }
};

class B : public A {
public:
  void hello() { cout << "My name is B." << endl; }
};

void main()
{
  B* obj = new B; // Create derived object
  A* ptr;         // base pointer
  obj->hello();
  ptr = (A*)obj;  // Convert to base pointer type
  ptr->hello();
}
```

This short program produces a hello() from *each* class—a different message from each class:

```
My name is B.
My name is A.
```

The operation of the function is similar to the slicing copies you dealt with earlier. Then, not everything got copied when the assignment operator was invoked; now, you may not be getting the function you actually wanted to call. Declaring the class A hello() member function *virtual*, however, guarantees that the derived class's copy will be executed—no matter how the object is accessed. The following rewrite of this short program adds the virtual keyword and fixes the problem:

```
#include <iostream.h>
#include <iomanip.h>

class A {
public:          // Look at the difference in hello()
  virtual void hello() { cout << "My name is A." << endl; }
};

class B : public A {
public:
  void hello() { cout << "My name is B." << endl; }
};

void main()
{
  B* obj = new B; // Create derived object
  A* ptr;         // base pointer

  obj->hello();
  ptr = (A*)obj;  // Convert to base pointer type
  ptr->hello();
}
```

Here the base class function has been declared virtual. This means that if there is a derived class function by the same name and signature, the derived class's copy will be selected to execute. That is exactly what happens, producing the following (correct) output:

```
My name is B.
My name is B.
```

Now that the hello() function is declared virtual in the base class, the derived class function is said to *override* the base class function. Therefore, the same copy of hello() is called whether through a pointer with the derived class type or with the base class type. Note that if the derived class's function differs in signature, the virtual function mechanism is bypassed: the derived class function hides the base class function (it can still be accessed with the scope resolution operator).

Thus, a virtual function can be defined as a function that *depends only on the type of object for which it is called*, not on the type of reference or pointer used to make the function call. Selection of the correct copy of one of several identically typed functions is called late, or *dynamic*, binding. In other words, it is not necessary to know, until it is determined at run time, which precise derived class type the function call belongs to.

This important feature of C++ is useful in defining interfaces to an object, the precise nature of which may not be completely known in a given context. If the interface is defined with virtual functions and the *base class* interface *is* known, all is well—a function call binds to the correct version no matter what.

The classic example is the shape base class from which is derived specific shape classes (square, circle, line, and so on). The shape base class has a draw() virtual function that is overridden in each derived class to satisfy specific drawing requirements. If a pointer to a derived class shape object has been passed to a function that does not know which particular shape it has received, it can still draw() the object with some confidence in the results because that function (presumably) knows of the base class drawing interface.

Looked at from another point of view, the virtual function mechanism supplies the capability to call *diverse functions through the same interface*. This characteristic is called *polymorphism* (different "shapes" in different contexts) and is considered by many to be the essence of object-oriented programming (as opposed to object-based programming).

Of course, there are some rules for the use of virtual functions. As you develop your base and derived classes by using virtual functions, be aware of the following points:

❑ *A virtual function must be a nonstatic member function of a class.* The whole point of virtual functions *is* membership (and selecting which class type to bind). A virtual function cannot be static either: binding for a virtual function depends on object type, so the function cannot be dissociated from particular objects of its class by being declared static.

❑ *An overriding function of a virtual function is itself virtual.* That is, the overriding function does not have to be explicitly declared virtual, because it is associated with a virtual function. You can declare an overriding function virtual if you want, but it is not necessary.

❑ *You can define a virtual function in a base class, but not in any derived class.* If there is no overriding function in the derived class, the base class function will be called. You might find yourself declaring base class functions virtual without overriding functions during program development, in anticipation of later interfaces being added.

❑ *The scope resolution operator defeats the virtual function mechanism.* Because the scope resolution operator is aimed at "manually" selecting the class type to bind in a base and derived class hierarchy, the virtual function mechanism does not apply.

❑ *A virtual function can be declared a friend by another class.* You will learn how to arrange this bit of esoterica immediately following this list.

❑ *A virtual function in a base class must be either defined by the base class or declared to be a pure virtual function.* This rule means that you can't just write a function prototype for a virtual function in the base class, providing a function *body* only for overriding functions. The reason is simply that the base class copy might actually be called. The significance of this rule is slightly different if the function is a pure virtual function. That subject is covered later in this chapter, in the discussion on abstract classes.

You can declare a virtual function in one class to be a `friend` of another class, as mentioned in the preceding list. Although you probably won't see or use this technique often, a simple example is provided here. Note the following short program that declares a virtual function `friend` in another class:

```
#include <iostream.h>
#include <iomanip.h>

class C;

class A {
public:
  virtual void report( C& );
};

class B : public A {
public:
  void report( C& );
};
class C {  // not a derived class, but declares friend
  int c_data;
public:
  friend virtual void A::report( C& );
  friend         void B::report( C& );
  C() { c_data = 37; }
};

void A::report( C& cobj) {
  cout << "Nothing happening here." << endl;
}
```

```
void B::report( C& cobj ) {
  cout << cobj.c_data << endl;
}

void main()
{
  B bobj;   // derived class object
  C cobj;   // accessed by B friends
  A* ptr = (A*)&bobj; // but get base pointer

  ptr->report( cobj );
}
```

Notice carefully in this short program how the declarations and function definitions are arranged. The order is not accidental: it is designed to prevent "You haven't declared that yet!" messages.

You should also notice that class C declares both the base and derived class report() functions as friends. This is necessary because *friends are not inherited*. That is, declaring the base class virtual function as a friend does not mean that the derived class virtual function is also a friend. In fact, it is not strictly necessary to declare the base class report() function a friend in this example; in other circumstances, however, the base class might be used to create an object directly, requiring the friend declaration. The declaration is included here to highlight this point.

The virtual function "pass through" mechanism works in this example as expected. In this short program, the base class virtual friend function is not used; the derived class virtual function is used. And as you can see, in the last line of main(), the derived class virtual function can still be accessed through a *base* class pointer causing the overriding function to be invoked. And because that function is a friend of class C, C's private data can be accessed by it.

Using Scope Resolution To Control Member Function Access

You learned in the preceding section that the scope resolution operator can be used to call a base class copy of a virtual function, but that this circumvents the virtual function mechanism. Scope resolution can also be used in a hierarchy of derived classes to select which copy of a redefined function is to be used in a function call (or which version of a hidden variable is to be accessed).

That a hierarchy of derived classes can exist implies, of course, that a derived class can act as a base class for yet another derived class. For example, you can build a hierarchy of classes A, B, and C:

```
class A { ... };
class B : public A { ... };
class C : public B { ... };
```

Each class in the hierarchy depends on the previous class to form its base class. This arrangement of derived classes introduces the notion of *direct* bases and *indirect* bases for derived classes. In the preceding code fragment, for example, A is the direct base for B, and B is the direct base for C, but A is an *indirect* base for C. The concatenation of subobjects in a hierarchy of derived classes is similar to that for single inheritance with one base class. Pointer casts to base classes are also the same, except that here a class C object pointer could be cast to either a B* or A* base class pointer. Virtual functions "cascade" down through the hierarchy, too, as long as there are properly formed overriding functions.

But note that a hierarchy of derived classes is *not* multiple inheritance. Each derived class here has only one direct base: multiple inheritance (discussed in the next section) involves defining multiple direct bases for a single derived class.

Returning now to the discussion of scope resolution, consider what happens when you have a hierarchy of derived classes, each of which redefines an identically typed function in its base class, as shown here:

```
class A { public: void func(); };
class B : public A { public: void func(); };
class C : public B { public: void func(); };
...
C someobj;
...
someobj.func();
```

In this code fragment, the class C object someobj seems to have no recourse but to use the class C copy of func(). The scope resolution operator can get you around this problem. With a fully qualified member function name, specifying the class whose copy you want to use is the simple solution:

```
someobj.B::func();   // Use class B copy
```

The scope resolution operator can also be useful in resolving ambiguous references in complicated derivations. Such complications are most likely to arise when you are using multiple base classes—which is the topic of the next section.

Using Multiple Base Classes

You are not restricted to using a single base class when deriving a new class. You can write a *base list* containing any number of direct base classes for the derived class. Deriving a class in this way is called *multiple inheritance*, or class derivation with *multiple base classes*.

Most of the knowledge you have just acquired in learning about single inheritance can be applied directly to multiple inheritance. There will, of course, be other considerations that arise for the first time when you are deriving classes with multiple base classes. One of the most important of these new considerations is the avoidance of ambiguous references, which are more easily created when you use multiple base classes instead of single base classes.

Deriving from More Than One Base Class

Suppose, for example, that you want to derive class C from classes A and B, making both base classes public (all the access specifiers still apply in the same ways you have just learned). The class declarations look like this:

```
class A { ... };
class B { ... };
class C : public A, public B { ... };
```

Thus, class C inherits public and protected members from both A and B: subobjects are constructed by the compiler just as they are for single inheritance, but the resulting class object now has three, not two, subobjects. Classes derived from multiple bases always have, by definition, proportionately more subobjects than classes derived from single bases. Figure 17.5 illustrates the subobject construction for the preceding code fragment.

Figure 17.5 also indicates that conversion of derived class pointers to base class pointers is possible, as it is for classes derived from single bases. As you can see, however, there are more valid base class pointers to which you can convert when you are deriving from multiple base classes.

The principles of virtual function declarations apply in multiple inheritance in the same way as in single inheritance. No matter which base class pointer is used to access the derived class object, a virtual function still correctly overrides any progenitor functions above it in the hierarchy.

Fig. 17.5. *Multiple bases mean multiple subobjects and the possibility of more than one valid cast to a base pointer type.*

```
class A { ... };
class B { .. };
class C: public A, public B { ... };
```

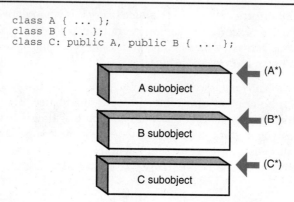

You can also use hierarchies of derived classes, one or more of which have multiple base classes. For example, you can write the following:

```
class A { ... };
class B : public A { ... };
class C { ... };
class D : public C { ... };
class E : public B, public D { ... };
```

Because the preceding derivation has no redundancy of base classes, there will be five subobjects in a class E derived class object. It is possible, however, to introduce a redundant (or possibly redundant) copy of a base class, if it is an *indirect* base class of a derived class more than once. Figure 17.6 illustrates how this can occur.

Notice carefully in figure 17.6 that no base class appears as the *direct* base for a derived class more than once: that is illegal. It is hardly possible, however, to outlaw the appearance of a class more than once as an indirect ancestor, because complicated derivations can conceivably make it impossible to proceed if such classes are not allowed. You might find yourself in a "you can't get there from here" design dilemma.

Having a class appear as an indirect base more than once does not necessarily introduce ambiguous names into the derived class. Suppose that classes B and C are both derived from class A, and that class D is derived from both classes B and C. Suppose further that class A has a member integer named `counter`. Now, because there are two class A subobjects in the resulting derived class, is it possible to use one of the `counter` member objects—or for that matter, to unambiguously reference either? It is possible, and you can do it with the scope resolution operator. The code looks something like this:

Fig. 17.6. A base class can be an indirect base for a derived class more than once, but its presence increases the number of subobjects present.

```
class common {...};

class A : public common {...};

class B : public common {...};

class C: public A, public B {...};
```

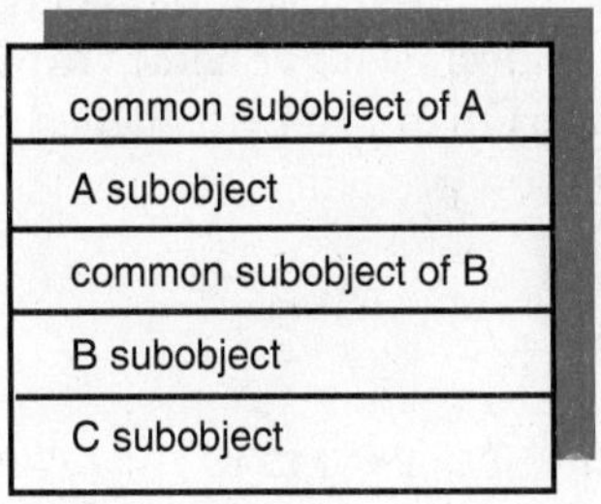

common subobject of A
A subobject
common subobject of B
B subobject
C subobject

```
class A {
public:
  int counter;
  ...
};
class B : public A { ... };
class C : public A { ... };
class D : public B, public C {
public:
  void report{
  cout << B::counter << endl; // Use A subobject of B
  cout << C::counter << endl; // Use A subobject of C
  }
};
```

Casts to base pointers can be especially tricky when a given class appears more than once as an indirect base class of a derived class. With the preceding code fragment in mind, the following casts to a base pointer (from a pointer to class D) are illegal because they are ambiguous:

```
D* d_ptr = new D;
...
A* a_ptr = d_ptr;  // Implicit cast is ambiguous - which A?
a_ptr = (A*)d_ptr; // Explicit cast is still ambiguous
```

In neither case in this code fragment is it possible for the compiler to sort out which class A subobject is meant. Is it the one belonging to B or C? There is no way to determine the answer.

That dilemma does not prevent you from accessing an A class subobject from the preceding example, but you have to approach it in the correct way. For example, you can write this:

```
A* a_ptr = (A*)(B*)d_ptr // Point to B's A subobject
d_ptr = (D*)(C*)a_ptr    // Point to D containing C's A
```

Problems with ambiguous references will probably plague you more often concerning *member names* than class names, however. There is a much greater likelihood that two base classes contributing to a derived class will contain identical member names (or member names that can be confused by the compiler) than that class names will conflict. Consider, for example, the following short program:

```
class A {
public:
  int a;
  int (A::* f1)();  // Notice how the pointer is declared
  int f2() { return 0; }
  int f3() { return 0; }
};

class B {
public:
  int a;
  int f1() { return 0; }
  int f2() { return 0; }
};

class C : public A, public B { };

void main()
{
  C c_obj;

  c_obj.f1 = f2;   // ERROR: f1 ambiguous and f2 undefined
  c_obj.a = 2;     // ERROR: A::a or B::a?
  c_obj.f2();      // ERROR A::f2 or B::f2?
  c_obj.f3();      // OK, not ambiguous
//
// Here is the correct way to do it:
//
  c_obj.A::f1 = A::f2;
  c_obj.B::a = 2;
  c_obj.A::f2();
}
```

Once more, the scope resolution operator is the answer to the problem. If you use the scope resolution operator and the name of the appropriate base class, all ambiguities are made to disappear.

Notice in the preceding short program that the member name ambiguities arise because the base classes are "siblings." If B had been derived from A (in a hierarchy, that is), the member identifier in the derived class would *dominate* the same identifier in the base class. You should understand that *dominance* is not the same thing as overloading, nor the same thing as overriding (which virtual functions do). There are conceptual similarities among the three terms—dominate, overload, and override—but they are different ideas, applying to different contexts.

Declaring and Using Virtual Base Classes

You have just seen the effects of designing a derived class for which an *indirect* base class was specified more than once. Because there are circumstances in which the repeated subobjects for that common base class are necessary, you need to know how to work with them.

In most cases, you will find that allowing a repeated indirect base to cause the construction of multiple subobjects is simply wasteful—only one such subobject is usually needed. There is a way to control such repetition of subobjects for a common indirect base class. You can declare *virtual base classes* and cause the construction of the derived class to contain only one unique subobject for each "parent" class. Here is a sample of the syntax required to create and use virtual base classes:

```
class A { ... };
class B : public virtual A { ... };
class C : public virtual A { ... };
class D : public B, public C { ... };
```

Without virtual base classes, an object of the derived class D would consist of five subobjects (counting the extra class A subobject). Using virtual base classes, there will be only four subobjects. Furthermore, there will be no possible ambiguities involved in casting to the common indirect base class. Note also that because the virtual keyword is used here with the *derived class declaration*, the "virtualness" of a base class is a characteristic of this kind of derivation, not something that inheres in a base class itself.

When not using virtual base classes, you can cast a derived class object pointer to a base class pointer, and you can cast it back again into a derived class pointer (as shown earlier). Using virtual base classes, however, you *can* cast from a derived class to a virtual base class, but you *cannot* cast from a virtual base class to a derived class. To allow this maneuver would require the compiler to develop lists of pointers to enclosing objects—in effect, converting from one kind of memory layout to another on the fly.

Finally, you can define virtual functions within virtual base classes. Doing this has the interesting result that you can arrange virtual functions and base pointers so that sibling base class subobjects can communicate with one another. Again, assume that both classes B and C are derived from the virtual base class A; derived class D is derived from B and C. Here is a short program in which the C subobject acquires information from the B subobject:

```
#include <iostream.h>

class A {
  int a_val;
public:
  A() { a_val = 0; }
  virtual int b() { return a_val; }
  virtual int c() { return a_val; }
};

class B : public virtual A {
  int b_val;
public:
  B() { b_val = 16; }
  virtual int b() { return b_val; }
};

class C : public virtual A {
  int c_val;
public:
  C() { c_val = 64; }
  virtual int c() { return c_val; }
};

class D : public B, public C { };

void main()
{
  D* d_obj = new D;     // Declare derived object
  C* c_obj = d_obj;     // cast to C base pointer
                        // Now call C path, get value from B path
  cout << c_obj->b() << endl;
}
```

When you run the preceding program, it appears that you are reaching the desired virtual function by entering through the C class "path"—and indeed you are. But the arrangement of virtual base class and virtual functions guarantees that you will actually execute the `B::b()` function. The value returned and displayed is therefore 16, as you should expect.

If that is not enough flexibility to suit your needs for building derived classes, there are abstract classes and pure virtual functions available for you. These are discussed next.

Deriving Classes from Abstract Classes

C++ has now evolved to the point where the notion of a completely generalized type is supported. The *abstract class* defines a concept or generalized type. An abstract class can be used *only* as a base class for another, derived, class. A few special rules apply to abstract classes:

❏ *An abstract class must have at least one pure virtual function.* Pure virtual functions are what give abstract classes their distinctive character. These functions are discussed in the section following this list.

❏ *An abstract class cannot be used as an argument type, a function return type, the type of an explicit conversion, or the type of an object.* That is, if `tree` is an abstract class, all of the following statements are illegal:

```
tree oak;              // tree cannot be object type
tree func();  // tree cannot be function return type
int numleaves(tree); // tree cannot be argument type
someptr = (tree*)otherptr; // cannot be used in explicit cvt
```

❏ *You can declare a pointer or reference to an abstract class.* The following statements are acceptable:

```
class oak : public tree{ ... };
...
oak* mytree = new oak;
tree* treeptr = mytree;
```

Because the essence of abstract classes is the pure virtual function, it is discussed first.

Understanding Pure Virtual Functions

Aside from being unavailable for creating objects, all abstract classes have one common characteristic: each has at least one pure virtual function. The formal definition of a *pure virtual function* is that it possesses the pure specifier, as shown here:

```
virtual type functionname( args ) = 0;
```

It is true that this is a peculiar syntax. But the whole point of abstract classes, and hence, virtual functions, is that they define a *concept*, not an object. This syntax suggests that (normally) a pure virtual function is a pathway to other, concrete, member functions serving real objects.

Implementing Pure Virtual Functions

You can always understand a strange concept more easily if you see it in action. The following short program defines the abstract class tree, mentioned earlier:

```
#include <iostream.h>
#include <string.h>

class tree {     // Declare an abstract TREE type
  char treehdr[30];
public:
  tree() { strcpy( treehdr, "This tree has no type." ); }
  virtual void saytree() = 0;  // <== pure virtual specifier
};

=class oak : public tree {  // Here is a class for a real tree
  char treehdr[30];
public:
  oak() { strcpy( treehdr, "This tree is an oak." ); }
  void saytree() {                 // <== NO pure virtual spec.
    cout << treehdr << endl;
  }
};

=void main()
{
  oak yardtree;  // Declare particular tree object
=  yardtree.saytree();
}
```

The class t r e e is used here just to define the concept of a tree. A real tree, an o a k in this case, has more specific attributes that the abstract class by definition cannot know about.

Pure virtual functions are inherited as pure virtual functions. Somewhere along the line, however, there has to be a function body for the function, or it could never do anything useful. This implies that a pure virtual function may have a function body. Note that a pure virtual function in an abstract class doesn't need to have a function definition unless you intend to call it directly by using the scope resolution operator to locate it. The following rewrite of the preceding program shows how to call a pure virtual function in an abstract class:

```
#include <iostream.h>
#include <string.h>

class tree {
  char treehdr[30];
public:
  tree() { strcpy( treehdr, "This tree has no type." ); }
  virtual void saytree() = 0 {   // <== pure virtual specifier
    cout << treehdr << endl;
  }
};

class oak : public tree {
  char treehdr[30];
public:
  oak() { strcpy( treehdr, "This tree is an oak." ); }
  void saytree() {               // <== NO pure virtual spec.
    cout << treehdr << endl;
  }
};

void main()
{

  oak yardtree;  // Declare particular tree

  yardtree.saytree();
  yardtree.tree::saytree();
}
```

This version of the program produces two messages: one message identifies the derived object as an o a k, and the second message calls the pure virtual function in the abstract class. The s a y t r e e ( ) function in the abstract class promptly demonstrates that it has no knowledge of specific trees.

Using Constructors and Destructors with Inheritance

As you might imagine, the use of constructor and destructor functions in derived classes—particularly the more complicated ones—is more complex than in simple classes.

This section discusses the differences involved in designing constructors and destructors for derived classes, and wraps up the chapter as well.

Initialization Code Is Not Inherited

Initialization code (as well as deinitialization code) is not inherited. You now have enough background in deriving C++ classes to understand why this is true.

Even though a derived class eventually acts as the type for a single unified object, a derived class consists of a number of subobject classes. Each of these classes (except for abstract classes) can also stand as the type definition for objects directly, as well as contribute to the structure of a derived class object. Thus, each base class has its own distinct initialization requirements.

The implication, of course, is not only that all classes coming together in a derived class have their own constructors and destructors, but also that all of these initialization functions are *executed*. That may sound like a trivial deduction, but you would be surprised at the trouble you can buy for yourself by forgetting it even momentarily.

Understanding the Order of Constructor and Destructor Calls with Inheritance

Because all the constructors for base and derived classes are executed when an object of the derived class is created, it may be important to the design of your derived class to understand their order of execution. Usually, certain things must happen in a certain order. Here is the order of constructor calls made when a derived class object is created:

❑ *All virtual base class constructors are executed first.* If there are multiple virtual base classes, their constructors are executed in the order in which they were declared.

❑ *All nonvirtual base class constructors are executed next.* The dependency of nonvirtual base classes on their virtual parents is obvious. If there are multiple nonvirtual base classes, their constructors are executed in the order in which they were declared.

❑ *The derived class constructor, or the only constructor when there is no hierarchy, is executed last.* There can be, by definition, only one of these in a hierarchy. That does not mean that there can be only one hierarchy, of course.

The order of destructor function calls made when an object is destroyed is simple: the order is exactly the reverse of that of constructor function calls.

Using Virtual Destructor Functions

Constructor and destructor functions cannot be inherited. Nor can a constructor function be a virtual function. But a destructor function *can* be virtual, and it is often a good idea to make a destructor function virtual.

To understand why this is advisable, recall the earlier discussion of the slicing copy operation that can result when you are defining an assignment operator for a derived class. If a base pointer is used to access a derived class object, and the assignment operator function is accessed through the base pointer path, not all members of the derived class will be copied. You learned how to get around that (and when to do so).

Something similar can happen to your destructor functions in a hierarchy of derived classes—a destructor can fail to be executed under the right circumstances. When can this happen? It is not uncommon when you have created a derived class object with `new`, placing the resulting pointer in a *base class* pointer, and then calling `delete` to destroy the object. Suppose, for example, that you have defined a `tree` base class and derived an `oak` class from it. The `oak` class constructor further acquires free store outside the object to hold an array of `leafdata`. Now consider what happens in the following short program:

```
#include <iostream.h>
#include <string.h>

class tree {
  char treehdr[30];
public:
  tree() { strcpy( treehdr, "This tree has no type." ); }

  ~tree() { cout << "Bye, bye!" << endl; }
```

```
    virtual void saytree() = 0 {   // <== pure virtual specifier
      cout << treehdr << endl;
    }
};

class oak : public tree {
  char treehdr[30];
  int* leafdata;             // pointer to fairly large array
public:
  oak() {
    strcpy( treehdr, "This tree is an oak." );
    leafdata = new int[1000];
  }
  ~oak() {                   // Derived destructor is virtual, too
    cout << "Releasing leaf storage." << endl;
    delete leafdata;
  }
  void saytree() {                    // <== NO pure virtual spec.
    cout << treehdr << endl;
  }
};

void main()
{
  tree* yardtree = new oak;  // Look at this one carefully!

  yardtree->saytree();
  delete yardtree;
}
```

When this program runs, you receive only the `Bye, bye!` message from the base class destructor. The `oak` destructor is not executed. This means that the 1,000-integer array `leafdata` allocated by the `oak` constructor is still in free store. If you allow the derived class destructor to be bypassed often in the same program, you will soon exhaust free store altogether. You can correct this problem by merely adding the `virtual` keyword to the `~tree()` destructor function, as shown here:

```
#include <iostream.h>
#include <string.h>

class tree {
  char treehdr[30];
public:
  tree() { strcpy( treehdr, "This tree has no type." ); }
  virtual ~tree() { cout << "Bye, bye!" << endl; }
```

```
    virtual void saytree() = 0 {   // <== pure virtual specifier
      cout << treehdr << endl;
    }
};

class oak : public tree {
  char treehdr[30];
  int* leafdata;                // pointer to fairly large array
public:
  oak() {
    strcpy( treehdr, "This tree is an oak." );
    leafdata = new int[1000];
  }
  ~oak() {                 // Derived destructor is virtual, too
    cout << "Releasing leaf storage." << endl;
    delete leafdata;
  }
  void saytree() {                     // <=== NO pure virtual spec.
    cout << treehdr << endl;
  }
};

void main()
{

  tree* yardtree = new oak;   // Look at this one carefully!

  yardtree->saytree();
  delete yardtree;
}
```

When this version of the program runs, you receive three messages on the system display:

```
This tree is an oak.
Releasing leaf storage.
Bye, bye!
```

You should draw two conclusions from this demonstration. First, because the destructor function names for the base and derived classes are *not the same* (but the technique still works), the destructor of a class derived from a class with a virtual destructor is *always virtual*. The function names don't matter here.

Second, you should notice that messages from *both* destructors appeared, even though all access was through a base class pointer. They appeared in the correct order too. Because the base *constructor* was called first, the base class *destructor* was called last.

Exercises

Derived classes are the essence of C++ object-oriented programming. The following exercises give you a chance to create and manipulate C++ derived classes.

1. Pick a simple type of object and write a class for it. Then reuse it first by composition with another class and then by deriving another class from it.

2. Create a hierarchy of derived classes, each having a single base class (that is, do not use multiple inheritance). Create an object of the derived class, using `new`, to get a pointer to it. Experiment with casting the derived class pointer to the various base class pointer types. Look carefully for such behavior as the slicing copy, which was discussed in this chapter.

3. Create another hierarchy of derived classes, this time using multiple base classes. Perform the same experiments on this class that you did in exercise 2.

4. Prove to yourself that virtual functions actually do what they are advertised to do. You can use pointer casts to test execution paths into the derived class objects you create. You can do the same thing with virtual base classes, by using the `sizeof` operator to measure the size of the resulting objects, compared to those created without virtual base classes. Hint: member functions don't contribute to the size of a class object, so be sure to include member *data* objects in all classes for this test.

Summary

Class derivation and virtual functions (through which C++ implements its brand of polymorphism) are considered by most C++ programmers to be the essence of object-oriented programming. These features of the C++ language also supply some of its most powerful features. This chapter covered the following important points:

❑ *C++ class code can be reused by class composition and by class derivation.* Class composition involves declaring an object of one class within another class. Composition allows code reuse with no modifications to existing code. Class derivation involves telling the compiler, "Create a new class that is just like the old class, with a few changes." Class derivation allows code reuse with stringently controlled changes to existing code.

❑ *A derived class can be defined with one base class.* Derivation using only one base class is also called *single inheritance*. Single inheritance allows the construction of hierarchies of derived classes, as long as every derived class has only one base.

❑ *A derived class can be defined with multiple base classes.* Derivation using multiple base classes is also called *multiple inheritance*. You can build hierarchies of derived classes with multiple base classes.

❑ *Virtual functions guarantee selection of the correct member function when identical function types appear under derivation.* The virtual function facility will select the correct member function for execution even when a pointer to a derived class object is cast to a pointer to a base class object. The ability to select among multiple functions at run time based on execution context is called *polymorphism* (also called *late binding*).

❑ *Virtual base classes eliminate duplicate base class subobjects.* Using virtual base classes does more than reduce the size of derived class objects: it also helps to eliminate possible ambiguity and confusion.

❑ *Abstract classes are used to define concepts, not objects.* An abstract class must have at least one pure virtual function. Although an abstract class can never be used to create a class object directly, you can directly call a pure virtual function defined within an abstract class (assuming that the pure virtual function does have a function body).

❑ *Class initialization code requires special handling under derivation.* Class constructors and destructors are called in a specific, predictable order under derivation that may affect the way you design your classes. It is very important to remember that initialization code is *not* inherited. You can, however, define virtual destructor functions. It is often wise to do so.

If you don't feel comfortable yet with single and multiple inheritance, virtual functions and virtual base classes, abstract classes and pure virtual functions, and object construction and destruction under derivation, don't feel bad—these are tough subjects. By all means, go back and review if you need to, but don't let this part of C++ get by you.

Object Control, Performance, and Future Directions

This chapter wraps up the discussion of Borland C++ object-oriented programming by considering a collection of miscellaneous C++ related topics. These topics are of interest to all C++ programmers, but some are difficult to group logically in other chapters. This chapter discusses the following:

❏ *User-defined type conversions*. Type conversions have been mentioned in other contexts in this book. This chapter reviews conversion methods, and takes a closer look at user-defined conversion functions implemented as class type-cast operators.

❏ *Generic classes and class abstraction*. You have already used generic classes when you wrote parameterized C++ stream manipulators (Chapter 16). Now you are shown how the techniques for using generic classes work, so that you can design and use your own generic classes.

❏ *Class object performance and friend functions*. You can use friend functions to increase object performance as well as class flexibility. Now you find out why this is so, and when to use friend functions to increase performance.

❑ *Future directions for C++*. The base document already contains material labeled "experimental," which concerns function templates and exception handling. This chapter briefly discusses the current development of these features.

In the following discussions, the `quad` sample class is mentioned occasionally. The `quad` class implements higher precision integers by using an array of two `long int` variables (plus two more for work and overflow area). The complete source file listings for the `quad` class and its test driver program are in Appendix D. Some of the code from the `quad` class source files is repeated here, as needed.

User-Defined Type Conversions

Without the capability to convert other types to a class type, C++ would not be a very useful language. A moment's reflection on the plain C programs you write will show you that implicit and explicit conversions are used frequently in normal code. The same thing is true of programming with classes.

The two main types of class-related conversion techniques were mentioned in previous chapters without focusing on the conversion processes themselves. There are two ways you can convert other types to a class type: by using *class constructor functions* and by writing *user-defined conversion functions* (overloaded cast operator functions).

Using Constructors To Convert Types

When you declare a class object, you usually expect to be able to provide initialization data for that object at the same time. You already know about writing object declarations with constructor function arguments. It is possible to write constructors that accept argument lists containing many parameters. In the special case in which a constructor function accepts a *single argument*, the constructor is said to specify a conversion from the argument type to the class type.

In addition to the default and copy constructors, the `quad` class contains two constructors that convert their arguments to the class type. The declarations in the header file (`quadword.hpp`) for those constructors are

```
quad( long );
quad( int );
```

These declarations permit you to declare `quad` objects with constructor type conversion like this:

```
int a;
long b;
...
quad qobj1( a );
quad qobj2( b );
```

These declarations are simple C++ code: there is nothing here that you have not already seen. Another syntax that is not so obvious, however, is equivalent to the preceding code fragment. You can also write the following:

```
int a;
long b;
...
quad qobj1 = a;
quad qobj2 = b;
```

Even though the assignment operator is used in this last code fragment, an overloaded `operator=()` function is not invoked. Instead, the constructor function is called immediately, as if you had specified the first form of declaration, because the last two lines *are* object declarations.

Even if the class has what appears to be an applicable `operator=()` function, it will *never* be used for an object declaration that invokes constructor type conversion. The `quad` class does have an assignment operator function, declared as follows:

```
quad& operator=( char* );
```

Nevertheless, the following short program misuses the class constructor and assignment functions, and will *not compile*:

```
#include <stdlib.h>
#include <stdio.h>

#include "quadword.hpp"

void main()
{
  quad X = "Hello!";
  printf( "%s\n", (char*)X );
}
```

If you try to compile this short program, an error message is produced, stating that the compiler cannot find a matching declaration for the called function `quad::quad(char*)`. No such constructor function exists, and there is no search for any other function.

Conceptually, the assignment of a string to a `quad` class object is very much a conversion task. You may find the conversion of a string to a numeric quantity interesting, so here is the code for the `operator=()` member function for the `quad` class:

```
quad& quad::operator=( char *s )
{
  int neg, i;
  if ( *s == '-' ) {
    neg = 1; s++;
  }
  else neg = 0;
  *this = 0;
  while ( *s ) {
    *this = *this * 10;      // Shift previous result left
    *this += (int)( *s++ - '0' ); // next partial product
  }
  if ( neg ) {    // Simulate 2's complement negation
    vdata[0] = ~vdata[0];
    vdata[1] = ~vdata[1];
    *this += 1;
  }
  return *this;
}
```

This function operates by "stepping down" the source string and subtracting an ASCII `'0'` character from each input character. The subtraction converts each digit from a display character to a `signed char`. Then as the previously developed result is shifted left out of the way, the new digit is simply added to the accumulating result. Finally, if a minus sign is detected at the beginning of the string, the result is negated using two's complement logic.

Even though assignment operators do perform a conversion task, it is important to remember that assignment *syntax* does not cause the compiler to convert constant or data types at compile-time: your assignment operator *function* does it at run-time.

Overloading Type Cast Operators

Other than using conversion by constructor function, you can only convert other data types to your class type by writing assignment operator functions (or explicit conversion functions—you could declare an `inttoquad( int )` function, for example). But how can you convert your class type to another data type? Neither conversion technique discussed in the previous section addresses that question.

Converting an object from your class type to another data type (including another class type) is a job for a *user-defined conversion function*, more descriptively called a user-defined cast operator function. The following short program shows the basic method of defining a class cast operator function:

```
#include <iostream.h>

class A {
  int dat;
public:
  A( int num = 0 ) : dat( num ) {}
  operator int() { return dat; }
};

class X {
  int dat;
public:
  X( int num = 0 ) : dat( num ) {}
  operator int() { return dat; }     // castop to int
  operator A() {                      // castop to class A
    A temp = dat;
    return temp;
  }
};

void main()
{
  X stuff = 37;
  A more = 0;
  int hold;

  hold = (int)stuff;
  cout << hold << endl;

  more = (A)stuff;  // convert X::stuff to A::more
  hold = (int)more; // convert A::more to int
  cout << hold << endl;

}
```

As the preceding short program demonstrates, cast operator functions are declared using the following syntax:

```
operator typename *opt();
```

You can convert your class object to another object type as specified by typename, or to a pointer to typename. The preceding short program also illustrates that a cast operator function must *return an object of the specified type* (or a pointer to such an object if the indirection operator was used).

User-defined cast operator functions have the following additional requirements and characteristics:

❏ *Cast operator functions must be nonstatic member functions.* These functions cannot be friend functions, nor can they be declared `static`.

❏ *The target type of the conversion cannot be an enumeration or a `typedef` name.* The reason for this restriction is obvious: enumerations and `typedef`s are not objects, so you cannot return one from the conversion function.

❏ *You cannot specify a return type.* The type of the object to be returned is given by the target `typename`, and thus cannot be specified again.

❏ *You cannot declare arguments for a cast operator function.* Function arguments for a conversion function are irrelevant. It is assumed that the function is dealing with `*this` as input. No other inputs are allowed because a cast operator is considered a unary operator acting upon your class object.

❏ *User-defined cast expressions can be used anywhere an ordinary cast is syntactically allowed.* If you have defined the greater-than operator (>) for your class, for example, you can write an expression like this:

```
class X { ... };
...
X a, b;
...
int biggest = (a > b) ? a: b;   // Pick the "largest"
```

❏ *Cast operator functions are inherited, and they can be virtual functions.* Nothing prevents the inheritance of a cast operator function, because by definition it deals only with data members from its own subobject type. It makes even more sense to allow cast operator functions to be virtual, because this is a function that *depends* on being bound to the correct subobject type.

❏ *User-defined cast operator functions are implicitly invoked if the conversion is not ambiguous, and if the containing expression requires such a conversion.* Your cast operators are not second-class citizens: they are invoked implicitly if expression syntax requires it, exactly as is done for basic (predefined) C types when conversion is indicated.

❑ *Only one cast operator function can be* implicitly *applied to a class object*. Plain C numeric types may undergo both conversion and promotion during expression evaluation, but your cast operator functions are not repetitively applied to a class object. This rule does *not* mean that the result of your cast operator function cannot be converted or promoted again. If you cast a class X object to int, for example, the resulting int can still be promoted to long if the expression containing it requires such promotion. Further, this rule does *not* prevent you from explicitly casting several times in one expression. For example, suppose you have declared classes A, B, and C, and created a C object. Then, if you have written all the required cast operator functions, you could write:

```
C cobj;
...
A aobj = (A)(B)cobj;
```

❑ *Cast operator functions cannot be overloaded*. If there is neither return type nor signature (as is the case here), a mangled function name cannot be developed, and overloading is impossible.

❑ *A cast operator function in a derived class hides a cast operator function in its base class only if the target type is exactly the same*. This was mentioned and explained in Chapter 17, but it is repeated here for completeness.

Cast operators can be designed in imaginative and useful ways. You have seen cast operator functions used to report errors in class states (the void* cast in stream, extended memory, and swap buffer classes). The most common and important use of cast operator functions, however, is changing data formats for input or output. For an example of this use of a cast operator function, here is the code for casting a quad class object to a string just before outputting a very long number:

```
static char outstr[81];
...
quad::operator char*()
{
   int neg, i;
   char *s, *p;
   quad VA = *this;

 s = outstr;
   if ( VA.vdata[1] & 0x80000000L ) {
     neg = 1;
     VA.vdata[0] = ~VA.vdata[0];
     VA.vdata[1] = ~VA.vdata[1];
```

```
        VA += 1;
      }
      else neg = 0;
      while( 1 ) {
        VA -= 10;
        if ( VA.vdata[1] & 0x80000000L ) break; // done
        VA += 10;
        *s++ = '0' + (int)( VA % 10 );
        VA = VA / 10;
      }
      VA += 10;                          // fixup from loop
      if ( (int)VA > 0 ) *s++ = (int)VA + '0';
      if ( neg ) *s++ = '-';
      *s = '\0'; // Terminate the string
      s = outstr;
      p = s + strlen( s ) - 1;
      while ( p > s ) {  // Reverse the string
        *s ^= *p; *p ^= *s; *s++ ^= *p--;
      }
      return outstr;
    }
```

The technique for converting a `quad` number to a string is simple in concept: continuously divide the number by 10, taking the remainder as the next output digit. When the number becomes less than 10, that is the last digit, and no further division is needed. This process develops the output string backwards, so you must reverse the string as the last step.

Using Generic Classes

In Chapter 16 you encountered stream applicator classes while learning about parameterized types for stream manipulators. That's quite a mouthful, and the implementation of such things is equally complicated. Still, the techniques you briefly encountered in Chapter 16 are important as a foundation for future language developments. This section discusses the more general theory behind parameterized types.

The applicator classes in Chapter 16 were instances of *control abstraction* put into practice. The sample code in this chapter primarily involves *type abstraction*. What are these things, and how do you put them into your programs? How do they relate to parameterized types? Before you can answer these questions, you must begin to shift your thinking toward the realm of abstract, generalized program design.

Understanding Abstraction and Generic Class Design

When you read about parameterized manipulators for stream classes, you were really learning how to devise a *generalized approach* to writing stream manipulators. There are only a handful of stream classes, but you can endlessly create parameterized manipulators.

The particular approach chosen in Chapter 16 for implementing parameterized manipulators seemed complicated, but that was due to the indirection of references required by generalizing the process. Parameterized manipulators of all kinds have a great deal in common, differing from one another in internal details but not in syntax. In other words, manipulators involve classes that are only trivial variations on a single theme.

This situation means that you can generalize the method of implementing a set of similar facilities. The idea of generalizing your code is best understood by thinking about generalized *types*, particularly class types. Class code that can be applied to a variety of different (but closely related) data types is said to be *generic*. The process of designing and writing generic classes is called *type abstraction*.

You have already started the process of moving toward generic classes by using class derivation and virtual functions. With a little more thought and effort, you can further generalize your classes without using any new techniques. You can do it by carefully designing a base class, such as a class for maintaining lists, then creating trivial derivations from the generalized (but not yet generic) base class. Listing 18.1 shows a LIST base class and the derivation of a LIST_String class. To simplify the example, the LIST base class provides member functions only for adding, deleting, and extracting list elements. The responsibility for displaying the list is shifted to the derived classes (LIST_String here).

Listing 18.1. genlist.cpp. *A generalized list base class.*

```
1   #include <string.h>
2   #include <iostream.h>
3
4   class LIST {
5     void* (*PtrList)[16]; // pointer to array of pointers
6     int Item;
7   public:
```

Listing 18.1. continues

Listing 18.1. continued

```
 8    LIST() {
 9      Item = -1;
10      PtrList = (void* (*)[16] ) new (void*)[16];
11    }
12    virtual ~LIST() { delete PtrList; }
13    virtual void Add( void* Elem, size_t Size ) {
14      ++Item;
15      if ( Item == 16 ) return;
16      (*PtrList)[Item] = new char[Size];
17      memmove( (*PtrList)[Item], Elem, Size );
18    }
19    virtual void Delete() {
20      if ( Item < 0 ) return;
21      delete (*PtrList)[Item];
22      --Item;
23    }
24    void* GetItem( int Elem = 0 ) {
25      if ( Elem > Item || Elem < 0 )
26        return NULL;
27      else return (*PtrList)[Elem];
28    }
29  };
30
31  typedef char* String; // typedefs for use in names
32  typedef int    Int;
33
34  size_t Size_String( String argument ) {
35    return strlen( argument ) + 1;
36  }
37  void Show_String( String argument ) {
38    cout << argument << endl;
39  }
40
41
42  class LIST_String : public LIST {
43    size_t (*ObjSize)(String);
44    void   (*Show)(String);
45  public:
46    LIST_String() {
47      ObjSize = Size_String;
48      Show = Show_String;
49    }
```

```
50    ~LIST_String();
51    void Add( String arg ) {
52      LIST::Add( (void*)arg, ObjSize( arg ) );
53    }
54    void Delete() {
55      LIST::Delete();
56    }
57    void Display();
58  };
59
60  LIST-String::~LIST_String() {  // out-of-line because of loop
61    while ( GetItem(0) ) Delete();
62  }
63
64  void LIST_String::Display() {  // out-of-line because of loop
65    int i = 0;
66
67    while ( GetItem(i) ) {
68      Show( (String)GetItem(i) );
69      ++i;
70    }
71  }
72
73  void main()
74  {
75    int i;
76    LIST_String X;
77
78    for ( i=0; i<16; ++i ) X.Add( "Hello" );
79    X.Display();
80  }
```

Both the LIST base class and the derived LIST_String classes in listing 18.1 have features dictated by the design decision to generalize the base class to allow simple derivation of other types. Most notably, a void pointer in the base class is used to locate a list of pointers outside the object's boundaries. Each of these pointers in turn locates an unspecified data area that will be dynamically acquired.

Using void pointers in this fashion allows a fair degree of generalization. The trade-off, however, is some added complexity in forming expressions dealing with pointers. The base pointer for the list is written

```
5    void* (*PtrList)[16]; // pointer to array of pointers
```

because the higher operator precedence of the subscript operator (`[]`) would have otherwise forced the interpretation of the expression as "array of 16 void pointers to pointer" and not "pointer to array of 16 pointers." Similarly, you have to use a peculiar pointer cast to get the pointer value returned from `new` to cooperate with your syntax, as follows:

```
10       PtrList = (void* (*)[16] ) new (void*)[16];
```

Because `PtrList` has type `void*(*)[16]`, you must use parentheses to access a single pointer in the list. The resulting expression, `(*PtrList)[Item]`, refers to a pointer, so you may be tempted to refer to a data area by writing `*(*PtrList)[Item]`. But that expression is illegal: you cannot dereference a `void` pointer. You would first have to cast the pointer extracted from the list to another type (`int*`, for example).

Next, notice the arrangement of virtual functions in the base and derived classes in listing 18.1. The `Add()` and `Delete()` base class member functions are made virtual to allow for future development of the classes into something more significant than sample code. The virtual destructors are quite important, however.

You can see in lines 60–62 that the derived class has the responsibility of stepping down the list and releasing memory for the data areas. The base class destructor (line 12) releases the array storage pointed to by `PtrList`. This arrangement allows the base class to remain as small and generalized as possible, but it places another burden on the class designer: both the base and derived class destructors must execute, and must execute in the correct order. The virtual destructors guarantee the correct execution of the destructor code.

Now reflect for a moment on the usefulness of writing generalized classes in this manner. Is it useful? Yes, but only in a restricted way. A generalized base class is good as far as it goes, but it requires that you design and code trivial derivations individually, for every type of list (in this case) you want to implement. Further, it does not smooth the path of another programmer who may need to derive classes from the generalized base—that programmer will have to know something about the internal logistics required by the base class, and spend time developing his or her own classes, as well.

It would be nice if you could write a single line of code, specifying a type parameter (sound familiar?), which automatically generates the desired type of class. It would also be nice if you could create objects of the new class without having to know internal naming schemes or structures.

Well, you can do all of that by writing generic classes and providing `declare()` and `implement()` macros for them. Generic classes are the subject of the next section.

Building Generic Classes

A generic class permits you to declare a parameterized type that generates a specific class declaration from the generic class. In the examples in this chapter, you develop a generic class named LIST, which you can use to declare specific classes such as LIST_String and LIST_Int by writing a single line of code (a macro call).

Building generic classes revolves around the ingenious use of the predefined token-pasting macros in the generic.h header. At this point, do not stop to inspect that header: read on a bit first, to get the outlines of the techniques required for building generic classes. The entire facility is founded on some powerful macros and can be confusing (because of the name indirection involved) if you begin by looking at implementation details. This chapter builds the details of those macros slowly, as you move through the discussion. You are introduced to three levels of concepts in this section:

❑ *How to use existing generic classes*. If you do not know what you want to do, it is difficult to understand how you should go about it. Seeing generic classes in action is therefore the first order of business.

❑ *Writing the generic class itself*. A generic class is written as a single (large) function-like macro. Creating a generic class is simple (aside from difficulties introduced by name indirection in the macros themselves) after you understand that one macro is at the bottom of it all.

❑ *Writing support macros and functions*. Some type-dependent activities require special handling (consider the difference between determining the length of a string and obtaining the size of an integer). Further, the generic class macro does not supply all the required user interfaces, so you must write a few macros.

These three stages of developing concepts may remind you of the procedures for writing parameterized stream types in Chapter 16. You will be doing much the same thing, using the same generic class facilities.

Look first, then, at listing 18.2 to see how the LIST generic class is used in action. This program uses the generic class to declare and then use both LIST_String and LIST_Int classes. Note how easy it is to declare and implement a specific class using a generic base class. (All the hard work is hidden at this level.)

```
1   #include "genlist.hpp"
2
3     // --------------------------------------------------------------
4     // The following macros declare classes for strings and ints
5     // The declare macros generate more macros with the syntax
6     //    LISTdeclare(type)
7     // matching our own declaration macro in GENLIST.HPP.
8     // Notice that these macros must be used at file scope.
9     // --------------------------------------------------------------
10
11    declare(LIST, String)
12    declare(LIST, Int)
13
14  void main()
15  {
16    int i;
17    char Message[] = "Hello";
18
19
20    // --------------------------------------------------------------
21    // Now implement (instantiate) a LIST of strings.
22    // --------------------------------------------------------------
23
24    implement(LIST, String) X;   // Do it once for strings.
25
26    for ( i=0; i<16; ++i ) X.Add( Message );
27    X.Display();
28
29    implement(LIST, Int) I;      // Do it again for integers.
30
31    for ( i=0; i<16; ++i ) I.Add( i );
32    I.Display();
33  }
```

Two classes are declared in lines 11 and 12, one for a list of strings and one for a list of integers. The parameterized nature of the declarations is apparent. Both declarations depend on the LIST generic class. The comments bear important messages: the most important is that you should use the declare() macro only at file scope. This is because the macro generates a class declaration, which is illegal in block scope (inside main(), for example).

The comments also indicate that the `declare()` macro generates another macro before final expansion. The `declare()` macro is defined in `generic.h`; in this case it will generate a token `LISTdeclare(String)`, which is a macro you must define. The `LISTdeclare(type)` macro defines the generic class. You will see how to code it shortly.

The `implement()` macro is used to define a class object of the desired target type. It, too, is defined in `generic.h` and generates another token, `LISTimplement(type)`. You must write a macro definition for this second name, as well. Because the `implement()` macro is used to instantiate an object, it can be used in block scope.

One of the main purposes of generic classes is to automate the production of trivial derivations from a base class. In these examples, the base class is `BASELIST` (renamed from the first version to avoid difficulties in naming macros). The `BASELIST` class is similar to the original `LIST` base class in listing 18.1. In addition, the pointer manipulations in `BASELIST` are simplified (there is enough complexity in the macro construction for this example). `BASELIST` is shown in listing 18.3.

Listing 18.3. `listbase.hpp`. *The header containing the* `BASELIST` *base class.*

```
1   #ifndef LISTBASE
2   #define LISTBASE
3
4   // ------------------------------------------------
5   // Base LIST class; not used alone
6   // ------------------------------------------------
7
8   class BASELIST {
9     char* PtrList[16];
10    int Item;
11  public:
12    BASELIST() {
13      int i;
14      Item = -1;
15    }
16    virtual ~BASELIST() {}
17    virtual void Add( char* Elem, size-t Size ) {
18      ++Item;
19      if ( Item == 16 ) return;
20      PtrList[Item] = new char[Size];
```

Listing 18.3. continues

Listing 18.3. continued

```
21        memmove( PtrList[Item], Elem, Size );
22      }
23      virtual void Delete() {
24        if ( Item < 0 ) return;
25        delete PtrList[Item];
26        --Item;
27      }
28      char* GetItem( int Elem = 0 ) {
29        if ( Elem > Item || Elem < 0 )
30          return NULL;
31        else return PtrList[Elem];
32      }
33    };
34
35    #endif
```

The BASELIST class is now contained in a header file to permit multiple uses of the LIST generic class code without introducing multiple declarations of the BASELIST class. Otherwise, it is essentially the same as before. Pointers to the unspecified data areas for list items now have type char*. This was done to simplify and speed debugging (you cannot directly view the contents of an area located by void* in Turbo Debugger, so the char* type was used). Debugging a program heavily populated with macros is often necessary and difficult. Be prepared.

Now the fun can begin. The generic LIST class must be defined, according to the second step of development. This is done by coding a LISTdeclare() function-like macro. The generic class macro definition, together with support macros, is shown in listing 18.4.

Listing 18.4. genlist.hpp. *The header file for the generic LIST class implementation.*

```
1    #ifndef GENLIST
2    #define GENLIST
3
4    #include <string.h>
5    #include <iostream.h>
6
7    // ------------------------------------------------
8    // Be sure to include generic.h.
```

```
 9   // And do not forget LISTBASE.
10   // -------------------------------------------------------
11
12   #include <generic.h>
13   #include "listbase.hpp"
14
15   // -------------------------------------------------------
16   // Typedefs and helper macros for the generic LIST classes
17   // -------------------------------------------------------
18
19   typedef char* String;
20   typedef int   Int;
21
22   #define Size_String(arg) strlen( arg ) + 1
23   #define Show_String(arg) cout << (String)arg << endl
24   #define AdrsOf_String(arg) (char*)arg
25
26   #define Size_Int(arg) sizeof(arg)
27   #define Show_Int(arg) cout << *(Int*)arg << endl
28   #define AdrsOf_Int(arg) (char*)&arg
29
30   // -------------------------------------------------------
31   // Macros for developing specific names from generic names
32   // -------------------------------------------------------
33
34   #define SIZE(type) _Paste2(Size_, type)
35   #define SHOW(type) _Paste2(Show_, type)
36   #define LIST(type) _Paste2(LIST_, type)
37   #define ADRS(type) _Paste2(AdrsOf_, type)
38
39   // -------------------------------------------------------
40   // Declare macro for generic LIST classes.
41   // -------------------------------------------------------
42
43   #define LISTdeclare(type)                               \
44   class LIST(type) : public BASELIST {                    \
45   public:                                                 \
46     ~LIST(type)();                                        \
47     void Add( type arg ) {                                \
48       BASELIST::Add( ADRS(type)(arg), SIZE(type)(arg) );  \
49     }                                                     \
```

Listing 18.4. continues

Listing 18.4. continued

```
50     void Delete() {                                    \
51        BASELIST::Delete();                             \
52     }                                                  \
53     void Display();                                    \
54   };                                                   \
55                                                        \
56   LIST(type)::~LIST(type)() {                          \
57     while ( GetItem(0) ) Delete();                     \
58   }                                                    \
59                                                        \
60   void LIST(type)::Display() {                         \
61     int i = 0;                                         \
62                                                        \
63     while ( GetItem(i) ) {                             \
64       SHOW(type)(GetItem(i));                          \
65       ++i;                                             \
66     }                                                  \
67   }                                                    \
68
69   #define LISTimplement(type) _Paste2(LIST_, type)
70
71   #endif
```

The generic LIST class macro is defined in lines 43–67 of listing 18.4. Again, the whole generic class definition is one macro. That is why the backslash continuation character (\) is used on all lines of the macro, except the last line.

Line 43 is the prototype part of the macro declaration. It consists of a preprocessing token composed of the generic class name (LIST) and the declare constant token, followed by the formal argument in parentheses. The formal argument is named type because during macro invocation the argument will be a type name. (typedef was used to define String in this file to simplify the handling of the char* type.) In the discussion of listing 18.2, it was mentioned that the declare() macro is expanded into another macro: LISTdeclare(type) is that macro. Figure 18.1 shows the progressive expansion of the declare() macro into a usable class declaration in your program.

Fig. 18.1. Expansion of the `declare()` *macro when declaring a specific class using generic class definitions.*

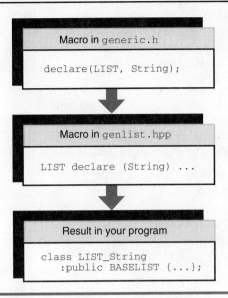

The `LIST declare()` macro contains the class declaration body, but there are support macros wherever a type-dependent name is required. How are specific names built from generic ones in the generic class definition macro? You use the `_Pastex` macros defined in `generic.h` to write the support macros, and build them from the type name argument pasted to the generic class name.

Four support macros are used for this purpose in `genlist.hpp` in listing 18.4: the `SIZE`, `SHOW`, `LIST`, and `ADRS` macros, found in lines 34–37. The `LIST` support macro is used only to construct the specific derived class name. Thus, coding a `declare(LIST, String)` macro invocation will expand line 44 to `LIST_String`.

The remaining three support macros in this first group deal with type-dependent operations. For example, the `SIZE(String)` macro call expands to an expression using the `strlen()` function (see line 22), and the `SIZE(Int)` macro call expands to an expression using the `sizeof` operator (see line 26).

In looking at these first four support macros, you can see clearly how name indirection is compounded when building generic classes. The

`SHOW(String)` macro call used in line 64, for example, expands to another macro name, `Show_String`, which is defined in line 23 (that expansion performs the display operation). The `Show_String` macro is one of a group of similar macros in lines 22–28 that form the next layer of support macros to be expanded. This second group of macros is not used directly by the generic `LIST` class definition. These macros are invoked only indirectly as a result of expanding a macro from the first group, or layer.

The proliferation of name indirection in layers of macros may be confusing, but such indirection is necessary to build abstract type definitions. This is particularly true because some degree of control abstraction is required to achieve genericness. To see why, look at the generic `LIST(type)::Display()` member function implementation:

```
60   void LIST(type)::Display() {       \
61     int i = 0;                        \
62                                       \
63     while ( GetItem(i) ) {            \
64       SHOW(type)(GetItem(i));         \
65       ++i;                            \
66     }                                 \
67   }
```

Notice that line 64 uses the `SHOW(type)` macro in the `LISTdeclare()` macro to generate the correct output statements. The only indication that there might be a type dependency in this function is the use of the formal argument `type`. Why go to such lengths to avoid type-specific code in the generic class? That is, why not rewrite line 64 as follows to simplify the output statements:

```
SHOW(type)((type*)GetItem(i));
```

You should avoid the temptation to perform the pointer cast to the correct type at this point in the code. The reason is that if you do not move type dependent code outside the generic class, and into the support macros and functions (that is, abstract the control functions for the class), you may lose control of the internal interfaces to the generic class.

Specifically, you can define several `Show_type` macros for the the `LIST` generic class. Because of the way this class is designed, all these macros expect to receive a `void` pointer to the object they will display, and to cast the pointer to the correct type for themselves. If the `Display()` function has already performed the cast (and possibly even dereferenced the pointer), there is no common protocol for invoking a `Show_type` macro. That is not much of a problem in the simple `LIST` class presented here, but code for production is often much more complicated.

Alternatively, you could write the necessary macro logic directly into the LISTdeclare() macro for all possible types (you should either do it or not, but be consistent—macro debugging can be tough). The drawback to this approach is that you will have to perform some fancy footwork with #if conditional logic, and that will require more #define support macros. You are already dealing with a complicated macro structure. Why make it worse?

Thus, it is better to abstract type-dependent statements or declarations into support macros. It will make your life easier, even if you must write a few more lines of code. And macros are generally the best method of dealing with abstracted logic. There are two reasons for using macros instead of functions in a generic class definition wherever possible: to simplify the resulting compilable code and to increase the performance of the final product.

As a rule of thumb, try to design your macros so that the resulting compilable code is as simple as possible. Otherwise, you may lose control of the coding process. A simple example will illustrate this point.

The Show_type macros could have been implemented as functions rather than macros. In that case, the SHOW(type) macros would have been expanded into functions, not inline code. That is fine for displaying data, because the output does not depend on the location of the data to be displayed. It is a different story, however, for the ADRS(type) macros.

Consider what happens if you define the ADRS(type) macros to expand into function calls. You pass a copy of the argument to the support function, which takes the argument's address at its stack location, not its original location, and returns the erroneous address to the caller. Trying to use an auto variable after its owner function has gone out of scope is a classic error. You won't get away with it in the LIST generic class because the PtrList array assumes that it is pointing to objects that stay put long enough to use them.

Designing ADRS(type) to expand to a support macro has the opposite and accurate effect. The resulting compilable code will contain the proper reference to the argument name substituted for the macro call. Not only does this work much better, it localizes the code to the class member function that uses it. You must keep in mind the difference between preprocessing time and compile time. Even though several macros are used in this example, dispersed throughout the generic class definition, the final result is one line of inline code to be compiled.

That last comment leads to the second reason for using support macros rather than support functions. Inline statements run faster (sometimes much faster) than function calls. You will often find that type-dependent statements, which must be abstracted from the generic code, require only trivial support functions, consisting of one or two lines of code in the function body. Repetitive calls to trivial functions greatly increase run-time overhead, and there is no point in deliberately designing a program that is inefficient.

The last support macro to discuss in this section is the LISTimplement(*type*) macro. Just as there is a macro definition in generic.h for declare() that expands into a macro call of LISTdeclare(*type*) (in the example), there is an implement() macro in generic.h. The implement() macro similarly expands into a macro call for LISTimplement(*type*) (again using the example's name), and you must define this last macro. Thus, when users of your LIST generic class want to create a LIST of integers named ilist, they can simply write:

```
implement(LIST, Int) ilist;
```

The macro definition in generic.h expands this macro call into another macro call, resulting in the following statement:

```
LISTimplement(Int) ilist;
```

Finally, the macro definition in genlist.hpp expands the new macro call into compilable code, as follows:

```
LIST_Int ilist;   // This statement creates a LIST_Int object
```

These macro manipulations make using generic classes seem like going around the block just to get next door. The complexity of the macros is probably the major drawback to using generic classes. Automating the derivation of repetitive and similar classes from a common base is not nearly as advanced as it could be, given more compiler support. Yet the macro preprocessing facility can get you a long way down the road to automation: the task of abstracting type-specific logic and names from the class declaration will remain for the programmer, even with more advanced compiler support.

Generic classes do serve a purpose, however, and can make life easier for the users of these classes, if not for their designers. Generic classes provide support for parameterized typing and help you avoid coding multiple trivial derivations. And perhaps most important, generic classes are all you have until later releases of C++ provide true parameterized types in the form of class templates. One of the reasons this discussion has been presented is to prepare you for the discussion of class templates later in this chapter. In the meantime, to use your generic classes, users need to know only how to use the declare() and implement() macros, the generic class name, and the interfaces to the classes you provide (that is, the callable functions and their arguments).

Controlling Object Behavior and Performance

You can wander into a lot of dark corners while writing C++ programs, unless you take the time to reflect on the significance of the programming tools you are using—how they affect expression evaluation, how they use storage, and what resources they use to get their assigned tasks done. In this section, you explore issues that deal with class object behavior and performance. The issues discussed here are examples of the kind of thinking you need to do when designing and writing C++ programs.

Using Friend Functions To Boost Efficiency

Friend functions are an important part of your toolkit for crafting C++ programs, so you should understand what they will, and will not, do for your programs.

You can use friend functions to increase the efficiency (speed) of your class objects. It is easy to imagine that defining a class support function as a friend rather than as a member could increase the class's efficiency simply because it reduces the class object's size. If that were the case, you could pass objects by value on the stack, for example, with less overhead in the movement of data.

But that is not the case. Neither friend functions nor member functions are physically part of a Borland C++ class object, so defining a function as a friend makes no difference in object size. You can use Turbo Debugger to see that there is internally no difference in the number of machine instructions required to access a class object for friends and members. Figure 18.2 proves this point. The figure shows the assembler code used to access a single object, once by a friend and once by a member. The instruction streams are identical.

So what can friend functions do to increase performance? Perhaps the most important aspect of using friends for performance is that they have access to all class members, including private ones. Thus, a friend function can be used as an interface to a class object in a direct fashion. One such friend function might replace several otherwise required member functions designed to provide a generalized user interface. Friends should be used also when you are tempted to write a global function as part of the programming interface to your class objects.

Fig. 18.2. *Machine instructions required by friends of a class to access its objects are the same as the instructions required by members.*

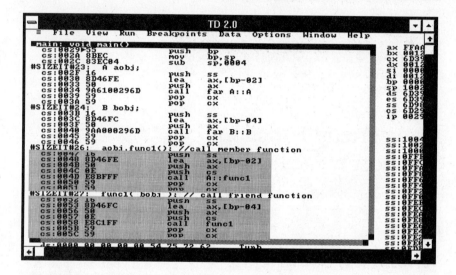

When you use friend functions (where possible) to provide programming interfaces to your classes, you reduce the number of function calls. Function calls can be surprisingly expensive in processing time, especially when they are made frequently. Reducing their number almost always leads to noticeable increases in the performance of your code.

Using Friend Functions To Control Object Syntax

Using friend functions to define overloaded operator functions for your class code can be an important way to control object syntax. *Object syntax* is the way the compiler handles your class objects in an expression (much as it handles numbers in an expression).

Expressions are parsed by the compiler according to the C rules for operator associativity and precedence, even if the expressions contain objects of your user-defined class. You need to understand how expressions are evaluated. Otherwise your class objects will not behave correctly.

The way you define operator functions for a class determines how objects of that class will behave in an expression. Specifically, the operator function definition determines where *lvalues* (object locators) can appear in the expression. The operator function definition also has an important bearing on how temporary class objects can be used internally during evaluation. The last point is considered in the next section, "Using the *static* Storage Class To Avoid Repetitive Instantiation." Class operator functions and their effect on lvalues and syntax are analyzed in this section.

Most operator functions can be written as either friend or member functions; the difference is in the argument types expected by the two kinds of functions. An example will illustrate this point. Listing 18.5 is a program with *two* operator+() member functions: one expects an integer argument, and the other expects a reference to an object of its own class. The goal is simply to be able to support the evaluation of the two expressions in lines 23 and 24. Look at the program, and see if you can determine why the compiler handles these two expressions as it does.

Listing 18.5. badop.cpp. *A program that will not compile, even with two defined operator functions.*

```
1    #include <iostream.h>
2
3    class A {
4      int val;
5    public:
6      A( int newval = 0 ) : val(newval) {}
7      A operator+( int rightop ) {
8        A TEMP;
9        TEMP = val + rightop;
10       return TEMP;
11     }
12     A operator+( A& rightop ) {
13       A TEMP;
14       TEMP = val + rightop.val;
15       return TEMP;
16     }
17   };
18
```

Listing 18.5. continues

Listing 18.5. continued

```
19  void main()
20  {
21    A a=2, b;
22
23    b = a + 3;  // This one is okay.
24    b = 3 + a;  // This one will fail.
25  }
```

Note the simplicity of the expressions in lines 23 and 24. But the expression in line 24 will not compile correctly. The compiler produces an error message stating that you cannot use those specific operands with those specific operators—although there are two operator functions, no `operator+()` function has been defined to cover the second case.

Neither of the operator functions in listing 18.5 can handle the expression in line 24 precisely because they are member functions, not friend functions. A member function (operator or otherwise) has an implied first argument: `this`. That is, both of these functions are expecting a left operand with type `A&`. Thus, when the compiler reaches the integer constant 3 in the expression in line 24, the compiler determines that it has encountered a type mismatch. End of attempted compilation.

The moral of this example is that when you define a member operator function, the parser requires an lvalue (an object locator of the class type) as the left operand. This is not a flexible arrangement, but you can avoid the problem by using a friend function to define the operator.

Listing 18.6 shows another version of the preceding sample program. The new version has two notable features: the operator function is a friend function, and only one operator function is required for the correct evaluation of both expressions. Look at this program for a moment and see if you can determine why.

Listing 18.6. `badop2.cpp`. *A program that compiles for multiple expressions with just one defined operator function.*

```
1  #include <iostream.h>
2
3  class A {
4    int val;
```

```
5   public:
6     A( int newval = 0 ) : val(newval) {}
7     friend A operator+( A& leftop, A& rightop );
8   };
9
10  A operator+( A& leftop, A& rightop ) {
11    A TEMP;
12    TEMP.val = leftop.val + rightop.val;
13    return TEMP;
14  }
15
16  void main()
17  {
18    A a=2, b;
19
20    b = a + 3;   // This one is okay.
21    b = 3 + a;   // This one is okay, too.
22  }
```

There is something sneaky about listings 18.5 and 18.6. Did you notice that the constructor functions take a single argument of another type, which makes them conversion functions? The capability of the class to convert integers to the class type is crucial to the correct functioning of the operator function in listing 18.6.

Here is why the second version works: because the operator function is now a friend, you explicitly specify arguments for both the left and right operands. Thus, implicit conversions can be performed on both arguments, and the order of appearance of types in the expression makes no difference. If an operand is an integer, the compiler now knows to apply an implicit conversion (provided by the constructor function) to the operand, creating an internal temporary object of the correct class type. That is, neither operand must be an lvalue. Either one can be a class object, an integer, or a subexpression that evaluates to one of those two types (this sample deliberately does not provide for other types).

In summary, use a member operator function definition when you want the expression syntax to require an lvalue for the left operand. (The assignment operator is a good example of an operator function that needs an lvalue on the left.) Otherwise, use a friend function that explicitly specifies *both* operands, to provide the maximum flexibility in evaluating expressions involving objects of your class type.

Using the *static* Storage Class To Avoid Repetitive Instantiation

This section deals with another aspect of evaluating expressions that contain class objects: the need for temporary objects, and the effect this has on class performance (speed, not syntax). To understand why you might need a temporary object during expression evaluation, think of an operator as something that has *inputs* (its operands), and an *output* (the resulting object or value). The catch is that the output of an operator may or may not be one of the inputs.

This view of an operator as something that has a target destination (an output) leads to a conceptual grouping of all the operators your class will use: some operators have a unary effect, and some have a binary effect. An operator in either category may use either a member or friend function (except assignment, which requires a nonstatic member function), depending on the syntactical flexibility you require. The unary or binary effect of an operator has a bearing on both the operator's return type and its need for an internal temporary holding object. Note the following rules:

❏ *Operators with a unary effect produce a result that replaces the value of the left operand object.* For example, in an expression such as ++i, the value of i is incremented, and put back into i. Operator functions with a unary effect typically return a *reference* to the modified operand (usually *this) after modifying its value. Further, these operator functions usually do not require the use of a temporary class object in the operator function body, because they modify the operand contents. Other operators in this class include unary plus and minus, and the compound assignment operators (for example, += and -=). Simple assignment is also in this category because the operator function modifies its left operand. (But the operator function must be a member function, not a friend, because the left operand must be an lvalue.)

❏ *Operators with a binary effect produce a result that must not modify either operand.* This category of operators includes the remainder of the true binary operators. The addition operator, for example, must not modify either operand, but instead should return a value that can be used to further parse the complete expression containing it. Further, because the result must be held somewhere, operators with binary effect typically require an internal temporary class object.

The second of these two rules determined the return type of the operator+() functions in listings 18.5 and 18.6, and also required the presence of the TEMP temporary variable.

Creating local class objects to hold temporary results, as was done in the two preceding programs, takes time. When evaluating more complex expressions, your class's operator functions are called more often (operator functions are often the hardest working functions in a class), so the time required for instantiating (creating) local temporaries can be high. Overhead devoted to temporary object control can be so time-consuming that some method is usually needed to control the amount of overhead time. One method is to assign a static storage class to internal temporary class objects.

A simple experiment will give you some idea of how much overhead can be saved by declaring temporaries as static. A static object is created once, then left alone. Listing 18.7 was designed to invoke the addition operator function frequently (it performs multiplication by repeated addition, which is not the usual method). The program in listing 18.7 assigns the static attribute to temporary class objects. You may want to enter this program in the IDE and compile and run it now to see what happens.

Listing 18.7. `tempvar.cpp`. *Using the static storage class to prevent the unnecessary creation of temporary objects.*

```
1    #include <iostream.h>
2    #include <time.h>
3
4    class Int1 {
5      long value;
6    public:
7      Int1( long newval = 0 ) { value = newval; }
8      Int1& operator=( Int1& other ) {
9        value = other.value;
10       return *this;
11     }
12     Int1  operator+( Int1& rightop );
13     Int1  operator*( Int1& rightop );
14   };
15
16   Int1 Int1::operator+( Int1& rightop )
17   {
18       static Int1 SUM(0);
19
20       SUM.value = value + rightop.value;
21       return SUM;
22   }
```

Listing 18.7. continues

Listing 18.7. continued

```
23
24   Int1 Int1::operator*( Int1& rightop )
25   {
26     long i;
27     static Int1 ACCUM(0);
28
29     for ( i=0; i<rightop.value; ++i )
30       ACCUM = ACCUM + *this;
31     return ACCUM;
32   }
33
34   void main()
35   {
36     Int1 a(0), b(2), c(100000);
37
38     clock-t time0, time1;
39     double seconds;
40
41     time0 = clock();
42     a = b * c;
43     time1 = clock();
44     seconds = (double)(time1-time0) / (double)CLK-TCK;
45     cout << seconds
46          << " seconds elapsed." << endl;
47   }
```

When the program in listing 18.7 runs, it requires 2.033 seconds to complete the long-winded multiplication on a 386DX running at 20 MHz (normal methods of multiplying numbers would run with normal speeds). To see how much time is required to build `auto` class local temporaries, just remove the `static` keyword, and recompile and rerun the program. It now requires 2.802 seconds, a 37.8 percent increase in execution time.

There is a trade-off to using `static` class temporary objects: they increase the memory requirements of your program. In the preceding sample program, the cost in memory is not high. The `quad` class presented in Appendix D has a lot more temporary objects, so the cost is higher. Even with the `quad` class, however, the cost is not too high, but it is something you should consider when designing class operator functions.

So far, the execution speed of the `tempvar.cpp` program has been improved by almost 40 percent, just by using the static storage class with temporary variables. Can you do better? Yes, by using references.

Using References and Pointers

When the temporary object used in the previous `operator+()` functions (listing 18.6) was an `auto` class object, the object had to be returned by value: other methods would not work (or even compile with Borland C++). Returning a result by value in this way means that intermediate results (such as an accumulating total) during the evaluation of an expression are copied back and forth to the stack. Intermediate results reside on the stack when temporary holding objects are `auto`.

In the next step (listing 18.7), the temporary object was made static. That improved performance considerably for the example class, mainly because temporary object creation is mostly eliminated in the operator function. That step eliminated many free store allocations and constructor function calls.

Now, as long as the temporary objects are `static` (so they will not go away), and you understand completely what you are doing, you can go one step further: you can return results by reference, so that intermediate values are not copied to the stack. Listing 18.8 shows the example program rewritten to do this.

Listing 18.8. `tempvar2.cpp`. *Returning a temporary value by reference from an operator function.*

```
1   #include <iostream.h>
2   #include <time.h>
3
4   class Int1 {
5     long value;
6   public:
7     Int1( long newval = 0 ) { value = newval; }
8     Int1& operator=( Int1& other ) {
9       value = other.value;
10      return *this;
11    }
12    Int1&  operator+( Int1& rightop );
13    Int1&  operator*( Int1& rightop );
14  };
15
16  Int1& Int1::operator+( Int1& rightop )
17  {
18      static Int1 SUM(0);
19
```

Listing 18.8. continues

Listing 18.8. *continued*

```
20     SUM.value = value + rightop.value;
21     return SUM;
22  }
23
24  Int1& Int1::operator*( Int1& rightop )
25  {
26    long i;
27    static Int1 ACCUM(0);
28
29    ACCUM.value = 0;
30    for ( i=0; i<rightop.value; ++i )
31      ACCUM = ACCUM + *this;
32    return ACCUM;
33  }
34
35  void main()
36  {
37    Int1 a(0), b(2), c(100000);
38
39    clock-t time0, time1;
40    double seconds;
41
42    time0 = clock();
43    a = b * c;
44    time1 = clock();
45    seconds = (double)(time1-time0) / (double)CLK-TCK;
46    cout << seconds
47         << " seconds elapsed." << endl;
48  }
```

The use of references as the return type from the `operator+()` function eliminates much copying of objects to and from the stack. How much does it eliminate? The previous version of the program ran in about 2.03 seconds; this version runs in about 1.76 seconds. You have increased the speed of the `operator+()` function by another 14 percent.

You must be very careful when returning operator function values by reference. Intermediate values are no longer on the stack; they are now in the static temporary variable for that operator. Care must be taken to ensure that the intermediate value is not accidentally destroyed. This is not as difficult to arrange as it might seem. Line 20 in listing 18.8, for example, makes it look like the previous value of SUM is being destroyed, but does not actually do so. Consider what happens when an expression such as a+b+c is evaluated.

First the subexpression a+b is evaluated, using the operator+() function. The intermediate result is stored in SUM, and a reference to SUM is returned. That reference now becomes the left operand in another call to operator+(), and c becomes the right operand. Thus, the operator+() function statement

```
20    SUM.value = value + rightop.value;
```

is, on this second pass through the function, equivalent to the statement

```
SUM.value = SUM.value + rightop.value;
```

This is exactly what is needed to preserve the intermediate result and continue to accumulate the total value.

So far, you have been provided with a workable, high-performance operator+() function that can handle a chain of additions (a+b+c+...) without upsetting intermediate values. But how will using reference return types and static temporaries affect more complicated expressions such as a=b+c*c*c+b? First, the operator*() function must be reworked into something fitting for the real world, because it was deliberately rigged to take a long time. The following code fragment is the rewritten function:

```
Int1& Int1::operator*( Int1& rightop )
{
   long i;
   static Int1 ACCUM(0);

   ACCUM.value = value * rightop.value;
   return ACCUM;
}
```

Replace lines 24–33 of listing 18.8 with the preceding lines. If you now compile and run the tempvar2.cpp program under Turbo Debugger, you will discover two things. The a=b+c*c*c+b expression evaluates to the correct answer, and intermediate results are distributed among the temporary objects they belong to.

That is, additive intermediate results reside in SUM, and multiplicative intermediate results reside in ACCUM. You need do nothing further to the operator functions to make them work correctly in arbitrarily complex expression evaluations (assuming that you provided any other necessary operator functions).

Using Inline Functions
To Eliminate Function Calls

In the `tempvarx.cpp` programs developed in this chapter, you may have noticed that the assignment operator function *definition* is written directly into the class declaration. When you write a member function definition in this way, it is implicitly considered to be an inline function. You can also explicitly request that a function body be expanded inline at the point where the function is called (something like a macro expansion) by using the `inline` keyword just before the function's return type specification.

If a function is expanded inline, all the overhead of a function call is eliminated. That could save considerable execution time for a function called frequently. The price, however, is a larger code segment in your program, particularly if the inline function is called in many different places.

There are some problems involved with using inline functions. You should write only the most trivial (very short) functions as inline functions, because of the severe restrictions on the kinds of statements that can be in an inline function. For example, in the preceding examples, you cannot use the `inline` keyword with the `operator+()` function because `static` variables cannot be declared in an inline function. Further, you cannot make the `operator*()` function inline either, because iteration control statements (`for`, `while`, and `do-while` statements) are not permitted in the body of an inline function.

Finally, Borland C++ regards the `inline` keyword as merely a suggestion, much as it does the `register` keyword. Even if you do explicitly declare a function inline, it may not be compiled as one.

Is there anything more you can do to improve the performance of these operator classes? There is one more thing, but it will help performance only very slightly. Because the temporary objects are declared static anyway, you might consider moving their declarations outside the member function body. That is, make the temporary object a global object.

There are sufficient objections to this maneuver that it is probably not worthwhile. One objection is that now you must be sure that you do not attempt to declare (for other purposes) another class object with the same name. The temporary object is no longer protected or hidden by the class scope. Second, the internal integrity of the class has been compromised because the temporary object is now global. Any nonmember (or member) function can manipulate the temporary object, destroying the validity of intermediate results.

Finally, because the object is `static`, it is created only once per program execution. Eliminating one constructor function call results in only a slight improvement in performance. If you are desperate to tune up your operator functions, however, you may still want to resort to this last-ditch option.

Directions in Class Object Control

C++ has a lot to offer the programmer who wants to develop sophisticated applications. Two of the weakest areas of the C++ language definition, however, are generic classes (currently implemented in preprocessing macros) and exception handling (currently not implemented).

Do not despair: new features addressing these areas are being developed (by Bjarne Stroustrup and others). They should be part of Borland C++ when their language definition is settled. This section outlines the broad strokes of the features so that you will be prepared when they do arrive.

Class and Function Templates

Expressing groups of related classes as parameterized versions of a generic type leads to generic classes. In this chapter, you saw the macro implementation of generic classes. You surely have seen enough to realize that the macro implementation of generic classes is awkward (but useful). There should be a better way to define parameterized types and avoid trivial class derivations.

Soon there will be a better way: class templates are currently being experimented with, and should ultimately supersede the macro-based generic class facility. A class template is similar to a generic class definition. More precisely, a *class template* is the declaration of the object structure and included operations for an unbounded set of related types. The syntax for declaring a class template will most likely look something like this:

```
template<class typename> class ptype {
    ...
};
```

typename is the user-defined type name used by the template, and *ptype* is the parameterized type name for the template.

Looking back to the LIST generic class in this chapter, for example, you might define a class template for the LIST parameterized type as follows:

```
template< class TYPE> class list {
  TYPE* Elements;
  int numentry;
public:
  list( int nument = 16 ); // constructor declaration
  TYPE* GetItem( int );
  ...
};
```

In this code fragment, list is the template name and TYPE is the type name used in the template declaration to refer generically to a type that will be made specific when an object of the class is defined. For example, with the preceding template definition you can now define and use a list of 64 integers as follows:

```
list<int> counters = 64;   // same as counters(64)
...
int* firstgroup;
...
firstgroup = counters.GetItem(0); // Get counter value
(*firstgroup)++;                  // and increment its value
```

So far, this is reminiscent of generic classes and their usage. Defining a member function of a template class is a little different, however. A definition for GetItem() might look like this:

```
template<class TYPE> TYPE* list<TYPE>::GetItem( int which ) {
  if ( which >= 0 && which < numentry )
    return &Elements[which];

}
```

You can also write templates for nonmember functions using a syntax similar to the syntax for member functions (nonmember functions do not require the fully qualified class::member name). The similarity of class and function templates to generic class definitions is almost complete (because the generic class facility was designed for an easy transition to templates). If you were able to understand the discussion of generic classes in this chapter, you will have no trouble with class and function templates when they appear in Borland C++.

Exception Handling

C++ has no built-in facility for handling exceptional conditions (errors). The proposed exception-handling mechanism will incorporate three new reserved words: `throw`, `catch`, and `try`.

When your code detects an error condition, it can use the `throw` keyword to trigger the exception handler. For example, suppose `main()` tries to call `GetItem()` for a list element that is out of range. The code for `GetItem()` and `main()` would look something like this:

```
...
template<class TYPE> TYPE* List<TYPE>::GetItem( int which ) {
if ( which >= 0 && which < numentry )
  return &Elements[which];
else
  throw
}
...
void main()
{
  List<int> counters(16);
  ...
  try {
    int* thisone;
    thisone = counters.GetItem(17); // subscript range error
  }
  catch ( List<int>& copy ) {
    // Use copy to examine error
    cout << "List range error." << endl;
  }
}
```

This code fragment shows that you do not call a function that might `throw` an exception; you `try` it, so that the exception handler defined by `catch` can be located correctly.

Exercises

The following exercises help you polish your understanding of class type conversions, generic classes, and methods for tuning the performance of class operator functions.

1. Design and write a class that has some distinctive numeric data element. Write conversion functions for the class that can cast a class object to various other numeric types, and to `char*` as well.

2. Add other data types to the `LIST` generic class. When you have added two or three other types, design your own generic class. For example, you could redesign the `lifo` generalized stack class into a true generic class. Remember that the original `lifo` class can handle different object types simultaneously; your generic class objects will handle only one type each.

3. Design and write a class that is rich in operator functions. Use Turbo Debugger to experiment with the various combinations of return types, `auto` and `static` temporary objects, and so on. It will be difficult to become accustomed to writing workable operator functions until you invest the time for this activity.

Summary

This chapter contains a miscellany of C++ related topics that are of great importance to all C++ programmers. The following topics were covered:

❏ *User-defined conversion functions*. User-defined cast operators are more important to a full-featured class than you might at first expect. Cast operator functions are distinctive in that they allow neither return types nor function arguments.

❏ *Generic classes*. Generic classes provide a means for you to abstract both data structure and control logic. Currently, generic classes are implemented with the macro preprocessor. This can be troublesome, but sometimes generic classes are worthwhile.

❏ *C++ class object performance and syntax issues*. Friend functions can be used to provide greater power and flexibility for your class designs, and for many class operator function definitions. Friend functions contribute nothing to object execution speed, however. Object execution speed is greatly influenced by your choice of operator function return types and the storage class of internal temporary objects.

❏ *C++ future trends*. Two developments are likely to appear in production compilers soon. These developments involve class templates and an exception-handling mechanism. Class templates promise to be an effective replacement for the macro-based generic class facility.

This chapter concludes the discussion of C++ and object-oriented programming. Part III introduces you to Borland's new high-end compiler product, Borland C++ 2.0, and the exciting (and very different) world of programming for the Windows 3.0 graphical environment. Hold on to your hats!

Part III

Using Borland C++ with Microsoft Windows

19

Introducing
Borland C++ 2.0

Borland C++ 2.0, Borland International's new high-end C++ development package, replaces the Turbo C++ Professional package. Like Turbo C++ Professional, Borland C++ includes a stand-alone debugger and profiler. The Borland C++ package includes many improvements, the most noticeable of which are protected mode operation and the capability to generate Microsoft Windows 3.0 executable files. You can also run the IDE under Windows, and Turbo Debugger 2.5 can debug Windows applications.

The big new feature of Borland C++ is the capability to create applications that can take advantage of all the features offered by Microsoft Windows 3.0. The Windows functions open up a new world for the programmer. With the Windows functions, you can easily create applications that use the Windows GUI (Graphical User Interface). The chapters in Part III give you a taste of the many new resources available with Windows applications.

To help you develop your new Windows applications, Borland has included the Whitewater Resource Toolkit with the Borland C++ 2.0 package. The Toolkit lets you build and modify the Windows resources for your programs. Also included are Turbo Debugger 2.5, Turbo Profiler 1.1, and Turbo Assembler 2.5. All of these packages have been upgraded, so they are easier to use and more productive.

This chapter is a quick tour of the new features of Borland C++ 2.0. You see how each of the pieces of the development package has been improved and how these improvements help you.

New Features and Utilities

As mentioned, the two biggest improvements in Borland C++ 2.0 are the capability to create Windows applications and run in the computer's protected mode. This section shows how these features can enhance your productivity and help you create better programs. Another neat, new feature of Borland C++ is the precompiled header file feature.

The programs you run under Windows 3.0 can be divided into two broad categories: Windows applications and non-Windows applications. A non-Windows application can run under DOS and Windows, but you cannot use any Windows features, and the application does not have the look and feel of a real Windows application.

A Windows application is designed to run under the Windows environment, so the application depends on the interface functions that Windows supplies. When you design a Windows application, you do not have to design and create the user interface. To create a professional, easy-to-use interface, you just call the right Windows functions. Windows keeps track of all the tedious details involved with running the Graphical User Interface. Figure 19.1 shows a Windows application that is created in Chapter 20.

***Fig. 19.1.** The* `fcwin.c` *program screen.*

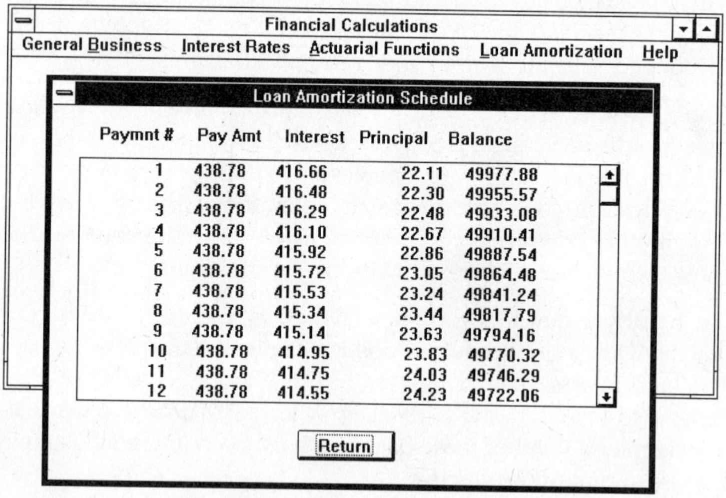
Financial Calculations
General Business
Interest Rates
Actuarial Functions
Loan Amortization
Help
Loan Amortization Schedule
Paymnt # Pay Amt Interest Principal Balance
1 438.78 416.66 22.11 49977.88
2 438.78 416.48 22.30 49955.57
3 438.78 416.29 22.48 49933.08
4 438.78 416.10 22.67 49910.41
5 438.78 415.92 22.86 49887.54
6 438.78 415.72 23.05 49864.48
7 438.78 415.53 23.24 49841.24
8 438.78 415.34 23.44 49817.79
9 438.78 415.14 23.63 49794.16
10 438.78 414.95 23.83 49770.32
11 438.78 414.75 24.03 49746.29
12 438.78 414.55 24.23 49722.06
Return

There are many advantages to creating Windows applications. The most obvious is the consistent user interface. Another big advantage is the speed with which you can put together a complex program that communicates with the outside world. Windows gives you support utilities that make it easy to use the video and other I/O ports on your computer. When you create a Windows application, you can control what happens when multiple copies of the program are started. Writing programs for Windows makes it possible to take advantage of Windows multitasking capabilities.

Chapters 20, 21, and 22 introduce you to programming in Windows. Windows programming is not very difficult, but if you have never programmed for a multitasking environment, it will take some practice.

Borland C++ can now run in protected mode, which is a special operating mode found on the 80286, 80386, and 80486 processor chips. Protected mode changes the way the computer's main memory is accessed; you can access more memory in protected mode than in real mode. Borland C++ uses the extra memory for its own code and the program you are working on. Because Borland C++ can store more data in memory when protected mode is activated, the linker can execute quickly.

You run the BCX.EXE program when you want to use the protected mode version of Borland C++. Although the standard and protected modes of Borland C++ are different internally, they look and are handled the same. The only difference between the two versions of the IDE is the way they use the computer's memory.

If you have ever been tired of sitting in front of your computer waiting for it to finish compiling your program, you will appreciate the new precompiled header file feature. With this feature, you can create and use precompiled header files. The following brief explanation of header files and the compilation process show you why this new feature is so helpful.

When you compile one of your programs, Borland C++ parses the header files that you have included. As the header files are parsed, a symbol table is created. The symbol table is used to record information about the declarations and definitions used in your programs. Without the precompiled header feature, a new symbol table is created each time a program is compiled, and thrown away after compilation.

With the precompiled header feature, you can specify that the symbol table created for a particular group of header files be kept when the compilation process is finished. The next time you compile a program that uses that group of header files, Borland C++ will read the stored symbol table from disk rather than create a new symbol table. Skipping the creation of the symbol table can save a lot of time during the program's compilation.

Just be aware that when you create a precompiled header file, the symbol table is stored on your disk. If you are running short of space, be careful about how many different symbol table images you create.

The following conditions must be the same in all the source files that will be using a particular precompiled header file:

❏ The same header files must be used in the same order. Further, the included header files must all have the same time stamp. Such headers can be included directly or indirectly (by being embedded in another #include).

❏ Macros must be defined with identical values.

❏ The same language must be used. That is, use C or C++, but do not change the language for the next compilation when using precompiled headers.

❏ Memory models must be the same.

❏ The underscores on externs should match.

❏ The target environment should be the same. With Borland C++ 2.0, you can choose the DOS standard, Windows executable, or Windows DLL target types.

❏ The Generate Word Alignment option must be set the same way.

❏ The Pascal type call style must be used in the same way.

❏ If enumerations were treated as integer values, they still must be treated this way.

❏ If the default char type was unsigned, make it so when using a precompiled header.

❏ You can generate smart, local, external, public, and far virtual tables when compiling C++ programs. Make sure you use the same options every time when using precompiled headers.

Running the Programmer's Platform

This section shows you how to run Borland C++ in the environment of your choosing: DOS or Windows. The first part shows you how to get Borland C++ running in Windows. The second part explains the command-line options you can use when you start Borland C++. These options are used mainly when the program is running in a regular DOS environment.

Running the Programmer's Platform under Windows

Although Borland C++ 2.0 is not a Windows application, you can easily run the package from Windows. To do so, you need to create a Program Information File (PIF) and add Borland C++ to a program group. The PIF is a special file used by Windows to set up and run an application in the Windows environment.

You create a PIF by using the Windows built-in PIF editor. When you start the PIF editor, choose the New option so you can create a PIF for Borland C++. You will see a screen like the one in figure 19.2.

Fig. 19.2. The 386 enhanced mode PIF Editor screen.

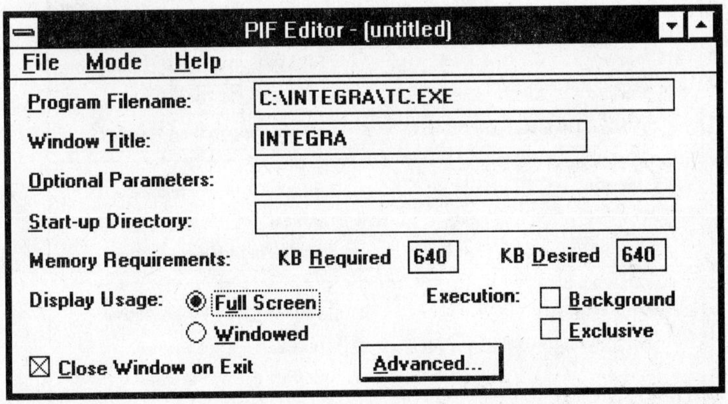

The PIF screen in figure 19.2 is the first of two PIF editor screens used in Windows 386 enhanced mode. (The standard mode screen is an abbreviated version of the enhanced mode screens.) The first field in the PIF editor screen is the Program Filename field. In this field, enter the complete path and file name for the BC.EXE file.

In the Window Title box, you enter the title that will appear on the Program Manager screen. The Optional Parameters and Start-up Directory fields are not required, but can be handy. If you are saving program source code in a directory other than the one BC.EXE resides in, you can specify that directory here.

The Memory Requirements field is important. If you specify 640K as the amount of memory required, you do not have to worry about the Desired memory field.

Because the Borland C++ IDE is not a real Windows application, it has to be run in a full-size screen. Running full size means that you cannot shrink the Borland C++ window the way you can shrink a Windows App window.

Clicking the Advanced button at the bottom of the 386 enhanced mode PIF editor screen will pop up another menu full of options. Figure 19.3 shows the second PIF editor screen.

Fig. 19.3. *The second PIF Editor screen.*

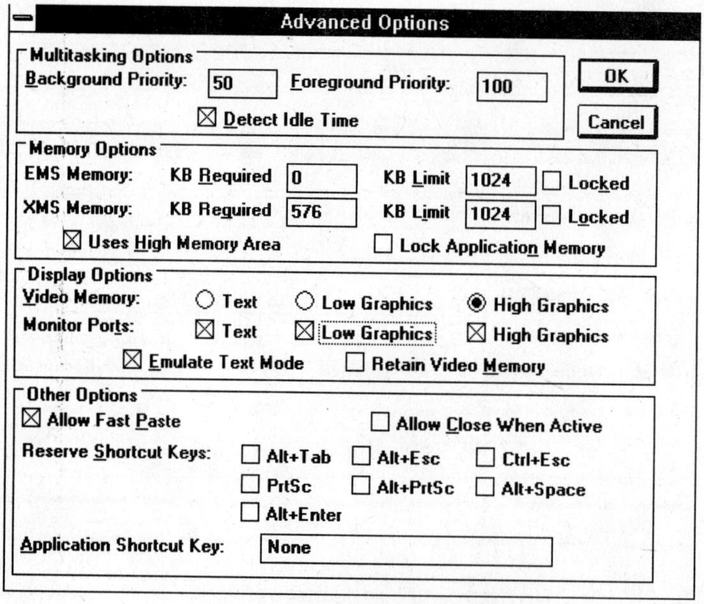

Unless you have a specific need, it is best to leave the Windows default settings for the Background Priority and Foreground Priority.

In the Memory Options box, you can choose how much memory and what kind of memory will be held for your application. EMS memory is expanded memory. XMS memory is extended memory found on 286 and 386 computers. The amount of memory you allocate for the use of Borland C++ depends on the amount of memory installed in your machine.

If you want to run the protected mode version of Borland C++ (TCX.EXE) under Windows, you have to run Windows in real or standard mode. You cannot use Windows enhanced mode and the protected mode IDE together.

When you run Borland C++ under Windows, you need to execute the TKERNEL.EXE program. When you run BCX.EXE under a DOS environment, TKERNEL is executed automatically. When you run BCX.EXE under Windows, however, you need to execute TKERNEL.EXE with the following parameters:

```
TKERNEL hi=yes kilos=nnnn
```

The *nnnn* parameter tells TKERNEL how many kilobytes of memory it will be able to manage. Borland recommends that the *nnnn* option be set to 2048. After you execute TKERNEL.EXE, you can start Windows in standard mode. All remaining extended memory is available for Windows use.

After you have created the PIF file for Borland C++, you can add the program to one of your Windows program groups. The first step in the process is to use the mouse to highlight the program group to which Borland C++ will be added. The second step is to choose the File | Add menu command from the Program Manager main menu. Third, select the Add Program Item radio button, because you are only adding a program to a group.

The fourth step is to fill in the next dialog box, which asks for the command line to start Borland C++. If Borland C++ was installed using default directory names, enter the following command line:

```
C:\BORLANDC\BIN\BC.PIF
```

This command line tells Windows to load the PIF file and execute the program described in the PIF file. (Use your own directory names, if they differ from this example.) You also need to give Windows a name for the new program item. You enter the item's name in the Description field of the dialog box.

When you finish entering all the information, Windows adds Borland C++ to the program group you specified. The next time you want to start Borland C++, just point to it and double-click the mouse. Windows will start the compiler with the options you specified in the PIF.

Options for Starting Borland C++

You can specify several command-line options when you start BC or BCX. The form of the command-line options follows:

BC | BCX $options_{opt} sourcename_{opt}$ | $projectname_{opt} sourcename_{opt}$

With the $sourcename$ and $projectname$ options, you specify which source file or project file will be loaded when Borland C++ is started. Specifying a file name or project name here saves you the effort of locating and opening files in the IDE (you can specify both a project and a file name, to open the project and load a file for editing).

The following list describes the command-line options available:

❑ The /b option causes Borland C++ to rebuild all the files in your project. Borland C++ will start, load either the current project or the project specified on the command line, recompile and relink all the files, and return to DOS.

❑ The /d option turns on dual monitor mode, but only if the needed hardware is detected. See Chapter 1 for more information on using Borland's compiler products and dual monitors.

❑ The /e option tells Borland C++ to swap to expanded memory. Usually, Borland C++ will swap to your hard drive when memory is allocated. But the /e option tells Borland C++ to swap to expanded memory instead of the hard drive. The format of the /e command is

/e=n_{opt}

where n is an optional value that is equal to the number of pages of expanded memory you want to use. Each page of expanded memory is equal to 16K.

❑ The /x option works like the /e command except that extended memory is used. The format for the /x command is

/x=r_{opt},n_{opt}

where r specifies the number of kilobytes of memory to reserve for other applications, and n specifies the number of kilobytes of memory to be allocated for swapping.

❑ The /h option lists all the available command-line options.

❑ The /l option starts Borland C++ in a video mode that can be seen on an LCD screen.

❏ The /m option causes Borland C++ to make all the files in your
project. Only the files that are out-of-date will be recompiled and
relinked. The /m option is the same as the /b option except that /m
recompiles and relinks only files that are out-of-date.

❏ The /p option controls palette swapping on EGA systems. If your
program modifies the EGA palette and the /p option is turned on,
the original palette is restored when the screen is swapped.

❏ The /r option tells Borland C++ to swap to your RAM drive instead
of the hard drive. The form of the /r option is

```
/r x
```

where x is the drive letter of your RAM disk. For example, /r e will
cause Borland C++ to swap to the E: RAM drive.

Turbo Debugger 2.5

The major upgrade in Turbo Debugger 2.5 is the capability to debug
Windows applications. Turbo Debugger has been upgraded so that it can be
used with Borland C++ 2.0.

Borland provides two versions of Turbo Debugger in the Borland C++
2.0 package. The first version, TD.EXE, is the regular version of Turbo
Debugger that can be run under DOS. The second version, TDW.EXE, is a
special version of Turbo Debugger designed to run under Microsoft Windows
3.0. Because Turbo Debugger for Windows is a Windows application, it needs
to be installed in a Windows program group.

Installing Turbo Debugger for Windows is easy. If you elected to install
the debugger, Turbo Debugger for Windows was automatically copied to your
hard disk with the rest of the Borland C++ package. By default, Turbo
Debugger for Windows is in the \BORLANDC\BIN subdirectory.

Because all Turbo Debugger for Windows files are already on your disk
drive, the only remaining task is to add Turbo Debugger to a Windows program
group. This takes three steps. First, use the mouse to select the program group
to which Turbo Debugger will be added. Second, choose the File | Add menu
selection from the Program Manager's main menu bar. Third, add a program
item to the current program group. When you add a program item, Windows
will prompt you for the name that appears in the program group and for the
command line to start the program. If Turbo Debugger is installed in the default
directory, the following command line can be used:

```
C:\BORLANDC\BIN\TDW.EXE
```

Because Turbo Debugger is a true Windows application, the icon for the program is stored in the TDW.EXE file. Instead of choosing one of Windows built-in icons, you can use Turbo Debugger's unique icon.

Using Turbo Debugger for Windows is much like using the regular debugger. The difference is that Turbo Debugger for Windows can display Windows-specific information. The Windows information includes:

❑ Messages passed among your application's windows.

❑ A complete listing of modules that comprise your program. The DLL (Dynamic Link List) modules are included.

❑ The local and global heap.

There are also several features that Turbo Debugger for Windows does *not* support, compared to DOS Turbo Debugger, because the features do not apply to the Windows environment. Note the following features:

❑ Hardware debugging is not supported.

❑ Debugging device drivers and TSRs are not supported.

❑ There is no option for keystroke recording.

❑ A DOS shell is not needed or available.

❑ You cannot quit TDW and leave it resident.

❑ Table Relocate is not supported because you cannot set the base segment of the symbol table.

❑ Switching from the application being debugged to TDW is accomplished with the Ctrl-Alt-SysReq key combination.

❑ Setting the Options | Path For Source also sets the startup directory.

You must have at least an 80286-based computer to run Turbo Debugger for Windows. TDW has to be run in Windows standard or enhanced mode, and these modes are available only on 286, 386, and 486 machines.

Using Turbo Assembler 2.5

The new Borland C++ 2.0 high-end package brings with it an array of new features. Not surprisingly, Turbo Assembler has not been left out of the general upgrade of functionality. Turbo Assembler 2.5 contains all the new features found in TASM 2.0, plus a few more significant features, which are mentioned in this section. The following changes in the package are discussed:

❏ *Compiler differences that affect TASM 2.5*. Some differences between Turbo C++ 2.0 and Borland C++ 2.0 will affect the way you interface C and assembly routines.

❏ *New MODEL identifiers for Windows 3.0 support*. The most significant new feature of the Borland C++ 2.0 package is support for Windows 3.0 application programming. TASM 2.5 accordingly has new features to allow you to mix assembly and C languages in the Windows environment.

❏ *Virtual segment support*. TASM 2.5 borrows a note from C++ with virtual segments. Virtual segments are assumed to belong to their enclosing segments, and to inherit the properties of their enclosing segments. (This will sound familiar to C++ fans.)

❏ *486 instruction support*. The Intel 80486 is making a strong appearance in the CPU marketplace. TASM 2.5 has new 486 instructions and assembler directives to support this more powerful CPU.

❏ *RETCODE directive*. This new directive generates near or far return instructions, based on the current memory model.

C Compiler Differences That Affect TASM

You need to be aware of several differences between Turbo C++ and Borland C++ 2.0 when mixing C and assembly code. These differences include the following new features and requirements.

Do not try to mix TASM 1.0 inline assembly statements in a Borland C++ 2.0 program. TASM 1.0 is too far out-of-date, and it may not be able to handle all the assembly statements generated by Borland C++ 2.0 inline assembly. But remember that Borland C++ 2.0 now has a built-in assembler; this restriction is meaningful only if you use the #pragma inline directive or –B compiler directive to explicitly invoke the external assembler.

In Chapter 10 you learned how to return a 3-byte or greater than 4-byte structure from assembly language to C. The rules in that chapter and in the *Turbo Assembler 2.0 User's Guide* state that you should copy such a structure to a global static area and return a pointer to the structure (in AX or DX:AX for small and large models).

Those rules are true as far as they go, but they do not go far enough. The on-disk README files for both Turbo C++ and Borland C++ 2.0 state that functions expected to return a struct are also passed a hidden pointer (it will always be a far pointer) to an area into which the function must copy the structure. You get garbage if you do not perform the copy, as well as return the pointer. The location pointed to is often on the stack.

To summarize: if the s t r u c t created by the assembly module is not in
a global static area, copy it to one. Return the address of the area pointed to by
the hidden argument to the caller—the caller's C code will probably expect to
copy the s t r u c t from that location again. For example, the following short
C++ program expects an assembly language module to create and return a
class s t r i n t object (which is, after all, a s t r u c t):

```
#include <iostream.h>

class strint {
  int a,b,c;
public:
  void show() {
    cout << a << ' ' << b << ' ' << c << endl;
  }
};

extern strint rsasm(); // Create and return class obj

void main()
{
  strint i;

  i = rsasm(); // Call TASM routine to build class obj
  i.show();
}
```

The following assembly language routine does the trick nicely. (Note that
the *mangled* function name is required.)

```
          DOSSEG
          .MODEL small

ISTRUCT   STRUC
int1      dw        0
int2      dw        0
int3      dw        0
ISTRUCT   ENDS
          .DATA
classobj ISTRUCT <2,3,4>        ; Create class object / struct
          .CODE
;
; Use C++ mangled function name.
;    Note that we do not use the C language spec. for the
;         PUBLIC or PROC directives so that underscores
```

```
;           will not be generated (C++ mangled names only)
;
            PUBLIC @rsasm$qv
@rsasm$qv PROC
            push bp
            mov  bp,sp
            lea  si,classobj   ; offset sender, DS already set
            push [bp+6]                  ; seg adrs of recv'g loc
            pop  es
            mov  di,[bp+4]     ; offset address of recv'g loc
            mov  cx,3                          ; copy 3 words
copyit:
            lodsw
            stosw
            loop copyit
            mov  ax,[bp+4]     ; small model ptr is just offset
            pop  bp
            ret                         ; and return to caller
@rsasm$qv ENDP
            END
```

With Turbo C++ 2.0, you can declare far functions and pointers. Now, with Borland C++ 2.0, you can declare far objects. Declaring an object as far places it in its own far segment (as if the huge model was being used). For example, the integers i and j in the code fragment

```
int far i = 0;
int far j;
```

create a separate far segment for each data object. You can also use the extern and static specifiers with far objects.

If you want, you can control the far segment's name, class, and group, with either command-line compiler (TCC) options or #pragma *option* compiler directives (or you can combine the two methods). The command-line options are these:

−zE*segname*

> Set the segment name to the declared value. This can be any legitimate segment name that TASM will accept.

−zF*classname*

> Set the segment class to the declared value. This has the same effect as declaring SEGMENT ... 'classname'.

```
-zHgroupname
```

Define a group to which the far segment belongs.

Command-line options allow you to define a far segment only once. By using the #pragma *option* C directive, however, you can place far objects in several different far segments, combining them in any way you want. For example, the code fragment

```
#pragma option -zEusrseg -zHusrgroup -zFusrclass
int far i;
int far j;
#pragma option -zEappseg -zHappgroup -zFappclass
int far k;
int far p;
#pragma option -zE* -zH* -zF*
```

places the far objects i and j in the usrseg far segment, and places the far objects k and p in the appseg far segment. The last line resets the far segment name, class, and group back to the default values.

New *MODEL* Identifiers for Windows 3.0 Support

Now that Borland C++ 2.0 supports the Windows 3.0 programming environment, there are corresponding additions to TASM 2.5. You should especially take note of the new keywords available in the PROC directive for generating Windows compatible prolog and epilog code. The general syntax of the PROC directive is

$modifier_{opt} language_{opt} NEAR|FAR_{opt} procname\ PROC\ language$
$modifier_{opt}\ language_{opt}\ NEAR|FAR_{opt}$

where the legal language modifiers can be NORMAL or WINDOWS. The NORMAL language modifier selects normal procedure entry and exit code sequences. The WINDOWS modifier selects entry and exit code sequences compatible with the Microsoft Windows programming environment.

The NORMAL and WINDOWS language modifiers can precede any legal language keyword. (Note that a language keyword can be used in .MODEL, EXTRN, GLOBAL, PUBLIC, PUBLICDLL, COMM, PROC, and CALL, but is used only by PROC.) The entry and exit code sequences generated for the NORMAL keyword are the following:

```
;Entry/exit sequences not generated if no args or locals.
;Note that the 186 version uses ENTER/LEAVE.
        push bp
        mov bp,sp
        sub sp,local_size  ; Do this if locals used
        [push uses registers here]
        ...                     ; User code goes here
        [pop uses registers here]
        mov sp,bp            ; Do this if locals used
        pop bp
        ret
```

The entry and exit code sequences generated for a Windows TASM application are the following:

```
        push ds
        pop ax
        xchg ax,ax
        inc bp
        push bp
        mov bp,sp
        push ds
        mov ds,ax
        sub sp,local_size    ; if local variables used
        [push uses registers here]
        ...                     ; User code goes here
        [pop uses registers here]
        sub bp,2             ; if local variables used
        mov sp,bp           ; if local variables used
        pop ds
        pop bp
        dec bp
        ret
```

The Windows environment permits the construction of Dynamic Link Libraries (DLLs), which have some special requirements for segment arrangements (see Chapter 22 for more on this subject). In particular, a DLL module has no stack of its own: it must use the stack of the application module that called it. The MODEL directive can now declare that the stack segment is not part of the data segment, as follows:

```
.MODEL SS_NE_DS LARGE    ; Equivalent to BC s large model
```

The SS_NE_DS modifier has the effect of declaring ASSUME SS:NOTHING, which means that the stack is not considered to be part of DGROUP.

Note that now there is also a WINDOWS.INC assembly include file for writing Windows applications in assembly language.

Virtual Segment Support

You can now declare a segment to be a VIRTUAL segment. (This was introduced in TASM 2.0, but is worth mentioning again.) A VIRTUAL segment is a common area that belongs to the segment enclosing it. The general syntax of a VIRTUAL segment declaration is

```
segname SEGMENT VIRTUAL      ; MASM mode
...
ENDS

SEGMENT segname VIRTUAL      ; Ideal mode
...
ENDS
```

A VIRTUAL segment is similar to a COMMON segment, except that it represents a pooling of data objects in a common area, rather than an overlay view of data as given by COMMON. Further, a VIRTUAL segment is ASSUMEd to be addressed by the segment register belonging to its parent (enclosing) segment.

486 Instruction Support

TASM 2.5 now supports the Intel 80486 CPU. The following directives and instructions have been added:

❑ .486, .486c

In MASM mode only, these directives enable the assembly of 80486 real mode nonprivileged instructions and floating-point instructions.

❑ P486N

Enables assembly of real mode nonprivileged instructions for the 486 processor.

❑ .486p

In MASM mode only, enables the assembly of all CPU and coprocessor instructions.

❏ `P486`

Enables assembly of all CPU and coprocessor instructions.

❏ `BSWAP <reg-32>`

This is the 486 byte-swap instruction.

❏ `XADD <r/m>,<reg>`

This is the 486 exchange-and-add instruction.

❏ `CMPXCHG <r/m>,<reg>`

This is the 486 compare-and-exchange instruction.

❏ `INVD`

This 486 instruction invalidates the data cache.

❏ `WBINVD`

This 486 instruction invalidates data cache after a write-back.

❏ `INVLPG <memptr>`

This 486 instruction invalidates the TLB entry for an address.

There are also three new test registers for the 80486 CPU. They are the `TR3`, `TR4`, and `TR5` registers.

RETCODE Instruction

TASM 2.5 now has a `RETCODE` instruction, which is the equivalent of a near or far return instruction (`RETN` or `RETF`). Whether a near or far return is generated depends on the current memory model being used. The general syntax for the `RETCODE` instruction is

`RETCODE expression`$_{opt}$

The optional `expression` specifies the number of bytes to pop off the stack before returning to the caller. You won't need this immediate operand when writing assembly language modules for C programs (the caller, not the called module, is responsible for cleaning up the stack).

TASMX.EXE and the Windows DPMI

TASM 2.5 can now run from the Windows 3.0 DOS prompt and use all of the 80386's (or 80486's) extended memory, when you run Windows in 386 enhanced mode. This is accomplished by running TASMX.EXE, rather than TASM.EXE.

TASMX.EXE can detect whether the Windows DPMI (DOS Protected Mode Support) feature is present. If it is, TASMX.EXE loads the DPMILOAD.EXE program, and uses that program to finish loading itself. Then TASM can use all of the system's memory by taking advantage of the capability of Windows to use the 386 paging registers to implement virtual memory.

The Whitewater Group Resource Toolkit

The Whitewater Group Resource Toolkit (WRT) is now part of the Borland C++ 2.0 distribution package. WRT is a complete replacement utility for the Microsoft Resource Toolkit (provided with the Microsoft Software Development Kit for the Windows programming environment) for use with Borland C++ 2.0 in developing Windows applications.

Using WRT, you can create every kind of resource you need for a Windows application. WRT supports the creation and maintainence of resources in separate files or directly in a Windows executable file. You can create and maintain seven different kinds of resources with WRT:

❏ *Keyboard accelerators*. A keyboard accelerator is a shorthand keystroke you can define to cause the input of a longer sequence of keystrokes. An accelerator, in other words, is a keyboard macro, designed especially for the Windows environment.

❏ *Bit maps*. A bit map is the default Windows graphics image format. You can display bit maps directly in a window with text or other graphics images (including icons). WRT supports the creation of bit maps up to 200-by-200 pixels.

❏ *Cursors*. If you already use Windows, you are familiar with the standard cursors: arrows, pointing hands, and a sand clock cursor, which indicates that the user should wait while the program performs its work. You can also edit and design your own cursors for use with your application programs.

❏ *Dialogs*. Turbo C++ IDE users are already familiar with dialog boxes. Windows has its own dialog facility, and its own kind of dialog box. You can use WRT to draw dialog boxes and the controls that go in them. You see much more about dialogs and dialog boxes in Chapters 21 and 22.

❏ *Icons*. An icon is a small graphic image that represents an entire application program. The Windows Program Manager displays an icon with every application program you can select from its window. Using WRT, you can design the icon that will be used by the Program Manager to display your application to the user, and you can design icons to be used directly by your application code.

❏ *Menus*. Windows menus consist of a menu bar displayed across the top of the application's window, and pop-up menus associated with every item on the menu bar. Menus are the norm in the Windows environment, and almost all applications use them, though that is not absolutely required. With WRT, you can draw your application's menus, and assign a control ID to every menu item.

❏ *Strings*. Strings are a resource and resemble C's object-like macros. You can use strings to reduce the amount of constant storage overhead in your application program's memory, and to streamline your program design. Strings defined as a Windows resource are assigned an integer control ID.

WRT displays all the editors for the different kinds of resources as pushbuttons you can click at the top of its window. The pushbuttons for WRT are shown in figure 19.4.

Fig. 19.4. The WRT main window, showing the editor buttons and the resource browser boxes.

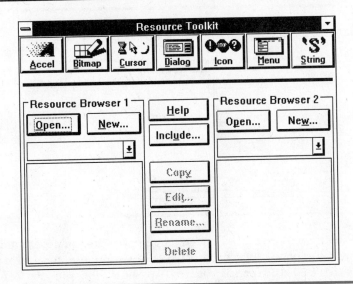

In addition to the resource editors, WRT provides two resource browsers for editing and maintaining existing resources. The resources that WRT can handle can exist in separate files (such as ICO files for icons), or they can exist in the Windows executable file for your application program. Some resources, particularly icons, should be created separately and copied into an executable file using the resource browsers.

To edit a resource using a resource browser, click the Open button for the browser you want to use (1 or 2). Then you can scroll the file-open selection window (displayed in a dialog box) and click the file containing the resource you want to edit. When the resources contained in that file have been loaded, you can use the browser's combo box to select the kind of resource and the list box to select the particular resource. Next, the appropriate editor for the selected resource is started, and the resource is loaded into it.

If you want to edit the window icon used by the Program Manager, for example, select PROGMAN.EXE from the file-open list box. Then select Icon from the combo box, and select the resource named 31944 from the resource list box. Figure 19.5 shows this icon about to be selected in Browser 1.

Fig. 19.5. Selecting the "window" icon belonging to `progman.exe`*.*

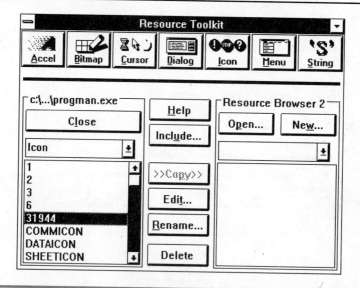

After the icon editor has loaded the resource, editing it is as intuitive as drawing with a pencil. In fact, that is what you do in the editor—the drawing tool is depicted as a pencil. Figure 19.6 shows the window icon from PROGMAN.EXE being edited. Although you can edit resources belonging to Windows itself, you will probably not do so.

Fig. 19.6. Editing the "window" icon belonging to `progman.exe`.

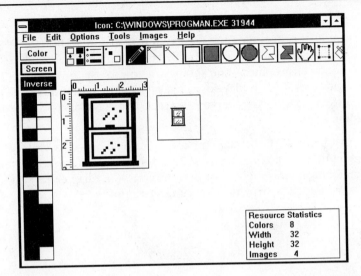

You can define any of these resources in text form in a resource script file (RS file), and use the resource compiler to build resource binary files (RES files) from them. This process is quite tedious. Fortunately, because Borland has packaged WRT with Borland C++ 2.0, you almost never need to resort to this archaic method.

You see more of the Resource Toolkit in Chapters 20-22. In those chapters, you take a grand tour of Windows application programming using Borland C++ 2.0 and related utilities. If you have never programmed in the Windows environment, these chapters should provide an eye-opening experience. If you have already experienced this programming environment, you may want to read on anyway, to get a first taste of the Turbo C++ tools available for this activity.

Few things stemming from this chapter could be presented as adequate practice problems, so there is no exercises section—just this once.

Summary

The Borland C++ 2.0 package includes a world of new features, and opens up a new world of programming: the Windows world. Nearly all the satellite programs (debugger, profiler, and assembler) have been updated to keep up with changing times (including 80486 support). The addition of

Windows support requires (and Borland provides) a new utility, the Whitewater Group's Resource Toolkit, for creating and maintaining Windows program resources.

Windows programming is the major new feature of Borland C++ 2.0, and the rest of this book is devoted to that topic. Chapter 20 introduces you to the Windows environment, and shows you how to use the Resource Toolkit. You begin to use WRT to develop some of the resources used by the sample programs in the following chapters. You also write your first, simple Windows program: `easy.c`.

In Chapters 21 and 22, you continue to see how to write Windows programs by designing and then writing a Windows application that helps you do something interesting—manage your money. In Chapter 22, you see also how to write a DLL (Dynamic Link Library) module.

20

Using Borland C++ 2.0 with Windows

This chapter deals with the most significant new feature in the Borland C++ 2.0 package: Windows 3.0 programming support. Added support for Windows 3.0 in Borland C++ 2.0 includes all the necessary changes to the compiler, linker, and IDE. The new utilities include the Whitewater Group Resource Toolkit (RT), a Resource Compiler (RC), and an import librarian (IMPLIB).

Before this time, few compiler products supplied all the resources required for Windows application development. The only significant player in the Windows programming market was Microsoft itself, with its Software Development Kit (SDK), which included versions of RT, RC, and IMPLIB.

The new Borland package is exciting and important for every Turbo C and C++ programmer in at least two ways. First, it means that Microsoft is serious about promoting the use of Windows (because they licensed sufficient proprietary information to make Windows development with Borland C++ possible). This means that more significant code will now support the Windows environment. This is an area of C programming you need to move into right now, unless you are content with writing code for only one of the currently important environments.

Second, it means that Borland plans to be a major player in Windows application program development. This, in turn, means that the price of tools for writing Windows applications will be affordable for the individual programmer (a practice for which Borland is famous).

It may not be accurate to say that slick Windows applications will become as common as grass in the pasture (Windows *is* a complex environment), but knowledge of Windows programming will proliferate among capable C and C++ programmers. Wouldn't you like to be in that group?

Is it worth the effort to learn a new programming regime, just to write Windows applications? That question sounds similar to the question asked about learning C++. It is definitely worth the effort to learn how to write Windows applications, now that the tools for doing so have become so readily available. And the reasons that it is worthwhile are much the same as they were for C++. You get added power and flexibility, and with the Windows Graphical User Interface (GUI), you get a quantum leap in the appearance of your programs. Even more, you will find that using a GUI such as Windows unexpectedly adds functionality to your programs, as a side effect.

The remainder of this book introduces Windows programming using the Borland C++ 2.0 compiler and tools. The discussion is directed to Windows users. If you are not a Windows user, you can easily remedy that. Windows 3.0 is not expensive, and only a little practice is required to become a fairly proficient Windows user.

Because Windows programming is an extensive and sometimes complicated subject, you are presented with only a brief tour of the subject. This tour, however, may kindle your interest in further study of Windows programming.

Understanding the Windows Programming Environment

Windows is a complicated programming environment primarily because programming for Windows is an all-or-nothing proposition. You can write a true Windows application program—one that handles all keyboard, screen, and printer I/O through Windows services—or you can write a DOS application. You cannot mingle the two modes of programming. (Some DOS programs can run under Windows in a virtualized DOS window, but this is not quite the same thing as a Windows program.)

In addition to performing all standard I/O only through Windows services (you can still use the same C file I/O functions for disk files), true Windows application programs must contend with two other factors. One, Windows application programs run in a *multitasking environment*, which requires some radical changes to the way you structure your programs. Two, Windows is an *object-oriented environment*. Thus, you must know how to deal with Windows objects and resources, and some of the techniques can be quite complicated. However, they can be quite rewarding, too.

Windows Is a Multitasking Environment

If you have read the previous parts of this book, you know something about dealing with objects. Thus, the object-oriented nature of Windows programming will not cause you grief when learning Windows programming. Rather, the multitasking environment—and the programming style it requires—may at first perplex you.

Do not be put off if multitasking programming stumps you momentarily. Multitasking, whether done on PCs or mainframes, has always confused programmers, at least temporarily. With a little patience and persistence, you will rapidly overcome the hurdles to a new way of perceiving the art of programming.

Windows handles its guest applications in different ways. DOS applications running under Windows often cannot be preempted, defeating the multitasking scheme of the environment. But true Windows applications, those using the Windows interfaces and protocols as they should, can run at the same time as other Windows applications. When dealing with true Windows applications, many programs can be running (and not just waiting to be swapped into memory) at the same time. The Task List dialog box of the Program Manager illustrates this point, as shown in figure 20.1.

As you can see in figure 20.1, Windows can load and run several native applications at once. Other applications may be running even though the main window for only one application program is visible. In figure 20.1, for example, only the Program Manager has a window visible on the screen. You can tell that other applications are present because their icons appear at the bottom of the screen. The Terminal application, however, could very easily be processing data from the communications ports in *background mode*, even though only its icon is visible at the moment.

Now, what kind of structural program changes does the multitasking environment require? The answer revolves around the fact that your program must now be designed to coexist with other active programs. For your program to exist cooperatively with Windows, a few things *must* be in your program, and other things *can* be in your program. Typically, you will write four kinds of functions in your Windows C programs: the main Windows interface function, the main window procedure (still a C function), other windows-oriented functions, and simple helper functions. The significance of these four kinds of functions follows:

Fig. 20.1. *Windows can run many application programs at the same time.*

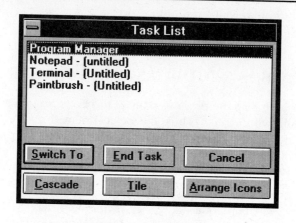

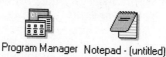
Program Manager   Notepad - (untitled)

Terminal - (Untitled)   Paintbrush - (Untitled)

❑ *The main Windows interface function is required and must be named* `WinMain()`. `WinMain()` is similar to the ordinary C function `main()`, in that it is required to get things rolling—it is the main entry point for the program (note that a Windows program does *not* have a `main()` function). The `WinMain()` function does three crucially important things:

1. `WinMain()` *registers the window class for the application's main window.* This simply means that the `WinMain()` function tells Windows what the characteristics of the main window will be (the name of the window procedure function, what icon to use to represent the application when its window is minimized, background color, what menu to use, and other things).

2. `WinMain()` *creates the application's main window.* `WinMain()` issues the `CreateWindow()` Windows function calls to create the main window for the application and to

display it on the screen. Function arguments to `CreateWindow()` include the application's Windows name; the caption text for the window; and the window's style, initial position, and menu name.

3. `WinMain()` *contains the application's main message loop.* The main message loop gets commands and data input from Windows and sends requests for certain services to Windows. The principal Windows function call in the main message loop is the `GetMessage()` function call, which requests and receives data and commands from Windows. When your program calls `GetMessage()`, Windows may decide to momentarily execute another application's program: this is the primary vehicle for implementing the Windows multitasking scheme. The main message loop is discussed in detail in Chapter 22.

❏ *The main window procedure is also required and is usually named* `WndProc()`. The `WinMain()` message loop indirectly invokes the main window procedure, but never calls it directly. The main window procedure processes and acts on Windows commands and messages received by the main message loop.

To understand this strange state of affairs, remember that Windows was told the name of the main window procedure when the window class was registered. When the main message loop gets a message from Windows, it performs any necessary translation of the message and dispatches the message back to Windows. Only at this point does Windows finally invoke the main window procedure, passing to it the message (data or commands) for action.

❏ *Other Windows-oriented functions may be required, depending on what Windows features you use.* Some functions are required only if you use certain features of the Windows environment. Creating, displaying, and handling a dialog box, for example, requires the use of a dialog function, whose name is made known to Windows (it too will be called directly by Windows, not by your program). In Chapters 21 and 22, you develop a sample application program, called FCWIN, that uses quite a few dialog boxes.

❏ *Simple helper functions may be needed to complement your program's work.* "Simple" helper functions mean non-Windows functions; they might be quite complex, depending on what your program does.

You will learn how to code these four kinds of functions in your Windows program as you develop the sample application code in Chapters 21 and 22.

For now, think about the fact that you will soon be programming in a new environment, and what that might mean. You need to see, at least briefly, a number of new concepts and tools before you tackle the program code for FCWIN.

Windows Is an Object-Oriented Environment

Having already taken on the task of learning C++ object-oriented programming, you will avoid the double culture shock of encountering object-oriented system *and* multitasking for the first time.

Windows is decidedly an object-oriented system, and Windows programming is definitely a form of object-oriented programming. You can probably think of one object present in the Windows environment: the window! A Windows window is handled very much like a C++ object. It has a user-defined type (remember registering the window class?), instances of the class (objects) are created at run time (`CreateWindow()`), and you handle objects by sending messages to them (with `GetMessage()` and `DispatchMessage()` functions). It all sounds familiar, doesn't it?

A window type object is not the only object type in Windows. There are many more, some of which are indicated in figure 20.2.

Windows programs routinely deal with such objects as bit maps, cursors, dialog boxes, icons, menus, and string resources. Most of these objects are easy to understand—you deal with them regularly in the Borland C++ 2.0 IDE, for example. Other resources, such as keyboard accelerators (tables defining application hot keys), may be familiar in concept, but implemented in new ways. That is all part of the fun of learning to write Windows applications: new toys are everywhere!

To briefly illustrate the concepts mentioned so far, the `easy.c` program is presented here. This program, which is the Windows equivalent of the ubiquitous "hello, world" introductory C program, does nothing but create a main window, with text for the caption bar and text in the client area of the window. All text lines are centered in the client area of the window. The appearance of the `easy.c` window is shown in figure 20.3.

Fig. 20.2. Windows deals with objects (such as windows!) and operates by routing messages between them.

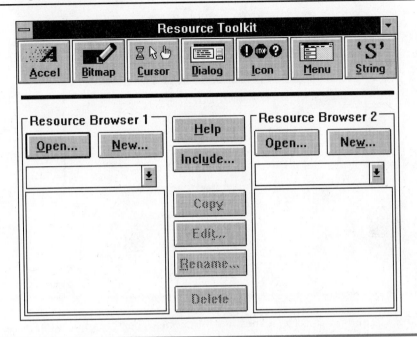

The interesting thing about easy.c is that its window can be dragged around the screen and sized to any proportions you like (within limits), and the text in the client area stays centered. How is this accomplished? Putting the easy.c Windows application together requires three source files, plus a project file, because the IDE is used to build the program. (It also requires the WINSTUB.EXE file, which is explained in the next chapter.) The project file is the easiest to build. You just open a new project, and insert the following files:

```
easy.c
easy.def
```

The nature of the easy.def file will become clear in just a moment. The easy.h header file is also quite simple; it consists of one line, as follows:

```
#define szAppName "EasyC"
```

Fig. 20.3. The easy.c *window, with caption bar and text in the client area.*

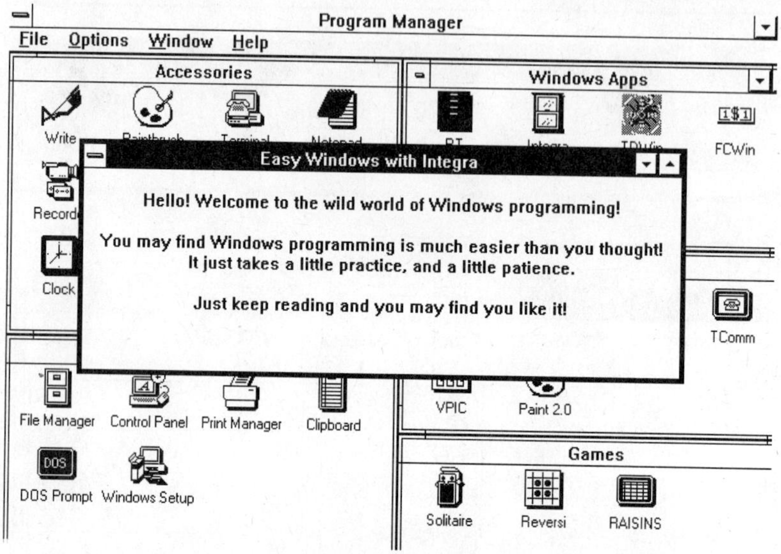

The szAppName macro defines a string containing the application name used to identify the application to Windows when the main window is created. You should #include the easy.h header at the beginning of the easy.c application program. Later, when you write a longer and more complex application, the application header file will contain quite a few macros (manifest constants) used to identify menu items and window components. Thus, although the easy.h header is ridiculously simple, the application header will play a serious role in the construction of a serious Windows application.

Now turn your attention to the easy.def file. Its contents are shown in listing 20.1.

Listing 20.1. easy.def. *The module definition file for* easy.c.

```
1   NAME          EasyC
2   DESCRIPTION   'First Windows application for UTC'
3   STUB          'WINSTUB.EXE'
4   CODE          PRELOAD MOVEABLE DISCARDABLE
5   DATA          PRELOAD MOVEABLE MULTIPLE
6   HEAPSIZE      8192
7   STACKSIZE     8192
8   EXPORTS       WndProc
```

The first thing you should know about DEF files is that they are called *module definition files.* A module definition file describes to the linkage editor the program's attributes and some resources it will need, so that the EXE module can be set up properly for the Windows environment. For this project, type the DEF file exactly as you see it in listing 20.1.

The second thing you should know about DEF files is that the Borland documentation says you can compile and link a Windows program without a module definition file. Our advice is to always provide one with your Windows application program. It documents your program's characteristics and could prevent the use of unwanted default characteristics.

The significance of the individual statements in the module definition file is explained in detail in Chapters 21 and 22, when you go through the development of a much larger project. Notice, however, that the EXPORTS statement names a function called WndProc (which will be the main window function for easy.c). This is how you tell the linker which functions can be called by Windows system code from outside your program.

The source code for easy.c is shown in listing 20.2. As you look through the program listing, notice that the WinMain() function and a main window procedure function named WndProc() are present, but the third and fourth categories of functions are not necessary in this short program.

Listing 20.2. easy.c. The Windows application program for the EASY window.

```
1    #include <string.h>
2    #include <windows.h> /* Declarations for Windows */
3    #include "easy.h"     /* Declarations for EASY.C */
4
5    char *HelloMsgs[] = {
6      "Hello! Welcome to the wild world of Windows programming!",
7      " ",
8      "You may find Windows programming is much "
            "easier than you thought!",
9      "It just takes a little practice, and a little patience.",
10     " ",
11     "Just keep reading and you may find you like it!",
12   };
13
14   long FAR PASCAL WndProc (HWND, unsigned, WORD, LONG) ;
15
16   int PASCAL WinMain(HANDLE hInstance, HANDLE hPrevInstance,
```

Listing 20.2. continues

Listing 20.2. continued

```
17                 LPSTR lpszCmdLine, int nCmdShow )
18  {
19      WNDCLASS    wndClass;
20      MSG         msg;
21      HWND  hWnd;
22
23      /*
24       * Register window class style if first
25       * instance of this program.
26       */
27      if ( !hPrevInstance )
28      {
29      wndClass.style          =CS_HREDRAW | CS_VREDRAW ;
30      wndClass.lpfnWndProc    =WndProc;
31      wndClass.cbClsExtra     =0;
32      wndClass.cbWndExtra     =0;
33      wndClass.hInstance      =hInstance;
34      wndClass.hIcon          =LoadIcon(NULL,
35                                        IDI_APPLICATION);
36      wndClass.hCursor        =LoadCursor(NULL,IDC_ARROW );
37      wndClass.hbrBackground=GetStockObject(WHITE_BRUSH );
38      wndClass.lpszMenuName =NULL;
39      wndClass.lpszClassName=szAppName;
40
41      if (!RegisterClass(&wndClass))
42       return FALSE;
43      }
44
45      hWnd = CreateWindow(szAppName,
46                      "Easy Windows with Integra",
47              WS_OVERLAPPEDWINDOW,
48              CW_USEDEFAULT,
49              CW_USEDEFAULT,
50              CW_USEDEFAULT,
51              CW_USEDEFAULT,
52                      NULL,
53                      NULL,
54                      hInstance,
55                      NULL);
56
57      ShowWindow(hWnd, nCmdShow);
```

```
58       UpdateWindow(hWnd);
59
60       while (GetMessage(&msg, NULL, 0, 0))
61       {
62           TranslateMessage(&msg );
63        DispatchMessage(&msg );
64       }
65       return msg.wParam;
66   }
67
68   long FAR PASCAL WndProc (HWND hWnd, unsigned Message,
69                   WORD wParam, LONG lParam)
70   {
71     static HANDLE hDc;
72     PAINTSTRUCT ps;
73     int LineWidth, LineSpace, xPos;
74     int i;
75     TEXTMETRIC TextMetric;
76     LONG dwExtent;
77     RECT rect;
78
79     switch(Message)
80     {
81
82       case WM_PAINT:
83         hDc = BeginPaint( hWnd, &ps );
84         GetTextMetrics( hDc, &TextMetric );
85         LineSpace = TextMetric.tmHeight
86                   + TextMetric.tmExternalLeading;
87         GetClientRect( hWnd, &rect );
88         LineWidth = rect.right - rect.left + 1;
89         for ( i=0; i<6; ++i ) {
90           dwExtent = GetTextExtent( hDc, HelloMsgs[i],
91                   strlen( HelloMsgs[i] ) );
92           xPos = ( LineWidth - LOWORD( dwExtent ) ) / 2;
93           TextOut( hDc, xPos, (i+1)*LineSpace,
94                   (LPSTR)HelloMsgs[i], strlen(HelloMsgs[i]) );
95         }
96         EndPaint( hWnd, &ps );
97         return 0;
98
```

Listing 20.2. continues

Listing 20.2. continued

```
 99
100      case WM_DESTROY:
101           PostQuitMessage(0);
102           return 0;
103    }
104    return DefWindowProc(hWnd,Message,wParam,lParam);
105  }
106
```

Lines 1–14 of listing 20.2 contain necessary preliminary statements. Notice that windows.h and easy.h are #included in lines 2 and 3. Other material in these lines include the array of pointers to the message strings that will be painted on the client area of the window, and a function prototype for the WndProc() main window procedure's function.

The required WinMain() function is found in lines 16–66 of listing 20.2. As mentioned, WinMain() does three important things: it registers the main window class, creates and displays the main window, and contains the main message loop.

In lines 29–43, you can see the process of registering the window class, which consists of assigning values to members of a window class structure (which has type WNDCLASS and is declared in windows.h) and calling the RegisterClass() Windows function. RegisterClass() is only one of hundreds of functions residing in Windows (not in your code) that constitute the programming interface to the Windows environment. As long as you remember to declare #include <windows.h>, all of these Windows functions and facilities are available without other preparatory action.

Registering the window class does not cause anything to happen on the system display, however. To create and display the window, you must use the CreateWindow() function, as seen in lines 45–58. CreateWindow() uses the szAppName macro declared in the easy.h header (line 45), and you can write the window caption text directly into the function call as a constant string (line 46).

Even after the CreateWindow() function has been called, the main window still exists only as an area of memory in Windows. To force the window to appear on the system screen, call the ShowWindow() function (line 57). To invoke the user code that paints the contents of the window's client area, call the UpdateWindow() function (line 58).

The main message loop (lines 60–65) is in the `WinMain()` function. It drives the whole application—without the main message loop, no Windows messages are received or dispatched. The main message loop is the indirect interface between Windows and your main window procedure. Chapter 22 covers the main message loop in more detail, but its three basic components are the following:

1. *The `while` loop controlled by the `GetMessage()` Windows function.* `GetMessage()` retrieves the next Windows message from your application's input message queue (by asking Windows to return it), and gives Windows the opportunity to select another application for execution (by simply giving control to Windows momentarily).

2. *The `TranslateMessage()` Windows function call in the `while` loop.* The `TranslateMessage()` function call is important for handling keyboard input, especially if you want your program to handle ANSI multibyte characters. This function translates keyboard scan and character codes into ANSI standard character codes (which may be ASCII single-byte characters on English-based systems).

3. *The `DispatchMessage()` Windows function call.* This function call passes the message—ready for dispatching—back to Windows. *Dispatching* means the process of routing the message to the window it belongs to. In `easy.c`, for example, there is only one active window (the main window), and its window procedure function is `WndProc()`. Windows therefore passes the message to `WndProc()` for handling any action.

The most important thing to remember about the main message loop is that you do not call a window procedure yourself. You let Windows route messages to the correct window, by simply giving the message back to Windows through `DispatchMessage()`. It is important to understand this idea, especially when you progress to writing applications using multiple windows.

Next, look at the main window procedure's function, `WndProc()`. Its code is found in lines 68–105. Remember that the main window procedure can have any valid name. In `easy.c`, the main window procedure name is identified during window class registration (line 30 of listing 20.2) as `WndProc`.

The main window procedure for `easy.c` handles two Windows messages: `WM_PAINT` and `WM_DESTROY` (both declared in `windows.h`). The names of these messages clearly show *what* they are, but not *when* they might be generated.

The WM_PAINT message is received any time the UpdateWindow() function is called, the window is moved, or the window is resized (by a Windows user). The code that handles the WM_PAINT message (see lines 82–97) has the primary responsibility of keeping the client area of the window painted correctly under all circumstances. This short piece of code (just 16 lines) clearly illustrates why there is a steep learning curve associated with Windows programming; the code contains seven calls to Windows functions. That is more than you might expect, when the objective is to put lines of text in the client area, centered in the window. The seven Windows functions and their uses are these:

❑ *BeginPaint() establishes the device context for the window.* Establishing a device context for the window display (or printer, or other device or resource) is similar to invoking the constructor for a C++ class object. It tells Windows what you are about to do, and where you are about to do it.

❑ *GetTextMetrics() acquires information about the font being used in the current device context.* easy.c needs this information to compute the height of a line of text. Remember that all window I/O is *graphics* I/O—that is one of the main reasons for the existence of Windows. The pixel-based dimensions of the text and window must be converted to text-based dimensions to keep track of the current text location.

❑ *GetClientRect() acquires information from Windows about the size (in pixels) of the client area of the window.* This action is necessary because you want to center every line of text in the client area. The only way to do that is to count pixels (especially because the default font for Windows 3.0 is a variable pitch font).

❑ *GetTextExtent() determines the line length, in pixels, of a line of text.* The line length is used with the client area dimensions to compute the starting horizontal position for each line of centered text.

❑ *LOWORD() extracts the low-order word from a double word object.* This function-like macro is used to extract the horizontal dimensions of the current line of text from the double word (DWORD) returned by GetTextExtent().

❑ *TextOut() paints the line of text in the client area in the desired location.* Using arguments computed by the previous logic and function calls, TextOut() positions the current text line in the client area.

❑ *EndPaint() both releases the device context and tells Windows that the window is now valid.* BeginPaint() and EndPaint() must always be used in pairs, to begin and end the painting process.

It might seem that seven Windows calls are excessive for putting text on the screen, but there is a good reason for the added complexity. The simplicity of the easy.c sample program is misleading in this case. More overhead is required to control a window than to display a string using puts(). But the overhead is both necessary and acceptable because Windows programs typically do much more than plain DOS-based programs, and do it much more attractively (with graphics, windows, dialogs, and so on).

The processing required for the WM_DESTROY message is simple compared to the preceding code. Windows sends the WM_DESTROY message to the window procedure when the user pulls down the system menu in the window and selects Close. Because you cannot exit() a Windows program to end it, the code for handling WM_DESTROY sends *back to Windows* a message indicating that the program is finished, using the PostQuitMessage() Windows function call. Windows then sends that message to the main message loop in WinMain(). This causes the GetMessage() function to return a NULL value, which ends the while loop, and hence ends the program also.

Finally, look at line 104 of listing 20.2. This line of code calls the DefWindowProc() Windows function if all case statements for processing the message fail (fall through). As the function name indicates, the DefWindowProc() call invokes the Windows default window procedure for any messages that your window did not process. You should always code this function call as the last line in the main window procedure.

Setting Up Borland C++ 2.0 for Windows Applications Building

The IDE for Borland C++ 2.0 differs from the IDE for Turbo C++ version 1.0 and Turbo C version 2.0, just as you would expect when dealing with the Windows environment.

Borland C++ 2.0 has new options in the IDE menu and new transfer links for the new utilities that are used to compile and link a Windows application program. This section explores these new features and their implications for building Windows applications. Also included is an explanation of how to build the easy.c Windows executable file.

The compiler's job in building a Windows application program is only slightly different from building plain C or C++ modules. The compiler has always generated *prologs* (entry initialization code) and *epilogs* (exit deinitialization code) for C and C++ functions. But, up until now, it has done so only for the DOS environment, building standard DOS OBJ modules.

The linker's job in building a Windows application is quite different, however. A new set of run-time code (object modules and run-time libraries) is involved in building a Windows application program. The linker must now access different libraries to provide Windows-oriented initialization and run-time library code. For a small model Windows application program, for example, the C0WS.OBJ initialization module and the CWINS.LIB run-time library are used. The original initialization modules and run-time libraries are still available for plain DOS projects.

Setting Up Transfer Options for the Resource Compiler and the Import Librarian

Additional facilities must be invoked for building Windows application programs. Two new programs must run together with the normal compiler and linker to build a Windows application program. These new programs are the Resource Compiler (RC) and the Import Librarian (IMPLIB).

Whether or not either of these two new programs is run at compile and link time depends on what resources your Windows program needs. If you have included a resource script (RC) file in the project file list, RC will be invoked to produce the RES resource file (a binary format file). RC will also be invoked again later in the process to combine the RES file with the EXE file built by the linker to produce the completed Windows EXE file. The `easy.c` program has no RC file, so the first invocation of RC is not needed for that application.

The use of the Import Librarian (IMPLIB.EXE) may be confusing, until you grow accustomed to the new environment. If you have poked around in the Borland C++ 2.0 directories, you may have noticed that a file named IMPORT.LIB is in the `\integra\lib` directory (using directory names as found on the test system for this book). IMPORT.LIB contains information to aid your program's access to Windows functions. It is tempting to jump to the conclusion that IMPLIB is used to input the information in IMPORT.LIB to the compile and link information. But that is the wrong conclusion.

IMPLIB is used to *create* import libraries for your application code. These import libraries are similar to the supplied IMPORT.LIB file in that they contain information allowing other programs to access their contents, but such import libraries are unique to your application. IMPLIB is usually used to create import libraries (which have the LIB file extension) when you are building Dynamic

Link Libraries (DLLs). Setting IDE options for building DLLs is discussed in this chapter in the section "Setting Up Compiler Options for Entry and Exit Code." Writing the source code for a DLL is discussed in Chapter 22.

Running the IDE Alone

RC.EXE resides in the \integra\bin directory, with the TC.EXE program file. If \integra\bin is the current directory, or is in the current PATH environment variable, you can make or build the application from the IDE with no trouble. When the IDE is *not* running under Windows, the Resource Compiler will be found without requiring you to take any other actions, because Borland C++ 2.0 installs a transfer link to RC by default.

If you are more than a casual C programmer, you probably created several subdirectories containing source code for different projects or groups of projects, rather than lumped all source files in the \integra\bin directory. In this book, for example, all Windows applications code was placed in the \integra\pgm subdirectory. When you arrange source code in this fashion, you can use a DOS batch file such as the following one to set the DOS environment correctly before running the IDE:

```
PATH;
SET LIB=
SET INCLUDE=
PATH=C:\;C:\DOS;C:\INTEGRA\BIN
SET LIB=C:\INTEGRA\LIB
SET INCLUDE=C:\INTEGRA\INCLUDE
CD \INTEGRA\PGM
```

With the preceding batch file, you can navigate to the source code subdirectory of your choice, and maintain access to the Resource Compiler and its companion utility, RC2MSG.EXE. Incidentally, the rc2msg.c source code file can be found in \integra\examples, in case you are interested in the methods used to send RC messages back to the IDE message window.

Running the IDE under Windows

In this section, you examine the requirements for running the Borland C++ 2.0 IDE under Windows to build Windows applications. For this discussion, it does not matter whether you start the IDE with the TC (real mode) or TCX (protected mode) command. The same considerations apply in either case.

The problem is to establish a directory environment under Windows in which the IDE can find everything it needs to build a Windows application program. You can start the IDE in four basic ways; each affects the resulting application directory structure slightly differently. The four methods for starting the IDE follow:

❏ *Invoke the IDE from the Program Manager's File | Run menu selection*. Simply click the Program Manager's File menu item, click Run, and type in the complete path and file specification for the TC.EXE file. For example:

```
c:\integra\bin\tc.exe
```

Using this method to invoke the IDE, you can use the File | Change dir menu options to set the source file directory (to \integra\pgm2, for example). The problem with using this method is that there is neither a PATH environment variable available nor a transfer link for the RC2MSG.EXE message filter. The make will fail when this utility cannot be found. The Import Librarian, used when building DLLs, has a similar message filter named IMPL2MSG.EXE that presents similar transfer problems.

You can still use this method successfully, however, if you copy the RC2MSG.EXE, RCPP.ERR, and IMPL2MSG.EXE files to the source file directory you are using (for example, to c:\integra\pgm). You must also edit the Resource Compiler's and Import Librarian's Program Path (in the Modify/New Transfer Item options dialog), as discussed immediately following this list.

❏ *Create a program item in a Program Manager group, and enter the path and EXE file name in the Command Line edit box of the Program Item Properties dialog*. This method allows you to click an icon on the Program Manager's window to invoke the IDE. The transfer programs will experience the same problems as with the first method, however. You can get around those problems in the same manner.

❏ *Create a program item in a Program Manager group, and enter the path and file name of a DOS batch file in the Command Line edit box of the Program Item Properties dialog*. You can place such a batch file in the Windows directory or in the source file directory you will be working with. You can use a batch file of this sort, for example, when you want to run Borland C++ 2.0 in black-and-white mode rather than color mode for capturing screen images. Here is a sample batch file you can invoke from Windows to start the IDE:

```
set PATH=C:\;C:\INTEGRA\BIN
cd \integra\pgm2
tc
PATH=
cd \
```

The nice thing about using a batch file such as the preceding one is that the IDE will behave exactly as if it were running stand-alone. There will be no transfer problems, and there is no need to copy the message filter modules to a source file directory.

❏ *Create a Windows PIF file for the IDE session, and specify the path for the source code directory (the location of your source programs) in the Start-up Directory edit box of the PIF dialog*. You can create a PIF file for Borland C++ 2.0's IDE as well, and name that PIF file in the Program Item Properties dialog as the command-line value. There is little operational difference, however, between this method and the first two methods discussed in this section. There are still transfer and directory problems (which can still be worked around in the same fashion).

Of the four methods for invoking the IDE, the third method is clearly the most trouble free. Yet you may still find occasion to use the other methods. If you do use one of the other methods, you will have to update the Program Path value in the Modify/New Transfer Item dialog of Options | Transfer for both the Resource Compiler and the Import Librarian.

The default value for the Program Path for these two Transfer Items is simply the program name RC or IMPLIB. You must supply the \integra\bin path specification, as shown in figure 20.4. Updating the Program Path values in this fashion carries out the transfer successfully but does not interfere with the stand-alone operation of the IDE.

Setting Up Compiler Options for Entry and Exit Code

Borland C++ 2.0 has all the facilities you need to build both normal Windows application programs and Windows Dynamic Link Libraries (DLLs). Each kind of executable module, however, has its own requirements for program attributes.

Fig. 20.4. Setting the path for the Resource Compiler (RC) under the Borland C++ 2.0 IDE.

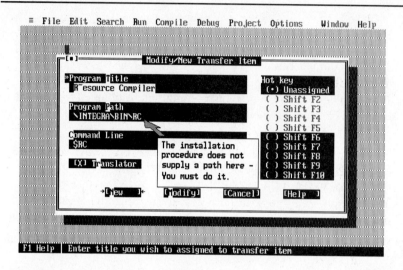

The main thing that the compiler must know is what kind of prolog and epilog (entry and exit code) to wrap around your program's functions. Any Windows program requires prologs and epilogs that differ from those used for DOS applications. Beyond that, Windows application programs require different prologs and epilogs from those needed by DLL functions. As you might imagine, incorrect settings for a program's compiler options will cause many problems, usually soon enough to prevent building the EXE file successfully.

You can use two methods to set the compiler and linker options for a Windows program or DLL. The first method involves setting every option individually, as follows:

❑ *Options | Compiler | Code Generation*

For a Windows program, use the Code Generation dialog box to choose the desired memory model. Do *not* use the tiny or huge memory model for any Windows executable file (either an application program or a DLL), but you *can* use the remaining memory models for both application programs and DLLs.

You should be aware that using the small memory model for building a DLL module is begging for trouble: a DLL module *must* address its data segment using far-sized addresses. As you will see shortly, Borland C++ 2.0 uses the compact memory model for DLLs when you let the IDE use default values, for this very reason.

❏ *Options | Compiler | Entry/Exit Code*

Choose either Windows Application or Windows DLL from this dialog box. *Be certain* not to allow DOS Standard or DOS Overlay to remain in effect when building a Windows application. If you do not select the correct type of prolog and epilog code for your program, it will not work correctly.

❏ *Options | Make*

The Make dialog box allows you to control whether to generate an import library for a DLL, and if so, where to collect the names of exported functions. You should probably set the Use DLL Exports option until you understand the process of building DLLs fairly well.

❏ *Options | Linker*

From the Linker dialog box you should select the Windows Application or Windows DLL option, as appropriate. Again, be sure that the DOS Standard or DOS Overlaid options are *not* selected for any Windows application.

Using the individual option settings gives you the most flexibility in setting up the IDE to build a Windows application. That method gives enough leeway, in fact, to foul things up considerably. There is a safer and quicker way to set the IDE options for a Windows application. This is the second method of setting the compiler and linker options, and it is to use the Options | Application menu selection. This selection pops up the Set Application Options dialog box, as shown in figure 20.5.

Fig. 20.5. Setting IDE options for compiling and linking a Windows application program using Set Application Options.

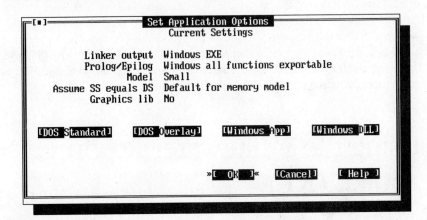

Figure 20.5 shows the Set Application Options dialog box with the Windows Application option selected. All you have to do is select that one option, and all the other required options (except memory model) are set to default values for you. There is not much room for errors here.

Setting up the IDE for a Windows DLL using the Set Application Options dialog box is equally simple. This selection is illustrated in figure 20.6.

Fig. 20.6. Setting IDE options for compiling and linking a Windows DLL file using Set Application Options.

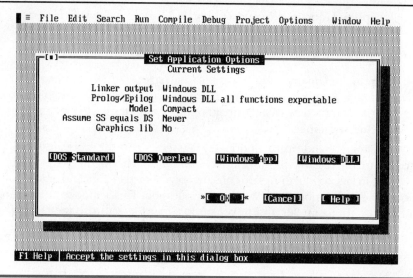

Notice that the memory model in figure 20.6 is set to Compact. This is the default for a Windows DLL because a DLL must access its data segment using far addresses—something that is difficult using the small memory model. Notice also that the Assume SS equals DS option is set to No. This is because a DLL module always uses its caller's stack so that the stack segment (SS) and data segment (DS) can never be the same. More information on this subject is in Chapter 22, when you are shown how to write a simple DLL.

Using the Whitewater Resource Toolkit (RT)

Because a Windows application is object-oriented, it uses a number of *resources* to accomplish certain tasks in the Windows environment. A Windows resource is both a *thing* and an *actor* (that is, a thing that can act on itself). This sounds a lot like C++ class objects, and Windows resources are a lot like class objects. A Windows menu, for instance, is a thing that displays options the user can choose in the window, and it can report to its owner program what the selected option was.

Windows resources include such things as memory, the display, the keyboard, the system printer, menus, icons, bit maps, strings, and keyboard accelerators (hot key definitions). To introduce you to the world of Windows resources in a concrete context, the remainder of this chapter describes the kinds of resources needed by a fairly lengthy Windows program called FCWIN (its project name), which is developed in detail in Chapters 21 and 22.

FCWIN is a financial calculator program that does a number of interesting and useful things with money calculations. FCWIN uses a Windows menu to detect the user's choices, and dialog boxes to input data and display results. The dialog boxes use such resources as edit boxes, static text, group boxes, list boxes, and pushbuttons. The system printer will be used, and you can use an icon (a dollar bill—what else?) to add FCWIN to a Program Manager group.

Further, the resources for FCWIN are presented in the context of the Whitewater Resource Toolkit (RT) that was used to create them. You won't write many Windows applications using Borland C++ 2.0 without RT, so this is a good place for an introduction to that indispensable utility.

Setting Up RT as a Windows Program Item

Windows resources are traditionally described as being created in source form (with a text editor) in an RC (resource script) file. The resource script is then compiled by the Resource Compiler into a RES (resource) file that can be incorporated into the Windows executable program file.

RT can short-circuit all that. With RT, you can create resources in a graphical Windows environment (by drawing them), and store them directly into a RES file. The FCWIN application has a resource file named FCWIN.RES. All of the resources described in the following sections were stored in the FCWIN.RES file. (FCWIN.RES is included in the program diskette for this book. The program diskette is offered separately: see the insert at the back of the book.)

RT can be run only under Windows, because it uses Windows' GUI. The first step, therefore, is to set up RT as a program item under Program Manager, so that you can run it by simply clicking its icon with the mouse. Figure 20.7

shows the Program Item Properties dialog box with the required inputs to define RT as a Windows application.

Fig. 20.7. Using the Program Manager's Program Item Properties dialog box to set up RT as a Windows application item.

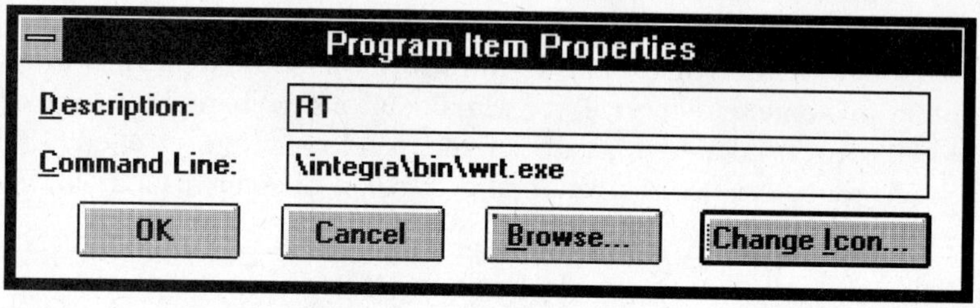

Notice that the executable file name for RT is WRT.EXE (*W*hitewater Group *R*esource *T*oolkit). The executable file resides in the `\integra\bin` subdirectory, together with TC and the other Borland C++ 2.0 utilities.

Resources Needed by the *fcwin.c* Sample Program

You may have already surmised that a single RES file can contain a number of different resources. That is the case with FCWIN.RES. The FCWIN.RES file contains 16 resources: 1 icon, 1 menu, and 14 dialog boxes (14 types of financial calculations are supported).

Each resource in a RES file has associated with it a *resource name*, an identifier by which it is made known to Windows. Table 20.1 lists all the resources used by FCWIN, along with their names, types, and uses.

This chapter won't show you a sample of every resource used by FCWIN, but will present an example of each significant kind of resource usage. (The binary format `fcwin.res` file is included on the program diskette offered at the back of the book. The resource scripts—in RC file format—for all the FCWIN resources are presented in Appendix E.) First, however, you need to know something about running and using RT.

Table 20.1. FCWIN resources and names.

Resource Name	Type Resource	Description
FCICON	Icon	The dollar bill icon for the application
FCMENU	Menu	The menu for the application, including the main menu bar pull-down entries
FCEFFCON	Dialog box	Dialog, effective interest rate with continuous compounding
FCEFFPER	Dialog box	Dialog, effective interest rate with periodic compounding
FCFVANN	Dialog box	Dialog, future value of an annuity
FCFVSIN	Dialog box	Dialog, future value of a single amount
FCLOANDA	Dialog box	Dialog, mortgage loan data entry
FCMKUPCO	Dialog box	Dialog, markup over cost
FCMKUPPR	Dialog box	Dialog, markup over price
FCMORTLS	Dialog box	Dialog, display amortization schedule in a scrollable list box
FCMORTPR	Dialog box	Dialog, setup and send amortization schedule to system printer
FCPAYOUT	Dialog box	Dialog, display loan payout analysis
FCPCTCG	Dialog box	Dialog, percent change in amount
FCPCTTO	Dialog box	Dialog, percent of total amount
FCPVANN	Dialog box	Dialog, present value of an annuity
FCPVSIN	Dialog box	Dialog, present value of stated amount

Running RT

Starting RT is quite simple: after you have set it up under Program Manager as described previously, just click RT's icon, and off you go.

Navigating RT's Main Window

When RT starts, its main window is displayed on the screen. The main window for RT was used in figure 20.2 to illustrate the object-oriented nature of Windows. Look at that figure again, and you will see that the RT main window has a row of seven pushbuttons across the client area of the window, one for each kind of resource that RT can create or edit.

When you want to create a new resource, click the pushbutton for that kind of resource, and a child window for the resource's editor will appear. How to use the editor windows will be covered in a moment. Right now, think about how you will create the RES file initially.

Each editor window has a menu structure that is familiar to Windows users. The first item on the menu bar is the File selection. Under the File selection, you will see the Save As option. You can create the resource file, and the first resource you want to store in it, using the Save As selection with the following procedure:

1. From RT's main window, click the pushbutton for the kind of re-source you want to create. This starts the editor for that resource. Edit the resource until you are finished creating it.

2. Click the File menu item and then click the Save As item. You are prompted for the file name in which to store the resource (the file will be created if necessary). The File dialog box has the directory and file name list boxes usual in Windows applications. Navigate to the desired directory and type in the resource file's name. Be sure that the file extension is RES. Click OK.

3. You are prompted to enter the resource's attributes. In most cases, you need to type only the resource name (such as one of those in table 20.1). Click OK again.

The named resource will be stored in the requested file, creating the file if necessary. Note that this procedure *replaces* an existing resource file if you select a file name that matches the existing file's name.

When you want to create a new resource and store it in an *existing* file (without replacing the entire file), you should use a similar procedure, but select the Save Into menu item rather than Save As:

1. From RT's main window, click the pushbutton for the kind of resource you want to create. This starts the editor for that resource. Edit the resource until you are finished creating it.

2. Click the File menu item, then click the Save Into item. You are prompted for the file name in which to store the resource. Use the directory and file name list boxes to locate the existing resource file. Click OK.

3. You are now prompted to enter the new resource's attributes. Click OK and the job is finished.

Using the Resource Browser

Now you know how to create new resources. What if you want to edit an existing resource in an existing RES file? That is where RT's *resource browsers* can be used. A resource browser opens a resource file and displays the types and names of the resources in that file in a drop-down combo list box.

Two resource browsers are on the main RT window (this is useful when you want to copy resources from one RES file to another). Each of the browsers has an Open and a New pushbutton. Click the Open pushbutton to pop up a directory-file list box, from which you can navigate to and select the resource file you want to edit.

Having opened the resource file, you will see a resource type in the drop-down box, and a list of resources in that file having the indicated type. Figure 20.8, for example, shows the FCWIN.RES file opened in Browser 1, with the Dialog type selected. The list box below the drop-down box has a scroll bar, indicating that there are more dialogs in FCWIN.RES than can be displayed at one time. To edit a resource, just scroll to it and click it, and then click the Edit pushbutton in the middle of the window. The editor for that resource type will be started, and the resource will be loaded, ready for modifications.

Fig. 20.8. The RT Browser showing a menu of dialog boxes for FCWIN.

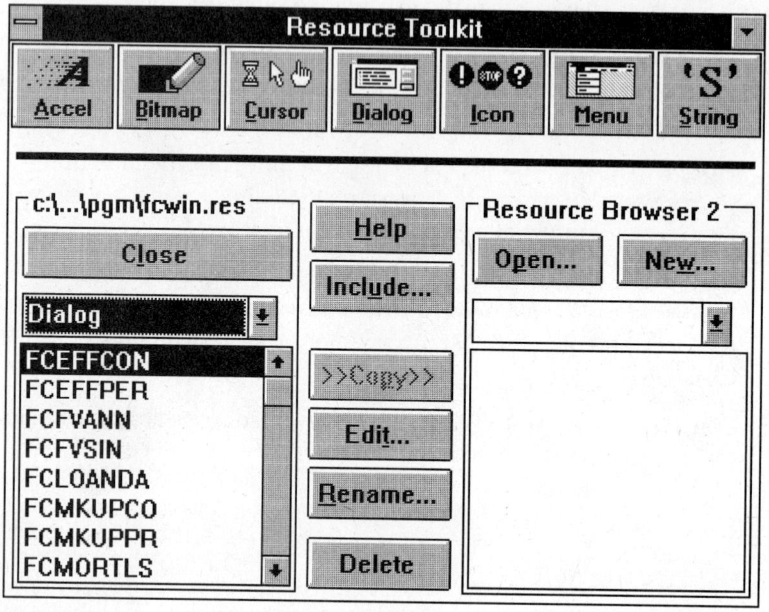

Creating and Editing Icons

The dollar bill icon (FCICON resource name) was the first resource created for FCWIN, using the first procedure previously described (that is, the procedure for creating a new resource and a new RES file). Figure 20.9 shows the icon editor with FCICON loaded and ready to be edited.

An icon is ridiculously simple to create. Just select the pencil tool and draw the icon by dragging the pencil. You can also click individual pixels to set them to the current drawing color. What you see is what you get.

Creating and Editing Menus

Before you look at the next figure, think about the structure of a Windows menu. The menu bar across the top of the client area contains a list of items, each of which is itself a pop-up menu.

Fig. 20.9. Using the Icon editor to create the dollar bill icon for FCWIN.

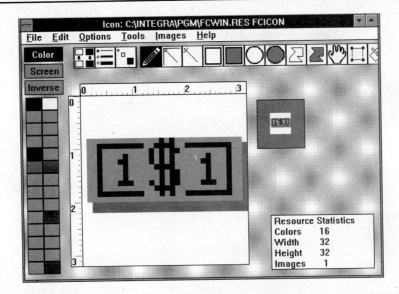

The first item on the menu bar of the FCWIN application, for instance, is General Business. Clicking this item will display a pop-up menu containing four more items (in a drop-down format). With that in mind, now look at how this menu structure is defined by the RT menu editor in figure 20.10.

Notice the two boxes in figure 20.10 labeled Item Text and Value. The Item Text field contains the text of the menu item as it will appear on the screen. The Value field contains an ordinal value, an integer, that will eventually be used to identify to your program which item was clicked by a user.

Next, notice that the ordinal value for General Business is zero. This, plus the fact that the item text is not indented, indicates that the text is the name of a pop-up menu. The four items following General Business are indented (to indent an item, use the arrow pushbuttons just above the Item Text box), and have nonzero ordinal values.

The unindented items (the ones with the zero values) in FCMENU are not reported to your program when they are clicked. Windows simply pops up the associated submenu (the following group of indented items). If a user should then click an item from the pop-up menu, Windows reports *that* to your program. It does so by sending a WM_COMMAND message to WndProc() (the main window procedure), and supplying a function argument that has the same value as the ordinal value of the menu item. You use a switch statement, similar to those you saw in listing 20.2, to interpret which menu item was selected.

Fig. 20.10. *Using the Menu editor to create the main menu and pull-down menus for FCWIN.*

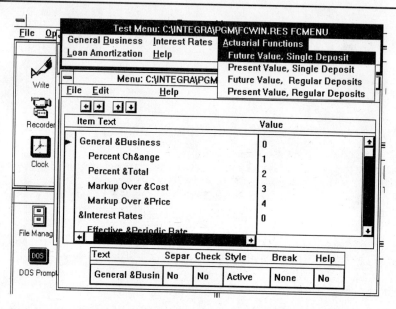

To show you the entire menu structure for FCWIN, and to demonstrate what it takes to define menus in a resource script file, FCMENU has been converted to a resource script file and is presented in listing 20.3. You can see in that listing all the pop-up menu items and the ordinal values for the selectable items. It is enough to make one glad that there is a tool like RT. Do not bother with RC files—use RT instead to create RES files directly. It will save you many hours of work, particularly when you are constructing other (more complicated) resources.

Listing 20.3. `fcmenu.rc`. *Resource script for the FCWIN menu.*

```
1   FCMENU   MENU PRELOAD MOVEABLE PURE DISCARDABLE
2   BEGIN
3     POPUP "General &Business"
4     BEGIN
5       MenuItem   "Percent Ch&ange", 1
6       MenuItem   "Percent &Total", 2
7       MenuItem   "Markup Over &Cost", 3
```

```
 8        MenuItem  "Markup Over &Price", 4
 9      END
10      POPUP "&Interest Rates"
11      BEGIN
12        MenuItem  "Effective &Periodic Rate", 5
13        MenuItem  "Effective &Continuous Rate", 6
14      END
15      POPUP "&Actuarial Functions"
16      BEGIN
17        MenuItem  "Future Value, Single Deposit", 7
18        MenuItem  "Present Value, Single Deposit", 8
19        MenuItem  "Future Value,  Regular Deposits", 9
20        MenuItem  "Present Value, Regular Deposits", 10
21      END
22      POPUP "&Loan Amortization"
23      BEGIN
24        MenuItem  "&Input Loan Data", 11
25        MenuItem  "Payout &Analysis", 12
26        MenuItem  "&Display Amortization Table", 13
27        MenuItem  "&Print Amortization Table", 14
28      END
29      POPUP "&Help"
30      BEGIN
31        MenuItem  "Percent Change", 15
32        MenuItem  "PerCent Total", 16
33        MenuItem  "Markup Percent of Cost", 17
34        MenuItem  "Markup Percent of Price", 18
35        MenuItem  "Effective Rate, Periodic", 19
36        MenuItem  "Effective Rate, Continuous", 20
37        MenuItem  "Future Value, Single Payment", 21
38        MenuItem  "Present Value, Single Payment", 22
39        MenuItem  "Future Value, Regular Deposits", 23
40        MenuItem  "Present Value, Regular Deosits", 24
41        MenuItem  "Input Loan Data", 25
42        MenuItem  "Payout Analysis", 26
43        MenuItem  "Display Amortization Table", 27
44        MenuItem  "Print Amortization Table", 28
45        MenuItem  " ", 0
46      END
47    END
```

Creating and Editing Dialog Boxes

Dialog boxes are the meat and potatoes of FCWIN. All the work is accomplished in a dialog box, whatever financial calculation is being performed. The reason for this approach is simple—it is the easiest way to get into some sophisticated Windows programming.

It is easy to pack a lot of function into a simple-looking dialog box. For example, look at figure 20.11, which shows the Percent Change dialog box being edited in RT.

Fig. 20.11. The Percent Change dialog box combines input fields, output fields, and pushbuttons.

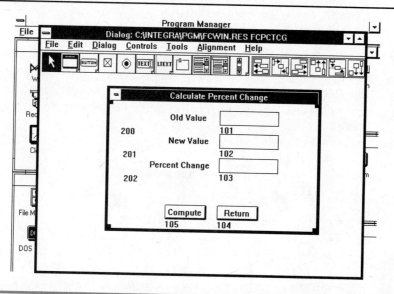

The Percent Change dialog has two edit boxes (numbers 101 and 102 in the figure 20.11) into which the user types the "old" and "new" amounts to be used in the computation. The last box (number 103) is an edit box, but attributes have been assigned to it so that it cannot be tabbed to or typed into. It is used strictly for displaying results. The edit boxes (and other items in the dialog box, too) are called controls, and the numbers shown with them are their ordinal values—like the values for menu items you just read about.

The nice thing about dialog boxes is shown in FCWIN: the application program can control the entire dialog box simply by watching for a WM_COMMAND message with an argument corresponding to the Compute pushbutton (value 105). When that message is detected, the dialog function (explained in Chapters 21 and 22) needs only to read the text in the edit controls, convert the input data to numeric values, compute, and place the answer in the Percent Change edit control (103). Similarly, when the Return pushbutton is detected (value 104), the dialog can end.

It should now be obvious that controlling menus and dialog boxes involves a lot of ordinal values. The application program must know about all these values to control processing logic. This requirement could result in a serious logistical problem, without some means of keeping track of all these numbers. That means is the application header file.

You may recall that the application header for the easy.c program was almost empty, but you were warned that larger programs utilize the header heavily. FCWIN is one of those larger programs (though still not very complicated). One of the first tasks in designing FCWIN was deciding which ordinal values would signify a particular control. The resulting value assignments are shown in table 20.2. The assignment of values is made by means of a #define object-like macro; the table shows macro names and corresponding values. Using the macro names in the program's source code instead of ordinal values makes it possible for the programmer to keep up with what is happening (as opposed to getting completely lost!).

Table 20.2. Ordinal value assignments used by FCWIN.

Control Macro Name	Ordinal Value Assigned
IDM_PCTCHANGE	1
IDM_PCTTOTAL	2
IDM_MKUPCOST	3
IDM_MKUPPRICE	4
IDM_EFFPER	5
IDM_EFFCONT	6
IDM_FVSINGLE	7
IDM_PVSINGLE	8
IDM_FVREGULAR	9
IDM_PVREGULAR	10
IDM_LOANDATA	11

Table 20.2. continues

Table 20.2. *continued*

Control Macro Name	Ordinal Value Assigned
IDM_PAYOUT	12
IDM_DISPAMORT	13
IDM_PRNTAMORT	14
HLP_PCTCHANGE	15
HLP_PCTTOTAL	16
HLP_MKUPCOST	17
HLP_MKUPPRICE	18
HLP_EFFPER	19
HLP_EFFCONT	20
HLP_FVSINGLE	21
HLP_PVSINGLE	22
HLP_FVREGULAR	23
HLP_PVREGULAR	24
HLP_LOANDATA	25
HLP_PAYOUT	26
HLP_DISPAMORT	27
HLP_PRNTAMORT	28
FCWIN_OLD	101
FCWIN_NEW	102
FCWIN_ANS	103
FCWIN_RETURN	104
FCWIN_COMPUTE	105
FCWIN_APR	106
FCWIN_AMT	107
FCWIN_YEARS	108

Control Macro Name	Ordinal Value Assigned
FCWIN_FREQ	109
FCWIN_LISTBOX	110
FCWIN_LEVELPAY	111
FCWIN_INTPAY	112
FCWIN_TOTPAY	113
FCWIN_BALLOON	114
FCWIN_START	115
FCWIN_CANCEL	116

You already know about the ordinal values assigned to menu selection items. But why are the values for edit boxes assigned beginning with 101? That is the default starting value used by the RT editors, and it was convenient to go along with it. Note that the values assigned to controls in different dialogs can be reused: the values 101–105 are almost always used in all 14 dialog boxes for FCWIN.

You may have noticed in figure 20.11 that the ordinal values for static text are assigned beginning with 200; in table 20.2, there are no macros for these items. This is because a control must have an ordinal value, but these values are not needed for FCWIN. Therefore, these values were conveniently separated from values actually used.

Some dialogs, such as the Mortgage Loan Data Entry dialog, do not display answers; they just collect input data. Figure 20.12 shows this dialog box under edit. The figure shows also how to assign the control attributes just mentioned.

To edit the attributes for a control, first click the RT editor's Controls menu item, popping up the Item Attributes dialog box (dialog boxes editing other dialog boxes!). Next click the Item Attributes Style push button, popping up the Styles dialog box for that control. In figure 20.12, the static text field *Mortgage loan amount* (number 200) is being styled.

Other dialogs have only output fields, such as the Payout Analysis dialog shown in figure 20.13. The edit boxes for output-only fields are styled Visible, Disabled (no input allowed), and the Tabstop checkbox is turned off.

Fig. 20.12. The Input Loan Data dialog box has only input fields and one push button.

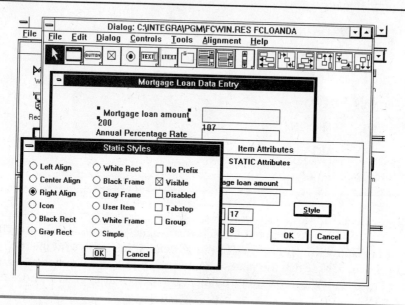

Fig. 20.13. The Payout Analysis dialog box has only output fields and one push button.

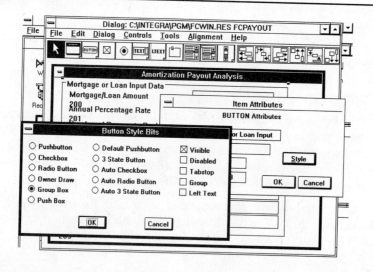

Notice that figure 20.13 shows the group box labeled *Mortgage or Loan Input Data* being styled. The RT editor indicates that the group box is a button, from the point of view of Windows administration of objects.

FCWIN uses another powerful window control, the list box. Figure 20.14 shows the Display Amortization Schedule dialog's list box being edited.

Fig. 20.14. *The Display Amortization Schedule dialog box has a Windows list box as it most important feature.*

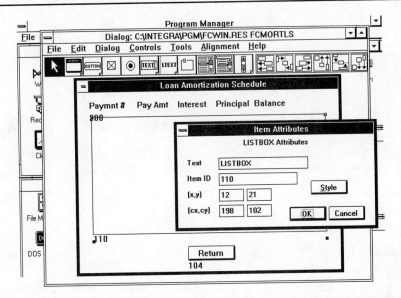

If you look at the program listing for fcwin.c (in Chapter 21, listing 21.2), you can see how the text strings are added to the list box. You can see also how little effort is required to control a list box's scrolling display. (No effort is required: Windows does it all!)

The visual effect of a list box is quite pleasing, making it an attractive feature for users of your program. Figure 20.15 shows the list box just edited in action, as FCWIN runs.

This has been a whirlwind tour of the resources used by the FCWIN project. If you want to get better acquainted with RT, there is only one good way to do so—go play with your new toy! The Windows graphical interfaces to the editors make the learning process easy and intuitive (the whole point of a GUI).

Fig. 20.15. *The Display Amortization Schedule dialog box in action, displaying a Windows list box.*

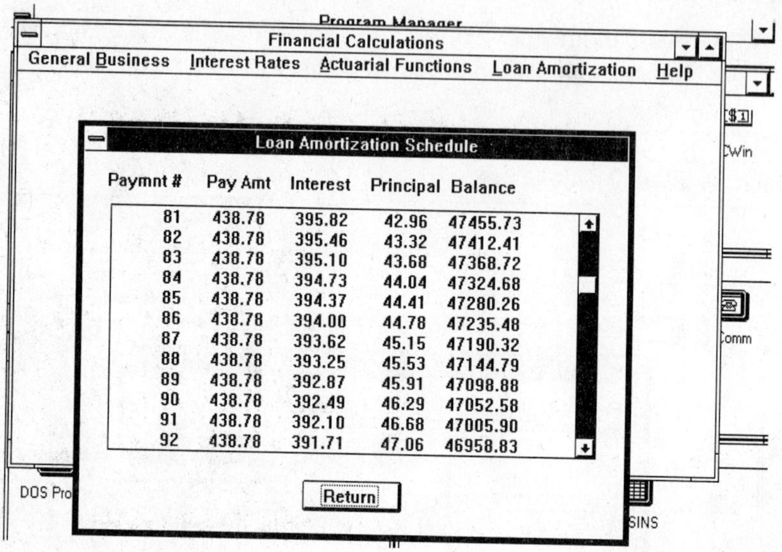

Exercises

The following exercises give you practice in working with Windows and developing code for the Windows environment.

1. Use the Resource Toolkit to create an icon for easy.c (just Save As an ICO file, for now). Use the icon to set up EASY as an item in a Program Manager group.

2. Use the easy.c source code as a skeleton for a program that paints your text in the client area of the window. Try writing the code so that only the first line of text is centered; left justify the remainder. Here is a tip for positioning the left-justified lines: assume a left margin of 40 pixels. This would require a TextOut() function like the following one:

```
TextOut( hDc, 40, (i+1)*LineSpace,
        (LPSTR)HelloMsgs[i], strlen(HelloMsgs[i]) );
```

You will need a project file to build the application's EXE file, as described in this chapter. The project file should contain references to `easy.c` and `easy.def`. Before making the project, do not forget to set IDE options correctly for a Windows application (the small memory model is fine for this exercise).

You will also need to consult the next chapter briefly to get the WINSTUB file, assemble it, and link it. WINSTUB.EXE is named in the `easy.def` file, and will have to be present to build the application.

Summary

This chapter introduced you to a number of new ideas. Before you read the next chapter, be sure you have grasped the following ideas:

❏ *The Windows Graphical User Interface (GUI) is different*. Windows is a multitasking, object-oriented environment. Your experiences as a C++ programmer should have helped prepare you for this new environment. Working with a GUI requires several important structural changes to your programs.

❏ *There are two required functions in a Windows application program*. The first is the `WinMain()` function, and it must have that name. The second required function is the main window procedure. It is usually named `WndProc()`, but you can choose another name. You tell Windows about the main window procedure during window class registration.

❏ *A Windows application program is driven by the main message loop*. The main message loop is the most critical part of your Windows program. It receives messages from Windows, translates them, and dispatches them. The main window procedure is reached only indirectly, through messages dispatched by the main message loop.

❏ *The main window procedure handles and acts on all messages for the main window*. You saw in this chapter how the `WM_PAINT` and `WM_DESTROY` messages are used. In the next two chapters (developing FCWIN), you will see how the `WM_CREATE` and `WM_COMMAND` messages can be used. The `WM_COMMAND` message identifies selected menu items to your application program.

❏ *Borland C++ 2.0's IDE must be properly configured to build Windows application programs*. In particular, you need to be sure that the Windows entry and exit code (prologs and epilogs) for functions is correct. DOS prologs and epilogs will not work in the Windows environment, and prologs and epilogs for Windows applications and Windows DLLs differ from each other, too.

❑ *The Resource Toolkit is the most important tool you have for creating resources for Windows programs.* With RT, you can draw resources quickly and easily. Do not waste time and energy writing resource script (RC) files; create resources with RT and build the RES file directly. RT's resource browsers also provide a means for easily editing existing resources.

21

Designing Windows Applications

The previous two chapters introduced you to the many new C and C++ features of Borland C++ 2.0 and showed you how to use the Whitewater Group Resource Toolkit (RT) to create and edit various resources for use by Windows applications programs. This chapter and the next guide you through the development of a Windows program written with Borland C++ 2.0. First, however, you need to understand the basic components of a Windows executable (EXE) file, and how Windows uses directories in storing and running its applications programs. The text is directed to readers who are familiar with the operation and handling characteristics of Windows from a user's point of view.

Setting Up the Windows Application Environment

Borland has done the work necessary for the IDE and Turbo Debugger to run under Windows, and has provided the tools for you to do program development for Windows *under* Windows. Some things remain, however, for you to do to prepare *your* program to run under Windows. You must provide a Windows stub program, and you must know where you can place your executable file, any DLLs you create, and other Windows resources that your program may need.

Building Your Own Windows Stub Executable File

What happens if you try to run a Windows application program without using Windows to run it? For example, suppose you change to the Windows directory and attempt to execute the Notepad program directly. You will receive the following message:

```
This program requires Microsoft Windows.
```

To understand what happened, you must understand that a Windows executable file contains a good deal more than a simple DOS program file. You can find out how much more if you own the Microsoft C 6.0 compiler and thus have access to the EXEHDR.EXE program. This program analyzes EXE files and reports their structure and contents (for Windows programs as well as DOS programs). Running EXEHDR against the NOTEPAD.EXE file in the Windows directory yields the following report:

```
Microsoft (R) EXE File Header Utility  Version 2.01
Copyright (C) Microsoft Corp 1985-1990.  All rights reserved.

Module:                  NOTEPAD
Description:             Microsoft Windows Notepad
                           Application (c)1989
Data:                   NONSHARED
Initial CS:IP:          seg   1 offset 19d4
Initial SS:SP:          seg   8 offset 0000
Extra stack allocation:  1000 bytes
DGROUP:                 seg   8

no. type address   file   mem    flags
  1 CODE 000007a0 032fb 032fb PRELOAD, (movable), (discardable)
  2 CODE 00003e00 0057a 0057a PRELOAD, (movable), (discardable)
  3 CODE 00004c20 0079d 0079e (movable), (discardable)
  4 CODE 00005500 00240 00240 (movable), (discardable)
  5 CODE 00005770 0066a 0066a (movable), (discardable)
  6 CODE 00005ec0 005f6 005f6 (movable), (discardable)
  7 CODE 00006580 0014a 0014a (movable), (discardable)
  8 DATA 00004480 00738 00738 PRELOAD, (movable)


Exports:
ord seg offset name
```

```
 1    1   0541   NPWNDPROC exported
 9    5   040b   FNABOUT exported
12    1   0a90   FNABORTPROC exported
11    1   0afe   FNABORTDLGPROC exported
10    6   00d6   DLGFNOPEN exported
14    1   10f7   PAGESETUP exported
 3    3   0000   FNSAVEAS exported
 8    5   0000   FNFIND exported
13    1   2864   DLGFNPRINTSETUP exported
```

Clearly, many kinds of information are recorded in a Windows program EXE file which are not found in a DOS EXE file. One important new item—which is not visible in the preceding report—is the Windows stub. The *stub* is itself an EXE program, but you connect it to your Windows application program. Its sole function is to produce a message (such as the one shown previously) when someone attempts to run the program without Windows and then to return to DOS. The stub is a required bit of protection present in *all* Windows programs.

Thus, you must provide a stub for your Windows programs too. The name of the stub program can be anything you want, but in this book it will be called WINSTUB (the traditionally used name). Borland does not supply a WINSTUB.EXE file with Borland C++ 2.0 (at least, not in the beta version used when this book was written), so you must supply your own. Fortunately, this is very easy to do. You can write the stub in C, but the resulting EXE file will be much larger than is needed. An assembler routine does the job just as well and is very short. Listing 21.1 is a `winstub.asm` source program you can use for this purpose.

Listing 21.1. `winstub.asm`. *Source code for your own Windows stub executable file.*

```
 1            .MODEL   small
 2            .STACK   100h
 3            .DATA
 4    HelloMessage DB 'This application requires Windows 3.x'
              DB 13,10,'$'
 5            .CODE
 6            mov   ax,@data
 7            mov   ds,ax        ; adrs of dseg in ds
 8            mov   ah,9         ; DOS print screen function
 9            mov   dx,offset HelloMessage
10            int   21h          ; call DOS
11            mov   ah,4ch       ; DOS terminate function
12            int   21h          ; call DOS
13            end
```

If you have the entire Borland C++ 2.0 package (including Turbo Assembler), this assembler program may look familiar. It should—it is a slightly modified version of the first sample program in the *Turbo Assembler User's Guide*.

Assemble and link the WINSTUB.ASM file, and place the EXE file in the same directory in which you keep the source code for your Borland C++ Windows programs. You do not need to add its name to a Project or MAKE file when building the complete program.

You *do* need to name the stub EXE file in the module definition file, which you create later in this chapter, in "Creating a Module Definition File." Then when you MAKE or Build the complete application's EXE file using the IDE, the Resource Compiler (RC) is invoked to combine the stub EXE with your Windows program's EXE file. You can build the WINSTUB.EXE file with the following simple commands:

```
tasm winstub
tlink winstub
```

Understanding Windows Directory Usage

You will use several disk directories when developing Windows applications. These directories and what can be placed in them are important. It is assumed in this discussion that Borland C++ 2.0 is installed in the \integra directory, and that Windows is in the \windows directory. The following directories and subdirectories are used by your program and Windows at run time:

❏ \integra\pgm

This is the current directory (the one that contains your program's source and EXE files). The current directory can be any directory you want. If your program has an associated DLL (dynamic link library), it can reside in the current directory also, but it is not required to reside there. Establishing a current directory while running under Windows is discussed after this list.

❏ \windows

This is the main Windows directory. You can place your application programs here, but you usually should not do so. If your program has an associated DLL, it can reside here if it is not in the same directory as your program's EXE file. The name of this directory does not have to be `windows`; its name can be obtained at run time by using the `GetWindowsDirectory()` Windows function.

❏ `\windows\system`

This is the Windows system subdirectory. It contains module and DLL files that are basic components of Windows. You usually should not place your program's EXE file here, though you might want to place an associated DLL in this directory. This subdirectory can also have a different name. The name of the Windows system subdirectory can be obtained at run time by using the `GetSystemDirectory()` Windows function.

❏ `PATH=\`*`directoryname`*

Both programs and DLLs can be placed in a directory named in the PATH environment variable. PATH is established before starting Windows.

❏ *A mapped network directory*

If you are running Windows on a network, directories are available from the network. Windows can search these directories for programs and other resources.

When Windows looks for a program or resource, the directories in the preceding list are searched in the order shown.

Of all the directories listed, the current directory may not be set in concrete—it can vary for different applications. Additionally, when you start Windows, the `\windows` directory is the DOS current directory. So what is the current directory as far as your program is concerned?

The current directory for your program is whatever path you specified to execute the program. You specify a path when you execute a program by selecting Program Manager | File | Run and typing in the execution name as follows:

```
c:\integra\pgm\fcwin.exe
```

The current directory for `fcwin.exe` is now `c:\integra\pgm`.

You do much the same thing when you install your program as a Program Item in a Program Manager group window. When you define the Program Item Properties of the item (your program), or when you create a PIF file for the program, you must still type the execution path. In all cases, when Windows runs your program, the specified execution path becomes the current directory for the duration of the program—but only for that program. Any programs running concurrently will probably have a different current directory.

Learn by Doing: Designing *fcwin.c*

Enough preliminaries: it is time to write some Windows code with Borland C++ 2.0. The sample code is borrowed from the `finance.c` financial calculator program, which was presented in *Using C*, published by Que Corporation. There is a twist, however. That simple program is recast into a Windows application that uses the Graphical User Interface (GUI) of Windows. The program has now become `fcwin.c`, and supports movable, sizable windows, with a complete pull-down menu system, fourteen dialogs for the various calculations, and a dynamic printer configuration dialog for spooled hard-copy output. The program also uses a DLL to support a complete help facility. Figure 21.1 shows a dialog box created by FCWIN.

Fig. 21.1. FCWIN uses the Windows GUI to create a finished, attractive application.

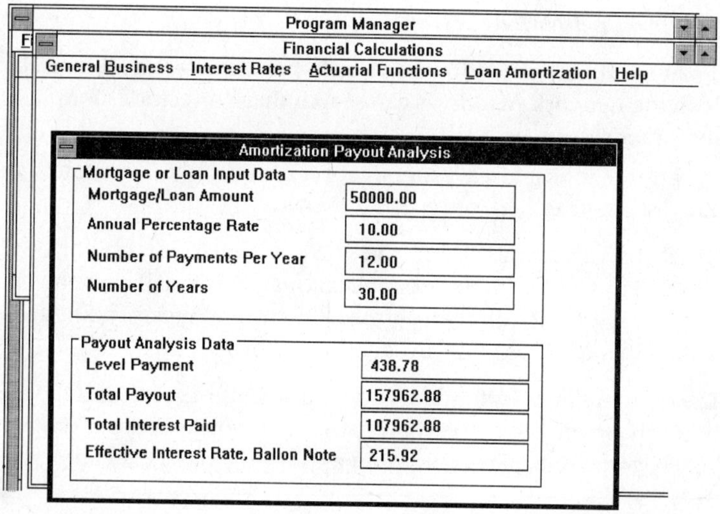

Although `fcwin.c` is lengthy, it is a straightforward program that uses only a limited number of Windows resources, and can be compiled using the small memory model (but this is about as large as you want a program to get with the small model). The remainder of this chapter and Chapter 22 examine the `fcwin.c` program, looking specifically at the following techniques:

❏ *Building the main program file and its support files*. It will probably not surprise you to learn that more is required of a program (and its programmer) in the Windows environment. You must add Windows support material to the source file, and modify the compile and link procedures. The remainder of this chapter presents most of the source files for the application, and begins to explain their uses. Because there is a lot of source code, the discussion of FCWIN is continued in Chapter 22. The help DLL source files are also presented and explained in Chapter 22.

❑ *Writing the main message loop*. The main message loop is required in every Windows program, and it must be coded in a function named `WinMain()`. The `WinMain()` function registers the window class (if this is the first execution instance of the program), creates the main window (the *frame* window), and then loops while dispatching messages it receives. Messages come from two sources: the window procedure you code or Windows itself.

❑ *Writing the window procedure*. The window procedure handles messages received, and can send messages back to `WinMain()` and Windows. This function is typically named `WndProc()`, and performs such functions as creating dialogs and child windows and calling support functions.

❑ *Setting up and writing dialog procedures*. A dialog invites user interaction, and is probably the easiest and quickest way to begin writing sophisticated Windows applications. A dialog procedure is a *callback* function, which means that the function is called by Windows, not from your code. You will be shown how to set this up, and how to utilize controls for the dialog (edit boxes, list boxes, static controls, and other things).

❑ *Using a Windows printer device*. Learning how to establish a device context for a device will prepare you for controlling the window display (or other devices, such as communications ports). Much of what you learn here about using GDI (Graphics Device Interface) calls can be applied directly to programming the window display.

❑ *Building and using a DLL*. A Dynamic Link Library can allow resources (such as common functions and bit maps) to be shared between several programs running concurrently, without duplicating those resources. A DLL can also help you simplify a program and control its size. FCWIN uses a DLL to implement the display of all the help message boxes. This moves both the logic for this task and the text associated with it out of the `fcwin.c` module.

The source code for `fcwin.c` is presented in listing 21.2. Much of what you see in listing 21.2 will be confusing if this is your first exposure to Windows programming, but it will become less confusing as you continue to read. Just remember that the results of writing Windows programs can be more than satisfying—they can be spectacular.

Listing 21.2. `fcwin.c.` *Financial calculator program using Windows 3.0 GUI.*

```
1    #include <stdio.h>
2    #include <string.h>
3    #include <stdlib.h>
4    #include <stdarg.h>
5    #include <math.h>
6    #include <windows.h> /* Declarations for Windows */
7    #include "fcwin.h"   /* Declarations for FCWIN    */
8
9
10   /* ------------------------------------------------------- */
11   /*   Declare pointers to all the exported functions.       */
12   /*       These are the functions that Windows will call    */
13   /*       from outside FCWIN  to support the main (frame)    */
14   /*       window with its menu, and the dialog functions.   */
15   /* ------------------------------------------------------- */
16
17   long FAR PASCAL WndProc (HWND, unsigned, WORD, LONG) ;
18   BOOL FAR PASCAL PopupMsg( int );        /* DLL Function */
19   BOOL FAR PASCAL DoPctChg( HWND, unsigned, WORD, LONG );
20   BOOL FAR PASCAL DoPctTot( HWND, unsigned, WORD, LONG );
21   BOOL FAR PASCAL DoPayOut( HWND, unsigned, WORD, LONG );
22   BOOL FAR PASCAL DoMkupCo( HWND, unsigned, WORD, LONG );
23   BOOL FAR PASCAL DoMkupPr( HWND, unsigned, WORD, LONG );
24   BOOL FAR PASCAL DoEffPer( HWND, unsigned, WORD, LONG );
25   BOOL FAR PASCAL DoEffCon( HWND, unsigned, WORD, LONG );
26   BOOL FAR PASCAL DoFvSin( HWND, unsigned, WORD, LONG );
27   BOOL FAR PASCAL DoPvSin( HWND, unsigned, WORD, LONG );
28   BOOL FAR PASCAL DoFvAnn( HWND, unsigned, WORD, LONG );
29   BOOL FAR PASCAL DoPvAnn( HWND, unsigned, WORD, LONG );
30   BOOL FAR PASCAL DoLoanDat( HWND, unsigned, WORD, LONG );
31   BOOL FAR PASCAL ListAmort( HWND, unsigned, WORD, LONG );
32   BOOL FAR PASCAL PrntAmort( HWND, unsigned, WORD, LONG );
33
34   /* ------------------------------------------------------- */
35   /*   Prototype declarations for FCWIN helper functions.    */
36   /*       These functions support pop-up message boxes for  */
37   /*       displaying help information, as well as           */
38   /*       financial computations.                           */
39   /* ------------------------------------------------------- */
40
41   void BuildTextMessage( char* szFormat, ... );
```

```
42    double SPFV( double apr, double freq, double periods );
43    double SPPV( double apr, double freq, double periods );
44    double USPV( double apr, double freq, double periods );
45    double USFV( double apr, double freq, double periods );
46
47    /* ------------------------------------------------------ */
48    /*  Declare global variables. Try to keep these to a     */
49    /*      minimum.                                         */
50    /* ------------------------------------------------------ */
51
52    char textmsg[256];
53    double apr = 10, years = 30, amt = 50000, freq = 12;
54    double levelpay, intpay, prinpay, numpay = 360, payno;
55    double bal, old, new, ans;
56    char instring[32];
57
58    /* ------------------------------------------------------ */
59    /*                                                        */
60    /*      CREATE FRAME WINDOW, DISPATCH WINDOWS MESSAGES    */
61    /*                                                        */
62    /*  WinMain() is required in every Windows program. It   */
63    /*      contains the main message loop. It is not        */
64    /*      exported; it is always assumed to be present.    */
65    /*                                                        */
66    /* ------------------------------------------------------ */
67
68    int PASCAL WinMain(HANDLE hInstance, HANDLE hPrevInstance,
69                       LPSTR lpszCmdLine, int nCmdShow )
70    {
71        WNDCLASS     wndClass;
72        MSG          msg;
73        HWND         hWnd;
74
75        /*
76         * Register window class style if first
77         * instance of this program.
78         */
79        if ( !hPrevInstance )
80        {
81            wndClass.style        =CS_HREDRAW | CS_VREDRAW ;
82            wndClass.lpfnWndProc  =WndProc;
```

Listing 21.2. continues

Listing 21.2. continued

```
 83            wndClass.cbClsExtra     =0;
 84            wndClass.cbWndExtra     =0;
 85            wndClass.hInstance      =hInstance;
 86            wndClass.hIcon          =LoadIcon(NULL,
 87                                          "IDI_APPLICATION");
 88            wndClass.hCursor        =LoadCursor(NULL,IDC_ARROW );
 89            wndClass.hbrBackground=GetStockObject(WHITE_BRUSH );
 90            wndClass.lpszMenuName ="FCMenu";
 91            wndClass.lpszClassName=szAppName;
 92
 93      if (!RegisterClass(&wndClass))
 94          return FALSE;
 95      }
 96
 97      /*
 98       * Create and display the window.
 99       */
100      hWnd = CreateWindow(szAppName,
101                      "Financial Calculations",
102                      WS_OVERLAPPEDWINDOW,
103                      CW_USEDEFAULT,
104                      CW_USEDEFAULT,
105                      CW_USEDEFAULT,
106                      CW_USEDEFAULT,
107                      NULL,
108                      NULL,
109                      hInstance,
110                      NULL);
111
112      ShowWindow(hWnd, nCmdShow);
113      UpdateWindow(hWnd);
114
115      while (GetMessage(&msg, NULL, 0, 0))
116      {
117          TranslateMessage(&msg );
118          DispatchMessage(&msg );
119      }
120      return msg.wParam;
121  }
122
```

```
123  /* ------------------------------------------------------ */
124  /*                                                         */
125  /*        PROCESS ALL MESSAGES FROM THE FRAME WINDOW       */
126  /*                                                         */
127  /*  WndProc() handles the processing of all messages      */
128  /*      dispatched by WinMain(). A pointer to this         */
129  /*      function was placed in the wndClass structure      */
130  /*      during registration of the frame window.           */
131  /*                                                         */
132  /* ------------------------------------------------------- */
133
134  long FAR PASCAL WndProc (HWND hWnd, unsigned Message,
135                           WORD wParam, LONG lParam)
136  {
137     static FARPROC lpfnDoPctChg;
138     static FARPROC lpfnDoPctTot;
139     static FARPROC lpfnDoMkupCo;
140     static FARPROC lpfnDoMkupPr;
141     static FARPROC lpfnDoEffPer;
142     static FARPROC lpfnDoEffCon;
143     static FARPROC lpfnDoFvSin;
144     static FARPROC lpfnDoPvSin;
145     static FARPROC lpfnDoFvAnn;
146     static FARPROC lpfnDoPvAnn;
147     static FARPROC lpfnDoLoanDat;
148     static FARPROC lpfnDoPayOut;
149     static FARPROC lpfnListAmort;
150     static FARPROC lpfnPrntAmort;
151     static HANDLE hInstance;
152
153     switch(Message)
154     {
155                 /* --------------------------------------- */
156                 /* Note which instance of FCWIN execution  */
157                 /* this is, and create instance thunks     */
158                 /* (connect dialog procs to instance).     */
159                 /* Note that several copies of FCWIN       */
160                 /* might be running at the same time.       */
161                 /* --------------------------------------- */
162
163     case WM_CREATE:
164         hInstance = ((LPCREATESTRUCT) lParam)->hInstance;
```

Listing 21.2. continues

Listing 21.2. continued

```
165        lpfnDoPctChg =
166                MakeProcInstance( DoPctChg, hInstance );
167        lpfnDoPctTot =
168                MakeProcInstance( DoPctTot, hInstance );
169        lpfnDoMkupCo =
170                MakeProcInstance( DoMkupCo, hInstance );
171        lpfnDoMkupPr =
172                MakeProcInstance( DoMkupPr, hInstance );
173        lpfnDoEffPer =
174                MakeProcInstance( DoEffPer, hInstance );
175        lpfnDoEffCon =
176                MakeProcInstance( DoEffCon, hInstance );
177        lpfnDoFvSin =
178                MakeProcInstance( DoFvSin, hInstance );
179        lpfnDoPvSin =
180                MakeProcInstance( DoPvSin, hInstance );
181        lpfnDoFvAnn =
182                MakeProcInstance( DoFvAnn, hInstance );
183        lpfnDoPvAnn =
184                MakeProcInstance( DoPvAnn, hInstance );
185        lpfnDoLoanDat =
186                MakeProcInstance( DoLoanDat, hInstance );
187        lpfnDoPayOut =
188                MakeProcInstance( DoPayOut, hInstance );
189        lpfnListAmort =
190                MakeProcInstance( ListAmort, hInstance );
191        lpfnPrntAmort =
192                MakeProcInstance( PrntAmort, hInstance );
193     return 0;
194
195                 /* ------------------------------------- */
196                 /* Process window commands. For FCWIN,   */
197                 /* this means noting which menu item     */
198                 /* was picked, and starting the dialog   */
199                 /* for it. The case values shown here    */
200                 /* are declared in FCWIN.H.              */
201                 /* ------------------------------------- */
202
203     case WM_COMMAND:
204         switch( wParam ) {
205           case IDM_PCTCHANGE:
```

```
206              if ( DialogBox( hInstance, "FCPCTCG",
207                             hWnd, lpfnDoPctChg ) )
208                  InvalidateRect( hWnd, NULL, TRUE );
209              return 0;
210
211          case IDM_PCTTOTAL :
212              if ( DialogBox( hInstance, "FCPCTTO",
213                             hWnd, lpfnDoPctTot ) )
214                  InvalidateRect( hWnd, NULL, TRUE );
215              return 0;
216
217          case IDM_MKUPCOST :
218              if ( DialogBox( hInstance, "FCMKUPCO",
219                             hWnd, lpfnDoMkupCo ) )
220                  InvalidateRect( hWnd, NULL, TRUE );
221              return 0;
222
223          case IDM_MKUPPRICE :
224              if ( DialogBox( hInstance, "FCMKUPPR",
225                             hWnd, lpfnDoMkupPr ) )
226                  InvalidateRect( hWnd, NULL, TRUE );
227              return 0;
228
229          case IDM_EFFPER :
230              if ( DialogBox( hInstance, "FCEFFPER",
231                             hWnd, lpfnDoEffPer ) )
232                  InvalidateRect( hWnd, NULL, TRUE );
233              return 0;
234
235          case IDM_EFFCONT :
236              if ( DialogBox( hInstance, "FCEFFCON",
237                             hWnd, lpfnDoEffCon ) )
238                  InvalidateRect( hWnd, NULL, TRUE );
239              return 0;
240
241          case IDM_FVSINGLE :
242              if ( DialogBox( hInstance, "FCFVSIN",
243                             hWnd, lpfnDoFvSin ) )
244                  InvalidateRect( hWnd, NULL, TRUE );
245              return 0;
246
247          case IDM_PVSINGLE :
```

Listing 21.2. continues

Listing 21.2. continued

```
248              if ( DialogBox( hInstance, "FCPVSIN",
249                              hWnd, lpfnDoPvSin ) )
250                  InvalidateRect( hWnd, NULL, TRUE );
251              return 0;
252
253          case IDM_FVREGULAR :
254              if ( DialogBox( hInstance, "FCFVANN",
255                              hWnd, lpfnDoFvAnn ) )
256                  InvalidateRect( hWnd, NULL, TRUE );
257              return 0;
258
259          case IDM_PVREGULAR :
260              if ( DialogBox( hInstance, "FCPVANN",
261                              hWnd, lpfnDoPvAnn ) )
262                  InvalidateRect( hWnd, NULL, TRUE );
263              return 0;
264
265          case IDM_LOANDATA :
266              if ( DialogBox( hInstance, "FCLOANDA",
267                              hWnd, lpfnDoLoanDat ) )
268                  InvalidateRect( hWnd, NULL, TRUE );
269              return 0;
270
271          case IDM_PAYOUT:
272              if ( DialogBox( hInstance, "FCPAYOUT",
273              hWnd, lpfnDoPayOut ) )
274                  InvalidateRect( hWnd, NULL, TRUE );
275              return 0;
276
277          case IDM_DISPAMORT:
278              if ( DialogBox( hInstance, "FCMORTLS",
279                              hWnd, lpfnListAmort ) )
280                  InvalidateRect( hWnd, NULL, TRUE );
281              return 0;
282
283          case IDM_PRNTAMORT:
284              if ( DialogBox( hInstance, "FCMORTPR",
285                              hWnd, lpfnPrntAmort ) )
286                  InvalidateRect( hWnd, NULL, TRUE );
287              return 0;
288
```

```
289            case HLP_PCTCHANGE:
290             PopupMsg( HLP_PCTCHANGE - HLP_PCTCHANGE );
291             return 0;
292
293            case HLP_PCTTOTAL:
294             PopupMsg( HLP_PCTTOTAL - HLP_PCTCHANGE );
295             return 0;
296
297            case HLP_MKUPCOST:
298             PopupMsg( HLP_MKUPCOST - HLP_PCTCHANGE );
299             return 0;
300
301            case HLP_MKUPPRICE:
302             PopupMsg( HLP_MKUPPRICE - HLP_PCTCHANGE );
303             return 0;
304
305            case HLP_EFFPER:
306             PopupMsg( HLP_EFFPER - HLP_PCTCHANGE );
307             return 0;
308
309            case HLP_EFFCONT:
310             PopupMsg( HLP_EFFCONT - HLP_PCTCHANGE );
311             return 0;
312
313            case HLP_FVSINGLE:
314             PopupMsg( HLP_FVSINGLE - HLP_PCTCHANGE );
315             return 0;
316
317            case HLP_PVSINGLE:
318             PopupMsg( HLP_PVSINGLE - HLP_PCTCHANGE );
319             return 0;
320
321            case HLP_FVREGULAR:
322             PopupMsg( HLP_FVREGULAR - HLP_PCTCHANGE );
323             return 0;
324
325            case HLP_PVREGULAR:
326             PopupMsg( HLP_PVREGULAR - HLP_PCTCHANGE );
327             return 0;
328
329            case HLP_LOANDATA:
```

Listing 21.2. continues

Listing 21.2. continued

```
330                    PopupMsg( HLP_LOANDATA - HLP_PCTCHANGE );
331                    return 0;
332
333                case HLP_PAYOUT:
334                    PopupMsg( HLP_PAYOUT - HLP_PCTCHANGE );
335                    return 0;
336
337                case HLP_DISPAMORT:
338                    PopupMsg( HLP_DISPAMORT - HLP_PCTCHANGE );
339                    return 0;
340
341                case HLP_PRNTAMORT:
342                    PopupMsg( HLP_PRNTAMORT - HLP_PCTCHANGE );
343                    return 0;
344            }
345            break;
346
347        case WM_DESTROY:
348            PostQuitMessage(0);
349            return 0;
350    }
351    return DefWindowProc(hWnd,Message,wParam,lParam);
352 }
353
354 /* ---------------------------------------------------- */
355 /*                                                      */
356 /*                  DIALOG PROCEDURES                   */
357 /*                                                      */
358 /* ---------------------------------------------------- */
359
360 BOOL FAR PASCAL DoPctChg( HWND hDlg, unsigned message,
361                          WORD wParam, LONG lParam)
362 {
363    switch ( message ) {
364
365      case WM_INITDIALOG:
366          SetFocus( GetDlgItem( hDlg, FCWIN_OLD ) );
367          return FALSE;
368
369      case WM_CLOSE:
370          EndDialog( hDlg, TRUE );
```

```
371            return TRUE;
372
373    case WM_COMMAND:
374      switch ( wParam ) {
375
376        case FCWIN_COMPUTE :
377            old = new = ans = 0.0;
378
379            GetDlgItemText( hDlg,FCWIN_OLD,instring,32 );
380            sscanf( instring, "%lf", &old );
381
382            GetDlgItemText( hDlg,FCWIN_NEW,instring,32 );
383            sscanf( instring, "%lf", &new );
384
385            if ( old != 0.0 )
386              ans = ((new-old)/old)*100.0;
387            sprintf( instring, "%7.2f", ans );
388
389            SetDlgItemText( hDlg,FCWIN_ANS,instring );
390            SetFocus( GetDlgItem( hDlg,FCWIN_OLD ) );
391            return FALSE;
392
393        case FCWIN_RETURN:
394            EndDialog( hDlg, TRUE );
395            return TRUE;
396      }
397    break;
398    }
399    return FALSE;
400 }
401
402 BOOL FAR PASCAL DoPctTot( HWND hDlg, unsigned message,
403                           WORD wParam, LONG lParam)
404 {
405    switch ( message ) {
406
407      case WM_INITDIALOG:
408            SetFocus( GetDlgItem( hDlg, FCWIN_NEW ) );
409            return FALSE;
410
411      case WM_CLOSE:
```

Listing 21.2. continues

Listing 21.2. continued

```
412                     EndDialog( hDlg, TRUE );
413                     return TRUE;
414
415          case WM_COMMAND:
416            switch ( wParam ) {
417
418              case FCWIN_COMPUTE :
419                     old = new = ans = 0.0;
420
421                     GetDlgItemText( hDlg,FCWIN_NEW,instring,32 );
422                     sscanf( instring, "%lf", &new );
423
424                     GetDlgItemText( hDlg,FCWIN_OLD,instring,32 );
425                     sscanf( instring, "%lf", &old );
426
427                     if ( old != 0.0 )
428                       ans = (new/old)*100.0;
429                     sprintf( instring, "%7.2f", ans );
430
431                     SetDlgItemText( hDlg, FCWIN_ANS, instring );
432                     SetFocus( GetDlgItem( hDlg, FCWIN_NEW ) );
433                     return FALSE;
434
435            case FCWIN_RETURN:
436                     EndDialog( hDlg, TRUE );
437                     return TRUE;
438          }
439        break;
440      }
441    return FALSE;
442  }
443
444  BOOL FAR PASCAL DoMkupCo( HWND hDlg, unsigned message,
445                             WORD wParam, LONG lParam)
446  {
447    switch ( message ) {
448
449      case WM_INITDIALOG:
450             SetFocus( GetDlgItem( hDlg, FCWIN_OLD ) );
451             return FALSE;
452
```

```
453      case WM_CLOSE:
454          EndDialog( hDlg, TRUE );
455          return TRUE;
456
457      case WM_COMMAND:
458        switch ( wParam ) {
459
460          case FCWIN_COMPUTE :
461              old = new = ans = 0.0;
462
463              GetDlgItemText( hDlg,FCWIN_OLD,instring,32 );
464              sscanf( instring, "%lf", &old );
465
466              GetDlgItemText( hDlg,FCWIN_NEW,instring,32 );
467              sscanf( instring, "%lf", &new );
468
469              if ( new != 0.0 )
470                ans = ((old-new)/new)*100.0;
471              sprintf( instring, "%7.2f", ans );
472
473              SetDlgItemText( hDlg, FCWIN_ANS, instring );
474              SetFocus( GetDlgItem( hDlg, FCWIN_OLD ) );
475              return FALSE;
476
477          case FCWIN_RETURN:
478              EndDialog( hDlg, TRUE );
479              return TRUE;
480          }
481        break;
482      }
483    return FALSE;
484  }
485
486  BOOL FAR PASCAL DoMkupPr( HWND hDlg, unsigned message,
487                            WORD wParam, LONG lParam)
488  {
489    switch ( message ) {
490
491      case WM_INITDIALOG:
492          SetFocus( GetDlgItem( hDlg, FCWIN_OLD ) );
493          return FALSE;
```

Listing 21.2. continues

Listing 21.2. continued

```
494
495        case WM_CLOSE:
496            EndDialog( hDlg, TRUE );
497            return TRUE;
498
499        case WM_COMMAND:
500          switch ( wParam ) {
501
502            case FCWIN_COMPUTE :
503                old = new = ans = 0.0;
504
505                GetDlgItemText( hDlg,FCWIN_OLD,instring,32 );
506                sscanf( instring, "%lf", &old );
507
508                GetDlgItemText( hDlg,FCWIN_NEW,instring,32 );
509                sscanf( instring, "%lf", &new );
510
511                if ( new != 0.0 )
512                  ans = ((old-new)/old)*100.0;
513                sprintf( instring, "%7.2f", ans );
514
515                SetDlgItemText( hDlg, FCWIN_ANS, instring );
516                SetFocus( GetDlgItem( hDlg, FCWIN_OLD ) );
517                return FALSE;
518
519            case FCWIN_RETURN:
520                EndDialog( hDlg, TRUE );
521                return TRUE;
522          }
523        break;
524    }
525    return FALSE;
526 }
527
528 BOOL FAR PASCAL DoEffPer( HWND hDlg, unsigned message,
529                             WORD wParam, LONG lParam)
530 {
531    switch ( message ) {
532
533      case WM_INITDIALOG:
534            SetFocus( GetDlgItem( hDlg, FCWIN_APR ) );
```

```
535             return FALSE;
536
537     case WM_CLOSE:
538             EndDialog( hDlg, TRUE );
539             return TRUE;
540
541     case WM_COMMAND:
542         switch ( wParam ) {
543
544             case FCWIN_COMPUTE :
545                 apr = freq = ans = 0.0;
546
547                 GetDlgItemText( hDlg,FCWIN_APR,instring,32 );
548                 sscanf( instring, "%lf", &apr );
549
550                 GetDlgItemText( hDlg,FCWIN_FREQ,instring,32 );
551                 sscanf( instring, "%lf", &freq );
552
553                 if ( freq != 0.0 && apr != 0.0 )
554                    ans = ( pow(1.0+apr/(100.0*freq),freq)-1 )
555                             * 100.0;
556                 sprintf( instring, "%7.2f", ans );
557
558                 SetDlgItemText( hDlg, FCWIN_ANS, instring );
559                 SetFocus( GetDlgItem( hDlg, FCWIN_APR ) );
560                 return FALSE;
561
562             case FCWIN_RETURN:
563                 EndDialog( hDlg, TRUE );
564                 return TRUE;
565         }
566      break;
567    }
568    return FALSE;
569 }
570
571 BOOL FAR PASCAL DoEffCon( HWND hDlg, unsigned message,
572                          WORD wParam, LONG lParam)
573 {
574    switch ( message ) {
575
```

Listing 21.2. continues

Listing 21.2. continued

```
576        case WM_INITDIALOG:
577            SetFocus( GetDlgItem( hDlg, FCWIN_APR ) );
578            return FALSE;
579
580        case WM_CLOSE:
581            EndDialog( hDlg, TRUE );
582            return TRUE;
583
584        case WM_COMMAND:
585          switch ( wParam ) {
586
587            case FCWIN_COMPUTE :
588                apr = ans = 0.0;
589
590                GetDlgItemText( hDlg,FCWIN_APR,instring,32 );
591                sscanf( instring, "%lf", &apr );
592
593                if ( apr != 0.0 )
594                   ans = ( exp(apr/100.0)-1 ) * 100.0;
595                sprintf( instring, "%7.2f", ans );
596
597                SetDlgItemText( hDlg, FCWIN_ANS, instring );
598                SetFocus( GetDlgItem( hDlg, FCWIN_APR ) );
599                return FALSE;
600
601            case FCWIN_RETURN:
602                EndDialog( hDlg, TRUE );
603                return TRUE;
604          }
605        break;
606      }
607    return FALSE;
608 }
609
610 BOOL FAR PASCAL DoFvSin( HWND hDlg, unsigned message,
611                    WORD wParam, LONG lParam)
612 {
613    switch ( message ) {
614
615      case WM_INITDIALOG:
616            SetFocus( GetDlgItem( hDlg, FCWIN_AMT ) );
```

```
617            return FALSE;
618
619     case WM_CLOSE:
620            EndDialog( hDlg, TRUE );
621            return TRUE;
622
623     case WM_COMMAND:
624        switch ( wParam ) {
625
626          case FCWIN_COMPUTE :
627              apr = amt = freq = numpay = ans = 0.0;
628
629              GetDlgItemText( hDlg,FCWIN_AMT,instring,32 );
630              sscanf( instring, "%lf", &amt );
631
632              GetDlgItemText( hDlg,FCWIN_APR,instring,32 );
633              sscanf( instring, "%lf", &apr );
634
635              GetDlgItemText( hDlg,FCWIN_FREQ,instring,32 );
636              sscanf( instring, "%lf", &freq );
637
638              GetDlgItemText( hDlg,FCWIN_YEARS,instring,32 );
639              sscanf( instring, "%lf", &years );
640
641              if ( apr != 0.0 && amt != 0.0
642                   && freq != 0.0 && years != 0.0 ) {
643                numpay = freq * years;
644                ans = amt * SPFV( apr, freq, numpay );
645              }
646              sprintf( instring, "%7.2f", ans );
647
648              SetDlgItemText( hDlg, FCWIN_ANS, instring );
649              SetFocus( GetDlgItem( hDlg, FCWIN_AMT ) );
650              return FALSE;
651
652          case FCWIN_RETURN:
653              EndDialog( hDlg, TRUE );
654              return TRUE;
655        }
656      break;
657    }
```

Listing 21.2. continues

Listing 21.2. continued

```
658      return FALSE;
659   }
660
661   BOOL FAR PASCAL DoPvSin( HWND hDlg, unsigned message,
662                       WORD wParam, LONG lParam)
663   {
664     switch ( message ) {
665
666       case WM_INITDIALOG:
667           SetFocus( GetDlgItem( hDlg, FCWIN_AMT ) );
668           return FALSE;
669
670       case WM_CLOSE:
671           EndDialog( hDlg, TRUE );
672           return TRUE;
673
674       case WM_COMMAND:
675         switch ( wParam ) {
676
677           case FCWIN_COMPUTE :
678               apr = amt = freq = numpay = ans = 0.0;
679
680               GetDlgItemText( hDlg,FCWIN_AMT,instring,32 );
681               sscanf( instring, "%lf", &amt );
682
683               GetDlgItemText( hDlg,FCWIN_APR,instring,32 );
684               sscanf( instring, "%lf", &apr );
685
686               GetDlgItemText( hDlg,FCWIN_FREQ,instring,32 );
687               sscanf( instring, "%lf", &freq );
688
689               GetDlgItemText( hDlg,FCWIN_YEARS,instring,32 );
690               sscanf( instring, "%lf", &years );
691
692               if ( apr != 0.0 && amt != 0.0
693                   && freq != 0.0 && years != 0.0 ) {
694                 numpay = freq * years;
695                 ans = amt * SPPV( apr, freq, numpay );
696               }
697               sprintf( instring, "%7.2f", ans );
698
```

```
699                SetDlgItemText( hDlg, FCWIN_ANS, instring );
700                SetFocus( GetDlgItem( hDlg, FCWIN_AMT ) );
701                return FALSE;
702
703          case FCWIN_RETURN:
704                EndDialog( hDlg, TRUE );
705                return TRUE;
706          }
707      break;
708      }
709    return FALSE;
710 }
711
712 BOOL FAR PASCAL DoFvAnn( HWND hDlg, unsigned message,
713                    WORD wParam, LONG lParam)
714 {
715    switch ( message ) {
716
717      case WM_INITDIALOG:
718            SetFocus( GetDlgItem( hDlg, FCWIN_AMT ) );
719            return FALSE;
720
721      case WM_CLOSE:
722            EndDialog( hDlg, TRUE );
723            return TRUE;
724
725      case WM_COMMAND:
726        switch ( wParam ) {
727
728          case FCWIN_COMPUTE :
729                apr = amt = freq = numpay = ans = 0.0;
730
731                GetDlgItemText( hDlg,FCWIN_AMT,instring,32 );
732                sscanf( instring, "%lf", &amt );
733
734                GetDlgItemText( hDlg,FCWIN_APR,instring,32 );
735                sscanf( instring, "%lf", &apr );
736
737                GetDlgItemText( hDlg,FCWIN_FREQ,instring,32 );
738                sscanf( instring, "%lf", &freq );
739
```

Listing 21.2. continues

Listing 21.2. continued

```
740                      GetDlgItemText( hDlg,FCWIN_YEARS,instring,32 );
741                      sscanf( instring, "%lf", &years );
742
743                      if ( apr != 0.0 && amt != 0.0
744                          && freq != 0.0 && years != 0.0 ) {
745                          numpay = freq * years;
746                          ans = amt * USFV( apr, freq, numpay );
747                      }
748                      sprintf( instring, "%7.2f", ans );
749
750                      SetDlgItemText( hDlg, FCWIN_ANS, instring );
751                      SetFocus( GetDlgItem( hDlg, FCWIN_AMT ) );
752                      return FALSE;
753
754              case FCWIN_RETURN:
755                      EndDialog( hDlg, TRUE );
756                      return TRUE;
757          }
758      break;
759  }
760  return FALSE;
761 }
762
763 BOOL FAR PASCAL DoPvAnn( HWND hDlg, unsigned message,
764                     WORD wParam, LONG lParam)
765 {
766   switch ( message ) {
767
768     case WM_INITDIALOG:
769             SetFocus( GetDlgItem( hDlg, FCWIN_AMT ) );
770             return FALSE;
771
772     case WM_CLOSE:
773             EndDialog( hDlg, TRUE );
774             return TRUE;
775
776     case WM_COMMAND:
777        switch ( wParam ) {
778
779          case FCWIN_COMPUTE :
780                  apr = amt = freq = numpay = ans = 0.0;
```

```
781
782             GetDlgItemText( hDlg,FCWIN_AMT,instring,32 );
783             sscanf( instring, "%lf", &amt );
784
785             GetDlgItemText( hDlg,FCWIN_APR,instring,32 );
786             sscanf( instring, "%lf", &apr );
787
788             GetDlgItemText( hDlg,FCWIN_FREQ,instring,32 );
789             sscanf( instring, "%lf", &freq );
790
791             GetDlgItemText( hDlg,FCWIN_YEARS,instring,32 );
792             sscanf( instring, "%lf", &years );
793
794             if ( apr != 0.0 && amt != 0.0
795                 && freq != 0.0 && years != 0.0 ) {
796              numpay = freq * years;
797              ans = amt * USPV( apr, freq, numpay );
798             }
799             sprintf( instring, "%7.2f", ans );
800
801             SetDlgItemText( hDlg, FCWIN_ANS, instring );
802             SetFocus( GetDlgItem( hDlg, FCWIN_AMT ) );
803             return FALSE;
804
805         case FCWIN_RETURN:
806             EndDialog( hDlg, TRUE );
807             return TRUE;
808         }
809     break;
810     }
811     return FALSE;
812 }
813
814 BOOL FAR PASCAL DoLoanDat( HWND hDlg, unsigned message,
815                    WORD wParam, LONG lParam)
816 {
817     switch ( message ) {
818
819             /* ------------------------------------ */
820             /* Prime the edit control boxes with    */
```

Listing 21.2. continues

Listing 21.2. continued

```
821                         /* initial values.                        */
822                         /* ------------------------------------- */
823
824     case WM_INITDIALOG:
825             sprintf( instring, "%7.2f", amt );
826             SetDlgItemText( hDlg, FCWIN_AMT, instring );
827
828             sprintf( instring, "%7.2f", apr );
829             SetDlgItemText( hDlg, FCWIN_APR, instring );
830
831             sprintf( instring, "%7.2f", freq );
832             SetDlgItemText( hDlg, FCWIN_FREQ, instring );
833
834             sprintf( instring, "%7.2f", years );
835             SetDlgItemText( hDlg, FCWIN_YEARS, instring );
836
837             SetFocus( GetDlgItem( hDlg, FCWIN_AMT ) );
838             return FALSE;
839
840     case WM_CLOSE:
841             EndDialog( hDlg, TRUE );
842             return TRUE;
843
844     case WM_COMMAND:
845       switch ( wParam ) {
846
847         case FCWIN_RETURN :
848             GetDlgItemText( hDlg, FCWIN_AMT, instring, 32 );
849             sscanf( instring, "%lf", &amt );
850
851             GetDlgItemText( hDlg, FCWIN_APR, instring, 32 );
852             sscanf( instring, "%lf", &apr );
853
854             GetDlgItemText( hDlg, FCWIN_FREQ, instring, 32 );
855             sscanf( instring, "%lf", &freq );
856
857             GetDlgItemText( hDlg, FCWIN_YEARS, instring, 32 );
858             sscanf( instring, "%lf", &years );
859
860             if ( apr != 0.0 && amt != 0.0
861                 && freq != 0.0 && years != 0.0 ) {
```

```
862                 numpay = freq * years;
863             }
864
865             EndDialog( hDlg, TRUE );
866             return TRUE;
867         }
868     break;
869     }
870   return FALSE;
871 }
872
873 BOOL FAR PASCAL DoPayout( HWND hDlg, unsigned message,
874                          WORD wParam, LONG lParam)
875 {
876   switch ( message ) {
877
878     case WM_INITDIALOG:
879         levelpay = 1 / USPV( apr, freq, numpay ) * amt;
880
881         sprintf( instring, "%7.2f", amt );
882         SetDlgItemText( hDlg, FCWIN_AMT, instring );
883
884         sprintf( instring, "%7.2f", apr );
885         SetDlgItemText( hDlg, FCWIN_APR, instring );
886
887         sprintf( instring, "%7.2f", freq );
888         SetDlgItemText( hDlg, FCWIN_FREQ, instring );
889
890         sprintf( instring, "%7.2f", years );
891         SetDlgItemText( hDlg, FCWIN_YEARS, instring );
892
893         sprintf( instring, "%7.2f", levelpay );
894         SetDlgItemText( hDlg, FCWIN_LEVELPAY, instring );
895
896         sprintf( instring, "%7.2f", levelpay*numpay );
897         SetDlgItemText( hDlg, FCWIN_TOTPAY, instring );
898
899         sprintf( instring, "%7.2f", levelpay*numpay-amt );
900         SetDlgItemText( hDlg, FCWIN_INTPAY, instring );
901
902         sprintf( instring, "%7.2f",
```

Listing 21.2. continues

Listing 21.2. continued

```
903                              ((levelpay*numpay-amt)/amt)*100.0 );
904                   SetDlgItemText( hDlg, FCWIN_BALLOON, instring );
905
906                   return TRUE;
907
908        case WM_CLOSE:
909                   EndDialog( hDlg, TRUE );
910                   return TRUE;
911
912        }
913     return FALSE;
914  }
915
916  BOOL FAR PASCAL ListAmort( HWND hDlg, unsigned message,
917                                    WORD wParam, LONG lParam )
918  {
919     HANDLE hWndCntrl;
920
921     switch ( message ) {
922
923       case WM_INITDIALOG:
924            hWndCntrl = GetDlgItem( hDlg, FCWIN_LISTBOX );
925
926            levelpay = 1 / USPV( apr, freq, numpay ) * amt;
927            payno = 0;
928
929            while ( payno < numpay ) {
930              ++payno;
931              intpay = levelpay
932                     * USPV( apr, freq, numpay-payno+1.0 )
933                     * (apr/freq/100.0);
934              prinpay = levelpay - intpay;
935              bal = levelpay * USPV( apr, freq, numpay-payno );
936              BuildTextMessage( "%12d%12.2f%12.2f%12.2f%12.2f",
937                               (int)payno, levelpay,
938                               intpay, prinpay,
939                               bal
940                             );
941              SendMessage( hWndCntrl, LB_ADDSTRING, NULL,
942                          (LONG)(LPSTR) textmsg );
943            }
```

```
944
945              SetFocus( GetDlgItem( hDlg, FCWIN_RETURN ) );
946              return FALSE;
947
948      case WM_CLOSE:
949              EndDialog( hDlg, TRUE );
950              return TRUE;
951
952      case WM_COMMAND:
953          switch ( wParam ) {
954
955          case FCWIN_RETURN  :
956                  EndDialog( hDlg, TRUE );
957                  return TRUE;
958          }
959        break;
960      }
961      return FALSE;
962 }
963
964 BOOL FAR PASCAL PrntAmort( HWND hDlg, unsigned message,
965                              WORD wParam, LONG lParam )
966 {
967
968                    /* ------------------------------------ */
969                    /* DeviceMode() not in windows.h file.  */
970                    /* Provide a typedef for the function.  */
971                    /* ------------------------------------ */
972
973      typedef VOID (FAR PASCAL *DEVMODEPROC)(HWND,HANDLE,
974                                  LPSTR,LPSTR);
975
976      HDC hPr;          /* Device context handle for printer */
977
978      char szPrinter[80];        /* Device info from WIN.INI */
979      char szDriverFile[16];  /* Name of prt driver DLL file */
980
981      HANDLE hLibrary;      /* Handle for prt driver DLL file */
982      DEVMODEPROC lpfnDM;    /* Pointer to DeviceMode() proc */
983
984      LPSTR szPrintType;              /* Printer type string */
```

Listing 21.2. continues

Listing 21.2. continued

```
985        LPSTR szPrintDriver;        /* Printer driver name string */
986        LPSTR szPrintPort;           /* Printer port name string */
987
988        int LineSpace, LinesPerPage, CurrentLine, LineLength;
989
990        POINT PhysPageSize;
991        TEXTMETRIC TextMetric;
992
993        switch ( message ) {
994
995          case WM_INITDIALOG:
996              SetFocus( GetDlgItem( hDlg, FCWIN_START ) );
997              return FALSE;
998
999          case WM_CLOSE:
1000             EndDialog( hDlg, TRUE );
1001             return TRUE;
1002
1003         case WM_COMMAND:
1004           switch ( wParam ) {
1005
1006             case FCWIN_START :
1007
1008                     /* ------------------------------------- */
1009                     /* Get the profile string for the       */
1010                     /* current printer and parse it.        */
1011                     /* ------------------------------------- */
1012
1013                 GetProfileString( "windows", "device", ",,,",
1014                             szPrinter, 80 );
1015             if ( (szPrintType   = strtok( szPrinter, "," )) &&
1016                  (szPrintDriver = strtok( NULL,       "," )) &&
1017                  (szPrintPort   = strtok( NULL,       "," )))
1018
1019                     /* ------------------------------------- */
1020                     /* Create a device context for the      */
1021                     /* printer.                             */
1022                     /* ------------------------------------- */
1023
1024                 hPr = CreateDC( (LPSTR)szPrintDriver,
1025                                 (LPSTR)szPrintType,
```

```
1026                          (LPSTR)szPrintPort,
1027                          NULL );
1028        else {
1029          MessageBox( hDlg, "Unable to start printing.",
1030                     NULL, MB_OK | MB_ICONHAND );
1031          DeleteDC( hPr );
1032          EndDialog( hDlg, TRUE );
1033          return TRUE;
1034        }
1035
1036             /* ------------------------------------- */
1037             /* This code loads the driver file from  */
1038             /* the DLL. Get the handle for the       */
1039             /* driver. Use the handle to get the     */
1040             /* address of its DeviceMode() function, */
1041             /* and invoke it using the pointer. This */
1042             /* is the code that causes the printer   */
1043             /* initialization dialog to pop up.      */
1044             /* ------------------------------------- */
1045
1046        strcat( strcpy( szDriverFile, szPrintDriver ), ".DRV" );
1047        hLibrary = LoadLibrary( szDriverFile ); /* get DLL mod */
1048        if ( hLibrary < 32 ) {
1049          MessageBox( hDlg, "Can't locate the driver\n"
1050                     "file for this printer.",
1051                     NULL, MB_OK | MB_ICONHAND );
1052          DeleteDC( hPr );
1053          EndDialog( hDlg, TRUE );
1054          return TRUE;
1055        }
1056        lpfnDM = GetProcAddress( hLibrary, "DEVICEMODE" );
1057        (*lpfnDM)( hDlg, hLibrary, (LPSTR)szPrintType,
1058                   (LPSTR)szPrintPort );
1059
1060             /* ------------------------------------- */
1061             /* Notify Print Manager that we are      */
1062             /* about to start spooling print using   */
1063             /* the STARTDOC Escape call.             */
1064             /* ------------------------------------- */
1065
1066        if ( Escape( hPr, STARTDOC, 11,
1067             "PrintAmort", 0L ) < 0 ) {
```

Listing 21.2. continues

Listing 21.2. continued

```
1068            MessageBox( hDlg, "Unable to start printing.",
1069                       NULL, MB_OK | MB_ICONHAND );
1070        DeleteDC( hPr );
1071        EndDialog( hDlg, TRUE );
1072        return TRUE;
1073    }
1074
1075            /* -------------------------------------- */
1076            /* Now calculate printing area parms    */
1077            /* using the GetTextMetrics() function  */
1078            /* and the GETPHYSPAGESIZE Escape call. */
1079            /* -------------------------------------- */
1080
1081    GetTextMetrics( hPr, &TextMetric );
1082    LineSpace = TextMetric.tmHeight
1083              + TextMetric.tmExternalLeading;
1084    Escape( hPr, GETPHYSPAGESIZE, NULL, NULL,
1085            (LPSTR)&PhysPageSize);
1086    LinesPerPage = ( PhysPageSize.y / LineSpace ) - 6;
1087    CurrentLine = LinesPerPage + 1;
1088
1089    levelpay = 1 / USPV( apr, freq, numpay ) * amt;
1090    payno = 0;
1091
1092            /* -------------------------------------- */
1093            /* Finally, loop and use TextOut() to    */
1094            /* spool print.                          */
1095            /* -------------------------------------- */
1096
1097    while ( payno < numpay ) {
1098      if ( ++CurrentLine >= LinesPerPage ) {
1099        Escape( hPr, NEWFRAME, 0, 0L, 0L );
1100        CurrentLine = 0;
1101        BuildTextMessage( "%s%s%s%s%s",
1102                          " Paymnt #  ",
1103                          " Level Pay ",
1104                          " Int Amt   ",
1105                          " Prin Amt  ",
1106                          " Balance   " );
1107        TextOut( hPr, 0, CurrentLine*LineSpace,
1108                 (LPSTR)textmsg, strlen(textmsg) );
```

```
1109                    ++CurrentLine;
1110                    BuildTextMessage( "%s%s%s%s%s",
1111                                      "-----------",
1112                                      "-----------",
1113                                      "-----------",
1114                                      "-----------",
1115                                      "-----------" );
1116                    TextOut( hPr, 0, CurrentLine*LineSpace,
1117                             (LPSTR)textmsg, strlen(textmsg) );
1118                    ++CurrentLine;
1119               }
1120               ++payno;
1121               intpay = levelpay
1122                        * USPV( apr, freq, numpay-payno+1.0 )
1123                        * (apr/freq/100.0);
1124               prinpay = levelpay - intpay;
1125               bal = levelpay * USPV( apr, freq, numpay-payno );
1126               BuildTextMessage( "%12d%12.2f%12.2f%12.2f%12.2f",
1127                                 (int)payno, levelpay,
1128                                 intpay, prinpay,
1129                                 bal
1130                               );
1131               TextOut( hPr, 0, CurrentLine*LineSpace,
1132                        (LPSTR)textmsg, strlen(textmsg) );
1133          }
1134
1135          Escape( hPr, NEWFRAME, 0, 0L, 0L );
1136          Escape( hPr, ENDDOC, 0, 0L, 0L );
1137          FreeLibrary( hLibrary );
1138          DeleteDC( hPr );
1139          EndDialog( hDlg, TRUE );
1140          return TRUE;
1141
1142     case FCWIN_CANCEL :
1143          EndDialog( hDlg, TRUE );
1144          return TRUE;
1145     }
1146     break;
1147  }
1148  return FALSE;
1149 }
1150 /* ----------------------------------------------------------- */
```

Listing 21.2. continues

***Listing 21.2.** continued*

```
1151   /*                                                              */
1152   /*                   HELPER ROUTINES FOLLOW                     */
1153   /*                                                              */
1154   /* ------------------------------------------------------------ */
1155
1156   void BuildTextMessage( char* szFormat, ... )
1157   {
1158     va_list ap;
1159
1160     va_start( ap, szFormat );
1161     vsprintf( textmsg, szFormat, ap );
1162     va_end( ap );
1163   }
1164
1165   double SPFV( double apr, double freq, double periods )
1166   {
1167     return( pow(1.0+(apr/freq)/100.0,periods) );
1168   }
1169
1170
1171   double SPPV( double apr, double freq, double periods )
1172   {
1173     return( 1.0 / SPFV(apr,freq,periods) );
1174   }
1175
1176   double USPV( double apr, double freq, double periods )
1177   {
1178     return( ( 1.0 - 1.0
1179               / SPFV(apr,freq,periods))
1180               / (apr/freq/100.0) );
1181   }
1182
1183   double USFV( double apr, double freq, double periods )
1184   {
1185     return( ( SPFV(apr,freq,periods)- 1.0) / (apr/freq/100.0) );
1186   }
1187
```

Creating Source Files for Windows Applications

A graphical user interface environment such as Windows is a complicated place because there is so much you can do with it and in it. This fact is highlighted by the contrast between the original `finance.c` program and the Windows version, `fcwin.c`. Both programs do similar things, but `fcwin.c` provides the user with a more pleasant appearance, more flexibility and utility in handling the windows (for editing, display, and so on), and greatly enhanced printing capability. All this is true just because FCWIN (referring to it by the project name) exists in a GUI.

The `finance.c` program consisted of a single source file capable of being compiled immediately and directly. But FCWIN consists of three ASCII text source files and a binary Windows resource file that must all be compiled, linked, and combined—in addition to the DLL file that must be produced to support the help facility (the original had no help facility).

Thus, much of the design of FCWIN must focus on the program's interface to the Windows environment. This section explains these design considerations. The discussion assumes that you have read the description of the `fcwin.res` resource file and its components in Chapter 20.

Understanding the Windows 3.0 Programming Environment

A number of things must come together correctly to create a Windows executable program file for even the simplest application program, such as FCWIN. Figure 21.2 shows the components that create the finished FCWIN application.

Figure 21.2 includes the `fcwin.res` resource file (containing menus, dialog boxes, and icons). If necessary, refer to Chapter 20 for a discussion of resource files, and `fcwin.res` in particular.

The main file is a standard C file, `fcwin.c`. The `fcwin.c` file, which was shown in listing 21.2, contains the logic that drives the entire application. The main source file cannot function without the module definition (DEF) file, but does not use it directly, as you will shortly see.

Fig. 21.2. *Source files, support files, and finished executable files for FCWIN.*

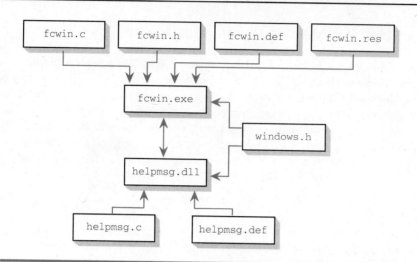

The main file does use the `fcwin.h` application header file, in that the program `#includes` the header, and depends on constant values `#defined` there. The main file also uses the resource (RES) file directly, in that it refers to objects located in the resource file by resource name. (A resource name is recorded in the RES file with each resource object.)

The manner in which the main source file depends on the contents of its support files is discussed in the remainder of this chapter. Chapter 22 explains the logical structure of the main program file, and discusses the construction and use of the help DLL.

Creating a Module Definition File

The *Borland C++ 2.0 User's Guide* states that a Windows application program can be compiled and linked without benefit of a module definition (DEF) file. This is true, but a number of things are taken for granted by the compiler and linker when you allow default actions to be taken, and may cause the resulting program to work differently from your expectations. More likely, the program will not work at all. Here is a general rule of thumb: write and use a module definition file. Having a DEF file gives you precise control of program characteristics, and documents them for later reference.

The module definition file describes for the compiler and linker the relationship of the main source file to the Windows environment. Listing 21.3 is the module definition file for FCWIN.

Listing 21.3. `fcwin.def`. *FCWIN module definition file.*

```
 1   NAME          FCCalcs
 2   DESCRIPTION   'Sample Windows application for UTC'
 3   STUB           'WINSTUB.EXE'
 4   CODE           PRELOAD MOVEABLE DISCARDABLE
 5   DATA           PRELOAD MOVEABLE MULTIPLE
 6   HEAPSIZE      8192
 7   STACKSIZE     8192
 8   EXPORTS       WndProc
 9                 DoPctChg
10                 DoPctTot
11                 DoMkupCo
12                 DoMkupPr
13                 DoEffPer
14                 DoEffCon
15                 DoFvSin
16                 DoPvSin
17                 DoFvAnn
18                 DoPvAnn
19                 DoLoanDat
20                 DoPayOut
21                 ListAmort
22                 PrntAmort
23   IMPORTS       HELPMSG.PopupMsg
```

The tokens coded in all uppercase are reserved words, and should be written as you see them here. The NAME statement (line 1) both defines the associated source file as a Windows application program and identifies the application to Windows. A program module must have a NAME statement, but the NAME field does not have to be the same as the program name.

The statements in lines 2–7 provide a description of the program module plus important information about how the module can be handled by Windows. Notice that the stub program is named here (line 3). Lines 4 and 5 tell Windows that both code and data should be preloaded when starting the application, and that they can be moved in memory during execution. Program code can even be thrown away and reloaded during execution (it is *discardable*). If multiple instances of the application are running concurrently, line 5 also tells Windows that each instance has its own data segment. Finally, notice that you can control the heap and stack size for the program (lines 6 and 7).

The EXPORTS statement (lines 8–22) identifies for Windows the functions in the main source file that Windows can call outside your program. For FCWIN, these functions include the WndProc() window procedure and the dialog procedures (functions called to control a dialog). There are fourteen dialogs in FCWIN, one for each kind of financial computation.

The IMPORTS statement in line 23 identifies the PopupMsg() function, which resides in the HELPMSG.DLL file. This declaration tells Windows where to locate the function when PopupMsg() is called. Building the DLL is discussed at the end of Chapter 22.

Designing the Program's Header File

The next step is coding the application program's header file, fcwin.h. The application header is used by only the main source file. An application header usually contains a macro defining the application name (this is used to register the window class) and manifest constants used by the program. The manifest constants correspond to the ordinal (integer) values of display windows and their controls that send messages to your program. The fcwin.h header is shown in listing 21.4.

Listing 21.4. fcwin.h. *FCWIN header file for the Windows environment.*

```
 1   #define  szAppName "FinancialCalcs"
 2
 3   #define  IDM_PCTCHANGE     1
 4   #define  IDM_PCTTOTAL      2
 5   #define  IDM_MKUPCOST      3
 6   #define  IDM_MKUPPRICE     4
 7   #define  IDM_EFFPER        5
 8   #define  IDM_EFFCONT       6
 9   #define  IDM_FVSINGLE      7
10   #define  IDM_PVSINGLE      8
11   #define  IDM_FVREGULAR     9
12   #define  IDM_PVREGULAR    10
13   #define  IDM_LOANDATA     11
14   #define  IDM_PAYOUT       12
15   #define  IDM_DISPAMORT    13
16   #define  IDM_PRNTAMORT    14
17
18   #define  HLP_PCTCHANGE    15
19   #define  HLP_PCTTOTAL     16
20   #define  HLP_MKUPCOST     17
21   #define  HLP_MKUPPRICE    18
```

```
22   #define HLP_EFFPER      19
23   #define HLP_EFFCONT     20
24   #define HLP_FVSINGLE    21
25   #define HLP_PVSINGLE    22
26   #define HLP_FVREGULAR   23
27   #define HLP_PVREGULAR   24
28   #define HLP_LOANDATA    25
29   #define HLP_PAYOUT      26
30   #define HLP_DISPAMORT   27
31   #define HLP_PRNTAMORT   28
32
33   #define FCWIN_OLD       101
34   #define FCWIN_NEW       102
35   #define FCWIN_ANS       103
36   #define FCWIN_RETURN    104
37   #define FCWIN_COMPUTE   105
38   #define FCWIN_APR       106
39   #define FCWIN_AMT       107
40   #define FCWIN_YEARS     108
41   #define FCWIN_FREQ      109
42   #define FCWIN_LISTBOX   110
43   #define FCWIN_LEVELPAY  111
44   #define FCWIN_INTPAY    112
45   #define FCWIN_TOTPAY    113
46   #define FCWIN_BALLOON   114
47   #define FCWIN_START     115
48   #define FCWIN_CANCEL    116
```

Line 1 in listing 21.4 defines a constant string containing the application name. The application name could have been declared directly in the main source file, but this place is better (that is, more visible).

Manifest constants of various sorts make up the rest of the FCWIN header. The macro name IDM_PCTCHANGE (line 3), for example, defines the ordinal value of the menu selection item for the Percent Change calculation. When a user clicks the Percent Change menu item, Windows sends a Windows message command (WM_COMMAND) to your window procedure (WndProc()) using that value as a subparameter. It is much easier to refer to the message ID by name rather than by the ordinal number.

The object-like macros in lines 33–48 serve a different purpose. These macros define ordinal values associated with window controls, such as edit boxes, list boxes, and pushbuttons. The FCWIN_COMPUTE macro, for example, is assigned an ordinal value of 105. Defining these constants is one of the most tedious parts of Windows programming, because you must be sure that the value matches the one you assigned to any Compute pushbutton in a dialog box. Control IDs are passed to the appropriate dialog procedure and acted upon there, in a fashion similar to the processing performed in the window procedure for the parent window.

Before compiling the program, be sure that your header is included in the main source file, together with the Windows header, as follows:

```
#include <windows.h>
#include "fcwin.h"
```

If you do not include both of these header files, the compile will fail miserably.

Creating a Project File for FCWIN

The application's project file is the first of two keys to building a Windows program, as opposed to just a C program. Using the IDE, open a new project and add to it the three files fcwin.c, fcwin.def, and fcwin.res. The presence of these last two files signals the compiler and linker that a Windows application is being built.

Before starting the Make or Build All, be sure to go to the Options | Application IDE menu and select the Windows Application option (this action is the second of the two keys to building a Windows program). Otherwise, the correct entry and exit code (prologs and epilogs) will not be used with the program's functions.

Having created a project file, select either Compile | Make or Compile | Build All from the IDE Compile menu. The FCWIN Windows application is built in the following steps:

❑ *Compilation of the source code to object code proceeds normally.*
The only visible difference between this and a normal C compilation is the presence of the windows.h header with its (large) collection of prototypes and declarations. (But remember that internally the entry and exit code generated is now specifically for Windows.)

❑ *The Turbo linker takes notice of the requested Windows environment.* At this point, things begin to happen differently from a normal C program build. First, the program needs different initialization code (the normal C0.OBJ code won't do; you need C0Wx.OBJ). Second, the prolog and epilog code normally wrapped around the library functions won't do either, so you need the Windows versions of the

Borland C++ libraries (CWINS.LIB for the small model). Last, the linker must use the information in IMPORT.LIB to provide access to the functions in Windows (such as creating a window or dialog) that you will use.

❏ *Finally, the Resource Compiler builds the completed application EXE file*. Even though the output from the previous step is an EXE file, it lacks the Windows stub and the resources (menus, icons, dialog boxes, and more) your program uses. All these things are packaged in the Windows executable file. Clearly, the result is not a normal DOS EXE file!

You can take full control of the application building process if you want. You can use the command compiler and linker, or you can write a MAKE file, to compile and link your Windows application program. Considering the depth and power of the Windows development tools provided by the combination of Borland C++ 2.0 and the Whitewater Group Resource Toolkit (RT), it is difficult to conceive of circumstances that would force you to abandon the convenience of the IDE.

Now you know everything there is to know about building a Windows application with Borland C++ 2.0—except, that is, how to write the code (and a few other variations and details). Constructing the logic for a Windows program is covered in the next chapter.

Exercises

Even though the discussion of FCWIN continues into the next chapter, you can begin *now* to practice writing Windows stubs and menus, by working the following exercises.

1. Write, assemble, and link your own Windows stub program. Call it WINSTUB or make up your own name. Put your own message in the stub program, and use it with the `easy.c` program shown in Chapter 20.

2. Use RT to create a menu for `easy.c`. Provide at least one pop-up menu. In the pop-up menu, provide an item that will start a dialog. You can look at the code for FCWIN to see how to hook the menu into `easy.c`.

Keep the menu you just created. In the next chapter you learn how to use the menu to start a dialog. Exercises in the next chapter complete the project started here.

Summary

This chapter gave you an introduction to the source files required to build a Windows application program, and a basic knowledge of the environment in which your application program will operate. You were introduced to the following topics:

❏ *How to write your own WINSTUB.EXE executable file, and how to understand the Windows directory structure.*

❏ *How to design and write the supporting source files for your Windows program.* These files include the module definition (DEF) file, your program's header (H) file, and the binary resource definition (RES) file.

❏ *How the support files are used by the compiler and linker to tailor your program to the Windows environment.*

This is not a good place to stop the discussion: all the pieces are not in place yet, so pausing here would leave many questions unanswered. Continue by reading Chapter 22 to see how your Windows program does its work in the Windows environment.

22

Writing Windows Applications with Borland C++ 2.0

In Chapter 21, you learned how to design and write the necessary source files for a Windows application program, and you learned about the environment in which the program will operate. This chapter is an extension of the same subject. It discusses the program logic required to interface your program with the Windows environment. The application used to illustrate these techniques is still FCWIN, the financial calculator program.

The program listing for `fcwin.c` (listing 21.2) is mentioned frequently in this chapter. In many places in this chapter, portions of the code are repeated, retaining the original line numbers from listing 21.2. You occasionally may want to glance at the entire source file, for a sense of context and continuity.

Designing Windows Interfaces

A number of things *must* be written into your Windows program, and many more things *can* be written into your Windows program. Necessary tasks include registering the window class, creating the main window, setting up the main message loop, and providing a window procedure to handle incoming messages. Some optional features used by FCWIN include establishing dialog boxes, controlling dialogs using callback functions, using message boxes, establishing a device context for the printer device, producing a report, and using a DLL module to provide a help facility. This section deals with these topics.

Just as there must be a `main()` function in a plain C or C++ program, a Windows application program has a required function that is the primary entry point. In the Windows environment, this required function is `WinMain()`, and it must have that name. Further, because the `WinMain()` function is called by Windows from outside your program, it must be exported. For the FCWIN application, the export is performed by writing the `EXPORT` statement in the DEF file, as follows:

```
EXPORT        WinMain
              ... ( other exports )
```

Any function that will be called by Windows management modules from outside your program must be exported—just add the function names to the `EXPORT` list in the DEF file. Such functions are termed *callback* functions because they are called from elsewhere in the environment.

The `WinMain()` function is where you write the code that drives the entire application. It is in this function that you must register the window class, create the main window, and establish the main message loop.

Registering the Window Class

Before you can create a window for FCWIN, you must tell Windows something about the attributes of the window. This action is called "registering the window class" and is performed in the `WinMain()` function (or in a function that `WinMain()` can call). In addition to registering the window class, you must make the program aware of which *instance* (that is, which execution) of the application owns the class: a window class needs to be registered only once, no matter how many concurrent copies are running. The following lines of code excerpted from listing 21.2 show how to register the window class:

```
68   int PASCAL WinMain(HANDLE hInstance, HANDLE hPrevInstance,
69                   LPSTR lpszCmdLine, int nCmdShow )
70   {
71       WNDCLASS      wndClass;
...
79       if ( !hPrevInstance )
80       {
81           wndClass.style          =CS_HREDRAW | CS_VREDRAW ;
82           wndClass.lpfnWndProc    =WndProc;
83           wndClass.cbClsExtra     =0;
84           wndClass.cbWndExtra     =0;
```

```
85          wndClass.hInstance      =hInstance;
86          wndClass.hIcon          =LoadIcon(NULL,
87                                            "IDI_APPLICATION");
88          wndClass.hCursor        =LoadCursor(NULL,IDC_ARROW );
89          wndClass.hbrBackground=GetStockObject(WHITE_BRUSH );
90          wndClass.lpszMenuName ="FCMenu";
91          wndClass.lpszClassName=szAppName;
92
93      if (!RegisterClass(&wndClass))
94          return FALSE;
...
121     }
```

The concept of *instance* is an important one in the Windows environment because several copies of the same program can be running at the same time. You must take care to register the window class only once, as shown in the preceding code fragment. Notice that `WinMain()` accepts the `hInstance` and `hPrevInstance` arguments. The class needs to be registered only if there is no previous instance (no other copy running yet—this one is the first). If there are no other instances, `hPrevInstance` is zero.

The window class is built in a structure with type `WNDCLASS`. Ten member data items must be filled in by the program:

❏ `wndClass.style = CS_HREDRAW | CS_VREDRAW;`

Assigning these attributes to the window's style tells Windows to redraw the window automatically if it is moved or resized by the user.

❏ `wndClass.lpfnWndProc = WndProc;`

This member variable informs Windows which function you will provide for the window procedure that interprets and acts upon Windows messages.

❏ `wndClass.cbClsExtra=0;`

The `cbClsExtra` member tells Windows how many extra bytes to allocate for this class structure. FCWIN needs none.

❏ `wndClass.cbWndExtra=0;`

The `cbWndExtra` member tells Windows how many extra bytes to allocate for all windows created with this class. FCWIN needs none.

❏ `wndClass.hInstance=hInstance;`

This member informs Windows which instance of FCWIN owns the window class ("this" one does—sounds a lot like the C++ `this` pointer, doesn't it?).

❑ `wndClass.hIcon=LoadIcon(NULL, "IDI_APPLICATION");`

The `hIcon` member specifies which icon will be used if the application's window is minimized by a user. `IDI_APPLICATION` specifies the built-in application icon.

❑ `wndClass.hCursor=LoadCursor(NULL,IDC_ARROW );`

`hCursor` specifies the cursor to use with the application. It is the normal mouse arrow cursor for FCWIN.

❑ `wndClass.hbrBackground=GetStockObject(WHITE_BRUSH );`

The `GetStockObject(WHITE_BRUSH )` Windows function causes the background for FCWIN to be painted white.

❑ `wndClass.lpszMenuName="FCMenu";`

You must specify the menu to be used with FCWIN. The string given here, `"FCMenu"`, must match the resource name of the menu created by RT and stored in the FCWIN.RES file.

❑ `wndClass.lpszClassName=szAppName;`

Finally, tell Windows the application's name. Remember that `szAppname` is a C macro in the `fcwin.h` header (line 1) and is equated to the `"FinancialCalcs"` string.

You use the `RegisterClass()` Windows function to register the window class (see lines 93 and 94 of listing 21.2). If the class cannot be registered, the program returns a `FALSE` value and ends the application.

After registering the window class, you must tell Windows to create the window. This is done with the `CreateWindow()` function, shown in lines 73–110 of listing 21.2 :

```
 73        HWND            hWnd;
 74

...
100        hWnd = CreateWindow(szAppName,
101                            "Financial Calculations",
102                            WS_OVERLAPPEDWINDOW,
103                            CW_USEDEFAULT,
104                            CW_USEDEFAULT,
105                            CW_USEDEFAULT,
106                            CW_USEDEFAULT,
107                            NULL,
108                            NULL,
109                            hInstance,
110                            NULL);
```

Line 73 declares a window *handle* (a unique integer that identifies *this* particular window, corresponding to *this* particular instance of program execution—using the word *this* in much the same sense as the C++ *this). The call to `CreateWindow()` in lines 100 –110 tells Windows how to go about initializing the window.

The first argument to the function is the application name string, followed by a string that is used as the window's title text. The next argument tells Windows that this is an overlapped window, meaning that it can be partially or wholly covered by another window, and must be refreshed if that occurs.

Next, four consecutive arguments specify `CW_USEDEFAULT`. This means that Windows is to build the FCWIN window with default values for the horizontal position, vertical position, window width, and window height, respectively.

The first `NULL` argument specifies that FCWIN's main window has no parent window (it *is* a parent window). The next `NULL` argument indicates that there is no override menu; the one given in the window class structure should be used.

Creating a window does not necessarily mean that it is yet visible on the screen. You should use the `ShowWindow()` function as soon as possible after creating the window to display it (line 112), as follows:

```
112        ShowWindow(hWnd, nCmdShow);
113        UpdateWindow(hWnd);
```

The `UpdateWindow()` function call in line 113 tells Windows that all or part of the window's client area is invalid, and that the `WM_PAINT` message should be issued to the window procedure.

Usually, the `WM_PAINT` message is very important for applications that paint information in the client area. FCWIN does not process this message in `WndProc()` because the application uses dialog boxes for everything—it does not matter whether the client area becomes invalid because there is nothing in it.

Setting Up the Main Message Loop

Your Windows program does not interact directly with the screen, keyboard, printer, or any other device. Windows does all that, and places the results in an application message queue (in a device-independent fashion). Messages from this queue are popped off and sent to your application's program for processing. Processing these messages is the business of the main message loop. Figure 22.1 compares the flow of execution in your program to the flow of message and data traffic from Windows to your program.

Fig. 22.1. *Messages and data flow from Windows queues to your program (bold line), while your program's message loop continuously checks the message queues and dispatches messages to* WndProc() *(light line).*

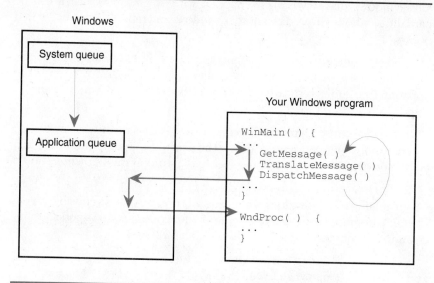

Although the arrangement depicted in figure 22.1 may seem awkward at first, it allows Windows to multitask several applications at the same time. It seems to your program as if the WinMain() procedure is the only one ever executed: it does not directly call any other function in the program. WinMain() *indirectly* invokes the WndProc() window procedure, but it must do so by dispatching messages to WndProc() *through Windows*. At this point, Windows has the opportunity to interleave the execution of other application programs. The following discussion looks at how this is done in more detail.

The main message loop for FCWIN is quite simple and is found in lines 115–120:

```
115        while (GetMessage(&msg, NULL, 0, 0))
116        {
117            TranslateMessage(&msg );
118            DispatchMessage(&msg );
119        }
120        return msg.wParam;
```

The `GetMessage()` returns a non-`NULL` value for every message except the quit message (you see how to generate a quit message in the next section). When `GetMessage()` gets a quit message, the loop ends and the application is finished. Note that a return value has been placed in `msg.wParam` by the quit procedure and should be returned from the `WinMain()`.

The `TranslateMessage()` Windows function passes along many messages as they are but also translates keyboard scan codes and character codes into ANSI character values. (An ANSI character can be an ANSI multibyte or wide character or an ASCII character.) If your program expects to receive keyboard input from the user, as FCWIN does, this function call should be present. Finally, `DispatchMessage()` sends the message to the appropriate window procedure. FCWIN uses the `WndProc()` main window procedure and a number of dialog procedures (a *dialog* is a special kind of child window), all of which must receive their messages at the proper time.

Writing the *WndProc()* Function

The `WinMain()` function is made known to Windows by exporting it. The *window procedure* (the function that receives and interprets all your program's messages from Windows), however, is identified by the `lpfnWndProc` member of the window class structure at registration time. After the window class has been registered, the window procedure is invoked each time the `DispatchMessage()` function is called in the main message loop. Note that, a little later on in program execution, it may be a dialog function which is dispatched—Windows keeps up with what part of your program is active at any given time, and forwards the dispatched message to the correct function. A Windows program can have several existing windows and dialogs at the same time.

The window procedure for FCWIN is in lines 134–352 of listing 21.2. This procedure processes the messages received from the main message loop, performing whatever action is indicated. The following partial listing of the FCWIN window procedure illustrates its generally required form:

```
134    Long FAR PASCAL WndProc (HWND hWnd, unsigned Message,
135                                WORD wParam, LONG lParam)
136    {
...
151        static HANDLE hInstance;
152
153        switch(Message)
154        {
```

```
 ...
 162
 163        case WM_CREATE:
 ...                             /* Perform setup tasks
 193           return 0;
 ...
 203        case WM_COMMAND:
 204            switch( wParam ) {
 205              case IDM_PCTCHANGE:
 206                  if ( DialogBox( hInstance, "FCPCTCG",
 207                                    hWnd, lpfnDoPctChg ) )
 208                    InvalidateRect( hWnd, NULL, TRUE );
 209                  return 0;
 ...
 344            }
 345            break;
 346
 347        case WM_DESTROY:
 348            PostQuitMessage(0);
 349            return 0;
 350    }
 351    return DefWindowProc(hWnd,Message,wParam,lParam);
 352 }
```

As you can see, WndProc() processes the WM_CREATE, WM_COMMAND, and WM_DESTROY messages. There are many more possible messages, but these are all that are needed by FCWIN.

The WM_CREATE message is the first message received by the window procedure and should be used to perform any final initialization tasks. FCWIN, for example, uses the WM_CREATE message as a signal that it is time to set up all the pointers to the dialog procedure functions.

A WM_COMMAND message is received each time the user clicks a menu item. When this happens, the wParam argument contains the ordinal value of the menu's control item. This is where all the macro names for the ordinal values become very handy. Without such names, it would be very difficult to determine whether the case statements are coded correctly.

The third and final Windows message processed by WndProc() is the WM_DESTROY message. Windows sends this message when a user pulls down the window's system menu (using the button in the top left corner of the main window frame) and clicks Close. When this happens, the WndProc() code uses the PostQuitMessage() Windows function to send the quit message (WM_QUIT) to the main message loop, as mentioned previously.

If all the `case` statements fail, `WndProc()` must pass along an unprocessed message to the default handlers in Windows. This is done by returning the value gotten from the `DefWinProc()` function (the default window procedure).

Setting Up Callback Functions for Dialogs

As mentioned, FCWIN does not use the client area of the main window directly to display information. All data input and display is handled by dialogs, because this is a good way to produce a sophisticated display quickly.

To use a dialog, your program must have available the dialog resources necessary to control the screen. These resources were created using the Whitewater Group RT, described in Chapter 20. Each dialog resource contains controls (edit boxes, list boxes, and static text) that are each associated with an ordinal value. Defining control IDs is a good place to use macros to define these ordinal values, as was done in the `fcwin.h` file. Without the macros, it would be difficult to keep track of which numbers indicate which controls.

In the main source file, you must set up and then control the dialog functions. You must provide Windows with pointers to the dialog functions (they are *callback* functions, and will be called by Windows from outside your program); you must create the dialog at the right moment; and you must provide the code for controlling and ending the dialog.

Creating Dialog Functions

Before your program can create a dialog, Windows must be informed of the location of the dialog procedure (function) that will control it. Therefore, the first step is to declare far pointers to the dialog functions. This is done in the `WndProc()` function, as follows:

```
134   long FAR PASCAL WndProc (HWND hWnd, unsigned Message,
135                                   WORD wParam, LONG lParam)
136   {
137      static FARPROC lpfnDoPctChg;
138      static FARPROC lpfnDoPctTot;
139      static FARPROC lpfnDoMkupCo;
140      static FARPROC lpfnDoMkupPr;
...   /* Other declarations */
352   }
```

There are two important things to note about these pointer declarations. First, be sure to declare them with the `static` storage class specifier (or perhaps make them global variables), so that the compiler will locate them in the data segment of the program. If you allow them to be compiled as `auto` variables, they will be destroyed before a dialog can be started. Second, always use the `FARPROC` Windows type name to declare the pointers to functions. The strange-looking prefix `lpfn` (*long pointer to function*) used with function names to form a pointer name is not required, but it is common practice to use it.

The next task is to initialize the pointers to the dialog functions. This is accomplished using the `MakeProcInstance()` Windows function, as follows:

```
163        case WM_CREATE:
164          hInstance = ((LPCREATESTRUCT) lParam)->hInstance;
165          lpfnDoPctChg =
166                MakeProcInstance( DoPctChg, hInstance );
```

Notice in line 163 that the `WndProc()` function does not automatically know which instance of the application it is serving at the moment. This must be determined by extracting the instance handle from the `lParam` argument of the `WndProc()` function. The resulting instance handle, `hInstance`, is in turn used as an argument to `MakeProcInstance()`, which returns the address of the current copy of the dialog procedure.

Now only the creation of the dialog remains. This is not done until a user clicks the corresponding menu item. At that time, the `DialogBox()` Windows function is given arguments for the instance and function pointer, and is called to create the dialog:

```
203        case WM_COMMAND:
204            switch( wParam ) {
205              case IDM_PCTCHANGE:
206                  if ( DialogBox( hInstance, "FCPCTCG",
207                                  hWnd, lpfnDoPctChg ) )
208                    InvalidateRect( hWnd, NULL, TRUE );
209                  return 0;
```

When the dialog returns to `WndProc()` immediately after the `DialogBox()` call, the dialog has run to completion (controlled by the dialog procedure described next). The call to the `InvalidateRect()` Windows function informs Windows that the screen area occupied by the dialog box is now invalid and needs repainting.

Controlling the Dialog

When Windows invokes the dialog procedure in response to the `CreateDialog()` call, it passes several parameters to the dialog. These parameters include a window handle for the dialog box (which is, after all, a special child window), a Windows message, and two more parameters, only one of which is used by FCWIN. Here is the dialog function for the Percent Change dialog:

```
360   BOOL FAR PASCAL DoPctChg( HWND hDlg, unsigned message,
361                             WORD wParam, LONG lParam)
362   {
363      switch ( message ) {
364
365         case WM_INITDIALOG:
366             SetFocus( GetDlgItem( hDlg, FCWIN_OLD ) );
367             return FALSE;
368
369         case WM_CLOSE:
370             EndDialog( hDlg, TRUE );
371             return TRUE;
372
373         case WM_COMMAND:
374           switch ( wParam ) {
375
376           case FCWIN_COMPUTE :
377               old = new = ans = 0.0;
378
379               GetDlgItemText( hDlg,FCWIN_OLD,instring,32 );
380               sscanf( instring, "%lf", &old );
381
382               GetDlgItemText( hDlg,FCWIN_NEW,instring,32 );
383               sscanf( instring, "%lf", &new );
384
385               if ( old != 0.0 )
386                 ans = ((new-old)/old)*100.0;
387               sprintf( instring, "%7.2f", ans );
388
389               SetDlgItemText( hDlg,FCWIN_ANS,instring );
390               SetFocus( GetDlgItem( hDlg,FCWIN_OLD ) );
391               return FALSE;
392
393           case FCWIN_RETURN:
394               EndDialog( hDlg, TRUE );
```

```
395                     return TRUE;
396            }
397        break;
398      }
399      return FALSE;
400    }
```

The first parameter a dialog procedure receives is a window handle, named hDlg here. This window handle is not for the main window; it is only for the dialog box (child window). This handle is used in several Windows function calls: to set the input focus to a particular control (item) in the dialog box, to get text from a dialog control, to place text in a dialog control, and to end the dialog.

A dialog does not receive a WM_CREATE message from Windows. Instead, it receives a WM_INITDIALOG message. The DoPctChg() dialog function sets the input focus to the top edit box in the dialog at this time (see lines 365–371).

The WM_CLOSE Windows message is received when a user has clicked Close in the dialog box's system menu. This signals to the dialog function that the dialog should be ended using the EndDialog() Windows function (see lines 369–371).

When a WM_COMMAND message is received, the third function argument, wParam, contains the ordinal value of the dialog control that was clicked by the user. Notice that DoPctChg() needs to detect only the FCWIN_COMPUTE control (which indicates that the user clicked the Compute pushbutton). When the FCWIN_COMPUTE control ID has been detected, you can use the GetDlgItemText() Windows function to retrieve text from the various edit boxes and the SetDlgItemText() Windows function to send text to the output control box.

Using *MessageBox()* for Pop-Up Help and Error Messages

There is another, even quicker way to get display information on the screen. You can use the MessageBox() Windows function to display text in a message box that has at least one built-in pushbutton button (which you do not have to control); an optional window caption (a message box is a window); and an optional icon, such as the exclamation point, hand, or stop sign. The following code fragment comes from the printer dialog function of fcwin.c in listing 21.2 and shows how to use a message box to produce an error message:

```
1024        hPr = CreateDC( (LPSTR)szPrintDriver,
1025                        (LPSTR)szPrintType,
1026                        (LPSTR)szPrintPort,
1027                        NULL );
1028    else {
1029        MessageBox( hDlg, "Unable to start printing.",
1030                    NULL, MB_OK | MB_ICONHAND );
1031        DeleteDC( hPr );
1032        EndDialog( hDlg, TRUE );
1033        return TRUE;
1034    }
```

In this code fragment, MessageBox() is used to display an error message when the function fails to correctly create the printer device context (which is explained shortly). The first argument must be either a window handle (hDlg is the dialog's window handle) or NULL if the message box does not have to be associated with a particular window.

The second argument for the MessageBox() function is a pointer to a string containing the message text (it can be a string literal here, as in most C code). The third argument, if present, is another pointer to a string containing caption text for the message box. This sample does not use a caption, but you will see how to supply that parameter in the discussion of the PopupMsg() help function for FCWIN in the section "Using Dynamic Link Libraries" at the end of this chapter.

The fourth argument is an integer containing bit flags that tell the MessageBox() procedure what kind of icon to use (if any) and which push buttons to use. The icon and push-button flags should be identified using only the Windows macro names, and the two kinds of flag should be ORed together, as shown in the preceding code fragment.

You can use the following macro names for the icon type: MB_ICONHAND, MB_ICONINFORMATION, MB_ICONEXCLAMATION, MB_ICONSTOP, or MB_ICONQUESTION. There is no default value for this flag: if you do not supply one, there will be no icon in the message box.

There are also several push-button macros with fairly self-explanatory names. These macros include MB_OK, MB_OKCANCEL, MB_YESNO, MB_YESNOCANCEL, MB_RETRYCANCEL, and MB_ABORTRETRYIGNORE. The macro name tells you what label will appear on the push button. There is a default for this value: it is MB_OK. You can specify only one of these macro names, so there can be at most three buttons in the message box (if you specify MB_ABORTRETRYCANCEL).

How can you tell which push button was activated? A return value from the `MessageBox()` call was not used in the preceding code fragment, but `MessageBox()` does return one of six ordinal values. The following code fragment shows you how to use the return value from `MessageBox()`:

```
switch( MessageBox( /* parms */ ) ) {
case IDOK:       /* Do something about OK status */
    break;
case IDCANCEL:   /* Do something about cancelling task */
    break;
case IDYES:      /* Do something about YES answer */
    break;
case IDNO:       /* Do something about NO answer */
    break;
case IDABORT:    /* Do something about aborting the task */
    break;
case IDRETRY:    /* Do something about retrying */
    break;
}
```

You see another use of the `MessageBox()` function in the discussion of the `PopupMsg()` DLL module later in this chapter, in the section "Using Dynamic Link Libraries."

Spooling Hard Copy to the Windows Print Manager

FCWIN can generate all kinds of useful financial information, including complete amortization schedules for your home loan. What good is an amortization schedule, however, if you cannot print and keep it? Because amortization information has limited usefulness without print capability, FCWIN has a dialog for spooling output hard copy to the Windows Print Manager (the normal method under Windows).

The `PrntAmort()` dialog procedure is the most complicated function in the FCWIN application. Therefore, the majority of its code will be discussed in sections. Lines 964–992 in listing 21.2, shown next, contain the dialog function's declaration part and variable declarations:

```
964   BOOL FAR PASCAL PrntAmort( HWND hDlg, unsigned message,
965                                   WORD wParam, LONG lParam )
966   {
967
968                   /* ------------------------------------- */
969                   /* DeviceMode() is not in windows.h file. */
970                   /* Provide a typedef for the function.    */
971                   /* ------------------------------------- */
972
973       typedef VOID (FAR PASCAL *DEVMODEPROC)(HWND,HANDLE,
974                                         LPSTR,LPSTR);
975
976       HDC hPr;          /* device context handle for printer */
977
978       char szPrinter[80];        /* device info from WIN.INI */
979       char szDriverFile[16];  /* name of prt driver DLL file */
980
981       HANDLE hLibrary;      /* handle for prt driver DLL file */
982       DEVMODEPROC lpfnDM;    /* pointer to DeviceMode() proc */
983
984       LPSTR szPrintType;              /* printer type string */
985       LPSTR szPrintDriver;     /* printer driver name string */
986       LPSTR szPrintPort;        /* printer port name string */
987
988       int LineSpace, LinesPerPage, CurrentLine, LineLength;
989
990       POINT PhysPageSize;
991       TEXTMETRIC TextMetric;
992
```

The `typedef` in the preceding code fragment is present because the printer driver's `DeviceMode()` function is called later, and there is no prototype for it in `windows.h`. The meaning and use of the other variables follow:

❑ `HDC hPr;          /* device context handle for printer */`

As with most things in Windows, you must establish a *context* to use a facility, and you must have a handle for that context. `hPr` stores the printer device context for the dialog. The context is deleted at the end of the dialog. You could compare creating a context to opening a file in plain C.

❏ `char szPrinter[80];`   `/* device info from WIN.INI */`

`szPrinter` holds the unparsed printer profile text string. This profile string is acquired from the WIN.INI Windows file using the `GetProfileString()` Windows function.

❏ `char szDriverFile[16];`   `/* name of prt driver DLL file */`

This string holds the name of the printer driver DLL file, after the DRV file extension has been concatenated to it.

❏ `HANDLE hLibrary;`   `/* handle for prt driver DLL file */`

A DLL file is a Windows resource, like everything else, so it will have a handle. The DLL handle is stored in the `hLibrary` variable in this application.

❏ `DEVMODEPROC lpfnDM;`   `/* pointer to DeviceMode() proc */`

`lpfnDM` is a far pointer to a function that will contain the address of the printer driver's `DeviceMode()` function. The `DeviceMode()` function pops up a printer configuration dialog box, the contents of which depend on the type of printer attached to the system.

❏ `LPSTR szPrintType;`   `/* printer type string */`

`szPrintType` is a string that contains a descriptive name for the system printer, such as "Epson 24 Pin". It is used in creating the printer device context.

❏ `LPSTR szPrintDriver;`   `/* printer driver name string */`

After parsing the profile string, the `szPrintDriver` string will hold the text string name of the printer driver module library (DLL). The printer that this dialog was tested on, for example, was an Epson LQ-800, so the driver file name is `EPSON24`. This string will also be used in creating the device context.

❏ `LPSTR szPrintPort;`   `/* printer port name string */`

This string is the third parameter used to create the printer device context. It contains the name of the printer port, such as "LPT1:".

❏ `int LineSpace, LinesPerPage, CurrentLine, LineLength;`

These integer variables contain the results of the text-dimensioning calculations performed to fit the output text on the printer page.

❏ POINT PhysPageSize;

The GETPHYSPAGESIZE escape call (described shortly) returns an object with type POINT. A POINT object contains two integers that reflect the number of horizontal and vertical printer pixels on a whole page.

❏ TEXTMETRIC TextMetric;

The TextMetric variable (a structure) contains detailed information about the dimensions of characters in the current font selected in the printer information context (which FCWIN does not attempt to change).

Normal start-up code for the dialog function appears next, and there is nothing unusual about it:

```
993     switch ( message ) {
994
995        case WM_INITDIALOG:
996            SetFocus( GetDlgItem( hDlg, FCWIN_START);
997            return FALSE;
998
999        case WM_CLOSE:
1000            EndDialog( hDlg, TRUE );
1001            return TRUE;
1002
1003        case WM_COMMAND:
1004            switch ( wParam ) {
1005
1006            case FCWIN_START :
1007
```

Now the real fun begins. The goal is to set up the printer context for whatever printer is attached to the system on which FCWIN is running at the time. This task involves getting the profile string for the printer from Windows, parsing it, and creating the device context. The device context handle will be needed later for sending text to the printer device. Here is the code for this activity:

```
1008                       /* ------------------------------------- */
1009                       /* Get the profile string for the       */
1010                       /* current printer and parse it.         */
1011                       /* ------------------------------------- */
1012
1013          GetProfileString( "windows", "device", ",,,",
1014                            szPrinter, 80 );
1015          if ( (szPrintType   = strtok( szPrinter, "," )) &&
1016               (szPrintDriver = strtok( NULL,      "," )) &&
1017               (szPrintPort   = strtok( NULL,      "," )))
1018
1019                       /* ------------------------------------- */
1020                       /* Create a device context for the      */
1021                       /* printer.                             */
1022                       /* ------------------------------------- */
1023
1024             hPr = CreateDC( (LPSTR)szPrintDriver,
1025                             (LPSTR)szPrintType,
1026                             (LPSTR)szPrintPort,
1027                             NULL );
1028          else {
1029          MessageBox( hDlg, "Unable to start printing.",
1030                      NULL, MB_OK | MB_ICONHAND );
1031          DeleteDC( hPr );
1032          EndDialog( hDlg, TRUE );
1033          return TRUE;
1034          }
1035
```

The GetProfileString() Windows function call in the preceding code fragment gets the printer profile string from the WIN.INI file and places it in szPrinter. The ordinary strtok() C library function is then used to parse the profile string into its component parts. Lines 1024–1027 call the CreateDC() Windows function to create the device context (once more, this is similar to opening a DOS file in C) and place the resulting device context handle in the hPr variable.

After the printer type, driver, and output port are established, the printer driver must be found and loaded (it is a DLL library). In addition, the address of the driver's DeviceMode() printer-setup dialog function is extracted, and then DeviceMode() is called using the resulting pointer to function. This is accomplished in the following code:

```
1036                          /* ----------------------------------- */
1037                          /* This code loads the driver file from */
1038                          /* the DLL. Get the handle for the      */
1039                          /* driver. Use the handle to get the    */
1040                          /* address of its DeviceMode() function, */
1041                          /* and invoke it using the pointer. This */
1042                          /* is the code that causes the printer   */
1043                          /* initialization dialog to pop up.      */
1044                          /* ----------------------------------- */
1045
1046                  strcat( strcpy( szDriverFile, szPrintDriver ),
1047                          ".DRV" );
                        hLibrary = LoadLibrary( szDriverFile );
1048                  if ( hLibrary < 32 ) {
1049                    MessageBox( hDlg, "Can't locate the driver\n"
1050                                "file for this printer.",
1051                                NULL, MB_OK | MB_ICONHAND );
1052                    DeleteDC( hPr );
1053                    EndDialog( hDlg, TRUE );
1054                    return TRUE;
1055                  }
1056                  lpfnDM = GetProcAddress( hLibrary, "DEVICEMODE" );
1057                  (*lpfnDM)( hDlg, hLibrary, (LPSTR)szPrintType,
1058                            (LPSTR)szPrintPort );
1059
```

Line 1046 in the preceding code fragment builds the driver library file name, complete with the DRV file extension. Line 1047 calls the Load Library() Windows function to load the printer driver DLL and place the resulting handle in the hLibary variable. (Nothing else is done with the library just yet.) The hLibrary handle is then used in line 1056 as a parameter for the GetProcAddress() Windows function to determine the address of the DeviceMode() printer driver function. Last, lines 1057 and 1058 show how the far pointer to the lpfnDM function is used to call the DeviceMode() function.

Using the printer driver's built-in DeviceMode() function lends a nice touch to the application, one that you do not have to write explicit code for. The DeviceMode() function starts a dialog for printer setup, using a dialog screen like the one shown in figure 22.2.

Fig. 22.2. *The* `DeviceMode()` *dialog screen for an Epson 24-pin printer.*

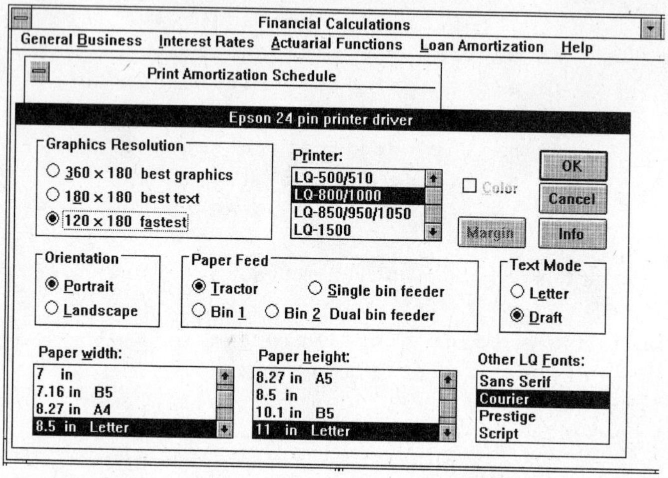

Now you can inform Windows that you are about to start sending output to the printer device context. Use the `Escape()` Windows function for this purpose, passing the `hPr` device context handle (see line 1024) and the `STARTDOC` flag as parameters to the function. The only complication here is detecting any errors resulting from the function call and displaying a message box notifying the user that a problem occurred. Here is the `StartDOC` escape sequence:

```
1060                    /* --------------------------------- */
1061                    /* Notify the Print Manager that we are */
1062                    /* about to start spooling print using */
1063                    /* the STARTDOC Escape call.           */
1064                    /* --------------------------------- */
1065
1066        if ( Escape( hPr, STARTDOC, 11,
1067             "PrintAmort", OL ) < 0 ) {
1068        MessageBox( hDlg, "Unable to start printing.",
1069                    NULL, MB_OK | MB_ICONHAND );
1070        DeleteDC( hPr );
1071        EndDialog( hDlg, TRUE );
1072        return TRUE;
1073        }
1074
```

Unlike DOS printer services, which view everything as a character stream, Windows views the printer as a graphics device similar to the system display—the printer is an integral part of the Windows GUI. Thus, a printer page is thought of as a graphics frame in much the same way as a window is perceived. Approaching printing tasks from this new perspective adds responsibilities to the programmer's workload.

Specifically, it is up to you (that is, the application program) to determine what can fit on a page, how it will be displayed (displaying printer graphics is nearly as easy as displaying printer text with Windows), and when to clear the current frame (printer page) to receive the next image. The printer dialog's next task, therefore, is to determine the size and characteristics of the printer page. This can be accomplished by using the GETPHYSPAGESIZE escape sequence to determine the printer page size in printer pixels, and the GetTextMetrics() Windows function to determine the dimensions of the current font's characters, also in printer pixels (FCWIN allows the printer's built-in text font to be used). From all this information, you can determine the number of text lines that will fit on one page, as follows:

```
1075        /* ------------------------------------- */
1076        /* Now calculate the printing area parms  */
1077        /* using the GetTextMetrics() function    */
1078        /* and the GETPHYSPAGESIZE Escape call.   */
1079        /* ------------------------------------- */
1080
1081     GetTextMetrics( hPr, &TextMetric );
1082     LineSpace = TextMetric.tmHeight
1083             + TextMetric.tmExternalLeading;
1084     Escape( hPr, GETPHYSPAGESIZE, NULL, NULL,
1085             (LPSTR)&PhysPageSize);
1086     LinesPerPage = ( PhysPageSize.y / LineSpace ) - 6;
1087     CurrentLine = LinesPerPage + 1;
1088
```

Notice especially in line 1086 that FCWIN does not allow the LinesPerPage variable to be as large as the theoretical maximum. Six lines are subtracted from the maximum to prevent printing down to the bottom perforation of the page. (Another reason, besides aesthetics, for preventing this will become clear shortly.)

Finally, the printer dialog function is ready to send the amortization schedule to the printer device. A while loop is used to do this, as follows:

```
1089              levelpay = 1 / USPV( apr, freq, numpay ) * amt;
1090              payno = 0;
1091
1092                  /* ------------------------------------- */
1093                  /* Finally, loop and use TextOut() to    */
1094                  /* spool print.                          */
1095                  /* ------------------------------------- */
1096
1097              while ( payno < numpay ) {
1098                if ( ++CurrentLine >= LinesPerPage ) {
1099                  Escape( hPr, NEWFRAME, 0, 0L, 0L );
1100                  CurrentLine = 0;
1101                  BuildTextMessage( "%s%s%s%s%s%s",
1102                                    "   Paymnt #   ",
1103                                    "  Level Pay   ",
1104                                    "    Int Amt    ",
1105                                    "  Prin Amt    ",
1106                                    "   Balance    " );
1107                  TextOut( hPr, 0, CurrentLine*LineSpace,
1108                           (LPSTR)textmsg, strlen(textmsg) );
1109                  ++CurrentLine;
1110                  BuildTextMessage( "%s%s%s%s%s%s",
1111                                    "-------------",
1112                                    "-------------",
1113                                    "-------------",
1114                                    "-------------",
1115                                    "-------------" );
1116                  TextOut( hPr, 0, CurrentLine*LineSpace,
1117                           (LPSTR)textmsg, strlen(textmsg) );
1118                  ++CurrentLine;
1119                }
1120                ++payno;
1121                intpay = levelpay
1122                        * USPV( apr, freq, numpay-payno+1.0 )
1123                        * (apr/freq/100.0);
1124                prinpay = levelpay - intpay;
1125                bal = levelpay * USPV( apr, freq, numpay-payno );
1126                BuildTextMessage( "%12d%12.2f%12.2f%12.2f%12.2f",
1127                                  (int)payno, levelpay,
1128                                  intpay, prinpay,
1129                                  bal
1130                                );
1131                TextOut( hPr, 0, CurrentLine*LineSpace,
```

```
1132                              (LPSTR)textmsg, strlen(textmsg) );
1133              }
1134
1135              Escape( hPr, NEWFRAME, 0, 0L, 0L );
1136              Escape( hPr, ENDDOC, 0, 0L, 0L );
1137              FreeLibrary( hLibrary );
1138              DeleteDC( hPr );
1139              EndDialog( hDlg, TRUE );
1140              return TRUE;
1141
```

Lines 1098–1119 of the preceding fragment of fcwin.c detect page breaks and format and print a header line for the report. The page is physically ejected by the NEWFRAME escape sequence, as seen in line 1099. The use of this escape sequence in the printer device context is important enough to discuss in more detail.

The NEWFRAME escape sequence is the same escape sequence you must use to clear a graphics frame (such as the client area of the main window) when painting in a display window. The behavior of this escape sequence in the printer device context is the other reason for not allowing printing to continue to the physical bottom of the page. If you allow this condition to occur, a strange thing happens when the Windows Print Manager sends the spooled print to the real device: it not only physically ejects the page, but also sends your page eject after it has automatically ejected the page, leaving a blank sheet of paper in the middle of your report. Furthermore, it *skips the data that goes with that page*. Therefore, it is a good idea to avoid the physical bottom of a printer page.

The TextOut() Windows function is used to send print to the Print Manager. Note that the BuildTextMessage() function is *not* a Windows function: it is a helper function written to facilitate the construction of strings that are sent to displays and printers by the dialog functions. The code for BuildTextMessage() appears in listing 21.2 beginning in line 1156.

When the entire amortization schedule is printed, execution falls out the bottom of the while loop. A final NEWFRAME escape sequence ejects the last page, and the ENDDOC escape sequence notifies Windows that printing is complete. Because the printer driver DLL was loaded earlier, the FreeLibrary() Windows function releases it (line 1137), and the DeleteDC() Windows functions deletes the printer device context.

Using Dynamic Link Libraries

Windows dynamic link libraries are very useful. They can contain code (functions), bit maps, icons, or just about anything else you want. The objects in a DLL reside in a file outside your main program, which helps save lines of code. FCWIN implements all the help dialogs using the `PopupMsg()` DLL module, as shown here:

```
289            case HLP_PCTCHANGE:
290                PopupMsg( HLP_PCTCHANGE - HLP_PCTCHANGE );
291                return 0;
```

In this section, you learn how to implement a simple function, the `PopupMsg()` function, in a DLL file named `HELPMSG.DLL`. This DLL and function are used in FCWIN to implement the help facility.

Understanding DLLs

A DLL is a library, but it is *not* like a DOS LIB file. A DLL can contain executable code and must be written in a source file, compiled, and linked much like your application's main source file.

Although a DLL file can have any file extension, using the DLL extension makes the DLL file implicitly available to your program. That is, you won't have to use the `LoadLibrary()` function as FCWIN did to get to the printer driver's DLL. However, you must still let the linker know that your program will be using a DLL module. This can be done with the `IMPORT` statement in your main program's DEF file. The last line of the FCWIN.DEF file (listing 21.3), for example, contains the following statement:

```
IMPORT         HELPMSG.PopupMsg
```

This `IMPORT` statement tells the linker that the `PopupMsg()` function in the `HELPMSG.DLL` file will be used by the program.

In the main source file, you should also provide a function prototype of the function that will be imported, as seen in line 18 of listing 21.2:

```
18  BOOL FAR PASCAL PopupMsg( int );            /* DLL function */
```

By now, you may be asking why, if a DLL module is not linked to the application until the application is running, the linker program needs to know about the DLL. What happens when the linker sees a reference to `PopupMsg()`, for example? It cannot generate a simple function call sequence because the function will never be in a predictable memory location at run time.

The linker uses supplied code (found in the IMPORT.LIB file in the \integra\lib directory) to generate Windows calls to get the address of the DLL module and call it. At this stage, the DLL module is identified only by the familiar ordinal value assigned to it when the DLL was compiled and linked.

How does the linker know the function's ordinal value? The linker can get this value by examining the HELPMSG.LIB import library (in this instance), which was generated when helpmsg.c was compiled and linked.

You should know about a few other oddities concerning DLLs. First, when an executable DLL module is called from the main program (as PopupMsg() will be), the called DLL function is considered logically part of the main application. The DLL program therefore uses the *calling program's stack*, even though the DLL is not part of the calling program. A DLL module has no stack of its own.

Second, a DLL can access data segment variables *using only far pointers*. The DLL's stack and data segment can never be in the same segment of memory because a DLL module has no stack of its own. Therefore, a DLL's data segment is allocated separately, in another segment of memory, and requires far pointers to be accessed. Consequently, Borland C++ 2.0 always uses the compact memory model to compile a DLL, because this makes pointers to the data segment use the far form. Much more complicated problems arise because of this situation, but they are beyond the scope of this book. For now, you can write DLL functions like the PopupMsg() function (presented in the next section) with little trouble. Just do not try to get fancy until you know a good deal more about DLL internals.

Writing a DLL Application

Because a DLL is a Windows file (potentially containing executable code), you should begin construction of the DLL by writing a module definition file for it. The HELPMSG.DEF file for use with FCWIN is shown in listing 22.1.

Listing 22.1. helpmsg.def. *The module definition file for the HELPMSG DLL.*

```
1   LIBRARY       HELPMSG
2   DESCRIPTION   'Sample DLL Module Def file'
3   EXETYPE       WINDOWS
4   CODE                  PRELOAD MOVEABLE DISCARDABLE
5   DATA                  PRELOAD MOVEABLE SINGLE
6   HEAPSIZE      4096
7   EXPORTS       PopupMsg
```

The first thing to notice about the `helpmsg.def` file is that, although there is a `HEAPSIZE` statement, there is no `STACKSIZE` statement. Again, a DLL module has no stack of its own.

The second thing to notice is the `LIBRARY` statement in line 1. This identifies the module definition file as belonging to a DLL, not to a Windows program. This statement is required and causes all sorts of confusion if you accidentally code a `NAME` statement instead.

Notice also the `EXETYPE` statement in line 3. This statement is present because the default target environment is OS/2 rather than Windows. This statement is especially important if you ever plan to migrate your Windows program to Microsoft C.

At this stage of development, all the facilities necessary for your main program and the DLL function to recognize each other are present, in the form of the `IMPORT` and `EXPORT` statements in the respective DEF files. Figure 22.3 illustrates this state of affairs.

Fig. 22.3. *IMPORT and EXPORT statements for the FCWIN and HELPMSG source files.*

Writing the source code for `helpmsg.c` is simplicity itself. The code for this file, including the `PopupMsg()` function, is shown in listing 22.2. Note that the `window.h` file must be included in this source file, just as it was in the main source file for `fcwin.c`.

Listing 22.2. `helpmsg.c`. *C source code that will compile and link to HELPMSG.DLL.*

```
1   #include <windows.h>
2
3   #define NUMMSG 14
4
5   struct {
6     char* caption;
7     char* body;
8   } Messages [] = {
```

```
 9      "General Business/Percent Change",
10          "Percent change calculates the\n"
11          "difference between the new amount\n"
12          "and the old amount as a percentage\n"
13          "of the old amount.",
14      "General Business/Percent of Total",
15          "Percent of total calculates the\n"
16          "partial amount as a percentage of\n"
17          "the total amount.",
18      "General Business/Markup Over Cost",
19          "Markup over cost calculates the\n"
20          "difference between the price and\n"
21          "the cost as a percentage of the cost.",
22      "General Business/Markup Over Price",
23          "Markup over price calculates the\n"
24          "difference between the price and\n"
25          "the cost as a percentage of the price.",
26      "InterestRates/Effective Periodic Rate",
27          "Effective periodic rate calculates\n"
28          "the effective interest rate with\n"
29          "periodic compounding of an APR, when\n"
30          "all interest is reinvested.",
31      "InterestRates/Effective Continuous Rate",
32          "Effective continuous rate calculates\n"
33          "the effective interest rate with\n"
34          "continuous compounding of an APR, when\n"
35          "all interest is reinvested.",
36      "Actuarial/Future Value Single Amount",
37          "Future value of a single amount calculates\n"
38          "the future value of a single deposit given\n"
39          "the initial amount, an APR, compounding\n"
40          "frequency, and the number of years.",
41      "Actuarial/Present Value Single Amount",
42          "Present value of a single amount calculates\n"
43          "the lump sum deposit you would have to\n"
44          "make now to grow to the requested amount\n"
45          "over the given time.",
46      "Actuarial/Future Value Regular Deposits",
47          "Future value of regular deposits (i.e.,\n"
48          "of an annuity) calculates the future total\n"
49          "value of a series of deposits of the reques-\n"
50          "ted amount over the given time.",
```

Listing 22.2. continues

Listing 22.2. continued

```
51      "Actuarial/Present Value Regular Deposits",
52          "Present value of regular deposits (i.e.,\n"
53          "of an annuity) calculates the equivalent\n"
54          "lump sum deposit you must make now to grow\n"
55          "to the same value as a series of deposits.",
56      "Amortization/Loan Data Entry",
57          "Enter the loan amount, precentage rate,\n"
58          "payment frequency, and number of years.\n"
59          "If you close the dialog without clicking\n"
60          "Return, no changes are made to variables.",
61      "Amortization/Payout Analysis",
62          "Payout analysis displays the level pay-\n"
63          "ment required, total dollars repaid, total\n"
64          "interest paid, and the eff. interest % for a\n"
65          "balloon note (the real cost of the loan).",
66      "Amortization/Display Amortization Sched",
67          "The complete amortization schedule for the\n"
68          "loan is displayed in a scrollable listbox.\n"
69
70      "Amortization/Print Amortization Sched",
71          "The complete amortization schedule for the\n"
72          "loan is sent to the Windows Print Manager.\n"
73          "A setup dialog box is displayed first, to\n"
74          "allow you to configure the printer.",
75  };
76
77
78  int FAR PASCAL LibMain( HANDLE hInstance, WORD wDataSeg,
79                          WORD wHeapSize, LPSTR lpszCmdLine )
80  {
81    if ( wHeapSize > 0 ) UnlockData( 0 );
82    return 1;
83  }
84
85  BOOL FAR PASCAL PopupMsg( int msgnum )
86  {
87    if ( msgnum >= NUMMSG ) return FALSE;
88    MessageBox( NULL, (LPSTR)(Messages[msgnum].body),
89                (LPSTR)(Messages[msgnum].caption),
90                MB_ICONINFORMATION | MB_OK );
91    return TRUE;
92  }
```

As you can see in listing 22.2, most of the source file is taken up by the array of structures containing caption and message text. The large amount of this material was the primary reason to move it out of fcwin.c and locate it elsewhere, but in a fashion still easily accessible to the program. A DLL is made to order for that kind of task.

Lines 78–83 contain the only required function in a DLL. There must be a LibMain() function in a DLL, just as there must be a WinMain() function in a Windows program, or a main() function in an ordinary C or C++ program. In the simple version of a DLL that FCWIN uses, it is necessary only to verify that a local heap is available, to call UnlockData() to tell Windows that the DLL's data segment can now be moved if necessary, and to return a TRUE (nonzero) value.

Locating the bulk of the help messages in the DLL is a good design decision. First, because the DLL can be shared by more than one copy of the application, the error message text needs to be loaded into memory only once, which reduces overhead. If all the help messages had been defined in fcwin.c, each instance of the application would load a fresh copy of all that text. Second, this arrangement allows Windows to move the data in memory, or swap it out to disk if necessary, to streamline multitasking operations. This makes FCWIN a more courteous "guest" of the system, capable of coexisting efficiently with other applications.

The use of the array of structures to access the help and caption text (lines 85–92) is ordinary, but there is something new in the way that the MessageBox() function is used (lines 88–91). Notice that the first argument for MessageBox() is not a window or dialog handle, as it was in fcwin.c when this function was used to display error messages. Unless you supply a window handle, PopupMsg() is not aware of which instance of FCWIN invoked it.

You do not have to know a particular handle to use MessageBox(). You can simply code NULL for the first argument, as was done here, so that the message box is not associated with any instance or window. The message box pops up in the middle of the screen, rather than aligns with a window boundary, but that does not hurt a thing for our purposes.

Before you compile and link a DLL source file using the Borland C++ 2.0 IDE, be sure to select the Options | Application | Windows DLL option. You must do this so that the correct Entry/Exit code for the DLL functions can be used, and also so that the import librarian can be invoked during the link edit process.

The function of the import librarian is to generate the HELPMSG.LIB file, in addition to the EXE file. This file is used by the linkage editor when processing fcwin.c to obtain the ordinal value of the PopupMsg() function mentioned previously.

Exercises

This chapter demonstrated the potential power of a fully developed Windows program. Although FCWIN is a simple sample program—much of its length is due to the large number of dialogs it supports—it does some interesting and useful things in a pleasing format.

There is enough information in this chapter to help you write some interesting, though simple, Windows programs, but much had to be omitted. You still have before you the majority of the learning curve required for full-fledged Windows programming. Accordingly, there are only two exercises for this chapter.

1. Use the menu you created in Chapter 21 for `easy.c` to allow a user to start a dialog. In the dialog, display a static text message of your own choosing in the dialog box. Hint: you will have to use RT again to create the dialog box and to identify the static text control. Do not forget to provide the necessary `#defines` in `easy.h`.

2. Read Charles Petzold's *Programming Windows*, Second Edition (Microsoft Press, 1990). The Borland documentation for Borland C++ 2.0 does not—and does not intend to—teach the extensive subject of Windows programming.

Summary

This has been quite a chapter. Although it is impossible to get a complete working knowledge of programming Windows applications from the whirlwind tour of the subject presented in this part of the book, perhaps your appetite for the subject has been whetted. The Borland C++ 2.0 integrated environment and toolset for Windows programming offers unprecedented access to the world of powerful, multitasking, graphically based applications in the Windows environment.

This chapter has given you just a taste of what you can do by writing Windows applications with Borland C++. Although getting to the Windows support functions is more difficult than it is in ordinary C or C++ programs, it is well worth the effort. This chapter introduced you to the following topics:

❏ *How to set up the Windows interfaces for your program.* This activity includes registering the window class and starting the main message loop, creating the main window, and setting up linkage between

Windows and your program's callback functions. In the `fcwin.c` sample program, you saw how to create and control dialogs with their callback functions.

❏ *How to use message boxes to display pop-up information, such as help information and error messages.*

❏ *How to write and use a dynamic link library (DLL).* The DLL is a central feature of the Windows programming environment. This powerful feature permits the construction of large application programs with a maximum of efficiency.

There is much, much more to Windows programming. If you read the entire book, you certainly covered a lot of ground. If you mastered it all, you can now write C++ programs that will astonish your friends.

Exciting and important things are going on in the world of C and C++ programming, including the recent open access policy of Microsoft concerning Windows. All of these things require greater programming expertise, utilizing all the new tools and working in the new environments. If this book has helped prepare you for the future of Turbo C and C++ programming, we have accomplished what we set out to do.

ASCII Charts

The original ASCII character set is composed of a 7-bit code, to avoid having the high-order bit turned on. The resulting possible decimal integer values for the ASCII character set are 0–127. If a byte is treated as an `unsigned char`, an additional 128 characters (decimal values 128–255) can be used. These characters, together with the original ASCII values, are called the IBM extended ASCII character set. This appendix shows the original codes and their corresponding characters, as implemented on an IBM PC or compatible, and the second group of 128 characters (the extended characters).

Char	Value	Char	Value	Char	Value	Char	Value
0	null	11	♂	22	▬	33	!
1	☺	12	♀	23	↨	34	"
2	●	13	♪	24	↑	35	#
3	♥	14	♫	25	↓	36	$
4	♦	15	☼	26	→	37	%
5	♣	16	►	27	←	38	&
6	♠	17	◄	28	∟	39	'
7	●	18	↕	29	↔	40	(
8	◘	19	‼	30	▲	41	)
9	○	20	¶	31	▼	42	*
10	◙	21	§	32		43	+

Char	Value	Char	Value	Char	Value	Char	Value
44	'	65	A	86	V	107	k
45	-	66	B	87	W	108	l
46	.	67	C	88	X	109	m
47	/	68	D	89	Y	110	n
48	0	69	E	90	Z	111	o
49	1	70	F	91	[	112	p
50	2	71	G	92	\	113	q
51	3	72	H	93	]	114	r
52	4	73	I	94	^	115	s
53	5	74	J	95	–	116	t
54	6	75	K	96	'	117	u
55	7	76	L	97	a	118	v
56	8	77	M	98	b	119	w
57	9	78	N	99	c	120	x
58	:	79	O	100	d	121	y
59	;	80	P	101	e	122	z
60	<	81	Q	102	f	123	{
61	=	82	R	103	g	124	¦
62	>	83	S	104	h	125	}
63	?	84	T	105	i	126	~
64	@	85	U	106	j	127	Δ

Char	Value	Char	Value	Char	Value	Char	Value
128	Ç	136	ê	144	É	152	ÿ
129	ü	137	ë	145	æ	153	Ö
130	é	138	è	146	Æ	154	Ü
131	â	139	ï	147	ô	155	¢
132	ä	140	î	148	ö	156	£
133	à	141	ì	149	ò	157	¥
134	á	142	Ä	150	û	158	Pt
135	ç	143	Å	151	ù	159	ƒ

Char	Value	Char	Value	Char	Value	Char	Value
160	á	184	╕	207	╧	231	τ
161	í	185	╣	208	╨	232	Φ
162	ó	186	║	209	╤	233	θ
163	ú	187	╗	210	π	234	Ω
164	ñ	188	╝	211	╙	235	δ
165	Ñ	189	╜	212	╘	236	∞
166	ª	190	╛	213	╒	237	ø
167	º	191	┐	214	╓	238	∈
168	¿	192	└	215	╫	239	∩
169	⌐	193	┴	216	╪	240	≡
170	¬	194	┬	217	┘	241	±
171	1/2	195	├	218	┌	242	≥
172	1/4	196	─	219	█	243	≤
173	¡	197	┼	220	▄	244	⌠
174	«	198	╞	221	▌	245	⌡
175	»	199	╟	222	▐	246	÷
176	░	200	╚	223	▀	247	≈
177	▒	201	╔	224	α	248	°
178	▓	202	╩	225	β	249	•
179	│	203	╦	226	Γ	250	·
180	┤	204	╠	227	π	251	√
181	╡	205	=	228	Σ	252	η
182	╢	205	=	229	σ	253	²
183	╖	206	╬	230	µ	254	■
						255	

B

Details on Using
printf( ) and *scanf( )*

Chapter 6 explained how to use the `printf()` and `scanf()` families of functions, but there was not enough room in the chapter to show all the format string options that can be used with these two functions. This appendix is a brief listing of those format string options. The first part covers the `printf()` functions, and the last part covers the `scanf()` functions.

The `printf()` format string specifiers have the form:

$$flags_{opt} width_{opt} \% \ flags_{opt} \ width_{opt}.prec_{opt} F|N|h|L|L_{opt} \ type$$

The percent sign (%) is a required part of the format specifier. The percent sign signals the `printf()` function that the information that follows is a conversion specification.

The optional *flags* specify how the data being displayed will be presented. Only one flag at a time can be used. The following list explains each of the flags.

Flag	Meaning
-	Left justification. The result is aligned on the left; the right is padded with blanks if needed. If the – flag is not used, `printf()` right justifies by default. (When right justified, the left side is padded with blanks or zeros as appropriate.)

Flag	Meaning
+	Specifies that signed conversion will begin with a plus sign (+) or minus sign (–).
blank	Tells `printf()` to begin nonnegative values with a blank character. Negative values are preceded with a minus sign (–).
#	This character signals that the argument will be converted using an alternate form, as follows:

Conversion Character	Conversion Alternate
c,s,d,i,u	The # flag has no effect on these conversion characters.
0	Prefixes a 0 to a nonzero argument.
x,X	Prefixes 0x or 0X to the argument.
e,E,f	Forces the floating-point number to display a decimal point.
g,G	This works the same as e or E except that any trailing zeros are not removed.

The optional `width` specification sets the minimum field width. The following list shows the ways the `width` argument can be specified.

Width Specifier	Effect of Specifier
n	Causes at least *n* number of characters to be printed. If *n* characters are not available, the result is padded with blanks.
0n	At least *n* characters are printed. If there are not *n* characters, the result is padded with zeros.

Width Specifier	Effect of Specifier
*	Tells `printf()` to look up the value for the new width specification. `printf()` gets the new width value from the next argument in the argument list.

The optional precision is noted by the `.prec` specification. In general, the `.prec` specifies how many digits are displayed for integer values or how many fractional digits are displayed for floating-point values. The beginning decimal point (`.`) in the precision specification option is mandatory even if the width is not specified. If both the width and precision are used in a conversion specifier, there cannot be any whitespace between them (for example, `%6 .2` is wrong; use `%6.2`). The following list shows how the precision specification is used.

Precision Specification	Effect of Specifier
.n	Prints *n* number of decimal places. When the value being displayed is larger than *n*, the type of the value determines whether the displayed value is truncated or rounded, as shown in the next table.
.0	For floating-point numbers of type `e`, `E`, and `f`, the fractional portion is suppressed. For integer type values `i`, `d`, `o`, `u`, and `x`, precision is set to default values.
*	Tells `printf()` to get the precision specification from the argument list. The argument that specifies precision should precede the value to be displayed.
none	Sets default precision values. For integer type values, precision is 1. For floating-point values, precision is 6. For `g` and `G` type values, all significant digits are displayed. With string types, all characters to the first null value are printed. There is no default for character type values.

The type of the value being displayed determines what effect the precision specification will have. The following list shows you how the precision specification affects each of the basic data types.

Date Type	Effect of Precision Specification (. n)
d,i,o,u,x,X	At least n digits are displayed. If the value does not contain enough digits to display, the display value is padded to the left with zeros. If the output value is larger than n, there is no truncation or rounding.
e,E,f	At least n fractional characters are displayed. The last digit to be displayed is rounded.
g,G	At most, n significant digits are printed.
s	No more than n characters are printed.
c	The precision specification has no effect on character data.

The input-size modifiers, [F|N|h|l|L], tell printf() what type of pointer or argument is in the argument list. The next list documents the type of value associated with each of the input-size modifiers.

Input-size Modifer	Type of Argument
F	far pointer
N	near pointer
h	short int
l	long int or double floating point
L	long double for floating point

The last part of a conversion specification is the type specification. The type specification tells printf() the data type of the information being displayed. The following list shows each type specification and the data type associated with the specification.

Type Specification	Data Type
d,i	signed int
o	unsigned octal int
u	unsigned int
x,X	unsigned hexadecimal int
e,E,f,g,G	signed floating point
c	char
s	string

The scanf() family of functions is used to input data. Like printf(), the scanf() functions have a format string and an argument list. The format of the conversion specifiers in the format string is

% *_{opt} widthopt F|N_{opt} h|l|L_{opt} type

The percent character (%) tells scanf() that it is about to encounter a conversion specification. The percent character is a required part of every conversion specification you include.

The asterisk (*) is an optional modifier that suppresses the assignment of the next input field. Although this assignment suppression option looks like a pointer operator, it is not.

The optional width value tells scanf() the maximum number of characters to read. When scanf() reads an input field, it reads as many characters as possible for the data type being converted, up to the number specified by width.

The input-size modifiers determine how scanf() interprets the address associated with a conversion specification. The next list shows the effect of the input-size modifiers.

Input-size Modifer	Effect
F	Tells scanf() that a far pointer argument is asssociated with the current conversion specification.
N	Tells scanf() that a near pointer argument is associated with the current conversion specification.

The argument-type modifiers indicate how input data will be converted. The following list shows the modifiers and their effects. If a type of conversion specifier is not listed with an argument-type modifier, the modifer has no effect on that conversion specifier.

Argument-type Modifier	Effect
h	With d, i, o, u, and x data types, the input data is converted to a short int and stored in a short type data object.
l	For the d, i, o, u, and i data types, the input is converted to a long int and stored in a long type data object.
	For the e, f, and g types, the input is converted to double and stored in a double type object.
L	The L format works with e, f, and g conversion specification types. The input value is converted to a long double and stored in a double type data object.

The *type* is a character that indicates the data type of the information that scanf() is reading. The following list shows the *type* specification and the data type for each of the characters.

Type Specifier	Data Type
d	decimal integer; pointer to int
D	decimal integer; pointer to long
o	octal integer; pointer to int
0	octal integer, pointer to long
i	decimal, octal, or hex; pointer to int
l	decimal, octal, or hex; pointer to long
u	unsigned decimal integer; pointer to unsigned int
U	unsigned decimal integer; pointer to unsigned long

Type Specifier	Data Type
x	hexadecimal integer; pointer to `int`
X	hexadecimal integer; pointer to `long`
e,E,f,g,G	floating point; pointer to `float`
c	character; pointer to `char`
s	string; pointer to array of `char`

C

Details on Using
exec...() and
spawn...()

The exec...() and spawn...() functions are used to run *child* processes. A child process is simply an executable program that is started from inside another executable program.

The exec...() and spawn...() families contain several functions. Each function in each family performs the same basic task, but each function works somewhat differently. This appendix lists each function and its distinctive features.

The exec...() family of functions consists of the following functions:

```
int execl( char *path, char *arg0, *arg1, ..., *argn, NULL );
int execle( char *path, char *arg0, *arg1, ..., *argn, NULL,
          char **env );

int execlp( char *path, char *arg0, *arg1, ..., *argn, NULL );
int execlpe( char *path, char *arg0, *arg1, ..., *argn, NULL,
          char **env );

int execv( char *path, char *argv[] );
int execve( char *path, char *argv[], char **env );

int execvp( char *path, char *argv[] );
int execv( char *path, char *argv[], char **env );
```

Each of the functions in the exec...( ) family is made by appending the letters l, p, e and v to exec. The following list gives the purpose of each of these suffixes.

exec...( ) *Suffix*	*Purpose*
l	Causes the argument pointers, *arg0*, *arg1,* and so on, to be passed as separate arguments. The l suffix is used when you already know how many arguments you will have to pass. Either this option or the v option is required.
v	Causes the argument pointers, *arg0*, *arg1,* and so on, to be passed to the child process as an array of pointers. The v option is used when you have a variable number of arguments to pass to the child process. Either this option or the l option is required.
p	Tells exec...( ) to search for the child process in the directories listed in the DOS path command.
e	The exec...( ) functions with the e option have the capability of sending a new *env* argument to the child process.

The *path* argument in the exec...( ) function call is the file name of the child process that is being started. The *argn* parameters are arguments passed to the child process. On the exec...( ) functions that support it, *env* is a list of new environment settings that can be used by the child process.

The exec...( ) functions must pass at least one argument to the child process. If you do not supply an argument, a copy of the *path* argument is passed to the child process.

If the exec...( ) function is successfully called, the function is unable to return a value. If exec...( ) fails, however, a value of –1 is returned and the errno variable is set. The following list shows the values that can be placed in errno if exec...( ) fails.

errno *Value*	*Meaning*
E2BIG	The argument list was too long.
EACCES	Permission was denied.

errno Value	*Meaning*
EMFILE	There are too many open files.
ENOENT	Either the path or file name was not found.
ENOEXEC	There was an exec format error.
ENOMEM	Not enough memory is left.

The spawn...( ) family of functions is also used to start one executable program from within another. The functions in the spawn...( ) family are

```
int spawnl( int mode, char *path, char *arg0, arg1, ..., argn,
        NULL );
int spawnle( int mode, char *path, char *arg0, arg1, ..., argn,
        NULL, char *envp[] );

int spawnlp( int mode, char *path, char *arg0, arg1, ..., argn,
        NULL );
int spawnlpe( int mode, char *path, char *arg0, arg1, ..., argn,
        NULL, char *envp[] );

int spawnv( int mode, char *path, char *argv[] );
int spawnve( int mode, char *path, char *argv[], char *envp[] );

int spawnvp( int mode, char *path, char *argv[] );
int spawnvpe( int mode, char *path, char *argv[], char *envp[] );
```

The mode argument determines what happens to the parent process after the spawn...( ) function is called. Following is a list of the possible values that can be used for the mode command.

Argument	*Effect*
P_WAIT	The parent process waits until the child process has completed execution.
P_NOWAIT	The parent process continues running while the child process is running. (Borland C++ provides this value for completeness; using it will cause an error because DOS cannot multitask.)
P_OVERLAY	Overlays the child process in the memory area formerly occupied by the parent process.

The *path* argument is the file name of the child process.

Each of the functions in the spawn...( ) family is made by appending the letters l, p, e and v to spawn. The following list shows the purpose of each suffix.

spawn...( ) Suffix	Purpose
l	Causes the argument pointers, *arg0, arg1,* and so on, to be passed as separate arguments. The l suffix is used when you already know how many arguments you will have to pass. Either this option or the v option is required.
v	Causes the argument pointers, *arg0, arg1,* and so on, to be passed to the child process as an array of pointers. The v option is used when you have a variable number of arguments to pass to the child process. Either this option or the l option is required.
p	Tells spawn...( ) to search for the child process in the directories listed in the DOS path command.
e	The spawn...( ) functions with the e option have the capability of sending a new *env* argument to the child process.

If the spawn...( ) function completes successfully, the exit status of the child process is returned. Normally, the exit status is 0. If spawn...( ) is unsuccessful, a value of −1 is returned and errno is set. The following is a list of the values spawn...( ) can store in errno.

Error Value	Meaning
E2BIG	The argument list was too long.
EINVAL	An invalid argument was used.
ENOENT	The path or file name was not found.
ENOEXEC	There was an exec format error.
ENOMEM	There was not enough memory.

Program Listings for
the *quad* Class

The quad class is similar to the vli (Very Large Integer) class presented in the book *Using C* (Que Corporation, 1990). The quad class is in fact a conversion of the vli class. The conversion is straightforward, but it is tedious and not trivial. (One reason for presenting the complete listings was to avoid conversion issues.) If you do not have a copy of *Using C*, and want to compare the two classes with an eye toward making your own conversions, you should do two things before you make any such attempt. First, understand thoroughly the physical formats used by the 80x86 CPU for storing data. Second, understand completely the arithmetic principles involved in performing multiplication and division by emulating hardware shift registers.

The quadword.hpp header file is shown in listing D.1. Note that the operators with binary effect (see Chapter 18) return by value rather than by reference in this version.

Listing D.1. quadword.hpp. *Header file for the* quad *class source file* quadword.cpp.

```
1   #include <stdlib.h>
2   #include <stdio.h>
3   #include <string.h>
4
```

Listing D.1. continues

```
 5   class quad {
 6     unsigned long vdata[4];
 7     int quadoflow;
 8     int quaduflow;
 9   public:
10     quad();
11     quad( quad & );
12     quad( long );
13     quad( int );
14     quad& operator=( quad& );
15     quad& operator=( long );
16     quad& operator=( int );
17     quad& operator=( char* );
18     operator long();
19     operator int();
20     operator char*();
21     friend quad operator+(  quad&, quad& );
22     friend quad operator+( quad&, long );
23     friend quad operator+( quad&, int );
24     friend quad &operator+=( quad&, quad& );
25     friend quad &operator+=( quad&, long );
26     friend quad &operator+=( quad&, int );
27     friend quad operator-( quad&, quad& );
28     friend quad operator-( quad&, long );
29     friend quad operator-( quad&, int );
30     friend quad &operator-=( quad&, quad& );
31     friend quad &operator-=( quad&, long );
32     friend quad &operator-=( quad&, int );
33     friend void shiftleft( quad& );
34     friend void shiftright(quad& );
35     friend quad operator<<( quad&, int );
36     friend quad operator>>( quad&, int );
37     friend quad operator*( quad&, quad& );
38     friend quad operator*( quad&, long );
39     friend quad operator*( quad&, int );
40     friend quad operator/( quad&, quad& );
41     friend quad operator/( quad&, long );
42     friend quad operator/( quad&, int );
43     friend quad operator%( quad&, int );
44   };
```

The `quad` class member functions are shown in listing D.2. Note that in this version, internal temporary `quad` objects are not `static`. Creating and destroying multiple temporary objects during the evaluation of an expression involving `quad` class objects can be expensive. You may want to try using the class as is, and also after making temporary objects static and changing the return type to a reference. The difference in execution speed can be considerable.

Listing D.2. `quadword.cpp`. *Member functions for the `quad` class.*

```
 1   #include "quadword.hpp"
 2
 3   static char outstr[81];
 4
 5   quad::quad()
 6   {
 7     int i;
 8
 9     for ( i=0; i<4; ++i ) vdata[i] = 0;
10     quadoflow = 0;
11     quaduflow = 0;
12   }
13
14   quad::quad( quad &old )
15   {
16     int i;
17
18     for ( i=0; i<4; ++i ) vdata[i] = old.vdata[i];
19     quadoflow = old.quadoflow;
20     quaduflow = old.quaduflow;
21   }
22
23   quad::quad( long value )
24   {
25     int i;
26
27     memset( (void *)vdata, 0, 16 );
28     vdata[0] = value;
29     if ( vdata[1] & 0x80000000L )
30       vdata[1]=0xFFFFFFFFL;
31     quadoflow = 0;
```

Listing D.2. continues

Listing D.2. continued

```
32     quaduflow = 0;
33   }
34
35   quad::quad( int value )
36   {
37     int i;
38
39     memset( (void *)vdata, 0, 16 );
40     vdata[0] = value;
41     if ( vdata[0] & 0x80000000L )
42       vdata[1]=0xFFFFFFFFL;
43     quadoflow = 0;
44     quaduflow = 0;
45   }
46
47   quad& quad::operator=( quad& other )
48   {
49     int i;
50
51     memmove( (void *)vdata, (void *)other.vdata, 16 );
52     quadoflow = other.quadoflow;
53     quaduflow = other.quaduflow;
54     return *this;
55   }
56
57   quad& quad::operator=( long value )
58   {
59     int i;
60
61     memset( (void *)vdata, 0, 16 );
62     vdata[0] = value;
63     if ( vdata[1] & 0x80000000L )
64       vdata[1]=0xFFFFFFFFL;
65     quadoflow = 0;
66     quaduflow = 0;
67     return *this;
68   }
69
70   quad& quad::operator=( int value )
71   {
72     int i;
```

```
73
74     memset( (void *)vdata, 0, 16 );
75     vdata[0] = value;
76     if ( vdata[1] & 0x80000000L )
77       vdata[1]=0xFFFFFFFFL;
78     quadoflow = 0;
79     quaduflow = 0;
80     return *this;
81   }
82
83   quad& quad::operator=( char *s )
84   {
85     int neg, i;
86     if ( *s == '-' ) {
87       neg = 1; s++;
88     }
89     else neg = 0;
90     *this = 0;
91     while ( *s ) {
92       *this = *this * 10;
93       *this += (int)( *s++ - '0' );
94     }
95     if ( neg ) {
96       vdata[0] = ~vdata[0];
97       vdata[1] = ~vdata[1];
98       *this += 1;
99     }
100    return *this;
101  }
102
103  quad::operator long()
104  {
105    return *(long *)vdata;
106  }
107
108  quad::operator int()
109  {
110    return *(int *)vdata;
111  }
112
113  quad::operator char*()
```

Listing D.2. continues

```
114  {
115     int neg, i;
116     char *s, *p;
117     quad VA = *this;
118
119     s = outstr;
120     if ( VA.vdata[1] & 0x80000000L ) {
121        neg = 1;
122        VA.vdata[0] = ~VA.vdata[0];
123        VA.vdata[1] = ~VA.vdata[1];
124        VA += 1;
125     }
126     else neg = 0;
127     while( 1 ) {
128        VA -= 10;
129        if ( VA.vdata[1] & 0x80000000L ) break; // done
130        VA += 10;
131        *s++ = '0' + (int)( VA % 10 );
132        VA = VA / 10;
133     }
134     VA += 10;                    // fixup from loop
135     if ( (int)VA > 0 ) *s++ = (int)VA + '0';
136     if ( neg ) *s++ = '-';
137     *s = '\0'; // terminate the string
138     s = outstr;
139     p = s + strlen( s ) - 1;
140     while ( p > s ) {  // reverse string
141        *s ^= *p; *p ^= *s; *s++ ^= *p--;
142     }
143     return outstr;
144  }
145
146  quad operator+( quad& a, quad& addend )
147  {
148     unsigned int* ADD1 = (unsigned int*)a.vdata;
149     unsigned int* ADD2 = (unsigned int*)addend.vdata;
150     unsigned long x, y;
151     unsigned carry = 0;
152     int i;
153     quad SUM;
154     unsigned int* ANS = (unsigned int*)SUM.vdata;
```

```
155
156     SUM = 0;
157     for ( i=0; i<4; ++i ) {
158       x = ADD1[i]; y=ADD2[i];
159       x += y + carry;                // add with carry
160       ANS[i] = x & 0x0000FFFF;       // store partial result
161       carry = (unsigned)( x >> 16 ); // save the carry
162     }
163     if ( carry ) SUM.quadoflow = 1; else SUM.quadoflow = 0;
164     return SUM;
165   }
166
167   quad operator+( quad& a, long addend )
168   {
169     quad SUML;
170
171     SUML = addend;
172     return a + SUML;
173   }
174
175   quad operator+( quad& a, int addend )
176   {
177     quad SUMI;
178
179     SUMI = addend;
180     return a + SUMI;
181   }
182
183   quad& operator+=( quad& a, quad& addend )
184   {          // compound assign needs assign back to this
185     return a = a + addend;
186   }
187
188   quad& operator+=( quad& a, long addend )
189   {
190     return a = a + addend;
191   }
192
193   quad& operator+=( quad& a, int addend )
194   {
195     return a = a + addend;
```

Listing D.2. continues

```
196   }
197
198   quad operator-( quad& a, quad& subt )
199   {
200     int i;
201     quad DIFF;
202
203     for ( i=0; i<2; ++i ) subt.vdata[i] = ~subt.vdata[i];
204     subt += 1;
205     DIFF = a + subt;        // perform subtraction
206     for ( i=0; i<2; ++i ) subt.vdata[i] = ~subt.vdata[i];
207     subt += 1;
208     return DIFF;
209   }
210
211   quad operator-( quad& a, long subt )
212   {
213     quad DIFFL;
214
215     DIFFL = subt;
216     return a - DIFFL;
217   }
218
219   quad operator-( quad& a, int subt )
220   {
221     quad DIFFI;
222
223     DIFFI = subt;
224     return a - DIFFI;
225   }
226
227   quad& operator-=( quad& a, quad& subt )
228   {
229     int i;
230
231     for ( i=0; i<2; ++i ) subt.vdata[i] = ~subt.vdata[i];
232     subt += 1;
233     a = a + subt;           // perform subtraction
234     for ( i=0; i<2; ++i ) subt.vdata[i] = ~subt.vdata[i];
235     subt += 1;
236     return a;
```

```
237   }
238
239   quad& operator-=( quad& a, long subt )
240   {
241     return a = a - subt;
242   }
243
244   quad& operator-=( quad& a, int subt )
245   {
246     return a = a - subt;
247   }
248
249   void shiftleft( quad& a )
250   {
251     int i, carry;
252
253     for ( i=3; i>=0; --i ) {
254       if ( a.vdata[i] & 0x80000000L ) carry = 1;
255       else carry = 0;
256       a.vdata[i] <<= 1;
257       if ( i < 3 ) a.vdata[i+1] |= carry;
258     }
259   }
260
261   void shiftright( quad& a )
262   {
263     int i;
264     unsigned long carry;
265
266     for ( i=0; i<4; ++i ) {
267       if ( a.vdata[i] & 0x00000001L ) carry = 0x80000000L;
268       else carry = 0;
269       a.vdata[i] >>= 1;
270       if ( i > 0 ) a.vdata[i-1] |= carry;
271     }
272   }
273
274   quad operator<<( quad& a, int dist )
275   {
276     int numbytes, numbits, i;
277     char *s;
```

Listing D.2. continues

Listing D.2. continued

```
278      quad SLEFT;
279
280      SLEFT = a;
281      dist = ( dist > 128 ) ? 128 : dist;
282      numbytes = dist / 8; numbits = dist % 8 ;
283      s = (char *)SLEFT.vdata;
284      if ( numbytes < 16 && numbytes > 0 )
285        memmove( &s[numbytes], &s[0],
286                 16 - numbytes );
287      for ( i=0; i<numbytes; ++i ) s[i] = 0;
288      for ( i=0; i<numbits; ++i ) shiftleft( SLEFT );
289      return SLEFT;
290    }
291
292  quad operator>>( quad& a, int dist )
293  {
294    int numbytes, numbits, i;
295    char *s;
296    quad SRIGHT;
297
298    SRIGHT = a;
299    dist = ( dist > 128 ) ? 128 : dist;
300    numbytes = dist / 8; numbits = dist % 8 ;
301    s = (char *)SRIGHT.vdata;
302    if ( numbytes < 16 && numbytes > 0 )
303      memmove( &s[0], &s[numbytes],
304               16 - numbytes );
305    for ( i=16-numbytes; i<16; ++i ) s[i] = 0;
306    for ( i=0; i<numbits; ++i ) shiftright( SRIGHT );
307    return SRIGHT;
308  }
309
310  quad operator *( quad& a, quad& mcand )
311  {
312    unsigned char mask;
313    unsigned char *m1;
314    int loop, inloop;
315    quad MUX;
316
317    MUX = 0; // init running total
318    m1 = (unsigned char *)a.vdata;
```

```
319     for ( loop=7; loop>=0; --loop )
320       if ( m1[loop] != 0 ) break; //skip leading 0 s
321     if ( loop < 0 ) return MUX;
322     for ( ; loop>=0; --loop ) { // process every byte
323       mask = 0x80;
324       for ( inloop=0; inloop<8; ++inloop ) {    // every bit
325         if ( m1[loop] & mask ) MUX += mcand;
326         mask >>= 1;                 // shift mask for next bit
327         shiftleft( MUX );            // adjust running sum
328       }
329     }
330     shiftright( MUX ); // put last shift back
331     return MUX;
332   }
333
334   quad operator *( quad& a, long mcand )
335   {
336     quad MUXL;
337
338     MUXL = mcand;
339     return MUXL * a;
340   }
341
342   quad operator *( quad& a, int mcand )
343   {
344     quad MUXI;
345
346     MUXI = mcand;
347     return MUXI * a;
348   }
349
350   quad operator/( quad& a, quad& div )
351   {
352     int i, aneg = 0, bneg = 0;
353     quad DIVIDEND;
354     quad DIVISOR;
355     quad FRAG;
356
357     DIVIDEND = a;                    // get a working copy of dividend
```

Listing D.2. continues

Listing D.2. continued

```
358    DIVISOR = div;              // get a working copy of divisor
359    DIVISOR -= 1;
360    if ( DIVISOR.vdata[1] & 0x80000000L ) // it was 0
361      return DIVIDEND;
362    DIVISOR += 1;
363    if ( DIVIDEND.vdata[1] & 0x80000000L ) { // any negatives?
364      aneg = 1;                       // dividend was negative
365      for (i=0;i<2;++i) DIVIDEND.vdata[i]=~DIVIDEND.vdata[i];
366      DIVIDEND += 1;
367    }
368    if ( DIVISOR.vdata[1] & 0x80000000L ) {
369      bneg = 1;                       // divisor was negative
370      for (i=0;i<2;++i) DIVISOR.vdata[i]=~DIVISOR.vdata[i];
371      DIVISOR += 1;
372    }
373
374    for ( i=0; i<64; i+=32 ) { // skip 0's in dividend
375      if ( DIVIDEND.vdata[1] != 0 )
376        break;
377      else DIVIDEND = DIVIDEND << 32;
378    }
379    if ( i == 64 ) return DIVIDEND;        // dividend was zero
380
381                    // the gyrations with FRAG are necessary
382                    // to allow arithmetic with the high order
383                    // part of DIVIDEND
384
385    for ( ; i<64; ++i ) {                     // do division
386      shiftleft( DIVIDEND );      // shift dividend left one bit
387      memmove( (void *)&FRAG.vdata[0],  // set up subtraction
388              (void *)&DIVIDEND.vdata[2], 8 );
389      FRAG -= DIVISOR;                        // trial subtraction
390      if ( FRAG.vdata[1] & 0x80000000L ) FRAG += DIVISOR;
391      else DIVIDEND.vdata[0] |= 0x00000001L;  // quotient bit
392      memmove( (void *)&DIVIDEND.vdata[2],       // restore it
393              (void *)&FRAG.vdata[0], 8 );
394    }
395
396    if ( aneg ^ bneg ) {        // make it negative if necessary
```

```
397        DIVIDEND.vdata[0]=~DIVIDEND.vdata[0];
398        DIVIDEND.vdata[1]=~DIVIDEND.vdata[1];
399        DIVIDEND += 1;
400    }
401    return DIVIDEND;
402 }
403
404 quad operator/( quad& a, long div )
405 {
406    quad DIVL;
407
408    DIVL = div;
409    return a / DIVL;
410 }
411
412 quad operator/( quad& a, int div )
413 {
414    quad DIVI;
415
416    DIVI = div;
417    return a / DIVI;
418 }
419
420 quad operator%( quad& a, int div )
421 {
422    int i;
423    quad MODULUS, FRAG;
424
425    MODULUS = div;
426    MODULUS = a / MODULUS;
427            // use this memmove to do the 128-bit
428            // shift quickly
429    memmove( (void *)&FRAG.vdata[0],
430      (void *)&MODULUS.vdata[2], 8 );
431    return FRAG;
432 }
```

Finally, a test driver program for the quad class is shown in listing D.3.

Listing D.3. `testquad.cpp`. *Test drive the* `quad` *class functions.*

```
1   #include <conio.h>
2   #include "quadword.hpp"
3
4   main()
5   {
6      quad X, Y, Z;
7
8      clrscr();
9      X = 2; Y = 3; Z = 4;
10     X = ( X * Y - Z ) / 2;
11     printf( "%ld\n", (long)X );
12     X = "-999999999";
13     printf( "%s\n", (char *)X );
14     X = ( X / 2 ) * 3;
15     printf( "%s\n", (char *)X );
16  }
```

If you want to use the `quad` class for serious purposes, you have to make temporaries static and use references wherever possible. You may also want to use other internal methods for performing the arithmetic to achieve good execution speeds. You might, for example, want to familiarize yourself with the 80x87 coprocessor and make use of its high-speed integer arithmetic capabilities.

E

Complete Listings of FCWIN Resources

I n Chapters 20 through 22, the FCWIN financial calculator application for Windows was developed in some detail. However, complete details on the Windows resources used by FCWIN were not presented there. For those of you who do not wish to obtain the FCWIN.RES binary file from the program diskette, the resources are provided here in resource *script* format. You can type them all into an FCWIN.RC file using the IDE and include the RC file in the FCWIN project file. Be careful, however, not to make any keystroke errors while typing!

The only resource which cannot be described in an RC file is the application icon. It is therefore shown in figure E.1, so that you can duplicate it using RT.

The FCWIN menu drives the entire application. Its structure is shown in listing E.1.

Fig. E.1. `fcicon.ico` *being edited by RT.*

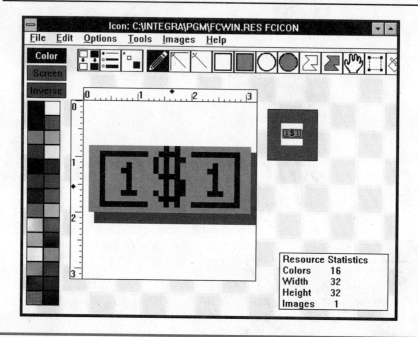

Listing E.1. `fcmenu.rc`. *The menu resource script for FCWIN.*

```
FCMENU    MENU PRELOAD MOVEABLE PURE DISCARDABLE
BEGIN
  POPUP "General &Business"
  BEGIN
    MenuItem   "Percent Ch&ange", 1
    MenuItem   "Percent &Total", 2
    MenuItem   "Markup Over &Cost", 3
    MenuItem   "Markup Over &Price", 4
  END
  POPUP "&Interest Rates"
  BEGIN
    MenuItem   "Effective &Periodic Rate", 5
    MenuItem   "Effective &Continuous Rate", 6
  END
  POPUP "&Actuarial Functions"
  BEGIN
    MenuItem   "Future Value, Single Deposit", 7
    MenuItem   "Present Value, Single Deposit", 8
```

```
        MenuItem  "Future Value,  Regular Deposits", 9
        MenuItem  "Present Value, Regular Deposits", 10
    END
    POPUP "&Loan Amortization"
    BEGIN
        MenuItem  "&Input Loan Data", 11
        MenuItem  "Payout &Analysis", 12
        MenuItem  "&Display Amortization Table", 13
        MenuItem  "&Print Amortization Table", 14
    END
    POPUP "&Help"
    BEGIN
        MenuItem  "Percent Change", 15
        MenuItem  "PerCent Total", 16
        MenuItem  "Markup Percent of Cost", 17
        MenuItem  "Markup Percent of Price", 18
        MenuItem  "Effective Rate, Periodic", 19
        MenuItem  "Effective Rate, Continuous", 20
        MenuItem  "Future Value, Single Payment", 21
        MenuItem  "Present Value, Single Payment", 22
        MenuItem  "Future Value, Regular Deposits", 23
        MenuItem  "Present Value, Regular Deosits", 24
        MenuItem  "Input Loan Data", 25
        MenuItem  "Payout Analysis", 26
        MenuItem  "Display Amortization Table", 27
        MenuItem  "Print Amortization Table", 28
        MenuItem  " ", 0
    END
END
```

The fourteen FCWIN dialog resource scripts are presented next. Dialog resource scripts appear without comment, other than the listing titles.

Listing E.2. `fceffcon.dlg`. *Dialog resource script for Effective Rate, Continuous Compounding.*

```
FCEFFCON DIALOG DISCARDABLE LOADONCALL PURE MOVEABLE 34, 43, 188, 81
STYLE WS_POPUP | WS_CAPTION | WS_SYSMENU | 0x80L
CAPTION "Effective Rate, Continuous Compounding"
```

Listing E.2. continues

Listing E.2. continued

```
BEGIN
  CONTROL "" 106, "EDIT", WS_CHILD | WS_VISIBLE | WS_BORDER |
          WS_TABSTOP, 111, 17, 54, 12
  CONTROL "" 103, "EDIT", WS_CHILD | WS_VISIBLE | WS_DISABLED |
          WS_BORDER, 111, 37, 54, 12
  CONTROL "Return" 104, "BUTTON", WS_CHILD | WS_VISIBLE |
          WS_TABSTOP, 101, 59, 40, 12
  CONTROL "Compute" 105, "BUTTON", WS_CHILD | WS_VISIBLE |
          WS_TABSTOP, 42, 59, 40, 12
  CONTROL "Annual Percentage Rate" 200, "STATIC", WS_CHILD |
          WS_VISIBLE | 0x2L, 11, 18, 84, 12
  CONTROL "Effective Periodic Rate" 201, "STATIC", WS_CHILD |
          WS_VISIBLE | 0x2L, 11, 37, 84, 12
END
```

Listing E.3. `fceffper.dlg`. *Dialog resource script for Effective Interest, periodic compounding.*

```
FCEFFPER DIALOG DISCARDABLE LOADONCALL PURE MOVEABLE 44, 45, 177, 106
STYLE WS_POPUP | WS_CAPTION | WS_SYSMENU | 0x80L
CAPTION "Effective Interest, Periodic Compounding"
BEGIN
  CONTROL "" 106, "EDIT", WS_CHILD | WS_VISIBLE | WS_BORDER |
          WS_TABSTOP, 111, 16, 54, 12
  CONTROL "" 109, "EDIT", WS_CHILD | WS_VISIBLE | WS_BORDER |
          WS_TABSTOP, 111, 35, 54, 12
  CONTROL "" 103, "EDIT", WS_CHILD | WS_VISIBLE | WS_DISABLED |
          WS_BORDER, 111, 53, 54, 12
  CONTROL "Return" 104, "BUTTON", WS_CHILD | WS_VISIBLE |
          WS_TABSTOP, 99, 86, 40, 12
  CONTROL "Compute" 105, "BUTTON", WS_CHILD | WS_VISIBLE |
          WS_TABSTOP, 40, 86, 40, 12
  CONTROL "Annual Percentage Rate" 200, "STATIC", WS_CHILD |
          WS_VISIBLE | 0x2L, 11, 18, 84, 12
  CONTROL "# Compounding Periods" 201, "STATIC", WS_CHILD |
          WS_VISIBLE | 0x2L, 11, 36, 84, 12
  CONTROL "Effective Periodic Rate" 202, "STATIC", WS_CHILD |
          WS_VISIBLE | 0x2L, 11, 54, 84, 12
END
```

Listing E.4. `fcfvann.dlg`. *Dialog resource script for Future Value of Regular Deposits.*

```
FCFVANN DIALOG DISCARDABLE LOADONCALL PURE MOVEABLE 10, 35, 235, 138
STYLE WS_POPUP | WS_CAPTION | WS_SYSMENU | 0x80L
CAPTION "Future Value of Regular Deposits"
BEGIN
    CONTROL "" 107, "EDIT", WS_CHILD | WS_VISIBLE | WS_BORDER |
            WS_TABSTOP, 127, 15, 65, 12
    CONTROL "" 106, "EDIT", WS_CHILD | WS_VISIBLE | WS_BORDER |
            WS_TABSTOP, 127, 32, 65, 12
    CONTROL "" 109, "EDIT", WS_CHILD | WS_VISIBLE | WS_BORDER |
            WS_TABSTOP, 127, 49, 65, 12
    CONTROL "" 108, "EDIT", WS_CHILD | WS_VISIBLE | WS_BORDER |
            WS_TABSTOP, 127, 66, 65, 12
    CONTROL "" 103, "EDIT", WS_CHILD | WS_VISIBLE | WS_DISABLED |
            WS_BORDER, 127, 83, 65, 12
    CONTROL "Compute" 105, "BUTTON", WS_CHILD | WS_VISIBLE |
            WS_TABSTOP, 66, 111, 44, 12
    CONTROL "Return" 104, "BUTTON", WS_CHILD | WS_VISIBLE |
            WS_TABSTOP, 123, 111, 44, 12
    CONTROL "Regular deposit amount?" 200, "STATIC", WS_CHILD |
            WS_VISIBLE | 0x2L, 18, 16, 98, 9
    CONTROL "Annual Percentage Rate" 201, "STATIC", WS_CHILD |
            WS_VISIBLE | 0x2L, 33, 33, 82, 8
    CONTROL "Number of Payments per Year" 202, "STATIC", WS_CHILD |
            WS_VISIBLE | 0x2L, 15, 50, 100, 9
    CONTROL "Number of Years" 203, "STATIC", WS_CHILD | WS_VISIBLE |
            0x2L, 52, 69, 63, 9
    CONTROL "Future Value of Deposits" 204, "STATIC", WS_CHILD |
            WS_VISIBLE | 0x2L, 30, 87, 85, 8
END
```

Listing E.5. `fcfvsin.dlg`. *Dialog resource script for Future Value of a Single Amount.*

```
FCFVSIN DIALOG DISCARDABLE LOADONCALL PURE MOVEABLE 10, 35, 235, 138
STYLE WS_POPUP | WS_CAPTION | WS_SYSMENU | 0x80L
CAPTION "Future Value of a Single Amount"
BEGIN
    CONTROL "" 107, "EDIT", WS_CHILD | WS_VISIBLE | WS_BORDER |
            WS_TABSTOP, 127, 15, 65, 12
    CONTROL "" 106, "EDIT", WS_CHILD | WS_VISIBLE | WS_BORDER |
```

Listing E.5. continues

Listing E.5. *continued*

```
            WS_TABSTOP, 127, 32, 65, 12
    CONTROL "" 109, "EDIT", WS_CHILD | WS_VISIBLE | WS_BORDER |
            WS_TABSTOP, 127, 49, 65, 12
    CONTROL "" 108, "EDIT", WS_CHILD | WS_VISIBLE | WS_BORDER |
            WS_TABSTOP, 127, 66, 65, 12
    CONTROL "" 103, "EDIT", WS_CHILD | WS_VISIBLE | WS_DISABLED |
            WS_BORDER, 127, 83, 65, 12
    CONTROL "Compute" 105, "BUTTON", WS_CHILD | WS_VISIBLE |
            WS_TABSTOP, 66, 111, 44, 12
    CONTROL "Return" 104, "BUTTON", WS_CHILD | WS_VISIBLE |
            WS_TABSTOP, 123, 111, 44, 12
    CONTROL "FV of what amount?" 200, "STATIC", WS_CHILD |
            WS_VISIBLE | 0x2L, 39, 17, 77, 8
    CONTROL "Annual Percentage Rate" 201, "STATIC", WS_CHILD |
            WS_VISIBLE | 0x2L, 33, 33, 82, 8
    CONTROL "Number of Payments per Year" 202, "STATIC", WS_CHILD |
            WS_VISIBLE | 0x2L, 15, 50, 100, 9
    CONTROL "Number of Years" 203, "STATIC", WS_CHILD | WS_VISIBLE |
            0x2L, 52, 69, 63, 9
    CONTROL "Future Value of Amount" 204, "STATIC", WS_CHILD |
            WS_VISIBLE | 0x2L, 30, 87, 85, 8
END
```

Listing E.6. `fcloanda.dlg`. *Dialog resource script for Mortgage Loan Data Entry.*

```
FCLOANDA DIALOG DISCARDABLE LOADONCALL PURE MOVEABLE 10, 35, 220, 113
STYLE WS_POPUP | WS_CAPTION | WS_SYSMENU | 0x80L
CAPTION "Mortgage Loan Data Entry"
BEGIN
  CONTROL "" 107, "EDIT", WS_CHILD | WS_VISIBLE | WS_BORDER |
          WS_TABSTOP, 127, 15, 65, 12
  CONTROL "" 106, "EDIT", WS_CHILD | WS_VISIBLE | WS_BORDER |
          WS_TABSTOP, 127, 32, 65, 12
  CONTROL "" 109, "EDIT", WS_CHILD | WS_VISIBLE | WS_BORDER |
          WS_TABSTOP, 127, 49, 65, 12
  CONTROL "" 108, "EDIT", WS_CHILD | WS_VISIBLE | WS_BORDER |
          WS_TABSTOP, 127, 66, 65, 12
  CONTROL "Return" 104, "BUTTON", WS_CHILD | WS_VISIBLE |
          WS_TABSTOP, 86, 88, 44, 12
  CONTROL "Mortgage loan amount" 200, "STATIC", WS_CHILD |
```

```
                WS_VISIBLE | 0x2L, 39, 17, 77, 8
    CONTROL "Annual Percentage Rate" 201, "STATIC", WS_CHILD |
                WS_VISIBLE | 0x2L, 33, 33, 82, 8
    CONTROL "Number of Payments per Year" 202, "STATIC", WS_CHILD |
                WS_VISIBLE | 0x2L, 15, 50, 100, 9
    CONTROL "Number of Years to amortize" 203, "STATIC", WS_CHILD |
                WS_VISIBLE | 0x2L, 4, 69, 111, 9
END
```

Listing E.7. `fcmkupco.dlg`. *Dialog resource script for Markup Over Cost.*

```
FCMKUPCO DIALOG DISCARDABLE LOADONCALL PURE MOVEABLE 43, 48, 193, 118
STYLE WS_POPUP | WS_CAPTION | WS_SYSMENU | 0x80L
CAPTION "Markup Over Cost"
BEGIN
    CONTROL "" 101, "EDIT", WS_CHILD | WS_VISIBLE | WS_BORDER |
                WS_TABSTOP, 107, 8, 66, 12
    CONTROL "" 102, "EDIT", WS_CHILD | WS_VISIBLE | WS_BORDER |
                WS_TABSTOP, 107, 38, 66, 12
    CONTROL "" 103, "EDIT", WS_CHILD | WS_VISIBLE | WS_DISABLED |
                WS_BORDER, 107, 66, 66, 12
    CONTROL "Return" 104, "BUTTON", WS_CHILD | WS_VISIBLE |
                WS_TABSTOP, 101, 91, 40, 12
    CONTROL "Compute" 105, "BUTTON", WS_CHILD | WS_VISIBLE |
                WS_TABSTOP, 40, 91, 44, 12
    CONTROL "Price of Item" 200, "STATIC", WS_CHILD | WS_VISIBLE |
                0x2L, 6, 10, 83, 12
    CONTROL "Cost of Item" 201, "STATIC", WS_CHILD | WS_VISIBLE |
                0x2L, 6, 39, 83, 12
    CONTROL "Markup % of Cost" 202, "STATIC", WS_CHILD | WS_VISIBLE |
                0x2L, 6, 67, 83, 12
END
```

Listing E.8. `fcmkuppr.dlg`. *Dialog resource script for Markup Over Price.*

```
FCMKUPPR DIALOG DISCARDABLE LOADONCALL PURE MOVEABLE 47, 44, 195, 114
STYLE WS_POPUP | WS_CAPTION | WS_SYSMENU | 0x80L
CAPTION "Markup Over Price"
BEGIN
    CONTROL "" 101, "EDIT", WS_CHILD | WS_VISIBLE | WS_BORDER |
                WS_TABSTOP, 109, 14, 64, 12
```

Listing E.8. continues

Listing E.8. *continued*

```
CONTROL "" 102, "EDIT", WS_CHILD | WS_VISIBLE | WS_BORDER |
        WS_TABSTOP, 109, 38, 64, 12
CONTROL "" 103, "EDIT", WS_CHILD | WS_VISIBLE | WS_DISABLED |
        WS_BORDER, 109, 64, 64, 12
CONTROL "Return" 104, "BUTTON", WS_CHILD | WS_VISIBLE |
        WS_TABSTOP, 109, 87, 40, 12
CONTROL "Compute" 105, "BUTTON", WS_CHILD | WS_VISIBLE |
        WS_TABSTOP, 50, 87, 40, 12
CONTROL "Price of Item" 200, "STATIC", WS_CHILD | WS_VISIBLE |
        0x2L, 9, 14, 82, 12
CONTROL "Cost of Item" 201, "STATIC", WS_CHILD | WS_VISIBLE |
        0x2L, 9, 40, 82, 12
CONTROL "Markup % of Price" 202, "STATIC", WS_CHILD |
        WS_VISIBLE | 0x2L, 9, 65, 82, 12
END
```

Listing E.9. `fcmortls.dlg`. *Dialog resource script for Loan Amortization Schedule (displayed in a list box).*

```
FCMORTLS DIALOG DISCARDABLE LOADONCALL PURE MOVEABLE 29, 31, 222, 149
STYLE WS_POPUP | WS_CAPTION | WS_SYSMENU | 0x80L
CAPTION "Loan Amortization Schedule"
BEGIN
  CONTROL "Return" 104, "BUTTON", WS_CHILD | WS_VISIBLE |
          WS_TABSTOP, 92, 128, 40, 12
  CONTROL "LISTBOX" 110, "LISTBOX", WS_CHILD | WS_VISIBLE |
          WS_BORDER | WS_VSCROLL | 0x41L, 12, 21, 198, 102
  CONTROL "Paymnt #     Pay Amt     Interest     Principal  Balance" 200,
          "STATIC", WS_CHILD | WS_VISIBLE, 10, 7, 187, 10
END
```

Listing E.10. `fcmortpr.dlg`. *Dialog resource script for Print Amortization Schedule.*

```
FCMORTPR DIALOG DISCARDABLE LOADONCALL PURE MOVEABLE 58, 37, 193, 80
STYLE WS_POPUP | WS_CAPTION | WS_SYSMENU | 0x80L
CAPTION "Print Amortization Schedule"
BEGIN
  CONTROL "Start" 115, "BUTTON", WS_CHILD | WS_VISIBLE |
          WS_TABSTOP, 111, 54, 36, 12
```

```
      CONTROL "Cancel" 116, "BUTTON", WS_CHILD | WS_VISIBLE |
              WS_TABSTOP, 46, 54, 36, 12
      CONTROL "Printing the amortization schedule for the current loan" 200,
              "STATIC", WS_CHILD | WS_VISIBLE, 10, 9, 177, 9
      CONTROL "data. Click Start to begin printing, and click Cancel" 201,
              "STATIC", WS_CHILD | WS_VISIBLE, 10, 17, 177, 9
      CONTROL "to change your mind." 202, "STATIC", WS_CHILD |
   WS_VISIBLE, 10, 25, 177, 9
   END
```

Listing E.11. `fcpayout.dlg`. *Dialog resource script for Amortization Payout Analysis.*

```
FCPAYOUT DIALOG DISCARDABLE LOADONCALL PURE MOVEABLE 10, 35, 252, 149
STYLE WS_POPUP | WS_CAPTION | WS_SYSMENU | 0x80L
CAPTION "Amortization Payout Analysis"
BEGIN
   CONTROL "Mortgage/Loan Amount" 200, "STATIC", WS_CHILD |
           WS_VISIBLE, 15, 11, 78, 9
   CONTROL "Annual Percentage Rate" 201, "STATIC", WS_CHILD |
           WS_VISIBLE, 15, 24, 79, 9
   CONTROL "Number of Payments Per Year" 202, "STATIC", WS_CHILD |
           WS_VISIBLE, 15, 38, 101, 9
   CONTROL "Number of Years" 203, "STATIC", WS_CHILD | WS_VISIBLE,
           15, 51, 58, 9
   CONTROL "Level Payment" 204, "STATIC", WS_CHILD | WS_VISIBLE,
           15, 85, 50, 9
   CONTROL "Total Payout" 205, "STATIC", WS_CHILD | WS_VISIBLE,
           15, 98, 43, 9
   CONTROL "Total Interest Paid" 206, "STATIC", WS_CHILD |
           WS_VISIBLE, 15, 111, 62, 8
   CONTROL "Effective Interest Rate, Balloon Note" 207, "STATIC",
           WS_CHILD | WS_VISIBLE, 15, 123, 117, 9
   CONTROL "" 107, "EDIT", WS_CHILD | WS_VISIBLE | WS_DISABLED |
           WS_BORDER | 0x2L, 131, 9, 76, 12
   CONTROL "" 106, "EDIT", WS_CHILD | WS_VISIBLE | WS_DISABLED |
           WS_BORDER | 0x2L, 131, 23, 76, 12
   CONTROL "" 109, "EDIT", WS_CHILD | WS_VISIBLE | WS_DISABLED |
           WS_BORDER | 0x2L, 131, 37, 76, 12
   CONTROL "" 108, "EDIT", WS_CHILD | WS_VISIBLE | WS_DISABLED |
           WS_BORDER | 0x2L, 131, 51, 76, 12
   CONTROL "Mortgage or Loan Input Data" 208, "BUTTON", WS_CHILD |
```

Listing E.11. continues

Listing E.11. continued

```
            WS_VISIBLE | 0x7L, 8, 0, 212, 69
    CONTROL "" 111, "EDIT", WS_CHILD | WS_VISIBLE | WS_DISABLED |
            WS_BORDER | 0x2L, 139, 82, 75, 12
    CONTROL "" 113, "EDIT", WS_CHILD | WS_VISIBLE | WS_DISABLED |
            WS_BORDER | 0x2L, 139, 95, 75, 12
    CONTROL "" 112, "EDIT", WS_CHILD | WS_VISIBLE | WS_DISABLED |
            WS_BORDER | 0x2L, 139, 108, 75, 12
    CONTROL "" 114, "EDIT", WS_CHILD | WS_VISIBLE | WS_DISABLED |
            WS_BORDER | 0x2L, 139, 121, 75, 12
    CONTROL "Payout Analysis Data" 209, "BUTTON", WS_CHILD |
            WS_VISIBLE | 0x7L, 8, 74, 212, 66
END
```

Listing E.12. `fcpctcg.dlg`. *Dialog resource script for Calculate Percent Change.*

```
FCPCTCG DIALOG DISCARDABLE LOADONCALL PURE MOVEABLE 60, 40, 177, 105
STYLE WS_POPUP | WS_VISIBLE | WS_CAPTION | WS_SYSMENU | 0xC0L
CAPTION "Calculate Percent Change"
FONT 10, "Symbol"
BEGIN
    CONTROL "Compute" 105, "BUTTON", WS_CHILD | WS_VISIBLE |
            WS_TABSTOP, 49, 85, 35, 12
    CONTROL "Return" 104, "BUTTON", WS_CHILD | WS_VISIBLE |
            WS_TABSTOP, 93, 85, 35, 12
    CONTROL "" 101, "EDIT", WS_CHILD | WS_VISIBLE | WS_BORDER |
            WS_TABSTOP | 0x82L, 94, 7, 50, 12
    CONTROL "" 102, "EDIT", WS_CHILD | WS_VISIBLE | WS_BORDER |
            WS_TABSTOP | 0x82L, 94, 26, 50, 12
    CONTROL "Old Value" 200, "STATIC", WS_CHILD | WS_VISIBLE |
            0x2L, 10, 9, 73, 12
    CONTROL "New Value" 201, "STATIC", WS_CHILD | WS_VISIBLE |
            0x2L, 12, 28, 73, 12
    CONTROL "Percent Change" 202, "STATIC", WS_CHILD | WS_VISIBLE |
            0x2L, 13, 48, 73, 12
    CONTROL "" 103, "EDIT", WS_CHILD | WS_VISIBLE | WS_DISABLED |
WS_BORDER | 0x2L, 94, 46, 50, 12
END
```

Listing E.13. `fcpctto.dlg`. *Dialog resource script for Percent of Total.*

```
FCPCTTO DIALOG DISCARDABLE LOADONCALL PURE MOVEABLE 44, 49, 173, 108
STYLE WS_POPUP | WS_CAPTION | WS_SYSMENU | 0x80L
CAPTION "Percent of Total"
BEGIN
   CONTROL "Partial Amount" 200, "STATIC", WS_CHILD | WS_VISIBLE |
         0x2L, 17, 14, 52, 12
   CONTROL "Percent Total =" 202, "STATIC", WS_CHILD | WS_VISIBLE |
         0x2L, 17, 56, 52, 12
   CONTROL "Total Amount" 201, "STATIC", WS_CHILD | WS_VISIBLE |
         0x2L, 17, 36, 52, 12
   CONTROL "" 102, "EDIT", WS_CHILD | WS_VISIBLE | WS_BORDER |
         WS_TABSTOP | 0x82L, 95, 12, 56, 12
   CONTROL "" 101, "EDIT", WS_CHILD | WS_VISIBLE | WS_BORDER |
         WS_TABSTOP | 0x82L, 95, 33, 56, 12
   CONTROL "" 103, "EDIT", WS_CHILD | WS_VISIBLE | WS_DISABLED |
         WS_BORDER | 0x2L, 95, 54, 56, 12
   CONTROL "Compute" 105, "BUTTON", WS_CHILD | WS_VISIBLE |
         WS_TABSTOP, 38, 87, 44, 12
   CONTROL "Return" 104, "BUTTON", WS_CHILD | WS_VISIBLE |
WS_TABSTOP, 92, 87, 40, 12
END
```

Listing E.14. `fcpvann.dlg`. *Dialog resource script for Present Value of Regular Deposits.*

```
FCPVANN DIALOG DISCARDABLE LOADONCALL PURE MOVEABLE 10, 35, 235, 138
STYLE WS_POPUP | WS_CAPTION | WS_SYSMENU | 0x80L
CAPTION "Present Value of Regular Deposits"
BEGIN
   CONTROL "" 107, "EDIT", WS_CHILD | WS_VISIBLE | WS_BORDER |
         WS_TABSTOP, 127, 15, 65, 12
   CONTROL "" 106, "EDIT", WS_CHILD | WS_VISIBLE | WS_BORDER |
         WS_TABSTOP, 127, 32, 65, 12
   CONTROL "" 109, "EDIT", WS_CHILD | WS_VISIBLE | WS_BORDER |
         WS_TABSTOP, 127, 49, 65, 12
   CONTROL "" 108, "EDIT", WS_CHILD | WS_VISIBLE | WS_BORDER |
         WS_TABSTOP, 127, 66, 65, 12
   CONTROL "" 103, "EDIT", WS_CHILD | WS_VISIBLE | WS_DISABLED |
         WS_BORDER, 127, 83, 65, 12
```

Listing E.14. *continues*

Listing E.14. continued

```
      CONTROL "Compute" 105, "BUTTON", WS_CHILD | WS_VISIBLE |
              WS_TABSTOP, 66, 111, 44, 12
      CONTROL "Return" 104, "BUTTON", WS_CHILD | WS_VISIBLE |
              WS_TABSTOP, 123, 111, 44, 12
      CONTROL "Regular deposit amount?" 200, "STATIC", WS_CHILD |
              WS_VISIBLE | 0x2L, 16, 17, 100, 8
      CONTROL "Annual Percentage Rate" 201, "STATIC", WS_CHILD |
              WS_VISIBLE | 0x2L, 33, 33, 82, 8
      CONTROL "Number of Payments per Year" 202, "STATIC", WS_CHILD |
              WS_VISIBLE | 0x2L, 15, 50, 100, 9
      CONTROL "Number of Years" 203, "STATIC", WS_CHILD | WS_VISIBLE |
              0x2L, 52, 69, 63, 9
      CONTROL "Present Value of Deposits" 204, "STATIC", WS_CHILD |
              WS_VISIBLE | 0x2L, 30, 87, 85, 8
END
```

Listing E.15. `fcpvsin.dlg`. *Dialog resource script for Present Value of a Single Amount.*

```
FCPVSIN DIALOG DISCARDABLE LOADONCALL PURE MOVEABLE 10, 35, 220, 136
STYLE WS_POPUP | WS_CAPTION | WS_SYSMENU | 0x80L
CAPTION "Present Value of a Single Amount"
BEGIN
   CONTROL "" 107, "EDIT", WS_CHILD | WS_VISIBLE | WS_BORDER |
           WS_TABSTOP, 129, 17, 65, 12
   CONTROL "" 106, "EDIT", WS_CHILD | WS_VISIBLE | WS_BORDER |
           WS_TABSTOP, 129, 34, 65, 12
   CONTROL "" 109, "EDIT", WS_CHILD | WS_VISIBLE | WS_BORDER |
           WS_TABSTOP, 129, 51, 65, 12
   CONTROL "" 108, "EDIT", WS_CHILD | WS_VISIBLE | WS_BORDER |
           WS_TABSTOP, 129, 68, 65, 12
   CONTROL "" 103, "EDIT", WS_CHILD | WS_VISIBLE | WS_DISABLED |
           WS_BORDER, 129, 85, 65, 12
   CONTROL "Compute" 105, "BUTTON", WS_CHILD | WS_VISIBLE |
           WS_TABSTOP, 64, 113, 44, 12
   CONTROL "Return" 104, "BUTTON", WS_CHILD | WS_VISIBLE |
           WS_TABSTOP, 121, 113, 44, 12
   CONTROL "PV of what amount?" 200, "STATIC", WS_CHILD |
           WS_VISIBLE | 0x2L, 41, 19, 77, 8
   CONTROL "Annual Percentage Rate" 201, "STATIC", WS_CHILD |
           WS_VISIBLE | 0x2L, 35, 35, 82, 8
```

```
CONTROL "Number of Payments per Year" 202, "STATIC", WS_CHILD |
        WS_VISIBLE | 0x2L, 17, 52, 100, 9
CONTROL "Number of Years" 203, "STATIC", WS_CHILD | WS_VISIBLE |
        0x2L, 54, 71, 63, 9
CONTROL "Present Value of Amount" 204, "STATIC", WS_CHILD |
        WS_VISIBLE | 0x2L, 32, 89, 85, 8
END
```

Index

N

O

P

Computer Books From Que Mean PC Performance!

Spreadsheets

1-2-3 Database Techniques	$29.95
1-2-3 Graphics Techniques	$24.95
1-2-3 Macro Library, 3rd Edition	$39.95
1-2-3 Release 2.2 Business Applications	$39.95
1-2-3 Release 2.2 PC Tutor	$39.95
1-2-3 Release 2.2 QueCards	$19.95
1-2-3 Release 2.2 Quick Reference	$ 8.95
1-2-3 Release 2.2 QuickStart, 2nd Edition	$19.95
1-2-3 Release 2.2 Workbook and Disk	$29.95
1-2-3 Release 3 Business Applications	$39.95
1-2-3 Release 3 Workbook and Disk	$29.95
1-2-3 Release 3.1 Quick Reference	$ 8.95
1-2-3 Release 3.1 QuickStart, 2nd Edition	$19.95
1-2-3 Tips, Tricks, and Traps, 3rd Edition	$24.95
Excel Business Applications: IBM Version	$39.95
Excel Quick Reference	$ 8.95
Excel QuickStart	$19.95
Excel Tips, Tricks, and Traps	$22.95
Using 1-2-3/G	$29.95
Using 1-2-3, Special Edition	$27.95
Using 1-2-3 Release 2.2, Special Edition	$27.95
Using 1-2-3 Release 3.1, 2nd Edition	$29.95
Using Excel: IBM Version	$29.95
Using Lotus Spreadsheet for DeskMate	$22.95
Using Quattro Pro	$24.95
Using SuperCalc5, 2nd Edition	$29.95

Databases

dBASE III Plus Handbook, 2nd Edition	$24.95
dBASE III Plus Tips, Tricks, and Traps	$24.95
dBASE III Plus Workbook and Disk	$29.95
dBASE IV Applications Library, 2nd Edition	$39.95
dBASE IV Programming Techniques	$24.95
dBASE IV Quick Reference	$ 8.95
dBASE IV QuickStart	$19.95
dBASE IV Tips, Tricks,and Traps, 2nd Edition	$24.95
dBASE IV Workbook and Disk	$29.95
Using Clipper	$24.95
Using DataEase	$24.95
Using dBASE IV	$27.95
Using Paradox 3	$24.95
Using R:BASE	$29.95
Using Reflex, 2nd Edition	$24.95
Using SQL	$29.95

Business Applications

Allways Quick Reference	$ 8.95
Introduction to Business Software	$14.95
Introduction to Personal Computers	$19.95
Lotus Add-in Toolkit Guide	$29.95
Norton Utilities Quick Reference	$ 8.95
PC Tools Quick Reference, 2nd Edition	$ 8.95
Q&A Quick Reference	$ 8.95
Que's Computer User's Dictionary	$ 9.95
Que's Wizard Book	$ 9.95
Quicken Quick Reference	$ 8.95
SmartWare Tips, Tricks, and Traps 2nd Edition	$24.95
Using Computers in Business	$22.95
Using DacEasy, 2nd Edition	$24.95
Using Enable/OA	$29.95
Using Harvard Project Manager	$24.95
Using Managing Your Money, 2nd Edition	$19.95

Using Microsoft Works: IBM Version	$22.95
Using Norton Utilities	$24.95
Using PC Tools Deluxe	$24.95
Using Peachtree	$27.95
Using PFS: First Choice	$22.95
Using PROCOMM PLUS	$19.95
Using Q&A, 2nd Edition	$23.95
Using Quicken: IBM Version, 2nd Edition	$19.95
Using Smart	$22.95
Using SmartWare II	$29.95
Using Symphony, Special Edition	$29.95
Using Time Line	$24.95
Using TimeSlips	$24.95

CAD

AutoCAD Quick Reference	$ 8.95
AutoCAD Sourcebook 1991	$27.95
Using AutoCAD, 3rd Edition	$29.95
Using Generic CADD	$24.95

Word Processing

Microsoft Word 5 Quick Reference	$ 8.95
Using DisplayWrite 4, 2nd Edition	$24.95
Using LetterPerfect	$22.95
Using Microsoft Word 5.5: IBM Version, 2nd Edition	$24.95
Using MultiMate	$24.95
Using Professional Write	$22.95
Using Word for Windows	$24.95
Using WordPerfect 5	$27.95
Using WordPerfect 5.1, Special Edition	$27.95
Using WordStar, 3rd Edition	$27.95
WordPerfect PC Tutor	$39.95
WordPerfect Power Pack	$39.95
WordPerfect Quick Reference	$ 8.95
WordPerfect QuickStart	$19.95
WordPerfect 5 Workbook and Disk	$29.95
WordPerfect 5.1 Quick Reference	$ 8.95
WordPerfect 5.1 QuickStart	$19.95
WordPerfect 5.1 Tips, Tricks, and Traps	$24.95
WordPerfect 5.1 Workbook and Disk	$29.95

Hardware/Systems

DOS Tips, Tricks, and Traps	$24.95
DOS Workbook and Disk, 2nd Edition	$29.95
Fastback Quick Reference	$ 8.95
Hard Disk Quick Reference	$ 8.95
MS-DOS PC Tutor	$39.95
MS-DOS Power Pack	$39.95
MS-DOS Quick Reference	$ 8.95
MS-DOS QuickStart, 2nd Edition	$19.95
MS-DOS User's Guide, Special Edition	$29.95
Networking Personal Computers, 3rd Edition	$24.95
The Printer Bible	$29.95
Que's PC Buyer's Guide	$12.95
Understanding UNIX: A Conceptual Guide, 2nd Edition	$21.95
Upgrading and Repairing PCs	$29.95
Using DOS	$22.95
Using Microsoft Windows 3, 2nd Edition	$24.95
Using Novell NetWare	$29.95
Using OS/2	$29.95
Using PC DOS, 3rd Edition	$24.95
Using Prodigy	$19.95

Using UNIX	$29.95
Using Your Hard Disk	$29.95
Windows 3 Quick Reference	$ 8.95

Desktop Publishing/Graphics

CorelDRAW Quick Reference	$ 8.95
Harvard Graphics Quick Reference	$ 8.95
Using Animator	$24.95
Using DrawPerfect	$24.95
Using Harvard Graphics, 2nd Edition	$24.95
Using Freelance Plus	$24.95
Using PageMaker: IBM Version, 2nd Edition	$24.95
Using PFS: First Publisher, 2nd Edition	$24.95
Using Ventura Publisher, 2nd Edition	$24.95

Macintosh/Apple II

AppleWorks QuickStart	$19.95
The Big Mac Book, 2nd Edition	$29.95
Excel QuickStart	$19.95
The Little Mac Book	$ 9.95
Que's Macintosh Multimedia Handbook	$24.95
Using AppleWorks, 3rd Edition	$24.95
Using Excel: Macintosh Version	$24.95
Using FileMaker	$24.95
Using MacDraw	$24.95
Using MacroMind Director	$29.95
Using MacWrite	$24.95
Using Microsoft Word 4: Macintosh Version	$24.95
Using Microsoft Works: Macintosh Version, 2nd Edition	$24.95
Using PageMaker: Macinsoth Version, 2nd Edition	$24.95

Programming/Technical

Assembly Language Quick Reference	$ 8.95
C Programmer' sToolkit	$39.95
C Quick Reference	$ 8.95
DOS and BIOS Functions Quick Reference	$ 8.95
DOS Programmer's Reference, 2nd Edition	$29.95
Network Programming in C	$49.95
Oracle Programmer's Guide	$29.95
QuickBASIC Advanced Techniques	$24.95
Quick C Programmer's Guide	$29.95
Turbo Pascal Advanced Techniques	$24.95
Turbo Pascal Quick Reference	$ 8.95
UNIX Programmer's Quick Reference	$ 8.95
UNIX Programmer's Reference	$29.95
UNIX Shell Commands Quick Reference	$ 8.95
Using Assembly Language, 2nd Edition	$29.95
Using BASIC	$24.95
Using C	$29.95
Using QuickBASIC 4	$24.95
Using Turbo Pascal	$29.95

For More Information, Call Toll Free!

1-800-428-5331

All prices and titles subject to change without notice.
Non-U.S. prices may be higher. Printed in the U.S.A.

Order Your Program Disk Today!

You can save yourself hours of tedious, error-prone typing by ordering the companion disk to *Using Borland C++*. The disk contains the source code for all complete programs and many of the shorter samples in the book.

You will get code that shows you how to use all the basic and advanced features of Borland C++ 2.0. Samples include code for graphics and screen control, VROOMM overlay management, C I/O, and mixing C and assembly language. C++ samples include classes for stacks, linked-lists, MS Mouse control, extended memory (XMS) use, and samples of derived classes and virtual functions, overloaded operators, and C++ generic classes. Windows 3.0 sample programs include window procedures, dialog procedures, DLL modules, and a complete, working Windows financial calculator application.

Disks are available in both 5-1/4" and 3-1/2" format. The cost is $10 per disk. (Foreign orders please add $5 for shipping and handling.)

Just make a copy of this page, fill in the blanks, and mail with your check or money order only to:

Using Borland C++ Diskette
Atkinson, Campbell Development
P.O. Box 8292
Jackson, MS 39284

Please **print** the following information:

Payment method: *Check:* _____ *Money order:* _____

Name: _____

Street Address: _____

City: _____ State: _____

Zip: _____

*Checks require 2 weeks to clear

Checks and money orders should be made payable to:

Atkinson, Campbell Development

(This offer is made by Atkinson, Campbell Development, not by Que Corporation.)